Experimenter Effects in Behavioral Research

ENLARGED EDITION

THE CENTURY PSYCHOLOGY SERIES

Gardner Lindzey, Kenneth MacCorquodale & Kenneth E. Clark
Editors

The late Richard M. Elliott, *Founding Editor*

Experimenter Effects in Behavioral Research

ENLARGED EDITION

ROBERT ROSENTHAL

HARVARD UNIVERSITY

IRVINGTON PUBLISHERS, Inc., New York

Halsted Press Division of
John Wiley & Sons

New York   London   Toronto   Sydney

Distributed by HALSTED PRESS
A division of JOHN WILEY & SONS,
New York

Library of Congress Cataloging in Publication Data

Rosenthal, Robert, 1933-
    Experimenter effects in behavioral research.
    Bibliography: p
    Includes indexes.
    1.   Psychological research, Experimenter effects in.
I.   Title.
BF76.5.R63   1976   150'.7'24   75-37669
ISBN 0-470-01391-5

PRINTED IN THE UNITED STATES OF AMERICA

Preface to the Enlarged Edition

Ten years have passed since the completion of the original edition of *Experimenter Effects in Behavioral Research,* and a follow-up is in order. Our focus will be on studies of interpersonal expectation effects as these occur both in laboratory settings and in everyday life. The ten year span has seen more than a ten-fold increase in research on interpersonal expectations, and there are now well over 300 studies specifically designed to investigate the occurrence, the importance, and the operating characteristics of interpersonal self-fulfilling prophecies. To summarize all this research in detail would require a book of its own rather than an epilogue and, indeed, someday I hope to write such a book. In our present epilogue there is space only for some summaries and some illustrations.
—R.R.

To my mother
Hermine Kahn Rosenthal

Preface

The effort to understand human behavior must itself be one of the oldest of human behaviors. But for all the centuries of effort, there is no compelling evidence to convince us that we do understand human behavior very well. The application of that reasoning and of those procedures which together we call "the scientific method" to the understanding of human behavior is of relatively recent origin. What we have learned about human behavior in the short period—let us say from the founding of Wundt's laboratory in Leipzig in 1879 until now—is out of all proportion to what we learned in preceding centuries. The success of the application of scientific method to the study of human behavior has given us new hope for an accelerating return of knowledge on our investment of time and effort. But most of what we want to know is still unknown. The application of scientific method has not simplified human behavior. It has perhaps shown us more precisely just how complex it really is.

In the contemporary behavioral science experiment it is the research subject we try to understand. He serves as our model of man in general, or at least of a certain kind of man. We know that his behavior is complex. We know it because he does not behave exactly as any other subject behaves. We know it because sometimes we change his world ever so slightly and observe his behavior to change enormously. We know it because sometimes we change his world greatly and observe his behavior to change not at all. We know it because the "same" careful experiment conducted in one place at one time yields results very different from the results of an experiment conducted in another place at another time. We know his complexity because he is so often able to surprise us with his behavior.

Most of this complexity of human behavior may be in the nature of the organism. But some of it may derive from the social nature of the psychological or behavioral experiment itself. Some of the complexity of man as we know it from his model, the research subject, resides not in the subject himself but rather in the particular experimenter and in the interaction between subject and experimenter.

That portion of the complexity of human behavior which can be attributed to the experimenter as another person and to his interaction with the subject is the focus of this book.

Whatever we can learn about the experimenter and his interaction with his subject becomes uniquely important to the behavioral scientist. To the extent that we hope for dependable knowledge in the behavioral sciences generally, and to the extent that we rely on the methods of empirical research, we must have dependable knowledge about the researcher and the research situation. In this sense the study of the behavioral scientist-experimenter is crucial; there are important implications for how we conduct and how we assess our research.

There is another sense in which the study of the experimenter and his interaction with his subject is important. In this sense it is not at all crucial that the experimenter happens to be the collector of scientific data. He might as well be a teacher interacting with his student, an employer interacting with his employee, a healer interacting with his patient, or any person interacting with another. In this sense, the experimenter himself serves as a model of man or of one kind of man. His subject also serves as a model, and the interaction between them, the situation arising from their encounter, serves as a model of other more or less analogous situations. From the behavior of the experimenter, we may learn something of consequence about human behavior in general.

This book is divided into three parts. The first deals with the general nature of the effects an experimenter may have on the results of his research. The second describes a program of research on the effects of a particular type of experimenter variable on the results of research. The third takes up some methodological implications of the data presented.

Part I consists of two sections. The first contains a discussion of those effects of the experimenter that do not influence the subject's response even though they may affect the results of the research. When the experimenter serves as observer of the subject's behavior, when he records the data, summarizes, analyzes, and interprets the data, he may err in significant ways but not by directly affecting the subject's response.

However, when the experimenter interacts with the subject, his own more enduring attributes, his attitudes, and his expectancies may prove to be significant determinants of the subject's behavior in the experiment. These effects of the experimenter are discussed in the second section of Part I.

The last chapter of Part I provides a historical introduction to the experimenter variable that is central to the second major part of this book. That variable is the experimenter's orientation toward the outcome of his research. The hypothesis is put forward that the experimenter's hypothesis, his expectancy, can be a significant determinant of the results of his research.

Part II begins with a presentation of the evidence that an experimenter's expectancy may serve as self-fulfilling prophecy of his subjects' responses when the subjects are either humans or animals. In these and in following chapters, evidence is presented in sufficient detail for the research to be critically evaluated by the reader without reference to papers published elsewhere. This seems particularly necessary in a work that purports to offer some suggestions for the further development of behavioral research methodology.

In the second section of Part II some factors are discussed that have been shown to augment, to neutralize, or to reverse the effects of the experimenter's expectancy on the results of his research. These factors include subjects' expectancies, the nature of data earlier obtained by the experimenter, the motive states aroused in the experimenter, and the subjects' view of the experimenter.

What are the factors that make possible the dramatic effects of the experimenter's expectancy? The third section of Part II is addressed to this question. Those characteristics and behaviors of the experimenter associated with greater exertion of unintentional influence are discussed. Those characteristics of experimental subjects associated with a greater susceptibility to the influence of the experimenter's hypothesis are presented. Finally, those cues that might serve to communicate the experimenter's expectancy to his subjects are considered.

The evidence put forth in Part II of the book has clear methodological implications for the behavioral researcher. But beyond the methodological implications there are substantive implications as well, for what is evidence for the effects experimenters can have on their subjects is also, more generally, evidence for the importance in human relations of unintentional interpersonal influence and, more specifically, the interpersonal influence that stems from one person's expectancy of another's behavior.

It seems not overly important that the possibility of unintentional influence has been demonstrated. No one will probably be very surprised. What does seem important is that the process of unintended social influence can be observed in the laboratory, and that its dynamics can now be more fully and more systematically investigated.

Part III deals with a number of methodological implications. In the first section of Part III the generality of experimenter effects is discussed and a conceptual schema presented which should make it easier to talk about the operating characteristics of experimenters. Also the general problem of replications and their assessment is related to the earlier sections of the book.

In the second section of Part III concrete proposals are offered which the behavioral scientist can employ to reduce and/or assess the effects of his and his surrogate's expectancies on the results of his research. An effort has been made to have these suggestions be useful, and they are offered with due regard for the practical problems of getting research done, getting it done expeditiously, and getting it done economically.

The suggestions made for the control of experimenter expectancy effects will not, in all probability, solve the problem of "experimenter bias." But that does not seem discouraging. In the short time that "scientific method" has been applied to the study of human behavior it has shown itself to be a good and robust teacher. There *are* things we have learned about human behavior in spite of the possible operation of experimenter expectancy effects. We may do still better by the addition of even imperfect safeguards.

Whether we will ever be able to account for all the sources of variance deriving from the experimenter remains a moot question. It does not differ in kind from the question of whether we will ever be able to account for all the sources of variance deriving from the subject. It is the question of whether the concept of indeterminacy applies because it is in the nature of the universe or whether it applies because of how much there is we do not yet know. Both views have been held by distinguished contributors to our understanding of nature. Thus, how each reader of this volume answers this question for himself may make little difference in terms of what we want to know and will be able to learn. The more meaningful question, perhaps, is whether we can account for increasing proportions of the total variance in experiments by a consideration of experimenter expectancy (and related) effects, and whether we can, by some form of intervention, reduce these sources of error.

I owe much to many people who, on many counts, contributed in one way or another to the thinking and to the research that resulted in this book. I cannot thank them all. The authors of a book or a paper read a decade ago—they will forgive me if I express their idea, and in less eloquent language than theirs and without acknowledgment, and for having forgotten that the idea was not mine in the first place. But there are those I can thank, and happily. Donald T. Campbell, Harold B. Pepinsky, and Henry W. Riecken all provided more intellectual stimulation and personal encouragement than I could hope to repay.

So many people, I cannot recall them all, have given of their time to make available to me reprints, their own and others, and references they knew would be of interest to me. None has been more generous than Professor William B. Bean, Head of the Department of Internal Medicine, State University of Iowa College of Medicine, and a wise and knowledgeable student of error in science.

This book would not have been written nor would it have been worth the writing without the research program that forms its core. This research was supported initially by a grant from the University of North Dakota Faculty Research Committee, and since 1961 by the Division of Social Sciences of the National Science Foundation (G-17685, G-24826, GS-177, GS-714). Without the support of the Foundation much of the research could not have been conducted. This book owes much to that support.

The research on which much of the book is based was not conducted by me alone. It owes much to the work of my colleagues both senior and junior. Reed Lawson, Edward Halas, and John Gaito were not only co-authors of joint research, but my tutors as well. Kermit Fode, Linda V. Kline, Gordon Persinger, and Ray Mulry collaborated for a period of years on our research—from their undergraduate days through various advanced degrees. Other collaborators included Jack Friedman, Paul Kohn, Patricia Greenfield, Mardell Grothe, and Noel Carota (all collaborators on several occasions) and Neil Friedman, Suzanne Haley, Daniel Kurland, Carl Johnson, Thomas Schill, and Ray White. All these collaborators would surely join me in thanking our far more numerous collaborators of a different kind: the many experimenters and the many subjects upon whose participation our research program was dependent, and whose behavior we were privileged to observe.

A number of people kindly read and commented on various portions of the manuscript: Elliot Aronson, Neil Friedman, David Marlowe, Fred Mosteller, Theodore Newcomb, Martin Orne, Karl Weick, and the following members of the latter's seminar in experimental social psychology: Gordon Fitch, I. Helbig, Michael Langley, Donald Penner, Dan Ray, Marion Reed, Edward Ypma, and Joseph Zuro. Kenneth MacCorquodale and Milton Rosenberg read and improved the entire manuscript. To them my debt is greater still. I want to thank each of these readers for his help, and absolve them of any responsibility for remaining errors and inelegancies of expression. These inelegancies would have been still more considerable had I not had the benefit of some earlier tutorials from that scholarly, wise, and kind tutor, E. G. Boring.

The typing of various parts of this manuscript and the consequent improvements of spelling and punctuation were expertly undertaken by Betty Burnham, Nancy Johnson, Susan Novick, and Kathy Sylva.

For endless putting aside of dishes and laundry to listen to an idea or a paragraph and typing it and improving it and for countless other assistances I thank my wife, Mary Lu. For being interested in their father's homework I thank Roberta, David, and Virginia.

R. R.

Contents

I

THE NATURE OF
EXPERIMENTER EFFECTS

EXPERIMENTER EFFECTS NOT
INFLUENCING SUBJECTS' BEHAVIOR

EXPERIMENTER EFFECTS
INFLUENCING SUBJECTS' BEHAVIOR

1

The Experimenter as Observer

It was the science of astronomy that made clear that the scientific observer was an imperfectly calibrated instrument. In the closing years of the eighteenth century, Maskelyne, the astronomer royal at the Greenwich Observatory, discovered that his assistant, Kinnebrook, was consistently "too slow" in his observation of the movement of stars across the sky. During the next six months, despite Maskelyne's admonition, Kinnebrook's recording continued to lag behind Maskelyne's own recording of the times of stellar transits. Maskelyne then felt forced to discharge Kinnebrook.

Some twenty years later, Bessel, the astronomer at Königsberg, studied this incident and concluded that Kinnebrook's "error" must have been beyond his control. Bessel then compared his own observations of stellar transits with those of other senior astronomers and discovered that differences in observation were the rule, not the exception. Furthermore, he found these differences or "personal equations" to vary over time. These important events in the history of the notation of observer error have been described and documented by Boring (1950).

THE GENERALITY OF OBSERVER EFFECTS

The plan of the next few pages is to indicate some of the disciplines that have shown a self-conscious awareness of the problem of observer effects. The intent is not to be exhaustive, but rather to be sufficiently representative to establish some consensus with the reader regarding the generality of the phenomena.

The Physical Sciences

Newton did not have much confidence in his own observational ability, and for at least one occasion, the lack of confidence seemed justified. Boring (1962a) noted that Newton did not see and report the absorption lines in the prismatic solar spectrum, which were visible with Newton's apparatus, because of his theoretically based expectations. Boring put it aptly and beautifully: "To the observing scientist, hypothesis is both friend and enemy" (p. 601). Boring's suggestion that observer effects may not be random with respect to the observer's hypothesis is agreed with by N. R. Hanson (1958) and E. B. Wilson (1952).

Another dramatic example of observer errors (errors that were both nonrandom and widespread among observers) has been reported by Rostand (1960). In 1903, Blondlot discovered "N-rays," which appeared to make reflected light more intense. This phenomenon was viewed by a great many observers, including many famous scientists of the day. Only a few were unable to detect the phenomenon, which later was evaluated as at least a colossal compounded observer error if not a downright fraud. Interestingly, as this evaluation became generally known, the effects of "N-rays" could no longer be observed.

Discussion of observer effects, especially as they have been operative in the physical sciences, often ends by reference to modern instruments which serve to eliminate observer effects. That these effects may be brought under partial control by mechanical means seems reasonable enough. That instrumentation may not eliminate observer effects must also be considered. If the instrument is a dial, it must be read by a human observer. If the instrument is a computer, the print-out must also be read by an observer. Observer effect, or variability in the reading of scales, has been noted by Yule, writing in the *Journal of the Royal Statistical Society* (1927). A general error tendency found was the inclination to read scales to quarters of intervals rather than to tenths. Empirical analysis of his own observer effect revealed to Yule his tendency to avoid the number 7 as a final digit and to favor the numbers 8, 9, 0, and 2. That this particular bias was not at all unique to Yule was demonstrated in a still earlier work by Bauch (1913). The digit preference phenomenon has also revealed itself in large sample data collection enterprises. In an age census conducted in England and Wales, both males and females showed a preference for the digit 0 and an avoidance of the digit 1 in the units place of their age statements.

Yule planned to investigate observer errors in scale reading in more systematic fashion but did not do so. His plan, revealing his awareness of the role of psychological factors in observer errors, was to relate the nature of the error or effect to the nature of the observer.

The Biological Sciences

The counting of blood cells is a routine and important procedure in biological research and in the practice of medicine. For many years the standard textbooks published data setting the "maximum allowable discrepancy" between blood cell counts of successive samples of blood. Then, in 1940, Berkson, Magath, and Hurn reported a way of counting blood cells more accurately than was ordinarily possible. Each blood cell was pierced by a stylus a single time, and each piercing was recorded electrically. After collecting many series of blood samples, the investigators were led to the inescapable conclusion that laboratory technicians had for years routinely reported blood cell counts that could have agreed with one another so well only 15 to 34 percent of the time. "Published studies involving erythrocyte counts, as well as standard texts, disallow discrepancies between successive counts so small that they would in most instances necessarily be exceeded as a matter of chance if counts were accurately made and faithfully recorded" (p. 315). The story has many similarities to the story of the "N-rays." Observations were made by many observers, over a long period of time, which were consistent with the observers' expectations but inconsistent with the realities of nature as subsequently defined.

In the field of agricultural statistics, observer effects have been well demonstrated by Cochran and Watson (1936). These investigators enlisted the aid of 12 experienced observers who believed themselves able to select young plants whose heights would vary in truly random fashion. When actually put to the task, it was found that observers selected plants or shoots that were neither representative nor random. Because these observer errors were not randomly distributed around the "true" values, the errors were appropriately defined as biased. Bias, it was found, did not remain constant from sampling unit to sampling unit. In the observation of shoot heights, as in the observation of stellar transits, observer effects were not easily predictable.

In the field of experimental genetics Fisher (1936) cites Dr. J. Rasmussen, who mentioned that in experimental genetics he, as well as his assistants, showed an unconscious bias to select the best plants first for observation. This type of observer effect, or more specifically "bias," like that shown in the selection of shoot heights and that shown to occur in other situations by Yule and Kendall (1950), has led these authors to propose that man may simply be unable to select random sets of events to be observed without such external aids as tables of random numbers.

Perhaps the most important case of observer effects in the history of experimental genetics is the one involving the work of Gregor Mendel. Mendel, it will be recalled, expected that when hybrid pea plants were self-fertilized 75 percent of the offspring would show the dominant phenotype and 25 percent would show the recessive phenotype. That, almost exactly, was what Mendel's observations subsequently showed. Considering the relatively small sample sizes reported, Fisher (1936), in a closely reasoned logical and statistical analysis, showed that Mendel could not reasonably have obtained the data he reported. The data were just too good to be likely. We may at least hypothesize the existence of an observer effect or, because of its directionality, a bias, in either Mendel, his assistant, or both. If the biased error was due to the work of an assistant, the case does not stand alone (Shapiro, 1959). Alfred Binet, of intelligence testing fame, working then in the area of physical anthropology, was forced to discharge a research assistant who made errors in cephalometric measurements (Wolf, 1961). These errors, too, were not randomly distributed but rather were in the direction of the hypothesis. These errors, like those possibly committed by Mendel's assistant, were not necessarily errors of observation. In any case we can see that the history of science has often repeated the Kinnebrook episode.

In a treatise on the octopus, Lane (1960) asserts that scientists may "equate what they *think* they see, and sometimes what they *want* to see, with what actually happens" (p. 85). W. B. Bean (1953), a thoughtful student of the role of error in science, presents the following data: In 1901, Leser claimed an association of cherry angioma, an easily observable skin condition, with malignant disease. Leser's first assistant, Müller, found that 49 of 50 cancer patients had cherry angiomas, but among a control series of 300 noncancer patients, he found only a handful. On the basis of theoretical considerations and especially the inability to replicate this result, it appeared most likely to have been a case of observer error. Bean wondered, "Was the wish father to the thought, was Müller a too avid helper or an unbelievably bad observer" (p. 241)? Bean has also called attention to the work of Feinstein (1960) and M. L. Johnson (1953). It was the former who pointed out the observer error involved in the use of the stethoscope in cardiac diagnostics. Feinstein asked that physicians as well as their stethoscopes be calibrated. Johnson cited the case of a radiologist who saw a button "on a vest" rather than in the throat where it lodged because, presumably, buttons occur more frequently on vests than in throats. In experiments on observer processes, Johnson found medical students observing quite inaccurately when presented with two x-rays of hands for study. Johnson, in this paper entitled "Seeing's Believing," was prompted to say, "Our assumptions define and limit what we see, i.e., we tend to see things in such a way that they will fit in with our assumptions even if this involves distortion or omission. We therefore may invert our title and say 'Believing Is Seeing' " (p. 79).

We might find it instructive to consider the data bearing on the question of the reliability of medical or psychological diagnoses. There is ample evidence that the diagnostic process has great unreliability, but this phenomenon does not quite fit our conception of observer error. In too many cases where the unreliability is great, the defining characteristics of the classes to which assignment is to be made are all too vague. We may therefore have interpretive errors or perhaps not even that. When nosological categories are carefully defined and objective criteria of inclusion are available, then, when error occurs we may more legitimately regard it as observer error. Bean (1948) found in nutritional examinations that experienced physicians disagreed in the diagnosis of nutritional deficiency even when objective standards were available. Speaking of observer errors, and of others as well, Bean stated, "Our aim must not be to deny error, but to learn from it, avoiding the stability it gets from repetition" (p. 54).

The Behavioral Sciences

Harry Stack Sullivan has called attention to the problem of observer effect on the social sciences generally and on the "social science of psychiatry" in particular (1936–37). More than most investigators, he was aware of the extent to which the observer entered into transaction with the object of the observation. Sullivan, of course, was not alone in this awareness, an awareness eloquently expressed by Wirth (1936), and somewhat later by Bakan (1962), Colby (1960), and Kubie (1956).

The psychotherapy relationship may be viewed appropriately as a data-collecting situation with the therapist in the position of observing his patient's responses. Both the lore of the practicing clinician and the evidence of more formal investigations point to the omnipresent effects of the clinical observer. Events occurring in the clinical interaction are often unobserved or at least unreported by the clinician. Events not occurring in the clinical interaction are sometimes reported erroneously by the clinician. And often, the errors may be shown to be related to the personal characteristics of the clinical observer, particularly to his personal "blind spots" (Cutler, 1958; Garfield & Affleck, 1960; Levitt, 1959; Sarason, 1951; Strupp, 1959; Wallach & Strupp, 1960; Zirkle, 1959).

The observation of planaria. Although observer effects may be less obvious in a laboratory than in a clinical setting, it is nevertheless clear that they do occur. A well-designed experiment by Cordaro and Ison (1963) nicely illustrates the fact. The behavior to be observed was the number of head turns and body contractions made by planaria (flatworms placed low on the phylogenetic scale). For half the worms, seven observers were led to expect a very high incidence cf turning and contracting. For the remaining worms the same observers were led to expect a very low incidence of turning and contracting. The worms observed under the two conditions of expectation were, of course, essentially identical. Results of this phase of the experiment showed that observers reported twice as many head turns and three times as many body contractions when their expectation was for high rates of response as when their expectation was for low rates of response.

The basic plan of this experiment was repeated employing a new set of ten observers. This time, however, half the experimenters were to observe only "high-response-producing" worms, and the remaining observers were given only "low-response-producing" worms. Again there was no real difference between the two "types" of worms. The results of this phase of the experiment found nearly five times as many head turns and twenty times as many contractions reported by the observers who expected high levels of responding as reported by observers expecting low levels of responding.

The observers employed in the experiments cited were undergraduate college students enrolled in an introductory psychology course. It may be, of course, that the degree of observer bias shown would not be found among more experienced observers, a possibility pointed out by Shinkman and Kornblith (1965) and by Cordaro and Ison themselves. Some data are available which have a bearing on this question.

In an experiment investigating "natural" individual differences among workers interested in planaria, it was found that differences among these experimenters in the number of turning, contraction, and other responses obtained were for the most part statistically significant (Rosenthal & Halas, 1962). This experiment differed from that of Cordaro and Ison in two ways. First, the experimenters were not given any false expectancies but were engaged in "actual" research on behavior modification in planaria. Second, all eight of these experimenters were more experienced than any of those employed by Cordaro and Ison. Half had master's degrees at the time, and the set of eight experimenters averaged just under three publications each. At least six of the experimenters are still active in psychological research and four have Ph.D.'s.

As might be expected, the absolute magnitudes of differences among experimenters in numbers of responses observed were not so large as those found by Cordaro and Ison. In no case did one observer report twice as many turns as another, although the differences obtained were statistically significant more often than not. Observations of body contractions, however, were subject to surprisingly large observer effects. The largest discrepancy occurred when one observer reported nearly seven times as many contractions as his comparison observer. The smallest discrepancy was one in which an observer reported nearly twice as many contractions as his comparison observer. Each of the results presented was based on a minimum of 900 trials (observations) per observer.

It seems reasonable to conclude that even experienced observers may differ in their perception of the behavior of planaria. A somewhat different but perhaps more serious problem, however, is that in which observer effects interact with experimental conditions (Rosenthal & Halas, 1962). Table 1-1 illustrates just this effect for those two experimenters for whom the most complete data were available. These experimenters were among the most academically advanced and the most experienced in research. Each experimenter tried to condition six planaria to respond by turning or contracting to a light which had been paired with an electric shock. As a control pro-

TABLE 1—1

Two Experiments in the Learning of Turning in Worms

	EXPERIMENTER I		EXPERIMENTER II	
	Experimental	Control	Experimental	Control
First block	10.5	11.5	9.0	8.0
Second block	10.0	9.0	11.0	11.0
Third block	11.5	9.5	15.0	10.5
Fourth block	12.5	9.0	15.5	11.0
Fifth block	9.0	12.0	17.0	11.0
Sixth block	8.0	9.5	16.0	11.5
Means	10.2	10.1	13.9	10.5
p (difference)	NS		.02	

cedure, each experimenter had six other planaria to which the light was administered without the shock.

The results of Table 1-1 show the mean number of turns for six blocks of 25 trials each. One experimenter obtained "conditioning" of turning responses, and one did not. Experimenter II not only obtained more turning in his experimental group than in his control group, but his experimental animals showed an increase in turning in each subsequent block. The correlation (rho) between number of turns per block and block order was .94, $p = .02$. However, the control group for this experiment also showed a tendency to turn more often on later trials (rho = .77, $p = .10$), although the rate of increase was much more gradual.

Table 1-2 shows the analogous data for body contractions. Once again there is no difference between the mean responses of the experimental and control groups for experimenter I, but there is a surprise in the difference between the mean number of contractions observed for the experimental and control groups by experimenter II. This time planaria in the control group responded more than planaria in the experimental group. This reversal of the results of experimenter II is the more surprising as turning and contracting responses have been found to be so well correlated that they are commonly added together to form a "total response" score.

For these experienced experimenters, therefore, it can be concluded that there are individual differences in the extent to which behavior modifications in planaria are observed and that the particular differences found are affected by the specific type of behavior being observed.

TABLE 1—2

Two Experiments in the Learning of Contraction in Worms

	EXPERIMENTER I		EXPERIMENTER II	
	Experimental	Control	Experimental	Control
First block	2.0	0.5	0.5	2.0
Second block	0.5	1.0	0.0	0.5
Third block	0.0	0.0	0.5	1.0
Fourth block	1.0	1.0	0.5	2.0
Fifth block	1.0	1.5	0.5	1.5
Sixth block	1.0	2.0	1.0	2.0
Means	0.9	1.0	0.5	1.5
p (difference)	NS		.005	

Although the foregoing data have been cited as evidence of observer effects, alternative explanations are possible. It could be that the effects arose by chance. That does not seem likely, however, since the animals were assigned to experimenters and to experimental conditions at random. The likelihood of the experimenter's effect being due to chance is given by the p values of Tables 1-1 and 1-2, and these p values are low. It could also be that the planaria behavior was correctly observed but incorrectly recorded. Recording errors of such magnitude, however, are too rare to serve as likely explanations, as will be shown in the next section of this chapter. Intentional errors are generally only a remote possibility and, on the basis of personal acquaintance, for these particular experimenters, a virtual impossibility. One remaining possibility is that in some way the experimenters' behavior affected the behavior of the planaria. This can be only a speculation, but it seems at least possible that one or the other of the two experimenters unintentionally treated his animals differentially as a function of whether they were in the treatment or control group. It cannot be assumed that experimenter II showed such a difference while experimenter I did not. It could as well be argued that, except for the programmed differences in treatment, experimenter II treated his animals identically and that the differences he obtained are those attributable only to the experimental conditions. Differential behavior toward the animals of the two groups of experimenter I might have "improperly" reduced the "true" difference between the experimental and control animals.

Research with rabbits, as with planaria, has shown significant effects associated with the particular experimenter employed. Brogden (1962) found that inexperienced experimenters required more trials in which to condition rabbits. As in the planaria research, the aim was to elicit an avoidance reaction to light which had been paired with an electric shock. Unlike the situation for the planaria research, however, the experimenter effect disappeared with further practice on the part of the inexperienced experimenters. Neither in the case of the rabbits nor in the case of the planaria can it be specified just what the experimenters did differently that could have led to such different records of animal learning. In a later chapter (Chapter 8) there will be occasion to discuss this problem again.

Recording errors. As experimenters observe the behavior of their subjects, their observations must in some way be recorded. It comes as no surprise that errors of recording have been demonstrated and that these errors are not always self-canceling. A self-canceling set of errors is one in which errors inflating a category are exactly offset by errors deflating that category. If an observer of the turning of worms records three turns that did not occur and fails to record three turns that did occur, he has committed six errors which have canceled each other out.

Kennedy and Uphoff (1939) performed a careful study of recording errors in experiments in extrasensory perception. Briefly, the task for the observers was to record the investigator's guesses as to the nature of the symbol being "transmitted" by the observer. The symbols employed were the standard ones used in such research and included circles, squares, stars, crosses, and wavy lines. Each trial consisted of 25 cards, five of each of the five symbols. Because the guesses made for the observers had been predetermined, it was possible to count the number of recording errors.

A total of 28 observers recorded a grand total of 11,125 guesses, of which 126, or 1.13 percent, were misrecorded. All observers made at least one error (one observer made 16), and the modal number of errors per observer was four. Some of the errors committed increased the telepathy scores (45.2 percent), some decreased it (21.4 percent), and some had no effect (33.4 percent). There was, then, a general tendency to make recording errors that increased the telepathy scores. Kennedy and Uphoff knew which observers had favorable attitudes to extrasensory perception and which had unfavorable attitudes. The analysis of errors by believers and disbelievers showed that each type of observer tended to err in the direction favorable to his attitude, though these biased errors were quite small. Believers in telepathy made 71.5 percent more errors increasing telepathy scores than did disbelievers. Disbelievers made 100 percent more errors decreasing the telepathy scores than did believers.

Very similar findings have been reported by Sheffield and Kaufman (1952). In an experiment in psychokinesis, they filmed the actual fall of the dice which subjects were trying to influence. They found subjects believing in the phenomenon to make more tallying errors in favor of the hypothesis. Subjects who disbelieved made more of the opposite type of tallying error.

Recording, as well as computational, errors by experimenters have also been studied in an experiment on the perception of people (Rosenthal, Friedman, Johnson, Fode, Schill, White, & Vikan, 1964). In that experiment, each subject wrote on a small writing pad his rating of the degree of success or failure experienced by persons pictured in photographs. The 30 experimenters of this study transcribed these ratings to a master data sheet. A comparison of the experimenters' 3,000 transcriptions with their subjects' recordings revealed that only 20 errors had occurred. The 0.67 percent rate of misrecording approached the 1 percent rate just exceeded (1.13 percent) by Kennedy and Uphoff. Probably because each of the experimenters of the experiment in person perception made only one fourth as many observations as did Kennedy and Uphoff's observers, 18 experimenters made no recording errors whatever.

Some experimenters had been given an expectation that they would obtain high ratings of the photos from their subjects, whereas some experimenters had been given the opposite expectation. Nine of the 12 experimenters who made any recording errors erred in the direction of their expectation, and their errors tended to be larger ($p = .05$).

The computational task for the experimenters in the study under discussion was simply to sum the 20 ratings given by each of their five subjects. Of the 30 experimenters, 18 made a computational error, and 12 of these erred in the direction of their expectation. Those experimenters who were more likely to make computational errors in the direction of their hypothesis also tended to make larger computational errors.

In this same experiment, all subjects rated their experimenters on the variable of "honesty" during the conduct of the experiment. This was a very impressionistic rating since the experimenters could not actually have been "dishonest" even if they had been so inclined. During the experiment, the co-investigators had all experimenters under surveillance (a fact apparent to all experimenters). In spite of the subjectivity of the ratings of the experimenters' honesty made by the subjects, these ratings predicted better than chance ($p = .02$) whether the experimenter would subsequently favor his hypothesis in the making of computational errors. It should be noted, however, that *all* experimenters were rated as being quite honest: +8.5 (extremely honest) was the mean rating assigned to experimenters who did not err in the direction of their expectation; +6.8 (moderately to highly honest) was the mean rating of experimenters who did err in the direction of their hypothesis.

In the same experiment it was possible to relate the occurrence of recording errors to the occurrence of computational errors. The correlation of .48 ($p = .01$) showed that experimenters who erred in data transcription tended to err in data processing. Somewhat surprisingly, however, those experimenters who erred in the direction of their expectancy in their recording errors were not any more likely (rho = .05) to err in the same direction in their computational errors. The making of numerical errors seemed, then, to be a consistent characteristic, but directionality of error vis-a-vis expectation did not.

We should note here that the overall effects of both recording and computational errors on the grand means of the different treatment conditions of the experiment reported were negligible. An occasional experimenter did have some real effect on the data he obtained; an effect that, at least in principle, could be serious if an entire experiment depended on an experimenter who was prone to err numerically.

In a recent experiment conducted by John Laszlo, three experimenters conducted the same basic experiment in person perception employing a total of 64 subjects. In this study, all three experimenters made computational errors. For the most accurate experimenter, 6 percent of his computations were in error. The other experimenters erred 22 and 26 percent of the time. The magnitudes of the errors were quite small, but for all three experimenters, a majority (75 percent overall) of the errors tended to favor the experimental hypothesis, though the frequency of these biased errors did not reach statistical significance. In spite of the apparent regularity of the occurrence of such errors, little attention has been given to real or alleged numerical errors in the scientific literature of psychology (Hanley & Rokeach, 1956; Wolins, 1962).

CONCEPTUALIZATION OF OBSERVER EFFECTS

In the mapping out of the generality of observer effects, we have had only broad hints at certain definitions and differentiations which must now be made more explicit. Later on, in Part III, we will consider these matters in greater detail. By "observer effects" or "observer error" we have referred to overstatement or understatement of some criterion value. When two observers disagree in an observation, each may be said to err with respect to the other. Both may be said to err with respect to some third observation which may, for various reasons, be a more or less usefully employed criterion. Given a population of observations, we may choose to define some central value (such as the mean or mode) as the "true" value and regard all observations not falling at that value as being more or less in error as a direct function of their distance from the central value.

Observer errors or effects may be distinguished from observer "bias" by the fact that observer errors are randomly distributed around a "true" or "criterion" value. Biased observations tend to be consistently too high or too low and may bear some relation to some characteristics of the observer (Roe, 1961), the observation situation (Pearson, 1902), or both.

In considering the act or sequence of acts constituting the observation in the scientific enterprise, we may distinguish conceptually among locations of error or bias. The error of "apprehending" occurs when there is some sort of misrecording between the event observed and the observer of the event. We may include here such diverse sources of apprehending error as differing locations of observers (Gillispie, 1960) or angles of observation (George, 1938), imperfections in the sensory apparatus, central relay systems, cortical projection areas, and the like. The error of recording may be distinguished conceptually from the apprehending error. In the case of recording error, we assume first an errorless act of apprehending followed by a transcription of the event (to paper, to the ear of another observer, or to another instrument) which differs from the event as correctly apprehended. In actual practice, of course, when an event or observation is recorded in error with respect to some criterion, we cannot locate the error as having occurred either in apprehending, in transcribing, or in both processes. There is no certain method for isolating an apprehending error unconfounded with a recording error, though introspective reports may be suggestive.

Computational errors are more clearly distinguishable from the foregoing errors since they involve the incorrect manipulation of recorded events. Incorrectness is usually defined here by the formal rules of arithmetical operations.

In some of the cases of "observer error," the criterion or "true" value of the observation is so vague and ephemeral that we cannot properly speak of errors of apprehending or recording (or computation). Such would be the case, for example, with psychiatric classification. When "error" occurs in this situation we may more appropriately speak of "error of interpretation." Interpretation effects will be discussed in the next chapter.

Finally, throughout this chapter the assumption has been made that the classes of errors discussed occurred without the intent of the observer. Those occasions when intent is involved in the production of an erring observation will be discussed in Chapter 3.

THE CONTROL OF OBSERVER EFFECT

A powerful, necessary, though insufficient, tool for the control of observer error is our awareness of the phenomenon. The role of various mechanical apprehenders and recorders in the reduction of observer error has been noted earlier. As Boring (1950) pointed out, these mechanizations do not replace the human observer; rather, they postpone human observation to some other, more convenient time and circumstance of reapprehension and rerecording. If mechanization reduces observer error—and it very likely does—there remain still subsequent errors of "re"-observation. Yule (1927) was relatively optimistic that observer training could eliminate observer error. This optimism seemed unshared by Fisher (1936) in citing Rasmussen.

The most critical control of observer error is probably woven into the fabric of science by the tradition of replication. Frequent replication of observations serves to establish the definition of observer errors. It does not, however, eliminate the problem, since replicated observations made under similar conditions of anticipation, instrumentation, and psychological climate may, by virtue of their intercorrelation, all be in error with respect to some external criterion (Pearson, 1902). An excellent example of this, as mentioned, is Rostand's (1960) discussion of the infamous N-rays. Perhaps the great contribution of the skeptic, the disbeliever, in any given scientific observation is the likelihood that his anticipation, psychological climate, and even instrumentation may differ enough so that his observation will be more an independent one. Error, in the sense of discrepancy, will then have a greater chance of being revealed. Which of two contradictory sets of observations will be regarded as error-free depends on sets of criteria subsequently adopted by the assessing community.

2

Interpretation of Data

Identical observations are often interpreted differently by different scientists, and that fact and its implications are the subject of this chapter. Interpretation effects are most simply defined as any difference in interpretations. The difference may be between two or more interpreters, or an interpreter and such a generalized interpreter as an established theory or an "accepted" interpretation of a cumulative series of studies. As in the observer effect, the interpreter effect, or difference, does not necessarily imply a unidirectional phenomenon. When observations are nonrandomly distributed around a true value, we refer to them as "biased observations." Similarly, when interpretations do not vary randomly—and usually they do not—we may refer to them as "biased." Note that we do not thereby imply that the biased interpreter is "wrong" with respect to some notion of "true interpretation," but only that his interpretation is predictable. It does not seem as reasonable to postulate the central value interpretation as the true interpretation as it does to postulate the central value observation as the true observation.

The distinction between an observation itself and the interpretation of an observation is not always simple. Some observations require a greater component of interpretation than others. If we observe the behavior of worms there seems to be less interpretation required to observe whether there is a worm present than to observe whether the worm is completely immobile. If we choose to observe a very small worm, however, even the observation of its presence or absence may require a larger interpretive element.

Interpretations or constructions of data have an enormous range of generality, from the interpretation of a speck as worm or not-worm, through the interpretation of a person's speech as schizophrenic or not schizophrenic, to the interpretation of measurements of the speed of light as damaging to or irrelevant to Einstein's theory of relativity.

At the lowest level of generality, differences in interpretation could easily be regarded as observer effects. At the highest level of generality, differences in interpretation are nothing more than differences in theoretical positions. Even at the higher levels of generality, however, differences in interpretation may affect the accuracy of observations. This can occur in two ways. First, a given theory or interpretive framework may affect the perceptual process in such a way as to increase errors of observation in the direction of greater consistency with the theory. Such effects are clearly implied by some of the evidence presented in the last chapter and by the extensive literature on need-determined perception (Dember, 1960; see also Campbell, 1958; Sanford, 1936; Stephens, 1936; Zillig, 1928). Second, a given interpretive framework may function to keep "off the market" data that may weaken the tenability of the theory. Such underrepresentation of data contradictory to prevailing theories would bias the "true" value of an observation. Since the "true" value of an observation was defined in terms of some central value of available observations, it seems obvious that by ignoring observations at variance with the existing central value that value will become more and more stable statistically and psychologically.

If in the history of science the proponents of a dominant theory have often thus shepherded the current central or true observation into the direction supporting their theory, they have also often been responsible for the fact that observations were being made at all. Theoretical biases are mixed blessings. They are selectively attentive to data that if completely unbiased by theory would not have been collected at all.

The Physical Sciences

In 1887 Michelson and Morley conducted their famous experiment on the speed of light. Their report showed that whether the light signals were sent out in the direction of the earth's motion or not, the speed was the same. It is said that this counterintuitive result was the stimulus for Einstein to develop his theory of relativity in 1905. The Michelson-Morley experiment was important to relativity theory, and, in fact, the result seemed required by it. But there are two facts that must be added. First, according to Einstein, the Michelson-Morley experiment had nothing to do with his original formulation of relativity theory. Second, the results of the Michelson-Morley experiment were probably in error, and there did appear to be an "ether drift." Defined by a difference in the speed of light as a function of the signal's direction in relation to the earth's motion, this "ether drift" could have jeopardized relativity theory. That it did not illustrates interpreter effects in science.

Michael Polanyi (1958) and Arthur Koestler (1964) have given the details. In 1902, some 15 years after the Michelson-Morley experiment,

W. M. Hicks showed some ether drift in their original observations. Then, from 1902 to 1926, D. C. Miller repeated the experiment with improved instrumentation thousands of times and consistently obtained a drift of from eight to nine kilometers per second. Still later, W. Kantor, using still more elegant instrumentation, also showed that the speed of light did depend on the motion of the observer. So well established was relativity theory that Miller's work was essentially ignored (though that was difficult, since he presented his complete evidence in 1925 to the American Physical Society, of which he was then president). It is true, as Polanyi tells us, that there was other evidence from different workers for the absence of ether drift as required by relativity theory. But that evidence was not available when Miller presented his data nor for the many years before that he had been making his observations. How do we decide whether there really was an artifact in Miller's work, so that people did well to ignore it? Is there a possibility that some physicist, had he been taught to take apparently sound data seriously, might, because of these inconsistent data, have so modified relativity theory that it would be more powerful by far? Such questions, if they are answerable at all, E. G. Boring would refer to history for verdict.

Miller's data were ignored but they were available. Sometimes the effects of interpretation of data are such as to keep those data unavailable. Bernard Barber (1961) tells of some well-known instances. One such was Lord Kelvin's interpretation of Roentgen's x-rays as a hoax, a kind of N-ray phenomenon in reverse. Several instances of workers' inability to publish papers that seemed to the judges to be paradoxical were also documented. The most interesting of these, because it represents a kind of controlled experiment, was the case of Lord Rayleigh. In 1886, he submitted a paper entitled "An Experiment to Show That a Divided Electric Current May Be Greater in Both Branches than in the Mains." He was, at the time, already well-known. In some way his name became detached from the paper, however, and it was rejected. Shortly afterward the name somehow became collated with the paper, which was then found to have sufficient merit for acceptance.

But perhaps the most useful illustration, for its recency and for its charm in the telling, is the case of Michael Polanyi himself and his theory of the adsorption (adhesion) of gases on solids (Polanyi, 1963). In 1914 he first published his theory and within a few years had adduced convincing experimental evidence on its behalf. But the then current conception of atomic forces made his theory unacceptable. Asked to state his position publicly, Polanyi was chastised by Einstein for showing a "total disregard" of what was then "known" about the structure of matter. Said Polanyi, "Professionally, I survived the occasion only by the skin of my teeth" (p. 1011). Polanyi, of course, was subsequently credited with having been correct. His analysis of the role of that orthodoxy in science which kept his evidence from being considered is remarkable for its balance, objectivity, and the lack of bitterness, a bitterness that characterized Planck's reaction to the resistance he encountered (Barber, 1961).

Polanyi felt that the rejection of his theory and his evidence was unavoidable and even proper given the state of knowledge at the time. Although recognizing the danger of orthodoxy in repressing contradictory evidence, he points out that the journals could easily become flooded with nonsense in the face of a too great tolerance of dissent. This moderate view of orthodoxy is much the same as that expressed by Florian Znaniecki in his classic work, *The Social Role of the Man of Knowledge* (1940).

The Biological Sciences

Mosteller put it well, ". . . perhaps sometimes the data are not ready to be looked at—and it is not that the anomalies aren't at all noticed, but that they aren't discussed much because no-one knows just what to say" (personal communication, 1964). Perhaps that is the reason why Mendel's now classic monograph, *Experiments in Plant-Hybridization,* first presented in 1865, had to wait to become important until de Vries, Correns, and Tschermak found something to say about it, all independently of each other, and all in 1900. Perhaps, too, less was found to say about Mendel's work because of his, for that time odd, applications of mathematics to botany, and because of Mendel's relative lack of scientific stature (Barber, 1961). Even after people found things to say about Mendel's data, however, no one looked at it closely enough because it was so easy to interpret in accordance with each one's own theoretical orientation. Fisher (1936) put it: "Each generation, perhaps, found in Mendel's paper only what it expected to find; . . . Each generation, therefore, ignored what did not confirm its own expectations" (p. 137).

Mendel's case is not unique in the history of biology. Darwin, Lister, Pasteur, Semmelweiss, and their observations tended to be ignored or rejected, and these are only some of the better-known cases. They and others, less well known, have been chronicled by Barber (1961), Fell (1960), Koestler (1964), and Zirkle (1960.)

Sometimes in science the situation is not that there is too little that can be said about the data but rather too much. A number of equally plausible interpretations are available, and that leads neither to rejecting the observations nor to ignoring them. It leads to an assimilation of the data to the various theoretical positions that can make use of them. Wolf (1959) gives us a good example based on Morris' data which found London tramway motormen with a higher incidence of coronary heart disease than tramway conductors. (The data may, for our purpose, be regarded as free from observer effect.) The original interpretation of these data was in terms of the relationship between sedentary occupations and heart disease, the motorman sitting while performing his task, the conductor moving about more. One alternative interpretation offered by Wolf was that motormen, because of their sedentary work, might be gaining weight faster and that it was the weight gain which led to a higher incidence of heart disease. Wolf presented the additional interpretation that the lessened social interaction with other people required by the motorman's job when compared to the conductor's job might also be the critical variable. Other interpretations are of course possible, including those which postulate that individuals prone to heart disease, because of their biological or psychological make-up, tend to select or be assigned to the front end of the trolley. Here, then, are alternative interpretations whose relative tenabilities could easily be established by further observation. The initial data were immediately important theoretically (and practically) because there were theories available that could make sense of the observations and could be tested further by performing the experiments implied by the various interpretations of the data. When the experiments are well designed and well executed the experimenter has a better chance to ". . . escape from his own preferences in interpreting his results" (Boring, 1959; p. 3).

The Behavioral Sciences

In the example of interpretation differences just given, it was assumed that there were no observer errors. Who is a motorman and who is a conductor seemed an easy observation on which to achieve consensus. The presence or absence of heart disease, however, is a somewhat more equivocal judgment (Feinstein, 1960). We are hard put to decide whether diagnostician differences are observer effects or interpretation effects. If we may assume that cardiologists hear the same "lub-dub" through their stethoscopes and see the same tracings of the electrocardiogram, we would be inclined to regard diagnostic variations as differences of interpretation.

In the applied behavioral sciences of psychiatry and clinical psychology, the diagnosis or categorization of behavior is a common enterprise. Differences in the interpretation of behavioral data are well illustrated by differences in diagnoses. The magnitude of such differences have been reported by Star (1950). During the second World War, psychiatric examiners interviewed army recruits for the purpose of rejecting any who might be too severely disturbed to function as soldiers. The most extreme difference in rate of rejection found one induction center rejecting 100 times more recruits than another. Although this magnitude of difference is unusual, the generality of differences in the interpretation of abnormal behavior seems well established (Hyman, Cobb, Feldman, Hart, & Stember, 1954).

In the diagnosis of abnormal behavior the large effects of interpreters are probably due to the vagueness of the defining characteristics of the various diagnostic categories. Of itself this would increase unreliability. If this source of unreliability were the only one, however, we would expect interpreter differences to be unbiased or unpredictable. But that is not the case. Robinson and Cohen (1954), for example, found that there were significant biases in the psychological evaluations of 30 patients by 3 psychological examiners. The authors related the biases in evaluation to the personality differences among the examiners, a relationship postulated by Henry Murray in 1937 and supported in a number of studies (e.g., Filer, 1952; Harari & Chwast, 1959; Rotter & Jessor, undated). In this discussion of interpreter effects among diagnosticians we have assumed that the examinee's behavior on which the interpretations were based was not itself affected by the examiner. Sometimes the examiner does affect the patient's behavior and markedly so. These effects will be discussed beginning with Chapter 4.

Before leaving the area of clinical diagnosis or interpretation it should be emphasized that diagnostic differences occur in other areas, perhaps even to as great an extent. Jones (1938), for example, has shown the degree of disagreement in the assessment of the nutritional health of school-children. Not only did diagnosticians disagree with one another, but they also differed from their own earlier assessments.

Sometimes in nutritional diagnosis, as in psychological diagnosis, we can speak of biased or directional or predictable differences among diagnosticians (Bean, 1948; Bean, 1959). An informal report by Wooster (1959) nicely illustrates such biased diagnosis. Wooster tells the possibly apocryphal story of 200 patients who were to be classified as obese, normal, or underweight. Leaner physicians tended to classify patients as more obese than did obese physicians.

One variable that has been shown especially likely to bias the assessment of behavior is the expectancy of the observer or interpreter. Rapp (1965) tells us about an especially carefully conducted experiment which demonstrates this expectancy bias. Rapp's experiment, it will be seen, could be equally well viewed as a study of observer effect or of interpreter effect. It deals with data falling in the range of experimenter effects that are difficult to categorize clearly.

The setting of the experiment was a nursery school, and the task for each of eight pairs of observers was to describe objectively the behavior of a single child as it occurred within one minute. One member of each pair of observers was led to believe that the child to be observed was feeling "under par." The other member of the pair of recorders was led to believe that the child was feeling "above par." Actually all the eight children included for observation had been selected so that their behavior would not show extreme behavior in either the above or below par direction. Results of this study showed that seven of the eight pairs of observers wrote descriptions of the children's behavior that were detectably biased in the direction of their expectation ($p = .003$).

An example of the biasing effect of expectations, one that seems to be more clearly an example of an interpreter effect, is given by Cahen (1965). His subjects, 256 prospective schoolteachers, were each asked to score several test booklets ostensibly filled out by children being tested for academic readiness. Each of the 30 test items was to be scored on a four-point scale using a scoring manual which gave examples of answers of varying quality. On each of the answer booklets to be scored some "background" information was provided for that child. This background information included an alleged IQ score, the purpose of which was to create an expectation in the scorer that the child whose booklet was being scored was (1) above average, (2) average, or (3) below average in intellectual ability. The scoring of the tests supported Cahen's hypothesis that children thought to be brighter would receive higher scores for the same performance than would children believed to be less able.

The assessment of cultures like the assessment of individuals is subject to widely divergent interpretations (Hyman et al., 1954). Oscar Lewis and Robert Redfield described the Mexican village of Tepoztlan in quite different ways. Redfield presented a picture of a highly cooperative, integrated, and happy society relative to Lewis' picture of an uncooperative, poorly integrated society whose members seemed anything but happy. Reo Fortune and Margaret Mead described the Arapesh in significantly different terms. For Mead, but not for Fortune, the Arapesh were a placid, domestic people characterized by a maternal temperament.

In such cases of anthropological disagreement we are hard put to account adequately for differing interpretations. It is important to know that such differences occur, but it would be most valuable to know why. If, for example, we could show a general tendency for female workers to perceive cultures as more peaceful, we could begin to write some general terms into the anthropological personal equations. In the absence of such data we are left with the unsatisfactory alternative of noting differences without adequately understanding them.

Sometimes an anthropological interpretive effect can be understood as an illustration of a well-known principle of perception. Such seems to be the case for data cited by Campbell (1959). The evaluation of the drabness or liveliness of Russian cities was found to depend on the order in which the cities were visited. Cities visited earlier on a tour were judged more drab than those visited later. "Against the adaptation level based upon experience with familiar U.S. cities, the first Russian city seemed drab and cold indeed. But stay in Russia modified the adaptation level, changed the implicit standard of reference so that the second city was judged against a more lenient standard" (1959, p. 11). (Here and elsewhere [1958] Campbell has provided inventories of sources of error relevant to our discussion of interpreter as well as observer effects.)

A major attempt to assess the biasing effects of different anthropological interpreters has been made by Raoul Naroll (1962). His method of data quality control is designed to compare anthropological reports made under more favorable conditions with reports made under less favorable conditions. Thus, staying in the field for over a year is associated with reports of higher rates of witchcraft attribution than staying in the field for less than a full year. Length of stay in the field is, then, a biasing factor but one for which it seems reasonable to assume that the longer stay gives a truer picture than does the shorter stay. Length of stay in a culture does not, however, bias reports of drunken brawling, so we see that conditions of observation or interpretation may bias reports of some behaviors but not others.

Another test of the quality of anthropological reports notes the investigator's knowledge of the native language. Whether he knows the language tends in fact to be related to his report, not only of witchcraft attribution, but of protest suicide as well. A third test described by Naroll is the distinction between a professional and nonprofessional investigator. The anthropologist is the former, and, in this context, the missionary the latter. Although in general we might expect professionals to be more accurate, Naroll suspects that, at least for reports of witchcraft attribution, missionaries may be more reliable than anthropologists. In summary, Naroll's method allows us not only to assess the extent of bias in a series of anthropological reports but to institute controls for these as well.

Perhaps more than any other, the survey research literature has shown a sophisticated awareness of interpreter and related effects; the already classic work of Hyman and his collaborators (1954) shows this fact most clearly. In their discussion of interviewer effects they describe the impact of interviewers' expectations on their interpretation of respondents' replies. Smith and Hyman (1950) provide the example. Recordings were made of two interviews. One of the respondents was a political isolationist described additionally as provincial and prejudiced. The other respondent, chosen to contrast markedly with the first, was an interventionist. In each interview, responses were included that objectively reflected equivalent sentiments on the part of both respondents. However, the interviewers were greatly affected by the respondent's overall orientation in assessing these matched replies. One of the questions dealt with the amount of money spent by the United States for European recovery. Answers to this question by the isolationist and interventionist both actually suggested that we were spending an appropriate amount. However, when these same answers were coded or interpreted by interviewers who had been given the isolationist vs. interventionist set, the results were dramatically altered. The isolationist's response was interpreted as meaning that we were spending too much for European recovery by 53 percent of the interpreters. The interventionist's response, which had been equated with the isolationist's response, was interpreted as meaning that we were spending too much by only 9 percent of the interpreters.

Another question on which the replies of the two respondents had been equated dealt with the respondents' interest in our policy toward Spain. Actually both respondents' replies indicated some interest, and 99 percent of the interpreters so coded the interventionist's reply. In contrast, however, only 76 percent of the coders so interpreted the isolationist's reply.

For our most recent examples of interpreter effects we turn to experimental research in psychology. A recent paper summarizes 25 experiments in which eyelid conditioning was related to the subjects' level of anxiety as measured by a paper and pencil test (Spence, 1964). Considerable theoretical importance is associated with the direction of this relationship, the more highly anxious subjects having been postulated to show the greater learning. In 21 of the 25 experiments the greater learning did in fact occur ($p = .002$) among the more anxious subjects, though the differences were not statistically significant for every individual comparison. The interpretive effects arise from the finding that 16 of the 17 studies carried out in the Iowa laboratory showed the predicted effect ($p < .001$), while in the other laboratories 5 out of 8 studies showed the predicted effect ($p > .70$). A great many differences in procedure and in sampling could, of course, easily account for these differences. One major interpretation offered to account for the differences, however, was that the studies not conducted at Iowa employed smaller sample sizes. Such an interpretation would simply be a restatement of the fact that the power of a statistic increases with the sample size if it were not for the fact that three of the eight smaller-sample studies showed mean differences in the unpredicted direction. In this case the interpretation that a larger sample size would lead to differences in the predicted direction can only be made if it assumes that later-run subjects differ significantly from earlier-run subjects and systematically so in the predicted direction. An example of an oppositely biased interpretation would be to suggest that if the eight experiments conducted at different laboratories had employed larger sample sizes their results would have been still significantly more different from the Iowa studies than they actually were. Other recent examples of interpreter differences may be found in discussions of extrasensory perception (Boring, 1962b; Murphy, 1962) and of social psychology (Chapanis & Chapanis, 1964; Jordan, 1964; Silverman, 1964; Weick, 1965).

Earlier in the discussion of the natural sciences, reference was made to the fact that sometimes interpreter differences lead to keeping data "off the market." This, of course, also occurs in the behavioral sciences. Sometimes it occurs directly, as in an explicit or implicit editorial decision to not publish certain kinds of experiments. Such decisions, of course, are inevitable given that the demand for space in scientific literature far exceeds the supply. Often the data thus kept off the market are negative results which are themselves often difficult to account for. (The problem of negative results will be discussed in greater detail in Part III.)

One good reason for keeping certain data off the market is that the particular data may be wrong. This suspicion may be raised about a particular observation within a series that is very much out of line with all the others. But the question of how to deal with such discordant data is not easily answered (Rider, 1933; Tukey, 1965). Kety's (1959) caution is most appropriate: ". . . it is difficult to avoid the subconscious tendency to reject for good reason data which weaken an hypothesis while uncritically accepting those data which strengthen it" (p. 1529). Wilson (1952) and Wood (1962) give similar warnings.

THE CONTROL OF INTERPRETER EFFECTS

Some interpreter effects are fully public events and some are not. If the interpretation of a set of public observations is uncongenial to our own orientation we are free to disagree. The public nature of these interpretive differences insures that in time they may be resolved by the addition of relevant observations or the development of new mental matrices which allow the reconciliation of heretofore opposing theoretical orientations (Koestler, 1964).

When interpreter effects operate to keep observations off the market, however, they are less than fully public events. If an investigator simply scraps one of his observations as having been made in error there is no one to disagree and attempt to use the discordancy in a reformulation of an existing theory or as evidence against its tenability. When negative results are unpublishable the fact of their negativeness is not a publicly available observation. When unpopular results are unpublishable they are kept out of the public data pool of science. All these examples are clear-cut illustrations of interpreter effects which reduce the "public-ness" of science. There are less clear-cut cases, however.

As in Mendel's case, the observations are sometimes available but so little known and so little regarded that for practical purposes they are unavailable publicly. Sometimes it is our unawareness of their existence that keeps them out of science, but sometimes they are known at least to some but ". . . they lie outside of science until someone brings them in" (Boring, 1962b, p. 357). That, of course, is the point made earlier, that we may know of the existence of data but not what can be said of them. When we speak, then, of the control of interpreter effects we do not necessarily mean that there should be none. In the first place, their elimination would be as impossible as the elimination of individual differences (Morrow, 1956; Morrow, 1957). In the next place their elimination would more likely retard than advance the development of science (Bean, 1958).

Only those interpreter effects that serve to keep data from becoming publicly available or those that are very close to being observer effects should be controlled. As for the interpreter effects of a public nature that involve the impassioned defense of a theory, Turner (1961a) put it thus: "In the matter of making discoveries, unconcern is not a promising trait. But the desire to gain the truth must be balanced by an equally strong desire not to be played false" (p. 585).

3

Intentional Error

Intentional error production on the part of the experimenter is probably as relatively rare an event in the psychological experiment as it is in the sciences generally (Wilson, 1952; Shapiro, 1959; Turner, 1961b). Nevertheless, any serious attempt at understanding the social psychology of psychological research must consider the occurrence, nature, and control of this type of experimenter effect.

The Physical Sciences

Blondlot's N-rays have already been discussed as a fascinating example of observer effect. Rostand (1960) has raised the question, however, whether their original "discovery" might not have been the result of overzealousness on the part of one of Blondlot's research assistants. Were that the case then we could learn from this example how observer or interpreter effects may derive from intentional error even when the observers are not the perpetrators of the intentional error. This certainly seemed to be the case with the famous Piltdown man, that peculiar anthropological find which so puzzled anthropologists until it was discovered to be a planted fraud (Beck, 1957).

A geologist some two centuries ago, Johann Beringer, uncovered some remarkable fossils including Hebraic letters. "The[se] letters led him to interpret earth forms literally as the elements of a second Divine Book" (Williams, 1963, p. 1083). Beringer published his findings and their important implications. A short time after the book's publication a "fossil" turned up with his name inscribed upon it. Beringer tried to buy back copies of the book which were by now circulating, but the damage to his reputation had been done. The standard story had been that it was Beringer's students who had perpetrated the hoax. Now there is evidence that the hoax was no schoolboy prank but an effort on the part of two colleagues to discredit him

(Jahn & Woolf, 1963). Here again is a case where interpreter effects on the part of one scientist could be in large part attributed to the intentional error of others.

A more recent episode in the history of archaeological research, and one far more difficult to evaluate, has been reported on the pages of *The Sunday Observer*. Professor L. R. Palmer, a comparative philologist at Oxford, has called into question Sir Arthur Evans' reconstruction of the excavations at Knossos (Crete). These reconstructions were reported in 1904 and then again in 1921. The succession of floor levels, each yielding its own distinctive type of pottery, was called by Palmer a "complete figment of Evans' imagination." Palmer's evidence came from letters that contradicted Evans' reconstruction—letters written by Evans' assistant, Duncan Mackenzie, who was in charge of the actual on-site digging. These letters were written after Evans had reported his reconstruction to the scientific public. Evans did not retract his findings but rather in 1921 he reissued his earlier (1904) drawing. Palmer felt that the implications of these events for our understanding of Greece, Europe, and the Near East were "incalculable" (Palmer, 1962). In subsequent issues of *The Observer* Evans had his defenders. Most archaeologists (e.g., Boardman, Hood) felt that Palmer had little reason to attack Evans' character and question his motives, though, if they are right, questions about Duncan Mackenzie's might be implied. The Knossos affair serves as a good example of a possible intentional error which could conceivably turn out to have been simply an interpreter effect—a difference between an investigator and his assistant. One thing is clear, however: whatever did happen those several decades ago, the current debate in *The Observer* clearly illustrates interpreter differences.

C. P. Snow, scientist and best-selling novelist, has a high opinion of the average scientist's integrity (1961). Yet he refers to at least those few cases known to scientists in which, for example, data for the doctoral dissertation were fabricated. In one of his novels, *The Affair,* he deals extensively with the scientific, social, and personal consequences of an intentional error in scientific research (1960). Other references to intentional error, all somewhat more pessimistic in tone than was C. P. Snow, have been made by Beck (1957), George, (1938), and Noltingk (1959).

The Biological Sciences

When, two chapters ago, observer effects were under discussion the assumption was made that intentional error was not at issue. Over the long run this assumption seems safely tenable. However, for any given instance it is very difficult to feel certain. We must recall: (1) Fisher's (1936) suspicion that Mendel's assistant may have deceived him about the results of the plant breeding experiments; (2) Bean's (1953) suspicion that Leser's assistant may have tried too hard to present him with nearly perfect correlations between harmless skin markings and cancer; (3) Binet's suspicion over his own assistant's erring so regularly in the desired direction in the taking of cephalometric measurements (Wolf, 1961).

One of the best known and one of the most tragic cases in the history of intentional error in the biological sciences is the Kammerer case. Kammerer was engaged in experiments on the inheritance of acquired characteristics in the toad. The characteristic acquired was a black thumb pad, and it was reported that the offspring also showed a black thumb pad. Here was apparent evidence for the Lamarckian hypothesis. A suspicious investigator gained access to one of the specimens, and it was shown that the thumb pad of the offspring toad had been blackened, not by the inherited pigment, but by India ink (MacDougall, 1940). There cannot, of course, be any question in this case that an intentional error had been perpetrated, and Kammerer recognized that prior to his suicide. To this day, however, it cannot be said with certainty that the intentional error was of his own doing or that of an assistant. A good illustration of the operation of interpreter effects is provided by Zirkle (1954) who noted that scientists were still citing Kammerer's data, and in reputable journals, without mentioning its fraudulent basis. More recently, two cases of possible data fabrication in the biological sciences came to light. One case ended in a public exposé before the scientific community (Editorial Board, 1961); the other ended in an indictment by an agency of the federal government (Editorial Board, 1964).

The Behavioral Sciences

The problem of the intentional error in the behavioral sciences may not differ from the problem in the sciences generally. It has been said, however, that at least in the physical sciences, error of either intentional or unintentional origin is more quickly checked by replication. In the behavioral sciences replication leads so often to uninterpretable differences in data obtained that it seems difficult to establish whether "error" has occurred at all, or whether the conditions of the experiment differed sufficiently by chance to account for the difference in outcome. In the behavioral sciences it is difficult to specify as explicitly as in the physical sciences just how an experiment should be replicated and how "exact" a replication is sufficient. There is the additional problem that replications are carried out on a different sample of human or animal subjects which we know may differ vary markedly from the original sample of subjects. The steel balls rolled down inclined planes to demonstrate the laws of motion are more dependably similar to one another than are the human subjects who by their verbalizations are to demonstrate the laws of learning.

In survey research the "cheater problem" among field interviewers is of sufficient importance to have occasioned a panel discussion of the problem in the *International Journal of Attitude and Opinion Research* (1947). Such workers as Blankenship, Connelly, Reed, Platten, and Trescott seem to agree that, though statistically infrequent, the cheating interviewer can affect the results of survey research, especially if the dishonest interviewer is responsible for a large segment of the data collected. A systematic attempt to assess the frequency and degree of interviewer cheating has been reported by Hyman, Cobb, Feldman, Hart, and Stember (1954). Cheating was defined as data fabrication, as when the interviewer recorded a response to a question that was never asked of the respondent. Fifteen interviewers were employed to conduct a survey, and unknown to them, each interviewed one or more "planted" respondents. One of the "planted" interviewees was described as a "punctilious liberal" who qualified all his responses so that no clear coding of responses could be undertaken. Another of the planted respondents played the role of a "hostile bigot." Uncooperative, suspicious, and unpleasant, the bigot tried to avoid committing himself to any answer at all on many of the questions. Interviews with the planted respondents were tape recorded without the interviewers' knowledge. It was in the interview with the hostile bigot that most cheating errors occurred. Four of the interviewers fabricated a great deal of the interview data they reported, and these interviewers tended also to cheat more on interviews with the punctilious liberal, although, in general, there was less cheating in that interview. Frequency of cheating, then, bore some relation to the specific data-collection situation and was at least to some extent predictable from one situation to another.

In science generally, the assumption of predictability of intentional erring is made and is manifested by the distrust of data reported by an investigator who has been known, with varying degrees of certainty, to have erred intentionally on some other occasion. In science, a worker can contribute to the common data pool a bit of intentionally erring data only once. We should not, of course, equate the survey research interviewer with the laboratory scientist or his assistants. The interviewer in survey research is often a part-time employee, less well educated, less intelligent, and less interested in the scientific implications of the data collected than are the scientist, his students, and his assistants. The survey research interviewer has rarely made any identification with a scientific career role with its very strong taboos against data fabrication or other intentional errors, and its strong positive sanctions for the collection of accurate, "uncontaminated" data. Indeed, in the study of interviewers' intentional errors just described, the subjects were less experienced than many survey interviewers, and this lack of experience could have played its part in the production of such a high proportion of intentional errors. In that study, too, it must be remembered, the design was such as to increase the incidence of all kinds of interviewer effects by supplying unusually difficult situations for inexperienced interviewers to deal with. However, even if these factors increased the incidence of intentional error production by 400 percent, enough remains to make intentional erring a fairly serious problem for the survey researcher (Cahalan, Tamulonis, & Verner, 1947; Crespi, 1945–46; Mahalanobis, 1946).

A situation somewhere between that of collecting data as part of a part-time job and collecting data for scientific purposes exists in those undergraduate science courses in which students conduct laboratory exercises. These students have usually not yet identified to a great extent with the scientific values of their instructors, nor do they regard their laboratory work as simply a way to earn extra money. Data fabrication in these circumstances is commonplace and well-known to instructors of courses in physics and psychology alike. Students' motivation for cheating is not, of course, to hoax their instructors or to earn more money in less time but rather to hand in a "better report," where better is defined in terms of the expected data. Sometimes the need for better data arises from students' lateness, carelessness, or laziness, but sometimes it arises from fear that a poor grade will be the result of an accurately observed and recorded event which does not conform to the expected event. Such deviations may be due to faulty equipment or faulty procedure, but sometimes these deviations should be expected simply on the basis of sampling error. One is reminded of the Berkson, Magath, and Hurn (1940) findings which showed that laboratory technicians were consistently reporting blood counts that agreed with each other too well, so well that they could hardly have been accurately made. We shall have occasion to return to the topic of intentional erring in laboratory course work when we consider the control of intentional errors. For the moment we may simply document that in two experiments examined for intentional erring by students in a laboratory course in animal learning, one showed a clear instance of data fabrication (Rosenthal & Lawson, 1964), and the other, while showing some deviations from the prescribed procedure, did not show any evidence of outright intentional erring (Rosenthal & Fode, 1963a). In these two experiments, the incidence of intentional erring may have been reduced by the students' belief that their data were collected not simply for their own edification but also for use by others for serious scientific purposes. Such error reduction may be postulated if we can assume that data collected only for laboratory learning are less "sacred" than those collected for scientific purposes.

Student experimenters are often employed as data collectors for scientific purposes. In one such study Verplanck (1955) concluded that following certain reinforcement procedures the content of conversation could be altered. Again employing student experimenters Azrin, Holz, Ulrich, and Goldiamond (1961) obtained similar results. However, an informal post-experimental check revealed that data had been fabricated by their student experimenters. When very advanced graduate student experimenters were employed, they discovered that the programmed procedure for controlling the content of conversation simply did not work.

Although it seems reasonable to assume that more-advanced graduate students are generally less likely to err intentionally, few data are at hand for documenting that assumption. We do know, of course, that sometimes even very advanced students commit intentional errors. Dr. Ralph Kolstoe has related an instance in which a graduate student working for a well-known psychologist fabricated his data over a period of some time. Finally, the psychologist, who had become suspicious, was forced to use an entrapment procedure which was successful and led to the student's immediate expulsion.

What has been said of very advanced graduate students applies as well to fully professional scientific workers. It would appear that the incidence of intentional errors is very low among them, but, again, few data are available to document either that assumption or its opposite. Most of the cases of "generally known" intentional error are imperfectly documented and perhaps apocryphal.

In the last chapter there was occasion to discuss those types of interpreter effects which serve to keep certain data off the market either literally or for all practical purposes. It was mentioned that sometimes data were kept out of the common exchange system because no one knew quite what to say about them. Sometimes, though, data are kept off the market because the investigator knows all too well what will be said of them. Such intentional suppression of data damaging to one's own theoretical position must be regarded as an instance of intentional error only a little different from the fabrication of data. What difference there is seems due to the "either-or-ness" of the latter and the "shades of grayness" of the former. A set of data may be viewed as fabricated or not. A set of legitimate data damaging to a theory may be withheld for a variety of motives, only some of which seem clearly self-serving. The scientist may honestly feel that the data were badly collected or contaminated in some way and may therefore hold them off the market. He may feel that while damaging to his theory their implications might be damaging to the general welfare of mankind. These and other reasons, not at all self-serving, may account for the suppression of damaging data. Recently a number of workers have called attention to the problem of data suppression, all more or less stressing the self-serving motives (Beck, 1957; Garrett, 1960; Maier, 1960). One of these writers (Garrett) has emphasized a fear motive operating to suppress certain data. He suggests that young scientists fear reprisal should they report data that seem to weaken the theory of racial equality.

Sometimes the suppression of data proceeds, not by withholding data already obtained, but by insuring that unwanted data will not be collected. In some cases we are hard put to decide whether we have an instance of intentional error or an instance of incompetence so magnificent that one is reduced to laughter. Consider, for example, (1) an investigator interested in showing the widespread prevalence of psychosis who chooses his sample entirely from the back wards of a mental hospital; (2) an investigator interested in showing the widespread prevalence of blindness who chooses his sample entirely from a list of students enrolled in a school for the rehabilitation of the blind; (3) an investigator interested in showing that the aged are very well off financially who chooses his sample entirely from a list of white, noninstitutionalized persons who are not on relief. The first two examples are fictional, the third, according to the pages of *Science,* unfortunately, is not. (One sociologist participating in that all too real "data"-collecting enterprise was told to avoid apartment dwellers.) A spokesman for a political group which made use of these data noted helpfully that the survey was supported by an organization having a "conservative outlook" (*Science,* 1960). The issue, of course, is not whether an organization having a "liberal outlook" would have made similar errors either of incompetence or of intent but rather that such errors do occur and may have social as well as scientific implications.

THE CONTROL OF INTENTIONAL ERROR

The scientific enterprise generally is characterized by an enormous degree of trust that data have been collected and reported in good faith, and by and large this general trust seems well justified. More than simply justified, the trust seems essential to the continued progress of the various sciences. It is difficult to imagine a field of science in which each worker feared that another might at any time contaminate the common data pool. Perhaps because of this great faith, science has a way of being very harsh with those who break the faith (e.g., Kammerer's suicide) and very unforgiving. A clearly established fraud by a scientist is not, nor can it be, overlooked. There are no second chances. The sanctions are severe not only because the faith is great but also because detection is so difficult. There is virtually no way a fraud can be detected as such in the normal course of events.

The charge of fraud is such a serious one that it is leveled only at the peril of the accuser, and suspicions of fraud are not sufficient bases to discount the data collected by a given laboratory. Sometimes such a suspicion is raised when investigators are unwilling to let others see their data or when the incidence of data-destroying fires exceeds the limits of credibility (Wolins, 1962). It would be a useful convention to have all scientists agree to an open-data-books policy. Only rarely, after all, is the question of fraud raised by him who wants to see another's data, although other types of errors do turn up on such occasions. But if there is to be an open-books system, the borrower must make it convenient for the lender. A request to "send me all your data on verbal conditioning" made of a scientist who has for ten years been collecting data on that subject rightly winds up being ignored. If data are reasonably requested, the reason for the request given as an accompanying courtesy, they can be duplicated at the borrower's expense and then given to the borrower. Such a data-sharing system not only would serve to allay any doubts about the extent and type of errors in a set of data but would, of course, often reveal to the borrower something very useful to him though it was not useful to the original data collector.

The basic control for intentional errors in science, as for other types of error, is the tradition of replication of research findings. In the sciences generally this has sometimes led to the discovery of intentional errors. Perhaps, though, in the behavioral sciences this must be less true. The reason is that whereas all are agreed on the desirability or even necessity of replication, behavioral scientists have learned that unsuccessful replication is so common that we hardly know what it means when one's data don't confirm another's. Always there are sampling differences, different subjects, and different experimenters. Often there are procedural differences so trivial on the surface that no one would expect them to make a difference, yet, when the results are in, it is to these we turn in part to account for the different results. We require replication but can conclude too little from the failure to achieve confirming data. Still, replication has been used to suggest the occurrence of intentional error, as when Azrin's group (1961) suggested that Verplanck's (1955) data collectors had deceived him. In fact, it cannot be established that they did simply because Azrin's group had been deceived by their data collectors. Science, it is said, is self-correcting, but in the behavioral sciences especially, it corrects only very slowly.

It seems clear that the best control of intentional error is its prevention. In order to prevent these errors, however, we would have to know something about their causes. There seems to be agreement on that point but few clues as to what these causes might be. Sometimes in the history of science the causes have been so idiosyncratic that one despairs of making any general guesses about them, as when a scientist sought instant eminence or to embarrass another, or when an assistant deceived the investigator to please him. Crespi (1945–46) felt that poor morale was a cause of cheating among survey research interviewers. But what is the cause of poor morale? And what of the possibility that better morale might be associated with worsened performance, a possibility implied by the research of Kelley and Ring (1961)? Of course, we need to investigate the problem more systematically, but here the clarion call for "more research" is likely to go unheeded. Research on events so rare is no easy matter.

There is no evidence on the matter, but it seems reasonable to suppose that scientists may be affected by the widespread data fabrication they encountered in laboratory courses when they were still undergraduates. The attitude of acceptance of intentional error under these circumstances might have a carry-over effect into at least some scientists' adult lives. Perhaps it would be useful to discuss with undergraduate students in the various sciences the different types of experimenter effects. They should, but often do not, know about observer effects, interpreter effects, and intentional effects, though they quickly learn of these latter effects. If instructors imposed more negative sanctions on data fabrication at this level of education, perhaps there would be less intentional erring at more advanced levels.

Whereas most instructors of laboratory courses in various disciplines tend to be very conscious of experimental procedures, students tend to show more outcome-consciousness than procedure-consciousness. That is, they are more interested in the data they obtain than in what they did to obtain those data. Perhaps the current system of academic reward for obtaining the "proper" data reinforces this outcome-consciousness, and perhaps it could be changed somewhat. The selection of laboratory experiments might be such that interspersed with the usual, fairly obvious demonstrations there would be some simple procedures that demonstrate phenomena that are not well understood and are not highly reliable. Even for students who "read ahead" in their texts it would be difficult to determine what the "right" outcome should be. Academic emphasis for all the exercises should be on the procedures rather than on the results. What the student needs to learn is, not that learning curves descend, but how to set up a demonstration of learning phenomena, how to observe the events carefully, record them accurately, report them thoroughly, and interpret them sensibly and in some cases even creatively.

A general strategy might be to have all experiments performed before the topics they are designed to illustrate are taken up in class. The spirit, consistent with that endorsed by Bakan (1965), would be "What happens if we do thus-and-so" rather than "Now please demonstrate what has been shown to be true." The procedures would have to be spelled out very explicitly for students, and generally this is already done. Not having been told what to expect and not being graded for getting "good" data, students might be more carefully observant, attending to the phenomena before them without the single set which would restrict their perceptual field to those few events that illustrate a particular point. It is not inconceivable that under such less restrictive conditions, some students would observe phenomena that have not been observed before. That is unlikely, of course, if they record only that the rat turned right six times in ten trials. Observational skills may sharpen, and especially so if the instructor rewards with praise the careful observation and recording of the organism's response. The results of a laboratory demonstration experiment are not new or exciting to the instructor, but there is no reason why they cannot be for the student. The day may even come when classic demonstration experiments are not used at all in laboratory courses, and then it need not be dull even for the instructor. That the day may really come soon is suggested by the fact that so many excellent teachers are already requiring that at least one of the scheduled experiments be completely original with the student. That, of course, is more like Science, less like Science-Fair.

If we are seriously interested in shifting students' orientations from outcome-consciousness to procedure-consciousness there are some implications for us, their teachers, as well. One of these has to do with a change in policy regarding the evaluation of research. To evaluate research too much in terms of its results is to illustrate outcome-consciousness, and we do it very often. Doctoral committees too often send the candidate back to the laboratory to run another group of subjects because the experiment as originally designed (and approved by them) yielded negative results. Those universities show wisdom that protect the doctoral candidate from such outcome-consciousness by regarding the candidate's thesis proposal as a kind of contract, binding on both student and faculty.

The same problem occurs in our publication policies. One can always account for an unexpected, undesired, or negative result by referring to the specific procedures employed. That this occurs so often is testament to our outcome-consciousness. What we may need is a system for evaluating research based only on the procedures employed. If the procedures are judged appropriate, sensible, and sufficiently rigorous to permit conclusions from the results, the research cannot then be judged inconclusive on the basis of the results and rejected by the referees or editors. Whether the procedures were adequate would be judged independently of the outcome. To accomplish this might require that procedures only be submitted initially for editorial review or that only the result-less section be sent to a referee or, at least, that an evaluation of the procedures be set down before the referee or editor reads the results. This change in policy would serve to decrease the outcome-consciousness of editorial decisions, but it might lead to an increased demand for journal space. This practical problem could be met in part by an increased use of "brief reports" which summarize the research in the journal but promise the availability of full reports to interested workers. Journals such as the *Journal of Consulting Psychology* and *Science* are already making extensive use of briefer reports. If journal policies became less outcome-conscious, particularly in the matter of negative results, psychological researchers might not unwittingly be taught by these policies that negative results are useless and might as well be suppressed. In Part III negative results will be discussed further. Here, as long as the discussion has focused on editorial policies which are so crucial to the development of our scientific life styles and thinking modes, it should be mentioned that the practice of reading manuscripts for critical review would be greatly improved if the authors' name and affiliation were routinely omitted before evaluation.[1] Author data, like experimental results, detract from the independent assessment of procedures.

[1] Both Gardner Lindzey and Kenneth MacCorquodale have advocated this procedure. The usual objection is that to know a man's name and affiliation provides very useful information about the quality of his work. Such information certainly seems relevant to the process of predicting what a man will do, and that is the task of the referee of a research proposal submitted to a research funding agency. When the work is not being proposed but rather reported as an accomplished fact, it seems difficult to justify the assessment of its merit by the reputation of its author.

4

Biosocial Attributes

In the last three chapters some effects of experimenters on their research have been discussed. These effects have operated without the experimenter directly influencing the organisms or materials being studied. In this chapter, and in the ones to follow, the discussion will turn to those effects of experimenters that operate by influencing the events or behaviors under study.

The physical and biological sciences were able to provide us with illustrations of those experimenter effects not influencing the materials studied. It seems less likely that these sciences could provide us with examples of experimenter effects that do influence the materials studied. The speed of light or the reaction of one chemical with another or the arrangement of chromosomes within a cell is not likely to be affected by individual differences among the investigators interested in them. As we move from physics, chemistry, and molecular biology to those disciplines concerned with larger biological systems, we begin to encounter more examples of how the investigator can affect his subject. By the time we reach the level of the behavioral sciences there can be no doubt that experimenters may unintentionally affect the very behavior in which they are interested.

Christie (1951) tells us how experienced observers in an animal laboratory could judge which of several experimenters had been handling a rat by the animal's behavior in a maze or while being picked up. Gantt (1964) noted how a dog's heart rate could drop dramatically (from 160 to 140) simply because a certain experimenter was present. The importance to an animal's performance of its relationship to the experimenter has also been pointed out for horses (Pfungst, 1911), sheep (Liddell, 1943), and porpoises (Kellogg, 1961). If animal subjects can be so affected by their interaction with a particular experimenter, we would expect that human subjects would also be, perhaps even more so. Our primary focus in this and in the following chapters will be on those characteristics of experimenters that have been shown to affect unintentionally the responses of their human subjects.

The study of individual differences among people proceeds in several ways. Originally it was enough to show that such characteristics as height, weight, and intelligence were distributed throughout a population and that the shape of the distribution could be specified. Later when the fact and shape of individual differences were well known, various characteristics were correlated with one another. That led to answers to questions of the sort: are men or women taller, heavier, brighter, longer-lived? From these studies it was learned which of the characteristics studied were significantly associated with many others. It was found that age, sex, social class, education, and intelligence, for example, were all variables that made a great deal of difference if we were trying to predict other characteristics. Always, though, it was a characteristic of one person that was to be correlated with another characteristic of that person. In undertaking the study of individual differences among experimenters, the situation has become more complex and even more interesting. Here we are interested in relating characteristics of the experimenter, not to other of his characteristics, but rather to his subjects' responses. The usual study of individual differences is not necessarily social psychological. The relationship between person A's sex and person A's performance on a motor task is not of itself social psychological. But the relationship between person A's sex and person B's performance on a motor task is completely social psychological. That person A happens to be an experimenter rather than a parent, sibling, friend, or child has special methodological importance but no special substantive importance.

It has special methodological importance because so much of what has been learned by behavioral scientists has been learned within the context of the experimenter-subject interaction. If the personal characteristics of the data collector have determined in part the subjects' responses, then we must hold our knowledge the more lightly for it. There is no special substantive importance in the fact that person A is an experimenter rather than some other person because as a model of a human organism behaving and affecting others' behavior, the experimenter is no more a special case than is a parent, sibling, friend, or child. Whether we can generalize from the experimenter to other people is as open a question as whether we can generalize from parent to friend, friend to child, child to parent.

There are experiments by the dozen which show that different experimenters obtain from their comparable subjects significantly different responses (Rosenthal, 1962). In the pages to follow, however, major consideration is given only to those studies showing that a particular type of response by an experimental subject is associated with a particular characteristic of the experimenter. Experimenter attributes that have been shown to be partial determinants of subjects' responses are sometimes defined independently of the experiment in which their effect is to be assessed. That is the case for such biosocial characteristics as sex, race, age, religion, and for such psychometrically determined variables as anxiety, hostility, authoritarianism, and need for social approval. Sometimes the relevant experimenter attributes can be defined only in terms of the specific experimental situation and the specific experimenter-subject interaction. Such attributes include the status of the experimenter relative to the status of the subject, the warmth of the experimenter-subject relationship, and such experiment-specific events as whether the experimenter feels himself approved by the principal investigator or whether the subject has surprised him with his responses.

Quite a little is known about the relationship between these different experimenter variables and subjects' behavior, but little is known of the mechanisms accounting for the relationships. For example, we shall see that male and female experimenters often obtain different responses from their subjects. But that may be due to the fact that males and females look different or that males and females conduct the experiment slightly differently, or both of these. Does a dark-skinned survey interviewer obtain different responses to questions about racial segregation because of his dark skin or because he asks the questions in a different tone of voice or because of both these factors? In principle, we can distinguish active from passive experimenter effects. Active effects are those associated with unintended differences in the experimenter's behavior that can be shown to influence the subject's responses. Passive effects are those associated with no such differences in the behavior of the experimenters and therefore must be ascribed to their appearance alone.

In practice, the distinction between active and passive effects is an extremely difficult one, and no experiments have yet been reported that would be helpful in making such a distinction. It may help illustrate the distinction between active and passive effects to describe a hypothetical experiment designed to assess the relative magnitudes of these effects. Suppose that female experimenters administering a questionnaire to assess anxiety obtain consistently higher anxiety scores from their subjects than do male experimenters. To simplify matters we can assume that the questionnaire is virtually self-administering and that the experimenter is simply present in the same room with the subject. Our experiment requires 10 male experimenters and 10 females, each of whom administers the anxiety scale individually to 15 male subjects. For one third of their subjects, the experimenters excuse themselves and say that their presence is not required during the experiment and that they will be busy with other things which take them to the other side of an obvious one-way mirror. From there they can from time to time "see how you are doing." Another one third of the subjects are told the same thing except that the experimenter explains that he has to leave the building. The light is left on in the room on the other side of the one-way mirror so that the subject can see he is not being observed. The final third of the subjects are contacted in the usual way with the experimenter sitting in the same room but interacting only minimally.

Table 4-1 shows some hypothetical results. Mean anxiety scores are

TABLE 4—1

Mean Anxiety Scores as a Function of Experimenter Sex and Presence

	SEX OF EXPERIMENTER			
	Male	Female	Difference	Sum
I Experimenter present	14	20	+6	34
II Experimenter absent but observing	18	22	+4	40
III Experimenter absent, not observing	23	23	0	46
Sum	55	65	10	120

shown for subjects contacted by male and female experimenters in each of the three conditions. Female experimenters again obtained higher anxiety scores but not equally so in each condition. We learn that when the experimenter is neither present nor observing, the sex-of-experimenter effect has vanished. The brief greeting period was apparently insufficient to establish the sex effect, but the physical presence of the experimenter appears to augment the effect. For convenience assuming all differences to be significant, we conclude that female experimenters obtain higher anxiety scores from their subjects only if the subjects feel observed by their experimenters. We cannot say, however, whether the greater sex-of-experimenter effect in the "experimenter present" condition was due to any unintended behavior on the part of the experimenters or whether their physical presence was simply a more constant reminder that they were being observed by an experimenter of a particular sex. If the results had shown no difference between Conditions I and II, we could have concluded that the sex effect is more likely a passive rather than an active effect. That seems sensible since the belief of being observed by an experimenter of a given sex, without any opportunity for that experimenter to behave vis-à-vis his subject, was sufficient to account for the obtained sex effects.

Often in our discussion of the effects of various experimenter attributes on subjects' responses we shall wish that data of the sort just now invented were really available. Sex, age, and race are variables so immediately assessable that there is a temptation to assume them to be passive in their effects. That assumption should be held lightly until it can be shown that the sex, age, and race of an experimenter are not correlated with specific behaviors in the experiment. Conversely, experimenter's "warmth" sounds so behavioral that we are tempted to assume that it is active in its effects. Yet a "warm" experimenter may actually have a different fixed appearance from a cooler experimenter.

The order of discussion of experimenter attributes proceeds in this and the following chapters from (1) those that appear most directly obvious (i.e., sex) to (2) those that are thought to be relatively fixed psychological characteristics (i.e., need for approval) to (3) those that seem quite dependent on the interpersonal nature of the experiment to (4) those that are very highly situational. This organization is arbitrary and it should be remembered that many of the attributes discussed may be correlated with each other.

Experimenter's Sex

A good deal of research has been conducted which shows that male and female experimenters sometimes obtain significantly different data from their subjects. It is not always possible to predict for any given type of experiment just how subjects' responses will be affected by the experimenter's sex, if indeed there is any effect at all. In the area of verbal learning the results of three experiments are illustrative. Binder, McConnell, and Sjoholm (1957) found that their attractive female experimenter obtained significantly better learning from her subjects than did a husky male experimenter, described as an "ex-marine." Some years later Sarason and Harmatz (1965) found that their male experimenter obtained significantly better learning than did their female experimenter. Ferguson and Buss (1960) round out this illustration by their report of no difference between a male and female experimenter. This last experiment also provides a clue as to how we may reconcile these inconsistent but statistically quite real findings. Ferguson and Buss had their experimenters behave aggressively to some of their subjects and neutrally to others. When the experimenter behaved more aggressively there was decreased learning. If we can assume that Binder and associates' ex-marine officer gave an aggressive impression to his subjects, their results seem consistent with those of Ferguson and Buss. However, we would have to assume further that Sarason and Harmatz's female experimenter was perceived as more aggressive by her subjects, and for this we have no good evidence. Another experiment by Sarason (1962), in any case, tends to weaken or at least to complicate the proffered interpretation. In this study, Sarason employed 10 male and 10 female experimenters in a verbal learning experiment. Subjects were to construct sentences and were reinforced for the selection of hostile verbs by the experimenter's saying "good" or by his flashing a blue light. More hostile experimenters of both sexes tended to obtain more hostile responses ($p < .10$). If we can assume that those experimenters earning higher hostility scores behaved more aggressively toward their subjects, then we have a situation hard to reconcile with the results presented by Ferguson and Buss. A further complication in the Sarason experiment was that the relationship between experimenter hostility and the acquisition of hostile responses was particularly marked when the experimenters were males rather than females.

Perhaps, though, the recitation of hostile verbs is a very special case of verbal learning, especially when it is being correlated with the hostility of the experimenters. One wonders whether more hostile experimenters would also be more effective reinforcing agents for first-person pronouns. Sarason and Minard (1963) provide the answer, which, though a little equivocal, must be interpreted as a "no." Hostility of experimenters neither alone nor in interaction with sex of experimenter affected the rate of selecting the first-person pronouns which were reinforced by the eight male and eight female experimenters of this study. Of very real interest to our general discussion of experimenter attributes and situational variables was the finding that the verbal learning of first-person pronouns was a complex function of experimenter sex, hostility, and prestige; subject sex, hostility, and degree of personal contact between experimenter and subject. It appears that at least in studies of verbal conditioning, when an experiment is so designed as to permit the assessment of complex interactions, these interactions are forthcoming in abundance. Only rarely, however, are most of them predictable or even interpretable.

In tasks requiring motor performance as well as in verbal learning, for young children as well as for college students, the sex of the experimenter may make a significant difference. Stevenson and Odom (1963) employed two male and two female experimenters to administer a lever-pulling task to children ages six to seven and ten to eleven. From time to time the children were rewarded for pulling the lever by being shown various pictures on a filmstrip. During the first minute, no reinforcements were provided in order that a base line for each subject's rate of pulling could be determined. Even during this first minute, significant sex-of-experimenter effects were found ($p < .001$). Subjects contacted by male experimenters made over 30 percent more responses than did subjects contacted by female experimenters. This large effect was the more remarkable for the fact that the experimenter was not even present during the subject's task performance. Experimenters left their subjects' view immediately after having instructed them.

Stevenson, Keen, and Knights (1963) provide additional data that male experimenters obtain greater performance than female experimenters in a simple motor task, in this case, dropping marbles in a hole. As in the other experiment, the first minute served as a base rate measure after which the experimenter began regularly to deliver compliments on the subjects' performance. This time the subjects were younger still, ages three to five. Subjects contacted by male experimenters dropped about 18 percent more marbles into the holes than did subjects contacted by female experimenters during the initial one-minute period ($p < .05$). As expected, female experimenters' subjects increased their rate of marble dropping after the reinforcement procedure began. Relative to the increasing performance of subjects contacted by female experimenters, those contacted by males showed a significant decrement of performance during the following period of reinforced performance ($p < .01$). The interpretation the investigators gave to the significant sex-of-experimenter effect was particularly appropriate to their very young subjects. Such young children have relatively much less contact with males, and this may have made them anxious or excited over the interaction with the male experimenter. For simple tasks this might have served to increase performance which then fell off as the excitement wore off from adaptation or from the soothing effect of the experimenter's compliments. The anxiety-reducing aspect of these statements might have more than offset their intended reinforcing properties.

We have already encountered the fact of interaction in the study of sex of experimenter in the work of Sarason (1962). One of the most frequently investigated variables, and one that often interacts with experimenter's sex, is the sex of the subject. Again we take our illustration from Stevenson (1961). The task, as before, is that of dropping marbles, and after the first minute the experimenters begin to reinforce the children's performance by regularly complimenting them. The six male and six female experimenters administered the task to children in three age groups: three to four, six to seven, nine to ten. Although the individual differences among the experimenters of either sex were greater than the effect of experimenter sex itself, there was a tendency for male experimenters to obtain slightly higher performance from their subjects ($t = 1.70$, $p < .10$, pooling individual experimenter effects and all interactions). When the experimenters began to reinforce their subjects' performance after the first minute, female experimenters obtained a greater increase in performance than did male experimenters, but only for the youngest (3–4) children. Among the oldest children (9–10) there was a tendency ($p < .10$) for a reversal of this effect. Among these children, male experimenters obtained the greater increase in performance. These findings show how sex of experimenter can interact with the age of subjects. It was among the middle group of children (age 6–7) that the sex of subjects became an interacting variable most clearly. Male experimenters obtained a greater increase of performance from their female subjects, and female experimenters obtained the greater increase from their male subjects. Although less significantly so, the same tendency was found among the older (9–10) children. Stevenson's alternative interpretations of these results were in terms of the psychoanalytic theory of development as well as in terms of the relative degree of deprivation of contact with members of the experimenter's sex.

The interacting effects of the experimenter's and subject's sex are not restricted to those studies in which the subjects are children. Stevenson and Allen (1964) had 8 male and 8 female experimenters conduct a marble sorting task with 128 male and 128 female college students. For the first 90 seconds subjects received no reinforcement for sorting the marbles by color. Thereafter the experimenter paid compliments to the subject on his or her performance. Once again, there were significant individual differences among the experimenters of both sexes in the rate of performance shown by their subjects. In addition, however, a significant interaction between the sex of subjects and sex of experimenters was obtained. When male experimenters contacted female subjects and when female experimenters contacted male subjects significantly more marbles were processed than when the experimenter and subject were of the same sex. This difference was significant during the first 30 seconds of the experiment and for the entire experiment as well. Even further support for the generality of the interaction of experimenter and subject sex was provided by Stevenson and Knights (1962), who obtained the now predicted interaction when the subjects were mentally retarded, averaging an IQ of less than 60.

In trying to understand their obtained interactions, Stevenson and Allen postulated that the effects could be due to the increased competitiveness, higher anxiety, or a greater desire to please when the experimenter was of the opposite sex. There is no guarantee, however, as Stevenson (1965) points out, that experimenters may not treat subjects of the opposite sex differently than subjects of the same sex. A little later in this section some data will be presented which bear on this hypothesis.

If the interaction between experimenter and subject sex is significant in such tasks as marble sorting and the construction of simple sentences, we would expect the phenomenon as well when the subjects' tasks and responses are more dramatic ones. Walters, Shurley, and Parsons (1962) conducted an experiment in sensory deprivation which is instructive. Male and female subjects were floated in a tank of water for three hours and then responded to five questions about their experiences during their isolation period. Half the time subjects were contacted by a male experimenter, half the time by a female. The questions dealt with (1) feelings of fright, (2) the most unpleasant experience, (3) sexual feelings, (4) anything learned about oneself from the experience, and (5) what the total experience was reminiscent of. All responses were coded on a scale which measured the degree of psychological involvement or unusualness of the phenomena experienced. If a subject reported no experience, his score was 0. If he reported hallucinations with real feeling, the response was scored 5, the maximum. Intermediate between these extremes was a range of scores from 1 to 4. For two of the questions the interaction between sex of experimenter and sex of subject was significant. To the question dealing with sexual feelings, subjects contacted by an experimenter of the same sex gave replies earning psychological "richness" scores three times higher than when contacted by an experimenter of the opposite sex. This was the most significant finding statistically and in terms of absolute magnitude. In a subsequent study, although in smaller and less significant form, the same effect was obtained (Walters, Parsons, & Shurley, 1964). This particular interaction seems less difficult to interpret than that found for the marble sorting experiment. Even in an experimental laboratory, subjects regard the "mixed company" dyad as not a place to discuss sexual matters freely.

In survey research, as in the experimental laboratory, the inhibiting effects of "mixed company" dyads have been demonstrated. Benney, Riesman, and Star (1956) reported that when given an opportunity to assess the cause of abnormal behavior, respondents gave sexual interpretations about 25 percent more often when their interviewer was of their own, rather than the opposite, sex. About the same percentage difference occurred when a fuller, frank discussion of possible sexual bases for emotional disturbance was invited. Interestingly, moralistic responses were more frequent when the interviewer and respondent were of the opposite sex. Apparently, then, in interviewer-respondent dyads, sex matters are less likely to be brought up spontaneously in mixed company, but if they are brought up by the interviewer, opposite-sexed respondents are more likely to take a negative, harsh, or moralistic stance than same-sexed respondents. Additional evidence for this interpretation has been presented by Hyman and co-workers (1954).

In projective methods of appraising personality, the sex of the experimenter has also been found to affect the subjects' responses—sometimes. Masling (1960) has summarized this literature which consists of some studies showing a sex effect, and some not.

Earlier in this chapter the question was raised whether the effects of experimenter attributes were passive or active. That is, do different experimenters elicit different responses because they have a different appearance, because they behave differently toward their subjects, or both? Some data relevant to, but not decisive for, these questions are available. The task was one of person perception. Subjects were asked to rate the degree of success or failure reflected in the faces of people pictured in photographs. The ratings of the photographs could range from −10, extreme failure, to +10, extreme success. The standardization of these particular photos was such that their mean rating was actually zero, or very neutral with respect to success or failure. There were 5 male and 5 female experimenters who contacted 35 female and 23 male subjects. About half the interactions between experimenters and subjects were filmed without the knowledge of either. Details of the procedure, but not the data to be reported here, have been described elsewhere (Rosenthal, Friedman, & Kurland, 1965). Table 4-2 shows the mean photo ratings obtained by the male and female experi-

TABLE 4—2

Mean Photo Ratings by Four of Subjects

		SEX OF EXPERIMENTER	
		Male	Female
SEX OF SUBJECT	Male	+0.14	+0.40
	Female	+0.31	−1.13

menters from their male and female subjects. Only the results from those 33 subjects whose interaction was filmed are included. Female subjects, when contacted by female experimenters, tended to rate the photographs as being of less successful persons than did the other three combinations of experimenter and subject sex ($p < .05$), which did not differ from one another. When the sex of subjects was disregarded it was found that male experimenters were significantly ($p < .05$) more variable ($\sigma = 1.97$) in the data they obtained from their subjects than were female experimenters ($\sigma = 0.61$). (A similar tendency was obtained by Stevenson [1961], though there the effect was not so significant statistically.) When the sex of the subjects was considered, it developed that when experimenters and subjects were of the same sex the variability of subjects' ratings ($\sigma = 1.68$) was significantly ($p = .06$) greater than when the dyads were composed of opposite-sexed persons ($\sigma = 0.78$).

Some data are available which suggest that the effects of experimenter sex are active rather than simply passive. It appears that male and female experimenters behave differently toward their subjects in the experiment. In connection with two other studies observations were made of the experimenters' glancing, smiling, posture, activity level, and the accuracy of his reading of the instructions (Friedman, 1964; Katz, 1964). Both workers kindly made their raw data available for this analysis. During the brief period preceding the experimenter's formal instructions to the subject, the experimenter asked the subject for such identifying data as name, age, class, and college major. In this preinstruction period there was no difference between male and female experimenters in the number of glances they exchanged with their subjects. However, experimenters tended to exchange more glances with their female subjects. When interacting with male subjects, 38 percent of the experimenters exchanged at least some glances, but when interacting with females 90 percent exchanged glances. The average number of glances exchanged with male subjects was .31 and with females .75 ($p < .10$). This finding that females drew about 2.4 times as many glance exchanges as males is close numerically to the ratio of 2.9 reported by Exline (1963), in spite of the differences in the group composition, experimental procedures, and measures of glancing behavior employed in his and the present study.

During the reading of the formal instructions to subjects, an interaction appeared in the glances exchanged. Now experimenters exchanged more than twice as many glances with subjects of their own sex (mean = 1.44) as with subjects of the opposite sex (mean = 0.62) ($p < .10$).

In this experiment, the subject's task was to rate the 10 photos in sequence, and during this rating phase of the experiment the experimenter's task was to present the photos in the correct order. Richard Katz made observations of the experimenters' glancing behavior separately for those times when the experimenter was actually presenting a photograph and when the experimenter was preparing to present the next stimulus. There was an interesting difference in the glancing behavior of experimenters as a function of the phases of the stimulus presentation. During the photo presentations male subjects were glanced at more (mean = 1.9) than female subjects (mean = 1.5), the difference not reaching significance ($p < .20$). During the preparation periods, however, male subjects were glanced at less (mean = 1.1) than female subjects (mean = 1.7). This interaction effect was significant ($p < .05$) and was shown by all but one of the experimenters. During the presentation period the subject is somewhat "on the spot." The experimenter is just sitting expectantly, and the subject has to do something and wants to do it well. It could easily be that during this mutually tense moment experimenters avoid eye contact with their female subjects in order to spare them any embarrassment. This seems an especially reasonable interpretation in the light of recent data provided by Exline, Gray, and Schuette (1965), who reported that eye contact was reduced during interviews creating greater tension.

In the moments following the subject's response the pressure is off. As the experimenters prepare their next stimulus for presentation, they need not fear for their female subjects' tension, and indeed their increased glancing at this point toward their female subjects may serve to reassure them that all is well. Looking at the subject during the rating period of the experiment is in fact correlated with smiling at the subject (rho = .63, $p = .10$), although smiling at the subject is very rare during this stage of the experiment and, during either the presentation or the preparation period considered separately, is not significantly related to glancing.

From these results, it can be seen that experimenters do in fact behave differently toward their subjects and that the differences are related sometimes to the sex of the subject, sometimes to the sex of the experimenter, and sometimes to both these variables. The particular pattern of experimenter behavior described suggests that at least in the psychological experiment, chivalry is not dead. Female subjects seem to be treated more attentively and more considerately than male subjects.

While discussing the differences in experimenter behavior during the stimulus presentation and stimulus preparation periods, another example of experimenter sex effect can be given. All five of the female experimenters showed more smiling during the preparation than the presentation period with an average 35 percent increase of smiles ($p < .05$). Among male experimenters, however, only one showed any increase, and the average increase was only about 2 percent. It appears that sometimes during those moments of the experimental procedure when the need for formality and austerity seems lessened, females, even when functioning as quite competent experimenters, behave more as females usually do. Those sociological writers who have been concerned with sex role differentiation would probably not be surprised either at these data or at their interpretation. Parsons (1955), Parsons, Bales, and Shils (1953), and Zelditch (1955) have all commented on the feminine role as that of greater socioemotional concern and the masculine role as that of greater concern with task accomplishment. The data presented so far and those to follow support this conception. Not only is the female more of a socioemotional leader when she is the leader but she seems much more to be led socioemotionally when she is the follower. For example, during the brief period preceding the formal instructions, the female subjects were smiled at significantly more often than were male subjects, regardless of the sex of the experimenter ($p < .05$). When contacting female subjects, 70 percent of the experimenters smiled at least a little, but when contacting male subjects only about 12 percent did so. The mean amount of smiling at female subjects by all experimenters was 0.50; at male subjects it was only 0.06. During the subsequent reading of the instructions, all experimenters showed less smiling and only 40 percent of the experimenters smiled at female subjects, but no experimenter smiled even a little at any male subject. Most of the smiling in this phase of the experiment was done by female experimenters (mean = 0.57) rather than males (mean = 0.10), though this difference was not very significant ($p = .15$). To summarize, female experimenters tended to smile more, and female subjects were recipients of significantly more smiles.

Although no one has written what Friedman (1964) calls an etiquette for the psychological experimenter, the reaction of most laboratory psychologists to these data has been to assume that female experimenters might be less competent at conducting experiments if they smile more than they "should." Smiling seems frivolous in such a serious interaction as that between experimenter and subject. But data are available which show that females, by an important criterion, are at least as competent as males. According to scoring categories developed by Friedman (1964), a scale of accuracy of instruction reading was developed. Errors in the reading of instructions would lower the score from the maximum possible value of 2.00. A more competent experimenter, as a minimum, should read the instructions to subjects as they were written. Accuracy of instruction reading, then, is an index of experimental competence, though not, of course, the only one. Table 4-3 shows the male and female experimenters' mean ac-

TABLE 4—3

Accuracy of Instruction Reading

| | | SEX OF EXPERIMENTER | | | |
		Male	Female	Difference	p
SEX OF	Male	1.62	2.00	+.38	.20
SUBJECT	Female	1.50	1.87	+.37	.12

curacy scores when the subjects were males and when they were females. For both male and female subjects, female experimenters read their instructions more accurately than did male experimenters (combined $p < .05$). Among female experimenters, 80 percent read their instructions perfectly to all subjects, whereas only 20 percent of male experimenters were that accurate. Considering the total number of times instructions were read to subjects, female experimenters read them perfectly to 88 percent of their subjects, whereas male experimenters read them perfectly only to 56 percent of their subjects.

There were no effects of experimenter's or subject's sex on the speed with which the experiment proceeded except during those periods of the rating task itself when the experimenter was preparing to show the next stimulus photo. Table 4-4 shows the mean time in seconds required during this part of the interaction by male and female experimenters when contacting male and female subjects. The only significant effect was of the interaction variety. Male experimenters were significantly slower in their preparation for presenting the next stimulus photo when the subjects were females than when they were males. Similarly female experimenters were slower when interacting with male rather than female subjects, although this tendency was

TABLE 4—4

Time Required for Stimulus Preparation

SEX OF EXPERIMENTER

		Male	Female	Difference	p
SEX OF SUBJECT	Male	33.2	45.4	+12.2	< .20
	Female	38.4	40.3	+ 1.9	> .20
	Difference	+5.2	−5.1		
	p	< .01	> .20		

not significant statistically. With the average male experimenter in his early twenties and the average female subject in her late teens, it appeared almost as though the male experimenters sought to prolong this portion of their interaction with their female subjects. This period of the experiment was earlier interpreted as having tension-releasing characteristics compared to the periods of tension increase (stimulus presentation) which preceded and followed these preparation periods. The few extra seconds of relaxed contact may have been stretched somewhat because of their intrinsic social interest when the dyads were of opposite-sexed members. Because the prerating periods were such busy times for the experimenter we would not expect him to utilize them for even covertly social purposes.

Observations were also available which told the degree to which the experimenter leaned in the direction of each of his subjects. Experimenters were seated diagonally across the edge of a table from their subjects so that the leaning was in a sideways direction that tended to bring experimenter and subject closer together. Table 4-5 shows the mean index numbers describing how much male and female experimenters tended to reduce the distances between themselves and their male and female subjects during the entire rating period. The results for the entire interaction are similarly significant, although the instruction-reading and preinstruction periods by themselves did not show significant effects. When female subjects were contacted there was no sex-of-experimenter effect. When subjects were males, however, male experimenters leaned closer than did female experimenters ($p < .05$). Relative to male experimenters, females may have been more bashful or modest in assuming any posture that would move them closer to their male subjects.

During the reading of the instructions male experimenters tended

TABLE 4—5

Degree of Leaning Toward Subjects

		SEX OF EXPERIMENTER	
		Male	Female
SEX OF SUBJECT	Male	1.35	0.75
	Female	0.99	0.96

($p < .10$) to show a higher level of general body activity (mean $= 6.2$) than did female experimenters (mean $= 4.4$). This was true regardless of the sex of the subjects contacted. Then, in the period during which subjects made their actual photo ratings, there was a tendency for all experimenters to show a greater degree of general body activity when their subjects were males (mean $= 4.4$) rather than females (3.9). This difference was not very significant statistically, however ($p = .15$). In our culture, general body activity is associated more with males (Kagan & Moss, 1962, p. 100); and male psychological experimenters, as any other members and products of their culture, do show more body activity in the experiment. That both male and female experimenters may show greater activity when contacting male subjects suggests that there may have been a kind of activity contagion and legitimation in the interactions with male subjects, who, we can only assume, were themselves more active during the experiment.

TABLE 4—6

Experimenter's Body Activity

		SEX OF EXPERIMENTER		
		Male	Female	Means
SEX OF SUBJECT	Male	4.6	4.3	4.45
	Female	4.1	3.8	3.95
	Means	4.35	4.05	4.20

Unfortunately, systematic observations have not yet been made of the subjects' activity level. Table 4-6 is relevant to the interpretation. Although none of the effects reach statistical significance, it can be seen that during the rating task on which these means are based, male experimenters move more, and most of all when contacting male subjects. Female experimenters move less, and least of all when contacting female subjects. Sex differences in the degree of motility of the experimenters seem to be well augmented by the hypothesized contagion and legitimation effects of being in interaction with people who very likely vary in their own degree of body motility.

Another line of evidence is available that male and female experimenters behave differently as they conduct their psychological experiments. Suzanne Haley kindly made the raw data available for this analysis. She had 12 male and 2 female experimenters administer the same photo-rating task to 86 female subjects. After the experiment, subjects were asked to rate their experimenters on how well they liked them and on 26 behavioral variables—e.g., degree of friendliness of the experimenter. Table 4-7 shows

TABLE 4—7

Ratings of Experimenters and Sex of Experimenter

SOURCE OF RATINGS

Ratings	Subjects		Observers	
	r_{pb}	p	r_{pb}	p
Friendly	+.32	.005	+.47	.05
Pleasant	+.37	.001	+.28	—
Interested	+.27	.02	+.36	—
Encouraging	+.27	.02	+.35	—
Enthusiastic	+.27	.02	+.41	.10
Pleasant-voiced	+.42	.001	−.11	—
Expressive-voiced	+.26	.02	+.20	—
Leg activity	+.30	.01	+.20	—
Body activity	+.23	.05	+.31	—
Median	+.27	.02	+.31	—

the ratings of the experimenter's behavior as a function of the sex of the experimenter. The correlations are point biserials and when positive in sign indicate that it was the male experimenters who were rated higher on the scales listed in the first column. The first column gives the correlations resulting from this analysis. It can be seen from the table that the female subjects of this experiment rated their male experimenters as more friendly in general, as having more pleasant and expressive voices, and as being more active physically. The nine correlations tabulated for this analysis were those significant at the .05 level out of the total of 26 possible. (As might be expected from the obtained correlations, male experimenters were also better liked, $r_{pb} = .34$, $p < .005$.) The magnitudes of the tabulated correlations tend to be conservative because only 10 of the 86 subjects were contacted by female experimenters. The median correlation of $+.27$ becomes $+.40$ when corrected for this imbalance.

Some additional preliminary data are available which suggest the stability of these correlations. The same photo rating task was administered by 15 male and 3 female experimenters to a total of 57 subjects; 40 females and 17 males. All these interactions were recorded on sound film and then rated by three observers for just the preinstruction-reading period on the dimensions listed in Table 4-7. The right side of the table gives the correlations. Male experimenters were judged more friendly and pleasant as before. With one exception, the correlations between the sex and behavior of the experimenter were similar to those obtained from the analysis of Haley's data. That exception was the variable of pleasantness of voice, which in this replication was reversed in sign though very small in magnitude. Since in this study only 16 df were available, only two of the correlations reached even the .10 level of significance.

From the results of both these studies it seems reasonable to conclude that, either by asking the subjects themselves or by asking observers who were not participants in the experiment, the behavior and manner of experimenters are associated with their sex. For the person perception task employed, and when interacting primarily with female subjects, male experimenters behave in a more friendly, personally involved, and physically active manner. Since two of the three observers who rated the experimenters were themselves females, this conclusion must be tempered by the possibility that female subjects or observers are biased to perceive male experimenters in the direction indicated.

For the 18 experimenters and 57 subjects whose interactions were recorded on film, there were consistent differences in the way experimenters were judged to behave when their subjects were males (N = 17) as compared to females (N = 40). For the preliminary data now available, the instruction-reading phase of the interaction was rated by one group of observers (N = 4) who could see the films but not hear the sound track. Another group of judges (N = 3) heard the sound track of the films but could not see the interaction. Table 4-8 shows the correlations between the sex of the subject contacted and the ratings of the experimenter separately for those observers who could see but not hear and those who could hear but not see the interaction between experimenters and subjects. Of 17 rat-

TABLE 4—8

Video and Audio Channel Ratings of Experimenters and Sex of Subject

OBSERVATION CHANNEL

Ratings	Video: r_{pb}	Audio: r_{pb}
Liking	−.29	−.39
Friendly	−.21	−.35
Pleasant	−.33	−.29
Encouraging	−.30	−.31
Honest	−.33	−.26
Relaxed	−.32	−.21
Median	−.31	−.30

ings that could be made under both conditions, 6 showed a correlation of ±.20 or larger under both conditions of observation. In every one of these 6 cases the direction of the correlation was the same under both conditions of observation, and the numerical values agreed closely. Judging both by looking at the experimenters and also by listening to their tone of voice, experimenters were more likable, pleasant, friendly, encouraging, honest, and relaxed when contacting female subjects than when contacting male subjects. The absolute size of the correlations would probably have been larger if there had been a more nearly equal division of male and female subjects (50:50 rather than 70:30) and if the reliability of the observers' judgments had been higher. The median reliability of the video variables tabulated was only .37 and of the audio variables it was .17. Corrected for attenuation the median of the correlations under the video condition becomes −.53, $p < .03$, and under the audio condition the median correlation becomes −.65, $p < .01$.

From the preliminary analysis of the filmed interactions between experimenters and subjects it seems that male experimenters behave more warmly than do female experimenters, at least when the subjects are primarily females. In addition, both male and female experimenters behave more warmly toward their female than toward their male subjects. The more molecular observations (e.g., glancing) reported earlier and made by Neil Friedman and Richard Katz, in general, tend to support these conclusions with one exception. That was the finding that female experimenters, at least sometimes, smiled more at their subjects than did male experimenters. The results for the effect on experimenter behavior of the sex of the subject contacted, however, are sufficiently stable to warrant retention of the conclusion that in the psychological experiment, a certain degree of chivalry is maintained.

Within the past few years a number of investigators have pointed out the interacting effects of experimental variables and the sex of subjects (Carlson & Carlson, 1960; Hovland & Janis, 1959; Kagan & Moss, 1962; McClelland, 1965; Sarason, Davidson, Lighthall, Waite, & Ruebush, 1960). Both simple, across-the-board sex differences and interacting sex differences may have multiple sources, including those that are genetic, morphological, endocrinological, sociological, and psychological. To this list must now be added the variable of differential treatment of male and female subjects. An experiment employing male and female subjects is likely to be a different experiment for the males and for the females. Because experimenters behave differently to male and female subjects even while administering the same formally programmed procedures, male and female subjects may, psychologically, simply not be in the same experiment at all. In order to assess the extent to which obtained sex differences have been due to differential behavior toward male and female subjects, it would be necessary to compare sex differences obtained in those studies that depended for their data on a personal interaction with the subject and those that did not. It would be reassuring to learn that sex differences obtained in a personal interaction between experimenter and subject were also obtained in mailed-out questionnaires and in experiments in which instructions to subjects were tape recorded and self-administered. In Part III such methodological implications will be considered in detail.

Experimenter's Age

As in the case of the experimenter's sex, the age of the experimenter can be readily judged, and fairly accurately, by the subject. There has been less work done to assess the effects of the experimenter's age on subjects' responses than has been the case for experimenter's sex. What work has been done suggests that, at least sometimes, the experimenter's age does affect the subject's response. One recent investigation was carried out by Ehrlich and Riesman (1961). Their analysis was of data collected from a national sample of adolescent girls and included the girls' responses to four questions of a more or less projective nature. One of these questions, for example, involved the presentation of a picture of a group of girls in which someone suggested they all engage in behavior that one of the girl's parents had forbidden. The respondent was to say what that particular girl's response would be to the group's suggestion. The answers to the four questions could be coded as to whether they would be socially acceptable or unacceptable by parental standards.

The interviewers in this survey were all women, primarily of middle-class background, and ranging in age from the early twenties to the late sixties. The most dramatic effects of the interviewers' ages were found to depend on the subjects' ages. Among respondents aged 15 or younger there was only the smallest tendency for younger interviewers to be given more "unacceptable" type responses. Interviewers under 40 received 6 percent more such replies than interviewers over 40. Among the older girls, however, those over 15, the younger interviewers evoked 44 percent more unacceptable responses than did the older interviewers. It was the older girls, then, who were more sensitive to the age differences among interviewers and who, perhaps, felt relatively freer to say "unacceptable" things to people closer to themselves in age. In the case of interviewer's age, then, the effects were found not to be simple but rather interactive. Often, as we saw earlier in this chapter, the effects of experimenter's sex were similarly interactive rather than simple.

The results just now reported tell us of the relationship between a data collector's age and the subjects' responses, but they do not tell us whether it is the age per se that makes the difference. Older interviewers differ in various ways from younger ones, and perhaps they behave differently toward their subjects as well. Just this question was raised by Ehrlich and Riesman. They had available some psychometric data on their interviewers, including scores on their ascendance or dominance. There was a tendency, though not statistically significant, for the older interviewers to score as more ascendant. Presumably this difference in personality test scores was reflected in differences in behavior during the interview. The less imposing behavior of the younger interviewers may have made it easier for the older girls to voice their less acceptable responses.

An analysis cited earlier in connection with the effects of experimenter's sex also provides evidence bearing on the effects of experimenter's age (Benney, Riesman, & Star, 1956). The data suggest that when the response required is a frank discussion of sexual maladjustment, the age of the data collector makes some difference, but particularly so when the age of the subject is considered. Among subjects under 40 there were 10.5 percent more frank responses to interviewers under 40 than to interviewers over 40. However, among respondents over 40 there were 52.2 percent more frank responses for the younger than for the older interviewers. Combining male and female interviewers and male and female subjects, when both participants are over 40, a frank discussion of sex matters is simply less likely to occur.

Experimenter's Race

The skin color of the experimenter may also affect the responses of the subject (Cantril, 1944; Williams, 1964), though not all types of responses are equally susceptible (Williams & Cantril, 1945). Some of the evidence for the survey research situation is provided by Hyman et al. (1954). Just as older interviewers tended to receive more "proper" or acceptable responses from some of their subjects, so did white interviewers receive more proper or acceptable responses from their Negro respondents than did Negro interviewers. The data cited were collected during World War II. Half the Negro respondents were interviewed by white, half by Negro, interviewers. One of the questions asked was whether Negroes would be treated better or worse by the Japanese in the event they won the war. When interviewed by Negroes, only 25 percent of the respondents stated that they would be worse off under Japanese than under American rule. When interviewed by whites, however, 45 percent stated that they would be worse off under Japanese rule ($p < .001$). When interviewed by whites, only 11 percent of the Negroes stated that the army was unfair to Negroes, but when the interviewers were Negroes, 35 percent of respondents felt the army was discriminatory ($p < .001$).

Additional evidence of this type is presented by Summers and Hammonds (1965), who also present some interesting data of their own. Their data, complementing the Hyman data, suggest further the interacting nature of the skin color of the experimenter and the skin color of the subject. In their survey research, the respondents were white and were contacted by a research team consisting sometimes of two whites and sometimes of one white and one Negro. The questionnaire was concerned with racial prejudice. When both investigators were white, 52 percent of the respondents showed themselves to be highly prejudiced. When one of the investigators was Negro, only 37 percent were equally prejudiced. These results ($p < .001$) are the more remarkable for the fact that subjects responded in writing and anonymously. Just as Negro respondents were shown to say the "proper" thing more often to a white interviewer, so too did white respondents say the "right" thing more often to Negro data collectors.

The experimenter's skin color also interacts with other characteristics of the subject to affect the subject's response. In the Summers and Hammonds study, those respondents whose father's income was higher showed a greater sensitivity to the race of the data collector. When father's income was below $5,000, 17 percent of the subjects decreased their stated degree of racial prejudice when one experimenter was Negro ($p < .50$). When father's income was over $5,000 but less than $10,000, 30 percent of respondents claimed less prejudice ($p < .005$). When father's income was over $10,000 there was a 38 percent reduction in admitted prejudice ($p < .005$). As socioeconomic status increases, the lessons of politeness and social sensitivity seem better taught and better learned. The same trend appears when church attendance is substituted for father's income. When church attendance is minimal, only 13 percent of subjects show a decrease in admitted racial prejudice when one investigator is Negro. When church attendance is moderate, 21 percent ($p < .05$) show a decrease of prejudice, and when church attendance is very regular, 44 percent ($p < .001$) show sensitivity to the race of the experimenter. In this case, the lessons of the church seem to be the same as the lessons of the social class.

Even when the response investigated is physiological, the race of the experimenter may affect that response. Rankin and Campbell (1955) showed that the galvanic skin response showed a greater increase if the experimenter adjusting the apparatus was Negro rather than white. More recently, Bernstein (1965) reported that basal skin impedance (measured in kilohms) was higher when the experimenter was white rather than Negro regardless of the race of the subject. In general, the effect of experimenter's race on subjects' physiological responses is poorly understood and, up to the present, little studied.

A number of studies are available which suggest that performance on various psychological tests may be affected by the race of the experimenter. Employing a test of expression of hostility, Katz, Robinson, Epps, and Waly (1964) carried out just such a study employing a white and Negro experimenter. Half the time the Negro subjects had their task structured as an affectively neutral research procedure, and half the time the task was structured as an intelligence test. When the task was presented as a neutral one there were no significant effects of the experimenter's race on subjects' hostility scores. However, when the task was structured as an intelligence test, significantly less hostility was obtained when the experimenter was white ($p < .01$). The authors' interpretation of this finding was that Negroes tended to control their hostility more when contacted by a white rather than a Negro experimenter. This interpretation is very much in line with that implied by the data from survey research studies in which Negroes gave more "proper" responses to their white as compared to Negro interviewers.

When the tests really are tests of intellectual functioning of various kinds, the race of the experimenter also has its effects. Thus, Katz and his co-workers describe an experiment in which the task was similar to one of the subtests of standard tests of intelligence, in this case digit-symbol substitution. When the task was structured as a test of coordination, the Negro subjects performed better for the white than for the Negro experimenter. It was as though the subjects were unwilling to demonstrate their "good sense of rhythm" to the Negro but quite willing to demonstrate it for the white experimenter who might, in their eyes, have expected it. When the same task was structured as an intelligence test, performance was relatively better with the Negro than with the white experimenter. Perhaps again these subjects were doing what they perceived to be the socially appropriate thing—in this case performing not so brightly for the white experimenter.

There are, too, studies that showed no effects of experimenter skin color on subjects' intellectual performance. In the same study described, for example, Katz and his associates found no effects of the experimenter's race on the adequacy of subjects' concept formation. Other examples of negative results are given by Canady (1936) and Masling (1960).

Experimenter's Religion

The experimenter's religion as a variable affecting subjects' responses has been investigated primarily in the area of survey research. Hyman and his collaborators (1954) give us one example. In 1943, over 200 subjects were interviewed by Jewish and Gentile data collectors who asked whether Jews had too much, too little, or the right amount of influence in the business world. Of the Gentile subjects contacted by Gentile interviewers, 50 percent felt that Jews had too much influence. When the interviewers were Jewish, however, only 22 percent thought so. Once again the respondents seemed to have said the right thing. One caution in the interpretation of these data was advanced by Hyman et al. In this study, interviewers were free to pick their own respondents within certain limits, so that Jewish interviewers might, perhaps unwittingly, have chosen more sympathetic Gentile respondents.

Robinson and Rohde (1946) varied both the appearance of Jewishness and the Jewishness of the interviewer's name in their study of the effect of perceived religion of the interviewer on the extent of anti-Semitic responses in public opinion research. When interviewers neither looked Jewish nor gave Jewish names, about 23 percent of respondents felt that Jews had too much power. When the interviewer was Jewish-appearing but did not give a Jewish name, about 16 percent of subjects felt Jews had too much power. When the interviewer looked Jewish and gave a Jewish name, only 6 percent of respondents felt Jews had too much power. In this study, the samples assigned the different types of interviewer were well matched, so that the results are more likely due to the respondent's perception of the interviewer rather than to a selection bias on the part of the data collector. Unlike the situation described earlier when race of experimenter was the variable, it was the lower economic status subjects who were more sensitive to the religion of the investigator.

Much of what has been learned about the effects of various biosocial attributes of the data collector on the responses obtained from subjects has come from the field of survey research. This seems natural enough as has been pointed out by Hyman et al. (1954) and by Mosteller in a personal communication (1964). In that field the numbers of data collectors are large enough to permit the systematic evaluation of interviewer differences with or without an attempt to relate these differences to specific attributes of the interviewer. But there is no reason to assume that the effects obtained in survey research of various experimenter attributes would not hold in such other data-collecting contexts as the laboratory experiment. Particularly for the variables of experimenter age and religion, however, there is little direct evidence to date that they operate in the laboratory as they do in the field.

The general conclusion to be drawn from much of the research reviewed here seems to be that subjects tend to respond in the way they feel to be most proper in the light of the investigator's attributes. That subjects in experiments as well as respondents in surveys want to do the right thing and want to be well evaluated has been suggested by Orne (1962), Riecken (1962), and Rosenberg (1965).

Before leaving the general topic of the biosocial attributes of the experimenter as determinants of subjects' responses, it would be well to repeat a caution suggested earlier. There is no way to be sure that any of the effects discussed so far are due to the physical characteristics of the experimeter rather than to some correlated variables. In fact, it was found quite likely, especially for the variable of experimenter's sex, that experimenters differing in appearance also behave differently toward their subjects. It could be this behavioral variation more than the variation of physical attributes that accounts for the effects on subjects' responses.

5

Psychosocial Attributes

The experimenter attributes discussed in the last chapter were all readily assessable by inspection. The experimenter attributes to be discussed now are also readily assessable, but not simply by inspection. The anxiety or hostility of those experimenters functioning well enough to be experimenters at all must be assessed more indirectly, sometimes by simply asking the experimenter about it, more often by the use of standard psychological instruments.

Experimenter's Anxiety

Winkel and Sarason (1964) have shown that the anxiety level of the experimenter may interact complexly with subject variables and with experimental conditions in determining the verbal learning of the experimental subjects. They employed 24 male experimenters, all undergraduates, half of whom scored high on a scale of test anxiety and half of whom scored low. Subjects were 72 male and 72 female students of introductory psychology. Half the subjects scored as high-anxious and half as low-anxious. Results showed that when the experimenters were more anxious there was no difference between male and female subjects in their performance on the verbal learning task. However, when the experimenters were less anxious, female subjects performed better than males. The optimal combination of the experimenter's anxiety and the subject's anxiety and sex was that in which the subject was a low-anxious female in contact with a low-anxious experimenter. In this condition performance was better than in any of the others. This interaction was further complicated by the still higher order interaction which involved the additional variable of the type of instructions given the subjects. When the experimenter attribute under investigation is anxiety, just as in the case of experimenter's sex, extremely complicated interactions tend to emerge if the experiment allows for their assessment.

Sarason (1965) describes an unpublished study by Barnard (1963) which showed that degree of disturbance of the experimenter as determined from a phrase association task was a predictor of the subjects' degree of disturbance in the same task.

When the task is the interpretation of ink blots rather than the learning of verbal materials, the anxiety level of the experimenter as defined by his own Rorschach responses also makes a difference. More anxious experimenters obtained from their subjects Rorschach responses interpreted as more hostile and more passive than the responses obtained by experimenters judged less anxious. In addition, the more anxious experimenters obtained from their subjects more fantasy material and a higher degree of judged self-awareness (Cleveland, 1951; Sanders & Cleveland, 1953).

When the task involved memory for digits, a subtest of many standard tests of intelligence, the degree of "adjustment" or anxiety of the experimenter affected subjects' performance (Young, 1959). The measure of adjustment, a variable correlated generally with anxiety, was based on the Worchel Self Activity Inventory administered to introductory psychology students. These students then served as experimenters and administered the digit span test to their peers. Subjects who were contacted by more poorly adjusted experimenters performed better at the task than did subjects contacted by the better adjusted experimenters. The results of this study are not consistent with those found by Winkel and Sarason (1964) for a verbal learning task. In that experiment, described above, anxiety of the experimenter was an effective variable only in interaction with subject variables or instruction variables. If anything, the more anxious experimenters tended to obtain less adequate performance. That seemed also to be the case for some data reported by McGuigan (1963). The more neurotic of his nine experimenters tended to obtain the poorer performance from their subjects in a learning task. From the studies considered, it seems safe to conclude that the experimenter's anxiety level (or perhaps adjustment level) may affect subjects' responses for a variety of tasks; but the nature of the effect is not predictable on the basis of our current knowledge. This conclusion is borne out by the results of the two experiments reported next.

In both studies, the task was that described earlier which required subjects to rate the success or failure of people pictured in photographs. In both experiments, the experimenters had been tested for anxiety level defined by the Taylor (1953) Scale of Manifest Anxiety. In one of these studies 40 experimenters administered the photo rating task to 230 subjects, half of whom were males, half females. In this study more anxious experimenters obtained higher ratings of success of the photos they asked their subjects to rate. The correlation was $+.48$, $p = .02$ (Rosenthal, Persinger, Vikan-Kline, & Mulry, 1963). In the other experiment, 26 experimenters administered the same photo rating task to 115 female subjects. In this experiment, it was the *less* anxious experimenters who obtained higher ratings of the success of the photos they presented to their subjects. The correlation this time was −.54, $p < .01$ (Rosenthal, Kohn, Greenfield, & Carota, 1965). Final evidence for the complexity of the relationship between experimenter's anxiety and subject's response comes from a study of verbal conditioning (Rosenthal, Kohn, Greenfield, & Carota, 1966). In that experiment 19 male experimenters conducted the verbal reinforcement procedures with 60 female subjects. Sentences were to be constructed by the subjects and each sentence was to begin with any one of six pronouns (Taffel, 1955). Whenever first-person pronouns were selected the experimenter said the word "good." The increase in the usage of first-person pronouns from the beginning to the end of the experiment was the measure of verbal conditioning. This time the high- and low-anxious experimenters did not differ from each other in the degree of verbal conditioning shown by their subjects. However, both high- and low-anxious experimenters obtained significantly more conditioning than did those experimenters who scored as medium-anxious ($p = .08$).

There is little information available to suggest what it is about the appearance or behavior of more or less anxious experimenters that might affect their subjects' responses. Only the barest clues are available from a preliminary analysis of the sound motion pictures mentioned earlier of experimenters interacting with subjects. Based only upon the ratings of the brief preinstruction phase of the experiment in which the experimenter asked for the subject's name, age, class, and major field, more anxious experimenters were judged to be more active in their leg movements ($r = +.42$, $p = .08$) and in the movement of their entire body ($r = +.41$, $p = .09$). These relationships tend only to add to the construct validity of the anxiety scale employed. We might expect that more anxious experimenters would be somewhat more fidgety in their interaction with their subjects. The movement variables mentioned were rated by four undergraduate observers who saw the films but did not hear the sound track. Three additional undergraduate observers listened to the sound track but did not see the films. Based on their ratings, those experimenters who scored as more anxious were judged to have a less dominant tone of voice ($r = −.43$, $p = .07$) and a less active tone of voice ($r = −.44$, $p = .07$).[1] More anxious experimenters, then, may behave toward their subjects in a way that communicates their tension through excessive fidgeting and a meeker, less self-assured tone of voice. (This impression is strengthened by some unpublished data kindly made available by Ray

---

[1] This general pattern of correlations between experimenter anxiety and experimenter behavior was also found on analysis of the instruction-reading period of the experiment. Some of the correlations became somewhat smaller, some became somewhat larger. During this period of the experiment, too, experimenters scoring as more anxious on the Taylor Scale were judged as more tense by the film observers. With or without benefit of sound track the correlation was the same: +.40 ($p < .10$).

Mulry. Analysis of these data showed more anxious experimenters to be rated more shy [$r = +.23$, $p = .06$] by their subjects during an experiment involving motor performance.) From the evidence presented, this constellation of experimenter behavior seems sometimes to increase, sometimes to decrease, and sometimes not to affect the subjects' performance at all. To make a notable understatement: more research is needed—much more.

Experimenter's Need for Approval

Crowne and Marlowe (1964) have shown that the need for social approval as measured by their scale (the Marlowe-Crowne Social Desirability Scale) predicts cautious, conforming, and persuasible behavior in a variety of experimental situations. Until recently only "subjects" had been administered this instrument, but now there are a few studies that have related the "experimenter's" need for approval to his subject's responses in various experimental situations. Mulry (1962), for example, employed 12 male experimenters to administer to some 69 subjects a pursuit rotor task requiring perceptual-motor skill. A number of tests, including the Marlowe-Crowne SD Scale, were administered to the experimenters. Mulry found a tendency for experimenters scoring higher on the need for approval to obtain superior performance on the pursuit rotor task. Experimenters higher in the need for approval obtained especially good performance from their male subjects when the experimenters had been led to believe that they themselves were good at a pursuit rotor task.

The unpredictability of the effects of the experimenter's anxiety on his subject's responses is matched by the unpredictability of the effects of experimenter's need for approval. Thus, in one experiment employing the person perception task described earlier, experimenters lower in need for approval obtained ratings of the photos as being of more successful people. The correlation was $-.32$, $p = .10$ (Rosenthal, Persinger, Vikan-Kline, & Mulry, 1963). In another experiment, also cited earlier, it was experimenters *higher* in need for approval who obtained more "success" ratings. That correlation was $+.38$, $p = .05$ (Rosenthal, Kohn, Greenfield, & Carota, 1965). Within a single experiment, Marcia (1961) obtained similarly unpredictable relationships. He employed seven male experimenters and six female experimenters to administer the same standard person perception task to subjects. Among male experimenters, the correlation between their need for approval scores and their subjects' ratings of "success" was $-.27$. Among female experimenters the analogous correlation was $+.43$. These two correlations, although not significantly different from zero, nor from each other for such small sample sizes, do suggest that the sex of the experimenter may interact with such experimenter attributes as need for approval to affect the subjects' responses.

In one of the experiments cited earlier, the experimenter's need for

approval was not related to the subject's susceptibility to the verbal reinforcements of the experimenter (Rosenthal, Kohn, Greenfield, & Carota,
1966). In that experiment, however, each experimenter was rated by each
of his subjects on his behavior during the interaction with that subject. Although the anxiety level of the experimenter was found to be unrelated to
any of the subjects' ratings, that was not the case for the experimenter's
need for social approval. Table 5-1 shows the correlations between subjects'

TABLE 5—1

Experimenter's Need for Approval and Experimental Behavior as Seen and Heard "Subjectively"

Behavior	Correlation	p
Personal	−.32	.02
Loud	−.27	.05
Enthusiastic	+.27	.05
Talkative	−.22	.10
Likable	−.22	.10

ratings of their experimenters and the experimenters' need for approval.
The pattern of correlations obtained apparently did not affect the subjects'
responses in this experiment on verbal conditioning. But presumably where
a quieter, more enthusiastic but less likable experimenter would affect his
subjects differently, we would expect the experimenter's need for approval
to affect his subjects by way of these different behaviors. That experimenters
higher in need for approval should be less well liked is predictable from the
work of Crowne and Marlowe (1964). However, that they should be less
personal does not seem to follow from what is known of the need for approval. If anything, these experimenters should try too hard to be friendly,
thereby becoming less popular with their subjects.

Once again we look to the preliminary analysis of the filmed interactions between experimenters and subjects as they transact their preinstructional business. The experimenters' need for approval was not found to be
related to any of the observations made of the films without benefit of the
sound track. When observers had access to both visual and auditory cues,
only three variables were found to be related to the experimenters' need for
approval. Experimenters higher in need for approval were judged to have a
more expressive face ($r = +.42$, $p = .08$), to smile more often ($r = +.44$, $p = .07$), and to slant their bodies more in the direction of their
subjects ($r = +.39$, $p = .10$). (Ratings of these last two variables were

made available by Neil Friedman and Richard Katz.) These findings are just what we would expect from the person higher in need for approval (Crowne & Marlowe, 1964).

It was the observations made of the sound track alone that yielded the most interesting information.[2] Table 5-2 shows the larger correlations be-

TABLE 5—2

Experimenter's Need for Approval and Experimental Behavior as Heard "Objectively"

Behavior	Correlation	p
Personal	+ .57	.02
Friendly	+ .47	.05
Dominant	+ .46	.05
Speaks distinctly	+ .46	.05
Expressive-voiced	+ .45	.06
Active	+ .41	.10
Likable	+ .40	.10
Enthusiastic	+ .39	.10
Pleasant-voiced	+ .39	.10

tween experimenter's need for approval and ratings by the "objective" observers—i.e., those who were not themselves subjects of the experimenter. These "tone-of-voice" variables partially agree with the observations made by subjects themselves in a different experiment and given a different task (Table 5-1). In both cases experimenters higher in need for approval were judged as more enthusiastic. In the verbal conditioning experiment, however, subjects found these experimenters less personal and less likable, whereas in the photo-rating experiment independent judges of the experimenters' tone found them more personal and more likable if they were higher in need for approval. It is pleasant to acknowledge the consistencies but difficult to account for the differences. The two experiments differed in the nature of the experimental tasks, the samples of experimenters, and the type of judgments made of the experimenter's behavior. The subject of the experiment is closer physically to the experimenter and may observe things not observable by the "objective" observer of the motion picture or sound track record. On the other hand, the interacting subject is much busier than the "objective" observer, who can attend completely to the experimenter's

[2] The same pattern of correlations was also obtained when the behavior during the instruction-reading period was analyzed, though fewer of the correlations reached the .10 level of significance.

behavior without having another task of his own to perform. A reconciliation of the differences is possible if we can assume that to be judged personal and likable from the tone of voice alone is not at all the same thing as to be judged similarly on the basis of all available sense modalities. What does seem clear is that experimenters higher or lower in need for approval are likely to behave differently in interaction with their subjects. Sometimes, but not always, this differential behavior is likely to affect the subject's response.

Experimenter's Birth Order

The order of birth within the family is not, in the usual sense, a psychological variable. It is not defined in terms of the subject's behavior except in the narrow sense that it is usually the subject's statement of his ordinal position, which is used as the operational definition of the variable. Since Schachter's already classic work (1959), birth order has been investigated by many workers and has been shown to bear significant relationships to other, more "properly" psychological variables.

One experiment shows that for the person perception task described earlier, firstborn experimenters tend to obtain higher ratings of the success of persons pictured in photos than do later-born experimenters ($x^2 = 5.85$, $p = .02$; Rosenthal, Kohn, Greenfield, & Carota, 1965). Another experiment, however, the one employing the verbal conditioning procedure, showed no effects on subjects' performance of the experimenter's birth order (Rosenthal, Kohn, Greenfield, & Carota, 1966). In that study, it may be recalled, subjects made judgments of their experimenter's behavior during the experimental transaction. Table 5-3 shows the correlations between these ratings of the experimenter's behavior and his birth order. The general picture that emerges is that, as experimenters, firstborns are faster but more reluctant speakers, employing fewer body and facial movements

TABLE 5—3

Experimenter's Earlier Birth and Behavior in a Verbal Conditioning Experiment

Behavior	Correlation	p
Talkative	−.37	.006
Slow-speaking	−.32	.02
Body activity	−.32	.02
Trunk activity	−.27	.05
Hand gestures	−.26	.05
Expressive face	−.24	.08

and expressions, than their later-born counterparts. In this verbal conditioning experiment, this combination of characteristics differentiating firstborn from later-born experimenters appeared to have no effect on subjects' responses; in other experiments it might.

In the experiment by Mulry (1962) already cited, there was no relationship between the birth order of the experimenter and the motor performance of his subjects. An analysis of the ratings these subjects made of their experimenters, however, showed that firstborn experimenters behaved differently during the experiment than did later-borns. Firstborn experimenters were rated as more mature ($r = +.24$, $p = .05$) and more defensive ($r = +.22$, $p = .07$) than later-borns, which seems consistent with the picture that emerges from Table 5-3 of firstborns as somewhat more staid and motorically controlled people. Further analysis of Mulry's data, however, revealed that firstborn experimenters were also rated as more talkative ($r = +.24$, $p = .05$) than later-borns. This is directly opposite to the relationship reported in Table 5-3 and is not easily reconciled by the fact that Mulry's task was motor while the other task was verbal.

A third experiment in which the birth order of the experimenter could be correlated with his behavior during the experiment was the study in person perception which had been filmed. In this experiment there was no relationship between the experimenter's birth order and the degree of success perceived by his subjects in the faces to be judged. However, during the instruction-reading phase of the interaction, firstborn experimenters were seen and heard to behave more actively and officiously than later-born experimenters. Table 5-4 shows the relevant correlations. Observations made during the brief preinstructional phase were not significantly correlated with the experimenter's birth order, though the correlations based on that phase were all in the same direction as those based on the instruction period. The results shown in Table 5-4 are opposite in direction to those

TABLE 5—4

Experimenter's Earlier Birth and Behavior in a Person Perception Experiment

Behavior	Correlation	p
Hand gestures	+ .50	.05
Body activity	+ .48	.05
Head activity	+ .47	.05
Arm gestures	+ .41	.10
Important-acting	+ .41	.10

obtained in the verbal conditioning study (Table 5-3). It cannot be said whether the difference is due to the different tasks employed in the two studies or to the fact that the observers in the one case were the subjects themselves rather than external observers of sound motion pictures. As for the variable of talkativeness which yielded opposite relationships in the verbal conditioning and the motor performance experiments, it was not significantly related to birth order in the filmed study. We are left with the unsatisfying conclusion that the birth order of the experimenter only sometimes affects the responses he obtains from his subjects; that more often his birth order is related to his behavior in the experimental interaction; and that the nature of this behavior seems to interact at least with the type of experiment he is conducting.

Experimenter's Hostility

The work of Sarason (1962) and of Sarason and Minard (1963) has already been cited in connection with the effects of experimenter's sex. It will be recalled that greater hostility of the experimenter was predictive of obtaining more hostile verbs in a sentence construction task (Sarason, 1962). This was especially the case when the subjects, too, tended to be more hostile. Among experimenters scoring low in hostility, those subjects scoring high in hostility emitted 9 percent fewer hostile verbs than did subjects scoring low in hostility. Among experimenters scoring high in hostility, those subjects scoring high in hostility emitted 17 percent *more* hostile verbs than did subjects scoring low in hostility. The interaction was significant at the .05 level.

When the experimenters reinforced subjects' use of first-person pronouns by saying "good," the hostility level of the experimenter was again found to make a difference, this time by affecting the increase in the use of the reinforced responses from earlier to later trials. Actually, it was the interaction of experimenter's hostility and his ascribed prestige that led to the dramatic effects obtained (Sarason & Minard, 1963). The increase in the use of the reinforced responses was only 4 percent when the experimenter was low in hostility and high in prestige and only 5 percent when he was high in hostility and low in prestige. The increase, however, was 47 percent when the experimenter was high in both hostility and prestige, and it was 52 percent when he was low in both hostility and prestige. Once again the complex nature of the effects of experimenter attributes on subjects' responses is demonstrated; and once again, the explanation is far from intuitively obvious.

Additional evidence is presented by Sarason (1965), who cites the unpublished work of Barnard (1963). Barnard administered a test of hostility to both subjects and experimenters and found that subjects contacted by less hostile experimenters showed a greater degree of disturbance on a phrase association test than did subjects contacted by more hostile experimenters.

The importance of distinguishing between overt and covert hostility levels of experimenters has been made clear by the work of Sanders and Cleveland (1953). Nine graduate students in psychology administered Rorschachs to a large sample of undergraduate students. Overt hostility was defined in terms of subjects' ratings of their experimenter. Covert hostility was defined in terms of the experimenter's own Rorschach responses. Subjects' responses reflecting hostility increased when experimenters were high on covert hostility but decreased when their experimenters were high on overt hostility. Overtly hostile experimenters may have intimidated their subjects into giving more benign responses, and covertly hostile experimenters may have legitimated subtly the expression of hostile responses. What seems especially needed at this time is information on the actual behavior of experimenters classified as high or low in hostility—behavior that presumably creates quite different standards for the appropriateness of subjects' responses.

Experimenter's Authoritarianism

On the basis of the California F Scale, Peggy Cook-Marquis (1958) obtained groups of experimenters and subjects who were high-authoritarian, low-authoritarian, and acquiescent. Experimenters administered tests of problem solving to their subjects. Performance on these problems was not related to experimenter personality. However, when attitudes toward different forms of teaching methods were assessed, it was found that high-authoritarian experimenters were less effective in influencing these attitudes than were the low-authoritarian or the acquiescent experimenters. The interpretation given these results by Cook-Marquis, with which it seems easy to agree, was that high authoritarians might not themselves believe in unstructured teaching techniques and that they were therefore less convincing in trying to influence their subjects to approve more of these techniques.

The work of Mulry (1962) has already been cited in connection with the need for approval and birth order variables. In his experiment, employing the pursuit rotor task, his twelve experimenters had also been assessed for authoritarianism by the use of the California F Scale. Authoritarianism of the experimenter was a factor in determining subjects' perceptual-motor performance only in interaction with the experimenter's belief about his own ability at the pursuit rotor task. Those experimenters who were low in authoritarianism and who felt themselves not to be good at the pursuit rotor task obtained superior performance from their subjects compared to the other combinations of experimenter's authoritarianism and perception of their own adequacy at the motor task they administered to their subjects.

Although Mulry's more authoritarian experimenters did not obtain significantly different data from their subjects (unless other variables were considered simultaneously), their subjects were affected differentially by contact with them. Thus, subjects contacted by more authoritarian experimenters described themselves as less satisfied with their participation in the experiment ($r = -.27$, $p = .03$) and as less interested in the experiment ($r = -.23$, $p = .06$). In addition, the more authoritarian experimenters were judged by their subjects to be less consistent in their behavior during the experiment ($r = -.27$, $p = .03$). Though it did not seem to occur in this study, it seems reasonable to suppose that there are experiments in which experimenters who thus affect their subjects' reactions will obtain different responses from them in the experimental task posed. There are some data that suggest that this is so.

From the analysis of sound motion pictures of experimenters administering the person perception task, it has been found that experimenters who are judged to be less consistent in their behavior tend to obtain ratings of the photos as of more successful people ($r = -.35$, $p < .01$). If more authoritarian experimenters are less consistent in their conduct of the person perception experiment, as they were in Mulry's motor performance experiment, we would expect that more authoritarian experimenters would obtain ratings of photos as being of more successful people. This prediction could be tested for only a small sample of six experimenters who had been administered the California F Scale and who also conducted a person perception experiment described in detail elsewhere (Rosenthal, Persinger, Mulry, Vikan-Kline, & Grothe, 1964a, p. 467). The mean rating of success obtained by the three more authoritarian experimenters was $+0.27$ and that obtained by the three less authoritarian experimenters was -1.06. The difference was significant at the .06 level ($t = 2.75$).

Experimenter's Intelligence

Perhaps because experimenters, even "student-experimenters," tend to be so highly selected for intelligence, there has been little effort expended to study the effects of experimenter's intelligence on subjects' responses. The restriction of the range of IQ scores found among a set of experimenters would tend to reduce dramatically the correlation between their IQ and their subjects' performance. In the Mulry (1962) experiment, no relationship was found between the intelligence test scores of the experimenter and his subject's perceptual-motor performance. There was a tendency, however, for experimenters' intelligence to interact with subjects' sex in such a way that male subjects earned particularly high performance scores when their experimenters scored lower on the Shipley-Hartford Test of intelligence. Once again, subjects' ratings of their experimenters were available.

Experimenters scoring higher in intelligence were rated by their subjects as more consistent in their behavior ($r = +.29$, $p = .02$) and more physically active as reflected in greater amount of body movements ($r = +.20$, $p = .10$). In addition, subjects contacted by brighter experimenters were more satisfied with their participation in the experiment ($r = +.26$, $p < .05$).

Experimenter's Dominance

Reference has already been made to the work of Ehrlich and Riesman (1961). They had available scores on a scale of ascendance or dominance earned by the interviewers employed in a study of adolescent girls. Those interviewers who were more ascendant and who appeared more task-oriented, as defined by a scale of "objectivity," obtained different responses from their subjects than did the remaining interviewers. Responses in this study were defined in terms of the social unacceptability of the reply. When interviewers scored high on both ascendance and objectivity, they obtained 38 percent fewer socially unacceptable responses than did interviewers scoring lower on these scales. No-nonsense type interviewers are, it would seem, more likely to draw no-nonsense type responses.

Sarason (1965) has summarized an unpublished dissertation by Symons (1964) which shows that subjects contacted by more dominant experimenters make more negative self-references than do subjects contacted by less dominant experimenters. There is also evidence that subjects contacted by more dominant experimenters make more negative references to *other* people. The correlation between ratings of the experimenter's dominance throughout an entire experiment and his subjects' rating other people as having experienced failure was $+.34$, $p < .005$. (This particular experiment is discussed further in the chapter dealing with the communication of experimenters' expectancies.) These findings make tempting the psychoanalytic interpretation that dominant experimenters evoke more hostility which, because it cannot be safely directed toward the source, is turned either inward, as in the Symons study, or against an external scapegoat. This interpretation is weakened somewhat by the fact that in data collected by Suzanne Haley, experimenters described as more "pushy" tended to obtain ratings of other people as more successful rather than more unsuccessful as we would have predicted from our interpretation.

To the extent that these definitions of dominance derive from the experimenter's behavior in the experiment rather than from standard psychological instruments, their further discussion seems best postponed until the next section. There will be found a more detailed consideration of other, more fully social psychological variables. One of these variables, that of experimenter status, seems particularly related to the variable of experimenter dominance as inferred from his behavior in the experiment.

SOCIAL PSYCHOLOGICAL ATTRIBUTES

The biosocial attributes of experimenters which have been discussed are, usually, immediately apparent to the subject. The psychological attributes discussed are not, usually, so immediately apparent to the subject, although as we have seen, there are often behavioral correlates of an experimenter's psychological characteristics. In this section the discussion turns more fully to those attributes of the experimenter that are defined neither by his appearance nor by his answers to items of a psychological test or questionnaire. Sometimes the definition of these social psychological attributes is directly and simply behavioral, as in the case of the attribute of "warmth." Sometimes the definition is only indirectly behavioral, as in the case of an experimenter's status, and not at all simple, in the sense that the relative status of an experimenter who is an army captain will be determined by whether the subject is an army private or a major.

Experimenter's Relative Status

In most laboratory research the subjects are undergraduates and the experimenters range in academic status from being advanced undergraduates, through the various levels of graduate students, all the way through the various status levels of the faculty, from new Ph.D. to senior professor. In military research settings, the status of the experimenter in terms of absolute rank is immediately apparent to the subjects, though an additional source of status, as we shall see, may derive from the setting in which the research is conducted. This effect of the setting or of the sponsorship of the research is well known to have an important influence in survey research (Hyman et al., 1954). Surveys conducted by the FBI are likely to earn a degree of cooperation quite different from that earned by a manufacturer of so-called washday products.

Regardless of how the experimenter derives his relative status or prestige in the eyes of his subject, that status often affects not only whether the subject will respond (Norman, 1948) but also how he will respond. An example of this has already been given in the discussion of experimenter's hostility. There we saw that the prestige of the experimenter interacted with his hostility level to serve as a determinant of subjects' susceptibility to verbal reinforcement (Sarason & Minard, 1963). Experimenter's prestige in that experiment was defined in terms of formality of dress, of manner, and of request for participation. Experimenter's prestige was found to interact with another variable—access to visual cues from the experimenter's face. When subjects could not see the experimenter's face and when he was in the low status condition, there was a decrease in the effect of his reinforcements on the subject's responses. Perhaps subjects felt that if the experimenter wasn't very serious and furthermore, wasn't even looking, it couldn't matter too much whether his verbal utterances of "good" were taken seriously or not. In this experiment 16 experimenters were employed; in general, Sarason and his collaborators have employed large samples of experimenters. For the experimenter attribute of status, most of the relevant studies are based on sample sizes of only two or three experimenters. Still, they may be usefully considered.

In a study of the control of verbal behavior of fifth-grade children, Prince (1962) employed two experimenters differing markedly in prestige. The more prestigious experimenter was more influential in controlling his subjects' responses. This is as we would expect and is consistent, generally, with the results of Sarason and Minard. However, just as other variables were found to interact with experimenter status in that study, so too do we find such interactions in the following. Ekman and Friesen (1960) employed two military experimenters to administer a photo judging task to army recruits. Sometimes the experimenters were presented to the subjects as officers, sometimes as enlisted men. Sometimes experimenters reinforced subjects for liking the persons pictured in the photos and sometimes for disliking them. The overall results, although not clear-cut, suggested that the officer-experimenter was more effective at increasing subjects' rate of disliking photographs, whereas the enlisted-man–experimenter was more effective at increasing subjects' rate of liking photographs. That is a result similar to the one found when photos were being rated for their success or failure and more dominant experimenters drew more failure ratings. The officer role seems a more dominant one than that of enlisted man. One plausible interpretation, related to that proposed earlier, of the present data is that the recruit-subjects were given the "go-ahead" by the officer to be aggressive when his presence might itself have made them feel aggressive. Here, in a sense, was a chance to combine the experimenter-required conformity with the subject-desired aggressiveness. When the experimenter was an enlisted man, as the subjects themselves were, they may have felt more friendly and, therefore, found it easier to increase their rate of liking the persons pictured in photos. In this particular experiment, the authors point out, the differences in status between the experimenters might have been diminished in their subjects' eyes because both were staff members of the high status organization carrying out the research.

In one experiment on verbal reinforcement the experimenter's status was defined in terms of his behavior during his interaction with the subject. It was assumed that a more professional, businesslike, less noisy, and more consistent experimenter would be ascribed a higher status by his subjects. The 19 male experimenters of this study said the word "good" whenever the subjects used first-person pronouns (Rosenthal, Kohn, Greenfield, & Carota, 1966). Table 5-5 shows the correlations between the increase in the use of first-person pronouns over the course of the experiment as a function of

TABLE 5—5

Experimenter's Status and Success at Controlling Subjects' Verbal Behavior

Variable	Correlation	p
Businesslike	+.43	.001
Professional	+.33	.01
Loud	−.31	.02
Behaved consistently	+.26	.05

subjects' perception of their experimenter's behavior during the experiment. Higher status experimenters, as defined by their subjects' perception of their behavior, were significantly more influential in changing their subjects' responses. In this particular study we cannot be certain that subjects' ratings of their experimenters actually reflected differences in that behavior. Possibly those subjects more susceptible to the influence of the experimenter only perceived him differently than did less influenceable subjects. It is also possible that having been influenced by an experimenter, subjects described that experimenter according to their conception of the sort of person by whom they would permit themselves to be influenced. Even if these more influential experimenters did not, in fact, behave as their subjects stated, it is instructive to note the pattern of characteristics ascribed to more influential experimenters. At least the stereotype of the behavior of more influential experimenters includes their being seen as behaving in a way associated with higher status.

We gain some support for the idea that experimenters who influence their subjects' responses more behave in a more professional way from a study by Barber and Calverley (1964a). In their experiment in hypnosis the single experimenter sometimes adopted a forceful, authoritative tone of voice and sometimes a lackadaisical one. Subjects accepted more suggestions when offered in the authoritative tone than when offered in a bored, disinterested tone. These variables of interest, enthusiasm, and expressiveness of tone were also employed in the verbal conditioning study cited, and in that study, too, were related to the experimenter's success at influencing verbal behavior. Experimenters who influenced their subjects more were rated by them as more interested ($r = +.43, p < .001$), more enthusiastic ($r = +.28, p < .05$), and more expressive-voiced ($r = +.24, p < .10$). The general impression obtained from the studies relevant to the experimenter's status is that when the subject's task involves conforming to an experimenter's influence (as in studies of verbal conditioning or hypnosis), higher status experimenters are more successful in obtaining such conformity. That seems to be the case whether the experimenter's status is defined in terms of such external symbols as dress or insignia or in terms of status-earning behaviors during the interaction with the subject. This conclusion seems consistent also with the general literature on social influence processes, though there the influencer is not usually an experimenter (e.g., Berg and Bass, 1961). Other investigators who have discussed the effect of the experimenter's status on subjects' susceptibility to his influence include Glucksberg and Lince (1962), Goranson (1965), Krasner (1962), and Matarazzo, Saslow, and Pareis (1960).

The effect of experimenter status can operate even when the subject's response is not a direct measure of social influenceability. Thus, Birney (1958) found that his two faculty experimenters obtained responses from subjects reflecting a higher need for achievement than did his student experimenter. Subjects may feel a greater need to achieve when in interaction with others who have probably achieved more; or at least subjects may feel it would be more proper to respond with more achievement responses in such company. The effect of the experimenter's being a faculty member, especially if he is known to the subject, has also been illustrated by McTeer (1953).

In many of the studies bearing on the effects of the experimenter's status, the samples of experimenters have been small, so that any number of factors other than status could have accounted for the differences obtained. Thus not only do faculty experimenters differ in status from student experimenters but they are likely to be older as well. In those studies where larger samples of experimenters were employed, the experimenters were usually aware that their status effects were being investigated, and this in itself might have made them perform the experiment somewhat differently. Where the subjects' perceptions of the experimenter's behavior were used to define status it was noted that the behavior that actually occurred was not necessarily the same as that reported by the subjects. What seems especially needed, then, is a study in which the status of the experimenter is varied without the experimenter's knowledge of this variation. Just such a study was carried out by John Laszlo, who made his data available for the analysis reported here. There were 3 experimenters who administered the photorating task to 64 subjects. Half the time the subjects were told they would be contacted by a prestigious investigator and half the time by "just a student." Each experimenter, then, obtained data from subjects when he "was" a higher status and a lower status person without his knowledge of that fact. Table 5-6 shows the tendency for experimenters who were ascribed the lower status to obtain ratings of the photos as being of more successful persons. Although this was not an experiment of verbal reinforcement, the results are reminiscent of those of Ekman and Friesen (1960), who also found a tendency for a lower status experimenter to obtain more favorable reactions to photographs. More directly analogous, for having employed

TABLE 5—6

Experimenter's Status and the Means of Subjects' Photo Ratings

	STATUS		
Experimenter	High	Low	Difference
A	−.58	−.18	+.40
B	−1.70	−.57	+1.13
C	−.69	−.56	+.13
Mean	−.99	−.44	+.55

the same task, are the two studies cited in the section dealing with experimenter's dominance. One of these studies yielded results just like those obtained by Laszlo, but the other obtained results in the opposite direction. In the Laszlo study, the results were not significant statistically, although all three experimenters showed the same tendency. In this experiment, too, another finding that did not reach statistical significance, but which is of interest, nevertheless, was that the effect of the experimenter's status was larger among subjects scoring higher on Rokeach's (1960) scale of dogmatism. These are just those subjects who would be expected to be more susceptible to the effects of the status of those with whom they interact. This finding receives support from the work of Das (1960), who employed four experimenters to administer a test of body sway suggestibility. The status of the experimenters varied from department chairman to attendant. Higher status experimenters obtained more body sway from their subjects ($p < .05$), but it was the more suggestible subjects who showed the effects of experimenter's prestige while the less suggestible subjects did not.

The data presented from Laszlo's study are supported by the results of another unpublished study employing the same photo-rating task. This is the study in which 19 experimenters contacted 57 subjects and were filmed during their interaction with the subjects. None of the ratings of the experimenter's behavior during the brief preinstruction period predicted subjects' judgments of the success of the persons pictured in the photos. However, ratings made during the instruction-reading phase of the experiment did. Table 5-7 shows the significant correlations between subjects' ratings of "success" and the ratings of experimenter's behavior made from simultaneously viewing the films and hearing the sound track. Other ratings were also significantly predictive of subjects' responses, but only those are listed here that may be used to define the status level of the experimenter. Those experimenters who behaved more professionally and consistently and showed

TABLE 5—7

Experimenter's Status and Subjects' Ratings of Photos as Successful

Variable	Correlation	p
Behaved consistently	−.35	.01
Professional	−.23	.10
Talkative	+.26	.05
Leg activity	+.29	.05
Trunk activity	+.24	.10

less body activity and talkativeness obtained lower ratings of success from their subjects. It seems reasonable to regard such experimenters as achieving higher status in their subjects' eyes by virtue of their behavior. In general, these results are very much in line with the trends obtained by Laszlo.

Experimenter's Warmth

An experiment by Ware, Kowal, and Baker (1963) is illustrative. Two experimenters alternated playing a warm, solicitous, democratic role and one that was cool, brusque, and autocratic. The task set for the military subjects of this study was one of signal detection. Regardless of the various conditions of environmental stimulation occurring during the signal detection task, those subjects who had been contacted by the warmer-acting experimenter detected signals significantly better than did those contacted by the cooler-acting experimenter ($p < .05$).

When the dependent variable was the production of verbal responses, the warmth of the experimenter was also an effective independent variable. Reece and Whitman (1962) defined "warm" experimenter behavior in terms of leaning toward the subject, looking directly at the subject, smiling, and keeping the hands still. Cold behavior was defined in terms of the experimenter leaning away from the subject, looking around the room, not smiling, and drumming his fingers. Subjects were, of course, able to judge correctly which was the warm and which the cold behavior, and this behavior affected their verbal output. Predictably, this was greater when the experimenter was warmer. This particular study is important not only because of its content but because of its method as well. Although there are a number of studies that manipulate warmth of experimenter, there are few that attempt to specify so carefully the motor behavior of the experimenter that is to be part of the picture of warmth.

In the area of projective testing, Masling (1960) has discussed the effects of the examiner's warmth on the subject's productions. In an experiment by Lord (1950), for example, three examiners administered the Rorschach under warm, cool, and neutral styles of interaction. Subjects contacted by examiners in the warm condition gave "richer," more imaginative Rorschachs than did subjects contacted under the cold condition. Interestingly, the differences among the three female examiners in the responses they obtained were greater than the differences among the three experimental conditions. Perhaps the "natural" warmth or coldness of the examiners was a more crucial variable than the role-played warmth or coldness.

A good illustration of the magnitude of difference in subjects' responses which may be associated with the experimenter's warmth or coldness comes from research by Luft (1953). He employed an undergraduate female experimenter who administered 10 home-made ink blots to 60 freshman subjects, half of them males, half females. The task for each subject was simply to indicate those of the blots that were liked and those that were disliked. Half the time the experimenter played a warm, friendly role. Half the time she played a cool, unfriendly role, which included asking the subjects some questions about current affairs which they were sure to be unable to answer accurately. Subjects contacted by the experimenter in the warm role liked 7.6 of the 10 blots. Those contacted by the cold-role experimenter liked 3.1 blots ($t = 9.7$). Among those subjects treated coldly, 57 percent disliked most of the cards; among those treated warmly, only a single subject (3 percent) disliked most of the cards. There was no effect of the sex of the subject by itself or in interaction with the experimental treatment. Luft's interpretation of the results bears repeating. "Like me and I will like your inkblots; reject me and I will reject them" (p. 491). Additional evidence that a cold examiner or experimenter may obtain different responses in storytelling tasks is available from the work of Bellak (1944) and of Rodnick and Klebanoff (1942). They found critical treatment of the subjects to increase the incidence of aggressive themes. Assuming cold experimenters to be relatively more stressful stimuli for their subjects, there is still more evidence that a cold experimenter may, by his coldness, alter the subject's responses in a variety of tasks. Masling (1960) gives an excellent summary of the relevant literature on projective testing.

Subjects' performance on an intelligence test may also be affected by the warmth of the examiner. Gordon and Durea (1948) administered the Stanford Binet Scale to 40 eighth-grade pupils. Half of these children were treated more coolly by the examiners. The result was that relative to the more warmly treated children, the coolly treated lost over six IQ points.

Some data supportive of this result were collected by Wartenberg-Ekren, who kindly made the data available for further analysis. In her experiment 8 male examiners administered a visual-motor test of intelligence (Block Design) to 32 male subjects. Each examiner was rated by his sub-

jects on his behavior during the administration of the test. The 21 scales
employed were similar to those used in other studies described in this
chapter. Two of the scales were significantly related to the subjects' performance. Examiners rated by their subjects as more casual ($p = .01$)
and as more talkative ($p = .02$) obtained superior performance on the
intelligence test administered. By themselves these variables do not seem
convincingly related to warmth. Table 5-8 shows the intercorrelations of
five of the variables on which examiners were rated as well as the correla-

TABLE 5—8

Examiner Warmth and Subjects' Intellectual Performance

DESCRIPTION OF EXAMINERS

	Casual	Talk- ative	Expressive Face	Encour- aging	Subjects' Performance
Casual	–				+ .83
Talkative	+ .76	–			+ .81
Expressive face	+ .75	+ .87	–		+ .61
Encouraging	+ .72	+ .71	+ .67	–	+ .52
Pleasant-voiced	+ .56	+ .66	+ .45	+.86	+ .44

tions of each with subjects' performance. The correlations are based on the
mean ratings ascribed to examiners and the mean performance each obtained. There being only eight examiners, a correlation of .62 is required
for significance at the .10 level and a .71 is needed for the .05 level. Because of the high intercorrelations, each examiner was given a cluster rating
by adding the individual ratings together. The correlation between these
cluster scores and subjects' performance was $+.79$, $p = .03$. It seems
reasonable to regard this cluster as one reflecting warmth. A word of caution is necessary, however. It is possible that subjects who performed more
adequately felt differently about their examiners because of it and rated
them differently, not because their behavior differed, but because of the
subjects' own improved mood. It is also possible that better performers at
this particular task simply rate other people higher on the particular variables in the warmth cluster. The interpretation that examiners did, in fact,
behave as described by their subjects, and that this casual, pleasant, encouraging syndrome fostered better performance, is not too far-fetched and
is consistent with the data from the Gordon and Durea experiment.

In a subsequent chapter dealing more thoroughly with problems of subjects' ratings of their experimenters, some evidence will be presented that suggests that subjects see their experimenters somewhat as their experimenters see themselves. This fact increases our confidence that what subjects say their experimenters did is, in fact, related to what their experimenters did do. There is evidence for this, too, from the survey research literature. One example relevant both to this point and to the attribute of warmth is a study by Brown (1955). He reported on a national survey conducted by the National Opinion Research Center in which subjects were to rate the interviewer's behavior during the data-collection transaction. Better rapport in the interview was associated with fewer avoidable "don't know" responses on the part of the subjects and with an increase in the number of usable responses given to open-ended questions. How the interviewer "really" behaved we cannot know. It is possible that more forthright subjects evaluate their questioners more favorably. It is also possible that after obtaining some forthright answers from subjects, data collectors in fact became more competent, or warmer, or happier, and that the subjects' record of the interviewer's behavior, although "accurate," has actually been determined by the subject's own behavior. All these processes may be operating, and yet there can be a kernel of correlation between the interviewer's actual behavior and his subjects' perception of that behavior. That, at least, is suggested by the data Brown obtained.

In some of the studies of the effects of the experimenter's warmth it was not the experimenter's behavior that was varied independently or even assessed as it occurred naturally. Rather, the set given the subject was varied in such a way that sometimes he expected the experimenter to be a warm, likable person and sometimes a cold, unlikable person. Though not originally employed to study experimenter-subject interaction, this manipulation has come to be associated with the earlier work of Back (1951). McGuigan (1963) describes an unpublished dissertation by Spires (1960) which employed just such a manipulation in a study of verbal conditioning. Spires found better conditioning to occur when subjects had been led to expect a warm experimenter, a finding borne out by Sapolsky's work (1960), which was conducted at about the same time. In Spires' study, most of the effect of the subject's set was actually associated with a particular personality characteristic of the subject. Subjects scoring higher on an "obsessive-compulsive" dimension, as defined by the Pt scale of the MMPI, were little affected by the set they had been given about the experimenter's warmth. However, subjects scoring high on an "hysteria" dimension, as defined by the Hy scale of the MMPI, showed a very large effect of the set they had been given. When experimenters believed to be warmer said "good" to reinforce subjects' responses, those scoring high on the Hy scale increased their use of the reinforced pronouns about 80 percent, whereas those scoring low on the Hy scale increased their use of these words only about 15 percent. From the results of the studies cited so far and from others (e.g., Sampson & French, 1960; Smith, 1961), it seems reasonable to conclude that when the subject's performance is a measure of influenceability, more influence is exerted by a warm, or warmly perceived, experimenter than by a cold, or coldly perceived, experimenter. The extent of the effect of experimenter warmth, however, appears to interact with subject variables and, very probably, with experimenter variables and situational variables as well.

TABLE 5—9

Experimenter Warmth and Subject's Performance in a Spool-Packing Task

		EXPERIMENTER BEHAVIOR		
		Warm	Cold	Mean
SUBJECT'S	Warm	+ 1.32	− .51	+ .405
EXPECTATION	Cold	− 1.32	+ .51	− .405
	Mean	0	0	

Some of the cited studies of experimenter warmth have defined warmth in terms of the experimenter's behavior, and others have defined warmth in terms of the subject's expectation of the experimenter's behavior. An experiment by Crow (1964) employed both definitions simultaneously. Although only a small study, employing 13 subjects and 4 experimenters, the results are instructive enough to warrant the telling of some of the details. Half the

TABLE 5—10

Experimenter Warmth and Subject's Performance in a Letter-Canceling Task

		EXPERIMENTER'S BEHAVIOR		
		Warm	Cold	Mean
SUBJECT'S	Warm	+ 1.53	− .33	+ .60
EXPECTATION	Cold	− 1.25	+ .05	− .60
	Mean	+ .14	− .14	

subjects had been found to have a conception of psychological experimenters as relatively warm in manner. The remaining subjects tended to expect experimenters to behave more coldly toward their subjects. Half the time experimenters played the part of a warm experimenter after the manner of Reece and Whitman (1962). That is, they smiled more at their subjects, leaned toward them, and looked at them more. Half the time experimenters played a cold role, defined by leaning away from their subjects, not smiling, avoiding eye contact, and drumming their fingers. Three tasks were administered to the subjects. One of these was a spool-packing task in which spools of thread were placed into an empty box, removed, repacked, removed, and so on for the duration of the task period. Another task called for the subjects to cross out all the W's on a page of randomly arranged letters. Both of these tasks have been employed or are similar to those employed by investigators interested in learning just how far subjects will go in cooperating with a psychological experimenter (e.g., Crowne & Marlowe, 1964; Orne, 1962). The third task administered to the subjects was a home-made version of a standard subtest of intelligence (digit symbol) which required the learning of a simple code for translating numbers into symbols. Tables 5-9, 5-10, and 5-11 give the mean performance

TABLE 5—11

Experimenter Warmth and Subject's Performance in a Digit Symbol Task

		EXPERIMENTER BEHAVIOR		
		Warm	Cold	Mean
SUBJECT'S	Warm	+1.43	−1.32	+.055
EXPECTATION	Cold	+.29	−.40	−.055
	Mean	+.86	−.86	

scores for each of the three tasks. The raw scores have been converted to standard scores from the raw data available in Crow's report.

Most of the results vary from task to task, except that in each case the performance was best when the experimenter behaved warmly and was contacting subjects who expected to be treated warmly. The average standard score for this subgroup was $+1.43$; that for the remaining subgroups was $-.48$ ($t = 3.62$, $p < .10$, $df = 2$). Closer study of the marginals of Tables 5-9, 5-10, and 5-11 suggests an interesting interaction effect involving the type of task and the relative effects of the experimenter's behavior compared to the effects of subjects' expectations. The lower marginals in Table 5-9, for example, show that for the spool-packing experiment there was no main effect for the experimenter's behavior. The right-hand marginals, however, show that the difference between the mean performances of subjects expecting warm treatment was superior by +.81 to that of subjects expecting cooler treatment. Table 5-12 gives the analogous values for each of the three tasks. A plus sign preceding the standard score data indicates that performance was superior in the warmer condition. For the spool-packing and letter-canceling tasks, the experimenter's actual

TABLE 5—12

Effects of Experimenter's Warmth Defined by Either Experimenter Behavior or Subject's Expectation

Task	Experimenter Behavior	Subject's Expectation	Difference
Spool-packing	.0	+.81	−.81
Letter-canceling	+.28	+1.20	−.92
Digit symbol	+1.72	+.11	+1.61
Mean	+.67	+.71	−.04

behavior made virtually no difference compared to the subject's expectation, which had a more substantial effect on the subject's performance. The situation was reversed for the digit symbol task. There, the subject's expectation made no difference but the experimenter's behavior made a good deal of difference in the subject's performance. The last column of Table 5-12 summarizes the interaction ($t = 25.9$, $df = 1$, $p < .05$).

For simple tasks with little meaning, subjects' expectations may assume a greater importance, because subjects who view experimenters more favorably may view his tasks more favorably, thereby transforming a compellingly inane procedure into one that simply "must" have more value. The experimenter's behavior may lose relative importance just because of the peculiarity of the task itself which absorbs the subject's attention. In the quasi-intelligence test, expectations about experimenters' behavior may become less salient because now the task is one like those the subject has been performing for years in school settings. The experimenter becomes more like those others in the student's life who have administered tests—usually teachers—and is to be evaluated more in terms of his actual behavior. The expectation of the experimenter's behavior becomes less important as soon as the subject finds the experimental situation to have required no special expectation at all because of its resemblance to the school situation. If that were the case, we might expect that expectations about the warmth of teachers would have been an effective determinant of subjects' performance. Those expecting teachers to be warmer should have performed better at the task most similar to that usually administered by teachers. Such data, unfortunately, are not available, and the interpretation offered remains an unsupported speculation. However, the fact that in an intelligence testlike task warmer-behaving experimenters obtained superior performance seems quite consistent with the data presented earlier.

In the discussion of the effects of experimenter warmth on responses to projective tests we encountered the work of Luft (1953). He had shown that subjects contacted by warmer experimenters were more favorably inclined toward ink blots. If a warmer experimenter draws more "liking" responses to blots we might expect that he would also draw more favorable responses to photos of people. Some indirect evidence is available from the experiment in person perception which had been filmed. Experimenters whose instruction-reading behavior was judged from both film and sound track to be more personal ($r = +.28$, $p < .05$) and more interested ($r = +.23$, $p < .10$) obtained ratings of photos as being of more successful people. These are weak findings, however, because for the variables "friendly" and "pleasant" the corresponding correlations were much lower than we would have expected ($rs = +.12$, and $+.09$) if warm experimenters dependably obtained more "success" ratings from their subjects. When subjects rated their experimenters on these same four variables in an experiment conducted by Suzanne Haley there was only the smallest trend for experimenters rated more positively by their subjects to obtain ratings of the photos as more successful.

Although we cannot always say exactly what the effect will be, the status and warmth of an experimenter often affect the responses given him by his subjects. Here, and elsewhere (Edwards, 1954; Rosenthal, 1963a), when that point was made, the emphasis has been on research employing human subjects. There appear to be no experiments on the effects of more enduring experimenter attributes on the performance of their animal subjects, but there are, nevertheless, sufficiently compelling anecdotes to make us suspect that even the performance of animals depends to some degree on the personality of the investigator (Christie, 1951; Maier, 1956; Pfungst, 1911; Rosenthal, 1965a).

To summarize, and in the process oversimplify grossly, what seems to be known about the effects of the experimenter's status and warmth: Higher status experimenters tend to obtain more conforming but less pleasant responses from their subjects. Warmer experimenters tend to obtain more competent and more pleasant responses from their subjects.

6

Situational Factors

More than an experimenter's score on a test of anxiety, his status and warmth are defined and determined in part by the nature of the experimental situation and the particular subject being contacted. The experimenter "attributes" to be considered now are still more situationally determined. That is, the degree of warmth an experimenter shows one subject may be correlated with the degree of warmth he shows other subjects. But whether he "accidentally" encounters a subject with whom he has had prior social contact seems less likely to be an enduring attribute and more purely situational. The distinction is, nevertheless, arbitrary. Experimenters who are acquainted with a subject may differ in associated personality characteristics which make them more likely to be acquainted with other subjects as well. The effects of prior acquaintanceship thus may be due not simply to the prior contact as such, but to correlated variables as well.

Experimenter's Acquaintanceship

When the experimenter has had prior contact with his subject, even when that contact is brief, the subject may respond differently in the experimental task. When the task was an intelligence test, the study by Sacks (1952) is the most interesting. Her subjects, 30 children all about three years old, were divided into three experimental groups. With the children of group A she spent one hour each day for 10 days in a nursery school, participating as a good, interested teacher. With the children of group B, she spent the same amount of time but her role was that of a dull-appearing, uninterested teacher. With the children of group C, she had no prior contact. The results were defined in terms of changes in intelligence test scores from before to after treatment. Group A gained 14.5 IQ points ($p < .01$), group B gained 5.0 IQ points ($p < .05$), while the no-contact control group gained only 1.6 IQ points. This study illustrates not only the effects of prior contact but also the effects of the warmth of that contact. When the experimenter had played a warmer role the gain in IQ was 9.5 IQ points greater than when she had played a cooler role ($p = .02$).

There may be an interaction between the effects of prior contact and the particular experimenter in determining the effects on children's intellectual performance. Marine (1929), for example, spent time with somewhat older schoolchildren and found this prior contact to have no effect on the children's gain in IQ points. Most clinicians feel that anxiety serves to lower intellectual performance under ordinary conditions. Prior contact with the experimenter may serve to lower any anxiety about being contacted by a stranger and thereby lead to a relative increase in IQ. When the experimenter, in addition, is warmer, anxiety may be still further reduced, thereby raising still more the level of intellectual performance. This interpretation could be tested by having subjects high and low on test anxiety and high and low in fear of strangers receive prior contact or no prior contact. Those more anxious over tests and those more fearful of strangers should profit most from prior contact with the experimenter, and probably also from contact with a warmer experimenter.

The effects of prior contact also seem to depend on the task set for the subject. When the task is a simple, repetitive motor task such as dropping marbles into holes, complete strangers seem to be more effective reinforcers than experimenters known to the subjects—in one case, the preschool subject's own parents (Stevenson, Keen, & Knights, 1963). This is just what we would expect on the basis of Hullian learning theory. When the response is a simple one, easily available to the subject, an increase in anxiety, such as we expect to occur in the presence of strangers, increases the performance level. When the response is a difficult one, not easily available to the subject, as in an intelligence test, an increase in anxiety makes these less available responses still less likely to occur because the more available responses, more often wrong, become more likely due to the so-called multiplicative effect of drive.

A recent experiment by Berkowitz (1964) is relevant. He employed 39 chronic schizophrenic and 39 medically hospitalized normals in a study of the effects of prior warm contact, prior cold contact, and no prior contact on reaction time scores. Early trials were not reinforced, but later trials were reinforced by the experimenter's complimenting the subject for his performance. Psychiatrically normal subjects who had prior contact, either warm or cold in character, were slower in reacting than were normal subjects who had no prior contact. Of the two prior contact groups, those subjects who had experienced a warmer interaction showed the slower reaction time. Berkowitz's interpretation of these results in terms of drive level fits well with the interpretation of the results of the Stevenson et al. study just mentioned. Because the task is a simple one, the less the anxiety or drive level, the poorer the performance. Prior contact, it was suggested earlier, reduces anxiety, and with a warm experimenter more so than with a cold one. In Berkowitz's study, the results for the schizophrenic patients were somewhat different. They, too, showed the slowest reaction time when their experimenter had been warm in prior contact. However, there was no difference between reaction times of subjects with cold prior contact and those with no prior contact. For schizophrenics, perhaps, cold prior contact does not reduce anxiety as it does for psychiatric normals.

With college students as subjects, Kanfer and Karas (1959) investigated the effects of prior contact on the conditioning of first-person pronouns. There were four groups of subjects; three had prior contact with the experimenter and the fourth did not. During their prior contact one group of subjects was made to feel successful at a brief intelligence test, another group was made to feel unsuccessful, and the third group was given no feedback. All three groups who had experienced prior contact with the experimenter conditioned faster than did the group with no prior contact. If it can be assumed that learning the contingency in a verbal conditioning experiment is somewhat challenging intellectually, then the results of this study seem consistent with those of Sacks (1952), who found intellectually challenging tasks to be performed better after prior contact with the experimenter.

Kanfer and Karas, however, found no difference in performance among the three groups who had prior contact with their experimenter. Such a difference might have been expected from the results of the studies described here. The lack of any difference might have been due to the fact that during the prior contact subjects took a brief IQ test, which might have made them all sufficiently anxious to weaken the effects of the different types of feedback received about their performance. The change to the simpler verbal conditioning task might have reduced the anxiety of all three groups to below the level of the control group, for whom the experimenter-subject interaction was new, strange, and therefore possibly more anxiety-arousing. There is also the possibility that the prior contact subjects retained their high anxiety levels through the verbal conditioning task and that more anxious subjects perform better at that task. That is what we expect if the task is not challenging intellectually. The two opposing interpretations must remain unreconciled for want of the relevant data. Even when anxiety is defined by a standard test such as the Taylor Scale of Manifest Anxiety or a near relative rather than by an experimental manipulation, it is not well established whether more or less anxious subjects show more or less verbal conditioning (Rosenthal, 1963d). Verbal conditioning may turn out to be less difficult than most items of an intelligence test but more difficult than such performances as reaction time or eyelid conditioning (Spence, 1964), and that may account for the equivocality of the data available.

There are some conclusions, though that can be drawn about the effects on the subject's performance of prior contact with the experimenter. Often, at least, such contact makes a difference (Krasner, 1962; Wallin, 1949). When the performance required is difficult, prior contact, especially when of a "warm" quality, seems to improve performance. When the task is simple, prior contact may worsen performance, although, it seems safe to assume, subjects may feel more relaxed about it. When the task is of medium difficulty, no clear prediction is possible except that how the subject is occupied during the prior contact may make the major difference.

Experimenter's Experience

It seems reasonable to suppose that a more experienced experimenter, one who has conducted more experiments or at last repeated a certain experiment more often, may behave differently in the experiment than a less experienced experimenter. This difference in behavior alters the stimuli offered the subject so that we might expect him to behave differently. We have already seen at least one experiment in which the experience of the experimenter seemed to affect the speed of learning of his subjects, and these subjects were rabbits (Brogden, 1962). The less experienced experimenter obtained a slower rate of learning than did more experienced experimenters. When the subject's task was to construct stories to TAT stimuli, there was a tendency for examiners who had administered fewer TAT's to elicit more storytelling material (Turner & Coleman, 1962). In the experiment in person perception, which was recorded on sound film, some of the 19 experimenters had prior experience. They had served in one of two other studies in which their task was also to present the photos of faces to their subjects and record subjects' ratings of success or failure. In this study, there was no effect on subjects' ratings of the stimuli associated with experimenters' having had prior experience in the experimenter role. However, from the analysis of the films and of the sound track, it was evident that the more experienced experimenters behaved differently during the course of the brief preinstructional period and during the reading of the instructions. Interestingly, it was in the sound track rather than in the film or in the film combined with sound track that the differences emerged. Table 6-1 shows the larger correlations between experimenters' behavior and their prior experience. During both the preinstructional period and the instruction reading itself, the more experienced experimenters spoke in a less personal tone of voice and less distinctly. They read the instructions with less expression and gathered the initial background information from the subjects in a less pleasant and less enthusiastic tone of voice. It may be that the nature of the task was such that having been through it all before, the more experienced experimenters were simply bored. The

TABLE 6—1

Experimenter's Experience and Behavior Observed
from Sound Track Only

PREINSTRUCTIONAL PERIOD

Variable	Correlation	p
Personal	−.56	.02
Enthusiastic	−.41	.10
Pleasant-voiced	−.41	.10
Speaks distinctly	−.50	.05

INSTRUCTIONAL PERIOD

Variable	Correlation	p
Personal	−.43	.08
Expressive-voiced	−.44	.07
Speaks distinctly	−.64	.005

boredom, however, if that is what it was, was revealed through tone of voice and not through motor behavior. It is of special interest to note that observers who had access to the sound track and also to the film could not make the tone of voice judgments as well. When the information is in the sound track rather than in the film, viewing the film while listening to the sound probably results in a decreased signal-to-noise ratio (Jones & Thibaut, 1958). The film then only distracts the judges. In this analysis there was even a trend for some of the correlations based on the judgments of the film to be opposite in direction from those based on judgments of the sound track.

Although the differences in vocal behavior between more and less experienced experimenters did not affect the subjects' responses in the present study, it is not difficult to imagine experimental tasks wherein such behavioral differences among experimenters could affect subjects' task performance. Studies in verbal conditioning are one such class of studies. Here the tone of the experimenter as he utters his "good's" and "um-hmm's" may make a substantial difference, and one wants to know whether more experienced reinforcers obtain better conditioning and, if they do, whether it is because their tone of voice is different.

Even when the experimenter has had no prior experience in that role, his experience changes during the course of his first experiment.

At the end of his first experiment he is more experienced than at the beginning. Sarason (1965) reports a finding from an unpublished study by Barnard (1963) which illustrates that even during the course of a single experiment, the behavior of the experimenter can change systematically. In the Barnard study experimenters administered a phrase association task to their subjects. The degree of associative disturbance shown by the subjects seemed to be related, at least sometimes, to the prior experience of the experimenter during this study. Barnard's experimenters also reported a drop in anxiety over the course of the experiment which might have accounted for the effects of experimenters' experience on subjects' degree of disturbance.

In the experiment recorded on film, the serial order in which each subject was seen was correlated with the experimenter's behavior. It was thereby possible to learn whether later-contacted subjects were meeting an experimenter whose behavior had changed from that shown earlier subjects. Considering only the preinstructional period, none of the ratings of the experimenters' behavior correlated "significantly" ($p < .05$) with the serial order of the subject contacted. Behavior during the instruction period, however, did seem to be affected by the number of subjects the experimenter had seen previously. Table 6-2 shows the larger correlations obtained when

TABLE 6—2

Serial Order of Subject Contacted and Experimenter's Behavior: Silent Film

Variable	Correlation	p
Active	−.32	.02
Body activity	−.32	.02
Trunk activity	−.32	.02
Leg activity	−.30	.03
Expressive face	−.24	.08

judgments were based on the observation of films without sound track. Table 6-3 shows the correlations obtained when the sound track was added to the films for a different group of observers. The general decrease of motor activity during the instruction period as successive subjects were contacted seems consistent with Barnard's report of decreased experimenter anxiety over the course of an experiment. Again, the addition of another channel of information resulted in a decrease of "correlational information" about these variables. When the sound track was added, only one of the variables shown in Table 6-2 remained significantly correlated with the

TABLE 6—3

Serial Order of Subject Contacted and Experimenter's Behavior: Film and Sound Track

Variable	Correlation	p
Interested	−.31	.02
Active	−.24	.10
Enthusiastic	−.23	.10
Encouraging	−.23	.10
Relaxed	+.26	.06
Leaning toward S	−.26	.06
Head nodding	−.25	.07
Accuracy	+.25	.07
Time	−.31	.03

serial order of subject contacted, and even that correlation was reduced substantially. Table 6-3 shows, however, that the addition of the sound track made possible the observation of different behaviors which were determined in part by the serial order of subjects contacted. Experimenters seemed to become less interested and less involved in their interaction with later-contacted subjects but more relaxed as well. They read their instructions more rapidly and more accurately to later than to earlier subjects, which suggests an expected practice effect. (Although not significant statistically, experimenters who had participated in an earlier experiment and thus were more experienced, by that definition, also tended to be more accurate $[r = +.26]$ and faster $[r = −.18]$ in reading their instructions.) In this experiment, as in Barnard's, experimenters seem to relax over the course of an experiment and, in this study, to become somewhat more bored though more proficient as well. Also, in this study, the behavior changes shown by the experimenters seemed to affect their subjects' responses to the photo-judging task. Later-contacted subjects tended to rate the photos as being of more unsuccessful people than did earlier subjects $(r = −.31, p < .02)$. It may be that over the course of an experiment the data collector acquires greater comfort and competence and thereby greater status. For the photo-rating task employed, it was shown earlier that experimenters judged to have higher status did tend to obtain ratings of photos as of more unsuccessful people.

From the evidence available it seems safe to conclude that the amount of experience of an experimenter may affect the responses collected from his subjects. This seems to be the case when experience is defined either over several experiments or within a single experiment.

Experimenter Experiences

Not only the amount of experience the experimenter has accumulated but also the experiences he has encountered in his role as data collector may affect his subjects' responses. Earlier, in discussing the effects of experimenter's warmth, it was suggested that the subject's response may affect the experimenter's behavior in his transaction with the subject. But, since the experimenter's behavior may influence the subject's response, it is easy to view the experimenter-subject system as one of complex feedbacks. The response given by the subject may itself affect his next response at the same time it affects his experimenter's response, which will also affect the subject's next response. Focusing on the experimenter, the same analysis is possible. His behavior affects his own subsequent behavior but also affects the subject's response, which, in turn, affects the experimenter's next response. The resulting complex of intertwining feedback loops may be incredibly complex but no more complex than that characterizing other dyadic interactions (Jones & Thibaut, 1958).

In this section the discussion will deal with such ongoing effects on the experimenter that have repercussions on the responses he obtains from his subjects. The subject's own effect on the experimenter will be considered as well as such other influences as the physical characteristics of the laboratory in which the experimenter works and the nature of his interaction with any principal investigator to whom he may be responsible.

Subjects' behavior. An experiment by Heller, Myers, and Kline (1963) demonstrates the effects of a subject's behavior on the interviewer's behavior. Each of 34 counselor-interviewers contacted 4 subject-clients in a clinical context. Actually, each counselor interviewed the same four "clients," who were accomplices of the investigators and trained to play one of four roles. Two clients played a dominant role, and one of these was friendly about it, the other hostile. The other two clients played a dependent role, one friendly, the other hostile. Observations of interviewer behavior revealed that contact with a dominant client led to interviewers' behaving in a more dependent manner (mean dominance score $= 12.1$), while contact with a more dependent client led to more dominant behavior (mean $= 15.2$, $p < .001$). When interviewers contacted more hostile clients they responded in a less friendly fashion (mean $= 11.4$) than when they contacted friendly clients (mean $= 21.4$, $p < .0005$). These results were just those the investigators had predicted. In this study it is reasonable to think of the actor-clients as the experimenters and the interviewers as the subjects. However, the interviewers' perceptions of their own role was more like that of data collector than of experimental subject. This may have reduced the obtained effects, since the role of subject is thought to include greater susceptibility to social influence than is the role of data collector, whether the collector be "experimenter," "examiner," "therapist," or "interviewer." When the task employed by the experimenters was the administration of an intelligence test, Masling (1959) found results analogous to those obtained by Heller, Myers, and Kline. Also employing actor-subjects, Masling found warmer subjects treated in more friendly fashion by the examiners.

For a situation in which the experimenter was trying to follow a more highly programmed procedure with his subjects, Matarazzo provides an illuminating anecdote (personal communication, 1964). The basic data are reported elsewhere (Matarazzo, Wiens, & Saslow, 1965), but briefly, the study was of the effect of the duration of an interviewer's utterance on the duration of the subject's utterance. The interviews were divided into three periods. During the first and third periods the interviewer tried to average utterances of five seconds. During the middle period he tried to average ten-second utterances. Regardless of the patterns employed (e.g., 5, 10, 5; 10, 5, 10; 5, 15, 5) the subject's average length of utterance was a function of the length of the interviewer's utterance. Matarazzo raised the possibility of a feedback effect upon the interviewer associated with the subject's length of utterance. Unless he paid strict attention to his average length of utterance, it seemed that his own length of utterance was being affected by the subject's length of utterance. Thus in one experiment, the interviewer overshot his target length of five seconds by only 6 percent in the first of the three periods; then, in the third period, after the subject had increased the length of his utterances in the second period, the interviewer overshot his target by 22 percent ($p < .01$). This effect disappeared completely when the investigator kept this phenomenon in mind. Subsequently, when not attentive to it, the hysteresis occurred again. This time the interviewer achieved the target length of five seconds perfectly in the first period of the interview. In the third period, however, after the increasing length of his subject's utterances in the second period, he overshot his target time by 10 percent ($p < .01$).

What happens to an experimenter during the course of his experiment may alter his behavior toward his subjects in such a way as to affect subjects' (1) judgments of the degree of success shown by standard stimulus persons, (2) responses on standard tests of personality, and (3) test-retest reliabilities of personality tests. In Part II of this book, Chapter 12, dealing with the effects of early data returns, will give the details. Briefly, for now, 26 experimenters administered the photo-judging task to a total of 115 female subjects. Half the experimenters were led to expect that their subjects would see the stimulus persons as successful and half were led to expect their subjects to see the stimulus persons as unsuccessful. Accomplices were trained to rate the photos sometimes as of successful people and sometimes as of unsuccessful people. Regardless of their initial expectancy, half the experimenters had their expectancies confirmed and half had their expectancies disconfirmed by their first two subjects who were the accomplices. That is, half of the experimenters who were expecting ratings of success ($+5$) obtained ratings of success, while the other half obtained ratings of failure (-5). Half the experimenters expecting ratings of failure (-5) obtained such ratings, and the other half obtained ratings of success ($+5$) from their "subjects." Subsequently, when the experimenters contacted real subjects, the mean rating of the photos obtained by experimenters whose expectations had been confirmed was -1.55; that obtained by experimenters whose expectations had been disconfirmed was -0.79 ($p = .05$). It may be that the confirmation of expectancies gave added confidence to these experimenters, a confidence reflected in a more professional, assured manner. Earlier, data were presented that suggested that such a more professional, prestigious experimenter was likely to obtain ratings of the photos as being of more unsuccessful people.

Before and after the experiment, subjects were tested with the Taylor Manifest Anxiety Scale and the Marlowe-Crowne Social Desirability Scale. Whether their experimenter had his initial expectations confirmed or disconfirmed did not affect subjects' level of anxiety. However, subjects whose experimenters had their expectancies confirmed showed a significant increase in their social desirability scores compared to the subjects whose experimenter's expectancies had been disconfirmed ($p < .05$). It can again be hypothesized that confirmatory responses increased the experimenter's self-confidence, leading to his behaving in a more professional manner. In the section dealing with the effects of experimenter status, we saw that increases in status and authority on the part of the experimenter lead to a greater degree of propriety in the responses he obtains from subjects. That seems to be what happened in this experiment as well.

Changes in test scores is a different matter from changes in test reliability. All subjects may earn higher or lower scores on a retest without the retest reliability being affected. The retest reliability of the subjects' scores on the social desirability scale was not affected significantly by the confirmation or the disconfirmation of their experimenter's expectation, though there was a slight decrease when the experimenter's hypothesis had been disconfirmed ($r = .74$ vs. $r = .66$). When their experimenter's expectation had been disconfirmed, the reliability of subjects' anxiety scores was lower ($r = +.80$) than when their experimenter's expectation had been confirmed ($r = +.90$, p of difference $= .06$). It is interesting to speculate on the possibility that the behavior of a more self-confident experimenter is such as to increase the retest reliability of his subjects' test scores. It may be that the general retest-taking set provided by such an experimenter is one for consistency of performance. This set could operate in spite of a general tendency for the experimenter's manner to affect subjects' retests uniformly, with the result being like that of adding a constant to an array of scores. Such a constant does not, of course, affect the correlation coefficient.

As mentioned, in experiments employing accomplices whose task it is to influence the interviewer, or the examiner, or the experimenter, it is sometimes useful to regard the accomplice as the experimenter and the data collector or clinician as the subject. In the experiment under discussion, the accomplices may be regarded as experimenters of a kind, since they were making the programmed responses. So, too, were the experimenters, but their behavior in carrying out the directions of the experiment could vary, within limits, without their being regarded as incompetent experimenters who were "spoiling" the experiment. There is no direct measure of the experimenters' behavior in this experiment, as it was not filmed, but there is good evidence that their behavior affected the performance of the accomplices. It will be remembered that half the time accomplices were to give $+5$ and half the time -5 responses to the photos presented by their experimenters. Sometimes these responses confirmed the experimenter's expectancy, sometimes they disconfirmed it. Accomplices did not, of course, know that they were confirming or disconfirming by their responses, or that the experimenters had any expectancy at all. All accomplices came close to giving their target ratings of $+5$ or -5 when considering that the photos' standardized value was approximately zero. The mean rating given (disregarding signs which, of course, were not disregarded by the accomplices) by accomplices in the four conditions described was 3.99, or about one scale unit too close to the neutral side of the scale of success or failure ($\sigma = .27$). Table 6-4 shows the mean absolute ratings

TABLE 6—4

Distance from Target Values of Ratings Made by Accomplices

	Experimenter's Expectancy	
	+5	−5
Confirmation	+.29	−1.70
Disconfirmation	+.63	+.78

given by accomplices to the experimenters of each of the four experimental conditions. The means have been converted to standard scores. If the numerical values given the experimenters had been equivalent in the four cells, all standard scores would have been close to zero. As it was, the accomplices assigned at random to the experimenters expecting and receiving ratings of the photos as failures gave ratings too close to the neutral end of the scale. In this they were significantly different from the accomplices in the other three conditions ($p < .02$). It must be emphasized that only the experimenters were given an expectancy and only the experimenters experienced confirmation or disconfirmation. In some way, the experimenter's behavior was such as to drive the accomplices' ratings off the target and into the direction of the neutral point if the experimenter expected and obtained negative ratings from the accomplice-subjects. Because there was no direct observation of the experimenter-accomplice interaction, the interpretation is speculative. It may be that experimenters expecting subjects to see failure in others feel sorry for such subjects. Under a hypothesis of projection, these subjects would be viewed as feeling themselves to be failures. When the experimenters expecting failure perceptions from their subjects have these expectancies disconfirmed, they need no longer feel sorry for their subjects. However, when they learn from the accomplices in the confirming condition that they do indeed see others as unsuccessful, they may react with special warmth and friendliness to these subjects suspected of feeling inadequate. This warmth, which has been shown to increase the perception of success of others, may similarly influence the accomplices in spite of the fact that they have learned a part to play and, most likely, are quite unaware of being so influenced by the experimenters they believe to be their "marks" or "targets." But if this interpretation were sound, what about those accomplices who also rate photos as unsuccessful for those experimenters expecting ratings of success? Would we not expect the experimenters to be warmer, too, to these failure perceivers? We would, ordinarily, but the effects of disconfirmation may be to disconcert the experimenter so that he cannot be an effective "therapist" for his unwilling and unneedful "client."

From the evidence presented in this section, it seems clear that the subject's behavior can affect the experimenter's behavior which, in turn, may have further effects on the subject's behavior. Each participant in the interaction affects not only the other but himself as well. The effect on the participant by the participant himself may be direct or indirect. It is direct when he recognizes the response he has made, and this recognition affects the probability of a subsequent response. It is indirect when his response alters the behavior of the other participant in such a way that the new response affects his own subsequent response. It makes no difference whether we speak from the viewpoint of the subject or of the experimenter. It makes no difference whether the experimenter is interacting with a bona fide subject or an accomplice. Experimenters do not simply affect subjects. Accomplices do not simply affect their targets. Subjects and targets both "act back."

Characteristics of the laboratory. Riecken (1962) has pointed out how much there is we do not know about the effects of the physical scene in which an experimental transaction occurs. We know little enough about how the scene affects the subject's response; we know still less about how the particular laboratory setting affects the experimenter. Riecken wondered about the effect on his subjects of the experimenter's white coat. Perhaps that makes him more of a scientist in his subject's eyes. Perhaps it does and perhaps, too, it makes him more of a scientist in his own eyes. If "clothes can make the man," then perhaps, too, a laboratory can make a scientist feel more the part. What impresses and affects the subject may impress and affect the experimenter. Perhaps the most senior of the laboratory directors is not susceptible to such effects. Even if he is not, however, we must ask what percentage of his laboratory's data he himself collects. It is perhaps more common for more data to be collected by less senior personnel who might be affected by the status of the setting in which they contact their subjects. So many psychology departments are housed in "temporary" buildings with space shortages that one wonders about the systematic effects possible if indeed the physical scene affected both subject and experimenter.

There is evidence that subjects' responses may be affected by the "laboratory's" characteristics. Mintz (1957) found that negative print photos of faces were judged more energetic and more pleased in a "beautified" room, more "average" in an average room, and less energetic and less pleased in an "uglified" room ($p < .01$). Observations of the two experimenters who administered the photo-judging tasks suggested that they, too, were affected by the rooms in which they conducted the experiments. Not only were their own ratings of the photos affected by their locale, but so too was their attitude toward the experiment and their behavior toward their subjects.

Some data collected together with Suzanne Haley show the effects of laboratory room characteristics on subjects and possibly their effects on experimenters' behavior. The experiment required subjects to rate photos of faces for degree of success experienced. There were 14 experimenters, 86 subjects, and 8 laboratory rooms. Experimenters and subjects were assigned to rooms at random. Each room was rated by 13 experimenters (not including the one who used that room) on the following four dimensions: (1) how professional the room was in appearance, (2) how high the status was of the room's characteristic user judging from the physical appearance, (3) how comfortable the room was, (4) how disorderly the room was. None of the room characteristics were significantly related to the subjects' ratings of the photos of faces. However, the characteristics of the rooms were significantly related to a large proportion of the 26 ratings subjects made of their experimenter's behavior. Table 6-5 shows the correlations between the experimenters' behavior as judged by their subjects and the room characteristics of "professional" and "disordered." The room characteristic of "status of the user" is omitted since its correlation with

TABLE 6—5

Experimenter Behavior and Characteristics of his Laboratory

Variable	PROFESSIONAL Correlation	p	DISORDERED Correlation	p
Talkative	+.24	.03	+.08	–
Loud	+.25	.02	+.09	–
Pleasant-voiced	+.04	–	+.19	.10
Expressive-voiced	+.22	.05	+.09	–
Hand gestures	+.32	.005	+.23	.05
Arm gestures	+.21	.05	+.11	–
Trunk activity	+.17	–	+.26	.02
Leg activity	+.31	.007	+.15	–
Body activity	+.22	.05	+.21	.05
Expressive face	+.32	.005	+.05	–
Encouraging	+.12	–	+.25	.02
Friendly	+.19	.10	+.07	–
Relaxed	+.20	.07	+.10	–
Interested	+.16	–	+.20	.07

"professional" was .98. The room characteristic "comfortable" is not listed because only one of the 26 judgments of experimenter behavior reached the .05 level. That one correlation showed the experimenters in more comfortable rooms to have a less pleasant voice ($r = -.24$, $p = .03$). Because it occurred as the only significant relationship in a set of 26 correlations, it is best mentioned and put aside.

When the room is a more professional-appearing locale for the experimental interaction, experimenters behave, or at least are seen as behaving, in a more motorically and verbally active manner. They are seen also to be somewhat more at ease and friendly. The pattern is not very different when the laboratory is described as more disordered, and that may be due to the substantial correlation of $+.41$ between the professionalness and disorderedness of the lab. There is no way to be sure whether the characteristics of the room affected only the subjects' judgments of their experimenters (as Mintz's subjects judged photo negatives of faces differently in different rooms) or whether experimenters were sufficiently affected by their surroundings to have actually behaved differently. Both mechanisms could, of course, have operated. If only the subjects' perceptions were affected, that still argues that we take more seriously than we have Riecken's (1962) invitation to study the effects of the physical scene on subjects' responses. If the experimenter appears differently to subjects as a function of the scene, subjects might respond differently for him in some experimental tasks, though in the present task of judging the success of others they did not.

There is one thin line of evidence that the behavior of the experimenters was, in fact, affected by the characteristics of the rooms to which they had been randomly assigned. All experimenters were asked to state the purpose of the experiment at its conclusion, in order that their degree of suspiciousness about the intent of the study might be assessed. In addition, their written statements were assessed for the degree of seriousness with which these graduate students appeared to take the experimenter role. Those experimenters who had been assigned to a more disordered room were less suspicious of the true intent of the experiment. The correlation obtained was $-.42$, but with the small number of experimenters (14) this was not statistically significant. How seriously the experiment was taken, however, did appear related to the rooms to which they had been assigned. If the room was more disordered, experimenters were more serious in their statements about their perception of the intent of the experiment ($r = +.39$). In addition, if the room was more comfortable, they were less serious in their written statements ($r = -.45$). These two findings taken together are unlikely to have occurred by chance, since the room characteristics of comfortable and disordered were positively correlated ($r = +.32$). The two room characteristics together predicted the seriousness of subsequent written statements with a multiple R of .73 ($p < .02$). Since the nature of the experimenter's room predicted his subsequent behavior, it seems more reasonable to think that it might have affected his behavior during the experiment as well. It is not too clear, however, why a more disordered, less comfortable room should make the experimenters view the experiment more seriously. Perhaps these graduate students, who were not in psychology, felt that a scientifically serious business was carried on best in the cluttered and severely furnished laboratory some of them may have encountered in the psychology departments of colleges at which they were undergraduates, and which seems to fit the stereotype of the scientist's ascetic pursuit of truth.

It seems, then, that the physical scene in which the subject interacts with his experimenter may affect the subject's response in two ways. First, the scene may affect directly the subject's response by making him feel differently. Second, the scene may affect the experimenter's behavior, which in turn affects the subjects' responses to the experimental task. Research on the physical scene as an unintended determinant of the subject's and experimenter's behavior is in its infancy. What data there are suggest the wisdom of collecting more.

The principal investigator. With more and more research carried out in teams and groups, the chances are increasing that any given experimenter will be collecting data not for himself alone. More and more, there is a principal investigator to whom the experimenter is responsible for the data he collects. The more enduring personal characteristics of the principal investigator as well as the content and style of his interaction with the experimenter can affect the responses the subjects give the experimenter.

In telling of the effects of the subjects' responses on the experimenter's behavior, an experiment was mentioned in which the expectation of the experimenter was confirmed half the time and disconfirmed half the time. In that same experiment, two other variables were studied, both relating to the effects of the principal investigator on the data obtained by the experimenters. One of these variables was the affective tone of the relationship between experimenter and principal investigator; the other was the individual differences between principal investigators. After the experimenters contacted their first few subjects (who were actually accomplices) they were given feedback by one of two principal investigators on how well they had done their work as experimenters. Half the experimenters were praised for their performance, half were reproved. Each of two principal investigators contacted half of the 26 experimenters and administered praise and reproof equally often. When the experimenters had been praised before contacting their real subjects, those subjects rated photos as being of more unsuccessful people (mean $= -1.60$) than when experimenters had been reproved (mean $= -.74$, $p < .05$). When experimenters had been *either* praised or reproved by one of the principal investigators, their subjects subsequently rated people as less successful (mean $= -1.57$) than when experimenters had been either praised or reproved by the other principal investigator (mean $= -.78$, $p < .05$). Both the kind of person the principal investigator is, as well as the content of his interaction with the experimenter, affect the responses subjects give their experimenter. Praising an experimenter (and contact with a certain type of principal investigator) may have the same effect on his behavior toward his subjects that confirming his expectation does. He feels, and therefore acts, in a more professional, self-confident manner, a pattern of behavior already shown to lead to ratings by subjects of others as less successful. A reminder is in order that we do not know the reasons for this reaction on the part of subjects to a more professional, confident, higher status experimenter. It has been suggested earlier that, in a military or an academic setting, a higher status experimenter may evoke more negative feeling which is displaced onto the stimulus persons. In the military setting, negative feeling toward an officer may be well institutionalized. In the academic setting, the higher status or more professional-acting experimenter may be seen as a more effective "poker and pryer" into the mind of the subject (Riecken, 1962); he is, therefore, more to be feared. It may even be that undergraduate subjects "know" or intuit something of Freud's concept of projection and feel that if they see too much success in photos they will be regarded as immodest by the higher status experimenter. As already shown, "proper" responses are more often given to data collectors of higher status in both laboratory and field research.

In the experiment described, subjects had been tested for anxiety and social desirability before and after the experiment. There were no effects on subjects' social desirability scores associated with which of the two principal investigators had contacted their experimenter early in the experiment. However, subjects whose experimenters had been either praised or reproved by one of the principal investigators showed a significantly greater increase in anxiety over the course of the experiment than did subjects whose experimenters had earlier been contacted by the other principal investigator ($x^2 = 7.71, p < .01$).

There is additional evidence of the effect of the principal investigator on the data obtained by his research assistants. In this experiment there were 13 principal investigators, each of whom was randomly assigned two research assistants (Rosenthal, Persinger, Vikan-Kline, & Mulry, 1963). Before the principal investigators received their "research grants," which allowed them to hire their research assistants, they had themselves served as experimenters in the person perception task. The principal investigators' scores on the Taylor Anxiety Scale correlated significantly with their subjects' ratings of the success of others (rho $= +.66, p = .03$). Remarkably enough, the principal investigators' anxiety also predicted the photo ratings their assistants obtained from their different sample of subjects (rho $= +.40, p < .07$). In "real-life" research situations, such a correlation could be enhanced by the possibility that principal investigators employ research assistants who are similar to themselves in personality. A correlation between an attribute of the principal investigator and his assistant's obtained data could then be nothing more than the effect of the assistant's personality on the subject's response. This has been well established by now and is not so intriguing. In the study described, however, assistants were assigned at random to their principal investigator. The correlation between the principal investigator's anxiety level and that of his assistants was only .02. Therefore, it must be that the nature of the principal investigator's interaction with his assistants altered their behavior in such a way as to affect their subjects' responses. The principal investigator affected the subject by affecting the data collector. It should be emphasized that the principal investigator never even saw the subjects who had been assigned to his research assistants.

In this same experiment, there was no effect of the principal investigator's need for social approval on the photo ratings obtained by his assistants, although that correlation ($-.16$) was in the same direction as that between the principal investigator's need for approval and his own subjects' perception of the success of persons pictured in photos ($-.49$). Finally, the correlation between the average "success" ratings obtained by any principal investigator and those obtained by his own research assistants from a different sample of subjects was $+.38$, which, for the sample of 13 principal investigators, was not significant. Omitting the three female principal investigators raised this correlation to $+.75$, $p < .02$, suggesting a possible interaction effect. Table 6-6 shows that such an interaction did occur. The mean photo ratings of success, in standard score form, obtained

TABLE 6—6

Experimenters' Data as a Function of Data Obtained by Their Male and Female Principal Investigators

PHOTO RATINGS OBTAINED
BY PRINCIPAL
INVESTIGATORS

		Success	Failure	Difference	t	p
SEX OF PRINCIPAL INVESTIGATOR	Male	+.63	−.54	+1.17	2.09	.07
	Female	−1.31	+1.22	−2.53	2.38	.05
	Difference	+1.94	−1.76	3.70		
	t	2.07	2.35		3.12	
	p	.08	.05			.02

by the experimenters are shown separately for those whose principal investigators had themselves obtained mean ratings of either success or failure from their own subjects. When the principal investigator was a male, his assistants obtained ratings significantly similar to those he had obtained. When the principal investigator was female, the assistants obtained data significantly opposite to the data she had obtained. The sample of female principal investigators, especially, is small but the data are clear. The responses a subject gives his experimenter depend not only, as we saw much earlier, on the sex of the experimenter, but on the sex of his experimenter's principal investigator as well.

Finally, there is an experiment in person perception in which, after training the experimenters, the principal investigators called their attention to the fact that only if they followed proper experimental procedures could the experimenters expect to obtain the results desired by the principal investigators (Rosenthal, Persinger, Mulry, Vikan-Kline, & Grothe, 1964b). There were 15 male experimenters who conducted the person perception experiment with a total of 60 female subjects. Those eight experimenters whose principal investigators had made them self-conscious about their procedure obtained ratings of persons as significantly less successful (mean =

—.57) than did experimenters who had not been made self-conscious (mean = +.37, $p < .06$), A subsample of the interactions had been filmed so that there were clues available as to how the more self-conscious experimenters might have behaved differently toward their subjects so as to obtain judgments of others as being more unsuccessful. The observations again come from three groups of observers. One group had access to the film and sound track, one group saw the film but did not hear the sound track, and one group heard only the sound track. None of the observations made by this last group of observers was related to the experimentally created self-consciousness of the experimenters.

During the brief preinstructional transaction, observers who saw only the film found a tendency for more self-conscious experimenters to behave more dominantly ($r = +.41$, $p < .10$). When the sound track was added to the films, these experimenters, who had been "put on the spot" by the principal investigators, were judged less relaxed ($r = -.45$, $p = .06$) and less courteous ($r = -.40$, $p < .10$). During the instruction-reading period, as Table 6-7 shows, the behavior of the more procedure-conscious experi-

TABLE 6—7

Instruction-Reading Behavior as a Function of Procedure Consciousness Induced by Principal Investigators

| | OBSERVATION CHANNELS | | | |
| | Sound Films | | Silent Films | |
Variable	r	p	r	p
Likable	−.45	.06	−.41	.10
Courteous	−.43	.07	−.15	—
Interested	−.07	—	−.40	.10
Slow-speaking	−.43	.07	—	—
Honest	−.42	.08	−.58	.01

menters was judged less likable from observing the films with or without the sound track. They were judged less courteous only when their tone of voice could be heard, less interested only when their tone could not be heard. Judged to be more slow-speaking from the observation of the sound film, that was not the case from a hearing of the sound track alone. Although the addition of information via a different sense modality does not always add usable information, it sometimes does, even when we would not expect it to. Finally, we note that more self-conscious experimenters are judged less honest. So the picture we have is of the principal investigator's admonition affecting the experimenter's behavior by making him less likable, less courteous in tone, faster speaking, and more "dishonest," by which is meant, probably, more subtly "pushy" or influential. (The particular subtle influence they were probably exerting on their subjects will be discussed later on in Part II. It has to do with the expectancy for particular responses from the subject.) In an earlier chapter, that which dealt with observer effects, we saw that subjects, as well as observers, could be quite sensitive to the "bias" of the experimenter and were likely to code this information into the category of "honesty." The general behavior shown by these experimenters is, as we have seen earlier, that kind of behavior which leads often, but not always, to subjects' responding with more negative ratings of the success of the stimulus persons.

The results of the last three studies described show that the interaction with the principal investigator can affect the experimenter's interaction with his subjects and, thereby, the responses he obtains from them. The precise direction of the effect, however, seems difficult to predict. In the first study described, the principal investigator's reproof led to the experimenter's obtaining ratings of others as more successful. In the second study, the more anxious the principal investigator was, the more successful were the perceptions of others obtained by his research assistants. An anxious principal investigator may affect the experimenter as a reproving one, so these two studies are not inconsistent. However, we cannot assume that the more anxious principal investigator simply made the experimenter more anxious and that this altered anxiety level affected the subjects so that they perceived more success in others. It must be remembered that in the discussion of the effects of experimenters' anxiety, one study showed that more anxious experimenters obtained ratings of others as more successful but another study showed the opposite effect.

In the third experiment, the only one in which we could see what happened in the experimenter-subject interaction, experimenters who were made more conscious of their procedures by their principal investigators obtained ratings of the stimulus people as less successful. The opposite result, although less intuitively appealing, would seem to have been more consistent with the results of the other two studies. More self-conscious experimenters should perhaps have been somewhat like reproved ones or like those in contact with an anxious principal investigator. We are left with little confidence that we can predict the specific effect on subjects' responses from a knowledge of the nature of the experimenter's interaction with the principal investigator. We can have considerable confidence, however, that the nature of the interaction between experimenter and principal investigator can affect the subjects' responses in some way.

Not all the evidence for this assertion comes from the person perception experiment. Mulry's experiment (1962) called for the experimenters to administer a pursuit rotor task to their subjects. Experimenters had been trained to administer this task by having themselves serve as subjects for the principal investigator. Half the experimenters were told by the principal investigator that they were very good at the perceptual-motor skills involved. Half the experimenters were led to believe their own performance was not a good one. There was no effect of this feedback on the performance of the experimenters' subjects. However, experimenters who had been complimented by their principal investigator were perceived quite differently by their own subjects than were the less fortunate experimenters. Complimented experimenters were seen to behave in a more interested ($r = +.31$, $p = .01$), more enthusiastic ($r = +.24$, $p = .05$), and more optimistic ($r = +.29$, $p = .02$) manner. From this it seems that even though the behavior of the experimenter is affected by his interaction with the principal investigator, that does not always affect the subject to respond differently. The next, and final, study to be considered shows an instance in which it does (Rosenthal, Kohn, Greenfield, & Carota, 1966).

The experimental task was a standard one for studies of verbal conditioning. Subjects constructed sentences and, after the establishment of a basal level, were reinforced by the experimenter's saying "good" whenever first-person pronouns were employed. There were 19 experimenters who contacted a total of 60 subjects. Before the experiment began, the principal investigators gave experimenters indirect and subtle personal evaluations. Half the experimenters were evaluated favorably, half were evaluated unfavorably. Within each of these conditions, half the evaluations dealt with the experimenter's intelligence, half with his influenceability. Thus, half the favorably evaluated experimenters were subtly informed that they were regarded as very intelligent by the principal investigators; half were evaluated as resistant to manipulation by others. Unfavorably evaluated experimenters were led to believe they were regarded by the principal investigators as either less intelligent or more manipulatable by others.

Experimenters who felt more favorably evaluated by their principal

TABLE 6—8

Conditioning Obtained by Experimenters as a Function of Their Principal Investigator's Evaluation

EVALUATION

Attribute	Favorable	Unfavorable	Difference	t	p
Intelligence	3.0	1.3	1.7	1.89	.10
Influenceability	3.1	0.8	2.3	2.56	.03

investigators were significantly more successful at obtaining increased use of first-person pronouns by their subjects. Table 6-8 shows the mean increase in the number of such words emitted from the operant level to the end of the experiment. There was no difference in the magnitude of the effect associated with the particular attribute evaluated. All ten of the experimenters who felt favorably evaluated obtained an increase in their subjects' use of the reinforced words ($p = .001$), but only five of the nine who felt unfavorably evaluated obtained any increase ($p = 1.00$).

An interesting additional finding was that even during the operant level of responding, before any reinforcements were provided, experimenters obtained a greater number of first-person pronouns (mean = 9.8) when their principal investigator's evaluation was favorable than when it was unfavorable (mean = 8.3, $p = .10$). This was not an artifact based on a relationship between the operant level and the operant to terminal block increase. The correlation between operant level and conditioning score was only $-.10$. Perhaps an experimenter who feels favorably evaluated by his supervisor makes his subjects more willing to make up more personal statements, quite apart from being a more effective reinforcer.

In this study, subjects were asked to describe their experimenter's behavior in a series of 28 rating scales. Table 6-9 shows the larger correla-

TABLE 6—9

Experimenters' Behavior as a Function of Favorable Evaluation by Their Principal Investigator

Variable	Correlation	p
Casual	+.33	.01
Courteous	+.27	.05
Pleasant	+.24	.08
Expressive-voiced	+.24	.08
Trunk activity	−.26	.05

tions between subjects' observations of the experimenter's behavior and the favorableness of his evaluation by the principal investigator. The correlations are what we would expect. Feeling more favorably evaluated, the experimenter is less tense and more pleasant, and these characteristics could reasonably make him a more effective reinforcer and a person for whom more "personal" (i.e., first person) sentences are constructed.

Earlier, the inconsistency of the effect of a principal investigator's interaction with the data collector on the subject's response was noted. It is interesting, however, that in those three studies in which the experimenter's behavior was observed, either by the subjects themselves or by external observers of the sound films, the results do show a certain consistency. Experimenters who, in their interaction with the principal investigator, were made to feel (1) less self-conscious, (2) more successful at the experimental task, and (3) more intelligent or less manipulatable, all seemed to behave toward their subjects in a more positive, likable, interpersonal style. In two of these three experiments, all employing different tasks, this behavior on the part of the experimenter probably affected the responses of the subjects in their performance of the experimental tasks.

CONCLUSION

From all that has been said and shown it seems clear that there are a great many variables that affect the subject's response other than those variables which, in a given experiment, are specifically under investigation. The kind of person the experimenter is, how he or she looks and acts, may by itself affect the subject's response. Sometimes the effect is a direct and simple one, but sometimes, too, the effect is found to interact with subject characteristics, task characteristics, or situational characteristics.

Not only the kind of person the experimenter "is" but the things that happen to him before and during the experiment affect his behavior in such a way as to evoke different responses from his subjects. The subject's behavior may have feedback effects on his own subsequent behavior not only directly but also by changing the experimenter's behavior, which then alters the subject's response.

The room in which the experiment is conducted not only may affect the subject's response directly but may affect it indirectly as well, by also affecting the behavior of the experimenter as he interacts with his subject. Such a change in experimenter behavior, of course, alters the experimental conditions for the subject.

The experimenter and the subject may transact the experimental business as a dyad, but often there is, in effect, a triadic business. The nonpresent third party is the principal investigator, who, by what he is, and what he does, and how he does it in his dyadic interaction with the experimenter, indirectly affects the responses of the subject he never comes to meet. He changes the experimenter's behavior in ways that change the subject's behavior.

Of all the possible variables associated with the experimenter, only those have been discussed for which enough evidence has been accumulated that we may say these often make a substantial difference. Probably they make less of a difference where the phenomena under investigation are very robust. There are experiments in psychophysics, learning, and psychopharmacology in which the average obtained responses may be only trivially (even if "significantly" in the statistical sense) affected by the experimenter's attributes. Increasing dosages of ether are more likely to produce unconsciousness, regardless of the attributes of the experimenter, though the shape of the curve may be altered by his unique characteristics and behaviors. Most of the behavioral science research carried out today is of the "50 subjects, $p = .01$" type. That means, of course, accounting for something like 13 percent of the variance in subjects' responses from a knowledge of our treatment conditions or a reduction in predictive errors of about 6 percent. Because the effects of our independent variables, though unquestionably "real," are usually so fragile, we must be especially concerned about the effects of experimenter attributes.

The methodological implications of the experimenter effects discussed will be treated more fully in Part III. Only a few points need be mentioned here. First, very little has been said so far about the effects of experimenter attributes on the "results of research." Generally the wording has been in terms of effects on the subject's response. Such effects may alter the the "results of research," but they may not. In that research which seeks to estimate a population mean from the mean of a sample, experimenter effects do change the "results of research." Examples include much of the work performed by survey research organizations. If we want to estimate the average degree of favorableness to a national policy, a well-dressed, high-status-appearing, older gentleman is likely to draw responses different from those obtained by a more shabbily dressed, bearded young man presumed to be from a nearby college. If we want to standardize a new test—i.e., estimate the national mean and standard deviation—or do sex behavior surveys, the results may be affected directly by the experimenter's effects on his subjects' responses. But much, perhaps most, psychological research is not of this sort. Most psychological research is likely to involve the assessment of the effects of two or more experimental conditions on the responses of the subject. If a certain type of experimenter tends to obtain slower learning from his subjects, the "results of his experiment" are affected not at all so long as his effect is constant over the different conditions of the experiment. Experimenter effects on means do not necessarily imply effects on mean differences.

In the survey research or test standardization type of research, the data tend to be collected by many different interviewers, examiners, or experimenters. We may be fortunate, and in the given sample of data collectors the various effects due to their characteristics or experiences may be canceled out. However, they may not be, as when there is a tendency for the data collectors to be selected on strict criteria, implicit or explicit, in such a way that the N different experimenters are more nearly N times the same experimenter. There will be more to say about this in Part III.

In the laboratory experiment, the effect of a given experimenter attribute or experience may interact with the treatment condition. We have seen earlier that this does happen when the experimenter is aware, and usually he is, which subjects are undergoing which different treatments. To use two experimenters, one for each treatment condition, of course, confounds any effects of the experimenter with the effects of the treatments, so that an assessment of treatment effects is impossible. Any method that makes it less likely that experimenter effects will interact with treatment conditions would reduce our problem of assessing adequately the effects of our treatment conditions. More will be said of this in Part III, but for now, the not very surprising conclusion is that for the control of the effects of experimenter attributes, as for the control of the other effects discussed in earlier chapters, we must rely heavily on the process of replication.

7

Experimenter Modeling

In this chapter the discussion will turn to an "attribute" of the experimenter which, like those considered just before, is also defined in terms of the particular experiment being conducted. That attribute is the performance of the experimenter himself of the same task he sets his subjects. For some experiments, then, this experimenter attribute will be a more enduring characteristic, such as intelligence or authoritarianism. For other experiments, this attribute will be a less enduring one, such as an opinion on a timely public issue, though such less enduring attributes may often be related to more enduring ones. When there is a significant relationship between the experimenter's own performance of the particular task he requires of his subjects and the performance he obtains from his subjects, we may speak of an experimenter's "modeling" effect. The evidence for this effect comes from the literature of survey research, clinical psychology, and laboratory experiments.

SURVEY RESEARCH

In the area of survey research, many investigators have assessed the effect of the interviewer's own opinion, attitude, or ideology on the responses obtained from respondents. The basic paradigm has been to ask the interviewers who are to be used in a given project to respond to the questionnaire themselves. The responses these interviewers subsequently obtain from their respondents are then correlated with their own responses. The correlation obtained becomes the estimate of opinion bias or ideology bias. The interpretation of such a correlation is not, however, always straightforward. If interviewers are allowed any choice in the selection of interviewees, they may simply be selecting like-minded respondents. If interviewers are not allowed any choice in interviewee selection but respondents are not randomly assigned to interviewers, the same problem may result. Thus, if interviewers are each assigned a sample of respondents from their home neighborhoods, the opinions of interviewers and respondents are likely to come precorrelated, because opinions are related to neighborhoods. If, however, respondents are randomly assigned to interviewers, and if errors of observation, recording, and coding can be eliminated, at least statistically, the resulting correlation between interviewers' opinions and their respondents' opinions provides a good measure of modeling effects. Evidence for the phenomenon of interviewer modeling effects has been discussed and summarized elsewhere (Hyman et al., 1954; Maccoby & Maccoby, 1954). Here it will do to note that, in some of the many relevant studies, modeling effects were found to occur and in others they were found either to occur not at all or only trivially. Where modeling effects have been found, they have ordinarily been positive. That is, the subjects' responses have tended to be similar in direction to those of the interviewer. In a minority of cases, however, the effects of the interviewer's own opinion or ideology have been negative, so that subjects responded in a direction significantly opposite to that favored by the interviewer himself (Rosenthal, 1963b).

An early study by Clark (1927), while not definitive, is illustrative of positive modeling effects. Two interviewers inquired of 193 subjects how much of their time was devoted to various daily activities. One of the interviewers was more athletically inclined than the other, and he found that his subjects reported a greater amount of time spent in athletic activities than did the subjects contacted by the less athletic interviewer. It is possible that the sampling problems mentioned or observer, recorder, or interpreter effects accounted for the obtained modeling effect. It seems equally reasonable to think that in the presence of the interviewer appearing and behaving more athletically, the respondents actually gave more athletic responses. Perhaps while in this interviewer's presence they were better reminded of the athletic activities in which they did engage. Or it could also have been that it seemed to respondents more "proper" to be more athletic in interaction with an athlete from a college campus. On many campuses, an athlete is attributed a higher status, and we have seen in our discussion of this attribute that subjects do tend to give more "proper" responses to higher status data collectors.

A more recent study reported by Hyman is equally interesting (1954). The data were collected by the Audience Research Institute in 1940. Respondents were given a very brief description of a proposed motion picture plot and were asked to state whether they would like to see such a movie. There were both male and female interviewers to contact the male and female subjects. Responses obtained by interviewers depended significantly ($p < .005$) on their sex and, perhaps, on the respondent's inference of what movies the interviewers would, because of their sex, themselves enjoy. One of the film plots described was that for "Lawrence of Arabia." When male and female subjects were asked about this film by interviewers of their own sex, male subjects were 50 percent more often favorable to the film than were female subjects. However, when the interviewer was of the opposite sex, male subjects responded favorably only 14 percent more often than female subjects. It appeared plausible to reason that subjects responded by "preferring" those movies which, judging from the sex of the interviewer, they thought would be preferred by them.

It is interesting to raise the question of whether subjects of field research or laboratory research tend, in general, to respond in such a way as to reduce the perceived differences between themselves and the data collector with whom they interact. No answer is available to this question at the present time, and surely it is highly oversimplified, as an assertion. It may, however, be a reasonable one if both the participants' attributes and the nature of the data collection situation are considered. From all we seem to know at present, these factors are all likely to interact with the subject's motives to be less different from the data collector. Two sources of such motives are obvious. One is the wish to be similar in order to smooth the social interaction. The other is the wish to be more like a person who very often enjoys, either continuously or at least situationally, a position of higher status. To "keep up with" that Jones who is a data collector, one must behave as one believes a Jones would behave in the same situation.

CLINICAL PSYCHOLOGY

It is often said of clinical psychological interactions that the clinician models his patients somewhat after his own image. When the clinical interaction is the protracted one of psychotherapy it seems especially easy to believe that such effects may occur. If it seemed plausible to reason that subjects in research tended to respond as they believed the experimenter would, then it is the more plausible to argue that such effects occur when the "subject" is a patient who may have all the motives of the experimental subject to respond in such a manner and, in addition, the powerful motive of hope that his distress may be relieved. Graham (1960) reports an experiment that is illustrative. Ten psychotherapists were divided into two groups on the basis of their own perceptual style of approach to the Rorschach blots. Half the therapists tended to see more movement in the ink blots relative to color than did the remaining therapists, who tended to see more color. The 10 therapists saw a total of 89 patients for eight months of treatment. Rorschachs administered to the patients of the two groups of therapists showed no differences before treatment. After treatment the patients seen by the relatively more movement-perceiving therapists saw significantly more movement themselves. Patients seen by the relatively more color-perceiving therapists saw significantly more color after treatment. This is exactly the sort of evidence required to establish modeling effects in the psychotherapeutic relationship. There is, of course, considerable literature on the effects of psychotherapy, and when changes have been shown to occur, the behavior of the patient becomes more like that of his therapist. This body of evidence is not directly relevant to a consideration of modeling effects. The reason is that assuming therapists' behavior to be more "normal" than their patients', and defining patient improvement as a change toward more normal behavior, it must follow that patients change their behavior in the direction of their therapist's behavior when they improve. Therefore, evidence of the kind provided by Graham is required. What must be shown is not simply that patients become more like therapists, but that they become more like their own particular therapist than does the patient of a different therapist.

Further evidence for modeling effects of the therapist comes from the work of Bandura, Lipsher, and Miller (1959), who found that more directly hostile therapists were more likely to approach their patients' hostility, whereas less directly hostile therapists tended to avoid their patients' hostility. The approach or avoidance of the hostile material, then, tended to determine the patient's subsequent dealing with topics involving hostility. Not surprisingly, when therapists tended to avoid the topic, patients tended to drop it as well.

The work of Matarazzo and his colleagues has already been cited (Matarazzo, Wiens, & Saslow, 1965) in connection with the effects of the subject on his experimenter's response. That, of course, was material quite incidental to their interest in the anatomy of the interview. The amount of evidence they have accumulated is compelling. It seems clear, as one example of their work, that increases in the speaking time of the interviewer are followed by increases in the speaking time of the subjects, who in this case were 60 applicants for Civil Service employment. Table 7-1 shows the increases and decreases in the average length of subjects' speaking time as a function of increases and decreases in the interviewer's speaking time. (The first column shows the target values the interviewer was trying to achieve, by and large very successfully.) The rank correlation between changes in the interviewer's length of utterance and his subjects' changes in length of utterance was $+.976$ ($p < .001$). On the average, subjects' length of utterances are five or six times longer than those of the interviewer. But clearly, from these data, patterns of behavior shown by the interviewer can serve as the blueprint for how the subject should respond.

Similar results have been reported by Heller, Davis, and Saunders (1964). There were 12 graduate student interviewers to talk with a total of 96 subjects. Half the interviewers were instructed to behave in a

TABLE 7—1

Subjects' Changes in Duration of Speech as a Function of Interviewer's Changes (After Matarazzo, Wiens, & Saslow, 1965, p. 199)

CHANGES IN SPEECH DURATION

Interviewer's Target	Interviewer	Subject
+200%	+204%	+109%
+100	+94	+111
+100	+87	+93
0	+4	+2
0	0	−8
−50	−38	−43
−50	−48	−45
−67	−64	−51

verbally more active manner, and half were instructed to be less active verbally. During every minute of the 15 minutes recorded, subjects spoke more if their interviewer had been more verbally active than if he had been less verbally active. Subjects contacted by more talkative interviewers spent about 16 percent more time in talk than did their peers assigned to more laconic interviewers ($p < .02$). In another connection we cited the work of Heller, Myers, and Vikan-Kline (1963). Now we need only a reminder of their findings relevant to the present discussion. Friendlier "clients" (experimenters) evoked friendlier interviewer (subject) behavior, an example of positive modeling effects. More dominant "clients" evoked less dominant interviewer behavior, an example not only of negative modeling effects but also of the fact that interviewers, and presumably also experimenters, may sometimes be modeled by their "clients" or subjects just as these are modeled by the interviewer or experimenter.

There is a sense in which the studies described so far are not true examples of modeling effects, though they are relevant to a consideration of such effects. The reason is that the therapists or interviewers were not assessed at exactly the same task or performance at which their patients, interviewees, or subjects were assessed, and not necessarily by the interviewer himself. These studies have all been instructive, however, in showing that the behavior of the interviewer along any dimension may affect the analogous behavior of the subject, though we are still unsure of the mechanisms by which these effects operate.

There is a difference, of course, in the degree of structure provided for therapists, interviewers, and experimenters as to how closely they must follow a given program or plan. In all the studies described so far, the clinicians were relatively free as to what they could say or do at any time. In the studies by Matarazzo and his colleagues only the length of each utterance was highly programmed, not the content of the utterance. In the studies by Heller and his colleagues the degree of dominance and friendliness was programmed into the stimulus persons, but they, too, were free to vary other aspects of their behavior as they felt it to be required. Of even greater relevance, then, to an understanding of the effects of the more highly programmed experimenter is the study of the effects of the psychological examiner. The manuals for the administration of psychological tests are often as explicit as the directions given to a psychological experimenter in a laboratory. The reduced freedom of the examiner and of the experimenter to behave as they would should reduce the magnitude of modeling effects, or so it would seem.

One experiment employing psychological examiners, and bearing on the consideration of modeling effects, was carried out by Berger (1954). All eight of his examiners had been pretested on the Rorschach. After each of the examiners had administered the Rorschach to his subjects, correlations were computed between the examiners' own Rorschach scores on 12 variables and the responses they had subsequently obtained from their subjects. Two of the 12 variables showed a significant positive correlation between the examiners' scores and their subjects' scores. Examiners who tended to organize their percepts into those very commonly seen obtained more such popular percepts from their subjects ($rho = +.86$, $p = .01$). Examiners who tended to use the white space of the ink blots more often, obtained from their subjects a greater use of such white space ($rho = +.80$, $p = .03$).

Another example of modeling effects in the more standard clinical interaction of psychological testing comes from the work of Sanders and Cleveland (1953). Again the Rorschach was the test administered. All 9 of the examiners were given the Rorschach, and they, in turn, administered the Rorschach to 30 subjects each. For each examiner and for each subject a Rorschach anxiety score and a Rorschach hostility score were computed. There was no relationship between the examiner's own anxiety level and the mean anxiety level reflected in the Rorschachs he obtained. However, those three examiners whose own hostility scores were highest obtained significantly higher hostility scores from their subjects (mean $= 16.6$) than did those three examiners whose own hostility scores were lowest (mean $= 13.5$, $p < .05$).

Two more informal reports conclude the discussion of modeling effects found in clinical settings. Funkenstein, King, and Drolette (1957) were engaged in a clinical experiment on reactions to stress in which it was necessary to test patients. Typically, patients showed anger in their responses. However, one of the experimenters found himself filled with doubts and anxieties about the studies undertaken. Every patient tested by this experimenter showed severe anxiety responses. Finally, the classic study of Escalona (1945) is cited to illustrate that the effects under discussion do not depend on verbal communication channels. The scene of the research was a reformatory for women in which the offenders were permitted to have their babies. There were over 50 babies altogether, and 70 percent of these were less than one year old. Part of the feeding schedule was for the babies to be given orange juice half the time and, on alternate days, tomato juice. Often the babies, many under four months of age, preferred one of these juices but disliked the other. The number of orange juice drinkers was about the same as the number of tomato juice drinkers. The ladies who cared for the babies also turned out to have preferences for either orange or tomato juice. When the feeders of the baby disliked orange juice, the baby was more likely to dislike orange juice. When the feeder disliked tomato juice, the baby similarly disliked tomato juice. When babies were reassigned a new feeder who preferred the type of juice opposite to the one preferred by the baby, the baby changed its preference to that of its feeder.

LABORATORY EXPERIMENTS

A number of laboratory studies mentioned earlier have suggested that even in these somewhat more highly structured interactions, modeling effects may occur. Thus Cook-Marquis (1958) found that high-authoritarian experimenters were unable to convince their subjects of the value of nonauthoritarian teaching methods. Presumably, such experimenters could not convincingly persuade subjects to accept communications they themselves found unacceptable. Barnard's work (1963) similarly suggested the operation of modeling effects. He used a phrase association task and found that subjects contacted by experimenters showing a higher degree of associative disturbance also showed a higher degree of disturbance than did subjects contacted by experimenters showing less such disturbance. Even before such experiments had been conducted, F. Allport (1955) had suggested that the experimenter might suggest to the subject, quite unintentionally, his own appraisal of the experimental stimulus and that such suggestion could affect the results of the experiment.

Similarly, in the area of extrasensory perception the work of Schmeidler and McConnell (1958) has raised the question that the experimenter's belief in the phenomenon of ESP could influence the subject's belief in ESP. In this area of research such belief tends to be associated with performance at ESP tasks. Subjects who believe ESP to be possible ("sheep") seem to perform better than subjects who believe ESP to be impossible ("goats").

From this it follows—and perhaps this should be more systematically investigated—that experimenters who themselves believe in ESP may, by affecting their subjects' belief, obtain superior performance at ESP tasks than do experimenters not believing in ESP.

Most of the research explicitly designed to assess the modeling effects of the data collector has come from the field of survey research, some has come from the area of clinical psychological practice, and, until very recently, virtually none has come from laboratory settings. In part, the reason for this may be the greater availability for study of the interviewers of field research and even of clinicians compared to the availability for study of laboratory experimenters. But that does not seem to be the whole story. There is a general belief, perhaps largely justified, that the greater "rough-and-tumble" of the field and of the clinic might naturally lead to increased modeling and related effects. The behavior of the interviewer and of the clinician is often less precisely programmed than the behavior of the experimenter in the laboratory, so that their unintended influences on their subjects and patients could come about more readily. In the laboratory, it is often believed, these unintended effects are less likely because of the more explicit programming of the experimenter's behavior. The words "experimenter behavior" are better read as "instructions to subjects," since this is usually the only aspect of the experimenter's behavior that is highly programmed. Sometimes, when the experimenter is to play a role, he is told to be warm or cold, and then other aspects of his behavior are more programmed, but still not very precisely so. Of course, we cannot program the experimenter so that there will be no unplanned influence on his subjects. We cannot do this programming because we do not know precisely what the behavior is that makes the difference—i.e., affects the subjects to respond differently than they would if the experimenter were literally an automaton. In the light of these considerations, we should not be too surprised to learn that modeling effects may occur in the laboratory as well as in the field and in the clinic. There is no reason to believe that even with instructions to subjects held constant, experimenters in laboratories cannot influence their subjects as effectively, and as unintentionally, as interviewers in the field or clinicians in their clinical settings. Furthermore, there is no reason to suppose that the interpersonal communication processes that mediate the unintended influence are any different in the laboratory than they are in the field, or in the clinic, or in interpersonal relationships generally. At present, we must settle for an evaluation of the occurrence of modeling effects in laboratory settings. For a full understanding of how these effects operate, we must wait for the results of research perhaps not yet begun.

There is a series of nine experiments specifically designed to assess the occurrence and magnitude of modeling effects in a laboratory setting. This series of studies, conducted between 1959 and 1964, employed the person perception task already described. Subjects were asked to rate a series of 10 or 20 photos on how successful or unsuccessful the persons pictured appeared to be. In all nine studies, experimenters themselves rated the photos before contacting their subjects. This was accomplished as part of the training procedure—it being most convenient to train experimenters by having them assume the role of subject while the principal investigators acted in the role of experimenter. For each study, modeling effects were defined by the correlation beween the mean rating of the photos by the different experimenters themselves and the mean photo rating obtained by each experimenter from all his subjects. The number of experimenters (and therefore the N per correlation coefficient) per study ranged from 10 to 26. The number of subjects per study ranged from 55 to 206. The number of subjects per experimenter ranged from 4 to 20, the mean falling above 5. In all, 161 experimenters and about 900 subjects were included.

All experimenters employed in the first eight studies were either graduate students or advanced undergraduate students in psychology or guidance. In the last experiment, there were two samples of experimenters. One consisted of nine law students, the other was a mixed group of seven graduate students primarily in the natural sciences. Subjects were drawn from elementary college courses, usually from psychology courses, but also from courses in education, social sciences, and the humanities. All of the experiments were designed to test at least one hypothesis about experimenter effects other than modeling effects—as, for example, the effects of experimenters' expectancy. All studies, then, had at least two treatment conditions, the effects of which would have to be partially transcended by modeling effects.

Table 7-2 shows the correlation (rho) obtained in each of the nine studies between the experimenters' own ratings of the photos and the mean rating they subsequently obtained from their subjects. The correlations are listed in the order in which they were obtained so that the experiment listed as No. 1 was the first conducted and No. 9 the last. There is a remarkable inconsistency of obtained correlations, the range being from $-.49$ to $+.65$. (Taken individually, and with the df based on the number of experimenters, only the correlation of $+.65$ [$p < .001$] differed significantly from zero [at $p < .10$]. This correlation of $+.65$, obtained in experiment No. 2 was not, however, available for closer study.) Employing the method described by Snedecor (1956) for assessing the likelihood that a set of correlations are from the same population, the value of x^2 was 23.52 ($df = 9$, $p = .006$). The same analysis omitting the data from experiment No. 2 yielded x^2 of 13.17 ($df = 8$, $p = .11$). It seems from these results that in different studies employing the person perception task there may be variable directions and magnitudes of modeling effects which, for any single study, might often be regarded as a chance fluctuation from a population correlation of zero. Disregarding the direction of the correlations

TABLE 7—2

Modeling Effects in Studies of Person Perception

Experiment	Correlation	N
1. Rosenthal and Fode (1963b)	+.52	10
2. Hinkle (personal communication, 1961)	+.65	24
3. Rosenthal, Persinger, Vikan-Kline, and Fode (1963a)	+.18	12
4. Rosenthal, Persinger, Vikan-Kline, and Fode (1963b)	+.31	18
5. White (1962)	−.07	18
6. Rosenthal, Persinger, Vikan-Kline, and Mulry (1963)	−.32	26
7. Persinger (1962)	−.49	12
8. Rosenthal, Persinger, Mulry, Vikan-Kline, and Grothe (1964a; 1964b)	+.14	25
9. Haley and Rosenthal (unpublished, 1964) I	−.18	9
Haley and Rosenthal (unpublished, 1964) II	+.54	7
Total		161

which turned out to be negative surprisingly often, we see that the proportions of variance in subjects' mean photo ratings accounted for by a knowledge of the experimenters' own responses to the experimental task varied from less than 1 percent to as much as 42 percent. Sometimes, then, modeling effects are trivial, sometimes large, a finding consistent with the results of the survey research literature. There the opinion of the interviewer sometimes makes a difference and sometimes not. When there is a difference, it is sometimes sizable, sometimes trivial.

Examination of Table 7-2 shows that for the first eight experiments, there is a fairly regular decrease in the magnitude of the correlations obtained $(p < .05)$. The interpretation of this trend holding for the first eight studies is speculative. Over the five years in which these experiments were conducted, the probability would seem to increase that experimenters might learn that they themselves were the focus of interest. This recognition may have led to their trying to avoid any modeling effects on their subjects. By trying too hard, they may have reversed the behavior that leads to positive modeling effects in such a way that negative modeling effects resulted. In a later chapter, dealing with the effects of excessive reward, some evidence will be presented that suggests that such "bending over backward" does occur.

The last study listed in Table 7-2 shows that, even within the same experiment, the use of different samples of experimenters can lead to different directions and magnitudes of modeling effects. Among the nine law students there were no large modeling effects, and the tendency, if any, was for negative effects. Among the seven graduate students, who were primarily in the physical sciences, the tendency was for larger and positive, though not significant, modeling effects. The two correlations could from statistical considerations alone have been combined, but because it was known that these two samples differed in a number of other characteristics, this was not done. The law student experimenters, for example, themselves rated the photos as being of more successful people ($r_{pb} = +.57$, $p < .05$), and from their written statements of the purpose of the experiment were judged more serious ($r = +.62$, $p < .02$) and less suspicious that their own behavior was under study ($r = -.74$, $p < .005$). This last finding argues somewhat against the earlier interpretation that as experimenters were more likely to be suspicious of being studied they would tend to bend over backward to avoid modeling their subjects.

The lawyers' behavior during the experiment also seemed to be different from that of the mixed sample of graduate students. Table 7-3 shows the larger point biserial correlations between subjects' ratings of their experimenters and experimenters' sample membership. The young attorneys were judged by their subjects to be friendlier and more active

TABLE 7—3

Experimenter Behavior Distinguishing Law Students
from Graduate Students

Variable	Correlation	p
Friendly	+.37	.001
Pleasant	+.26	.02
Likable	+.23	.05
Interested	+.30	.01
Pleasant-voiced	+.43	.001
Loud	+.24	.05
Hand gestures	+.24	.05
Head activity	+.27	.02
Leg activity	+.30	.01

and involved both vocally and motorically. It seems well established that, at least for these particular samples, the lawyers and graduate students treated their subjects differently; but there is nothing in the pattern of differences to tell us how it may have led to differences in modeling effects. Later, in Part II, we shall see that, if anything, this pattern of behavior is associated with greater unintended effects of the experimenter, though those effects are not of modeling but of the experimenter's expectancy.

Among the first eight experiments there was one (No. 8) that had been filmed. Unfortunately, this was an experiment that showed virtually no modeling effects. Still it might be instructive to see what the behavior was of experimenters who themselves rated the photos as being of more successful people. At least in some of the studies such behavior may affect the photo ratings of the subjects.

During the brief preinstructional period of the experiment, there was little experimenter behavior from which one could postdict how he had rated the success of photos of others. Those who had rated the photos as more successful were judged from the film alone to behave less consistently ($r = -.40, p < .10$) than those who had rated photos as of less successful people. Such a single relationship could easily have occurred by chance, however. During the instruction-reading phase of the experiment, observers who saw the film but heard no sound track judged more success-rating experimenters as less enthusiastic ($r = -.42, p = .08$). These experimenters were judged from the sound track alone to behave in a more self-important manner ($r = +.41, p < .10$). Observers who had access

TABLE 7—4

Experimenter Behavior and the Perception of Success of Others

Variable	Correlation	p
Personal	−.42	.08
Interested	−.40	.10
Expressive face	−.44	.07
Fast speaking	+.51	.03

to both the film and sound track made the most judgments found to correlate with the experimenter's own perception of the success of others. Table 7-4 shows the larger correlations. Relatively more success-perceiving experimenters seemed less interested, less expressive, and faster speaking than their less success-perceiving colleagues. Ordinarily we expect such behavior to result in subjects subsequently rating photos of others as less successful, and if that had occurred there would have been a negative modeling effect. Instead, there was virtually none at all, a little positive if anything. In the study conducted in collaboration with Haley, these general results were reversed. At least as defined by subjects' ratings, those experimenters who rated the photos as more successful behaved in a more friendly ($r = +.25$, $p = .02$) manner. We are left knowing only that the behavior of experimenters rating photos as of more successful persons differs significantly, but not consistently, from the behavior of less success-perceiving experimenters. Tritely but truly put, more research is needed.

There is a more recently conducted experiment, in which the task was to construct sentences beginning with any of six pronouns (Rosenthal, Kohn, Greenfield, & Carota, 1966). The procedures called for the experimenter's saying "good" whenever the subject chose a first-person pronoun. But before these reinforcements began, subjects were permitted to generate sentences without reinforcements, in order that an operant or basal level could be established. Before experimenters contacted their subjects, they, too, constructed sentences without receiving any reinforcements. Modeling effects are defined again by a correlation coefficient, this time between the experimenter's operant level of choosing to begin sentences with first-person pronouns and his subjects' subsequently determined operant levels. This was the experiment, described earlier, in which the experimenters were subtly evaluated by their principal investigator. Half the experimenters were evaluated on their intelligence, half on their influenceability. Within each of these groups half the experimenters were evaluated favorably, half unfavorably. Table 7-5 shows the correlations representing modeling effects for each of the four groups of experimenters. There was a general tendency for experimenters who had been favorably evaluated

TABLE 7—5

Modeling Effects of Experimenters as a Function of Their Principal Investigator's Evaluation

EVALUATION

Attribute	Favorable	Unfavorable	z difference	p
Intelligence	−.88*	+.997**	3.58	.0005
Influenceability	−.74	+.03	.98	—
Mean	−.81*	+.52	2.24	.03

* $p \leq .05$
** $p \leq .005$

to show negative modeling effects and for experimenters who had been unfavorably evaluated, especially as to their intelligence, to show positive modeling effects. (In the earlier discussion of the effects of evaluation by the principal investigator, it was mentioned that, in this particular experiment, the favorably evaluated experimenters were the ones who also obtained the significantly greater amount of conditioning from their subjects).

The experiment under discussion and that conducted with Haley are the only ones within which comparisons are made between different sets of experimenters. The favorably evaluated experimenters of the one study, and the lawyers of the other study, both showed negative modeling effects, and both were evaluated by their subjects as more interpersonally pleasant. The unfavorably evaluated experimenters and the natural scientists both showed positive modeling effects and were both evaluated generally as less pleasant. This consistency between the two studies was especially heartening in view of the fact that the two studies employed different tasks, sentence construction in the one case, person perception in the other.

It may be that subjects evaluate as more pleasant those experimenters who are not unintentionally influencing their subjects to respond as they would themselves respond. Or it may be that experimenters who are "really" more pleasant interpersonally, either characteristically or because they have been made that way by their interaction with the principal investigator, bend over backward to avoid modeling their subjects, while less favorably evaluated experimenters and those characteristically less pleasant interpersonally behave in such a way as to obtain positively modeled responses. This interpretation can be applied to the series of person perception studies which showed modeling effects to become more negative over time. In most of these studies there were one or more principal investigators who were involved with several of the studies. Perhaps as the principal investigators gained more experience in conducting such experiments they became more relaxed and pleasant toward the experimenters, so that, unintentionally, experimenters of the later studies felt less tense and less "on the spot" than experimenters of the earlier studies. Such unintentionally increased comfort on the part of the experimenters in later studies could account for an increase in their pleasantness toward their subjects, an increase that, in one way or another, seems to lead to negative modeling effects.

From all the evidence considered, it seems sensible to conclude that modeling effects occur at least sometimes in psychological research conducted in field or laboratory. We find it difficult, however, to predict the direction and magnitude of modeling effects. In survey research, they tend usually to be positive but variable as to magnitude. In laboratory studies, modeling effects are variable not only in magnitude but in direction as well. The interpretation of the variability of direction of modeling effects that is best supported by the evidence, though still not well established, is that a happier, more pleasant, less tense experimenter seems to model his subjects negatively. The less pleasant, more tense experimenter seems to model his subjects positively. Just why that should be is not at all clear.

Problems in the control of modeling and of related effects of the experimenter will be treated in Part III. One methodological implication follows from the possible relationship between the direction of modeling and the pleasantness of the experimenter's behavior. If a pleasant experimenter models negatively and an unpleasant experimenter models positively, then perhaps a more nearly neutral experimenter models not at all. If research were to show that this were the case, we could perhaps reduce modeling effects either by the selection of naturally neutral experimenters or by inducing more randomly selected experimenters to behave neutrally. If our selection of experimenters were fairly random with respect to the characteristic of pleasantness, and if we did not systematically change our assistants' degree of pleasantness in our interaction with them, we might hope for the modeling effects of the more and less pleasant data collectors to cancel each other out. Replication, therefore, is required for the assessment and control of an effect of the experimenter.

8

Experimenter Expectancy

The preceding chapters have dealt with the effects of various attributes of the experimenter on the responses he obtains from his subjects. Some of these attributes were quite stable (i.e., the sex of the experimenter) and some were quite situational (i.e., the experiences the experimenter encountered while conducting his experiment). In this chapter, the discussion turns to another "attribute" highly dependent on the specific experiment being conducted—the expectancy the experimenter has of how his subjects will respond. Much of the remainder of this book deals with this variable. In Part II the emphasis will be on the experimental evidence that supports the proposition that what results the experimenter obtains from his subjects may be determined in part by what he expects to obtain. In Part III, the emphasis will be on various methodological implications of this proposition, including what may be done to minimize the unintended effect of the experimenter's expectancy.

The particular expectation a scientist has of how his experiment will turn out is variable, depending on the experiment being conducted, but the presence of some expectation is virtually a constant in science. The independent and dependent variables selected for study by the scientist are not chosen by means of a table of random numbers. They are selected because the scientist expects a certain relationship to appear between them. Even in those less carefully planned examinations of relationships called "fishing expeditions" or, more formally, "exploratory analyses" the expectation of the scientist is reflected in the selection of the entire set of variables chosen for examination. Exploratory analyses of data, like real fishing ventures, do not take place in randomly selected pools.

These expectations of the scientist are likely to affect the choice of the experimental design and procedure in such a way as to increase the likelihood that his expectation or hypothesis will be supported. That is as it should be. No scientist would select intentionally a procedure likely to show his hypothesis in error. If he could too easily think of procedures that would show this, he would be likely to revise his hypothesis. If the selection of a research design or procedure is regarded by another scientist as too "biased" to be a fair test of the hypothesis, he can test the hypothesis employing oppositely biased procedures or less biased procedures by which to demonstrate the greater value of his hypothesis. The designs and procedures employed are, to a great extent, public knowledge, and it is this public character that permits relevant replications to serve the required corrective function.

In the behavioral sciences, especially, where statistical procedures are so generally employed to guide the interpretation of results, the expectation of the investigator may affect the choice of statistical tests. Unintentionally, the investigator may employ more powerful statistical tests when his hypothesis calls for his showing the untenability of the null hypothesis. Less powerful statistics may be employed when the expectation calls for the tenability of the null hypothesis. As in the choice of design and procedure, the consequences of such an unintentional expectancy bias are not serious. The data can, after all, be reanalyzed by any disagreeing scientist. Other effects of the scientist's expectation may be on his observation of the data and on his interpretation of what they mean. Both these effects have already been discussed in the opening chapters of this book.

The major concern of this chapter will be with the effects of the experimenter's expectation on the responses he obtains from his subjects. The consequences of such an expectancy bias can be quite serious. Expectancy effects on subjects' responses are not public matters. It is not only that other scientists cannot know whether such effects occurred in the experimenter's interaction with his subjects; the investigator himself may not know whether these effects have occurred. Moreover, there is the likelihood that the experimenter has not even considered the possibility of such unintended effects on his subjects' response. That is not so different from the situations already discussed wherein the subject's response is affected by any attribute of the experimenter. Later, in Part III, the problem will be discussed in more detail. For now it is enough to note that while the other attributes of the experimenter affect the subject's response, they do not necessarily affect these responses differentially as a function of the subject's treatment condition. Expectancy effects, on the other hand, always do. The sex of the experimenter does not change as a function of the subject's treatment condition in an experiment. The experimenter's expectancy of how the subject will respond does change as a function of the subject's treatment condition.

Although the focus of this book is primarily on the effects of a particular person, an experimenter, on the behavior of a specific other, the subject, it should be emphasized that many of the effects of the experimenter, including the effects of his expectancy, may have considerable generality for other social relationships.

That one person's expectation about another person's behavior may contribute to a determination of what that behavior will actually be has been suggested by various theorists. Merton (1948) developed the very appropriate concept of "self-fulfilling prophecy." One prophesies an event, and the expectation of the event then changes the behavior of the prophet in such a way as to make the prophesied event more likely. Gordon Allport (1950) has applied the concept of interpersonal expectancies to an analysis of the causes of war. Nations expecting to go to war affect the behavior of their opponents-to-be by the behavior which reflects their expectations of armed conflict. Nations who expect to remain out of wars, at least sometimes, manage to avoid entering into them.

EXPECTANCY EFFECTS IN EVERYDAY LIFE

A group of young men, studied intensively by Whyte (1943), "knew how well a man should bowl." On some evenings the group, especially its leaders, "knew" that a given member would bowl well. That "knowledge" seemed predictive, for on such an evening the member did bowl well. On other evenings it was "known" that a member would bowl poorly. And so he did, even if he had been the good bowler of the week before. The group's expectancy of the members' performance at bowling seemed, in fact, to determine that performance. Perhaps the morale-building banter offered that one who was expected to perform well helped him to do so by reducing anxiety, with its interfering effects. The communication to a member that he would do poorly on a given evening may have made his anxiety level high enough to actually interfere with his performance.

Although not dealing specifically with the effects of one person's expectancy on another's behavior, some observations made at the turn of the century by Jastrow (1900) are relevant. He tells of the bicycle rider who so fears that he may fall that his coordination becomes impaired and he does fall. "So in jumping or running and in other athletic trials, the entertainment of the notion of a possible failure to reach the mark lessens the intensity of one's effort, and prevents the accomplishment of one's best." We may disagree with Jastrow over his interpretation of the effects of expectancy on performance but that such effects occur seems well within common experience. In these examples Jastrow did not specify that the expectancy of falling or of failing came from another person, but as we saw in the example provided by Whyte, they often do.

Jastrow also gives the details of a well-documented case of expectancy effects in the world of work. The setting was the United States Census Bureau in 1890. The Hollerith tabulating machine had just been installed. This machine, something analogous to a typewriter, required the clerks to learn some 250 positions compared to the two-score positions to be learned in typing. All regarded the task as quite difficult, and Hollerith himself estimated that a trained worker should be able to punch about 550 cards per day, each card containing about 10 punches. It took two weeks before any clerk achieved that high a rate, but gradually, the hundreds of clerks employed were able to perform at even higher levels but only at great emotional cost. Workers were so tense trying to achieve the records established that the Secretary of the Interior forbade the establishment of any minimum number of cards to be punched per day.

At this point two hundred new clerks were brought in to augment the work force. They knew nothing of the work and, unlike the original group, had no training nor had they ever seen the machines. These workers' chief asset was that no one had told them of the task's great "difficulty." Within three days this new group of clerks was performing at the level attained by the initial group after five weeks of indoctrination and two weeks of practice. Among the initial group of workers, those who had been impressed by the difficulty of the task, many became ill from overwork when they achieved a level of 700 cards per day. Needless to say there was no such illness among the group of workers who had no reason to believe the task to be a difficult one. Within a short time, one of these new clerks was punching over 2,200 cards per day.

The effects on a person's behavior of the expectancies others had of that behavior is further illustrated in an anecdote related by the learning theorist E. R. Guthrie (1938). He told how a shy, socially inept young lady became self-confident and relaxed in social contacts by having been systematically treated as a social favorite. A group of college men had arranged the expectancies of those coming in contact with her so that socially facile behavior was expected of her. In a somewhat more scholarly report, Shor (1964) showed that in automobile driving, one driver's expectancy of another's behavior was communicated to that driver automotively in such a way as to increase the likelihood that the expected behavior would occur.

Education is one of the socially most important areas of everyday life in which expectancy effects have been regarded as central. With increasing concern over the education of economically, racially, and socially disadvantaged children, more and more attention has been paid to the effect of our expectancy of a child's intellectual performance on that child's performance. MacKinnon (1962) put it this way: "If our expectation is that a child of a given intelligence will not respond creatively to a task which confronts him, and especially if we make this expectation known to the child, the probability that he will respond creatively is very much reduced" (p. 493). The same position has been stated also by Katz (1964), Wilson (1963), and Clark (1963), who speaks of the deprived child becoming "the victim of an educational self-fulfilling prophecy" (p. 150). Perhaps the most detailed statement of this position is that made by the authors of *Youth in the Ghetto* (Harlem Youth Opportunities Unlimited, Inc., 1964).

In this report considerable evidence is cited which shows that the culturally deprived child shows a relative drop in academic performance and IQ as he progresses from the third to the sixth grade. Until recently, however, there has been no experimental evidence that teachers' expectations of a child's performance actually affect that performance. Now there are data that show quite clearly that when teachers expect a child's IQ to go up it does go up. The effect is consistent, not always large, but sometimes very dramatic (e.g., 20-point IQ gains). The data, not yet fully analyzed, were collected in collaboration with Lenore Jacobson and will be reported fully elsewhere.

EXPECTANCY EFFECTS IN SURVEY RESEARCH

Perhaps the classic work in this area was that of Stuart Rice (1929). A sample of 2,000 applicants for charity were interviewed by a group of 12 skilled interviewers. Interviewers talked individually with their respondents, who had been assigned in a wholly nonselected manner. Respondents ascribed their dependent status to factors predictable from a knowledge of the interviewers' expectancies. Thus, one of the interviewers, who was a staunch prohibitionist, obtained three times as many responses blaming alcohol as did another interviewer regarded as a socialist, who, in turn, obtained half again as many responses blaming industrial factors as did the prohibitionist interviewer. Rice concluded that the expectancy of the interviewer was somehow communicated to the respondent, who then replied as expected. Hyman and his colleagues (1954) disagreed with Rice's interpretation. They preferred to ascribe his remarkable results to errors of recording or of interpretation. What the correct interpretation is, we cannot say, for the effects, if of observation or of expectancy, were private ones. In either case, of course, the results of the research were strikingly affected by the expectancy of the data collector.

One of the earliest studies deliberately creating differential expectancies in interviewers was that conducted by Harvey (1938). Each of six boys was interviewed by each of five young postgraduates. The boys were to report to the interviewers on a story they had been given to read. Interviewers were to use these reports to form impressions of the boys' character. Each interviewer was given some contrived information about the boys' reliability, sociability, and stability, but told not to regard these data in assessing the boys. Standardized questions asked of the interviewers at the conclusion of the study suggested that biases of assessment occurred even without interviewers' awareness and despite conscious resistance to bias. Harvey felt that the interviewers' bias evoked a certain attitude toward the boys which in turn determined the behavior to be expected and then the interpretation given. Again, we cannot be sure that subjects' responses were actually altered by interviewer expectancies. The possibility, however, is too provocative to overlook.

Wyatt and Campbell (1950) trained over two hundred student interviewers for a public opinion survey dealing with the 1948 presidential campaign. Before collecting their data, the interviewers guessed the percentage distribution of responses they would obtain to each of five questions. For four of the five questions asked, interviewers tended to obtain more answers in the direction of their expectancy, although the effect was significant in the case of only one question. Those interviewers expecting more of their respondents to have discussed the campaign with others tended to obtain responses from their subjects that bore out their expectancy ($p = .02$). Interviewers had also answered the five questions themselves, so that an assessment of modeling effects was possible. These effects were not significant.

More recent evidence for expectancy effects in survey research comes from the work of Hanson and Marks (1958), and a very thorough discussion can be found in Hyman et al. (1954).

EXPECTANCY EFFECTS IN CLINICAL PSYCHOLOGY

Though it was the sociologist Merton who developed the concept of the self-fulfilling prophecy, particularly for the analysis of such large-scale social and economic phenomena as racial and religious prejudice and the failure of banks, the concept was applied much earlier and in a clinical context. Albert Moll (1898) spoke specifically of clinical phenomena in which "the prophecy causes its own fulfillment" (p. 244). He mentioned hysterical paralyses cured at the time it was believed they could be cured. He told of insomnia, nausea, impotence, and stammering all coming about when their advent was most expected. But his particular interest was in the phenomenon of hypnosis. It was his belief that subjects behaved as they believed they were expected to behave. Much later, in 1959, Orne showed that Moll was right, and still more recent evidence (Barber & Calverley, 1964b) gives further confirmation, though Levitt and Brady (1964) showed that the subject's expectation did not always lead to a confirming performance.

In the studies just now cited we were not dealing specifically with the hypnotist's expectancy as an unintended determinant of the subject's response. It was more a case of the subject's expectancy as a determinant of his own response. As yet there have been no reports of studies in which different hypnotists were led to have different expectations about their subjects' performance. That is the kind of study needed to establish the effects of the hypnotist's expectation on his subject's performance. Kramer and Brennan (1964) do have an interpretation of some data that fits the model of the self-fulfilling prophecy. They worked with schizophrenics and found them to be as susceptible to hypnosis as college undergraduates. In the past, schizophrenics had been thought far less hypnotizable. Their interpretation suggested that, relative to the older studies, their own approach to the schizophrenics communicated to them the investigators' expectancy that the patients could be hypnotized.

In the area of psychotherapy, a number of workers have been impressed by the effects of the self-fulfilling prophecy. One of the best known of these was Frieda Fromm-Reichmann (1950). She spoke, as other clinicians have, of iatrogenic psychiatric incurabilities. The therapist's own belief about the patient's prognosis might be a determinant of that prognosis. Strupp and Luborsky (1962) have also made this point. These clinical impressions are supported to some extent by a few more formal investigations. Heine and Trosman (1960) did not find the patient's initial expectation of help to be related to his continuance in treatment. They did find, however, that when the therapist and patient had congruent expectations, patients continued longer in treatment. Experimental procedures to help ensure such congruence have been employed by Jerome Frank and Martin Orne with considerable success (Frank, 1965).

Goldstein (1960) found no client-perceived personality change to be related to the therapist's expectancy of such change. However, the therapist's expectancy was related to duration of psychotherapy. Additionally, Heller and Goldstein (1961) found the therapist's expectation of client improvement significantly correlated (.62) with a change in the client's attraction to the therapist. These workers also found that after fifteen sessions, the client's behavior was no more independent than before, but that their self-descriptions were of more independent behavior. The therapists employed in this study generally were favorable to increased independence and tended to expect successful cases to show this decrease in dependency. Clients may well have learned from their therapists that independent-sounding verbalizations were desired and thereby served to fulfill their therapist's expectancy. The most complete discussion of the general importance to the psychotherapeutic interaction of the expectancy variable is that by Goldstein (1962).

But hypnosis and psychotherapy are not the only realms of clinical practice in which the clinician's expectancy may determine the outcome. The fatality rates of delirium tremens have recently not exceeded about 15 percent. However, from time to time new treatments of greatly varying sorts are reported to reduce this figure almost to zero. Gunne's work in Sweden summarized by the staff of the *Quarterly Journal of Studies on Alcohol* (1959) showed that *any* change in therapy led to a drop in mortality rate. One interpretation of this finding is that the innovator of the new treatment expects a decrease in mortality rate, an expectancy that leads to subtle differential patient care over and above the specific treatment under investigation. A prophecy again may have been self-fulfilled.

Greenblatt (1964) describes a patient suffering from advanced cancer who was admitted to the hospital virtually dying. He had been exposed to the information that Krebiozen might be a wonder drug, and some was administered to him. His improvement was dramatic and he was discharged to his home for several months. He was then exposed to the information that Krebiozen was probably ineffective. He relapsed and was readmitted to the hospital. There, his faith in Krebiozen was restored, though the injections he received were of saline solution rather than Krebiozen. Once again he was sufficiently improved to be discharged. Finally he was exposed to the information that the American Medical Association denied completely the value of Krebiozen. The patient then lost all hope and was readmitted to the hospital, this time for the last time. He died within 48 hours. Such an anecdote might not be worth the telling were it not for the fact that effects almost as dramatic have been reported in more formal research reports on the effects of placebo in clinical practice. Excellent reviews are available of this literature (e.g., Honigfeld, 1964; Shapiro, 1960; Shapiro, 1964; Shapiro, 1965), which show that it is not at all unusual to find placebo effects more powerful than the actual chemical effects of drugs whose pharmacological action is fairly well understood (e.g., Lyerly, Ross, Krugman, & Clyde, 1964).

In his comprehensive paper, Shapiro (1960) cites the wise clinician's admonition: "You should treat as many patients as possible with the new drugs while they still have the power to heal" (p. 114). The wisdom of this statement may derive from its appreciation of the therapeutic role of the clinician's faith in the efficacy of the treatment. This faith is, of course, the expectancy under discussion. The clinician's expectancy about the efficacy of a treatment procedure is no doubt subtly communicated to the patient with a resulting effect on his psychobiological functioning.

EXPECTANCY EFFECTS IN EXPERIMENTAL PSYCHOLOGY

There is an analysis of 168 studies that had been conducted to establish the validity of the Rorschach technique of personality assessment. Levy and Orr (1959) categorized each of these studies on each of the following dimensions: (1) the academic vs. nonacademic affiliation of the author; (2) whether the study was designed to assess construct or criterion validity; and (3) whether the outcome of the study was favorable or unfavorable to the hypothesis of Rorschach validity. Results showed that academicians, more interested in construct validity, obtained outcomes relatively more favorable to construct validation and less favorable to criterion validation. On the basis of their findings these workers called for more intensive study of the researcher himself. "For, intentionally or not, he seems to exercise greater control over human behavior than is generally thought" (p. 83). We cannot be sure that the findings reported were a case of expectancy effect or bias. It might have been that the choice of specific hypotheses for testing, or that the choice of designs or procedures for testing them, determined the apparently biased outcomes. At the very least, however, this study accomplished its task of calling attention to the potential biasing effects of experimenters' expectations.

Perhaps the earliest study that employed a straightforward experimental task and directly varied the expectancy of the experimenter was that of Stanton and Baker (1942). In their study, 12 nonsense geometric figures were presented to a group of 200 undergraduate subjects. After several days, retention of these figures was measured by five experienced workers. The experimenters were supplied with a key of "correct" responses, some of which were actually correct but some of which were incorrect. Experimenters were explicitly warned to guard against any bias associated with their having the keys before them and thereby unintentionally influencing their subjects to guess correctly. Results showed that the experimenter obtained results in accordance with his expectations. When the item on the key was correct, the subject's response was more likely to be correct than when the key was incorrect. In a careful replication of this study, Lindzey (1951) emphasized to his experimenters the importance of keeping the keys out of the subjects' view. This study failed to confirm the Stanton and Baker findings. Another replication by Friedman (1942) also failed to obtain the significance levels obtained in the original. Still, significant results of this sort, even occurring in only one out of three experiments, cannot be dismissed lightly. Stanton (1942a) himself presented further evidence which strengthened his conclusions. He employed a set of nonsense materials, ten of which had been presented to subjects, and ten of which had not. Experimenters were divided into three groups. One group was correctly informed as to which ten materials had been exposed, another group was incorrectly informed, and the third group was told nothing. The results of this study also indicated that the materials that the experimenters expected to be more often chosen were, in fact, more often chosen.

An experiment analogous to those just described was conducted in a psychophysical laboratory by workers (Warner & Raible, 1937) who interpreted their study within the framework of parapsychological phenomena. The study involved the judgment of weights by subjects who could not see the experimenter. The latter kept his lips tightly closed to prevent unconscious whispering (Kennedy, 1938). In half the experimental trials the experimenter knew the correct response and in half he did not. Of the 17 subjects, only 6 showed a large discrepancy from a chance distribution of errors. However, all 6 of these subjects made fewer errors on trials in which the experimenter knew which weight was the lighter or heavier. At least for those 6 subjects who were more affected by the experimenter's knowledge of the correct response, the authors' conclusion seems justified ($p = .03$). As an alternative to the interpretation of these results as ESP phenomena, they suggested the possibility of some form of auditory cue transmission to subjects.

Among the most recent relevant studies in the area of ESP are those by Schmeidler and McConnell (1958). These workers found that subjects who believed ESP possible ("sheep") performed better at ESP tasks than subjects not believing ESP possible ("goats"). These workers suggested that an experimenter, by his presentation, might affect subjects' self-classification, thereby increasing or decreasing the likelihood of successful ESP performance. Similarly, Anderson and White (1958) found that teachers' and students' attitudes toward each other might influence performance in classroom ESP experiments. The mechanism operating here might also have been one of certain teachers' expectancies being communicated to the children whose self-classification as sheep or goats might thereby be affected. The role of the experimenter in the results of ESP research has been discussed recently by Crumbaugh (1959), and much earlier by Kennedy (1939), as a source of evidence against the existence of the phenomenon. No brief is filed here for or against ESP, but if, in carefully done experiments, certain types of experimenters obtain certain types of ESP performances in a predictable manner, as suggested by the studies cited, further evidence for experimenter expectancy effects will have been adduced (Rhine, 1959).

In a more traditional area of psychological research—memory—Ebbinghaus (1885) called attention to experimenter expectancy effects. In his own research he noted that his expectancy of what data he would obtain affected the data he subsequently did obtain. He pointed out, furthermore, that the experimenter's knowledge of this expectancy effect was not sufficient to control the phenomenon. This finding, long neglected, will be discussed further in Part II when the question of early data returns is taken up.

Another possible case, and another classic, has been described by Stevens (1961). He discussed the controversy between Fechner and Plateau over the results of psychophysical experiments designed to determine the nature of the function describing the operating characteristics of a sensory system. Plateau held that it was a power function rather than a log function. Delboeuf carried out experiments for Plateau, but obtained data approximating the Fechnerian prediction of a log function. Stevens puzzled over these results which may be interpretable as experimenter expectancy effects. Either by implicitly expecting the Fechnerian outcomes or by attempting to guard against an anti-Fechnerian bias, Delboeuf may have influenced the outcome of his studies.

It would appear that Pavlov was aware of the possibility that the expectancy of the experimenter could affect the results of experiments. In an exchange of letters in *Science,* Zirkle (1958) and Razran (1959), in discussing Pavlov's attitude toward the concept of the inheritance of acquired characteristics, give credence to a statement by Gruenberg (1929, p. 327): "In an informal statement made at the time of the Thirteenth International Physiological Congress, Boston, August, 1929, Pavlov explained that in checking up these experiments, it was found that the apparent improvement in the ability to learn, on the part of successive generations of mice, was really due to an improvement in the ability to teach, on the part of the experimenter! And so this 'proof' of the transmission of modifications drops out of the picture, at least for the present."

Probably the best-known and most instructive case of experimenter expectancy effects is that of Clever Hans (Pfungst, 1911). Hans, it will be remembered, was the horse of Mr. von Osten, a German mathematics teacher. By means of tapping his foot, Hans was able to add, subtract, multiply, and divide. Hans could spell, read, and solve problems of musical harmony. To be sure, there were other clever animals at the time, and Pfungst tells about them. There was "Rosa," the mare of Berlin, who performed similar feats in vaudeville, and there was the dog of Utrecht, and the reading pig of Virginia. All these other clever animals were highly trained performers who were, of course, intentionally cued by their trainers.

Mr. von Osten, however, did not profit from his animal's talent, nor did it seem at all likely that he was attempting to perpetrate a fraud. He swore he did not cue the animal, and he permitted other people to question and test the horse even without his being present. Pfungst and his famous colleague, Stumpf, undertook a program of systematic research to discover the secret of Hans' talents. Among the first discoveries made was that if the horse could not see the questioner, Hans was not clever at all. Similarly, if the questioner did not himself know the answer to the question, Hans could not answer it either. Still, Hans was able to answer Pfungst's questions as long as the investigator was present and visible. Pfungst reasoned that the questioner might in some way be signaling to Hans when to begin and when to stop tapping his hoof. A forward inclination of the head of the questioner would start Hans tapping, Pfungst observed. He tried then to incline his head forward without asking a question and discovered that this was sufficient to start Hans' tapping. As the experimenter straightened up, Hans would stop tapping. Pfungst then tried to get Hans to stop tapping by using very slight upward motions of the head. He found that even the raising of his eyebrows was sufficient. Even the dilation of the questioner's nostrils was a cue for Hans to stop tapping.

When a questioner bent forward more, the horse would tap faster. This added to the reputation of Hans as brilliant. That is, when a large number of taps was the correct response, Hans would tap very, very rapidly until he approached the region of correctness, and then he began to slow down. It was found that questioners typically bent forward more when the answer was a long one, gradually straightening up as Hans got closer to the correct number.

For some experiments, Pfungst discovered that auditory cues functioned additively with visual cues. When the experimenter was silent, Hans was able to respond correctly 31 percent of the time in picking one of many placards with different words written on it, or cloths of different colors. When auditory cues were added, Hans responded correctly 56 percent of the time.

Pfungst himself then played the part of Hans, tapping out responses to questions with his hand. Of 25 questioners, 23 unwittingly cued Pfungst as to when to stop tapping in order to give a correct response. None of the questioners (males and females of all ages and occupations) knew the intent of the experiment. When errors occurred, they were usually only a single tap from being correct. The subjects of this study, including an experienced psychologist, were unable to discover that they were unintentionally emitting cues.

Hans' amazing talents, talents rapidly acquired too by Pfungst, serve to illustrate further the power of the self-fulfilling prophecy. Hans' questioners, even skeptical ones, expected Hans to give the correct answers to their queries. Their expectation was reflected in their unwitting signal to Hans that the time had come for him to stop his tapping. The signal cued Hans to stop, and the questioner's expectation became the reason for Hans' being, once again, correct.

Not all of Hans' questioners were equally good at fulfilling their prophecies. Even when the subject is a horse, apparently, the attributes of the experimenter make a considerable difference in determining the response of a subject. On the basis of his studies, Pfungst was able to summarize the characteristics of those of Hans' questioners who were more successful in their covert and unwitting communication with the horse. What seemed important was:

1. That the questioner have ability and "tact" in dealing with animals generally.
2. That he have an air of quiet authority.
3. That he concentrate on the correct answer, both expecting and wishing for it.
4. That he have a facility for motor discharge or be gesturally inclined.
5. That he be in relative good health.

Pfungst summarized eloquently the difficulties of uncovering the nature of Clever Hans' talents. Investigators had been misled by "looking for, in the horse, what should have been sought in the man." Additional examples of just such looking in the wrong place and more extensive references are to be found elsewhere (Rosenthal, 1964b; Rosenthal, 1965a).

There is a more recent example of possible expectancy effects, and this time the subjects were humans. The experiment dealt with the Freudian defense mechanism of projection (Rosenthal, 1956; Rosenthal, 1958). A total of 108 subjects was composed of 36 college men, 36 college women, and 36 hospitalized patients with paranoid symptomatology. Each of these three groups was further divided into three subgroups receiving success, failure, or neutral experience on a task structured as and simulating a standardized test of intelligence. Before the subjects' experimental treatment conditions were imposed, they were asked to rate the degree of success or failure of persons pictured in photographs. Immediately after the experimental manipulation, subjects were asked to rate an equivalent set of photos on their degree of success or failure. The dependent variable was the magnitude of the difference scores from pre- to post-ratings of the photographs. It was hypothesized that the "success" treatment condition would lead to greater subsequent perception of other people's success, whereas the "failure" treatment condition would lead to greater subsequent perception of other people's failure as measured by the pre-post difference scores.

An analysis (which was essentially unnecessary to the main purpose of the study) was performed which compared the mean *pre*-ratings of the three experimental treatment conditions. These means were as follows: success, -1.5; neutral, -0.9; failure, -1.0. The pre-rating mean of the success treatment group was significantly lower ($p = .01$) than the other means. In terms of the hypothesis under test, a lower pre-rating by this group would tend to lead to significantly different difference scores even if the post-ratings were identical for all treatment conditions. Without the investigator's awareness, the cards had been stacked in favor of obtaining results confirming the hypothesis under test. It should be emphasized that the success and failure groups' instructions had been identical, verbatim, during the pre-rating phase of the experiment. (Instructions to the neutral group differed only in that no mention was made of the experimental task, since none was administered to this group.)

The investigator, however, was aware for each subject which experimental treatment the subject would subsequently be administered. "The implication is that in some subtle manner, perhaps by tone, or manner, or gestures, or general atmosphere, the experimenter, although formally treating the success and failure groups in an identical way, influenced the success subjects to make lower initial ratings and thus increase the experimenter's probability of verifying his hypothesis" (Rosenthal, 1956, p. 44). As a further check on the suspicion that success subjects had been differently treated, the conservatism-extremeness of pre-ratings of photos was analyzed. The mean extremeness-of-rating scores were as follow: success, 3.9; neutral, 4.4; failure, 4.4. The success group rated photos significantly ($p = .001$) less extremely than did the other treatment groups. Whatever the manner in which the experimenter differentially treated those subjects he knew were destined for the success condition, it seemed to affect not only their mean level of rating but their style of rating as well.

It was these puzzling and disconcerting results that led to the experiments to be described in Part II.

II

STUDIES OF EXPERIMENTER EXPECTANCY EFFECTS

EXPERIMENTAL DEMONSTRATION OF EXPERIMENTER EXPECTANCY EFFECTS

FACTORS COMPLICATING EXPERIMENTER EXPECTANCY EFFECTS

VARIABLES RELEVANT TO THE COMMUNICATION OF EXPERIMENTER EXPECTANCY EFFECTS

9

Human Subjects

The evidence presented up to this point that the expectancy of the experimenter may in part determine the results of his research has been at least somewhat equivocal. Some of the evidence has been anecdotal. Some has required the untenable assumption that the expectancy of the experimenter, and not some correlated variable, had led to the effects observed. That is the case in any study in which the data collector estimates beforehand the data he will obtain and then obtains data significantly in that direction. In such cases it could be that experimenters who expect certain kinds of data differ in other attributes from their colleagues and that it is these attributes, rather than the expectancy, that influence the subjects' response. The most clear-cut evidence for the effects of the experimenter's expectancy, therefore, must come from experiments in which experimenters are given different expectancies. Of the studies examined, that by Stanton and Baker (1942) comes closest to meeting this requirement of the experimental induction of an expectancy. That study does require, however, the assumption that experimenters will expect the subjects to answer correctly the items being presented. The same assumption is required to interpret the case of Clever Hans as an experiment in expectancy effects. The studies to be described now seem to be fairly straightforward tests of the hypothesis of the effects of the experimenter's expectancy on his research results.

THE PERSON PERCEPTION TASK

In earlier chapters there has been occasion to refer often to the person perception task. The details of the standardization should be described. Fifty-seven photographs of faces ranging in size from 2×3 cm to 5×6 cm were cut from a weekly news magazine and mounted on 3×5 in. white cards. These were presented to 70 male and 34 female students, enrolled in an introductory psychology class at the University of North Dakota. Subjects were instructed to rate each photo on a rating scale of success or failure. The scale, shown in Figure 1, ran from −10, extreme failure; to +10, extreme success; with intermediate labeled points. Each subject was seen individually by the author who read to each the following instructions:

FIGURE 1

THE EMPATHY TEST RATING SCALE

Extreme	Moderate	Mild	Mild	Moderate	Extreme
Failure	Failure	Failure	Success	Success	Success

−10 −9 −8 −7 −6 −5 −4 −3 −2 −1 +1 +2 +3 +4 +5 +6 +7 +8 +9 +10

Instructions to Subjects. I am going to read you some instructions. I am not permitted to say anything which is not in the instructions nor can I answer any questions about this experiment. OK?

We are in the process of developing a test of empathy. This test is designed to show how well a person is able to put himself into someone else's place. I will show you a series of photographs. For each one I want you to judge whether the person pictured has been experiencing success or failure. To help you make more exact judgments you are to use this rating scale. As you can see the scale runs from −10 to +10. A rating of −10 means that you judge the person to have experienced extreme failure. A rating of +10 means that you judge the person to have experienced extreme success. A rating of −1 means that you judge the person to have experienced mild failure, while a rating of +1 means that you judge the person to have experienced mild success. You are to rate each photo as accurately as you can. Just tell me the rating you assign to each photo. All ready? Here is the first photo. (No further explanation may be given, although all or part of the instructions may be repeated.)

From the original 57 photos, 10 were selected for presentation to male subjects and 10 were selected for presentation to female subjects. All 20 photos were rated on the average as neither successful nor unsuccessful, and for each the mean rating evoked fell between +1 and −1. The distributions of ratings evoked by each of the photos were also symmetrical. The 10 photos composing the final sets of stimuli for male subjects and the 10 for female subjects were rated on the average as exactly zero.[1]

---

[1] Four years later, at the same university, a sample of 14 experimenters administered the photo-rating task to a sample of 28 female subjects. Each experimenter contacted 2 subjects. The grand mean photo rating obtained was −.004. It should be noted, however, that the demonstration of expectancy effects does not depend on the "validity" of the standardization. The standardization sample was useful to determine the characteristics of the stimuli, but it is not employed as a comparison or control group in any of the experiments described in this book.

THE FIRST EXPERIMENT [2]

Ten of the eleven students in a class in undergraduate experimental psychology served as experimenters. All were psychology majors, and three of them were first-year graduate students in psychology. All but two of the experimenters were males. Subjects were 206 students enrolled in a course in introductory psychology (92 males and 114 females). Because subjects were given class credit for participating in the experiment, most of the class volunteered, thus reducing the selective effect of using volunteer subjects (Rosenthal, 1965b). Each experimenter contacted from 18 to 24 subjects.

The experimenters' task was structured as a laboratory exercise to see whether they could replicate "well-established" experimental findings as "students in physics labs are expected to do." Experimenters were told to discuss their project with no one and to say nothing to their subjects other than what was in the *Instructions to Subjects*. All experimenters were paid a dollar an hour except that if they did a "good job" they would be paid double: two dollars an hour. All ten experimenters received identical instructions except that five experimenters were told that their subjects would average a $+5$ rating on the ten neutral photos. The other experimenters were told that their subjects would average a -5 rating. Thus the only difference between the two groups of experimenters was that one group had a plus mark written in front of the "5" while the other group had a minus mark written in front of the "5." As a part of the experimenters' training, each of them also rated the standardized set of ten photos. The exact instructions to experimenters were as follows:

Instructions to Experimenters. You have been asked to participate in a research project developing a test of empathy. You may have seen this project written up in the campus newspaper. There is another reason for your participation in this project—namely, to give you practice in duplicating experimental results. In physics labs, for example, you are asked to repeat experiments to see if your findings agree with those already well established. You will now be asked to run a series of Ss and obtain from each ratings of photographs. The experimental procedure has been typed out for you and is self-explanatory. DO NOT DISCUSS THIS PROJECT WITH ANYONE until your instructor tells you that you may.

You will be paid at the rate of $1.00 per hour for your time. If your results come out properly—as expected—you will be paid $2.00 instead of $1.00. The Ss you are running should average about a $(+$ or $-)5$ rating.

Just read the instructions to the Ss. Say *nothing* else to them except hello and goodbye. If for any reason you should say anything to an S other than what

[2] This study and the first replication have been reported earlier (Rosenthal & Fode, 1961; Rosenthal & Fode, 1963b).

is written in your instructions, please write down the exact words you used and the situation which forced you to say them.

GOOD LUCK!

The results of this experiment are shown in Table 9-1. Each entry represents the mean photo rating obtained by one experimenter from all his subjects. The difference between the mean ratings obtained by experimenters expecting success $(+5)$ ratings and those expecting failure (-5) ratings was significant at the .007 level (one-tailed p, $t = 3.20$, $df = 8$). All ex-

TABLE 9—1

Experimenters' Expectancy and Their Subjects' Mean
Ratings of Success

EXPECTANCY

	+5	−5
	+.66	+.18
	+.45	+.17
	+.35	+.04
	+.31	−.37
	+.25	−.42
Means	+.40	−.08

perimenters expecting success ratings obtained higher ratings than did any experimenter expecting failure ratings. Such nonoverlapping of distributions occurs only rarely in behavioral research and has a probability of .004 (one-tailed, for $N_1 = N_2 = 5$). The mean ratings obtained by the two female experimenters, one in each treatment condition, did not differ from the mean ratings obtained by the male experimenters of their respective experimental conditions. The grades earned by all experimenters in their experimental psychology course were not related to either the mean photo ratings obtained from subjects or the magnitude of the biasing phenomenon.

THE FIRST REPLICATION

The magnitude of the expectancy effects obtained was not readily believable, and a replication was performed by Kermit Fode (1960). There were other reasons for this study, which will be discussed in the chapter dealing with the communication of the experimenter's expectancy. Here, only those portions of the study are reported that served the replication function.

Twelve of the 26 male students enrolled in an advanced undergraduate course in industrial psychology were randomly assigned to serve as experimenters. In this sample of experimenters, few were psychology majors; most were majoring in engineering sciences. Subjects were 86 students enrolled in a course in introductory psychology (50 males and 36 females). These subjects were also given class credit for participating in the experiment. Each experimenter contacted from 4 to 14 subjects.

The procedure of this experiment was just as in the preceding study with the exception that experimenters did not handle the photos. Instead, each set of ten photos was mounted on cardboard and labeled so that subjects could call out their ratings of each photo to their experimenter. It was thought that less handling of the photos might serve to reduce the effects of experimenters' expectancies on the data obtained from subjects. There were two reasons for this thinking. First, if the experimenter did not hold each stimulus photo, the subject would have the experimenter in his field of vision much less often and the number of cues observed by the

TABLE 9—2

Experimenters' Expectancy and Subjects' Mean Ratings: Replication

	EXPECTANCY	
	+5	−5
	+3.03	+1.00
	+2.76	+0.91
	+2.59	+0.75
	+2.09	+0.46
	+2.06	+0.26
	+1.10	−0.49
Means	+2.27	+0.48

subject should be reduced. That had been Pfungst's experience with Clever Hans. The second reason, related to the first, was the suspicion that the movements of the hand in which the experimenter held the stimulus photo might serve a cueing function. (This was the thinking about the one change in procedure, but the change itself was not one of the variables investigated formally. Rather, the change was required so that the two replication groups would not differ from other experimental groups of the experiment in procedure.)

The results of the replication are shown in Table 9-2. As in the original experiment, half the experimenters had been led to expect ratings of success (+5) and half had been led to expect ratings of failure (−5). The difference between these two groups of experimenters in the responses they obtained from their subjects was again significant, this time at the .0003 level (one-tailed p, $t = 4.99$, $df = 10$). Once again, all experimenters expecting ratings of success obtained ratings of the photos as more successful than did any of the experimenters expecting failure ratings.

THE SECOND REPLICATION

There is one more experiment by Fode (1965) which is sufficiently similar to the two described already to be usefully regarded as another replication. Later, in the chapter dealing with experimenter characteristics associated with greater and lesser expectancy effects, other aspects of that study will be considered. Here, we consider only the two most relevant groups employed by Fode.

There were eight experimenters, all advanced undergraduate students in industrial psychology, the same course from which the experimenters of the first replication were drawn, but, of course, in a different year. The 90 subjects were all enrolled in an introductory psychology course (55 males and 35 females). Each experimenter contacted from 9 to 13 subjects. The procedure was as in the original experiment. The major difference between this and the original experiment was that experimenters had

TABLE 9—3

Experimenters' Expectancy and Subjects' Mean Ratings: Second Replication

	EXPECTANCY	
	+5	−5
	+1.51	−0.31
	+0.64	−0.49
	+0.47	−0.65
	+0.13	−1.02
Means	+0.69	−0.62

been selected for their characteristic level of anxiety defined by the Taylor Scale of Manifest Anxiety. The eight experimenters whose results will be described were all medium anxious. Half were randomly assigned to a group led to expect success ($+5$) ratings, and half were assigned to a group led to expect failure (-5) ratings.

The results of this second replication are shown in Table 9-3. Once again, experimenters expecting ratings of people as more successful obtained ratings of higher success than did experimenters expecting ratings of people as failures, this time with an associated p value of .005 (one-tailed, $t = 3.96$, $df = 6$). Once again, too, the distributions did not overlap. Every experimenter expecting positive ratings obtained positive ratings, and every experimenter expecting negative ratings obtained negative ratings. Table 9-4 gives a summary of the magnitude of expectancy effects obtained in each of the three experiments described. Employing Stouffer's method suggested by Mosteller and Bush (1954) gave a combined probability for the three experiments of one in about two million.

TABLE 9—4

Summary of Three Basic Replicates

	EXPECTANCY					One-Tail
Experiment	+5	−5	Difference	t	df	p
I	+0.40	−0.08	+0.48	3.20	8	.007
II	+2.27	+0.48	+1.79	4.99	10	.0003
III	+0.69	−0.62	+1.31	3.96	6	.005
Means	+1.12	−0.07	+1.19			

SOME DISCUSSION

It seems reasonable to conclude from these data that the results of an experiment may be determined at least in part by the expectations of the experimenter. Since the experimenters had all read from the identical instructions, some more subtle aspects of their behavior toward their subjects must have served to communicate their expectations to their subjects. From experimental procedures and from more naturalistic observation of experimenters interacting with their subjects, some things have been learned about the communication of expectancies. What is known of this communication will be discussed in a subsequent chapter. We may note in passing, however, that of the studies described just now, one (II of Table 9-4) in which the experimenters were less often in the subjects' field of vision, and in which experimenters did not handle the stimulus photos, did not show a decrement in the biasing effect of the experimenter's expectancy. Surprisingly, that study was the one to show the greatest magnitude of biasing effect. It may at least be concluded that the communication of the experimenter's expectancy does not depend either on his handling of the stimulus materials or on his being within the subject's constant view. From this alone, it seems that the communication processes involved are not quite like those discovered by Pfungst to apply to Clever Hans. Hans, it will be recalled, did suffer a loss of unintended communication when he lost visual contact with his experimenter.[3]

In the first few chapters of this book there was a discussion of a number of effects of experimenters which did not affect their subjects' responses but which could affect the results of their research. It should be considered whether errors of observation or interpretation, or even intentional errors, could have accounted for the findings reported. Errors of observation and of interpretation are hard to discriminate in these experiments. The subject calls out a number and the experimenter records it as he hears it. We do know that errors of recording occur and that they tend to occur in the direction of the experimenter's expectancy. But the evidence presented in earlier portions of this book suggests that the magnitude of such errors is most often trivial. Intentional errors could have occurred, but they, too, are unlikely to have led to three sets of nonoverlapping distributions.

The hypotheses of recording errors and of intentional errors seem further weakened by the microgeography of the experimental interactions. The subjects sat in such relation to the experimenter that they could see what the experimenter recorded on his data sheet. For either recording errors or intentional errors, therefore, the subject was in a position to correct the experimenter's entry.[4]

---

[3] There was another effect possibly due to the different conditions of experiment II. All experimenters of this study tended to obtain ratings of photos as more successful, regardless of their expectancy, than did the experimenters of the other two studies ($p < .01$, $x^2 = 6.8$, $df = 1$). It is possible that experimenters of study II, having less to do during their interaction with the subjects, were perceived by them as less important or of lower status. In the chapter dealing with the effects of the experimenter's status, some evidence was presented which suggested that lower status experimenters did tend to obtain ratings of these photos as being of more successful people.

[4] We know from the observation of other experiments employing the same task that occasionally subjects do correct their experimenter's data entry. We cannot be absolutely certain, however, that subjects generally do not let errors observed by them go by without comment. Possibly those of our subjects who corrected their experimenter were unusual. Perhaps they were lower in the need for social approval. An interesting experiment would be to have a sample of experimenters intentionally misrecord their subjects' responses in plain view of their subjects. One wonders how

Finally, from the filmed and direct observations of other experiments in progress, it could be determined that experimenters do record the response as given by the subject. In the filmed studies, not all responses could be checked, however, because there were places where the sound track was too poor to be sure what response the subject had given.

In the experiments described, the experimenters were offered extra pay for "a good job." Perhaps the expectancy effect depends on such extrinsic incentives. On the basis of just these experiments no answer is possible. Later, however, there will be experiments that did not offer such additional incentives to experimenters to obtain biased responses. In fact, we shall encounter evidence suggesting that with increased incentive, the effects of expectancy are reduced or even thrown into a reversal of direction.

Questions of the generality of expectancy effects have been discussed in the preceding chapter. In Part III there will be a detailed statement of the generality of expectancy effects based on the research program designed specifically to investigate them. For now, however, we should consider the task employed. On first glance it would seem that neutral photos would, because of their neutrality, make subjects especially watchful of cues from the experimenter to guide them in their ratings. If the photos could "be" anything, successful or unsuccessful, then even minor cues should make it easy to influence the subject's response. It must be considered, however, that the meaning of neutral is not "anything." The stimulus value, the "reality" of the stimulus, is a specific numerical value, zero. For one group of subjects to rate the photos as significantly different from that zero value, or from the value established by a control group of subjects, is not, therefore, a trivial deviation.

In the three experiments described there was a source of ecological invalidity which should be discussed. That was the fact that experimenters contacted subjects under only a single condition of expectancy. Subjects were expected to be either success perceivers or failure perceivers. In "real" research it is more common for the same experimenter to contact the subjects of both the experimental and the control groups. The question must therefore be raised whether expectancy effects occur also when the same experimenter contacts subjects for whom he has differing expectancies. An experiment that is similar to the ones described so far and which sheds light on this matter is one conducted by Laszlo. He employed three male experimenters to administer the photo-rating task to 64 female subjects. Each of the experimenters contacted from 18 to 23 subjects. For half these subjects the experimenters were led to expect positive ratings of the success of others ($+5$), and for half they were led to expect negative ratings (-5). The order in which experimenters contacted each "type" of subject was random. Table 9-5 shows the mean photo ratings obtained by each

often these "errors" will be called to the experimenter's attention, under what conditions, and by what type of subject.

TABLE 9—5

Experimenters' Expectancy and Subjects' Mean Ratings: Alternating Expectancies

EXPECTANCY

Experimenter	+5	−5	Difference
A	−.13	−.67	+.54
B	−.51	−.72	+.21
C	−.96	−1.59	+.63
Means	−.53	−.99	+.46

experimenter under each type of expectancy. All three of the experimenters obtained higher ratings of success when expecting such ratings than when not expecting such ratings ($p = .04$, one-tailed, $t = 3.61$, $df = 2$). The mean magnitude of the expectancy effect was $+.46$, which was very close to the value of $+.48$ obtained in the original experiment (I of Table 9-4). In Laszlo's study there was also no extra pay offered to experimenters for obtaining the expected data. Apparently neither the extra incentive offered for "good" data nor the holding of only a single expectancy for all subjects could account for the results of the three experiments described earlier. It should be noted, however, that in the Laszlo study, the distributions of mean photo ratings obtained under the two conditions of expectancy did overlap. In that sense at least, the results are less dramatic than those of the other three studies. Whether this was due to some dampening effect of the expectancies' varying for the experimenters cannot be determined. The Laszlo study differed also in that half the time a higher status was ascribed the experimenter, and half the time a lower status. This procedural difference might also account for the possibly weakened effect of the experimenter's expectancy. In a subsequent chapter dealing with the personal characteristics of more successful unintentional influencers, some additional evidence is presented which also shows that the effects of experimenters' expectancies do not depend upon their contacting subjects under only a single condition of expectancy.

Another question that must be raised is the extent to which the expectancy effects demonstrated were due, not to the expectancy of the experimenters, but to the expectancy of the author. If that were entirely the case it would not, of course, eliminate the evidence for the effects of the experimenter's expectancy. It would, however, reduce considerably the number of cases in the sample of experimenters studied from several hundred to one. We would have, then, a longitudinal case study of the expectancy effects of a single investigator, the author. In some of the early studies in the research program such effects of the principal investigator cannot be ruled out. Thus there were studies in which the author ushered subjects into the experimenters' rooms without being blind to the experimenters' expectancies. Knowing that a given subject was destined for a "success"-expecting experimenter may have led the author to treat these subjects differently, in such a way as to affect their photo ratings. Even when the walk with the subject from waiting room to laboratory is short, such effects cannot be ruled out. Later studies in the research program eliminated these potential effects. The details of the safeguards against the principal investigator's expectancy will be given in later chapters. For now it should be mentioned that in many of the studies conducted the investigators did not know which experimenters had what expectancies until the experiment was completely finished.

A point to be developed later is that ten experiments performed in a single laboratory may be worth less than the same ten experiments conducted in ten different laboratories. Most of the experiments reported in this book were conducted in a single "laboratory," or at least involved one common investigator. For this reason it is especially important to look to other laboratories for evidence to support or to infirm the hypothesis of the expectancy effect of the psychological experimenter. Some such evidence was reported in the last chapter, and a few more recent reports are relevant.

In a demonstration employing the same task described here, Karl Weick had two experimenters conduct the person perception experiment in front of his class in experimental social psychology. One experimenter was led to expect success ratings from his five subjects; the other was led to expect failure ratings from his five subjects. The results are given in more detail in the chapter dealing with the communication of expectancies. Briefly the experimenter expecting positive ratings obtained a mean rating of $+1.18$, whereas the experimenter expecting negative ratings obtained a mean rating of -0.50. The difference was significant at the .01 level, one-tailed.

There is a very recent experiment by Masling (1965) in which he gave "special training" to a group of 14 graduate students in a "new method of learning the Rorschach procedure." Half the examiners were led to believe that experienced examiners obtained a relatively greater proportion of human percepts in the ink blots. The remaining examiners were led to believe that experienced examiners obtained relatively more animal percepts from their subjects. All the examiner-subject interactions were tape-recorded. Examiners led to believe that more experienced examiners obtained relatively more human percepts obtained a ratio of 1.8 animal percepts to each human percept. Examiners led to believe that obtaining animal percepts was more desirable obtained an animal-to-human percept ratio of 2.4 ($p = .04$). If these examiners also expected to obtain the responses they probably desired, this experiment would be an excellent demonstration of expectancy effects. Even if they did not, however, this study illustrates, with data from a different laboratory, that cognitions of the experimenter may affect the subject's response by shepherding it into the desired (and perhaps the expected) direction. Interestingly, the analysis of the tape recordings of the examiner-subject interactions revealed no differential reinforcements of subjects' responses that could account for the differences obtained by the two groups of examiners.

Still more recently and even more directly, Marwit and Marcia (1965) tested the effects of experimenter expectancies on their subjects' responses to a Rorschach-like task. They employed 36 undergraduate students of experimental psychology to administer a modified Holtzman inkblot test to a total of 54 students enrolled in introductory psychology. Half the experimenters were asked to evolve their own hypotheses as to whether normal college students would give many or few responses to the inkblot stimuli. The remaining experimenters were given "ready-made" hypotheses as to whether subjects would give many or few responses. About two thirds of the experimenters evolving their own hypotheses expected their subjects to give many responses and one third expected few responses. About two thirds of the experimenters given ready-made hypotheses were, therefore, led to expect many responses to the inkblot stimuli, and one third were led to expect few responses.

The results of the Marwit and Marcia study showed that it made no difference whether experimenters evolved their own hypotheses or were given ready-made hypotheses. In both cases, experimenters expecting more responses to inkblots obtained more responses to inkblots. Among experimenters who originated their own hypotheses, those who expected more responses obtained 52 percent more responses than did those expecting fewer responses. Among experimenters who were given their expectations by the principal investigators, those led to expect more responses obtained 55 percent more responses than did experimenters led to expect fewer responses. For both groups of experimenters combined, these numerically large expectancy effects were also very significant statistically ($p = .00025$, one-tail, $t = 3.76$, $df = 50$).

Marwit and Marcia had felt that the number of questions asked by the experimenters of their subjects might serve to communicate their expectation to their subject. That, they found, was not the case. Whereas greater questioning of subjects was associated with significantly more responses from subjects among experimenters who evolved their own hypotheses, exactly the opposite relationship was found among experimenters who had been given "ready-made" expectancies. There was a general tendency, too, for expectancy effects to increase during the course of the interaction with each subject. Although this trend cannot establish that experimenters were employing any system of differential reinforcement, this learning curve at least suggests that such reinforcement was a possibility. Alternatively, it might have been the subject who reinforced the experimenter's unintentional communication behavior. This possibility will be discussed in more detail in the chapter dealing with the communication of expectancy effects.

Troffer and Tart (1964) reported on some relevant experimenter effects obtained from a sample of eight experimenters. The sample was particularly interesting in that these experimenters were fully aware of the problem of "experimenter bias." The experiment called for subjects to be tested on the Stanford Hypnotic Susceptibility Scale (Weitzenhoffer & Hilgard, 1962). Half the time the experimenters administered the scale after an hypnotic induction procedure. Half the time they administered the scale without having attempted any hypnotic induction. All experimenter-subject interactions were tape-recorded, and the experimenters knew that these recordings were being made. The very first item of the suggestibility tests was found to have been read differently to subjects depending on whether the experimenter had or had not gone through the induction procedure. Judges listening to the tapes rated experimenters as speaking in a more relaxed, somnolent, solicitous, and convinced tone when they had gone through the hypnotic procedure before testing their subjects. Whatever the precise cues, judges could correctly assess whether the experimenter had or had not carried out the induction procedure prior to his administration of item No. 1 of the Stanford Scale. Excluding one judge who could not differentiate better than chance, the remaining six judges were correct 73 percent of the time, where 50 percent would have been expected by chance ($p < .005$). As it happened, that one judge who performed only at a chance level was the only one who felt that the experiment would not turn up anything.

The authors of this report provide two interpretations, either or both of which might have accounted for the results. The first interpretation suggests that the act of having gone through an induction procedure essentially "warms up" the experimenter and makes him a more effective hypnotist. The second interpretation, more relevant to our immediate concern, suggests that experimenters expected better performance in the condition involving hypnotic induction. Expecting such better performance led them to put more into their reading of the item to their subjects. It should be noted that all eight of the experimenters favored the first, or "warm-up," interpretation over the second, or "expectancy," interpretation. So although we cannot be sure that we have here a case of expectancy effects, we do have excellent evidence that even seasoned experimenters, cautioned to treat their subjects identically, were unable to do so. Instead, these "bias-wise" experimenters treated their subjects as they would have to be treated to increase the likelihood of the confirmation of the hypothesis.

Smallest in sample size, but perhaps the most "lifelike," of the relevant studies from other laboratories is a study by Rosenhan (1964). There will be occasion to cite his work again when the topic of expectancy control groups is treated in Part III. Briefly, Rosenhan had established through correlational research a certain complex pattern of relationships between hypnosis and various types of conformity behavior. Then he and a research assistant set out independently to replicate these findings. Before beginning the replication, Rosenhan showed the assistant the pattern of correlations he had originally obtained; only he reversed the sign of every correlation coefficient. Thus the larger positive correlations became the larger negative correlations, the negatives became the positives. The data the assistant subsequently obtained from her subjects were significantly different from those obtained by Rosenhan in his own replication. In most cases, he reports, the correlations obtained by the assistant were opposite in sign to those obtained by him, but were, of course, in line with the correlations she had been led to expect.

In spite of identically programmed procedures, two "real" experimenters obtained significantly opposite data; to each came what was expected. Rosenhan points out that the two experimenters differed in more ways than just in the nature of the expectancy held by each. There were differences in sex, age, status, and experience, and any or all of these could have contributed to the obtained reversals. Rosenhan's conclusion, however, was that compared to the possible effects of these correlated variables, "It seems far more likely that the differences obtained in the hypnosis-conformity study were a function of the different expectations and hypotheses held by the experimenters" (p. 27).[5]

The basic experiments designed to test the hypothesis of the effect of the experimenter's expectancy require one additional comment. That has to do with the fact that in every case deception was involved. There was deception of the subjects in their being told that their task was a test of empathy. There was deception of the experimenters in their not being told that it was their behavior which was of the greatest interest, and in their being given false information about the subjects in order that expectancies could be induced.

Deception is a necessary commonplace in psychological research. One does not give subjects the California F Scale and ask them to "fill out this test which tells how authoritarian you are." Though that might make an interesting experiment, it is just not the way the instrument can be employed.

---

[5] Rosenhan (1964) also describes and analyzes another case which could be interpreted as a case of the experimenter's expectancy determining his behavior toward the subject in such a way as to fulfill his experimental prophecy. These data, which will not be described here, are especially interesting in that they involve a report by a co-author of a technical paper of an experimenter's behavior toward that co-author at a time when he was a bona fide subject. It represents, therefore, a sophisticated subject's eye-view of unintended experimenter behavior.

If it and many psychological techniques are to be used at all, the purpose must be disguised, and that, of course, is deception. The problem will be discussed again in Part III. For now the fact of deception must be accepted, and the hope must be that the knowledge acquired through this necessary deception is worth the price of having deceived.

10

Animal Subjects

In the last chapter a question was raised as to the generality of the effects of the experimenter's expectancy. The experiments to be described in this chapter were designed to extend the generality of these effects. It was felt that a major gain in the generality of the phenomenon depended on the demonstration that expectancy effects might operate with different species of subjects. Accordingly, the subjects of these experiments were rats rather than humans.

There were differences other than the change in subjects' species between these experiments and the original ones employing human subjects. In the animal studies, as in some of the later human studies, the experimenters were offered no special incentives for obtaining data consistent with the experimental hypothesis. In addition, in both the studies to be described now, closer supervision was possible of the experimenter's conduct of his experiment. There was, therefore, greater opportunity to note instances of error of observation, recording, and response interpretation as well as any intentional errors.

MAZE LEARNING

In the first experiment employing animal subjects, the experimenters were 12 of the 13 students enrolled in a laboratory course in experimental psychology. All the experimenters had been performing laboratory experiments with human subjects during the entire semester. The present study was arranged as their last experiment of the term, and the first to employ animal subjects. The following written instructions were given to each experimenter (Rosenthal & Fode, 1963a):

Instructions to Experimenters. The reason for running this experiment is to give you further experience in duplicating experimental findings and, in addition, to introduce you to the field of animal research and overcome any fears that you may have with regard to working with rats.

This experiment is a repetition of work done on Maze-Bright and Maze-Dull rats. Many studies have shown that continuous inbreeding of rats that do well on a maze leads to successive generations of rats that do considerably better than "normal" rats. Furthermore, these studies have shown that continuous inbreeding of rats that do badly on a maze leads to successive generations of rats that do considerably worse than "normal" rats.

Thus, generations of Maze-Bright rats do much better than generations of Maze-Dull rats.

Each of you will be assigned a group of five rats to work with. Some of you will be working with Maze-Bright rats, others will be working with Maze-Dull rats.

Those of you who are assigned the Maze-Bright rats should find your animals on the average showing some evidence of learning during the first day of running. Thereafter performance should rapidly increase.

Those of you who are assigned the Maze-Dull rats should find on the average very little evidence of learning in your rats.

The experiment itself will involve a discrimination learning problem. The animals will be rewarded only if they go to the darker of two platforms. In order that the animals do not simply learn a position response, the position of the darker platform will be varied throughout each day's running.

The apparatus employed by the experimenters was a simple elevated T-maze described by Ehrenfreund (1952) and built to his specifications. The two arms of the maze were interchangeable; one was painted white, the other a dark gray.

For the experimenters' use at the conclusion of the experiment, a questionnaire was constructed on which could be rated their satisfaction with the experiment, their feelings about the subjects, and a description of their own behavior during the experiment. Each scale ran from -10 (e.g., extremely dissatisfied) to $+10$ (e.g., extremely satisfied) with intermediate labeled points. On this questionnaire form, space was also provided for each experimenter to describe how he felt before, during, and after the experiment.

The subjects of this experiment were 65 naïve, Sprague-Dawley albino rats which ranged in age from 9 to 15 weeks. Thirteen groups of five each were formed in such a way as to make differences in mean age per group a minimum. Each group was composed of two male and three female animals and ranged in mean age from 12 to 13 weeks. Each group was housed in two cages, segregated by sex, and, several days before the beginning of the experiment, placed on 23-hour food deprivation.

The experimental procedure was described briefly in the instructions to experimenters. On the day the course instructor announced the details of the final experiment of the semester, the laboratory assistant entered the classroom announcing that the "Berkeley Rats" had arrived. Instructions were read to the experimenters and explained further where necessary. Each experimenter was then asked to rate on a 20-point scale how much he or she thought they would like working with the rats. None had any prior experience with animal subjects. On the basis of these ratings, six pairs of experimenters were formed, matched on their estimated liking of the rats. For each pair, one member was randomly assigned a group of subjects that had been labeled "Maze-Bright," while the other member of the pair was assigned a group labeled "Maze-Dull." Thus, the experimental treatment was the information that an experimenter's rats were Maze-Bright or Maze-Dull. Actually, of course, the groups had been labeled bright or dull randomly but with the restriction that differences in mean age per group per matched pair be at a minimum.

Before actually running any subjects, each experimenter was asked to rate on a 20-point rating scale ($+10$, extremely well, to -10, extremely poorly) exactly how well he thought his animals would perform. Each subject received one hour of handling and maze experience before being run in the maze. During the maze experience, subjects could obtain food from either arm of the T-maze.

Each subject was run ten times a day for five days. For each trial the experimenter recorded whether it was correct or incorrect as well as the time required to complete the response. The darker arm of the maze was always reinforced and the white arm was never reinforced. The darker arm appeared equally often on the right and on the left, although the particular patterning of correct position was developed randomly for each day of the experiment and followed by all experimenters.

It was mentioned that 12 of the 13 students in a particular course served as the experimenters. The thirteenth student was an undergraduate research assistant who had worked for almost a year on the program of research of which this experiment was a part. Although it seemed unlikely that any of the students in that class knew about the existence of this research project, and of the thirteenth student's connection with it, steps were taken to minimize the likelihood that such a connection could be made. The undergraduate research assistant therefore participated in the experiment just as any other experimenter but with the fully conscious motivation to get as good performance from her animals as possible without violating the formally programmed procedures. An advantage of her being in this class was that since the course instructor rarely observed the actual conduct of the course experiments, she could serve as an observer of the experimental procedures actually employed without arousing the self-consciousness that might have been incurred had the course instructor observed the experimental procedures. After the end of the semester during which this experiment took place, one of the experimenters became associated with the research program. He was thus also able to give valuable information on actual procedures employed by the experimenters during the conduct of the experiment. All reports made by these assistants were held in confidence and at no time was the name of a specific experimenter mentioned.

TABLE 10—1

Mean Number of Correct Responses

Experimenter Sample	DAYS					
	1	2	3	4	5	Mean
Research assistant	1.20	3.00	3.80	3.40	3.60	3.00
"Maze-Bright"	1.33	1.60	2.60	2.83	3.26	2.32
"Maze-Dull"	0.73	1.10	2.23	1.83	1.83	1.54
"Bright" > "Dull"	+0.60	+0.50	+0.37	+1.00	+1.43	+0.78
t	2.54	1.02	0.29	2.28	2.37	4.01
p (one-tail)	.03	.18	.39	.04	.03	.01

Table 10-1 shows the mean number of correct responses per subject for those six experimenters who believed they were running Maze-Bright rats, for the six who believed they were running Maze-Dull rats, and for the research assistant who was aware that the rats were neither bright nor dull but who was trying to obtain maximum performance from them. Performance of the animals run by experimenters believing them to be bright was significantly better on the first, fourth, and fifth days. In addition, when the data from all five days of the experiment were combined, t was again significant, this time with a one-tailed p of .01.

Inspection of the day by day means for each group of experimenters shows that the "bright" animals' performance increased monotonically as might be expected if learning were occurring. The obtained monotonic increase could be expected by chance only six times in a hundred. The "dull" animals' performance, on the other hand, increased only to day three, dropping on the fourth day and not changing on the fifth. The differences in obtained functions as well as the differences between performance means suggest that learning was less likely among rats run by experimenters believing them to be dull.

Table 10-1 also shows that, except for the first day of the experiment, the experimenter who was a research assistant and trying explicitly to obtain good performance from her rats did obtain better performance than did the experimenters believing their animals to be bright ($p < .05$, one-tail, $t = 2.38$). While her obtained performance function was not a monotonically increasing one, interpretation of this seems restricted by the fact that she ran relatively few animals compared to the number in the two experimental groups. Interpretation of the obtained t suggests that an experimenter who is explicitly "biased" to obtain good performance from animal subjects obtains even better performance than do experimenters who are biased to expect good performance but not explicitly instructed to obtain it.

Of the 300 occasions when subjects were run (60 subjects $\times$ 5 days) there were 60 occasions when the animal made no response at all. On the average, then, one out of every five sessions the animals refused to make a choice. This relatively poor performance may have been due to the difficulty of the discrimination problem, the limiting of pretraining to one hour, or the inexperience of the experimenters in running animals. At any rate, these no-response occasions were not equally distributed between the experimental groups. There were 17 such occasions among the "bright" subjects and 43 among the "dull," a division significant at the .001 level.

Since the "dull" animals made fewer responses, it was possible that the results shown in Table 10-1 were confounded, as animals responding more are likely to respond correctly more often. In order to partial out the effects of greater nonresponding among the "dull" rats, the mean time in minutes required to make only correct responses was computed for each day separately for the two experimental groups. The obtained mean times are shown in Table 10-2. Although for any given day the running times

TABLE 10—2

Time Required to Make Correct Responses

Experimenter Sample	DAYS					
	1	2	3	4	5	Mean
Research assistant	5.45	1.63	2.04	0.74	0.68	2.11
"Maze-Bright"	3.13	2.75	2.05	2.09	1.75	2.35
"Maze-Dull"	3.99	4.76	3.20	2.18	3.20	3.47
"Bright" < "Dull"	+0.86	+2.01	+1.15	+0.09	+1.45	+1.12

did not differ significantly between the two treatment groups, the difference for the entire experiment was found to be significant ($p < .02$, one-tail, $t = 3.50$). Thus, animals run by experimenters believing them to be bright made their correct choices more rapidly than did the rats run by experimenters believing their rats to be dull.

Inspection of the day-by-day means for the two treatment groups shows that the "bright" animals tended to improve more steadily than did the "dull" animals. The related question may be raised of whether "bright" rats simply ran faster or whether they actually improved their performance compared to the "dull" rats. Comparing the running time of the "dull" animals on their first and fifth days yielded a t of less than one, suggesting that this group did not improve their performance significantly. The comparable t for the "bright" animals was 1.77, which has a p of .06 (one-tailed test), suggesting that this group probably did improve their performance during the course of the experiment.

Table 10-2 also shows that the experimenter who was actually a research assistant obtained the shortest mean running time per correct response. Except for day one, on which her animals ran slowest of any group, her rats performed better than those run by experimenters believing their rats to be bright. This trend serves to support the earlier interpretation that an experimenter who is explicitly "biased" to obtain good performance from animal subjects obtains better performance than do less explicitly "biased" experimenters. (It is also possible, of course, that by chance this particular experimenter was the most competent.)

To what extent could the obtained results have been due to intentional or other errors on the part of the experimenters? The two experimenters who subsequently worked with the research program on experimenter expectancy had been in a position to observe most, but not all, of the actual experimental procedures. There were no observed instances of rats not actually being run or of the making of incorrect entries on the data sheets. There was, however, a total of five observed instances of deviation from programmed procedure when experimenters prodded subjects to run the maze. Two of these instances occurred among experimenters running "bright" rats while three occurred among experimenters running "dull" rats. It appears unlikely from this distribution of instances of procedural deviation that the differences obtained between the treatment groups could be ascribed to gross procedural or intentional errors on the part of the experimenters. In addition, the superior performance of the animals run by the research assistant shows that intentional errors are not needed to explain the good performance of animals run by experimenters believing them to be bright.

A question of some interest deals with whether both groups of experimenters were biased by their expectation or whether only one of the groups was actually biased, with the other group obtaining data no different from what they might have obtained had they been given no expectation. Prior to running their animals, all experimenters had been asked to predict the performance they would obtain from their animals. It was possible, therefore, to compute a correlation between the data the experimenter expected to obtain and the data he subsequently obtained. Such a correlation can serve as an index of the degree of expectancy effect. In this experiment there was a shrinkage of the correlations due to the experimenters within each condition having predicted what they were led to expect. This decreased the variation of predictions and, therefore, the correlations obtained. The rank correlation between expected and obtained performance was $+.43$ for the experimenters running "bright" rats and $+.41$ for those running "dull" rats. Since there were only six experimenters in each group, these correlations did not reach statistical significance (although when the correlations were combined, the one-tailed p ranged between .12 and .007 depending on the method of combination). These findings suggest that the two groups of experimenters were probably biased by their expectations to about the same degree, although of course in opposite directions.

At the conclusion of the experiment, each experimenter made ratings of his subjects, of his satisfaction with the experiment, and of his behavior during the experiment. These ratings were designed to suggest the mechanisms whereby the experimenters unintentionally influenced their animals to perform as the experimenter expected. The mean ratings on these scales are shown separately for each group of experimenters in Table 10-3. Only those scales have been listed which differentiated experimenters with

TABLE 10—3

Descriptions of Subjects' and of Experimenters' Behavior

	BELIEF ABOUT SUBJECT			Two-Tail
	"Bright"	"Dull"	t	p
Subjects' Behavior				
1. Bright	4.2	−3.0	2.94	.04
2. Pleasant	4.8	0.0	1.77	.15
3. Likable	4.8	2.2	0.92	.40
Experimenters' Behavior				
1. Satisfied	3.0	2.5	2.10	.10
2. Relaxed	8.7	4.8	5.11	.005
3. Pleasant	6.7	2.8	2.56	.05
4. Friendly	5.3	1.3	2.61	.05
5. Enthusiastic	5.5	0.2	1.51	.19
6. Nontalkative	6.2	3.2	1.19	.29
7. Gentle handling	6.5	2.7	1.95	.11
8. Much handling	5.2	0.3	1.17	.30

different expectancies in both the experiments described in this chapter. Experimenters who expected good performance from their animals saw them as brighter, somewhat more pleasant, and more likable. These experimenters were more satisfied with their participation in the experiment and felt more relaxed in their contacts with the rats. They described their behavior toward their animals as more pleasant, more friendly, somewhat more enthusiastic, and less talkative.

Of course, we cannot be sure of the sense modality by which the experimenter's expectancy is communicated to the subject. Rats are sensitive to visual, auditory, olfactory, and tactual cues (Munn, 1950). These last, the tactual, were perhaps the major cues mediating the experimenter's expectancy to the animal. The attitudinal ratings described, which differentiated the two groups of experimenters, may well have been translated into the quantity and quality of their handling of the animals. Table 10-3 suggests that experimenters expecting and obtaining better performance handled their rats more and also more gently than did the experimenters expecting and obtaining poorer performance. After a description of the second experiment employing rat subjects, further evidence will be presented that increased handling can improve performance (e.g., Bernstein, 1957).

At the end of each experimenter's questionnaire, space was provided for any comments he might wish to make. These comments suggested that the experimenters were unaware of their differential handling of the animals as a function of their expectancy. In addition, these comments made it appear still more unlikely that there were intentional errors being committed. Nine of the 12 experimenters spontaneously reported feeling good when the animals performed well, and feeling badly when they performed poorly. These comments were equally distributed between the experimental groups, four in the "dull," five in the "bright." Since even the experimenters expecting poor performance stated that they felt better if subjects performed better, it seems unlikely that they would have done anything to worsen their subjects' performance, at least intentionally. In fact, because it was academically important to the experimenter that he demonstrate the "laws of learning" in his experiment, the pressures on the experimenters expecting poor performance were to get good performance, and good learning. Any intentional errors, if they did occur, should therefore have operated to reduce those effects of the experimenters' expectancy that were demonstrated in this study.

OPERANT LEARNING

The second experiment designed to demonstrate the effects of the experimenter's expectancy on his animal subjects was conducted at the Ohio State University in the laboratory of Professor Reed Lawson, at his invitation (and has been reported earlier, Rosenthal & Lawson, 1964). A considerable gain in generality accrues from this fact. It was hinted at earlier and will be discussed in detail in Part III, but for now it is enough to make the point that replications conducted in a different laboratory are worth more than those conducted in one's own. Other gains in generality deriving from this second experiment with animal subjects will be mentioned shortly when this experiment is compared more systematically to the one already described.

In this experiment there were 30 male and 9 female students enrolled in a course in experimental psychology to serve as the experimenters. At the very beginning of the course all experimenters were given the following written instructions:

Instructions to Experimenters. The reason for running these experiments is to give you experience in duplicating experimental findings and, in addition, to introduce you to the field of animal research and overcome any fears you might have with regard to working with rats.

The experiments are all repetitions of work done recently on Skinner Box–Bright and Skinner Box–Dull rats. Many studies have shown that continuous inbreeding of rats that do well on Skinner box problems, such as those you will be running, leads to successive generations of rats that do considerably better than "normal" rats. Furthermore, these studies have shown that continuous inbreeding of rats that do badly on Skinner box problems, such as those you will be running, leads to successive generations of rats that do considerably worse than "normal" rats.

Thus generations of Skinner Box–Bright rats do much better than generations of Skinner Box–Dull rats.

Each of you will be assigned to a group to work with. Some groups will be working with Skinner Box–Bright rats, others will be working with Skinner Box–Dull rats.

Those of you who are assigned the Skinner Box–Bright rats should find your animals on the average showing some evidence of learning during even the early stages of each of your experiments. Thereafter, performance on each of your experiments should rapidly increase.

Those of you who are assigned the Skinner Box–Dull rats should find on the average very little evidence of learning in your rats. You should, however, not become discouraged, since it has been found that even the dullest rats can, in time, learn the required responses.

If you are interested in learning more about the details of the experiments on breeding rats for brightness and dullness, your lab instructors can give you references to the work done by Tryon and others at the University of California at Berkeley and elsewhere.

The animals employed in this experiment were 16 female laboratory rats (all 80 days old) drawn from the animal colony maintained by The Ohio State University Department of Psychology. They were randomly assigned to one of two groups. One group of eight rats was assigned to home cages which had been labeled "Skinner Box–Bright," while the other group was assigned to home cages which bore the labels "Skinner Box–Dull." Early in the course, two of the animals labeled "Dull" died, so that the maximum number available for the subsequent experiments was eight rats labeled "Bright" and six labeled "Dull." All were on a feeding regimen of one-half hour ad lib access to food daily throughout the eight weeks of the study.

The basic equipment employed in the studies were commercially made (Scientific Prototype Co.) demonstration Skinner boxes with feeders that dispensed 45-mg P. J. Noyes pellets.

Experimenters followed the laboratory manual of Homme and Klaus (1957), except that food pellets were used instead of water as reinforcement.

The questionnaire employed in the last study, in which experimenters could rate their satisfaction with their participation in the experiments, their feelings about their animals, and their description of their own behavior during the conduct of the experiments, was again administered at the conclusion of the study. A few new scales were added to this questionnaire.

At the beginning of the study each experimenter was assigned to one of five laboratory periods, to each of which had been assigned one or two "bright" and one or two "dull" rats. Assignment to laboratory sections could not be random, since there were only certain times that certain experimenters were able to schedule their laboratory section. Within each laboratory section, however, experimenters were randomly assigned to the animals to be run during that section. At least two experimenters were assigned to each subject, and the mean number of experimenters per subject was 2.7.

Each laboratory team performed three different functions during each of the experiments—that of experimenter, timer, and recorder. These functions were rotated among the members of each laboratory team. For those teams consisting of only two members, the functions of timer and recorder were usually performed by the same person.

A total of seven experiments was performed, each of which is described in detail in the manual mentioned earlier (Homme & Klaus, 1957). A brief description of each follows:

1. Magazine Training. Training the rat to run to the magazine and eat whenever the feeder was clicked. Latencies were recorded for each click, and the dependent variable was defined as the mean latency on the first and last ten clicks of the session.

2. Operant Acquisition. Training the rat to bar-press. Number of bar-pressing responses per minute was recorded, and the dependent variable was defined as the mean number of responses during the first and last ten minutes of the session.

3. Extinction and Spontaneous Recovery. Number of responses per minute was again recorded, and the dependent variable was defined as the number of minutes elapsed until the animal showed two response-free minutes. Data were analyzed separately for the two parts of this experiment.

4. Secondary Reinforcement. In this experiment the animals' responses were reconditioned and partially reextinguished. Subsequent responses were reinforced by the clicking sound without presentation of food. The dependent variable was again defined as the number of minutes elapsed until the animal showed two response-free minutes, while getting click reinforcements.

5. Stimulus Discrimination. Training the rat to bar-press only in the presence of a light and not in the absence of the light. For each trial of this experiment the experimenters recorded the latency for the reinforced response and the number of responses occurring under the nonreinforced condition until a criterion of 30 seconds of no responding had been reached. The dependent variable was defined as the ranks of the mean latencies of the first and last ten trials added to the ranks of the mean number of nonreinforced responses during these same trials.

6. Stimulus Generalization. Demonstrating that animals trained to respond only in the presence of a 110-volt light would show a decrease in response rate as the voltage was decreased to 70 v, to 35 v, and finally to 0 v. For each of the four test periods, the number of responses was recorded, and the dependent variable was defined as the probability for each subject that his response decrements as a function of stimulus decrements could have occurred by chance. The ranks of these probabilities would, of course, be identical, or nearly so, with the ranks of any other index of monotonic decrease.

7. Chaining of Responses. Conditioning a loop-pulling response which was followed by the light which signaled the animal that a bar-press would produce a food pellet. The number of complete chains per minute was recorded and the dependent variable was defined as the mean number of completed chains during the first and last ten minutes.

The students were expected to complete each of these studies in one 2-hour period each week, excepting the stimulus discrimination study, which was allotted two periods to complete. If a team did not complete a study within the scheduled time, they had to return to the laboratory in their free time and continue working until their subject was ready to go on to the next scheduled experiment. Even more than in the last experiment, then, the experimenters were all well motivated to have their animals learn as well as possible.

Comparison with the maze learning experiment. There were several differences between this and the first study. The studies were done at different universities using different learning tasks and apparatus. In this study there were fewer subjects, 14 compared to 60, but more experimenters, 39 instead of 12. In addition, this was a longitudinal study lasting about 8 weeks and a minimum of 14 hours spent with each animal, while the earlier study lasted 1 week with only 5 hours spent with each group of animals. In the present study, in spite of rotating their team functions, all experimenters spent a minimum average of four hours working with their rat, whereas in the earlier study no experimenter spent more than one hour with any one of his five animals.

In the earlier study experimenters worked alone and were much of the time unobserved by the laboratory supervisor. Whereas those instances of procedural deviation that came to light were found to be randomly distributed over the two treatment conditions, the present study provided better control over this possibility, since a laboratory instructor was present during each of the laboratory periods. Perhaps more important than the control of procedural deviation was the control of gross cues to the animals. Thus, if an experimenter, because of his belief that a rat was dull, handled the animal roughly, the laboratory instructor was there to point out to the experimenter that his rat would never learn unless he were better treated. In the present study, too, the motivations of the experimenters were quite different. In the earlier study it was found that experimenters felt better when their rats learned well but there was no external sanction for their learning well. In the present situation the rat in effect *had* to learn in order that the experimenter could write a report, get a grade, and go on to the next study.

An additional motivational difference was possibly associated with the differing roles of the laboratory instructors in the earlier and the present study. In the earlier study, the lone laboratory instructor reinforced the experimenters' beliefs that poor performance was accounted for by the rats' "dullness." As it happened, and not by design, in the present study, only one of the three laboratory instructors did so. Another instructor, as it happened, evaded any reference to the rats' brightness or dullness, while the third instructor told his students that there was no such thing in the final analysis as a dull rat, only a dull experimenter! Quite accidentally, then, a small sample of "climates" was acquired apparently more or less favorable to the occurrence of experimenter expectancy effects. This variation in "climates" would serve to increase somewhat the generality of any obtained findings. Any one team of experimenters performed their experiments in only one of these three climates.

Preliminary inspection of the results revealed that for several of the experiments there were such extremely deviant scores that the use of interval scale statistics seemed inappropriate. Therefore, in each experiment, the obtained scores were converted to ranks and the treatment effect evaluated by means of the Mann-Whitney U test. Since on the average each experiment was not conducted by some team of experimenters from each treatment condition, the mean raw rank for each treatment group was not comparable from experiment to experiment. In order to achieve comparability of mean ranks across experiments, and to legitimize their addition, all ranks were converted to Guilford's (1954) C-scale scores.

Table 10-4 shows these normalized mean ranks for each treatment

TABLE 10—4

Mean Ranks of Operant Learning for Seven Experiments

Experiment	BELIEF ABOUT SUBJECT		One-Tail p	Correlation with Preceding Experiment
	"Bright"	"Dull"		
I Magazine training	4.4	5.8	.13	–
II Operant acquisition	4.3	6.2	.09	.25
III				
A Extinction	4.2	5.8	.12	.08
B Spontaneous recovery	4.6	5.0	.48	.25
IV Secondary reinforcement	4.7	5.5	.17	.37
V Stimulus discrimination	4.0	6.3	.008	.38
VI Stimulus generalization	4.3	5.8	.02	.59 (p < .05)
VII Response chaining	5.8	3.8	.92	.45
Means (Total)	4.5	5.5	.015	.35

group as well as the rank correlation of the performances in that experiment with the performances of the preceding experiment. A lower mean rank is assigned to a superior performance. The overall probability that the superior learning shown by the rats labeled as "Bright" could have occurred by chance was .015 (one-tail). Inspection of the mean ranks for all eight comparisons shows that in every case but one, performance was superior when the experimenters expected a superior performance. It appears likely then that experimenters' belief or expectation about the performances of their animals was responsible in part for the performances obtained.

Inspection of the p levels for the eight comparisons suggests no trend for subsequent treatment effects to become either more or less significant. The combined p level for the first four comparisons was .035, and for the last four comparisons it was .025.

The question of correlated performances should be raised. That is, did the differences between the treatment groups arise during the first experiment and then simply maintain themselves over subsequent experiments? The answer to this question will tell us in part whether the seven experiments were nothing more than a single experiment replicated seven times. In Table 10-4 the last column shows that in most cases less than 15 percent of the variance of performances in any experiment could be accounted for by the performances in the preceding experiment. Only the correlation between performances in the experiments on stimulus discrimination and generalization was significant at the .05 level, one-tail test. A good illustration that the degree of interexperimental correlation was not sufficient to regard the seven experiments as only a single experiment is provided by examination of the results of the response-chaining experiment in Table 10-4. In that experiment subjects' performances correlated .45 with their performances in the preceding experiment, this correlation accounting for about 20 percent of the variance. Yet in spite of this, the obtained mean differences in performance differed significantly from each other and were in the opposite directions.

Although the animals' performances from experiment to experiment were not accounting for much of the variance of subsequent experiments, there was a tendency for later performances to be better predictors of subsequent performances. This increase over time of these correlations was significant at the .01 level ($rho = +.90$). Such an increase suggests that, over time, the animals may have been more and more "permanently" affected by their experimenters' differential treatment.

The original assignment of subjects to treatment conditions had been random, but the question may fairly be asked whether by chance animals labeled "Bright" might not in fact have been brighter, especially in view of the small sample size.[1] This question cannot be answered directly, but the likelihood of this factor accounting for the obtained results can be evaluated. If the obtained results had been due to preexperimental differences among the animals rather than to the labeling treatment, we would have expected correlations differing significantly from zero between subjects' performance in an experiment and their performance in the subsequent experiment. As an additional check on this question, the following comparison was made. Those four "dull" rats who participated in both experiments I and II were

[1] Max Bershad and Leon Pritzker pointed out this problem and clarified some of the issues involved.

matched with those four "bright" rats who also performed in both experiments and whose performances in experiment I were most similar to those of the "dull" rats. The mean normalized rank of performance in experiment I for the four "dull" rats was 5.5, while for the four "bright" rats the mean was 5.8. The mean normalized rank of performance in experiment II was 6.0 for these "dull" rats and 3.8 for these "bright" rats, the difference being significant at the .10 level, one-tail U test. Thus, when considering experiment I as the basis for "preexperimental" matching, the subsequent experiment showed no change in the direction of difference, or the degree of its significance, from what was obtained without preexperimental matching. It seems reasonable, then, to assume that if preexperimental differences in ability favored the "bright" animals, this could at most have affected only the results of experiment I.

It was mentioned earlier that all animals had been assigned to one of five laboratory periods, one or more of which were supervised by one of three laboratory instructors. It was also mentioned that each of these instructors appeared to provide a somewhat different "climate," which might be interpreted as more or less favorable to the occurrence of experimenters' expectancy effects. Table 10-5 shows the normalized mean ranks for all

TABLE 10—5

Mean Ranks of Operant Learning for Five Laboratories

| Laboratory | BELIEF ABOUT SUBJECT | | One-Tail |
	"Bright"	"Dull"	p
A	4.3	5.3	.08
B	4.9	6.5	.07
C	5.1	5.8	.25
D	3.7	4.6	.21
E	4.1	6.0	.07
Means	4.4	5.6	.02

the experiments combined for each treatment group listed by laboratories. In all five laboratories the treatment effects were in the predicted direction, with p levels ranging from .07 to .25 and the combined $p < .005$. The differences in obtained p levels for such a small sample of laboratories do not seem to warrant elaborate interpretation, although it seems safe to say that "climates" or lab periods did not seem to make much difference.

At the conclusion of the experiments, each experimenter filled out the questionnaire described earlier. Table 10-6 shows the mean rating for each treatment condition on each of the scales for which the results were given for the maze learning experiment. The last two scales were new for this experiment and the "amount of handling" ratings were made separately for handling before each experiment and after each experiment.

TABLE 10—6

Descriptions of Subjects' and of Experimenters' Behavior

Subjects' Behavior	BELIEF ABOUT SUBJECT		One-Tail	Both Studies Combined
	"Bright"	"Dull"	t	p	p
1. Bright	5.0	−2.6	2.64	.02	.002
2. Pleasant	5.2	3.7	1.07	.16	.05
3. Likable	4.1	2.2	1.28	.12	.08
Experimenters' Behavior					
1. Satisfied	9.1	6.6	4.40	.0005	.0003
2. Relaxed	6.3	6.1	—	—	.03
3. Pleasant	6.4	5.3	2.04	.04	.005
4. Friendly	5.8	3.9	1.31	.11	.02
5. Enthusiastic	4.2	1.9	1.31	.11	.04
6. Nontalkative	−0.2	−2.7	1.11	.15	.07
7. Gentle handling	5.8	5.7	—	—	.13
8. Much handling	(−1.0)	(−2.8)	—	—	(.10)
a. before experiments	−1.2	−2.3	—	—	.14
b. after experiments	−0.8	−3.3	1.17	.14	.07
9. Watching subjects	9.3	8.3	2.16	.03	—
10. Talking to subjects	−3.1	0.7	2.41	.02	—

In this study, too, experimenters believing their rats to be bright were significantly more satisfied with their participation in the experiments than were those believing their animals to be dull. However, even these latter experimenters were remarkably satisfied (6.6) compared to either the experimenters running "bright" rats (3.0) or those running "dull" rats (2.5) in the earlier study. This much greater satisfaction of the experimenters in the later study may have been due in part to the nature of the experiments performed. These experiments were an integral part of the course content, and the principles they were designed to demonstrate were covered in lectures by the course instructor. In the earlier study there was relatively much less relationship of the experiment to the content of the course. Furthermore, in the earlier study, although the "bright" rats learned faster, none really learned well. In the later study, although "bright" rats again learned faster, almost all animals did learn eventually.

The overall descriptions which differentiated the two groups of experimenters were much the same as in the first animal study. The last column of Table 10-6 shows the combined probabilities derived from both experiments. For both experiments, experimenters believing their subjects to have been bred for good learning judged their rats' behavior to be brighter, more pleasant, and more likable. These experimenters were also happier about their conduct of the experiment, and more so in this than in the preceding study. That makes sense, because in the present study, experimenters had much to be dissatisfied about if their animal learned poorly. They had to come in after hours and get their animal "caught up."

In both studies, experimenters assigned "bright" rats felt more relaxed in their contacts with their animals and felt their own behavior showed a more pleasant, friendly, and enthusiastic approach. These more global attitudes may have been translated more specifically into a less talkative "interaction" with the animal (one wonders what experimenters might have been saying to their "dull" rats), more handling, and more gentle handling.

As we would expect, the absolute amount of handling was considerably less in the operant learning experiments than in the maze learning study, regardless of the experimenters' belief about their animals' ability. What handling took place in the operant learning studies was confined to conveying animals from home cage to Skinner box and back again. In the maze learning study the animals were similarly handled in transport but also were handled after each trial when they were returned to the starting box of the T-maze. In the operant learning study separate descriptions were given of handling of animals before and after the experiments. Table 10-6 shows that experimenters expecting better performance handled their animals about 33 percent more after each experiment, whereas experimenters expecting poorer performance handled their animals about 44 percent *less* after each experiment. Handling in this experiment was generally quite gentle, even among experimenters expecting poor performance. That was not true for the first experiment and may have been due to the presence of the laboratory instructor, who could note and call attention to any rough handling. Therefore, most of the handling of this second experiment may have been positively reinforcing to the animals. Experimenters expecting good performance may have rewarded their rats tactually after a good performance, and such reward may have improved the animals' performance in the subsequent experiment. Experimenters expecting poor performance withheld their positive tactual reinforcement more after each experiment, perhaps because there was little to be even unintentionally reinforcing about.

We cannot decide easily whether this differential postexperimental reinforcement was only a consequence of the subjects' performance or whether
it was a partial determinant of that performance. It might well have been
both.

Also in the operant learning study, experimenters kept a closer watch
on their rats' behavior if they expected better performance, although all
experimenters watched their animals very closely. In operant learning
studies, closer observation of the subject may lead to more appropriate
and more rapid reinforcement of the response desired. So the closer watching, perhaps due to the expectation that there would be more promising
responses to be seen, may have made better "teachers" of the experimenters
expecting good performance.

The last item on each questionnaire was an open-ended one asking
each experimenter to say in his own words how he felt about the experiments. Nineteen completed questionnaires were obtained from those who
had worked with "bright" rats, and 17 were received from those who had
worked with "dull" rats. Table 10-7 shows the percentage of each group

TABLE 10—7

Spontaneous Comments by Experimenters

Comments	BELIEF ABOUT SUBJECT		One-Tail
	"Bright"	"Dull"	p
1. Beneficial experience	63%	41%	.16
2. Interesting experience	53%	18%	.04
3. Uneducable subject	5%	47%	.007
4. No comments made	0%	12%	.22

of experimenters who spontaneously mentioned (1) the benefit they derived from the experiments, (2) how interesting the experiments were,
(3) the difficulties of getting their animals to learn anything. The pattern
of spontaneous responses follows closely the pattern we expect from the
analysis of the more formally coded responses.

One of the open-ended comments was especially interesting: "Our rat, number X, was in my opinion, extremely dull. This was especially evident during training for discrimination. Perhaps this might have been discouraging but it was not. In fact, our rat had the 'honor' of being the dullest in all the sections. I think that this may have kept our spirits up because of the interest . . . in [our] rat." As a matter of fact, the animal in question was one of the two animals performing at the median level on the discrimination problem as well as for all the experiments taken as a whole. The cited comment serves to point out anecdotally the importance to the experimenters of the type of rat they were running. None of the 34 written comments even remotely suggested that any experimenter was aware that the subjects had not been specially bred. The impression of the three laboratory instructors confirmed this lack of suspicion on the part of the experimenters.

On the last day of the course, after the experiments and questionnaires had been completed, the entire study was explained to all the experimenters. There appeared to be great interest and animation on their part. One reaction, though, was surprising, and that was the sudden increase in sophistication about sampling theory in the experimenters who had been assigned "dull" rats. Many of these experimenters pointed out that, of course, by random sampling, the two groups of rats would not differ *on the average*. However, they continued, under random sampling, some of the "dull" rats would *really* be dull by chance and that *their* animal was a perfect example of such a phenomenon.

SOME DISCUSSION

The results of the experiments reported suggest that experimenters' expectancies may be significant determinants of the results of their research employing animal subjects. The overall combined probability that the results of the two experiments could have arisen by chance was .0007.

The conditions of the second experiment, particularly, suggest that the mediation of this expectancy biasing phenomenon may be extremely subtle. It appears unlikely that nonsubtle differences in the treatment and handling of the animals would have gone unnoticed and uncorrected by the various laboratory instructors whose task it was to supervise the learning of the experimenters via the learning of the subjects. The question occurs, however, whether the laboratory instructors might not have been biased observers. That is a possibility, but it will be recalled that the three instructors seemed to have different biases or orientations toward the experiment; yet in each one's laboratory, the results were quite comparable. In addition, the teaching function of the laboratory instructors was such as to diminish the effects of their students' expectancies. That was because they tended to give more help and advice to the experimenters whose animals were performing more poorly, a fact that would tend, of course, to offset the treatment effects.

What can be said specifically about the several operant learning experiments showing greater or lesser expectancy bias? Are certain types of tasks that rats may be called upon to perform more susceptible to the biasing effects of the experimenter's hypothesis? It seems doubtful that the data can answer this question. We may feel most confident in the experimenters' tendency to obtain biased data on stimulus discrimination and generalization type experiments. However, it might prove most useful, for the present at least, to regard the median obtained p level of .13 as our best estimate of the median p level to be obtained, with similar sample sizes, if we were to continue sampling the population of operant learning experiments. Taking this view, our more extreme p levels, those closer to zero and those closer to one, would be regarded as sampling fluctuations.

Later in Part II some evidence will be presented that suggests that experimenters' descriptions of their own behavior during the experiment are borne out rather well by their subjects' descriptions of that behavior. In these studies employing animal subjects there was no independent check from the subjects as to how they were treated by their experimenters. But as a source of possible interpretations of the results obtained, it can do no harm to assume the veridicality of the experimenters' self-descriptions.

Shall we, then, regard the experimenters' behavior toward their subjects as antecedents or as consequents of the subjects' performance? Perhaps it makes most sense to regard experimenters' behavior as both. Thus, initially, those experimenters expecting their animals to perform poorly treated them in some subtle fashion such as to produce dull behavior, whereas those experimenters expecting bright performance treated their rats accordingly. Those initial differences in the treatments accorded the animals might have led to different performances by subjects which could, in turn, reinforce experimenters' expectations about their animals and maintain the subtle differences in the treatment of the "bright" and "dull" rats.

The specific cues by which an experimenter communicates his expectancy to his animal subjects probably varies with the type of animal, the type of experiment, and perhaps even the type of experimenter. With Clever Hans as subject, the cues were primarily visual, but auditory cues were also helpful. That seemed also to be true when the subjects were dogs rather than one unusual horse.

The experiments were carried out by H. M. Johnson (1913), who knew of Pfungst's work with Clever Hans. Johnson believed that the alleged auditory discriminations shown by dogs were due to the experimenter's unintentional communication to the animals of the expectancy that such discrimination was possible. Just as Hans' questioners betrayed their expectancy of the horse's ability to answer questions, so did experimenters betray to their canine subjects how they should respond to confirm the experimenter's expectancy. The specific cues, Johnson felt, were the experimenter's posture, respiration, and the pattern of strain and relaxation of the muscles of the head and body. Just as in the case of Hans' questioners, such cues were obviously of an unintended, involuntary nature. As a control for the Clever Hans phenomenon, Johnson conducted the standard series of experiments on discrimination, but with the modification that the dogs could not see him at all. To control auditory cues at least partially, Johnson suggested that the experimenters not watch the dogs' responses so that they could not respond differentially and involuntarily as a function of whether the dog's response was the expected one. When all the appropriate controls had been employed, Johnson found that dogs could no more perform the discriminations with which they had been credited than Hans could solve problems of calculus.

When the subjects are rats instead of horses or dogs, the unintended cues from the experimenter might also be visual or auditory, but they could also be olfactory for all the little that is known of the matter at the present time. The best hypothesis to account for the results of the two experiments described in this chapter is probably that the quality and quantity of handling communicated the experimenters' hypotheses. In the study of operant learning, closer observation of the rats' response could have led to more clever teaching of the animals believed to be brighter. But that explanation would not do for the maze learning experiment. Handling differences seem the best explanation for both experiments. Animals believed to be brighter and more pleasant may well be handled more "pleasantly," and less fearfully, more gently and more often. Such handling could alter the animals' behavior and lead to still greater changes in handling patterns. Christie (1951) has told that he and others have been able to postdict which experimenter had handled an animal by observing the rat's behavior while in a maze or while being picked up. Support for these and similar informal observations is available from more formally collected data which show that rats that are handled more learn better (Bernstein, 1952; Bernstein, 1957). From the experiments described in this chapter, we cannot be certain of the role of handling patterns as the mediators of the experimenters' expectancies, nor of whether such other channels as the visual, olfactory, and auditory were involved. Experiments are needed, and could be performed, that would clear up the matter.

Earlier when the discussion was of observer errors, an experiment by Cordaro and Ison (1963) was described. That experiment employed the same paradigm as that described in this chapter, but this time the subjects were flatworms (planaria). Experimenters obtained responses from their planaria which were dramatically in the direction of their expectations. The results, very reasonably, were interpreted as due to biased observations of the worms' responses. It cannot be ruled out as an alternative interpretation, however, that the subjects' responses might have been affected by the experimenters' expectations. Visual, olfactory, auditory, and tactual cues do not seem likely candidates as the channels of unintended influence of an experimenter on his worm subjects. But perhaps changes in respiration of the experimenter affected the turbulence of the water medium in which the planaria swam and influenced them to respond differentially. That the experimenter's respiration may be affected by his expectation was pointed out, of course, by Johnson, though for his dogs such changes meant visual cues, rather than mechanical stimulation.

What seems to be needed in the area of research with planaria is an experiment suggested by Wernicke and described by Moll (1910) (for use with human subjects) in which a glass partition is placed between the experimenter and, in this case, his worm, to see whether this reduces the amount of "observer" error. If it does, it may well mean that the behavior of planaria can, like that of horses, dogs, and rats, be affected by the unintended communication of the experimenter's expectancy.

This chapter may be concluded by recalling a clinical and clever observation by Bertrand Russell, who, however, was referring more to the effects of the programmed experimental procedures than to the unprogrammed effects of the experimenter's expectancy (1927, pp. 29–30).

The manner in which animals learn has been much studied in recent years, with a great deal of patient observation and experiment. Certain results have been obtained as regards the kinds of problems that have been investigated, but on general principles there is still much controversy. One may say broadly that all the animals that have been carefully observed have behaved so as to confirm the philosophy in which the observer believed before his observations began. Nay, more, they have all displayed the national characteristics of the observer. Animals studied by Americans rush about frantically, with an incredible display of hustle and pep, and at last achieve the desired result by chance. Animals observed by Germans sit still and think, and at last evolve the solution out of their inner consciousness.

11

Subject Set

"Did I do right?" That was the question in the mind of one of the subjects. She had rated the standard 10 photos and, along with other subjects, had been asked to tell her feelings about the experiment. She did not mean by this question that she worried whether she earned a good score on the "empathy test," though that might have been part of it. She was more worried whether she had performed properly her role as "Subject of a Psychological Experiment." Another subject verbalized it, "I was wondering if I was doing the experiment the way it should be done." That subjects in psychological experiments think and worry about such matters has been pointed out increasingly in the last few years. "Part of the experimental task," says Joan Criswell, "relates to performing adequately as an experimental subject" (1958, p. 104). In this chapter the discussion will be of various subject sets as they complicate the effects of the experimenter's expectancy.

Martin Orne (1962) has shown the lengths to which subjects will go to give adequate performances. For some years he has been trying to find experimental tasks so tedious, dull, or meaningless that experimental subjects would refuse to do them or would soon discontinue them. No such tasks have been found. Subjects want to be good subjects; they don't want to waste their own time or the experimenter's. For Orne, being a good subject means ultimately that the subject wants to validate the experimental hypothesis. Such a motive on the part of the subject would help answer a question that may have occurred to some readers of this book. Granted that experimenters can communicate their expectations to their subjects, why do subjects act so as to confirm these expectations? Orne's answer seems to do partially for this question, but there are others. There seem to be too many subject pools where subjects seem too indifferent, or too disturbed, or too distracted, or too giggly for these scientific motivations to be always the primary ones. Orne lists motives for subjects' participating in experiments other than the advancement of science. These include the fulfilling of course requirements, pay, or the hope of improving personal adjustment.

Criswell (1958) lists these motives and adds curiosity about research, boredom, less pleasant alternative pursuits, and a need to ingratiate oneself with the experimenter. This last motive also helps explain why subjects who correctly "read" the experimenter's unintentionally communicated expectancy generally go along with it rather than choosing to disregard it or to defy it. (Jones [1965] has pointed out that successful ingratiation requires some subtlety rather than simple compliance. Simple compliance leads to a relative loss of esteem. In the experimenter-subject interaction, the subject's going along can hardly be called simple compliance, since the "requests" for certain responses are unintended or covert.) Going along with the experimenter's covert request satisfies the ingratiation motive subtly while at the same time satisfying the motive to make a useful contribution by confirming the experimenter's hypothesis, as Orne suggested.

Other workers have stressed the social nature of the psychological experiment (e.g., Bakan, 1953; Friedman, 1964; Mills, 1962; Tuddenham, 1960). One of the most important and one of the most systematic analyses of the social nature of the psychological experiment was that by Riecken (1962). After describing the features characteristic of experiments, Riecken notes three aims of the subject. The first of these is the attainment of those rewards he feels his due from having accepted the invitation to participate. These rewards may include course credit, money, and psychological insight. The second aim of the subject is to "penetrate the experimenter's inscrutability and discover the rationale of the experiment." The third aim of the subject, for which the second aim is instrumental, is to "represent himself in a favorable light" or "put his best foot forward." This third aim of the experimental subject is also discussed in detail by Rosenberg (1965), who has shown the systematic effects that "evaluation apprehension" may have on the outcome of the experiment.

The task the experimenter formally sets for the subject is only one problem the subject must solve. Riecken called attention also to the subject's "deutero-problem," the problem of "doping out the experiment" so his performance can be an appropriate one, and one that will lead to favorable evaluation. The solution to the subject's deutero-problem comes from his preconceptions of psychological research, from the formally programmed procedures of the experiment, from the physical scene, and from the unprogrammed "procedures" such as the experimenter's unintended communications. A good example of the possible effects of the physical scene on the subject's solution of his deutero-problem comes from a comment by Veroff (1960). In reviewing a research program on affiliative behavior, he wondered whether the amount of such behavior might not be affected by the sign which read "Laboratory for Research in Social Relations." Such scene effects are likely to be constant for all conditions of an experiment, so that the inferences drawn about experimental effects need not be affected. Nevertheless, it would be interesting to change the signs from time to time to see to what extent affiliative behavior occurs in "The Laboratory for the Study of Social Conformity."

Such cues to the solution of the deutero-problem have been called the "demand characteristics" of the experimental situation by Orne (1962). He has shown in his research program that in a variety of experiments, subjects perform as they believe they are expected to perform. Thus if subjects believe that hypnosis implies catalepsy of the dominant hand, they show such catalepsy when hypnotized. If they are not led to believe such catalepsy to be part of hypnosis, they do not show it when hypnotized (Orne, 1959).

EXPERIMENTER EXPECTANCY AND SUBJECT SET

One purpose of the experiment to be described now was to learn of the effects of demand characteristics operating independently of but jointly with experimenters' expectancies. A second purpose was to test the generality of the effects of experimenters' expectancies. The studies reported so far have established the occurrence of the phenomenon in the research domains of human perception and animal learning. Here the occurrence of the phenomenon is examined in a different but equally lively area of research. Such an area is that of verbal conditioning (Krasner, 1958), and one of its more hotly debated aspects is the question of the role of awareness in successful verbal conditioning (Dulany & O'Connell, 1963; Eriksen, 1960; Eriksen, 1962; Spielberger & DeNike, 1966). It should be emphasized that the purpose of this study was *not* to answer the question of whether such learning without awareness can occur. The purpose, rather, was to learn whether studies of the role of awareness in learning might be affected by the phenomena of experimenter expectancy effects and the effects of demand characteristics or subjects' set.

One provocative hint as to the possible role of demand characteristics in determining rates of awareness in studies of verbal conditioning is provided by Krasner (1958). He told of a subject who, during the course of a verbal conditioning experiment, spontaneously verbalized the correct contingency. On the subsequent inquiry for awareness, however, this same subject gave perfectly "unaware" responses. This interesting occurrence might be accounted for by the subject's perception of the demand characteristics of the situation as being, "You ought not to be aware of the contingency if you wish to regard yourself as a 'good subject.' "

The experiment has been described elsewhere (Rosenthal, Persinger, Vikan-Kline, & Fode, 1963b). Briefly, there were 18 graduate students to serve as experimenters, all enrolled in a graduate course in educational psychology, and all but one were males. There were 65 subjects, 57 of them females, most of whom were freshmen or sophomores.

Each experimenter presented to each of his subjects individually the standardized series of 20 photos of faces described earlier. Subjects were asked, as before, to rate each photo on the apparent success or failure that the person pictured had been experiencing. This time, however, experimenters were instructed to reinforce all positive ratings made by their subjects. Each experimenter was individually trained by an investigator, who did not know to which treatment condition the experimenter would be assigned. The exact instructions to experimenters and the instructions they were to read to their subjects were mimeographed and given to each experimenter at the conclusion of his training session.

Instructions to Experimenters. You have been asked to participate in a research project studying the phenomena of conditioning. The reason for your participation in this project is to standardize results of experiments dealing with conditioning. There is the problem in psychological research of different examiners getting somewhat different data on the same tests as a function of individual differences. Therefore, to standardize the tests it is better methodological procedure to use *groups* of experimenters.

You will now be asked to run a series of subjects and obtain from each ratings of photographs. The experimental procedure is as follows:

After recording the data from each subject at the top of the recording sheet, and reading the instructions to the subject, you are ready to begin.

Take photo #1 and say: "This is photo #1," and hold it in front of the subject until he tells you his rating, which you will write down on the recording sheet. Continue this procedure through the 20 photos. Do not let any subject see any photo for longer than 5 seconds.

After each subject, total the ratings of the 20 photos and find the average (mean).

Previous research in verbal conditioning has shown that subjects may be conditioned to give a certain number by verbal reinforcement. In this study we want you to say "good" after *every* plus rating up to the number five $(+5)$, and "excellent" after every rating of plus five and over. Do not say anything for minus ratings. As you would suspect, you should shortly be receiving very high ratings from your subjects, about a $+5$ or higher.

The Marlowe-Crowne Social Desirability scores of your subjects are such that they, on a postexperimental interview, will (not) [1] very likely be *aware* of having been *conditioned*. That is to say, this test (the Marlowe-Crowne) is able to predict beforehand which subjects will be aware of having been conditioned. The present study is designed to verify the reliability of the Marlowe-Crowne.

Just read the instructions to the subjects. Say nothing else to them except hello and goodbye and "excellent" and/or "good." If for any reason you should say anything to a subject other than that which is written in your instructions, please write down the exact words you used and the situation which forced you to say them. Good Luck!

Instructions to Subjects. I am going to read you some instructions. I am not permitted to say anything which is not in the instructions, nor can I answer any questions about this experiment. OK?

[1] This word was inserted in the instructions to half of the experimenters.

[2] Immediately after this experiment is over, you will be asked the purpose of this experiment, i.e., what is really going on. See how perceptive you can be in determining the *true* intent of this experiment.

Now I will show you a series of photographs. For each one I want you to judge whether the person pictured has been experiencing success or failure. To help you make more exact judgments you are to use this rating scale. As you can see, the scale runs from −10 to +10. A rating of −10 means that you judge the person to have experienced extreme failure. A rating of +10 means that you judge the person to have experienced extreme success. A rating of −1 means that you judge the person to have experienced mild failure, while a rating of +1 means that you judge the person to have experienced mild success. You are to rate each photo as accurately as you can. Just tell me the rating you assign to each photo. All ready? Here is the first photo. (No further explanation may be given, although all or part of the instructions may be repeated.)

The instructions given the experimenters carried one of the treatment dimensions. Half were led to expect that their subjects would subsequently be aware of having been conditioned, and half were led to believe that their subjects would not be aware. The instructions read to subjects by their experimenter were designed so that half the subjects would view it as a "good subject" performance to be aware of having been conditioned, and half the subjects would not be given such a set.

After the subjects had been contacted by their experimenter they were given two questionnaires to be filled out in succession. The first questionnaire was the one used by Matarazzo, Saslow, and Pareis (1960). It asked simply two questions: (1) "The purpose of this experiment was:" and (2) "My evidence for this is:". About a half page of space was provided for the answers to each of these questions. Orne (1962) has suggested that subjects agree to a "pact of ignorance" to not "see through" the ostensible purposes of the experiment. The experience of the research program under discussion supports this view. For this reason, it was felt that a very vague, general inquiry for subjects' awareness, with no incentives offered for reports of awareness, would be favorable to low rates of awareness among the subjects. An inquiry that offers many suggestions to subjects about what may have been going on in the experiment was felt to create a set favorable to seeing through the experiment. This is probably due not so much to the cues provided by the questions themselves, though that is a factor. More important, probably, is the general set given the subject that it must be acceptable role performance to have a lot of hunches and suspicions if the investigators themselves expect it enough to print up forms with questions that hint at seeing through.

The second questionnaire was patterned after Levin's (1961) and was chosen to elicit higher rates of awareness. It is as follows:

[2] For half of the subjects the sentence, "We are in the process of standardizing a test," was substituted for this paragraph.

The Second Questionnaire.
1. Did you usually give the first number which came to your mind?
2. How did you go about deciding which of the numbers to use?
3. Did you think you were using some of the numbers more often than others? Which numbers? Why?
4. What did you think the purpose of this experiment was?
5. What did you think about while going through the photos?
6. While going through the photos did you think that you were supposed to rate them in any particular way?
7. Did you get the feeling that you were supposed to change the ratings of the photos as you were giving them?
8. Were you aware of anything else that went on while you were going through the photos?
9. Were you aware of anything about the experimenter?
10. Were you aware that the experimenter said anything? If so, what?
Note: Answer the following questions only if you were aware of anything said by the experimenter.
11. What did the saying of the word or words by the experimenter mean to you?
12. Did you try to figure out what made the experimenter say anything or why or when he did?
13. How hard would you say that you tried to figure out what was making the experimenter say the word or words?

          very hard   fairly hard   not hard at all
14. What ideas did you have about what was making the experimenter say the word or words?
15. While going through the photos did you think that what the experimenter said had anything to do with the way that you rated the photos? How?

All awareness-testing questionnaires were scored blindly, independently, and without pretraining by two psychologists according to the criteria set forth below as modified for this study from the criteria employed by Matarazzo, Saslow, and Pareis (1960). The scoring weights were constructed by asking judges to arrange the five criteria, typed on small cards, along a yardstick with the distances between cards to represent differences in degree of awareness. Five faculty members and two graduate students involved in dissertation research served as judges and the following scores represent the median yardstick points assigned to each criterion (divided by three).

Criteria for Scoring Awareness

Score	Criterion
0	*S* had no idea of the purpose of the experiment, or had a completely wrong hypothesis, or made absolutely no mention of *E*'s reinforcing verbalizations.
3	*S* mentioned the reinforcement, but did not connect it with a specific

class of ratings; or *S* brought up the *possibility* of certain ratings being reinforced (including the correct response class), but in conjunction with other incorrect hypotheses.

6   *S* stated that some specific class of ratings was being reinforced, but names the wrong response class; or he states the correct response class but does so along with an incorrect hypothesis.

10   *S* correctly stated the specific response class being reinforced, and did not state an incorrect hypothesis in addition.

12   *S* correctly stated the specific response class being reinforced, stated no incorrect hypothesis, and correctly differentiated the use of "good" from the use of "excellent" as reinforcers.

Reliability of scoring was nearly perfect for questionnaire number one ($r = .99$), and adequate for questionnaire number two ($r = .87$). Both correlations were based on an N of 63 subjects who completed the questionnaires. The two subjects who did not complete the questionnaires were excused when they began using terms like "contingency" and all but argued the merits of open-ended versus structured interviews to tap awareness! As it developed, both had run a verbal conditioning study of their own the preceding semester as part of an undergraduate research program. As far as could be determined, there were no more than these two sophisticates.

In all cases where the two scorers' ratings of a questionnaire differed, the mean of the two ratings was the final score assigned that questionnaire.

Questionnaire effects. Questionnaire number two (Q2) evoked much higher awareness than did questionnaire number one (Q1). On Q1, 70 percent of all subjects earned awareness scores of zero while on Q2 only 2 percent earned zero scores. On Q1, 19 percent of the average experimenter's subjects earned awareness scores of 8 or higher, whereas on Q2, 56 percent earned such scores. Of all subjects, 78 percent earned a different awareness score on Q2 than they had on Q1, and 100 percent of these scored more aware on Q2 (binomial *p* less than .00001).

The correlation (rho) between experimenters' obtained rate of awareness on Q1 and Q2 was $+.58$ (one-tail $p = .01$, $df = .16$). The correlation (phi) between subjects' Q1 and Q2 awareness scores was $+.50$ ($p < .0001$).

The bimodal distribution of awareness scores, especially on Q1 where the distribution was markedly discontinuous and asymmetrical, suggested that for practical purposes the awareness scale was a two-point rather than a five-point scale. Accordingly, in all subsequent analyses a subject was defined as aware if his awareness score was 8 or higher. This number was chosen because it represented the lower limit of the upper distribution of scores on Q1.

Treatment effects. Tables 11-1 and 11-2 show the percentage of the average experimenter's subjects within each experimental condition who

TABLE 11—1

Percentage of Subjects Judged Aware: Questionnaire 1

		EXPERIMENTER'S EXPECTANCY		
		Awareness	Nonawareness	Means
SUBJECT'S	Awareness	31	13	23
SET	Nonawareness	24	10	14
	Means	28	11	19

were judged aware by Q1 and Q2. Analysis of the data from both questionnaires showed that experimenters expecting their subjects to be aware obtained higher rates of awareness than did experimenters expecting their subjects to be unaware ($p = .07$, one-tail). Subjects given the set to see through the experiment tended to be aware more often than the remaining subjects, though this difference was not reliable statistically. For both questionnaires, however, the most statistically significant differences were found to exist between the conditions where experimenter expectancy and subject set were both favorable to increased awareness and the conditions where both were unfavorable to awareness ($p = .02$, one-tail, $t = 2.46$).

What we do not know, but what must be learned, is how an experi-

TABLE 11—2

Percentage of Subjects Judged Aware: Questionnaire 2

		EXPERIMENTER'S EXPECTANCY		
		Awareness	Nonawareness	Means
SUBJECT'S	Awareness	78	40	62
SET	Nonawareness	55	47	50
	Means	68	43	56

menter who expects awareness from his subjects treats them compared to the way an experimenter who does not expect awareness treats his subjects. Perhaps experimenters expecting their subjects to be aware are less subtle in their reinforcement of subjects' responses. Perhaps, too, they convey a conspiratorial impression of "we both know what's going on here." Such an attitude may legitimate the subject's subsequent verbalization of what he knows.

In order to determine the effect of experimenters' reinforcement of higher ratings, it was necessary to employ an additional control group of experimenters which, like the experimental groups, expected high photo ratings but, unlike the experimental groups, was not programmed to reinforce them. Four additional experimenters, drawn from the same class as the other experimenters, were accordingly led simply to expect high photo ratings. These experimenters contacted a total of 26 subjects

TABLE 11—3

Mean Photo Ratings

| | | EXPERIMENTER'S EXPECTANCY | | |
		Awareness	Nonawareness	Means
SUBJECT'S	Awareness	.58	.63	.60
SET	Nonawareness	1.24	1.20	1.22
	Means	.91	.92	.91

drawn from the same class from which the other subjects had been drawn. These subjects were given no set to "see through" the experiment. Table 11-3 shows the mean photo ratings obtained by experimenters in the four experimental groups. The mean photo rating obtained by experimenters of the control group was $+.49$. Those subjects given a set to "see through" the experiment gave photo ratings that were no different from those given by the control group subjects. They were, however, significantly lower than those given by reinforced subjects with no set to "see through" the experiment ($p = .02$, two-tail). All experimental groups and the control group showed approximately linear curves of acquisition of positive ratings, all having about the same slope (35 degrees). Degree of awareness as judged from Q2 was found to be unrelated to photo ratings given. These results suggest that whether or not a subject may be judged aware of having been verbally reinforced for a certain response, he is significantly less likely to make the desired responses when he has been given a set to "see through" an experimental procedure. The set to "see through" may well carry an implication of "don't go along."

The question of whether any of the groups showed verbal conditioning must remain unanswered. All groups showed similar acquisition curves, but this may have been due, in part, to a photo order effect. An earlier study showed that experimenters biased to expect negative data also obtained linear acquisition curves of positive ratings (Rosenthal, Fode, Vikan-Kline, & Persinger, 1964).

THE PHENOMENOLOGY OF THE SUBJECT

Riecken stated that one of the experimental subject's major aims in the experiment is to "penetrate the experimenter's inscrutability and discover the rationale of the experiment" (1962). Even a cursory reading of the 60 questionnaires (Q1 and Q2 combined) confirms this hypothesis. After more careful study, each of the 60 questionnaires was assigned to one of the following three categories: (1) Subject stated that the purpose of the experiment was to standardize a test, and there was no indication of any other suspicion on his part. (2) Subject stated or implied that the purpose was to assess the role of reinforcement in changing responses with or without mentioning standardization of the "empathy" test. (3) Subject stated or implied that the purpose was really in some way to assess the subject other than by (or in addition to) simply trying to reinforce certain responses. Only 17 percent of the questionnaires fell into group 1, whereas 42 percent fell into each of the other two categories. Thus two out of five subjects held hypotheses about the rationale of the experiment which had little to do with this particular study but which sampled fairly well the kind of thing that contemporary research psychologists might very well be after. Several subjects thought they were being assessed for degree of conformity or resistance to conformity. Several hypothesized that we were measuring their degree of racial prejudice based on the fact that one of the photos was of a Negro. Perhaps the most common hunch was that the pictures were really "projective" devices designed to tap everything from self-concepts to optimism or pessimism. This finding lends support to Riecken's formulation that subjects tend to see the psychologist-researcher as a "poker" and a "pryer" into one's inner recesses (1962). All in all, subjects were quite actively engaged in formulating hypotheses, some of which would imply a fairly high level of sophistication.

Whereas on Q2 most subjects were aware, a number made specific reference to their handling of this information. One subject, who had not been rated as aware, said she was sure her experimenter was trying to get her to change her ratings, but she knew that since this was a rigorous standardization situation, this could not possibly be the case. One clearly aware subject manifested unmistakable signs of guilt over ruining the study through her being aware, while several mentioned the contingency and their decision to go along or not go along.

Perhaps the most striking illustration of the complexity of the problem of *our* penetrating the *subject's* inscrutability came from a questionnaire which in reply to Q1 stated: "The purpose of this experiment was to standardize a test. They used a standardized rating scale and the person administrating [sic] the test was not allowed to say anything. This kept his influence out. The fact that we all make our judgment on the pictures would give returns which would show the standardization of them." Not five seconds later this same subject on Q2 replied to the same question about the purpose of the experiment: "To see how much the words given by the tester influenced me."

In this study the experimenter-subject interactions lasted as little as five minutes. This seems to be an unusually short period for the development of "transference" reactions toward an experimenter. Nevertheless, one of our subjects made very clear reference to the sexual implications of being alone with an experimenter in a small room and described some of her experimenter's characteristics in inordinate detail. Even if such responses were quite rare, they would nevertheless serve to remind us that subjects are far from being the automated data production units that Riecken (1962) has suggested is a frequent current view of the subject. But such "transference" reactions are not all that rare. In the research program under discussion one or two such responses are obtained in every experiment. This is the more remarkable not only for the brevity of the experimenter-subject interaction but also because there is very little getting acquainted possible. The tasks chosen for this research program were intentionally designed to minimize experimenter-subject interactions so that it would be difficult to get the unintentional influencing we might more readily expect in more elaborate experimenter-subject interactions or in clinical interactions.

In a study of verbal conditioning employing a more standard sentence-construction task there was further evidence that subjects are sometimes interested in their experimenter as a person rather than simply as an inscrutable scientist-psychologist (Rosenthal, Kohn, Greenfield, & Carota, 1966). In that study 20 percent of the subjects made some reference to one or more physical characteristics of their experimenter which were "irrelevant" to the experimenter's role performance. References were made to the experimenter's posture, clothing, facial blemishes, eyeglasses, dental condition, and relative attractiveness.

When the research is somewhat more clinical we expect more of the "transference" reactions to the experimenter, and we get them. Klein (1956) has discussed this problem, and Whitman (1963) gives a more recent illustration. The research was in the area of dreaming responses. There were 10 volunteer subjects who were wakened and asked to report their dreams whenever their eye movements suggested to the monitors that dreaming might be going on. About one third of the dreams dealt overtly with the experimental situation, about one third dealt covertly with the experimental situation, and about one third did not appear to deal at all with the experimental situation. There was the predictable evaluation apprehension Rosenberg has described (1965) and a great variety of emotionally significant reactions to the experimenter. Female subjects tended to view him as more seductive, males as more sadistic. Some dreams found him incompetent; some found him potentially therapeutic but not helpfully motivated; some found him a cold, exploiting scientist, or even quite unscrupulous. This more clinical research may evoke stronger reactions to the experimenter, but from the evidence presented earlier we must conclude that such reactions may also occur in less psychodynamically loaded interactions, though perhaps to a lesser degree.

SOME RECAPITULATION AND DISCUSSION

The data suggest that in studies of verbal conditioning concerned with the role of awareness, the experimenter's expectancy of awareness can significantly affect the rates of awareness he will obtain. In addition, subjects' perceived demand characteristics of the experimental situation appear to play a role in the determination of subsequent awareness rates, although to a smaller and less reliable degree. Furthermore, the form of inquiry for awareness makes a significant difference in obtained awareness rates. However, when an experimenter expects more awareness from his subjects at the same time that his subjects have a positive sanction to see through the experiment, he tends to obtain higher rates of awarenesss from his subjects than when the converse conditions are true, regardless of the form of inquiry employed in this study. Although none of the obtained p levels was striking, the magnitude of the effects was. Thus on Q1, three times as many subjects of one condition were aware as were aware in the opposite treatment condition. This magnitude of effect may have been even greater had it not been for an unplanned-for difficulty in the experimental procedure. Many of the subjects in the standard set condition were able to see some earlier contacted subjects filling out the questionnaires. It seems likely that this might have established demand characteristics among the standard set subjects favorable to greater attentiveness and seeing through, sets reasonably to be expected from the subjects' prospect of having to answer questions about the experimental procedure.

Krasner (1958), in his review of 31 articles on verbal conditioning, found that over one half of them reported no awareness at all on the part of any subject. In all these studies, only 5 percent of all subjects were reported to be aware. In the present study, even on the crude Q1 19 percent of the subjects were aware, and on Q2 about 56 percent were aware. The reason for this discrepancy is not entirely clear. The possibility that all our subjects had perceived the demand characteristics as generally favorable to awareness cannot be ruled out. Communication among subjects was possible and likely, but this is probably true for most verbal conditioning studies (and other studies as well, though it is rare to find the problem taken seriously). In addition, it must be admitted that the author's expectation was for a high rate of awareness; and although it was possible to remain blind for membership in treatment conditions, subjects did have to be contacted by members of the research group, however briefly, so that they could be directed to the proper laboratory rooms and, later, have the questionnaires administered.

In another verbal conditioning experiment, the one employing a sentence construction task, the rates of awareness obtained were somewhat lower (Rosenthal, Kohn, Greenfield, & Carota, 1966). In that study 17 percent of the subjects were clearly aware, 8 percent were somewhat aware, and 75 percent were clearly unaware. In this experiment, as in the one described in detail, several aware subjects noted their difficulty in trying to decide whether to go along with the experimenter's attempt to influence their response. Subjects can sometimes verbalize their deutero-problem very well.

We cannot tell from answers to an awareness questionnaire whether the subject, if "aware," was aware during the experiment. We cannot tell whether the subject, if "unaware," is responding as unaware because he thinks that is the proper thing to do. There is a kind of subject especially interested in saying and doing the proper thing, and that is the subject who scores high on the Marlowe-Crowne Scale of Social Desirability (Crowne & Marlowe, 1964). In the sentence construction experiment, subjects scoring high in this scale gave significantly less aware responses ($r = -.30$, $p = .02$), and so did more anxious subjects ($r = -.22$, $p = .10$). These more anxious subjects and those higher in the need for approval may well have viewed the good subject role as that which permits no "seeing through." That they show their desire to please the experimenter in other ways is suggested by the fact that subjects higher in need for approval arrive earlier at the site of the experiment ($r = +.40$, $p = .003$).

The results of the qualitative analyses of the awareness questionnaires of this second study of verbal conditioning yielded much the same sort of information as the first. Subjects often did not believe the formal explanations offered them. Riecken (1962) was right to call for a more systematic investigation of subjects' perceptions of experimental situations.

The kinds of hunches subjects had about the true purposes of the two experiments, although frequently wrong for these particular studies, were uncomfortably accurate in assessing the kinds of research in which contemporary psychologists were likely to ask them to participate. The day of the naïve sophomore may rapidly be drawing to a close.

CONFLICTING EXPECTATIONS

In an experiment by C. R. White (1962), the expectations of the experimenters were varied as in other studies, but subjects were given varying expectations about the stimuli they would be asked to judge. His experimenters were 18 graduate students in counseling and guidance, and his subjects were 108 undergraduates enrolled in educational psychology.

In earlier studies in this research program there had always been only two expectancies. Thus, when the task was that of judging the success or failure of persons pictured in photos, half the experimenters were led to expect success ratings and half were led to expect failure ratings. White, however, employed six different expectancies, to each of which three experimenters were assigned at random. These six expectancies were not single numbers but rather a set of overlapping ranges of expectancies, the means of which were −6, −3, −0.5, +0.5, +3, and +6. Within each of these conditions of experimenter expectancy, subjects were divided into six groups, each with one of the expectancies analogous to those induced in the experimenters. These expectancies were induced by telling subjects that the particular photos they would be shown had been found earlier to evoke ratings of about −6 (or −3, −0.5, +0.5, +3, +6). The six conditions of experimenter expectancy, each with six conditions of subject expectancy, were analyzed by means of a 6 × 6 analysis of variance design.

Results of the analysis revealed a significant interaction effect ($p = .001$) between experimenters' and subjects' expectancies. Table 11-4 shows the mean ratings obtained by experimenters expecting either positive or negative ratings for subjects for whom either positive or negative ratings had been suggested. The data support the interpretation of contrast effects (Helson, 1964; Sherif & Hovland, 1961). Subjects predisposed to rate low, when contacted by experimenters expecting to obtain high ratings, gave the lowest ratings ($p = .01$), suggesting a kind of opinion entrenchment. Similarly, when subjects were given sets to rate high but were confronted by experimenters expecting low ratings, they gave the highest ratings, though this finding was statistically less significant.

White kindly made his data available for this further analysis. In addition to the "entrenchment" effect shown by subjects contacted by experimenters with contrasting expectations, another factor was found to contribute to our understanding of the interaction effect. Table 11-5 shows quartiles of subjects arranged in descending order of discrepancy between

TABLE 11—4

Mean Photo Ratings as a Function of Experimenter and Subject Expectancies

		EXPERIMENTER'S EXPECTANCY		
		Positive	Negative	Means
SUBJECT'S	Positive	.59	.81	.70
EXPECTANCY	Negative	−.43	.42	.00
	Means	.08	.62	.35

their own expectancy and their experimenter's expectancy. The correlation between discrepancy of expectations and mean photo rating was −.96 ($p = .05$). Regardless of the direction of experimenters' and subjects' expectations, subjects tended to rate the photos as more successful when their expectancy and that of their experimenter were in greater accord. It may be that when experimenters and subjects had similar expectancies, their experimental interaction was a smoother, more pleasant experience, with less conflict for the subject over whether to be influenced by the investigator who had induced the subject's expectancy or to be influenced by the subtle cues of his own experimenter. The lack of conflict may have been reflected in his perceiving others more cordially—i.e., as more successful.

The experiments described in this chapter have served in part to extend the generality of the effects of the experimenter's expectancy. More particularly they have shown the combined effects of the experimenter's expectancy and the subject's set or his perception of the demand character-

TABLE 11—5

Mean Ratings as a Function of Discrepancy Between Experimenters' and Subjects' Expectancies

Quartiles	Mean Discrepancy	Mean Rating
1	9.2	.35
2	5.3	.43
3	2.7	.50
4	0.3	.59

istics of the experimental situation (Orne, 1962). The examination of such joint effects is only just now being mapped out for inquiry. But from what data there are, both quantitative and qualitative, the conclusion seems warranted that what is in the head of the subject and in the head of the experimenter can unintentionally affect the results of psychological research.

12

Early Data Returns

In the last few chapters the effects of the experimenter's expectancy on his subjects' responses have been considered. In the present chapter, to some extent, we reverse the direction of the predictions and consider the effects of the subjects' responses on the experimenter's expectancy. Except in the most exploratory of experimental enterprises, the experimenter's expectancies are likely to be based upon some sort of observed data. These data need not have been formally acquired. They may derive from quite casual observations of behavior made by the experimenter himself or even by another observer. Since some sort of data are the most likely determinants of experimenter expectancies, we may fairly ask: what about the data obtained early in an experiment? What are their effects upon data subsequently obtained within the same experiment? Perhaps early data returns that confirm the experimenter's hypothesis strengthen the expectancy and thus make it more likely that subsequent data will also be confirmatory. Perhaps early data returns that disconfirm the experimenter's expectancy lead to a revision of the expectancy in the direction of the disconfirming data obtained, thereby making it more likely that subsequent data will continue to disconfirm the original hypothesis but support the revised hypothesis.

That the "early returns" of psychological research studies can have an effect on experimenters' expectancies was noted and well discussed by Ebbinghaus (1885). After saying that investigators notice the results of their studies as they progress, he stated: "Consequently it is unavoidable that, after the observation of the numerical results, suppositions should arise as to general principles which are concealed in them and which occasionally give hints as to their presence. As the investigations are carried further, these suppositions, as well as those present at the beginning, constitute a complicating factor which probably has a definite influence upon the subsequent results" (p. 28). He went on to speak of the pleasure of finding expected data and surprise at obtaining unexpected data, and continued by stating that where "average values" were obtained initially, subsequent data would tend also to be of average value, and where "especially large or small numbers are expected it would tend to further increase or decrease the values" (p. 29).

Ebbinghaus was, of course, speaking of himself as both experimenter and subject. Nevertheless, on the basis of his thinking and of the reasoning described earlier, it was decided to test Ebbinghaus' hypothesis of the effect of early data returns on data subsequently obtained by experimenters. There was also an interest in learning whether the male experimenters would have a greater biasing effect upon their female subjects than upon their male subjects. This seemed reasonable in view of the general finding in the literature that female subjects are more susceptible to interpersonal influence processes. Finally, there was interest in whether the effects of early data returns would operate uniformly throughout the series of subjects contacted by experimenters or whether earlier- or later-contacted subjects would be more affected.

THE EFFECTS OF EARLY RETURNS

The experiment has been described in more detail elsewhere (Rosenthal, Persinger, Vikan-Kline, & Fode, 1963a). Briefly, there were 12 male graduate students in education to serve as experimenters. The subjects were 55 undergraduates, mostly freshmen and sophomores, enrolled in beginning courses in psychology and education. About half were males and half were females. In this experiment, as in others investigating some factors complicating the effects of the experimenter's expectancy, it was decided that the same task as that employed in the original studies demonstrating expectancy effects should be used. Since the purpose of these studies was not simply to replicate the basic findings but to learn more about the variables affecting the operation of expectancy effects, the studies were kept comparable with respect to the basic task employed.

In the present study, therefore, each experimenter presented to each of his subjects individually the standardized series of 20 photos of faces and asked that the subject rate each photo on the apparent success or failure that the person pictured had been experiencing. Subjects were to use the rating scale described earlier to help them make their judgments.

Before contacting his subjects, each experimenter was individually instructed and briefly trained as to the experimental procedure. The exact instructions to experimenters were mimeographed and given to the experimenter when he came in for his training session. These instructions, as well as the instructions each experimenter read to his subjects, were similar to those presented in earlier chapters. It should be noted that the investigator who instructed the experimenters did not know into which treatment group any experimenter would be assigned.

The overall design of the experiment was to randomly establish three groups of four experimenters each, all with a bias, expectation, or hypothesis to obtain high positive ratings from their subjects. For one group of experimenters this bias, expectation, or hypothesis was to be confirmed by their first two pretest ("good data") subjects. For a second group this bias, expectation, or hypothesis was to be disconfirmed by their first two subjects ("bad data"). The third group of experimenters was to serve as a control group ("normal data").

The first group to be run was the control group of four experimenters, each of whom contacted six naïve subjects. Of those eight subjects who were run as the pretest subjects by the control experimenters, four were selected on the basis of their having free time when the remaining experimenters were to contact their subjects. These four subjects agreed to serve as accomplices and were instructed to give average ratings of $+5$ to the photo-rating task for the "good data" experimenters and -5 for the "bad data" experimenters. Each of the accomplices then gave "good data" to two experimenters and "bad data" to two experimenters. Accomplices appeared equally often as the first-run and second-run subject.

Treatment groups of experimenters were thus defined: the "good data" group experimenters each contacted two accomplices who gave them the expected data, followed by four subjects who were naïve. The "bad data" group experimenters each contacted two accomplices who gave them data opposite to that expected, followed by four subjects who were naïve. The "normal data," or control group, experimenters each contacted six naïve subjects. The dependent variable was defined as the mean of the photo ratings given by the last four subjects contacted by each experimenter in each condition. All these subjects were, of course, naïve, and it was hypothesized that the experience of having obtained "good data" should lead those experimenters to obtain "better" subsequent data, whereas the experience of having obtained "bad data" should lead those experimenters to obtain "worse" subsequent data in relation to the control group. Except for the accomplices, all subjects were randomly assigned to experimenters with the necessary restriction that they have free time during experimenters' available free time. One experimenter contacted only three test subjects instead of four.

Treatment effects. Table 12-1 shows the mean rating obtained by each experimenter and each treatment group, from their two pretest subjects and their four test subjects. For the "good" and "bad" data groups the two pretest subjects were, of course, the accomplices. Although none of the pairs of accomplices actually gave mean ratings of either $+5$ or -5 as

TABLE 12—1

Mean Photo Ratings

Treatment	Experimenter	Pretest Subjects	Test Subjects
"Good data"	E_1	3.68	0.51
	E_2	3.45	1.19
	E_3	2.03	0.83
	E_4	1.90	0.68
	Mean	2.77	0.80
Control	E_5	1.30	1.24
	E_6	0.43	0.80
	E_7	0.18	0.34
	E_8	−0.70	−0.06
	Mean	0.30	0.58
"Bad data"	E_9	−2.38	0.16
	E_{10}	−3.08	0.55
	E_{11}	−3.83	−0.09
	E_{12}	−4.38	0.10
	Mean	−3.42	0.18

they had been instructed, the treatments were considered adequate, since none of the groups' pretest ratings showed any overlap.

Table 12-2 summarizes the analysis of variance of the means of the mean ratings obtained by each of the experimenters from his four test

TABLE 12—2

Analysis of Variance of Mean Photo Ratings

Source	df	MS	F
Early returns	2	(0.4324)	(2.74)
Linear regression	1	0.7750	4.91
Deviation	1	0.0898	
Error	9	0.1577	

subjects. The obtained F of 4.91 for linear regression was significant beyond the .03 level (one-tail), the ordering of means having been predicted. The difference between the means of the two experimental groups was significant at the .01 level (one-tail, $t = 3.14$, $df = 6$).

Sex effects. Table 12-3 shows the mean obtained ratings, considering male and female subjects separately within treatments. The grand mean rating by males of $+.49$ did not differ from the grand mean rating by fe-

TABLE 12—3

Mean Photo Ratings by Sex of Subject

Treatment	Male Subjects	Female Subjects
"Good data"	.61	.99
Control	.52	.62
"Bad data"	.35	.08

males of $+.56$. Inspection of the treatment means suggests that the treatment effect may have been more powerful in its action upon female than upon male subjects. The differences between the means of the control and experimental groups were greater for the female than for the male subjects ($t = 7.21$, $df = 1$, $p = .10$, two-tail). The remaining analyses were carried out on male and female subjects combined, since it was found that the random assignment of subjects to experimenters had resulted in a proportional sex distribution for both treatments and order of test subjects. (In a subsequent chapter dealing with expectancy effects as a function of subject characteristics there will be a fuller discussion of the relevance of subjects' sex.)

Order effects. In order to determine whether the effects of "early returns" showed an order effect, the mean of the first two test subjects was compared to the mean of the second two test subjects for each group. Although these trends were not very significant statistically ($p = .13$, two-tail, $t = 5.42$, $df = 1$), they seem to be worth noting. Whereas the control group showed a mean rating change of only $+.02$, the "bad data" group showed a mean rating change of $-.59$ and the "good data" group showed a shift of $+.44$, suggesting that the effect of early returns becomes more marked later in the process of gathering subsequent data. After having run only the first of two test subjects, the mean obtained ratings were barely different from each other, although they were in the predicted directions (Table 12-4).

TABLE 12—4

Mean Photo Ratings by First and Last Two Test Subjects

Treatment	First Subjects	Last Subjects	Difference
"Good data"	0.58	1.02	0.44
Control	0.57	0.59	0.02
"Bad data"	0.47	-0.12	-0.59

Further support for a hypothesis of a "delayed action effect" can be seen in the sequence of correlations between the mean pretest ratings and the ratings obtained from the first-run test subjects, then the second-, third-, and fourth-run test subjects. This sequence of correlations (rhos) was .04, —.07, .43, .41. The last two correlations were significantly higher than the first two ($p = .02$, two-tail, $t = 8.20$, $df = 2$). Thus, considering subjects in order, it appears that the later-contacted subjects account for more of the correlation found overall and reported next. The correlation (rho) between the data that experimenters obtained from their two pretest subjects and that obtained from all four of their test subjects was $+.69$ ($p < .01$, one-tail, $t = 3.02$, $df = 10$). This correlation is identical with the one obtained if data from the control group experimenters are omitted. The effect of "early returns" of data, then, may have been great enough to account for up to 47 percent of the variance of the data obtained from the four subsequent subjects.

In order to learn of the relative contribution to this correlation of the first-run pretest subject alone, and the second-run pretest subject alone, analogous correlations were computed between the data they gave their experimenter and the data that experimenter subsequently obtained from his four test subjects. For the first-run pretest subject, the rho obtained was $+.55$, ($p < .05$), whereas for the second-run pretest subject, rho was $+.74$, ($p < .01$). The difference between these rhos did not even approach statistical significance, and therefore we cannot conclude that the effect of "good" or "bad" early returns is strengthened by adding more early returns. What is of real interest, however, is the possibility that the data from only one subject may have such a marked effect on subsequently obtained data. This interpretation, or rather speculation, must be tempered by the fact that all experimenters did in fact have two pretest subjects and that the effect on subsequent test subjects might have been quite different had only one pretest subject been employed.

One other factor complicates the interpretation of these obtained correlations. Rather than the early returns affecting subsequently obtained data, it may be that the experimenter, by virtue of his personality and technique in a given situation, tends to elicit similar responses from all his subjects, thus tending to inflate the obtained correlations. This possibility is most obvious for the control group experimenters who contacted only naïve subjects from the very beginning. However, it is also possible that the experimenter affects even the accomplices in a systematic way. Table 12-1 shows that there was considerable variability in the ways in which the accomplices were able to comply with the request to give +5 or —5 ratings to their experimenters. Whether the accomplice-within-treatments variability was due to initial accomplice variance, effect-of-experimenter variance, or an interaction variance remains an interesting question subject to further study. At any rate, this question does make any simple interpretation of the obtained correlations tenuous.

Examination of the rank correlation between pretest and test data for the control group alone shows it to be unity. In addition, the first-run pretest subject means correlated perfectly with the second-run pretest subject means. We are faced with the same difficulty in interpretation: was it experimenter effect or subject effect? Thus, although these subjects were not accomplices, their ratings may have served to give the experimenter hypotheses which he then went on to confirm.

SOME RECAPITULATION AND DISCUSSION

The data suggest that Ebbinghaus' hypothesis—that early data returns can affect subsequently obtained data—was correct not only in the situation where the experimenter serves as his own subject as Ebbinghaus originally formulated it, but also in the situation in which the experimenter is contacting others as his subjects. When the first one or two subjects give "good" or expected data, data obtained from subsequently contacted subjects tends also to be "good." When the first one or two subjects give "bad" or unexpected data, data from subsequent subjects tends also to be "bad." For the male experimenters employed in this study, it appears that the effect of early returns may operate more powerfully upon female than upon male subjects. The possibility was also suggested that the effect of early returns may not make itself immediately apparent, but that the effect may be delayed or cumulated to somewhat later-contacted subjects.

The finding that nearly half the variance of the test subjects' photo ratings could be accounted for by a knowledge of the pretest subjects' ratings was mentioned as difficult to interpret. It might well be that some portion of this variance is due to the effect of early returns and some to more enduring experimenter effects, such as his personality × technique × experimental-situation interaction, which effects might be distributed similarly over all the subjects contacted by the experimenter.

How might the effects of early data returns on subsequent data be explained? When the early returns of an experiment are "good," the hypothesis with which the experimenter undertook the study is partially confirmed in his own mind and thereby strengthened, with a possible increase in the biasing phenomenon for subsequent subjects. The experimenter's mood may also be considerably brightened (Carlsmith & Aronson, 1963), and this might lead him to be seen as a more "likable," "personal," and "interested" person in his interaction with subsequent subjects. There is some evidence, to be presented in subsequent chapters, which suggests that such experimenter behavior increases the effects of his expectancy on his subjects' responses.

That the flow of incoming data can indeed effect changes in an experimenter's mood has been suggested by Wilson (1952) and has been recently, charmingly, and autobiographically documented by Griffith (1961). He told how, as the data came in, "Each record declared itself for or against . . . [me] . . . and . . . [my] . . . spirit rose and fell as wildly as does the gambler's whose luck supposedly expresses to him a higher love or rejection" (p. 307).

The situation for the experimenter whose early returns are "bad" may be similarly analyzed, although the situation may be more complicated in this case. If the "bad" early returns are perceived by the experimenter as disconfirmation of his hypothesis, he may experience a mood change making him less "likable," "personal," and "interested," thereby possibly decreasing his effectiveness as an expectancy biasing experimenter. It may also be that for some experimenters the "bad" early returns form the basis for a revised hypothesis, confirmation of which is then obtained from subsequently contacted subjects.

A SECOND STUDY OF THE EFFECTS OF EARLY RETURNS

Essentially, then, two major variables have been proposed to help us understand the effects of early data returns. The more cognitive one has been called "hypothesis confirmation," the more affective one has been called "mood." It was suggested that the former implies an experimenter mood change; but, of course, mood change does not imply hypothesis confirmation or disconfirmation. Interest in the experiment reported now was in the relative proportion of variance of the early returns effect which could be ascribed to the operation of mood alone.

In the first experiment reported in this chapter, data were defined as "good" if they represented higher ratings of success of the persons pictured in the photos. In order that the definition of "good," or expected, data not be equated with higher ratings of the photos, the nature of the initial expectancy was also varied in the second study. Half the experimenters were thus led to expect +5 (success) ratings, as in the earlier study, but half the experimenters were led this time to expect —5 (failure) ratings from their subjects.

Hypothesis confirmation or disconfirmation was again varied by the use of accomplices serving as the first two subjects. These accomplices gave data either in accord with or opposite to the experimenters' expectancy or hypothesis.

Mood or hedonic tone was experimentally varied by having one of the investigators praise or reprove experimenters for their technique of "running subjects" after the accomplices had performed the experimental task but before the "real" subjects had been through the procedure. Praise was designed to induce a good mood in experimenters, reproof a bad mood.

The details of the experiment have been reported elsewhere (Rosenthal, Kohn, Greenfield, & Carota, 1965). The experimenters were 26 Harvard College seniors, all but one of whom was writing an undergraduate thesis in the Department of Social Relations. Experimenters administered the photo-rating task to 115 female subjects, all of whom were enrolled as undergraduates in a college of elementary education. Experimenters were trained in the experimental procedures by an investigator who did not know to which experimental conditions experimenters would be assigned.

The accomplices who served as the first two "subjects" were students at another women's college and were selected on the basis of "trustworthiness." That is, they were well known to one of the investigators before the experiment began. Twelve accomplices in all participated in the experiment, which was conducted on two evenings. Eight were used each evening, and six participated both evenings. Each accomplice served as "subject" for three or four experimenters an evening. Each was instructed to give photo ratings averaging as close to +5 or —5 as possible without using the same numbers suspiciously often. In half the conditions these ratings confirmed the expectancy previously induced in experimenters ("good" early returns). In the other half, the accomplices' ratings disconfirmed the initial expectancy ("bad" early returns).

After experimenters had contacted their first two subjects (accomplices), one of the two male investigators serving as critics entered each experimental room and either praised or reproved the experimenter.

In the praise conditions, the critic entered, picked up the experimenter's data sheets, studied them first with wrinkled brow and then with an increasingly pleased expression, and, smiling, finally said approximately the following:

Your data follow an almost classical pattern. Haven't seen results that good in a long time. I'd tell you more specifically what's so good about them, except that it wouldn't be really cricket to do that now—perhaps later. Anyway, I'm sure you must be running things very competently to draw data patterns like that. Obviously, you've run subjects before this. Well, keep up the good work with the rest of them. See you later.

In the reproof conditions, the critic entered, picked up the experimenter's data sheets, studied them with a wrinkled brow for about thirty seconds, began to frown, and then said approximately the following:

Your data certainly follow a strange pattern. Haven't seen results like *those* in a long time. I'd tell you more specifically what bothers me except that it wouldn't be really cricket to do that now—perhaps later. Anyway, I'm sure you must be doing something strange to draw data patterns like that! I don't imagine you've run subjects before this. Maybe empirical research is not your cup of tea. Well, please try to be very careful for the rest of them. See you later.

Then each experimenter contacted from three to six "real" subjects in succession. After they had completed their portion of the experiment, experimenters who had been reproved were told that they really had done a very good job.

Combination of the four variables described above—(1) +5 or −5 initial expectancy, (2) confirmation or disconfirmation of expectancy (i.e., "good" or "bad" early returns), (3) praise or reproof, (4) critic 1 or critic 2—yielded 16 experimental conditions (arranged in a 2 × 2 × 2 × 2 factorial design).

Experimenters, accomplices, and research rooms were randomly assigned to conditions. Both critics were also randomly assigned to conditions, except that the number of praises and reproofs that each administered was equalized as closely as possible. The accomplices did not know what the treatment conditions of the experiment were, and the critics were blind as to the particular conditions in which they were carrying out their praise or reproof.

Effects of early returns. Table 12-5 shows that expectancy effects, defined as the difference between data obtained when expecting +5 ratings

TABLE 12—5

Mean Photo Ratings by Initial Expectancy and Early Returns

Expectancy	"Good Data"	"Bad Data"
+5	−1.16	−0.96
−5	−1.94	−0.62
Difference	+0.78	−0.34

and when expecting −5 ratings, were greater when the early data returns were "good" ($p = .05$, one-tail, $t = 1.71$) and that they were smaller and in the wrong direction when early returns were "bad" ($p > .50$). Table 12-5 also shows an unexpected main effect on subjects' ratings of the nature of the experimenter's early data returns. Subjects tended to rate photos as being of more successful people when their experimenter's early returns were disconfirming. This particular result has been discussed earlier in the chapter dealing with situational factors affecting subjects' responses. When the effects of early data returns were considered separately for those experimenters contacted by critic 1 and those contacted by critic 2, a significant difference emerged. For experimenters contacted by critic 1, the effects of early returns were marked, whereas for experimenters contacted by critic 2 there were no effects of early returns, only a tendency for all experimenters to obtain data consistent with their initial expectancy. The personality of the principal investigator who interacts with the experimenter can, therefore, affect the relationship between early returns and subsequent subjects' responses. That the principal investigator can serve as a "moderator variable" (Marks, 1964) was suggested and discussed in the chapter dealing with situational influences on experimenter effects.

Effects of mood. Whether experimenters were praised or reproved did not affect the magnitude of their expectancy effects, nor did it affect the magnitude of the early returns effect. There was, however, an interaction between the effects of praise or reproof on expectancy effects as a function of which of the two critics had contacted the experimenters ($p = .10$). Experimenters contacted by critic 1 showed greater expectancy effects when praised rather than reproved. Experimenters contacted by critic 2 showed greater expectancy effects when reproved rather than praised. Such an interaction makes it virtually impossible to draw any conclusions about the effects of mood, as induced in this study, on experimenter expectancy effects. Who does the praising or reproving is more important than the fact of praise or reproof.

Early returns as sources of expectancy. When early returns confirmed initial expectancies, experimenters showed the greatest expectancy effects. There was also a tendency, when expectancies were disconfirmed, for experimenters to obtain data opposite to those expected initially. From this it might be inferred that the disconfirming early returns formed the basis for a revised expectancy. This inference would have an increased plausibility if it could be shown that early returns within treatment conditions often predicted the data subsequently obtained from real subjects. Some relevant data are available from the study described.

Within each of the eight conditions shown in Table 12-6, a correlation (r) was computed between the magnitude of the mean ratings given the

TABLE 12—6

Correlations Between Early Returns and Subsequent
Subjects' Responses

Evaluation	Expectancy	"Good Data"	"Bad Data"
Praise	+5	+.67*	+.88
Praise	-5	+.73	+.06
Reproof	+5	+.69*	-.76
Reproof	-5	+.999	+.44
Weighted mean		+.96	+.23

* Four experimenters per cell; all other cells had three
experimenters per cell.

experimenters by their first two subjects (accomplices) and the magnitude
of ratings subsequently obtained from real subjects. That such correlations
could be other than trivial in magnitude seemed unlikely in view of the
very restricted range of early returns within any conditions. All accomplices
within any of the experimental conditions had, of course, been programmed
to give the same responses. The average deviation of the early data given
experimenters by the accomplices within the eight conditions was only
0.5. Table 12-6 shows the obtained correlations; only one was not positive
(binomial $p < .04$, one-tail). The mean z transformed correlation was
+.79 ($p = .002$, one-tail, $df = 10$). Inspection of Table 12-6 suggests
that this overall correlation may mask a difference between those correlations obtained when accomplices were confirming as opposed to disconfirming the experimenters' initial hypotheses or expectations. When initial
expectancies were being confirmed the mean r was +.96 ($p < .0005$, one-
tail, $df = 6$). However, when experimenters' initial expectancies were being
disconfirmed, the mean r (+.23) was not significantly greater than zero.
It was, however, significantly lower than the mean r of +.96 ($z = 2.57$,
$p = .01$, two-tail). At least those experimenters, then, whose initial expectancies were confirmed by their early data returns tended to obtain data
from subsequent subjects that were similar to the data obtained from
earlier contacted subjects; and this in spite of an artificially restricted range
of early data returns. However, two quite different factors may have been
operating to bring this about: (1) an experimenter personality factor or
(2) an expectancy factor. If the personality factor were operant, experimenters would have affected the accomplices in the same way in which
they subsequently affected their real subjects. Accomplices were, after all,

free to vary at least a little in the ratings they produced. If, on the other hand, the expectancy factor were operating, the data produced by the accomplices would serve to modify the original expectancy—by a good deal when early returns were disconfirming, and by just a little when early returns were confirming. (The fact that the correlations were larger when the early returns were more similar to the initial expectancies seems best understood as an instance of "assimilation effects" as described by Helson [1964] and Sherif and Hovland [1961]. In psychophysics and attitude change alike, small deviations are often more accommodated to than large changes.)

If the personality factor were operative, one would expect experimenters to have a relatively constant effect on the responses obtained from accomplices and from real subjects regardless of order. Therefore, the correlation between responses obtained from accomplices and those obtained from subjects contacted later should be no higher than the correlation between responses obtained from real subjects contacted early and real subjects contacted later. The correlation between responses given to experimenters by accomplices and those given by real subjects subsequent to the first two was $+.85$ ($p = .005$, one-tail, $df = 6$). The correlation between responses given by the first two real subjects and those given by subsequently contacted real subjects was only $+.16$, a correlation not significantly greater than zero but appreciably lower than $+.85$ ($p = .06$, two-tail). These findings seem inconsistent with the hypothesis of experimenter personality effect but consistent with the hypothesis of experimenter expectancy. The earliest collected data, if they are not too inconsistent with the initial expectancy, may serve to modify or to specify more precisely the experimenter's expectancy.

Delayed action effect. In the earlier experiment on the effect of early data returns there was a "delayed action effect," with accomplices' data affecting later-contacted real subjects more than earlier-contacted real subjects. In the second study no such effect was found. There was, however, a tendency for experimenters' initial expectancies to become more effective for later than for earlier contacted subjects. Initial expectancies ($+5$ vs. -5) had no effect on data obtained from the first two real subjects. Among subsequently contacted real subjects, however, those contacted by experimenters initially expecting $+5$ ratings gave higher ratings ($-.35$) than did (-1.21) subjects contacted by experimenters expecting -5 ratings ($t = 1.73$, $p = .09$, two-tail, $df = 83$).

AN INCREASE IN GENERALITY

The data reported by Ebbinghaus and those reported in this chapter are not the only evidence relevant to the hypothesis of early returns as determinants of subsequent data. There is a recent study by McFall (1965) that is at least suggestive. Working in a different laboratory and at another university, McFall employed 14 experimenters to administer the photo-rating task to 56 subjects. (The particular photos employed were different from those employed in the earlier studies.) From half the subjects experimenters were led to expect +5 ratings of success and from half they were led to expect −5 ratings. Within each condition of experimenter expectancy half the subjects were given a set to respond to the stimulus photos with very fast responses. This set was induced by the use of conspicuous timing devices, and it led to the elimination of expectancy effects. McFall reasoned that the greater the number of subjects who had this set for speed who were contacted by experimenters, the more disconfirming returns would be obtained. He therefore analyzed the effects of experimenter expectancy separately for two stages of the experiment differing in the amount of disconfirming data obtained. When a good deal of disconfirming data had been obtained, experimenters showed no expectancy effects whatever. However, when there had been less disconfirming data, significant expectancy effects were obtained ($p < .05$). Table 12-7 shows the magnitude

TABLE 12—7

Expectancy Effects as a Function of Amount of Expectancy Disconfirmation (After McFall, 1965)

	EXPECTANCY				
Disconfirmation	+5	−5	Difference	t	p<
Less	+.51	−.40	+.91	1.86	.05
More	−.06	+.04	−.10	−	−
Mean	+.22	−.18	+.40	1.04	.15

of these effects. McFall replicated this experiment, but with half the experimenters expecting a shorter reaction time and half expecting a longer reaction time. When the experimenters' expectancies were of reaction times rather than magnitude of ratings, hardly any expectancy effects emerged ($p < .30$).

From the experimental results presented in this chapter it seems that Ebbinghaus was right. The data obtained early in an experiment may be significant determinants of the data obtained later in the same experiment. The methodological implications of these findings will be discussed in more detail in Part III. For now it is enough to raise the question of whether it might not be useful to try to remain uninformed as to how the data are turning out until the experiment is completed. That would mean that the experimenter collecting the data would have to be kept uninformed about what data are "good" and what data are "bad." But even if the data collector were uninformed of this at the beginning, there would be the difficulty of keeping him uninformed. If the experimenter reported the early returns to the principal investigator, there would probably be more or less subtle reactions to this report, reactions that might cue the experimenter as to whether data were falling well or poorly. If the data seemed to be coming well, judging from the principal investigator's reaction, the data collector might make a point of not modifying his behavior toward his subjects. The data might, therefore, continue to come in as before. If the data seemed to be coming poorly, judging from the principal investigator's reaction, the data collector might make a point, even if not consciously, of modifying his behavior toward his subsequently contacted subjects. Such a change in behavior, midway through an experiment, might lead to troublesome interactions of experimental treatment conditions with the number of subjects contacted. Later-collected data might turn out to support the experimental hypothesis because of the unintended change in the experimenter's behavior.

13

Excessive Rewards

Little has been said so far about the effects of the experimenter's motives on the operation of expectancy effects. From studies employing animal subjects it appeared that the experimenter's expectancy might be a more important determinant of the results of the experiment than the experimenter's motives. In these studies experimenters were motivated to have all their animal subjects learn rapidly; yet the animals' learning was impaired when the experimenter expected poor performance.

In some of the earlier studies employing human subjects, experimenters were offered a special incentive to obtain data consistent with their expectancy. In a few studies they were promised two dollars instead of the standard one dollar for their participation if their "data came out as expected." In these studies there were no control groups to show whether these incentives increased the effects of the experimenter's expectancy, although it is known from other studies that such incentives are not necessary for the demonstration of expectancy effects. Shortly, more formal evidence will be presented which shows the complicating effects of varying types and sizes of incentives on the operation of expectancy effects.

For any scientist to carry on any research, he must be motivated to do so, and probably more than casually so. It is, after all, a lot of trouble to plan and conduct an experiment. The motivation to conduct research is usually related to certain motivations associated with the results of the research. Rarely is the investigator truly disinterested in the results he obtains from his research, but very likely some scientists are more disinterested than others. The same scientist may be more or less disinterested in the results of his research on different occasions (Roe, 1961).

A number of workers have discussed the implication for science of the motivation of the experimenter vis-à-vis the results of his research. In his preface to Mannheim's *Ideology and Utopia,* Wirth spoke of the personal investment of the scientist in his research. Though he spoke more directly to the problem of interpreter effects than to the problem of expectancy effects, his remarks bear repeating: "The fact that in the realm of the social the observer is part of the observed and hence has a personal stake in the subject of observation is one of the chief factors in the acuteness of the problem of objectivity in the social sciences" (1936, p. xxiv). Similarly, Beck (1957, p. 201) has stated: "Each successive step in the method of science calls forth a greater emotional investment and adds to the difficulties of remaining objective. When the ego is involved, self criticism may come hard. (Who ever heard of two scientists battling to prove the other right?)"

More recently Ann Roe (1959; 1961) discussed the scientist's commitment to his hypothesis and suggested that creative advance may depend on it. She went on to caution us, however, to be aware of the intense bias that accompanies our involvement. (In an effort to implement this caution against bias, Roe devised the "Dyad Refresher Plan" for checking biases in clinical work. Lamentably this plan, which suggests periodic recalibration of the clinician, has not been well accepted.)

Motivational factors in the scientist affecting the work he does have been discussed by others as well (Barzun & Graff, 1957; Bingham & Moore, 1941; Griffith, 1961; Reif, 1961). But perhaps the most eloquent and most balanced brief statement on this topic was that by William James: ". . . science would be far less advanced than she is if the passionate desires of individuals to get their own faiths confirmed had been kept out of the game. . . . If you want an absolute duffer in an investigation, you must, after all, take the man who has no interest whatever in its results: he is the warranted incapable, the positive fool. The most useful investigator, because the most sensitive observer, is always he whose eager interest in one side of the question is balanced by an equally keen nervousness lest he become deceived" (1948, p. 102).

THE FIRST EXPERIMENT: INDIVIDUAL SUBJECTS

In the first experiment to investigate the effects of varying incentives on experimenter expectancy effects, 12 graduate students in education served as the experimenters (Rosenthal, Fode, & Vikan-Kline, 1960). They administered the standard photo-rating task to a total of 58 undergraduate students, of whom 30 were males and 28 females. Instructions read to subjects were those described in the preceding chapters. All experimenters were led to expect mean ratings of about $+7$ from all their subjects.

The motivation level of the experimenters was defined by the incentive offered for a "good job"—i.e., obtaining high ratings of photos from their subjects. The more moderately motivated group of six experimenters was told that the rate of pay would be two dollars per hour for a "good job," exactly as in some of the earlier described studies. The more highly motivated group of six experimenters, however, was told that the rate of pay would be five dollars for a good job.

In addition to the feeling that more highly motivated experimenters would show more biasing effects, it was also felt that subjects' motivation level might be an important variable affecting experimenter expectancy bias. Accordingly, all subjects were randomly assigned to a paid or an unpaid group. All experimenters contacted paid and unpaid subjects alternately. Paid subjects were told that they would receive fifty cents for their five minutes of participation.

In connection with another study, each subject and each experimenter was asked to fill in a lengthy questionnaire concerning their reaction to the experiment after their part in it was finished. In addition, before each experimenter contacted any subjects he was asked to predict as accurately as possible the average rating he would actually obtain from his subjects.

All experimenters were told to leave the doors to their research rooms open, as one of the research supervisors might drop in at any time. It was hoped that this might minimize the possibility of actual cheating by the more motivated experimenters.

In this study, magnitude of expectancy effect was defined in two ways. Higher mean obtained ratings—i.e., those closer to $+7$—were regarded as more biased. In addition, a higher positive correlation between the data specifically predicted by experimenters and the data subsequently obtained by them was regarded as an index of greater expectancy effect. Since experimenters had been led to expect a mean rating of $+7$, their specific predictions tended to cluster around that value. Consequently, correlations should underestimate the "true" correlations between predicted and obtained data because of the restriction of range of the experimenters' predictions.

Table 13-1 shows the mean ratings obtained by the more and less rewarded experimenters, each contacting paid and unpaid subjects. The

TABLE 13—1

Mean Photo Ratings

		EXPERIMENTER'S MOTIVATION	
		High ($5)	Moderate ($2)
SUBJECT'S	High (paid)	.96	.99
MOTIVATION	Moderate (unpaid)	1.24	2.28

analysis of variance revealed no differences in data obtained as a function of either of the treatments operating alone. The mean rating obtained by the more moderately motivated experimenters, when contacting unpaid subjects, did seem to be more biased than did the other three means of Table 13-1 ($p = .03$, two-tail, $t = 6.94$, $df = 2$). This was surprising, since it had been thought that the more highly motivated experimenters, especially when contacting paid subjects, would show the greatest expectancy effects. This first hint that an increase in motivation level (especially of experimenters, but of subjects as well) might *decrease* the effects of the experimenter's expectancy was further checked.

TABLE 13—2

Correlations Between Experimenters' Predicted and Obtained Ratings

		EXPERIMENTER'S MOTIVATION	
		High ($5)	Moderate ($2)
SUBJECT'S MOTIVATION	High (paid)	−.60	+.24
	Moderate (unpaid)	−.31	+.84*
	All subjects	−.31	+.99**

$^{*}p = .04$ (two-tail)
$^{**}p = .01$

Table 13-2 shows the correlations (rhos) between the data experimenters had specifically predicted they would obtain and the data they subsequently did obtain. This criterion (or definition) of experimenter expectancy effect correlated $+.80$ with the definition of expectancy effect based on photo ratings obtained (Table 13-1). Only among moderately motivated experimenters contacting moderately motivated subjects was the magnitude of expectancy effect significantly greater than zero. Disregarding motivation of subjects, it was found that the more moderately motivated experimenters biased their subjects' responses more than did the more highly motivated experimenters. The latter group, in fact, tended to show a negative or "reverse" expectancy effect, though this was not statistically significant.

The results just described led to a further investigation of the effect of the experimenter's motivation level. There was curiosity at this point, too, about two other variables. One was the degree of explicitness of the instructions to obtain expectancy biased data. Heretofore these had all been relatively implicit. The other variable of interest was whether expectancy effects could occur in the situation wherein an experimenter contacts a number of subjects simultaneously (Rosenthal, Friedman, Johnson, Fode, Schill, White, & Vikan-Kline, 1964).

THE SECOND EXPERIMENT: SUBJECTS IN GROUPS

In this second experiment 30 advanced male undergraduates, primarily from the College of Engineering, served as experimenters. With the modifications to be noted, they administered the photo-rating task to a total of 150 subjects, 90 males and 60 females, all of whom were students of introductory psychology.

Experimenters were divided into five treatment groups of six experimenters each. Four of the treatment groups were led to expect high positive ratings ($+5$) of the photos from their subjects, and the remaining group was led to expect high negative ratings (-5) from subjects. In order to test the effect of reward or motivation, half of the experimenters expecting high positive ratings from their subjects were given a dollar bill and told that if they did a "better" job—i.e., obtained closer-to-expected ratings— than an unknown partner, they could keep their dollar and get their partner's dollar as well. However, they were told that if their partner did a better job, he would get their dollar. The other half of the experimenters expecting high positive ratings were not involved in this betting situation and were thus considered the less motivated or less rewarded group. In order to test the effect of the explicitness of instructions to bias their subjects' responses, half the experimenters expecting to obtain high positive ratings were told to do whatever they could to obtain the expected data, but without deviating from the written instructions to subjects. The other half of the experimenters expecting high positive ratings were simply led to expect these ratings, and were thus considered to be less explicitly biased. The six experimenters expecting high negative ratings were given the more explicit instructions to bias their subjects and were also given the two-person sumzero game condition of motivation.

The entire experiment was carried out in a single evening. The locale was an armory in which 30 tables were arranged in a roughly circular pattern. Experimenters sat on one side of the table, and their five subjects sat across from them. Each photo was presented to each of the five subjects in turn. Subjects recorded their ratings on a small pad, and these pads were shown to the experimenter so that only he could see them. The purpose of having this double recording of ratings was to provide a check on any recording errors experimenters might make.

The treatment conditions were actually imposed by differential wording of "last-minute instructions," which experimenters found at their tables the night of the experiment. Each of the treatments was represented equally often in the different parts of the armory. Order of arrival then determined assignment of experimenters to tables, with earlier and later arrivers represented equally often among treatments.

Subjects were similarly assigned to experimenters, except that each table had three male and two female subjects. Positions of males and females vis-à-vis the experimenter were systematically varied within treatments.

Each experimenter was asked to predict the specific mean photo rating he would obtain. After the photos had been rated, each subject filled out a series of 20-point rating scales describing his experimenter's behavior during the course of the experiment. Each scale ran from -10 (e.g., extremely unfriendly) to $+10$ (e.g., extremely friendly). Experimenters also rated their own behavior on the same set of rating scales.

Table 13-3 shows the mean ratings obtained by the more and less motivated experimenters under more and less explicit instructions to obtain

TABLE 13—3

Mean Photo Ratings

		EXPERIMENTER'S MOTIVATION	
		High	Moderate
INSTRUCTIONS	Explicit	$-.23*$	$-.02$
	Implicit	$-.35$	$-.17$

* $+.14$ was the comparable mean obtained by experimenters expecting "-5" ratings.

expectancy biased data. More motivated experimenters tended to show less expectancy effect than did less motivated experimenters ($p = .05$). Explicitness of instructions to obtain biased data had at best only an equivocal effect. Table 13-4 shows the correlations between data experimenters had specifically predicted they would obtain and the data they subsequently did obtain. None of these correlations was significantly different from zero.

The analogous treatment conditions from the two experiments described here were those in which more and less motivated experimenters were implicitly set to bias the responses of unpaid subjects. Table 13-5 shows that rather similar correlations were obtained under the analogous

TABLE 13—4

Correlations Between Experimenters' Predicted and
Obtained Ratings

		EXPERIMENTER'S MOTIVATION	
		High	Moderate
INSTRUCTIONS	Explicit	.00*	−.10
	Implicit	−.21	+.59

* −.21 was the comparable correlation among experimenters expecting
"−5" ratings.

conditions of the two studies. Considered together, these studies suggest
that "excessive" rewards for expectancy effects actually led to decreased
expectancy effects under the particular conditions of the two experiments
described. The more explicitly instructed-to-bias and more highly motivated
experimenters expecting "−5" ratings obtained ratings *higher* than those of
any treatment condition imposed on experimenters expecting "+5" mean
ratings. This finding (two-tail, $p = .13$), together with the negative correlations representing magnitude of expectancy effects in the more highly
motivated treatment conditions, suggest the possibility that these experimenters were actively biased into a reversed direction.

In an earlier chapter, the finding that experimenters' computational
errors in data processing were not randomly distributed was reported. It

TABLE 13—5

Correlations Between Experimenters' Predicted and
Obtained Ratings for Analogous Treatment Conditions of Two Studies

	EXPERIMENTER'S MOTIVATION		p Difference
	High	Moderate	(Two-Tail)
Study I	−.31	+.84	.06
Study II	−.21	+.59	.27
Means	−.26	+.74	.05

can be reasoned that those more motivated experimenters whose computational errors favored the induced expectancy might also have biased their subjects' responses into the direction of the induced expectancy. By similar reasoning, those more motivated experimenters whose computational errors did not favor the induced hypothesis should not have biased their subjects' responses into the direction of their expectancy. This latter group of experimenters might be the one most likely to show a "reverse bias" effect. Among the less motivated experimenters there was no difference in data obtained by experimenters erring computationally in the direction of the hypothesis (+5) and those erring in the opposite direction. Among the more motivated experimenters, however, this difference was significant at the .10 level (two-tail). The mean photo rating obtained by more motivated experimenters subsequently erring computationally in the direction of their hypothesis (+5) was +.23, whereas the mean obtained by those not erring in this direction computationally was −.55 (These means, of course, were corrected for the effect of the errors themselves.) The effect of excessive reward seems to be to increase the variability of data obtained ($p <$ .05). Some experimenters appear to be significantly more biased by excessive reward, whereas some experimenters appear to be significantly less, or even negatively, biased.

SOME DISCUSSION

Why might one effect of excessive incentive to bias subjects' data be to reduce or even to reverse the expectancy effect of the experimenters? In a postexperimental group discussion with the experimenters of the second study, many of them seemed somewhat upset by the experimental goings-on. Several of them used the term "payola," suggesting that they felt that the investigators were bribing them to get "good" data, which was, in a sense, true. Since money had been mentioned and dispensed to only the more motivated experimenters of this study, it seems likely that they were the ones perceiving the situation in this way. Kelman (1953) found that subjects under higher motivation to conform to an experimenter showed less such conformity than did subjects under lower conditions of motivation. One of several of Kelman's interpretations was that the subjects who were rewarded more may have felt more as though they were being bribed to conform for the experimenter's own benefit, thus making subjects suspicious and resentful, and therefore less susceptible to experimenter influence. This interpretation fits the present situation quite well.

Ferber and Wales (1952) concluded from their data that in the interviewing situation if the interviewer is biased and knows it, he may show a "negative" bias as part of an overreactive attempt to overcome his known bias. Although this was not found consistently in their study, it seems to help in the interpretation of the "reverse" bias phenomenon. Dr. Raymond

C. Norris (in a personal communication) has related an anecdote that seems to illustrate nicely this bending over backward to insure freedom from bias:

Briefly, the situation involved an experiment in which the faculty member took a rather firm position consistent with Hullian theory and the student, being unschooled in Hullian theory, took a directly contradictory point of view based on some personal experience he had had in a similar situation. They discussed the expectations at some length and each experimenter was familiar with the point of view that the other was advancing. However, each felt some very deep commitment to his own expectations. When the results of the experiment were analyzed it was found that there was a significant treatment-by-experimenter interaction. Further analysis demonstrated that this interaction consisted of each experimenter producing the results that the other expected. Through some deep soul searching and interrogation both the experimenters became convinced that they had bent over backwards to avoid biasing the results in the direction of their prediction and consequently produced results antagonistic to their predictions.

Mills (1958) found that honest sixth graders became more anti-cheating under conditions of high motivation to cheat. In addition, he found that under conditions of high restraint against cheating, subjects became more anti-cheating than did similarly highly motivated subjects under conditions of low restraint against cheating. Mills interpreted this finding on the basis of the high-restraint group's feeling perhaps more suspected and therefore denouncing cheating more vehemently. During the conduct of both experiments reported in this chapter, experimenters had good reason to feel suspected. In the first study experimenters were asked to keep the doors to their research rooms open so the principal investigators might check up on them. In the second study a corps of eight researchers was in constant circulation about the armory in order to detect and correct any procedural deviations. The more highly motivated experimenters may have felt that their behavior in particular was being evaluated because of their higher stakes. This may have led many of them to bend over backward to avoid appearing in any way dishonest by biasing their subjects.

Festinger and Carlsmith (1959) found that subjects under conditions of lower reward, when forced to behave overtly in a manner dissonant from their private belief, changed their private beliefs toward their publicly stated ones more than did subjects under conditions of higher reward. This finding and those of Kelman (1953) and of Mills (1958) have been interpreted within the framework of Festinger's theory (1957) of cognitive dissonance. The finding from the present studies, that more motivated experimenters tend to show a reverse bias effect, is consistent with the studies reviewed and may also be interpreted within the framework of dissonance theory (Rosenthal, Friedman, Johnson, Fode, Schill, White, & Vikan-Kline, 1964).

Perhaps the most parsimonious interpretation of the reversal of expectancy effects is in terms of Rosenberg's concept of evaluation apprehension (1965 and in personal communication). The experimenters of the
studies described were, of course, a special kind of subject who may well
have experienced some apprehension about what the principal investigators
might think of them. Both the autonomy and honesty of the experimenters
may have been challenged by offering large incentives for affecting the results of their research. By bending over backward, the experimenters could
establish that they would not be either browbeaten or bribed to affect their
subjects' responses as their principal investigators had "demanded." Such
an interpretation speaks well of the integrity of the experimenters, but it
must be noted that the results of the research were still affected, though in
this case in the direction opposite to that expected.

No single interpretation of the results of these studies is entirely satis-
factory. That is because the locus of the reversal of expectancy effects cannot be determined from the data available. The interpretations offered so
far have assumed the locus to fall within the experimenter. In view of the
experimenters' very obvious concern with the question of bribery, the assumption seems reasonable. It is also possible, however, that the locus of
the reversal of expectancy effects falls within the subject. That is what we
would expect if the more motivated experimenter tried too hard to influence
his subjects. The subjects feeling pushed by an experimenter who "comes on
too strong" may resist his efforts at influencing their responses. This self-
assertion through noncompliance may operate in the service of evaluation
apprehension if the subject feels that the experimenter would think the less
of him if he complied.

Orne (1962), Schultz (1963), and Silverman (1965) have all suggested that when influence attempts become more obvious, subjects become less influenceable. This may be a trend of the future as much or more
than a fact of the past. As more and more subjects of psychological experiments become acquainted with the results of the classic research in
conformity (e.g., Asch, 1952) there may be more and more determination
to show the experimenter that the subject is not to be regarded as "one of
those mindless acquiescers" which instructors of elementary psychology
courses are likely to teach about. As likely as not, in the studies described
in this chapter, the locus of the reversal of expectancy effects is to be found
both in the experimenters (who were subjects) and in the subjects of these
"subjects."

SUBJECTS' PERCEPTION OF THEIR EXPERIMENTER

At the conclusion of the first experiment described in this chapter,
each subject was asked to fill out a questionnaire describing the behavior of
his experimenter during the course of the experiment. Experimenters com-

pleted the same forms describing their own behavior during the experiment. Neither experimenters nor subjects knew beforehand that they would be asked to complete these questionnaires, and no one save the investigators saw the completed forms (Rosenthal, Fode, Friedman, & Vikan-Kline, 1960). These forms consisted of 27 twenty-point rating scales ranging from −10 (e.g., extremely discourteous) to +10 (e.g., extremely courteous). The more desirable-sounding poles of the scales appeared about equally often on the right and left of the page. All scales were completed by all 12 experimenters and by 56 of the 58 subjects.

Table 13-6 shows the mean ratings of the experimenters by their sub-

TABLE 13—6

Mean Ratings of Experimenters' Behavior

Rating Scale	By Subjects	By Experimenters
Satisfied with experiment	1.44	5.09
Liking	5.16 (of E)	5.00 (of S)
Honest	7.56	8.55
Friendly	5.50	4.82
Personal	−0.36	1.45
Quiet (nontalkative)	1.89	4.73
Relaxed	5.82	4.73
Quiet (nonloud)	2.79	2.55
Casual	5.80	5.36
Enthusiastic	2.49	3.45
Interested	4.12	5.09
Courteous	6.89	7.09
Businesslike	5.45	6.36
Professional	4.66	5.45
Pleasant-voiced	7.39	6.27
Slow-speaking	1.55	2.45
Expressive-voiced	3.16	2.18
Encouraging	3.53	4.27
Behaved consistently	6.31	6.82
Pleasant	6.40	5.82
Use of hand gestures	−2.02	2.18
Use of head gestures	−0.72	−0.36
Use of arm gestures	−2.18	−2.27
Use of trunk	−2.75	−2.27
Use of legs	−2.86	−2.55
Use of body	−1.27	−0.09
Expressive face	2.57	0.73

jects and by themselves. Both sets of ratings reflected very favorably on the experimenters. The profile of the experimenters as they were viewed by subjects showed remarkable similarity to the profile of the experimenters as viewed by themselves. The rank correlation between profiles was .89, $p < .0005$. (It has been shown elsewhere that such correlations are increased by the commonly shared stereotype of the psychological experimenter [Rosenthal & Persinger, 1962].) To summarize and facilitate interpretation of the obtained ratings, all variables were intercorrelated and cluster-analyzed. Table 13-7 defines the four clusters that emerged. The associated B-coefficients are all considerably larger than generally deemed necessary to establish the significance of a cluster (Fruchter, 1954). For mnemonic purposes we may label Cluster I as "Casual-Pleasant," Cluster II as "Expressive-Friendly," Cluster III as "Kinesic" or "Gestural Activity," and Cluster IV as "Enthusiastic-Professional." The only scale not accommodated within any cluster was "quiet (nonloud)."

TABLE 13—7

Cluster Analysis of Subjects' Perceptions of Experimenters' Behavior

Cluster I: $B = 6.48$	Cluster II: $B = 3.97$
Honest	Liking
Casual	Friendly
Relaxed	Personal
Pleasant	Interested
Courteous	Encouraging
Businesslike	Expressive face
Slow-speaking	Expressive-voiced
Pleasant-voiced	Use of hand gestures
Behaved consistently	Satisfied with experiment
Mean rating = 5.91	*Mean rating* = 2.57

Cluster III: $B = 9.10$	Cluster IV: $B = 3.55$
Use of head gestures	Enthusiastic
Use of arm gestures	Professional
Use of trunk	Quiet (nontalkative)
Use of body	
Use of legs	
Mean rating = −1.96	*Mean rating* = 3.01

Table 13-7 also shows the subjects' mean rating of their experimenters for each of the four clusters. The mean rating on the "Casual-Pleasant" cluster was significantly higher ($p = .002$) than the mean rating on the "Expressive-Friendly" and the "Enthusiastic-Professional" clusters, which were not significantly different from each other. The mean rating on these latter two clusters, in turn, was significantly higher than the mean rating on the "Kinesic Cluster" ($p = .002$).

The 12 experimenters rated for their dyadic behavior had not uniformly influenced the responses they obtained from their subjects. We turn now to the question of whether those experimenters who showed greater positive expectancy effects were perceived by their subjects as in any way different in their experimental interaction from those experimenters who showed less or even a reversal of expectancy effects.

In order to answer this question, all experimenters were ranked according to the magnitude of their expectancy effect. For this purpose, magnitude of expectancy effect was defined as the discrepancy between the data an experimenter specifically predicted he would obtain and the data he actually did obtain. The smaller this discrepancy, the greater the expectancy effect; the greater this discrepancy, the less the expectancy effect.

Table 13-8 shows the correlations (rhos) between each of the behavioral variables and magnitude of expectancy effect. The median magnitude of the obtained correlations was .35 ($p = .02$, two-tail). Considering only those correlations reaching a $p = .10$, experimenters showing greater positive expectancy effects were viewed by their subjects as more interested, likable, and personal; as slower speaking and more given to the use of hand, head, and leg gestures and movements. As some of these relationships may have occurred by chance because of the number of correlations computed, we may obtain a more stable picture of the relationship between subjects' perceptions of their experimenter and the magnitude of his expectancy effects by looking at the four obtained clusters rather than at the 27 variables.

The median correlations with magnitude of expectancy effect of the variables in Clusters I and IV were .26 and .21, respectively; neither was significantly greater than a correlation having a $p = .50$. The median correlations with magnitude of expectancy effect of the variables in Clusters II and III were .47 and .43, respectively. Both of these median correlations were significantly greater than a correlation to be often expected by chance (ps were .04 and .01, respectively, two-tail). More expectancy biased experimenters, then, were characterized by higher loadings on the "Expressive-Friendly" and the "Kinesic" clusters. These findings suggested that kinesic and possibly paralinguistic (e.g., tone of voice) aspects of the experimenter's interaction with his subjects served to communicate the experimenter's expectancy to his subjects. Further evidence bearing on this formulation will be presented in the following chapters.

TABLE 13—8

Perceptions of Experimenters' Behavior and Magnitude of Expectancy Effects

Variables	Correlation
Satisfied with experiment	.17
Liking	.56*
Honest	.06
Friendly	.15
Personal	.53*
Quiet (nontalkative)	−.09
Relaxed	.31
Quiet (nonloud)	−.41
Casual	.35
Enthusiastic	.39
Interested	.71***
Courteous	−.04
Businesslike	.26
Professional	.21
Pleasant-voiced	.43
Slow-speaking	.64**
Expressive-voiced	.47
Encouraging	.12
Behaved consistently	.23
Pleasant	.24
Use of hand gestures	.61**
Use of arm gestures	.34
Use of head gestures	.52*
Use of trunk	.34
Use of legs	.55*
Use of body	.43
Expressive face	.39

* $p \leq .10$
** $p \leq .05$ (two-tail)
*** $p \leq .01$

PREDICTING COMPUTATIONAL ERRORS

The particular experimenters under discussion were those who participated in the first study described in this chapter. In the second study described, the subjects were also asked to make ratings of their experimenter's behavior during the conduct of the experiment. Eleven of the experimenters in that study made computational errors in their data processing in the direction of their hypothesis. These experimenters were rated an average of $+6.8$ on the scale of "honesty" by their 55 subjects. The 65 subjects of the remaining 13 experimenters rated them as $+8.5$, on the average, on the same scale. The difference between these mean ratings was significant at the .02 level (two-tail, $t = 2.67$, $df = 22$). Thus, whereas all experimenters were rated as quite honest (whatever that word might have meant to the subjects), those experimenters who later made computational errors in their hypothesis' favor were seen as somewhat less honest. Just how subjects were able to predict their experimenters' computational errors from their judgments of experimenters' behavior during the experiment is a fascinating question for which we presently have no answer. Clearly, however, subjects learn a good deal about their experimenter in the brief interaction of the person-perception experiment conducted. When a subject rates the behavior of an experimenter, we may do well to take his rating seriously.

14

Structural Variables

Are there some experimenters who, more than others, unintentionally affect the results of their research? Are there some subjects who, more than others, are susceptible to the unintentional influence of their experimenter's expectancy? The present chapter is addressed to these questions. The answers to these questions should increase our general understanding of the effects of the experimenter's expectancy and perhaps provide us with some clues to the effective control of these effects. In addition, the answers to these questions may suggest to us whether the unintentional influence processes under study are facilitated by factors similar to those that facilitate the more usually investigated processes of social influence.

EXPERIMENTER AND SUBJECT SEX

A number of studies have been conducted to learn the role of experimenter and subject sex in the operation of experimenter expectancy effects. In the two experiments to be described first there was an additional purpose to be served (Rosenthal, Persinger, Mulry, Vikan-Kline, & Grothe, 1964a). Most of the experiments described up to now had suffered from a certain nonrepresentativeness of design. The experimenters employed had expected all their subjects to give them a specific type of response. In "actual" psychological experiments, experimenters normally expect two or more *different* kinds of responses from their subjects, depending upon the experimental condition to which the subject has been assigned. In some psychological experiments, experimenters first collect data from subjects in one experimental condition and then later from subjects in the other condition(s). In other experiments, data from subjects representing all conditions are collected on the same occasion, with the order of appearance of subjects from different conditions either systematically or randomly varied.

The additional purpose of the experiments to be reported, then, was to learn whether the effects of experimenter expectancy might be generalized to include the two data collection situations described. Accordingly, in the first experiment, experimenters collected data from subjects under one condition of expectancy; then, some time later, these same experimenters collected data from a fresh sample of subjects under an opposite condition of expectancy. In the second experiment, experimenters collected all their data on a single occasion but with opposite expectancies of the responses to be obtained from subjects randomly distributed through the series. If experimenter expectancy effects could occur under these conditions, it would lend further support to the suggestion made in an earlier chapter that experimenters' hypotheses about subjects' responses might change in the midst of an experiment, and still serve as self-fulfilling prophecies.

The First Experiment

Three male and two female graduate students in counseling and guidance served as experimenters. The subjects were 52 undergraduate students enrolled in various elementary courses; 23 were males, 29 were females. Each experimenter presented to each of his subjects individually the standard 10-photo rating task. All experimenters were, as before, to read identical instructions to all their subjects. Experimenters were individually trained, and the importance of their role in the experiment was impressed upon them.

Each experimenter was randomly assigned an average of 10 subjects. In the first stage of this study, three experimenters were told that personality test data available from the subjects he would be contacting suggested that they would give mean photo ratings of about +5. The remaining two experimenters (one male, one female) were led to expect opposite results, mean ratings of −5. At this time each experimenter collected data from about five subjects. Several weeks later, each experimenter contacted about five more subjects. This time those experimenters who had earlier been led to expect mean ratings of +5 were led to expect ratings of −5. The expectancies of those experimenters initially expecting −5 ratings were similarly reversed. Explanations to experimenters were simply that this second set of subjects had opposite personality characteristics.

For each subject, magnitude of experimenter expectancy effect upon that subject was defined as the difference score between that subject's mean photo rating and the mean of the ratings by subjects contacted under the opposite condition of expectancy. A plus sign meant that the direction of difference was the predicted one—i.e., subject's rating was higher if the experimenter expected him to rate +5 or lower if the experimenter expected him to rate −5. The analysis of variance of the effects of experimenter expectancy as a function of experimenter and subject sex yielded only a

TABLE 14—1

Expectancy Effects as a Function of Sex of Experimenter and Subject

E Sex	S Sex	Mean	t	df	p (Mean = 0)
Male	Male	+1.33	3.01	16	.01
	Female	+.78	1.54	14	.16
Female	Male	−.25	.47	5	.66
	Female	+1.22	2.11	13	.06

significant interaction ($F = 3.05$, $p = .10$). Table 14-1 shows the mean expectancy bias score for each sex of experimenter by each sex of subject. For each of the four conditions the tabulated ps represent the likelihood that for the particular combination of experimenter and subject sex the magnitude of expectancy effect could have occurred by chance. Among the female experimenters contacting male subjects there was a nonsignificant trend for the data obtained to be opposite to that expected. Among the three remaining groups the combined p of experimenters' expectancy affecting subjects was .0005 ($z = 3.39$).

The Second Experiment

Six advanced undergraduate and beginning graduate students enrolled in psychology courses served as experimenters; three were females. All had served as experimenters in an earlier experiment and were familiar with the experimental procedure (Persinger, 1962). The subjects were 35 undergraduate students enrolled in various elementary courses; 22 were females, and 13 were males.

The experimental task and general instructions to experimenters were as in the first experiment. Each experimenter collected data from about six randomly assigned subjects, seen consecutively in a single session. Experimenters were told that their subjects were of two personality types and that some would therefore average +5 photo ratings while others would average −5 ratings. Before meeting each subject, the experimenter was told to which "group" that subject belonged. Experimenter expectancies thus were varied randomly on what amounted to a roughly alternating schedule. In order to detect gross, intentional procedural deviations, however, all experimenters were observed during their contacts with all subjects. About half these transactions were permanently recorded on 16 mm sound film. Neither experimenters nor subjects were aware of this monitoring, and no intentional procedural deviations were noted.

The analysis of variance yielded significant main effects of experimenter and subject sex. Male experimenters obtained more biased responses than did female experimenters ($F = 4.20$, $p = .05$). Female subjects were more susceptible to experimenter expectancy effects than were male subjects ($F = 7.67$, $p = .01$). The interaction was, however, somewhat too large to ignore entirely ($F = 1.79$, $p = .20$).

TABLE 14—2

Expectancy Effects as a Function of Sex of Experimenter and Subject: Second Experiment

E Sex	S Sex	Mean	t	df	p	p (Both Experiments)
Male	Male	+.72	.94	5	.40	.01
	Female	+1.54	2.17	10	.06	.01
Female	Male	−1.37	3.70	6	.01	.03
	Female	+.99	3.41	10	.01	.001

Table 14-2 shows the mean expectancy bias score for the four treatment combinations. In this experiment the tendency found earlier for female experimenters contacting male subjects to obtain responses opposite to those expected was found again and more markedly so ($p = .01$). For both experiments together the combined p for this reversal was .03 ($z = 1.93$). In this second study the combined p of the predicted effects' occurrence among the other three conditions was $< .002$ ($z = 3.06$); for both experiments $p < .0001$ ($z = 4.55$).

Considering the results of both experiments together it appears that male experimenters may unintentionally bias the data collected from both male and female subjects. For female experimenters, on the other hand, the situation is more complex. Influencing their female subjects to give predicted responses, they seem to obtain opposite results from their male subjects. It appears from this significant reversal that the subtle influence process that mediates experimenter expectancy effects is perceived accurately enough by the male subjects; otherwise we would have expected no expectancy effects at all. Male subjects, however, may feel somehow they ought not to let female experimenters influence them in this way. In response, they may then tend to give their female experimenters data opposite to that subtly requested as a demonstration of their masculine independence.

The results of these two experiments also extend the generality of earlier findings bearing on the effects of experimenter expectancies on the responses obtained from their subjects. The plausibility of the earlier suggestion that experimenters may alter their hypotheses in midexperiment and then obtain data in accord with the revised expectancy seems somewhat increased.

A subsequent study was undertaken to further evaluate the effects of subjects' sex (Rosenthal, Persinger, Mulry, Vikan-Kline, & Grothe, 1964b). The procedure in this study was very similar to that of the study just reported. Eight male experimenters conducted the photo rating experiment with 32 female subjects. Another 5 male experimenters conducted the same experiment with 13 male subjects. Each experimenter was led to expect about half his subjects to make photo ratings of $+5$; the remaining subjects were expected to make ratings of -5. Only 38 percent of the male subjects gave ratings in the expected direction, whereas 69 percent of the female subjects gave such biased ratings. For this sample of male experimenters, then, female subjects were clearly more susceptible to the biasing effects of their experimenters' hypotheses ($p < .05$, two-tail).

Data presented by Marcia (1961) were analyzable for differential biasing effects of male and female experimenters. Among his female experimenters the correlation between the experimenters' expectancy and the data subsequently obtained was only $-.34$. Among male experimenters the analogous correlation was $+.62$. However, because the total number of experimenters was only 13, the difference between these rhos was not very significant statistically ($p = .16$, two-tail).

An experiment conducted by Persinger (1962) also investigated sex of experimenters and of subjects as factors in the operation of expectancy effects. We shall have occasion to refer to his study in more detail later in this chapter. For now we may simply state that the combination of experimenter and subject sex showing the most extreme biasing effects was that wherein male experimenters contacted female subjects ($p = .07$, two-tail).

One other experiment also suggested that female subjects were more susceptible ($p = .10$, two-tail) to the expectancy effects of their experimenters. This experiment was summarized in an earlier chapter (Rosenthal, Persinger, Vikan-Kline, & Fode, 1963a). The overall picture that seems now to emerge is that, in general, male experimenters show more significant expectancy effects than do female experimenters. This finding, a fairly consistent one, may be due in part to the specific inability of female experimenters to bias the data given them by male subjects. One possible reason for this was advanced earlier.

A number of studies have been conducted in which no differences were found between male and female subjects in their susceptibility to experimenter expectancy effects. We have never found, however, a situation wherein male subjects were significantly more susceptible. With one exception, it does seem safe to conclude that where a sex difference does occur it is the female subjects who show the greater susceptibility. The possible exception to this has just been reported by Silverman (1965). He studied the effects of experimenters' expectancies on subjects' latencies in a word association task. The results suggested that male experimenters unintentionally influenced their female subjects more and that female experimenters influenced their male subjects more. This interaction may be specifically associated with the task employed by Silverman.

The susceptibility under discussion is to a subtle, unintended form of social influence. We have no empirical basis for assuming that those characteristics increasing susceptibility to experimenter expectancy effects should be the same characteristics found to increase susceptibility to other, more commonly investigated forms of social influence. Should this prove to be the case, however, we may entertain the hope of a "bootstrap" operation. That is, the results may extend the generality of the research findings in the area of social influence processes while at the same time finding a conceptual niche within that somewhat well-articulated area of investigation. In the question of relating subject sex to susceptibility to interpersonal influence, we find ourselves fortunate indeed. For a variety of situations of less subtle forms of influence, female subjects have consistently been found more influenceable (Aas, O'Hara, & Munger, 1962; Coffin, 1941; Crutchfield, 1955; Hovland & Janis, 1959; Jenness, 1932; London & Fuhrer, 1961; Simmons & Christy, 1962).

To expect a sex-linked genetic determination of response to specific situations by college sophomores would no doubt be to expect too much. To the extent that sex predicts susceptibility to interpersonal influence we may postulate that cultural sanctions are operating which serve to approve women's influenceability more than men's. Some interesting data tend to bear this out for the situation wherein a biased experimenter is the source of influence (Rosenthal & Fode, 1963). More influenceable, or more successfully biased, female subjects were better liked by their influencing experimenters (rho = +.59). More influenceable, or more biased, male subjects were very significantly *less* liked by their influencing experimenters (rho = −.54). In this experiment, in which all experimenters were male, subjects may have been liked to the degree to which their experimenter felt they fit their culturally prescribed roles of female-acquiescence and male-autonomy.

That females may prove to be more docile subjects from an experimenter's point of view has been interestingly if only accidentally reported. Foster (1961) briefly discussed attrition rates of subjects due to their suspicion that his Asch-type conformity (1952) situation was rigged. About 32 percent of his male subjects were suspicious enough to warrant their being dropped from the experiment, whereas only about 13 percent of his female subjects claimed this degree of suspicion. A fascinating if moot question might be: were the girls actually less suspicious or did they by virtue of some greater degree of acquiescence simply have the greater "decency" not to report to an experimenter something that they believed he might not wish to hear?

If female experimenters were usually less successful in the unintentional influencing of their male subjects, we might also expect that female experimenters would be less successful in influencing their male research assistants to obtain the data predicted. One experiment, which has been cited earlier and will be discussed again later, could be analyzed to help answer this question (Rosenthal, Persinger, Vikan-Kline, & Mulry, 1963). There were 10 male experimenters and 3 female experimenters who were given one of two opposite expectancies for responses to the photo-rating task. Table 14-3 shows the magnitudes of expectancy effects defined as the

TABLE 14—3

Expectancy Effects of Experimenters and of Their Research Assistants as a Function of Experimenter's Sex

| | EXPERIMENTER'S SEX | | | One-tail |
	Male	Female	Difference	p
Experimenter's subjects	+.37	+.30	+.07	NS
Assistants' subjects	+.32	−.07	+.39	.07
Difference	+.05	+.37		
One-tail p	NS	.10		

mean difference in ratings obtained under each of the two expectancies. A plus sign means that the difference was in the direction of the expectancy. The first row of Table 14-3 shows that female experimenters affected their own subjects' responses almost as much as did the male experimenters. Each experimenter then served as principal investigator and trained two research assistants. Experimenters were told not to tell their assistants what data the experimenter was expecting them to obtain. The second row of Table 14-3 shows that male experimenters were able to communicate their expectancy to their male research assistants in some covert manner. Female experimenters, however, were significantly less successful at influencing their male research assistants to obtain the data they expected the assistants to obtain from their new samples of subjects. Among male experimenters there was a correlation of +.66 ($p < .05$, two-tail) between the magnitude of an experimenter's expectancy effects on his own subjects and the magnitude of his research assistants' expectancy effects on their subjects. Among the female experimenters the correlation was in the opposite direction (rho = −1.00, p = .33, two-tail), though with so few female experimenters the correlation could not reach significance. The results are at least suggestive. Male principal investigators tend to influence their male research assistants to influence their subjects unintentionally to about the same degree as they themselves influenced their own subjects. Female principal investigators do not show this tendency. In fact, they tend to show a reversal of this effect. Just as male subjects may resist the unintentional influence attempts of their female experimenters, male research assistants may resist the unintentional influence attempts of their female principal investigators.

EXPERIMENTER AND SUBJECT ANXIETY

An experiment conducted by Fode (1965) was designed specifically to show whether experimenters' or subjects' anxiety level might be related to the occurrence of expectancy effects. He employed a total of 16 experimenters each of whom administered the standard photo-rating task to an average of 10 subjects. Some experimenters were led to expect positive ratings of the photos and some were led to expect negative ratings. Anxiety level was defined by scores on the Taylor Manifest Anxiety Scale (MAS). Magnitude of expectancy effects was defined by the difference scores between ratings obtained under the two conditions of expectancy. A plus sign preceding this difference score means that higher ratings were obtained by experimenters expecting higher rather than lower ratings. Table 14-4 shows the results of the Fode experiment. Examination of the marginals shows that medium-anxious experimenters exerted the greatest expectancy effects upon their subjects. Similarly, more medium-anxious subjects showed the greatest susceptibility to experimenter expectancy effects.

Six additional experiments (94 experimenters; 432 subjects), all em-

TABLE 14—4

Expectancy Effects at Three Levels of Experimenter and Subject Anxiety (After Fode, 1965)

| | | EXPERIMENTER'S ANXIETY | | | |
		High	Medium	Low	Mean
SUBJECT'S ANXIETY	High	+1.17	+1.23	+0.04	+0.82
	Medium	+0.72	+2.13	+1.85	+1.57
	Low	+0.23	+0.08	−0.18	+0.04
	Mean	+0.71	+1.15	+0.57	+0.81

ploying the same task, were designed in part to bring further evidence to bear on the question raised by Fode. In these studies, anxiety was also defined by MAS scores or by a near relative. Experimenters and subjects were again classified as high, medium, or low anxious if they fell into the top, center, or bottom third of their sample's distribution of anxiety scores.

TABLE 14—5

Anxiety Levels Maximizing Expectancy Effects

	EXPERIMENTERS			SUBJECTS		
Investigators	N	Level	p	N	Level	p
Fode, 1965	16	Medium	.001	167	Medium	.04
Persinger, 1962	12	Low	.05	43	Low	.07
RR, GP, KF, 1962	10	High	.13	–	–	–
RR, GP, LVK, RM, 1963	29	High	.05	200	High	.12
RR, PK, PG, NC, 1965	14	Medium	.08	28	High and low	.05
RR, GP, RM, LVK, MG, 1962	29	Medium	.08	86	High	.10
Vikan-Kline, 1962	–	–	–	75	Medium	.06

Table 14-5 summarizes the results of all seven studies. In three samples of experimenters, medium anxiety level was associated with the greatest effect of experimenter expectancy. In two samples, high anxiety level and in one sample low anxiety level were associated with greatest expectancy effects. Most of these findings must be regarded as significant statistically in spite of their remarkable inconsistency. A similarly chaotic pattern emerges when we consider the results for samples of subjects. Those subjects found to be most susceptible to experimenter expectancy effects were found to be high-anxious in three samples, medium-anxious in two samples, and low-anxious in two samples. All these results also tended to be statistically significant. We can safely conclude only that experimenters' and subjects' level of anxiety are significantly (but very unpredictably) related to the occurrence of expectancy effects.

If the results bearing on the relationship between subjects' anxiety level and susceptibility to subtle, unintended, interpersonal influence are confusing, they are at least matched in equivocality by the results from other areas of research on susceptibility to interpersonal influence.

The relationship of anxiety, also usually defined by scores on the MAS or a next of kin, to influenceability has been rather frequently investigated.

More-anxious subjects have been found more susceptible to interpersonal influence in "conditioning" situations by a number of workers (Gelfand & Winder, 1961; Haner & Whitney, 1960; Sarason, 1958; Taffel, 1955), although others have not found anxiety to be a relevant variable in the same situation (Buss & Gerjuoy, 1958; Dailey, 1953; Eriksen, Kuethe, & Sullivan, 1958; Matarazzo, Saslow, & Pareis, 1958).

More-anxious subjects were found more influenceable by persuasive communication (Fine, 1957; Janis, 1955), and more-conforming subjects were characterized as more anxious under conditions of stress by Crutchfield (1955); Goldberg, Hunt, Cohen, and Meadow (1954) found more-anxious females to be more conforming. On the other hand, several studies have shown more-anxious subjects to be *less* persuasible, a contradictory finding which was reviewed and partially reconciled by Cervin, Joyner, Spence, and Heinzl (1961). These workers showed that more-emotional subjects were indeed more persuasible when under conditions of public commitment. Their study, and others requiring subjects to make their responses publicly, seem most relevant to our interest in the social psychology of the psychological experiment, since in most experimental situations the subject's response is made in the presence of his minimum public of the experimenter. Left unexplained are data obtained by Kuethe (1960). In his classroom drama situation, more-acquiescent and less-anxious subjects were more susceptible to social influence. Goldberg et al. (1954) found their less-anxious male subjects to be more influenceable.

In a review of the relationship between postural sway suggestibility and neuroticism or anxiety, Heilizer (1960) summarized the equivocal findings obtained, and found in his own study, utilizing a more precise measure of postural sway, no relationship between suggestibility and either neuroticism or anxiety. In attempting to summarize the relationship between anxiety and susceptibility to interpersonal influence for a variety of situations we must settle for the unsatisfying conclusion that anxiety often makes a difference but we cannot accurately predict whether more or less anxious subjects will be the more influenceable.

One factor in the equivocality of the obtained relationships between anxiety and susceptibility to social influence processes, generally, may be the curvilinear nature of the underlying relationship. This curvilinearity appears clearly in our own data (Table 14-5), although admittedly we may be dealing with a special case of interpersonal influenceability. Another factor possibly contributing to the obtained equivocality of relationships is the anxiety level of the experimenter. Inspection of Table 14-5 suggests that the particular level of subject anxiety associated with greatest susceptibility to the influence of experimenter expectancy may depend on the anxiety level of the experimenter. When the experimenter showing greatest expectancy effects is high-anxious, chances are that the most susceptible subjects will also be high-anxious. When the experimenter showing greatest expectancy effects is low-anxious, chances are that the more susceptible subjects will also be low-anxious. The correlation (rho) between the level of anxiety characterizing most biasing experimenters and the level of anxiety characterizing most susceptible subjects was +.64. Although this correlation was not significant statistically ($p = .18$, two-tail), based as it was on only six samples, the potential implications are important enough to warrant further consideration. In research on experimenter expectancy effects and possibly in other research dealing with more traditional situations of interpersonal influence, the influence process may proceed most effectively when the source and target of influence are more alike in level of anxiety. Anxiety similarity or perhaps nondissimilarity may be a correlate of rapport just as racial and religious similarity often seem to be (Hyman et al., 1954). When the variables of experimenter and subject hostility were employed, Sarason (1962) also found the greatest influence exerted upon subjects when experimenters and subjects were similar. He too employed an interpretation of experimenter-subject similarity. Even if the hypothesis of similarity or of nondissimilarity were upheld by further research, we would be left with the problem of accounting for the differences in the absolute level of anxiety associated with maximal interpersonal influence. We could easily posit gross situational variables that might account for these differences, except that in the studies reported in Table 14-5 the situation was about as "uniform" as it is likely to be in social psychological research.

In time, we can hope for a developing structuring of the complex relationships between social influence processes and the anxiety status of the participants. It seems, however, from a research logistics point of view, that we should not expect any one or two or three experiments to provide the necessary integrating information. When seven experiments yield only an equivocal hypothesis, how many more may be required to impose a meaningful structure on a domain of data characterized by such complexity?

One of the reasons that the subject's level of anxiety is only a poor predictor of susceptibility to social influence may be that experimenters find it hard to treat subjects with differing levels of anxiety in even a roughly equivalent manner. There may be some experimenters who are sufficiently perceptive to be able to differentiate the anxiety levels of their subjects and to treat them differently as a function of their involuntary assessment of their anxiety level. If subjects differing in level of anxiety (or in other characteristics) are not treated similarly, they cannot be said to be in the same experiment, an argument that has been made in earlier chapters. An experiment by Pflugrath (1962) suggests that at least some experimenters do treat their subjects differently as a function of their perceived anxiety level.

The basic purpose of Pflugrath's study was to find out whether experimenter expectancy effects could operate under conditions of group personality testing. Because group testing situations minimize personal contact between experimenter and subject and maximize the physical distance between them, it was thought that expectancy effects would be, at most, trivial. Pflugrath employed nine experimenters, all graduate students in counseling and guidance, to administer the Taylor Manifest Anxiety Scale (MAS) to 142 students enrolled in introductory psychology, all of whom had already taken the MAS on an earlier occasion. Three of the experimenters were told the subjects they would be testing were highly anxious. Three were told their subjects were quite nonanxious, and three were told nothing about their subjects. Each experimenter administered the MAS to two groups of randomly assigned subjects. Number of subjects in each group ranged from 5 to 10 with a mean of 8. Instructions to experimenters explained that their subjects had been seen in the student counseling center, a fact that may assume some importance in our interpretation of Pflugrath's data.

The overall analysis of the results showed no significant differences in anxiety scores earned by the subjects of the three groups of experimenters. Among the subjects of the control group, 47 percent showed a decrease in anxiety score from their pretest level ($p > .70$). Among the subjects whose experimenters believed them to be nonanxious, 57 percent showed a decrease in anxiety ($p = .30$). Among the subjects whose experimenters believed them to be highly anxious, 70 percent showed a decrease in anxiety ($p < .005$). When we recall that the experimenters were counselors-in-training this result seems reasonable. Told that they would be testing very anxious subjects who had required interpersonal assistance at the counseling center, these experimenters may well have brought all their counseling skills to bear upon the challenge of reducing their subjects' anxiety. This unprogrammed "therapy" by psychological experimenters may operate more frequently in behavioral research than we may like to believe. In a good deal of contemporary behavioral research, subjects are exposed to conditions believed to make them anxious. What might be the effect, on the outcome of experiments of this sort, of the covert therapeutic zeal and/or skill of various investigators carrying out this research? Might certain investigators typically conclude "no difference" because they unwittingly tend to dilute the effects of treatment conditions? And conversely, might others be led to conclude "significant difference" by their unintentionally increasing the anxiety of subjects known to belong to the "more anxious condition" of an experiment? Clearly these are not necessarily effects of experimenters' expectancies, but they are effects of experimenter attributes which may have equally serious implications for how we do research.

EXPERIMENTER AND SUBJECT NEED FOR APPROVAL

A very extensive series of experiments by Crowne and Marlowe (1964) and their co-workers has shown the importance of the approval motive to our understanding of susceptibility to interpersonal influence. Higher need for social approval as defined by scores on the Marlowe-Crowne Social Desirability Scale (M-C SD) and related measures (Ismir, 1962; Ismir, 1963) usually (Buckhout, 1965), but not always (Spielberger, Berger, & Howard, 1963), characterizes those subjects who comply more with experimentally varied situational demands.

The eight samples of experimenters for whom expectancy effects were correlated with need for approval (M-C SD) are identified in Table 14-6.

TABLE 14—6

Need for Approval and Expectancy Effects at Three Levels of Anxiety

	ANXIETY LEVEL					
	High		Medium		Low	
Investigators	N	Rho	N	Rho	N	Rho
Fode, 1965	4	−.25	8	+.80	4	−.80
Marcia, 1961	−	−	13	+.74	−	−
Persinger, 1962	−	−	12	+.58*	−	−
RR,GP,KF, 1962	4	0.00	4	+.95	4	−.40
RR,GP,LVK,RM,1963						
Sample I	4	−.40	4	+.65	4	−.85
Sample II	5	+.07	7	+.15	5	+.13
RR,PK,PG,NC,1965	(14)	(−.55)**	14	−.55	(14)	(−.55)**
RR,GP,RM,LVK,MG, 1962	6	−.60	9	+.21	10	+.25

* For an atypical sample of subjects personally acquainted with their experimenter, the analogous correlation was −.34, p = .15.

** At each level of anxiety the relationship was similar.

Early in the series of studies, it became evident that the nature of the relationship depended upon the experimenter's level of anxiety. In Table 14-6, therefore, the correlations between degree of experimenter expectancy effects and M-C SD scores are tabulated separately for high, medium, and low levels of experimenter anxiety. In a few cases, this method of analysis was not possible, and the entire sample of experimenters was then classified as medium anxiety.

Considering only the medium-anxious samples of experimenters, all but one of the correlations was positive ($p < .05$, two-tail). Considering the high- and low-anxious samples of experimenters, however, the correlations tended to be more negative than positive ($p < .05$, two-tail). Experimenters at a medium or unclassified level of anxiety thus showed greater expectancy effects if they scored higher on need for approval (median rho $= +.62$), whereas experimenters at either high or low anxiety levels showed just the opposite relationship (median rho $= -.40$). Why this should be is not at all clear, and just as in the case of experimenter and subject anxiety discussed in the preceding section, we may guess that it will take considerable effort to impose a structure upon this complex array of data. At any rate, our findings do suggest that, at least for some situations, the predictive power of the M-C SD scale may be still further increased by controlling for the influencer's level of anxiety.

Let us suppose for a moment that our data had more clearly shown us that experimenters scoring higher on a scale of approval need biased their subjects' responses more. (Such a finding has in fact been reported by Buckhout [1965] for a situation in which the influence attempt was quite intentional.) Even then the interpretation would not be straightforward. These experimenters might affect their subjects more in order to please the investigators who created demands upon them. Alternatively, these experimenters might simply be more effective unintentional influencers without their necessarily wanting to please the principal investigators any more than the lower need approval experimenters. Either or both of these mechanisms might reasonably be expected to operate.

It could well be argued, on the basis of the literature relating need approval to social influenceability, that we should not have expected any particular correlation between experimenters' expectancy effects and M-C SD scores. In the more usual experiment, it is the high-need-approval subject who makes the conforming response for the experimenter. In our studies, the experimenter-subject, in order to conform to our demands, must successfully influence other, subordinate subjects. He is able to conform, then, only in an indirect and extremely complicated way.

Given samples of experimenters who do influence their subjects' responses, we might expect that those subjects scoring higher in need for approval would be more influenceable. In *none* of our samples of subjects was this hypothesis confirmed. Subjects' need for approval has consistently been found unrelated to degree of susceptibility to experimenter expectancy effects. It appears that susceptibility to the subtle, unintended social influence of a biased experimenter is not as predictable from subjects' need for approval as is susceptibility to more clearly intended forms of interpersonal influence.

EXPERIMENTER-SUBJECT ACQUAINTANCESHIP

Were there such a thing as a typical psychological experiment it would be likely to involve an experimenter who was unacquainted with all or most of his subjects. There are numerous situations, however, when a major proportion of the subjects are acquaintances of the experimenter. This is often the case with pilot studies and follow-up studies. It is also likely to be the case where an experimenter-teacher employs his intact classes as subjects or when the experimenter is located at a smaller college, clinic, hospital, or industrial setting from which he will draw his subject samples. Granting only that experimenters sometimes contact acquainted subjects, it would be worthwhile to know whether this changes the likelihood of the operation of expectancy effects. This question would, in fact, be of interest even if no experimenter ever contacted a prior-acquainted subject. Acquaintanceship, itself, is an inevitable result of an experimenter-subject interaction, and the degree of acquaintanceship varies directly with the time and intensity of the experimenter-subject interaction sequence. The longer an experiment lasts and the greater the information exchanged, the more acquainted will the participants be at some point in the sequence, e.g., its half-life.

Although acquaintanceship cannot readily be eliminated, it can and has been experimentally varied. In an earlier chapter several such studies were cited, and it was found that subjects' performance might be affected by prior acquaintance with the data collector. The study by Kanfer and Karas (1959) is most relevant to our interest here. They found that prior acquaintance with the experimenter increased subjects' susceptibility to the influence of the experimenter's reinforcing verbal behavior. These findings, together with the comprehensive work of Newcomb (1961), suggest that those subjects who are more acquainted with their experimenters should be more susceptible to expectancy effects. This might be even more true in the case of less obvious, unintended influence processes. Where the cues to the subject are only poorly programmed, the acquainted subject would seem to have the better chance of accurately "reading" the unintended signals sent by the experimenter.

The first data obtained bearing on the relationship between acquaintanceship and magnitude of expectancy effects were incidental to another purpose to be described later (Rosenthal, Persinger, Vikan-Kline, & Mulry, 1963). In that study, experimenters were asked to predict what sort of photo ratings of success or failure they would subsequently obtain from their six randomly assigned subjects. Magnitude of expectancy effect was defined by the correlation (rho) between ratings experimenters expected to obtain and the data they later did obtain. A subsample was available of 10 male experimenters who had been previously acquainted with one or more of their subjects and unacquainted with one or more of their subjects. Based only on data obtained from unacquainted subjects, the correlation defining expectancy effects was $-.05$. The analogous correlation based on these experimenters' acquainted subjects was $+.69$ ($p = .04$, two-tail). Thus expectancy effects operated for this subsample of experimenters only when their subjects were acquaintances. The effects of acquaintanceship in this analysis were, if anything, underestimated because of the tolerant definition of "acquainted." An experimenter who had only said "hello" to a subject on some earlier occasion was classified as acquainted. Even passing acquaintanceships may be nonrandom in origin, and it may be that willingness to be influenced by the acquaintance is a factor in the origination of the relationship. This selective factor, together with the greater reinforcement value of an acquaintance demonstrated by Kanfer and Karas (1959) and the possibly greater ability of acquainteds to "read" each others' interpersonal signals, may best account for the data reported here.

A subsequent experiment was designed to deal more explicitly with the relationship between acquaintanceship and experimenter expectancy effects (Persinger, 1962). Five male and seven female advanced undergraduate students served as experimenters, and 83 beginning undergraduate students served as subjects in a photo-rating experiment. Half the experimenters were led to expect ratings of success, and half were led to expect ratings of failure of the persons pictured in the photos. Each experimenter contacted both male and female subjects and had prior acquaintanceship with half his subjects.

The results of this study again showed that male experimenters exerted significantly greater expectancy effects upon acquainted than upon unacquainted subjects ($p = .005$, one-tail, $t = 2.64$, $df = 29$). This did not hold for female experimenters, however. In fact, there was a tendency, though not significant, for female experimenters to show greater expectancy effects with unacquainted subjects. The interpretation of acquaintanceship dynamics offered earlier, therefore, may be applicable only to male experimenters, though Silverman (1965) has recently reported a case in which a female experimenter, working in the area of angle estimation, had her hypothesis confirmed by acquainted subjects, her own students, but disconfirmed, and significantly so, by unacquainted subjects.

EXPERIMENTER STATUS

Data in the social sciences may be collected by experimenters differing greatly in the status or prestige ascribed them by their subjects. The distinguished professor, the new instructor, the graduate research assistant, the able undergraduate, all represent points on a scale of status consensually ascribed them by virtue of their position within the academic world. Similar status scaling for potential data collectors in clinical, industrial, military, and survey research settings would not be difficult. The general question of concern here is whether the experimenter's status makes a difference with respect to the results of his research. In an earlier chapter dealing with several experimenter attributes, some evidence was presented that suggested that experimenter status could, in fact, be a partial determinant of the data he obtained from subjects. The more specific question then becomes whether experimenter status is a factor in the operation of experimenter expectancy effects. Do higher status experimenters obtain data more in accord with their expectancy than do lower status experimenters? It was to this question that the following study by Vikan-Kline (1962) was addressed.

Six male faculty members and six male graduate students served as experimenters. Since all were psychologists familiar with research on experimenter expectancy effects, the expectancy-inducing procedure employed in earlier studies could not be used. Instead all experimenters were asked to somehow subtly influence half their subjects to rate photos as successful and influence half their subjects in the opposite direction. There was a total of 85 introductory psychology students who served as subjects. About half were males.

Before any subject was ushered into the research room, the experimenter was informed whether he should try to influence that subject to give ratings of success or of failure. No instructions were given as to how to influence the subjects. Indeed such instructions could not be given, since no one knew how this subtle form of interpersonal influence was mediated. It was hoped that subsequent to the data collection, experimenters' verbal reports of how they tried to influence subjects could be used as a source of hypotheses for further research. Perhaps those who proved to be more successful influencers would be able to tell us of having used different techniques of influence. Although this study differed from others in the program in that experimenters were fully aware of trying to influence their subjects, it was hoped that the mechanisms employed by unintentional influencers might be similar if less overt.

From the subjects' point of view, most of whom knew neither the faculty nor graduate student experimenters, the definition of status was a name card placed on each experimenter's desk. The graduate students had the words "psychology grad. student" written under their names. The faculty experimenters had the words "professor of psychology" written under their names. All experimenters had been rated as to apparent age by a sample of 14 colleagues; the apparent age (late twenties to early thirties) of the Ph.D group members was higher than that of any member of the graduate student group (early to mid-twenties). All experimenters dressed similarly—i.e., white shirts, ties, and jackets.

Results showed that the faculty experimenters were more successful at influencing their subjects to yield the desired data, but only among subjects contacted later in the experiment. In fact, Table 14-7 shows that early in the series of subjects, the faculty experimenters were, if anything, less successful influencers than the graduate student experimenters. Although the graduate students never did influence their subjects much, there was a tendency for them to grow less influential later in the series of subjects con-

TABLE 14—7

Expectancy Effects as a Function of Experimenter's Status

		EXPERIMENTER STATUS			
		Student	Faculty	Difference	p
ORDER OF SUBJECT	First half	−.12	−.88	−.76	NS
	Last half	−.75	+2.42	+3.17	.01
	Difference	−.63	+3.30		
	Two-tail p	NS	.01		

tacted. This trend can be interpreted within the framework of the data presented in the earlier chapter on the effects of early data returns. Having obtained initially "poor" data these experimenters went on to collect "worse" subsequent data. The studies of the early returns effect had been based on samples of graduate student experimenters. The early returns effect may be less likely to occur for faculty experimenters. Possibly they were less threatened by their earlier inability to produce the desired effects and were thus freer to learn from their early subjects what techniques of influence might be most effective.

What techniques were employed? Experimenters tended to employ several. In reading the instructions they tried to emphasize that portion of the description of the photo-rating scale which contained reference to the desired responses. If they were trying to influence positive ratings, they were friendlier in general, smiled more, and were more "accepting." They behaved in cooler fashion when trying to obtain negative ratings. When they obtained responses of the desired type they were more likely to look interested and pleasant, sometimes even smiling. This sort of reinforcement behavior was not so consistent nor so blatant, however, that we can regard this study as one of typical operant conditioning. Unfortunately no differences in self-description of attempted influencing behavior were found between those experimenters who were and those who were not successful influencers.

In general, the results of this study agree quite well with the general literature relating status to influential behavior (Coffin, 1941; Cole, 1955; Goranson, 1965; Homans, 1961; Hovland & Weiss, 1951; Lefkowitz, Blake, & Mouton, 1955; Mausner, 1953, 1954; Mausner & Bloch, 1957; Raven & French, 1958; Wuster, Bass, & Alcock, 1961). For a variety of situations, some of which were summarized in an earlier chapter, people with higher status are more likely to influence others successfully. If we can generalize from this literature and from the experiment reported, it appears that the higher status experimenter, in part because of his greater competence, more markedly affects his subjects' responses into the direction of his hypothesis. We shall have more to say about this formulation a little later. For now it is interesting to note that Pfungst (1911) had also found a relationship between the questioner's status or "air of authority" and the likelihood of his getting the correct response from Clever Hans. Even with a horse as subject, unintentional influence was more likely when the experimenter was more self-assured.

In the experiment by Vikan-Kline the status ascribed the experimenters was confounded with their age, with their actual status, and possibly with the techniques of influence employed. It would be useful to a clearer understanding of the effects of status per se to have an experiment in which the status of the same experimenter was varied experimentally and without his knowledge. The experiment by John Laszlo, referred to in an earlier chapter, employed three experimenters to administer the photo-rating task to 64 subjects. Half the time experimenters were led to expect ratings of success ($+5$), and half the time they were led to expect ratings of failure (-5). Half the subjects in each of these conditions were told that their experimenter was "just a student," and the remaining subjects were led to believe the experimenter was of higher status. The subjects had all been administered Rokeach's (1960) scale of dogmatism. Table 14-8 shows the

TABLE 14—8

Expectancy Effects as a Function of Experimenter's
Status and Subjects' Dogmatism

| | | EXPERIMENTER STATUS | | |
		High	Low	Difference
SUBJECTS'	High	+.83	+1.69	−.86
DOGMATISM	Low	−.88	+ .09	−.97
	Difference	+1.71	+1.60	

magnitude of expectancy effect as a function of the status ascribed to the experimenter and the subject's level of dogmatism. More-dogmatic subjects showed a greater susceptibility to the experimenter's unintended influence, as had been expected ($p < .05$, two-tail). Surprisingly, however, it was the experimenters with lower ascribed status who showed the greater expectancy effects, regardless of the level of their subjects' dogmatism ($p < .05$, two-tail).

Perhaps the subjects of this experiment felt sorry for the experimenter who was "just a student" and, therefore, were more willing to be influenced by him. In any case, it appears from this study that the status effects obtained by Vikan-Kline were probably not due to the labeling of her experimenters as students or as professors. More likely, the different appearance of her high and low status experimenters and possibly differences in the degree of self-assurance shown by her faculty and student experimenters accounted for her findings.

CHARACTERISTICS OF THE LABORATORY

Riecken (1962) has pointed out the potential importance to the results of psychological research of the characteristics of the laboratory in which the experiment is conducted. It seems reasonable to suggest that the room in which the subject is contacted by his experimenter will convey information to the subject about the sort of person the experimenter might be. If a tour is undertaken of research rooms and offices used by graduate students and faculty members in a university setting, great individual differences may be observed. Some rooms look impressive, some look very professional, some very comfortable, some inordinately neat or bare. While room characteristics may reflect the status of the occupant, the occupant may also derive certain characteristics in the eyes of his subjects from the scene in which the experimental contact occurs. The experiment to be reported now, conducted in collaboration with Suzanne Haley, was designed in part to vary characteristics of experimenters by the variation of the scenes in which they contacted their subjects.

A total of 16 experimenters administered the standard person perception task to a total of 72 female undergraduate subjects. Most of the experimenters were males and enrolled either in the Harvard Law School ($N = 9$) or in the Harvard Graduate School in the area of the natural sciences ($N = 7$). Each experimenter expected half his subjects to perceive the photos of faces as quite successful and expected half his subjects to perceive them as quite unsuccessful. In an effort to reduce the overall magnitude of experimenter expectancy effects, a screen was placed between experimenter and subject so that during the course of the data collection they could not see each other. In order to control for experimenter recording errors, subjects recorded their own responses. Finally, in order to eliminate the effects of early data returns, experimenters were not permitted to see the responses made by any of their subjects.

The experimental interactions took place on a single evening in eight different rooms to which experimenters were randomly assigned. Most of these rooms served as offices for psychology graduate students and faculty members. Each room was rated after the experiment by all 16 experimenters on the following dimensions:

1. How *professional* is the room in appearance?
2. How impressive is the room, i.e., what is the *status* of the person who normally occupies it?
3. How *comfortable* is the room, especially from the subjects' point of view?
4. How *disorderly* is the room?

Ratings were made on a scale ranging from zero (e.g., not at all professional) to 10 (e.g., maximally professional). The first three scales were found to be highly intercorrelated (mean rho $= +.78$), and a single scale of status was constructed by summing the scores on all three scales for each room. The mean reliability of these three scales was .89. The scale of disorder showed a correlation of only $+.29$ with the combined status scale and showed a reliability of $+.99$.

Table 14-9 shows the correlations of room status and room disorder

TABLE 14—9

Correlations Between Room Characteristics and Expectancy Effects

Experimenters	No. of Rooms	Status	Disorder
Law students	7	+.64	+.61
Graduate students	6	+.48	+.89
Means		+.58	+.77
Two-tail p		.10	.02

with magnitude of experimenter expectancy effect. Magnitude of expectancy effect was defined, as before, as the difference between mean ratings obtained from subjects believed to be success perceivers and those believed to be failure perceivers. The law student and graduate student experimenters are listed separately because the latter group showed significantly greater expectancy effects that did the former. For both samples of experimenters, the higher the status of the room in which the subject was contacted, the greater were the expectancy effects. This finding adds to our confidence in the hypothesis that, with the exception noted earlier, the higher the status of the experimenter, the greater his unintended influence on his subjects. For both samples of experimenters, the greater the disorder in the experimental room, the greater were the effects of the experimenters' expectancy. We saw in the last chapter that expectancy effects were likely to be greater when the experimenter was perceived as more likable and more personal. The disorderliness of an experimental room may have relevance to this dimension of interpersonal style. None of the rooms were disorderly to a chaotic degree. Within these limits the more disorderly room may be seen as reflecting the "living" style of a more likable and more personal experimenter.

At the conclusion of this experiment, the experimenters were told about the phenomenon of expectancy effects, shown published articles describing some of the earlier studies, and asked to repeat the experiment with a different sample of 86 female subjects. In this repetition of the experiment no screens were placed between the experimenters and their subjects. Half the experimenters were asked to try to avoid the operation of expectancy effects, half were asked to try to maximize them. Within each of these conditions, half the experimenters were told that in the original study they had shown significant unintended influence. The remaining experimenters were told that they had shown no real expectancy effects. Table 14-10 shows the mean increase of expectancy effect for each of the

TABLE 14—10

Increase in Expectancy Effects for Four Kinds of Experimenters

	ORIENTATION TO EXPECTANCY EFFECT		
Influence "History"	Maximize	Minimize	Difference
"Successful" influencer	+1.08	+0.23	+.85
"Unsuccessful" influencer	+1.33	+0.41	+.92
Difference	−.25	−.18	

four experimental conditions from the first study to the replication. Experimenters who were trying to influence their subjects showed significantly greater expectancy bias than did experimenters trying to avoid expectancy effects ($p < .05$, two-tail). (Somewhat surprisingly, however, even the experimenters trying to avoid them showed a tendency to increase their expectancy effects when the screens had been removed, $p < .20$.)

Those experimenters who had been told that they had shown no expectancy bias tended to show a greater increase in expectancy effects than did the experimenters who were told they had shown expectancy bias ($p = .11$, two-tail). Perhaps those experimenters who believed they had biased the results of their first study felt chastised for it and made some special efforts to retard the communication of their expectancy to their second set of subjects, even when they had been instructed to maximize expectancy effects.

When the changes in magnitude of expectancy effect from the original to the replication study were examined separately for law student and graduate student experimenters, an interesting difference emerged. Among law student experimenters, 66 percent of the subjects were more influenced in the second study than in the first ($p = .02$, $x^2 = 6.25$), disregarding the particular experimental conditions. Having learned about subtle communication processes between the time of the first and second samples, young lawyers may have felt it desirable for attorneys to be able to communicate subtly with other people.

Among the graduate students, most of whom were in the sciences, the subtle communication process may have been not only less prized but perhaps even abhorred as a cause of spoiling experiments. Regardless of their experimental condition, these young scientists showed a significant decrease in expectancy effects in the second study. Of their subjects, 73 percent were less biased than were the subjects of their first sample ($p < .05$, $x^2 = 4.54$).

In the second stage of this experiment, laboratory room characteristics were again correlated with magnitude of expectancy effects. As can be seen from Table 14-11, the correlations obtained earlier were not replicated under the conditions of the second phase of the study. Among the law student

TABLE 14—11

Room Characteristics and Expectancy Effects: Second Sample of Subjects

Experimenters	No. of Rooms	Status	Disorder
Law students	7	−.07	+.25
Graduate students	5	−.30	−.90*

* $p < .05$, two-tail.

experimenters the correlations tended simply to go toward zero. Among the graduate students, however, they tended to go into the opposite direction. If it is reasonable to think that our more science-oriented graduate students were trying to avoid the spoiling effects of their expectancy bias, the reversals of the correlations make sense. The higher status and more disordered rooms, then, still predicted the biasing effects of the experimenter's expectancy, only now the science-oriented graduate students expected, and hoped, to obtain data opposite to that which they had been led to expect. Their "real" expectancy may have become that which would avoid the effects of the induced expectancy, and subjects were more inclined to go along with these, now reversed, unintended communications in the higher status, more disordered laboratories.

15

Behavioral Variables

In the last chapter a number of experimenter characteristics were shown to be related to the operation of experimenter expectancy effects. The particular characteristics discussed could all be assessed before the experimenter entered his laboratory. In this chapter, the discussion of experimenter variables will continue, but now the emphasis will be on the experimenter's behavior in his interaction with the subject. Much earlier, in Part I, we saw that various structural variables such as the sex of the experimenter were correlated with the behavior of the experimenter as he interacts with his subjects. The behavioral variables to be discussed in this chapter, therefore, are not independent of the more structural variables discussed in the last chapter, but they do warrant special attention. The communication of expectancy effects to subjects must depend on something the experimenter does. If experimenters of a certain kind, as measured before the experiment begins, exert greater expectancy effects on their subjects, it is very likely due to their behaving differently toward their subjects. The observations of the experimenter's behavior to be discussed now come from two major sources. The first of these sources is the direct observation of experimenter behavior usually by the subject himself. The second of these sources is the observation of experimenter behavior by a variety of observers of sound motion pictures of experimenters interacting with subjects.

DIRECT OBSERVATIONS OF EXPERIMENTER BEHAVIOR

In the chapter dealing with the effects of excessive rewards, some preliminary data were presented which gave some idea of how subjects perceived the behavior of their experimenter. The subjects' ratings of their experimenter's behavior were intercorrelated and cluster analyzed (Fruchter, 1954). In three subsequent experiments, this procedure was repeated.

TABLE 15—1

Cluster Analyses of Four Samples of Subjects' Perceptions of their Experimenter's Behavior

	CLUSTERS			
	I	II	III	IV
	Casual	Expressive	Kinesic	Enthusiastic
Investigators	Pleasant	Friendly	Cluster	Professional
RR,KF,JF,LVK,1960	6.48	3.97	9.10	3.55
RR,GP,LVK,RM,1963				
Sample I	4.43	3.00	-3.77	-0.58
Sample II	1.69	2.33	4.86	0.33
RR,JF,CJ,KF,TS,RW,				
LVK,1964	0.67	6.01	9.12	-2.73
Mean	3.32	3.83	4.83	0.14

Table 15-1 lists the clusters and B-coefficients of the original study as well as those of the later experiments. A B-coefficient greater than 1.5 may be interpreted as indicating a significant cluster, and a B-coefficient of 3.0 indicates a relatively tightly intercorrelated set of variables. The mean B-coefficients for the four studies show that the first three clusters held up quite well, but Cluster IV, composed as it was of only three variables, tended to vanish. The first three clusters may prove to be a useful way of organizing subjects' perceptions of their experimenter's behavior in future studies. They may also be of value in other investigations of interpersonal perception. They have not, however, proved themselves related to magnitude of experimenter expectancy effects in most of the studies carried out.

For five samples of experimenters, their subjects' perceptions of their behavior were correlated with the degree to which the experimenters exerted expectancy effects upon their subjects. Experimenters who obtained data closest to that which they had been led to expect were ranked as most biased. Those who obtained data most unlike that which they had been led to expect were ranked as least biased. Three samples of experimenters employed the photo-rating task in which each experimenter contacted his subjects individually (Rosenthal, Fode, Friedman, & Vikan-Kline, 1960; Rosenthal, Persinger, Vikan-Kline, & Mulry, 1963). The data for the first sample were those presented in the chapter dealing with the effects of excessive reward. A fourth sample of experimenters also employed the photo-rating task, but the experimenter contacted subjects in groups of five (Rosenthal, Friedman, Johnson, et al., 1964). The fifth study employed a standard verbal conditioning paradigm, in which subjects were rewarded with a "good" for the correct choice of pronoun in forming a sentence. Although differential expectancies were created in experimenters leading them, presumably, to emit unintended cues to their subjects, they also were intentionally trying to influence their subjects by their contingent saying of "good." In this experiment, therefore, both intentional and unintentional influence processes were operating (Rosenthal, Kohn, Greenfield, & Carota, 1966). In this study, each experimenter contacted his subjects individually. The average sample size for each of the five experiments was about 20 experimenters and about 100 subjects.

TABLE 15—2

Subjects' Ratings of Their Experimenter's Behavior and Magnitude of Expectancy Effect: Applicable Under All Conditions

Behavior	r	df	p Two-Tail
Businesslike	+.31	105	.005
Expressive voice	+.26	105	.01
Professional	+.25	105	.01
Use of legs	+.22	105	.03

Table 15-2 shows the four variables that were least situation-specific in their correlation with magnitude of expectancy effect. None of the correlations was impressively high, though all held up statistically significantly over five replications. Also heartening was the fact that each of the four variables represented a different cluster. As we would expect, therefore, the intercorrelations among these variables were generally low. The only exception to this was the mean correlation of +.40 between professional and businesslike. Considering these two variables together it appears that for a variety of situations of unintended and intended influence, of individual and group contact with subjects, in person perception and verbal conditioning tasks, the experimenter with the more professional manner is more likely to exert his influence on his subjects. This finding is consistent with those presented in the preceding chapter in which experimenters with higher status, as independently determined, showed greater influencing of their subjects' responses.

An interesting extension of this finding was possible from one of our studies. Subjects' ratings of how professional their experimenter appeared correlated significantly (+.59, $p = .05$, two-tail) with the degree of expectancy effect exerted by the investigators who had trained these experimenters. It may be that more professional-mannered experimenters train their assistants to be more professional-mannered and therefore more influential. In this study, which has already been referred to (Rosenthal, Persinger, Vikan-Kline, & Mulry, 1963), research assistants were randomly assigned to investigators. In the real-life situation, selection factors no doubt combine with training effects to make research assistants and other colleagues more like each other than would be true of any random set of experimenters. This diminished variability due to selection and training may serve to make the results of research coming from any laboratory less variable than we would expect from randomly chosen experimenters, even with techniques of research held constant.

The correlation between experimenter expectancy effects and "expressive voice" suggests that part of the communication to the subject of what it is the experimenter expects him to do is carried by the inflection and tone given to the verbal instructions to subjects. Similarly, the correlation between experimenters' expectancy effects and use of legs suggests that movement or kinesic patterns also play a role in the mediation of experimenter expectancy effects (and in other situations of interpersonal influence as well, as Birdwhistell, 1963, has suggested). Why leg movements in particular should serve this function is not at all clear. All experimenters have been rated by their subjects as showing relatively few movements of any sort. In particular, leg movements are the least frequent of the infrequent movements. Perhaps because they are rare, very minor leg adjustments are more noted by subjects and responded to. Exactly what sort of leg adjustments are employed unintentionally by the experimenters, and what their immediate effect on the subject might be, is a question for further research.

The variables just discussed were those which held across all five samples of experimenters. When we omit the verbal conditioning sample, leaving us only those samples in which experimenter influence was more likely to be purely unintentional and in which the photo-rating task was employed, several additional variables become signficant. Table 15-3 shows these additional characteristics. That experimenters who are perceived as acting more important should show greater unintended influence is related to the more general finding of professional-mannered experimenters' exerting greater influence. The mean correlation of this variable with the variable "professional" for these samples was +.42. For the person perception task, the use of head movements became an additionally possible source of cues to subjects. For these samples the mean correlation between use of head and leg movements was only +.26 suggesting that it was not simply greater movement but differential movement of body areas that served as sources of information to subjects as to what it was the experimenter expected from them. For these samples of experimenters, those who appeared more relaxed (vs. nervous) were more effective expectancy com-

TABLE 15—3

Subjects' Ratings of Their Experimenter's Behavior
and Magnitude of Expectancy Effect: Applicable
When Influence is Unintentional Only

Behavior	r	df	p Two-Tail
Important-acting	+.33	39	.04
Relaxed	+.27	48	.07
Head gestures	+.23	48	.11

municators. Freedom from tension is consistent ($r = +.56$) with the picture of the more professional, higher status experimenter. In addition, however, this finding suggests that the movement patterns we have discussed were not gross, random activity patterns, as we might expect from an anxious experimenter, but rather more finely differentiated patterns of kinesic activity. The mean correlation between "relaxed" and use of head gestures was only —.06.

When we omit from our five samples only that sample in which experimenters contacted subjects in a group situation, the additional variables shown in Table 15-4 emerge as significant. When contact between experimenter and subject is one-to-one, those experimenters showing greater interest influence their subjects more, regardless of which task was employed and regardless of the degree of intentionality of the influence process. The slower-speaking experimenter probably can better give differential emphasis to the instructional proceedings, thereby giving subjects more information from which to "decide" what responses are expected by the experimenter. None of the experimenters are perceived as being very enthusiastic, but those who are somewhat more so, influence their subjects more. This would probably not be true for samples of overenthusiastic experimenters, who

TABLE 15—4

Subjects' Ratings of Their Experimenter's Behavior
and Magnitude of Expectancy Effect: Applicable
Only When Interaction is Dyadic

Behavior	r	df	p Two-Tail
Interested	+.42	84	.001
Slow-speaking	+.28	84	.01
Enthusiastic	+.20	84	.07

would likely be seen by their subjects as not too businesslike or professional. At lower levels of this variable, enthusiasm is related strongly to degree of experimenter interest ($r = +.58$) and significantly, but less strongly, to professional manner ($r = +.35$).

When we consider only those three samples of experimenters who influenced their subjects only unintentionally and in a face-to-face interaction, two additional variables emerge as related to degree of expectancy effects. The more important of these was the variable "personal-impersonal." Most experimenters are rated as neither very personal nor very impersonal, but a bit toward the latter end of the scale. Among these samples of experimenters, those who exerted more unintended interpersonal influence were perceived as significantly more personal ($r = +.46$, $df = 27$, $p = .02$). That more "personal" experimenters should be more influential makes rather good sense, given the face-to-face nature of the interaction in these experiments. A less sensible finding was that experimenters seen as more courteous tended to influence their subjects a little less ($r = -.30$, $df = 27$, $p = .11$). On the average all experimenters were viewed as very courteous, and ratings on this variable showed the lowest variability (S.D. $= 2.2$) of all 27 variables. Given this high general degree of courtesy it may be that extreme courtesy was perceived as aloofness by subjects who were more readily influenced by a more personal experimenter.

In two of the three samples of experimenters we have just been discussing, the interaction between experimenters and subjects was monitored by another experimenter who had trained the data collector. This observer simply sat in on the interaction and rated the experimenter's behavior on the same variables employed by the subjects. Table 15-5 shows the only

TABLE 15—5

Observers' Ratings of Experimenter's Behavior and Magnitude of Expectancy Effect: Applicable Only When Interaction is Dyadic

Behavior	r	df	p Two-Tail
Arm gestures	−.41	18	.08
Behaved consistently	+.39	18	.10
Slow-speaking	+.36	18	.13

three variables that gave promise of showing a relationship with the magnitude of experimenter expectancy effects. Most surprising was the finding that those experimenters who were rated as using fewer arm movements influenced their subjects more. The surprise was due to the generally high

positive correlations among all the movement variables, two of which had
already been shown to be positively related to experimenter expectancy
effects. A tentative explanation of this finding is that, to an external observer of the dyadic interaction, excessive movement by the experimenter
is interpreted as nonpurposive and, therefore, a reflection of both tension
and an unprofessional manner. Behaving consistently in interaction with
subjects is one of the qualifications of a competent, professional experimenter. The obtained correlation of +.39 between behaving consistently
and exerting expectancy effects upon subjects further strengthens the
emerging picture of the more competent, professional experimenter's showing the greater expectancy effects. The slower-speaking experimenter's
greater opportunity to convey information to the subject about the experimenter's expectancy has already been discussed. This hypothesis appears
to hold up regardless of whether the observation of "slow-speaking" is
made by a participant-observer subject or by an external observer. Before
leaving this section, it must be emphasized that these external observations
were made in the situation of face-to-face contact between experimenter and
a single subject and might not hold for the situation in which several subjects are contacted as a group.

Because our external observers were older, more sophisticated, and
more professional, we might be tempted to regard their observations of the
experimenters' behavior as somewhat more "valid" than the observations
made by the participant-observer subjects. At this stage of our knowledge
to make such an assumption seems unwarranted. Perhaps because of their
greater direct involvement and perhaps because of their less sophisticated,
more implicit theories of human interaction, the subjects' perceptions of
their experimenters may be, in a sense, even more valid than the external
observers'. Phenomenologically, the subjects were more really present
during the interaction with their experimenter.

Returning now to subjects' assessments of experimenters' behavior, we
find two additional variables to bear a relation to degree of expectancy effects. In the situation wherein groups of subjects are contacted by an experimenter, greater body movement by the experimenter is associated with the
exertion of greater unintended influence ($r = +.43$, $df = 22$, $p = .04$).
Whereas subtle movements of the legs and head may be sufficient to carry
information to the subject when he is alone in his interaction with the experimenter, the more gross cues of total body movements may be required to
convey equivalent information in the group situation. Individual subjects
may not see the experimenter quite as well in the group situation, and, in
addition, subjects may be emitting significant interpersonal messages to each
other via their movement patterns which serve to distract attention away
from signals emitted by the experimenter.

In the group situation as in the dyadic, subjects rate all their experimenters as very honest. Those experimenters, however, who influenced

their subjects more were seen as somewhat less honest than the less influential experimenters ($r = -.33$, $df = 22$, $p = .12$). In some way, subjects seem able to sense the process of unintended interpersonal influence and evaluate it as undesirable.

In the verbal conditioning study wherein experimenters were in part intentionally attempting to influence their subjects, several additional variables bore a relation to degree of experimenter influence (Table 15-6).

TABLE 15—6

Subjects' Ratings of Experimenter's Behavior and Magnitude of Experimenter Influence: Applicable When Influence is at Least Partially Intentional

Behavior	r	df	p Two-Tail
Loud	−.27	58	.04
Behaved consistently	+.24	58	.07
Important-acting	−.22	58	.10

In this situation, compared to the person perception task employed in the other samples, all experimenters were very active. They talked ("good") during the process of the subjects' responding, whereas in the person perception studies, experimenters served only as recorders during the data production phase. Under these conditions of experimenters' fairly obvious attempts to influence subjects' responses, a louder experimenter might have been viewed as a brow-beating influencer who could best be dealt with by negative conformity. The more consistent behavior of the more influential experimenter is in accord with our evolving view of the more effective influencer as the more competent, professional experimenter. The most interesting correlation may be the negative relationship between experimenter's influence and the degree to which he acts importantly. This relationship is opposite to that obtained under conditions of unintended influence. When the experimenter has already assumed the role of important reinforcer of desired responses, the still more important-acting experimenter may be seen as overbearing rather than simply important or high status. The "overinfluencer," the experimenter who seems to push too hard, may be a less successful influencer than the more modest, professional experimenter who more quietly communicates his wishes to his subjects. For this sample of experimenters the correlation between "loud" and "important-acting" was $+.40$ ($p < .005$).

From all the data available based on subjects' perceptions of their experimenters, four dimensions emerge that seem relevant to distinguishing experimenters who are more or less likely to exert the unintended influence of their expectancy upon their subjects:

1. *Professional status.* Experimenters who are more important, professional, businesslike, and consistent exert greater expectancy effects upon their subjects.
2. *Interpersonal style.* Experimenters who are more relaxed, interested, enthusiastic, and personal exert greater expectancy effects upon their subjects, but probably only so long as they maintain a professional manner, and do not permit the experiment to become a "social hour."
3. *Kinesic communication.* Experimenters who employ subtle kinesic signals from the leg and head regions exert greater expectancy effects upon their subjects. These kinesic signals may still be effective at higher levels of overtness if subjects are not paying full attention to the experimenter. However, if the kinesic signals become very obvious, they are likely to lead to a diminution of expectancy effects, because they will detract from the professional demeanor of the experimenter.
4. *Paralinguistic communication.* Experimenters who speak slowly and in an expressive, nonmonotonous tone exert greater expectancy effects upon their subjects. The way in which the experimenter delivers his programmed input (instructions, greeting, leavetaking) probably serves to communicate his expectancy to his subject.

It is through the kinesic and paralinguistic channels of communication that the experimenter may convey the information to the subject as to what responses are expected. The greater professional status of the experimenter who unintentionally influences his subjects more may serve to legitimize for the subject his conformity to the experimenter's expectancy. The more personal interpersonal style of the more influential experimenter may motivate the subject to want to fulfill the status-legitimized expectancy of the experimenter. If the experimenter becomes subtly bored, tense, or distant, the subject may subtly retaliate by disconfirming the experimenter's expectancy, even though it may be perceived as legitimate. If the experimenter lacks professional status in the eyes of the subject, it may be irrelevant that he is interested and personal; he may be viewed as having no right to expect the subject's conformity to his expectancy. If a high status, personal, interested experimenter cannot communicate effectively through the kinesic and/or paralinguistic channels, his influence will fail simply because the subject cannot learn what it is the experimenter really expects him to do. It seems likely that some experimenters communicate more effectively via the kinesic and some via the paralinguistic channels. Similarly, some subjects may be more influenceable simply because they are more accurate decoders of signals sent via the experimenter's particular channel of "choice."

One difficulty with the data based on subjects' perceptions of experimenters' behavior must be emphasized. In all these studies, subjects assessed their experimenter's behavior after they had made their responses for the experimenter. It is possible, then, that those subjects who felt they had been influenced by their experimenter went on to describe their experimenter, not as he was, but as he ought to have been for them to have been influenced by him. If this were the case we would have learned, not what sorts of experimenters influence subjects unintentionally, but rather what sorts of characteristics people ascribe to experimenters to justify their having been influenced. This too would, of course, be worth knowing. In any case, there is no way out of the dilemma created by asking subjects to assess their experimenters. If we asked subjects to describe their experimenter before they respond for him, the characteristics ascribed might easily serve as a basis for subjects' "deciding" whether or not to accept the influence of the experimenter. The act of having ascribed high status and personalness to an experimenter may be reason enough for subjects to behave as though these attributes had a validity independent of their own assessment. Dissonance reduction cuts both ways.

FILMED OBSERVATIONS OF EXPERIMENTER BEHAVIOR

Useful as it was to have subjects serve as observers of their experimenter's behavior, it became apparent that external observers would be needed to tell us how the experimenters "really" behaved when interacting with their subjects. These external observations would be important in their own right, and, in addition, they could serve to validate or invalidate the hypotheses generated from the subjects' observations of the behavior shown by experimenters exerting greater or lesser expectancy effects.

From sitting in on experimenter-subject interactions it became clear that only a fraction of the behavior of an experimenter could be observed, recalled, and reported. Pfungst's (1911) experience in tracking down the cues that questioners gave to his clever friend, Hans the horse, suggested too that "just watching" might be too coarse a methodological sieve with which to strain out the possibly tiny cues that communicated the experimenter's expectancy to his subject. What seemed most needed was the opportunity to observe the experimenter-subject interaction, the possibility of reobserving it, and, then, observing it again. Sound motion pictures seemed to provide the best permanent record of how the experimenter behaved vis-à-vis his subject. Reference to the sound films taken has already been made in earlier chapters. Now some of the details of the filming procedure are reported (Rosenthal, Persinger, Mulry, Vikan-Kline, & Grothe, 1962).

There were five different samples of experimenters whose interactions with their subjects were filmed. All had in common that they employed the photo-rating task but differed in the specific hypotheses to which the studies were addressed. Not including an analysis of the films, the substantive results of these studies have been reported in the appropriate chapters of this book and, in somewhat different form, elsewhere (Rosenthal, Persinger, Mulry, Vikan-Kline, & Grothe, 1964a; 1964b).

Altogether there were 24 male and 5 female experimenters who administered the photo-rating task to 164 subjects, of whom about 75 percent were females. Of the 29 experimenters, 24 were graduate students enrolled in a course in advanced educational psychology. The other 5 experimenters (2 males, 3 females) were advanced undergraduates enrolled in psychology courses. The subjects were undergraduates enrolled in elementary courses in psychology, education, English, history, and government. For the students enrolled in psychology courses, serving as subjects was a course requirement. Subjects from other courses were encouraged by their instructors to volunteer but were not required to participate. The subject population, therefore, was a mixed group of volunteers and nonvolunteers. Each experimenter contacted from three to eight subjects, and the mean number of subjects per experimenter was between five and six.

Experimental Groups

Table 15-7 presents a summary of the characteristics of each of the five experimental samples, including the number of experimenters and sub-

TABLE 15—7

Characteristics of Five Filmed Experiments

| | EXPERIMENT | | | | | |
	A_1	A_2	B_3	B_4	B_5	Total
Experienced experimenter	yes	yes	no	no	no	mixed
Ego-involved experimenter	no	no	no	yes	yes	mixed
Subjects' sex	mixed	mixed	female	female	male	mixed
N of experimenters	4	6	7	8	4	29
N of subjects	23	37	40	48	16	164
N of filmed interactions	15	24	20	22	10	91

jects involved in each and the number of dyadic interactions that were filmed. A description of the five experimental groups follows.

Group A₁. These experimenters had served as experimenters in an earlier study (Rosenthal, Persinger, Vikan-Kline, & Mulry, 1963). In that experiment some experimenters had been led to expect *either* ratings of success or of failure from their subjects. In the present study, those experimenters who had earlier been led to expect mean photo ratings of +5 were led to expect mean ratings of −5. Those experimenters earlier led to expect ratings of −5 were now led to expect ratings of +5.

Group A₂. These experimenters had also served as experimenters in an earlier study (Persinger, 1962). Some had been in a +5 expectancy condition, others in a −5 expectancy condition. In the present study, these experimenters were led to expect that some of their subjects would give photo ratings of +5, whereas other subjects would give photo ratings of −5. This condition and the preceding one had in common the fact that the experimenters had served as data collectors before in the same task. On the average, these experimenters had contacted about six subjects in their earlier data collection. The subjects contacted by these experimenters had all seen the photos to be rated when they were part of a standardization group. In the standardization study, subjects were shown the photos in their classrooms by means of an opaque projector.

Group B₃. These experimenters had not served before in the role of data collector. Each experimenter's group of subjects was divided into thirds. For the first third of his subjects contacted, each experimenter was given no expectation as to the photo ratings likely to be obtained from his subjects. The second third of these subjects were contacted with half of the experimenters led to expect +5 and half led to expect −5 ratings. For the final third of the subjects, each experimenter was led to expect ratings opposite to those he had expected from the second third of his subjects. All subjects in this group were females.

Group B₄. This group was identical with the just preceding group except that when their expectations of +5 or −5 data were induced, these experimenters were told that the "prediction" of subjects' ratings depended on the experimenter's following instructions and proper experimental procedure. This sentence was intended as a very mildly ego-involving manipulation. All subjects in this group were also females.

Group B₅. This group was identical with the one just preceding except that all the subjects were males rather than females. For all groups, the experimental manipulation of experimenters' expectancies was as follows:

According to several personality tests we have given the (next) subject(s), we are able to predict how they will rate the photos.[1] Some of these subjects tend to rate the photos, on the average, extremely high; and some tend to rate them, on the average, extremely low. The (next) subject(s) that you will run should average a +5 (or −5) which is a pretty high (or low) average.

The experimenters serving in groups B_3, B_4, and B_5, were assigned to these groups at random. Within all groups subjects were randomly assigned to their experimenters.

The Filming Procedure

All experimenters contacted all subjects in the same experimental room. This room was very large, measuring about 50 by 20 feet. Experimenters and subjects sat near the entrance to this room near one of the 20-foot walls. Their chairs were arranged so that they would be partially facing each other and partially facing the far 20-foot wall. At a point about 10 feet from this far wall a sound-insulated wall was constructed, shortening the experimental room and creating a smaller room for the placement of a camera.

A Bach Auricon Pro-600 sound movie camera employing Kodak Tri-X Reversal Film, tripod-mounted, and equipped with a Pan Cinor "zoom lens" was the recording instrument. The camera was focused on the experimenter and subject some 30 feet distant through an 8 by 8 inch double-glassed window built into the specially erected wall. This window was equipped with a wooden shutter which was operated from the observation room. In the experimental room the window was camouflaged by a glass-front, false-backed bookcase containing both books and old empty picture frames. These frames were intended to simulate the frame of the observation window and to give the impression that old frames were simply being stored in the old bookcase.

A microphone, connected to the camera audio system, was concealed in the false motor case of an 8-inch electric fan fastened to the ceiling directly above the table at which the experimenter and subject sat. The coaxial cable connecting the microphone to the camera equipment was made to appear as an extension cord from the fan to a wall socket. This was accomplished by connecting a false cable between the point where the true cable entered the camera room wall and a nearby wall socket.

In order to provide a system of communication between investigators in the camera room and those controlling the flow of subjects and experimenters, two army surplus field telephones were used. One telephone was located in the camera room and was positioned in such a way that the

[1] For the ego-involving manipulation, the following sentence was inserted here: "That is, if the experimenter follows his instructions and proper experimental procedure."

camera operator was able to manipulate the camera and telephone at the same time. The other telephone was located in a small room off the subjects' waiting-room area, and both the telephone operator and the telephone were concealed from the subjects' vision and hearing.

For the purpose of testing the success of the camouflaging of the camera and microphone, a number of graduate students and faculty members sat in the chairs intended for experimenters and subjects, and tried to locate the camera and microphone. None were able to do so. When permitted to approach within a few feet of the window, however, they were able to see the camera through the window if the window shutter was fully open. For this reason, a number of tables were placed between the experimental chairs and the observation window so that if an experimenter wandered around the room between subjects, he could not approach too close to the window.

As it turned out, few experimenters left their chairs, and none came close to the window. Out of the 91 experimenter-subject interactions filmed, in whole or in part, there were 4 or 5 subjects whose eyes dwelled on the bookcase long enough to make us fear their suspicions. When this occurred, the camera operator telephoned the subject router to conduct a postexperimental interview with that subject. These interviews suggested that while subjects were suspicious that the real intent of the experiment was being withheld, none hinted at a suspicion of being observed. Following these instances of overattention to the bookcase that camouflaged the window, we watched for an increased rate of looking at the bookcase by subsequent subjects. We could detect no such increase. Of course, had experimenters and subjects been aware that they were being observed, their behavior in the brief data-collecting interaction would no doubt have been affected.

All experimenters contacted all their subjects at a single sitting. The film capacity of the camera was such that not all the dyadic interactions could be filmed. Systematic sampling of the interactions was undertaken with an effort made to film the contact with one subject from the first third, one from the second third, and one from the final third of subjects contacted by each experimenter. This resulted in a good, though not perfect, distribution of subjects contacted by the experimenter with a +5, a −5, or no expectancy.

The experimenter was the focus for the camera, and virtually every frame shows his or her face and trunk. Most of the time the subject's face and trunk were also on camera, but whenever the camera "zoomed" in for a tighter close-up of the experimenter, the subject could not be seen. Because of the finding from subjects' observations of their experimenter that leg movements might be important sources of cues, the camera moved back from time to time so that full length pictures of the experimenter and subject could be obtained.

Most of the 91 interactions were filmed in their entirety, but sometimes the film ran out before the experimenter could finish obtaining the
photo ratings from the last subject scheduled to be filmed. Sometimes, too,
an experimenter was very slow, or a subject was, so that to film the entire
interaction would have meant losing the subsequent interaction with a subject of the opposite expectancy. Since one of the main reasons for this filming was to learn what experimenters did differently in their interaction with
subjects from whom they expected different ratings, very lengthy interactions were interrupted. Sometimes, for example, an experimenter would
make small talk before or after recording the "face sheet" data from the
subject. Such small talk was sometimes not filmed. When subjects were
very slow in making their ratings, the rating period was sometimes interrupted. There was good reason to believe that the communication of the
experimenter's expectancy occurred before the subject made his first response, the evidence for this to come in the next chapter. Therefore, inter-
rupting the rating period was felt to be particularly preferable to losing the
prerating period with another subject.

A Preliminary Analysis

There were 15 experimenters for whom films were available of their
interaction with subjects for whom they had been given no expectancy.
Experimenters' behavior in interaction with these subjects, therefore, reflected their "typical" behavior in the experiment uncomplicated by the
addition of any formal, uniform experimental hypothesis. To be sure, each
experimenter may have entertained hypotheses about the responses to be
obtained from each of these "practice" subjects, but these idiosyncratic
expectancies were probably fairly randomly distributed among the experimenters.

The five investigators served as the first observers and independently
rated each experimenter contact on the following variables:

1. *Dominance:* the extent to which the experimenter was clearly in
   charge of the situation.
2. *Liking:* the extent to which the observer liked the experimenter.
3. *Activity:* the extent to which the experimenter manifested gross and
   nonessential movements.
4. *Professional:* the extent to which the experimenter showed professional "good form" in his role as experimenter.
5. *Friendly:* the extent to which the experimenter was friendly to his
   subjects.

For each variable, ratings could range from 1 (least possible) to 10
(most possible). No effort was made to be more precise in either the definitions of the variables or the rating scale. At most, these observations of

experimenters' behavior were designed to serve as sources of hypotheses. All five observers had been involved in the collection of this data, and there was no way of assessing the degree to which any of them might not be blind to (1) the experimental condition under which each subject had been contacted, and (2) the magnitude of any experimenter's expectancy effect defined by the difference between data obtained from subjects under each condition of expectancy. All observers reported that "as far as they could tell" they were blind.

TABLE 15—8

Observations of Experimenter Behavior and Magnitude of Expectancy Effect

Behavior	Expectancy Effect	Dominant	Liking	Activity	Professional
Dominant	+.53**				
Likable	+.54**	+.38			
Activity	−.48*	−.44*	+.12		
Professional	+.63***	+.38	+.36	−.65***	
Friendly	−.03	+.12	+.60***	+.59***	−.19

* $p \leq .10$

** $p \leq .05$

*** $p \leq .02$

Table 15-8 shows the correlation between the mean of the observers' ratings and magnitude of expectancy effects as well as the intercorrelations among the ratings. In this analysis, the degree of expectancy effects may safely be regarded as the dependent variable, even though the subjects' responses could be observed, since these observations of the experimenters were all made while practice subjects were being contacted—i.e., no expectancies had as yet been induced in the experimenters.

Greater expectancy effects were shown subsequently by those experimenters who were judged as more professional, more in charge of the situation, less hyperactive, and who were better liked by the observers. The intercorrelations among the ratings suggest that several of these four variables tend to cluster together. Hyperactive experimenters were seen as less professional and less in charge of the experimental situation. These three variables seem to constitute the professional status dimension discussed earlier (mean intercorrelation $= +.50$). Observers' liking of experimenters shows a lower mean correlation with the professional status variables ($+.29$) and may be related to the interpersonal style dimension discussed earlier. Somewhat inconsistent was the finding that the variable of friendliness to subjects, which was correlated significantly with the liking variable, showed no relationship to magnitude of expectancy effects. Friendliness was significantly positively associated for this sample with hyperactivity and negatively, but not significantly, with professionalness. It may be that friendliness as judged by the observers was a hyperfriendliness which interfered with the professional business of the interaction. Some support for the finding, though not necessarily for its interpretation, comes from the recent report by Silverman (1965) that subjects are less responsive to the demands of a possibly too-friendly experimenter.

The possibility that the data presented here might be contaminated by the observers' exposure to criterion information was raised earlier. Some evidence is available, however, which suggests that these observers' ratings may yet have a measure of validity. Subsequent blind observations of the films were carried out by Neil Friedman (1964) and Richard Katz (1964). Some of these observations served to anchor our cruder observations to more precise, uncontaminated ones. Thus, the more "dominant" of this sample of 15 experimenters observed when contacting subjects in the "no expectancy" condition were found to be significantly older and therefore higher status (Vikan-Kline, 1962) ($r = +.54$), less likely to show gross body activity ($r = -.57$), and more expeditious in instructing their subjects ($r = +.40$). More "professional" experimenters were found to make significantly fewer errors in reading their instructions to their subjects ($r = -.57$). More "active" experimenters were found to show more gross body activity ($r = +.63$). Better liked experimenters looked ($r = +.64$) and smiled ($r = +.51$) more at their subjects throughout the experiment. Finally, more "friendly" experimenters smiled more at their subjects during the entire experiment ($r = +.87$). The nature and magnitude of these correlations suggests that the more global and possibly contaminated observations might, after all, be reasonably valid, especially in view of the fact that every one of the correlations with the "anchoring" variables reported was higher than the highest interobserver reliability of the more global variables ($r = +.34$).

In all the subsequent analyses of the filmed sessions, observers were kept uninformed as to the particular expectancy the filmed experimenter held for the responses of any of his subjects. All observations made of the films subsequently were made separately for the three stages of the experimental interactions. The first or preinstructional phase required the experimenter to obtain and record the subject's name, age, sex, marital status, year in school, and major field of study. The second stage required the experimenter to read the standard instructions to his subject. The third stage was that during which the experimenter presented each of the 10 photos to his subjects and recorded their response for each. Very roughly, the first or preinstructional phase lasted only about half a minute; the instruction reading lasted only about a minute; and the rating period about a minute and a half. Table 15-9 shows the mean time in seconds required

TABLE 15—9

Mean Duration of Three Stages of Experimental Interactions

	STAGES			
	Preinstructional	Instructional	Rating	Total
Mean duration	36.4	67.7	94.6	196.1
Standard deviation	8.8	10.8	34.3	42.3
Number of interactions	80	85	65	65

for each stage of the experiment. The standard deviations are also given as well as the number of dyadic interactions upon which each mean and standard deviation are based.

More Molecular Variables

Neil Friedman (1964) and Richard Katz (1964) undertook a very careful analysis of the appearance and behavior of the experimenters. Friedman observed for each experimenter the sort of clothing he wore, how often he smiled and glanced at his subject, how often he exchanged glances with the subject, how accurately he read the instructions to the subject, and how long each phase of the interaction lasted. Katz observed for each experimenter his smiling, glancing, direction of gaze, head and body activity, body position relative to the subject, and the manner of holding the stimulus photo during the rating period. For most of the variables, observations were made not only for each of the three stages of the experiment but at many specific points within each of the stages. Therefore, the total number of observational variables involved was well over 200. Two separate analyses were made by both Friedman and Katz; one for the first two samples of experimenters combined (A_1 and A_2) and one for the last three samples of experimenters combined (B_3, B_4, B_5).

From the analyses completed so far of these data (Friedman, 1964; Friedman, Kurland, & Rosenthal, 1965; Katz, 1964; Rosenthal, Friedman, & Kurland, 1965), it appeared that the behavior of the experimenter during the instructional period was the best predictor of the magnitude of his subsequent expectancy effects. The degree to which each subject was influenced by his experimenter's expectancy was defined as follows: When the experimenter's expectancy was for a $+5$ response, the subject's magnitude of influenceability was his mean rating of the photos minus the grand mean photo rating of *all* subjects (not only those who had been filmed) for whom that experimenter had an expectancy for a -5 response. When the experimenter had an expectancy for a -5 response, the subject's "bias" score was his mean photo rating subtracted from the grand mean photo rating of all subjects for whom that experimenter had an expectancy for a $+5$ response.

For just those experimenters of conditions B_3, B_4, and B_5, all of whom were males, all of whom had no prior research experience, and all of whom contacted either male or female subjects but never both, only a single cluster of behaviors, all of them during the instruction period, predicted subsequent expectancy effects. Experimenters showed greater subsequent expectancy effects if they exchanged fewer glances with their subject ($r = -.41$, $p = .02$), read their instructions with fewer errors ($r = -.42$, $p = .02$), and required less time to read the standard instructions, particularly the first short paragraph ($r = -.43$, $p = .02$). The mean intercorrelation of this cluster of variables was $+.37$. This more businesslike, no-nonsense experimenter is just the kind we would expect, on the basis of all the earlier evidence, to be the more effective unintentional influencer (Friedman, Kurland, & Rosenthal, 1965).

The male and female experimenters of conditions A_1 and A_2 had all had prior research experience, and all contacted both male and female subjects. Correlations between these experimenters' behavior and their subsequent expectancy effects were computed separately for male and female experimenters. Among male experimenters, those who exchanged fewer glances with their subjects ($r = -.59$, $p = .02$) and required less time to read the instructions ($r = -.52$, $p < .05$) subsequently showed greater expectancy effects. These findings and the fact that the more unintentionally influential experimenters showed less gross body activity ($r = -.66$, $p < .01$) support still further the hypothesis that more professional experimenters show greater expectancy effects. In this replication, however, there was an unexpected reversal of the relationship between the accuracy of instruction reading and subsequent expectancy effects. Now it was the experimenters who made more errors in reading their instructions who subsequently showed greater expectancy effects ($r = +.65$, $p < .01$). A number of hypotheses were suggested to account for this reversal in terms of the different characteristics of the samples of experimenters, but none were tenable after further analyses (Rosenthal, Friedman, & Kurland, 1965).

Among female experimenters of these same experimental conditions, none of the behaviors during the instruction-reading period predicted significantly the subsequent magnitude of expectancy effect. Compared to male experimenters there was a significant reversal of direction, however, in the correlations between their behavior and their subsequent expectancy effects. Female experimenters who exchanged more glances with their subjects ($r = +.45$) and were slower in reading their instructions ($r = +.36$) showed greater expectancy effects on their subjects' subsequent responses. (There was no relationship between their accuracy in reading the instructions and subsequent expectancy effects.) Although the sample of female experimenters was too small to make much of this reversal, it may be reasonable to expect that female experimenters show more effective interpersonal influence when they are more interpersonally oriented. That would be consistent with those theoretical formulations (Parsons & Bales, 1955) and those summaries of relevant data (McClelland, 1965) that suggest that men function more typically and effectively by a greater stress on task orientation relative to women, who function more typically and effectively by a greater stress on socioemotional orientation. "Average" subjects in "average" experiments may be better able to respond to the subtle cues of experimenters who are playing out their socially expected role behaviors. These subtle biasing cues may tend to be overshadowed and obscured by any behavior that, by its unexpectedness, calls for all of the subject's attention.

More Molar Variables

For the most part, the relatively more molecular observations described above were extremely reliable. The interobserver reliabilities showed a median correlation of over .80, with many of the variables showing nearly perfect (1.00) reliabilities (e.g., accuracy, speed of instruction reading, glancing at subjects). The analysis of all these data is far from complete and they have already shown their value. Yet, the utility of these more molecular variables as predictors of subsequent expectancy effects was somewhat disappointing in view of the relatively few correlations that reached significance out of the hundreds computed. It seemed likely that the more molecular variables were missing qualitative aspects of experimenters' behavior which might have interpersonal communication value. A glance is not just a glance, in interpersonal communication, but rather a friendly glance, a dominating glance, an interested glance, an encouraging glance. Too little is known at the present time about the exact features of a facial expression or a body movement that make one glance or one smile different from another glance or another smile. But ordinary people in everyday life seem able to make these judgments.

It was, therefore, decided to employ a sample of undergraduate students as paradigm observers. As members of the culture, they should be able to make the required judgments, not perfectly, but well enough. The particular judgments they were asked to make were the same global judgments that subjects had been making for some years about their experimenter's behavior. These judgments, made on 20-point rating scales, had proven to be useful; and in any case, it would be good to know whether external observers of an experimenter's behavior could predict his expectancy effect as well as subjects could postdict it. The basic variables were those presented in the chapter dealing with the effects of excessive reward. Four additional variables were employed: "active," "dominant," "important-acting," and "speaks distinctly." The first two were added because they had been employed in the preliminary analysis of the films and had been found promising. The third was added because it had been employed in earlier studies and seemed relevant; the last was added for these analyses.

A total of ten undergraduate students, six females and four males, rated each experimenter's behavior separately for the preinstructional period, the instruction-reading period, and the period in which the subject made his ratings of the level of success of the stimulus person. Three observers (one male, two females) made their ratings while watching the film and hearing the sound track. Four observers (one male, three females) made their ratings while watching the film but without hearing the sound track. Three observers (two males, one female) did not see the film at all but made their ratings solely from listening to the sound track.

The reason for the last two groups of observers was the thought that the meaning of a gesture or a tone might be thrown into bolder relief if it were not cross-referenced by another channel of communication. Single channel (i.e., visual or auditory) judgments could also be examined for discrepancy, and "channel discrepancy" has long been thought to be an important factor in normal and abnormal human communication (Allport & Vernon, 1933), though the evidence for this assumption has been at the anecdotal level (Bateson, Jackson, Haley, & Weakland, 1956; Ringuette & Kennedy, 1964).

Of the 29 experimenters whose interactions with their subjects had been filmed, only 19 (16 males and 3 females) were filmed in interaction both with subjects from whom they expected +5 ratings and with subjects from whom they expected −5 ratings. These 19 experimenters were observed in sessions with 48 subjects (33 females, 15 males) for whom they had one of these two opposite expectancies. We shall consider first the behavior of the experimenter during just the instruction-reading period as a predictor of his subsequent expectancy effects.

The first look was at the interobserver reliability within each of the

TABLE 15—10

Some Median Interobserver Reliabilities Under Three Conditions of Observation of Instructional Behavior

COMMUNICATION CHANNELS

Reliability	Visual plus Auditory (30 Variables)	Visual Only (24 Variables)	Auditory Only (23 Variables)
Lowest	−.12	−.26	−.10
Median	+.28	+.27	+.12
Highest	+.50	+.55	+.32

three conditions of observation. Table 15-10 shows some of the median reliability coefficients (r) of the sets of observers under each condition of observation. For the 30 observations made with access to both communication channels, the highest median reliability obtained was only +.50, and the median of the 30 median reliabilities was only +.28. Because some of the observations were impossible under the other two conditions of observation (e.g., loudness of voice in the absence of sound track) the numbers of reliability coefficients possible for each channel are shown in Table 15-10. In all conditions of observation there were some negative reliabilities. The median reliabilities were similarly depressing, and the maximum reliabilities were reminiscent more of validity than of reliability coefficients.

In spite of these unencouraging findings, the means of the observers' judgments within each condition were correlated with the experimenters' subsequent expectancy effects. The results were surprising. Of the 77 correlations, 17 (or 22 percent) were significant at the .05 level $(r \geq .29)$. The correlations predicting expectancy effects from experimenter behavior were clustered separately within each condition of observation. Table 15-11 shows the variables constituting each of the five clusters obtained. Every variable included in any cluster showed a significant correlation with expectancy effect $(p < .10)$, and each of these correlations is shown in Table 15-11. Table 15-12 shows for each of the five clusters its mean correlation with every other cluster, the strength or unity of the cluster expressed by the mean intercorrelation of the cluster's variables with each other, and the mean correlation of the cluster of behavioral ratings with the magnitude of subsequent expectancy effects.

The most significantly predictive cluster (I) might be labeled as the behavior of the likable-professional as perceived by paradigm observers judging only his visually communicated behavior. The likable-professional was relaxed (not tense), gave an honest visual impression, and was casual ("not pushy") in his approach to his subjects. This constellation of be-

TABLE 15—11

Clusters of Experimenter Instructional Behaviors Predicting Subsequent Expectancy Effects

OBSERVATION CHANNEL

Visual		Auditory		Visual plus Auditory	
Cluster I		Cluster IV		Cluster V	
Relaxed	+.56	Pleasant	−.33	Leg gestures	−.44
Likable	+.46	Honest	−.30	Hand gestures	−.37
Professional	+.45	Expressive voice	−.30	Arm gestures	−.34
Honest	+.40	Active	−.25	Body gestures	−.32
Casual	+.29	Friendly	−.25	Trunk gestures	−.31
		Personal	−.25	Head gestures	−.30
Cluster II		Not acting		Nervous	−.30
Dominant	+.32	important			
Cluster III					
Businesslike	+.33				
Arm gestures not used	+.25				

haviors is just the one we would expect on the basis of (1) our possibly contaminated preliminary analysis, (2) the data available from subjects' perceptions of their experimenter, and (3) the more experimental evidence available from this research program and those of others.

Clusters II and III, based also on the visual channel, strengthen our

TABLE 15—12

Intercorrelations Among Clusters of Experimenter Instructional Behavior

Clusters	II	III	IV	V	Mean r Intracluster	Mean r Expectancy Effects
I	+.13	+.19	.00	−.29	+.65	+.43
II	—	+.03	+.12	+.04	+1.00	+.32
III		—	−.10	−.46	+.51	+.29
IV			—	+.07	+.59	−.28
V				—	+.51	−.34

overall impression of the competent, professional experimenter as the one who shows greater expectancy effects, although both these clusters are independent of Cluster I and of each other. Cluster IV, based as it was on only the sound track of experimenters reading the same written instructions to subjects, reflected the behavior of a pleasant, expressive-voiced experimenter. Such experimenters tended to show less expectancy effects, perhaps because such a tone made the interaction into more of an amiable social situation rather than a more task-oriented one. It was suggested earlier that such a too-friendly tone may interfere with the unintentional influence exerted by the experimenter. Cluster V was a "nervous activity" cluster; and behaviorally tense, hyperactive experimenters showed less expectancy effect. Such experimenters could hardly be viewed as professional and competent, and we have seen that lacking this perception of the experimenter, subjects are unlikely to be influenced by their experimenter's expectancy. The correlation between this nervous activity cluster and the "likable-professional" cluster was not high ($r = -.29$), so that it was possible to be professional and yet nervous. Such experimenters probably were also unable to influence their subjects' responses unintentionally. The nervous hyperactivity would probably interfere with the subject's decoding of the unintended message by providing a context of excessive "noise" or distracting inputs.

One of the reasons for having observers judge the behavior of experimenters using only a single channel of communication was to learn about the effects of channel discrepancy. Of the total of 30 variables on which behavior was judged there were 17 for which judgments were available from both groups of single-channel judges. Relaxed-nervous, for example, could be judged from silent films or sound track. The remaining 13 variables could be judged from only one of the two single-channel conditions of observation (e.g., expressive voice or leg activity).

For each of the 17 variables judged from both visual cues alone and from auditory cues alone, a channel discrepancy score was computed simply by subtracting the mean rating assigned an experimenter in the auditory channel from the mean rating assigned that experimenter in the visual channel. A large discrepancy score on any variable simply means that the experimenter is rated higher on that variable in the visual than in the auditory modality. Table 15-13 shows those 7 of the 17 possible correlations between magnitude of channel discrepancy and magnitude of subsequent expectancy effects that reached a $p < .10$. All seven of these variables were highly intercorrelated, forming a cluster with a mean intercorrelation of $+.52$. This cluster is very similar to the likable-professional cluster reported earlier when the visual channel was considered by itself rather than in relation to the auditory channel. Apparently the most effective unintentional influencer must "look" like a likable-professional but must, in addition, *not* sound like one, perhaps because a too likable tone of voice while reading the instructions would detract from the task orientation of the interacting

TABLE 15—13

Visual Minus Auditory Channel Discrepancies in Experimenter Instructional Behavior and Subsequent Expectancy Effects

Behavior	r	p
Likable	+.44	.003
Relaxed	+.44	.003
Pleasant	+.42	.005
Honest	+.41	.007
Professional	+.33	.03
Casual	+.28	.07
Friendly	+.26	.08
Mean	+.37	.01

dyad. The subject is watching the experimenter, usually, while the instructions are being read, but the subject's main task is to hear and understand these instructions.

These channel discrepancies in behavior may have a very different meaning depending on the sex of the experimenter and the sex of the subject (Rosenthal, 1965c). Future work will be done in this area, but for now it may be interesting to see the effects of the subject's sex in the channel discrepancies of these primarily male experimenters. The point biserial correlations between the sex of the subject and the degree to which the

TABLE 15—14

Visual Minus Auditory Channel Discrepancies in Experimenter Instructional Behavior and Sex of Subject

Behavior	r	p
Dominant	+.53	.0001
Enthusiastic	+.35	.01
Interested	+.26	.06
Personal	+.25	.07
Professional	+.22	.10
Mean	+.32	.02

experimenter shows a given behavior more in the visual than in the auditory channel were computed. For this analysis interactions with 57 subjects were available, and there were 17 possible correlations. Table 15-14 shows the five correlations with $p \leq .10$. All five of these variables were highly inter-correlated, forming a cluster with a mean intercorrelation of $+.63$. These experimenters showed greater "dominant-enthusiasm" in the visual than in the auditory mode when interacting with male subjects. When interacting with female subjects, they showed their enthusiastic-dominance relatively more in the auditory than in the visual channel. One wonders whether such a relationship may have relevance not only for a better understanding of the social psychology of the psychological experiment but also for a better understanding of interpersonal communication in general.

At least we know that the results obtained and just reported are not a unique function of the instruction-reading situation in a psychological ex-periment. Channel discrepancies of behavior in the half minute of the pre-instructional period were also computed. This was that brief and more informal period during which the experimenter asked for and recorded the subject's name, age, and other such data. Channel discrepancies were again correlated with the sex of the subject. For this analysis 50 subjects were available, and again there were 17 possible correlations. Table 15-15 shows the seven correlations with $p \leq .10$. Again these variables were highly inter-correlated, and the cluster's mean intercorrelation was $+.45$. Although this cluster of behaviors was not the same as that found during the instruction reading period, it is similar enough that it may be regarded also as a "dominant-enthusiasm" cluster. Even during this brief period experimenters showed greater enthusiastic-dominance in the visual than in the auditory

TABLE 15—15

Visual Minus Auditory Channel Discrepancies in Ex-perimenter Preinstructional Behavior and Sex of Subject

Behavior	r	p
Dominant	+.36	.02
Active	+.34	.03
Relaxed	+.31	.03
Enthusiastic	+.30	.04
Interested	+.27	.06
Businesslike	+.26	.07
Friendly	+.24	.10
Mean	+.30	.04

mode when contacting male subjects, whereas with female subjects they showed relatively greater enthusiastic-dominance in the auditory channel.

When channel discrepancy in the preinstructional period was employed as a predictor of subsequent expectancy effects, the results were less impressive than when channel discrepancy in the instruction-reading period had been employed. Still, the results were consistent, if less striking. Experimenters who showed greater interest in the visual than in the auditory mode exerted greater subsequent expectancy effects ($r = +.30$, $p = .06$). Experimenters who showed a more businesslike manner in the auditory than in the visual channel showed greater expectancy effects ($r = -.30$, $p = .06$). Although these correlations were not very significant statistically, they suggest an early form of the pattern which emerges more clearly in the instructional period. (The correlation between these variables was $+.11$, which makes the multiple correlation $+.45$, $p = .02$.)

When speaking of "channel discrepancy" the "discrepancy" has always been taken by subtracting the mean rating of an experimenter's behavior judged only from the sound track from the mean rating of his behavior judged only from the silent film. Therefore, channel discrepancy has been a directional discrepancy. In clinical lore the importance of communication channels' carrying opposite messages does not depend on a given direction of difference. It seemed interesting to see whether disregarding the direction of channel discrepancy would teach us something about the unintentional influence of an experimenter's expectancy. We turn now to the correlation between the absolute discrepancy between the visual and auditory channels, sign of difference disregarded, and the magnitude of expectancy effects.

Considering the experimenter's behavior during the brief preinstructional phase we find, in Table 15-16, that channel discordance in three behavioral variables (out of a possible 17) significantly predicted subsequent expectancy effects. Regardless of which modality, the visual or the auditory, conveyed the greater interest, enthusiasm, or professionalness of

TABLE 15—16

Absolute Channel Discordance in Preinstructional Behavior and Subsequent Expectancy Effects

Behavior	r	p
Interested	+.46	.005
Enthusiastic	+.41	.01
Professional	+.35	.03
Mean	+.41	.01

manner, the greater the disagreement between channels, the greater the subsequent expectancy effects. Perhaps such channel discordance so confuses the subject, perhaps even without his awareness, that he tries especially hard to "read" the unintended messages from the experimenter so that he may better learn what really is expected of him. The particular variables shown in Table 15-16 were well clustered, with a mean intercorrelation of $+.53$.

When we turn to the instructional period for an examination of the absolute channel discordance as a predictor of expectancy effects we again find three significant predictors. Table 15-17 shows them, and we note

TABLE 15—17

Absolute Channel Discordance in Instructional Behavior and Subsequent Expectancy Effects

Behavior	r	p
Relaxed	$-.37$	.01
Enthusiastic	$-.36$	.02
Honest	$+.26$	.08

that two of them, "relaxed" and "honest," were also significant predictors when their algebraic channel discrepancies were considered. The correlation between the algebraic and absolute discrepancy for the variable "honest" was $+.65$, so perhaps this variable does not mean anything different from what we have seen before. However, the correlation between algebraic and absolute channel discrepancy for the variable "relaxed" was only $-.07$, so in this case we do have a different variable. During the instruction period experimenters who show less discordance of the visual and verbal channels in their tension level and in their enthusiasm level go on to exert greater expectancy effects. (The correlation between these variables was only $+.18$.) Perhaps during the instruction period, too much channel discordance, of a less systematic sort than is implied in algebraic discrepancy, confuses the subject at the very moment he is to receive the experimenter's unintended cues to what the "right" answer might be. Unsystematic channel discordance may be a good way to get a subject to be attentive, but when it serves as background to unintended specific communications, it may serve as just so much noise.

Although we have discussed the question of channel discrepancies in the preinstructional behavior of the experimenter, we have not yet considered the preinstructional behaviors in each of the three conditions of ob-

TABLE 15—18

Some Median Interobserver Reliabilities Under Three
Conditions of Observation of Preinstructional Behavior

COMMUNICATION CHANNELS

Reliability	Visual plus Auditory (30 Variables)	Visual Only (24 Variables)	Auditory Only (23 Variables)
Lowest	−.16	−.12	−.23
Median	+.16	+.20	+.08
Highest	+.39	+.41	+.45

servation that predict subsequent expectancy effects. Table 15-18 shows the highest, midmost, and lowest median reliability coefficient (r) of the sets of observers within each condition of observation. As in the case of the interobserver reliabilities of the rating of instructional behavior, the correlations are so low that one wonders how such variables can be predictive of anything. It should be kept in mind that the mean of the observers' ratings is a much more stable estimate of the experimenter's behavior than is the rating of any single observer. Individual observer idiosyncrasies are probably canceled out in taking the mean observation as the definition of the experimenter's behavior.

In the preinstructional period none of the behavior observations made from the sound track alone were predictive of subsequent expectancy effects. Table 15-19 shows for the visual channel and for the visual-plus-auditory channels the clusters of behaviors predicting subsequent expectancy effects. All the variables shown predict expectancy effects at $p < .10$, and the magnitude of the predictive correlation is given for each variable. Table 15-20 shows the intercorrelations among the five predictive clusters which emerged, the mean intercorrelation of the variables forming a cluster (cluster unity), and the mean correlation of each cluster of behaviors with subsequent expectancy effects. Although the preinstructional behavior of the experimenter showed five clusters predicting expectancy effects, just as did the experimenter's instructional behavior, the clusters were not quite the same, nor were they composed of as many variables. (The comparison is between Tables 15-19 and 15-11.)

In the visual mode, compared to his instructional behavior, the experimenter's preinstructional behavior was as relaxed and likable but less professional, less dominant, and less "honest," or scrupulous. The preinstructional period was less clearly defined for the experimenter than the instruction-reading period, and the general impression is that the more ef-

TABLE 15—19

Clusters of Experimenter Preinstructional Behaviors
Predicting Subsequent Expectancy Effects

OBSERVATION CHANNEL

Visual		Visual Plus Auditory	
Cluster I		Cluster IV	
Likable	+.39	Relaxed	+.42
Relaxed	+.34	Dominant	+.31
Personal	+.30	Active	+.29
Enthusiastic	+.24		
		Cluster V	
Cluster II		Leg gestures	−.31
Honest	−.25	Trunk gestures	−.25
Cluster III			
Not acting			
important	−.37		

fectively influential experimenter is less formal during this less formal stage
of the experiment than he will later become. In the visual-plus-auditory
mode the more unintentionally influential experimenter again showed his
lack of tension as well as showing that he was very much in charge of the
situation.

The overall impression we have of the behavior of the experimenter

TABLE 15—20

Intercorrelations Among Clusters of Experimenter
Preinstructional Behavior

Clusters	II	III	IV	V	Mean r Intracluster	Mean r Expectancy Effects
I	−.06	−.26	+.25	.00	+.54	+.32
II	—	+.36	.00	+.21	1.00	−.25
III		—	−.30	+.34	1.00	−.37
IV			—	−.17	+.46	+.34
V				—	+.42	−.28

who shows greater expectancy effects is that he is professional, competent, likable, and relaxed, particularly in his movement patterns, while avoiding an overly personal tone of voice that might interfere with the business at hand. When his interactions with the subject are not highly programmed by the design of the experiment, he relaxes his professional demeanor a bit, and perhaps engages his subject's attention more by showing discrepancies between his movement patterns and his tone of voice. When his interactions with the subject are more formally programmed, he becomes more formal in manner and sends more congruent messages through his movement patterns and his tone of voice.

The behavioral variables considered in this chapter, and the more structural variables considered in the last chapter, which are predictive of experimenter expectancy effects, may not be so different from the variables that predict other forms of interpersonal influence. Perhaps unintended social influence processes are governed by the same principles that govern intentional interpersonal influence. The major differences between intentional and unintentional influence processes may turn out to be associated with the system of communication or signal transmission employed. When the influence is intentional, as in studies of compliance, persuasive communication, or verbal conditioning, the signals of the influencer are both highly programmed and overt. When the influence is unintentional, the signals of the influencer are less overt and probably occur in a context of greater noise. In the next chapter we shall discuss the problem of signal transmission in the experimental situation.

16

Communication of
Experimenter Expectancy

There is now a good deal of evidence bearing on the question of what structural and behavioral characteristics of the experimenter tend to increase the operation of expectancy effects. But perhaps the most important question of all remains to be answered. That question, of course, is how does the experimenter inform his subject what it is he expects the subject to do? Data from several studies including the leisurely analysis of films suggests that no gross errors are responsible. Experimenters do not tell their subjects in words or even in any obvious gestures what it is they expect from them. Errors of observation and of recording, although they do occur, occur so rarely as to be trivial to any explanation of experimenter expectancy effects.

INTENTIONAL COMMUNICATION OF EXPECTANCIES

If experimenters were asked to communicate their expectancy to their subjects we might hope that the cues they employ intentionally might be simple exaggerations of cues employed unintentionally in the real experimental situation. As a first step, however, it would be necessary to learn whether observers could accurately "read" the expectancy intentionally being communicated by the experimenter.

Six graduate students and one faculty member of our research group served as the subjects of the first study. One of the graduate students administered the photo-rating task to the remaining subjects. The experimenter chose a number between −10 and +10 as the expectancy he would try to communicate to the subjects. The subjects' task was to try to "read" the experimenter's expectancy. Table 16-1 shows the results of two such attempts to read an intentionally communicated expectancy. Observers' ac-

TABLE 16—1

Subjects' "Readings" of Experimenter Expectancies

EXPERIMENTER'S EXPECTANCY

	−4.0	+3.5
	+7.0	+5.5
	−2.0	+4.5
	−2.0	+4.0
	−2.0	+4.0
	−3.0	+3.5
	−3.0	+3.0
Means	−0.83	+4.08

curacy was significantly better than chance ($p = .007$, one-tail). Only 1 of the 12 judgments was seriously in error.

The observers were unable to verbalize the source of the cues they had employed in making what were regarded as uncanny judgments. The possibility of extrasensory perception was somewhat lightly raised, and this possibility was tested. A standard deck of Rhine ESP cards was employed, but in the short runs employed no evidence for ESP emerged. No extended series of runs was required, since the ESP effect would have to emerge as significantly as our "reading" of experimenter cues if it were to serve as an explanation of these "readings." Subsequent conversation with J. B. Rhine (April 4, 1961) revealed that he did not feel that ESP was a strong enough or predictable enough phenomenon to account for the communication of experimenters' expectancies to their subjects.

The study just described was not, of course, a fair test of our general hypothesis. It included only a single experimenter who was free to choose expectancies that might well have been biased in some way. It became necessary, therefore, to employ more experimenters and to assign their expectancies at random. In addition, in order to permit more leisurely study of the communication of cues, a sound film record of the experimenters' behavior was desirable.

The first film made was of three experimenter-subject interactions. Expectancies between −10 and +10 were randomly assigned to experimenters who tried to influence their subjects to rate the standard photos in the desired way but without being too obvious about it. This film was viewed by 52 observers who tried to read the experimenters' expectancy and state their reason for their judgment. Three of the observers were faculty members, one was a representative of a publishing firm who happened by, and the rest were graduate students from a midwestern and an eastern university.

The second film was of five experimenter-subject interactions. Expectancies were again assigned at random. This film was viewed by 11 observers. One observer was a faculty member, one a wife of a faculty member, and the rest were graduate students. Three of these had served as observers of the first film; otherwise there was no overlap of observers for the two films.

Table 16-2 shows for each film the experimenter's randomly assigned

TABLE 16—2

Observers' "Readings" of Experimenters' Randomly Assigned Expectancies

EXPECTANCIES

	Experimenters'	Guessed (Mean)
Film I	−10.0	−4.6
	−1.0	+1.3
	+2.0	+2.5
Film II	+7.0	+6.1
	+5.0	−1.5
	+3.0	−0.4
	−9.0	−5.3
	−9.0	−2.2

expectancy and the mean "reading" of that expectancy by the observers. For each film, a correlation (rho) was obtained between each observer's "reading" of the experimenters' expectancies and the actual expectancies. The median of the 52 correlations thus obtained for film I was $+.88$ ($p < .00001$). The median of the 11 correlations obtained for film II was $+.72$ ($p < .001$). These results leave little doubt that observers can "read" experimenters' expectancies with great accuracy, at least when these are being deliberately communicated.

It might be expected that when observers can agree so well on experimenters' expectancies they would agree on the channel by which these expectancies were communicated. This was not at all the case, however. The numerous hypotheses advanced by the observers showed little agreement among themselves. Two major dimensions emerged, however, along which differences in hypotheses could be ordered: temporality and sense modality. Thus about half the hypotheses emphasized the experimenters' reaction to subjects' responses. For these observers, expectancy communication occurred only after subjects began responding and followed a differential reinforcement paradigm. For the other observers, expectancy communication occurred before the subject made even his first response. Within each of these schools of thought or observation there were some observations favoring a visual-kinesic mode and some favoring an auditory-paralinguistic mode of communication.

Table 16-3 summarizes the specific observations of behaviors that were

TABLE 16—3

Differential Reinforcers of Desired and Undesired Responses

REINFORCERS

Positive	Negative
Smiling	Head shaking
Head nodding	Raising eyebrows
Looking happier	Looking surprised
Looking more interested	Looking disappointed
Recording response more	Repeating response
vigorously	Pencil tapping
	Holding photo up longer
	Tilting photo forward
	"Throwing" photo down

hypothesized by our "reinforcement theorists" to increase the likelihood of desired responses and decrease the likelihood of undesired responses. Observers agreed that no two experimenters seemed to show the same patterns of differential reinforcement. In addition, it was their impression that the same experimenter employed different patterns as a function of the sex of subjects.

Those observers who felt that experimenters communicated their expectancies to their subjects before subjects began responding produced two types of hypotheses. The first of these emphasized the manner of delivering instructions about the rating scale subjects were to use. When experimenters mentioned the anchoring points in the region of the expected data they were said to use greater emphasis, to stammer, to speak more slowly, to speak faster, to make more reading errors, and to point a little longer at the region of the scale including the desired data. The second type of hypothesis held by these observers emphasized the general atmosphere created by experimenters even before they came to the critical section of the instructions.

Specific examples included the creation of a "positive" tone by experimenters who expected positive ratings and a "negative" tone by those who expected negative ratings. These observers also reported greater looking at subjects by experimenters who expected positive ratings and greater eye avoidance by experimenters who expected negative ratings. Table 16-4 gives a summary of the six most common "theories" of expectancy communication on the basis of the three major dimensions that differentiate them.

TABLE 16—4

Six Theories of Expectancy Communication

DIMENSIONS OF THEORIES

Theories	Temporality	Modality	Specificity
I	After subject's response	Visual	Specific cues
II	After subject's response	Auditory	Specific cues
III	Before subject's response	Visual	Specific cues
IV	Before subject's response	Auditory	Specific cues
V	Before subject's response	Visual	General atmosphere
VI	Before subject's response	Auditory	General atmosphere

Additional data, bearing this time on the unintentional communication of experimenter expectancies, were kindly made available by Karl Weick (1963). He employed two experimenters, each of whom administered the photo-rating task to five introductory psychology students. One experimenter was led to expect positive ratings; the other was led to expect negative ratings. The entire experiment was conducted in front of Weick's class in experimental social psychology. Table 16-5 shows the results of this study. The experimenter expecting higher ratings obtained higher mean ratings than did the experimenter expecting lower ratings ($t = 2.93, p = .01$, one-tail). For one of the experimenters, the classroom observers were unable to offer any clear hypotheses. For the other experimenter, the observers felt that when he obtained expected data he recorded them very rapidly but that he was slow to record unexpected responses. In addition, he was observed to "really stare" at his subjects in response to unexpected data. For one of these experimenters, then, the cues observed when the expectancy was communicated unintentionally were similar to those observed (at least by holders of Theory I, see Table 16-4) when the communication was deliberate.

The data presented so far which suggest that small cues from the ex-

TABLE 16—5

Weick's Classroom Demonstration of Experimenter
Expectancy Effects

EXPECTANCY

	+5	−5
	+2.20	−1.35
Subjects'	+0.50	+1.10
Mean	+0.75	−1.35
Ratings	+1.85	−0.65
	+0.60	−0.25
Mean	+1.18	−0.50

perimenter serve to communicate his expectancy to the subject are not without precedent. In an earlier chapter we discussed some of these now classic cases. There was Clever Hans (Pfungst, 1911), who could read the experimenter's expectancy from his head, eyebrow, and nostril movements. There was the phenomenon of unintentional whispering to subjects in ESP research (Kennedy, 1938). A short time later Kennedy (1939) suggested that involuntary movements by experimenters in ESP research might provide subjects with kinesthetic, tactual, auditory, and visual cues to the expected response. Much earlier, Moll (1898) had discussed Wernicke's warning of the involuntary cueing by muscle tremors of subjects in experiments in clairvoyance. The reading by subjects of cues in ESP research could apparently occur without their awareness and even at normally subthreshold values of illumination (Miller, 1942).

There have been several serious investigations of the dramatic cue-reading ability of apparently hypersensitive individuals. Foster (1923) summarized five experiments designed to test the ability of a "sensitive" who could locate hidden materials by means of a divining rod. The results of these studies suggested that when all possible sources of cues from the experimenter and from observers were removed, the subject was no longer able to locate hidden items such as watches, coins, and water mains. The eliminated cues included those of the visual-kinesic and auditory-paralinguistic modes.

Stratton (1921) reported an extensive series of experiments conducted on a famous "muscle reader," Eugen de Rubini. Both E. Tolman and W. Brown were present during most of the series. The subject's task was to select 1 of 10 books which had been chosen by one of the experimenters. Contact between this experimenter (guide) and the subject was established by a slack watch chain held by both. Although no observing experimenter could detect any sensory cue emitted by the guide to the subject, Rubini was able to select the correct item significantly (100 percent) more often than could be accounted for by chance. Even when the watch chain was not employed, the subject's performance was 50 percent better than chance alone. When possible auditory cues were reduced, the subject's performance actually improved, but when visual cues were reduced his performance deteriorated. Only when all visual and auditory cues were reduced drastically, however, was the subject's performance clearly no better than chance. An unexpected finding was that when the guide tried consciously to help Rubini, the latter's performance fell off. Apparently those cues actually used by this subject were not easily inferred, a finding in accord with the data presented earlier in this chapter.

Other workers have also suggested the importance to the experimental situation of unintended cues given off by the experimenter (Edwards, 1950). In his critique of Kalischer's research with dogs, Johnson (1913) suggested that the animals could correctly anticipate the experimenter's responses from his posture, muscle tonus, and respiratory changes. Johnson employed a control series in which the dogs could not see the experimenter. These controls led to the disappearance of the animals' alleged discriminatory ability.

Among fifth-grade children, Prince (1962) found that a not so subtle marking of the experimenter's data sheet served as a reinforcer of verbal behavior. A more subtle and unintended data-recording cue was reported by Wilson (1952). In a task requiring the discrimination of the presence and absence of a light, it was found that subject performance varied as a function of the data-recording system. That system yielding the best "discrimination" was one in which a longer pen scratch by the experimenter was associated with one of the alternatives. (A fuller discussion of some of these cases of communication by means of small cues is available elsewhere [Rosenthal, 1965a].)

EXPERIMENTAL RESTRICTION OF COMMUNICATION

In the preceding section we saw the potential relevance for the communication of experimenter expectancies of the visual-kinesic and auditory-paralinguistic modalities. In this section data will be presented that were in part designed to show which of these two channels of communication might be the more important (Fode, 1960; Rosenthal & Fode, 1963).

The standard photo-rating task was administered to 103 male and 77 female students in introductory psychology classes by 24 male advanced undergraduate engineers. In this study experimenters did not show each of the 10 photos to their subjects. Instead the entire set of photos was mounted on a rectangular board so that subjects could rate aloud the success or failure of the persons pictured without experimenters' handling the photos.

Six of the experimenters were randomly assigned to the control group and were led to expect photo ratings of −5 from their subjects. The remaining experimenters were all led to expect ratings of +5 and were randomly assigned to one of the following three experimental groups: (1) *Visual cues.* These six experimenters were fully visible to their subjects but remained entirely silent after greeting subjects and handing them their written instructions. (2) *Auditory cues.* These six experimenters were permitted to read their instructions to their subjects but were shielded from subjects' view by sitting behind a screen immediately after greeting their subjects. (3) *Visual plus auditory cues.* These six experimenters read their instructions to their subjects and remained in full view throughout the experiment. This group was identical with the control group in procedure and differed only in the induced expectancy. Each experimenter contacted an average of 7.5 subjects.

Magnitude of expectancy effect was defined as the difference between the mean photo rating obtained by each experimenter of the experimental groups (+5) and the mean of the mean photo ratings obtained by the experimenters of the control group (−5).

Table 16-6 shows the magnitude of expectancy effect for each experimenter of each experimental condition. Negative numbers indicate that those experimenters' obtained ratings were in the direction opposite to their expectancy. The experimenters of the visual cue group showed no effect of experimenter expectancy. The auditory cue group of experimenters showed significant expectancy effects ($t = 3.19$, $p = .005$). The visual plus audi-

TABLE 16—6

Magnitude of Expectancy Effects Under Three Conditions of Cue Communication

COMMUNICATION CHANNEL

	Visual	Auditory	Visual Plus Auditory
	.57	1.35	2.55
	.42	.98	2.28
	.09	.83	2.11
	−.16	.79	1.61
	−.64	.62	1.58
	−.71	.47	0.62
Means	−.07	.84	1.79

tory group of experimenters showed much more significant expectancy effects, and the magnitude of these effects was significantly greater than those of the auditory cue group ($t = 2.63$, $p = .02$). This finding suggests that a combination of the visual-kinesic and auditory-paralinguistic channels is most effective in the communication of experimenter expectancies. As to the differential effectiveness of the visual and auditory modalities, the data are equivocal. One interpretation suggests that auditory cues alone are more important than visual cues alone. (By "auditory" is meant, of course, the noncontent or paralinguistic aspects of speech, since all experimenters gave identical instructions to their subjects.) An alternative interpretation, however, suggests that the visual cue group's mute behavior in their experimental sessions may have struck their subjects as so peculiar and "unnecessarily" unfriendly that they reacted with a negative conformity to their silent experimenters' expectancy. Both of these alternative interpretations must at this time be regarded as more or less speculative. (We do know, however, from the work of Troffer and Tart [1964] that the auditory channel can be sufficient to communicate the expectancy of experimenters in hypnosis research.)

TEMPORAL LOCALIZATION

In the preceding section we discussed the role of two sense modalities in the communication of experimenter expectancy effects. Both modalities had been emphasized by observers of films of intentional cue production. In this section the question of *when* expectancy effects are communicated will be discussed. Some of the observers had suggested that the communication of expectancies occurred very early in the experimenter-subject negotiation. Others felt that this communication occurred only after the subjects began making their responses. These observers were essentially suggesting an operant conditioning paradigm with positive reinforcers emitted by experimenters in response to subjects' emission of expected responses. Negative reinforcers were thought to follow the occurrence of unexpected responses. In the films in question these events undoubtedly did occur, since the experimenters were intentionally trying to influence their subjects and consciously employed nonverbal reinforcements. The purpose of the data analysis to be presented here was to learn whether under the more ecologically valid or more representative conditions of unintended influence, operant conditioning was necessary for the operation of experimenter expectancy effects (Rosenthal, Fode, Vikan-Kline, & Persinger, 1964).

From the experiments completed at the time, those three were selected for analysis that met the following criteria: (1) that experimenters contacted their subjects individually using the same photo-rating task and identical instructions, (2) that experimenters and subjects be in full view of each other throughout the experiment, and (3) that there be one group of experimenters led to expect photo ratings of +5 while another group was led to expect ratings of −5.

To test the hypothesis that operant conditioning, as commonly defined (e.g., Krasner, 1958; Krasner, 1962), was necessary for the operation of experimenter expectancy effects, the following analysis was made. For each of the three experiments, the mean photo ratings obtained of the *first photo only* were compared for the +5 and −5 expecting experimenters. If the differences in ratings obtained by the oppositely outcome-biased experimenters were as great on the first photo as for all ten photos, we could reject the "theories" of expectancy communication which require operant conditioning as a necessary condition, since no reinforcement was possible until *after* this first rating.

To test the hypothesis that operant conditioning augments experimenter expectancy effects, the following analysis was made. For each of the three experiments the mean ratings obtained by experimenters of each treatment condition were plotted for each of the ten photos in sequence. Magnitude of experimenter expectancy effects, defined as the difference in mean rating, should show an increase over time if operant conditioning served to augment the phenomenon.

Table 16-7 shows the magnitude of experimenter expectancy effect

TABLE 16—7

Effect of Experimenter Expectancy on Ratings of the First Photo Alone and of All Ten Photos

Experiment	I	II	III
N of Es	10	12	8
N of Ss per E	21	7	11
	First Photo Only		
Mean difference	0.71	2.16	0.89
t	1.76	1.50	0.74
p	.08	.08	.25
	All Ten Photos		
Mean difference	0.50	1.79	1.30
t	2.19	4.97	3.94
p	.03	.0005	.005

(mean difference) for the first photo alone, and for all ten photos together, for each of the three experiments. In addition, Table 16-7 shows, for each experiment, the *t* and *p* level (one-tail) as well as the number of experimenters and the mean number of subjects contacted by each.

In the two studies having the larger number of experimenters, the magnitude of expectancy effect (mean difference) was somewhat greater for the first photo alone than for all ten photos combined. For all three studies combined, the grand mean difference based on the first photo alone was 1.34, and that based on all ten photos was 1.23. This finding clearly indicates that operant conditioning is not necessary for the communication of expectancy effects. Masling (1965), in his study of examiner effects in influencing subjects' Rorschach responses, was also unable to show that it was a pattern of examiner reinforcement that accounted for subjects' biased responses.

Comparison of the *t*s shown in Table 16-7 and their associated *p* levels does show that expectancy effects are more statistically significant when comparisons are based on the differences in ratings of all ten photos. This was due to the increased stability of the mean differences, resulting from their being based on ten times as many actual raw scores. The combined *p* of the mean differences based on first photos alone was < .03 (*z* = 2.01).

Figure 16-1 shows the grand mean photo ratings for each treatment

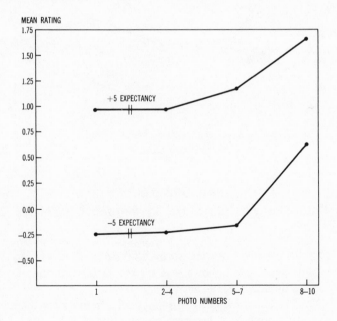

FIGURE 16-1
Mean Photo Ratings Obtained in Sequence

condition for photos grouped in sequence, for all three experiments combined (unweighted). Inspection of this figure shows that magnitude of experimenter expectancy effects, defined as the difference in mean rating, changed very little over time ($p > .50$), suggesting that verbal conditioning need not serve to augment expectancy effects.

In our earlier discussion of Weick's classroom experiment on expectancy effects we noted that the observers' reports suggested the operation of differential reinforcement of expected and unexpected responses by subjects. It is of special interest, therefore, to note that in this study, too, significant experimenter expectancy effects emerged before any reinforcement was possible. The magnitude of expectancy effect on the very first photo was $+5.00$ ($p < .02$, one-tail, $t = 2.84$, $df = 8$).

Figure 16-2 illustrates that for Weick's experiment the very first responses were more affected than were the subsequent responses. Magnitude of expectancy effect, after the first response, was fairly stable through-

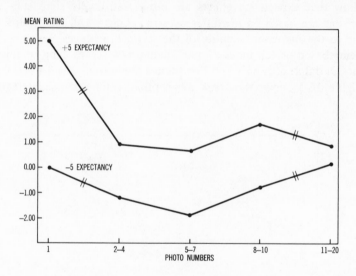

FIGURE 16-2
Mean Photo Ratings Obtained in Sequence (Weick's Data)

out the first 10 photos. In this study the standard 20-photo set was employed, and Figure 16-2 shows that for the last 10 photos, expectancy effects tended to diminish significantly ($p = .08$).

The fact that experimenter expectancy effects manifest themselves so early in the data collection process has important implications for the further study of the mediation of expectancy effects. It suggests that during the very brief period in which the experimenter greets, seats, and instructs his subject, the results of the experiment may be partially determined. The very special importance of the first few moments of the experiment has also been suggested by Kimble (1962) in experiments on eyelid conditioning and by Stevenson and Odom (1963), who found that the sex of the experimenter affected the subjects' performance even though the experimenter left the subject after giving instructions and before the subject began responding. From what we now know about the "when" of the communication of expectancies it seems that in future studies we must focus our attention on the brief predata-collection phase of the experimental interaction in order to discover the "how" of the communication of expectancies.

THE PROBLEM OF SIGNAL SPECIFICATION

Even if we knew the precise moment, if there were one, when the experimenter unintentionally signals his subject to respond in a certain way, and even if we could specify with near-certainty which experimenters would successfully influence their subjects' responses, we would still be left with the basic riddle of the Clever Hans phenomenon. Exactly what does the experimenter do differently when he expects a certain response compared to what he does when he expects the opposite response?

No upward movement of the head, or eyes, no dilation of the nostrils, have yet been shown to be the critical signals to subjects as they were in the case of Clever Hans. Nor should we push that analogy too far. Hans, after all, had only to receive a signal to stop a repetitive movement, the tapping of his foot. A simple signal by our experimenters to their subjects that they were responding "properly" would not do as a hypothesis, since we saw earlier that the crucial communication occurs before the subjects' first response.

The first attempt to see what experimenters did differently when interacting with subjects for whom they held opposite expectancies employed the original five molar variables described in the last chapter. For each of his interactions with a subject, each experimenter had been rated on his dominance, likability, activity, professional manner, and friendliness. The ratings made by the five original observers of an experimenter's interaction with a subject from whom he expected negative ratings of the success of others (−5) could be subtracted from the ratings made of his behavior when contacting a subject from whom he expected positive ratings (+5). These difference scores tended to be quite small compared to the differences found among different experimenters. Table 16-8 illustrates this fact by showing for each variable the *greatest* obtained difference between the means of different experimenters and the greatest difference obtained by any single experimenter between subjects under the two experimental conditions. Those variables showing the greatest within-experimenter variation were

TABLE 16—8

Maximum Obtained Differences in Experimenter Behavior

Behavior	Within Experimenters	Between Experimenters
Dominant	.60	3.70
Likable	.80	4.20
Activity	.90	4.00
Professional	1.60	4.95
Friendly	2.00	4.80
Means	1.18	4.33

also those showing the greatest between-experimenter variation ($r = .91$, $p = .03$).

Table 16-9 shows the mean differences in experimenter behavior vis-à-vis those subjects from whom photo ratings of +5 were expected and those from whom ratings of −5 were expected. These mean differences

TABLE 16—9

Differences in Experimenter Behavior as a Function of Expectancy

MAGNITUDE OF EXPECTANCY EFFECTS

Behavior	Positive Effect N = 8 Mean*	t	p	No Effect N = 8 Mean*	t	p	Negative Effect N = 7 Mean*	t	p
Dominant	+.04	–	–	−.18	1.94	.10	−.24	1.98	.09
Likable	−.25	1.68	.15	+.14	1.76	.13	−.19	1.66	.15
Activity	−.11	–	–	+.04	–	–	+.36	2.27	.06
Professional	+.19	–	–	−.20	1.11	–	−.31	1.55	.17
Friendly	−.52	1.60	.16	+.44	1.81	.12	−.11	–	–

* (Mean rating under "+5" expectancy condition) minus (mean rating under "−5" expectancy condition).

are tabulated separately for experimenters showing large positive expectancy effects ($> +1.00$), those showing no expectancy effects ($< +1.00$,
> -1.00), and those showing large negative or reverse expectancy effects
(< -1.00). None of these mean differences was significant at the .05 level
for any of the variables listed. However, since 9 of the 15 ts computed had
an associated $p < .20$ (too many to be reasonably ascribed to chance), it
appears that on the whole experimenters behaved differently toward their
subjects depending on whether they believed them to be success- or failure-
perceiving subjects. The profile of difference scores of the positively biased
experimenters was significantly opposite to the profile of the unbiased
experimenters (rho $= -1.00$, $p = .02$), and tended to be opposite to the
profile of the negatively biased experimenters (rho $= -.70$, $p = .20$). The
profile of difference scores of this latter group did not differ from the profile
of the unbiased group (rho $= +.70$, $p = .20$). Thus positively biased
experimenters behaved in a relatively less professional but more friendly
and likable manner toward those subjects they believed to be failure perceivers ("-5's"). The unbiased experimenters showed just the opposite
configuration of behavior and, in addition, behaved somewhat more dominantly toward their "-5" subjects. It appeared almost as though the positive biasing experimenters were trying to be especially nice to the subjects
they believed to be failure perceivers, while the unbiased experimenters were
just the opposite—perhaps from trying too hard to avoid treating their subjects differentially. The behavior of negative biasing experimenters seemed
to vary most as a function of their expectancy. Like the unbiased experimenters, they were relatively less dominant and professional toward their
"$+5$" subjects. But like the positively biased experimenters, they were also
less likable toward their "$+5$" subjects. Unlike either of the other groups of
experimenters, the reverse biasers behaved more actively vis-à-vis their
"$+5$" subjects. The differential behavior of this group of experimenters
might have been due either to their efforts to avoid affecting their data
and/or to "faulty" cueing behavior toward their subjects.

It seems unlikely that a simple increase in "friendliness," for example
toward a "-5" subject, leads to obtaining the lowered photo ratings we
would expect if bias were to occur. Table 16-10 shows the correlations
between subjects' photo ratings and the mean of their experimenter's rated
behavior. Higher ratings (disregarding expectancy) were obtained by experimenters who were more active, more friendly, less dominant, and less
professional (findings consistent with those reported in Part I of this book).
It may well be that changes in experimenter behavior have entirely different
meanings to their subjects depending on the usual behavior of that experimenter. We saw in an earlier chapter that more positively biased experimenters were different from less biased experimenters before they even
began their experiment. With respect to the behavioral variables being considered here, the more biased experimenter is ordinarily more professional,

TABLE 16—10

Correlations Between Subjects' Photo Ratings and
Their Experimenter's Typical Behavior

Behavior	r	p
Dominant	−.34	.005
Likable	+.08	−
Activity	+.18	.13
Professional	−.24	.05
Friendly	+.20	.09

dominant, likable, and less active. On the basis of the data presented in this section, we still cannot say how changes in experimenter behavior lead to changes in their subjects' responses. Of considerable interest, however, was the finding that experimenters' expectancies lead to changes in their own behavior regardless of whether they bias their data positively, negatively, or not at all.

Given that a more dominant experimenter subsequently exerts greater expectancy effects on his subjects, as we saw in the last chapter, if he becomes somewhat less dominant vis-à-vis a subject from whom he expects +5 ratings, that subject will tend to rate the photos as less successful, thereby leading toward negative or reversed expectancy effects. This can be seen from Table 16-9. Perhaps a simpler way of expressing this relationship is to give the correlation between the difference in behavior manifested toward subjects from whom different responses are expected and the difference in the responses subsequently obtained from them. For the behavior "dominant" this correlation was $+.47$, $(p = .03, df = 21)$, which means that if an experimenter was more dominant toward a "+5" than toward a "−5" subject he tended to obtain higher ratings from his "+5" than from his "−5" subjects. Of the five behavioral variables under discussion this was the only one that reached statistical significance. Although more-dominant experimenters generally tend to obtain lower photo ratings from their subjects, when they show an increase in dominance they tend to obtain higher photo ratings. Why this should be is far from clear, but it does suggest the possible importance of the effects of the subject's adaptation level (Helson, 1964).

The five behavioral variables being discussed were based on the judgments of five investigators whose ratings might have been contaminated. It was, therefore, important to see whether other observers who could not have been contaminated would make observations that would show similar correlations. In the last chapter, observations by uncontaminated observers were described. For the five behaviors we have been discussing, the mean ratings of experimenters contacting "−5" subjects were subtracted from the mean ratings of experimenters contacting "+5" subjects. These difference scores were correlated, as before, with the photo ratings made by "−5" subjects subtracted from photo ratings made by "+5" subjects. When judgments of experimenter behavior were made of only the brief preinstructional period, none of the correlations were significant, regardless of whether the behavioral observations were based on the silent films, the sound track, or the sound films. When judgments of experimenter behavior were made of the instructional period, by observers of the sound film, the only correlation to reach significance was the same one that reached significance when the possibly contaminated observers had been employed. Experimenters showing more-dominant behavior toward their "+5" subjects tended to obtain the expected higher photo ratings from them. The correlation was +.50 ($p = .04$, $df = 16$), very close to the value of +.47 obtained by the original observers. When the observations were based on the silent films alone, experimenters showing in their motor behavior an increase in professional manner toward their "+5" subjects relative to their "−5" subjects, obtained the expected higher photo ratings from them ($r = +.64$, $p = .008$, $df = 15$). None of the differential behaviors of the experimenters toward their "+5" or "−5" subjects as judged from sound track alone predicted significantly the differential photo ratings subsequently obtained from "+5" and "−5" subjects.

It may be recalled that these samples of observers had made ratings of other aspects of the experimenter's behavior than just those five we have been discussing. Table 16-11 shows the significant correlations ($p \leq .10$)

TABLE 16—11

Differential Instructional Behavior of the Experimenter as Predictor of Subjects' Differential Responding

OBSERVATION CHANNEL

Visual		*Visual Plus Auditory*	
Professional	+.64	Talkative	+.63
Not acting important	+.50	Dominant	+.50
Honest	+.43	Dishonest	+.43
Courteous	+.41		
Mean r = +.50		Mean r = +.52	
Mean intercorrelation = +.41		Mean intercorrelation = +.27	

between differences in instructional behavior vis-à-vis "+5" and "—5" subjects and differences in photo ratings subsequently obtained. None of the correlations based upon observations of experimenter behavior in the auditory channel alone reached a $p \le .10$.

Within each of the other two channels of observation the variables predicting subjects' differential responses as a function of experimenter expectancy were not well clustered. Within each channel the mean correlation predicting expectancy effect was higher than the mean intercorrelation. Judging from the visual-plus-auditory channel, experimenters who behaved in a more talkative, dominant, and "dishonest" way toward subjects from whom they expected +5 responses tended to obtain such responses. Judging from the visual channel alone, experimenters who acted in a more professional, more courteous, less important, and more "honest" manner toward their "+5" subjects tended to obtain the expected responses from them. The most puzzling aspect is the very different meaning of "honest" when it is judged from the visual channel alone compared to the visual-plus-auditory channel. As we would expect from the opposite directions of the correlations between honesty and subjects' responses, treating a subject in a more honest way judging from the visual channel alone is seen as treating him in a less honest way judging from the visual-plus-auditory channel ($r = -.62$, $p < .01$). These findings do not solve our problem of finding the key to the communication of expectancies, but there is a lesson for future studies of interpersonal communication. Adding a channel of communication does not simply strengthen the meaning of a message—it may, in fact, reverse that meaning.

Table 16-12 shows the significant ($p \le .10$) correlations between the differential preinstructional behavior shown vis-à-vis "+5" and "—5" subjects and the differential responses subsequently shown by these subjects. Judged from the visual-plus-auditory channels, experimenters who showed more hand gestures and whose speech was more "loud and clear" toward their "+5" than toward their "—5" subjects obtained more positive ratings from them than from their "—5" subjects. Again we find a judgment of behavior reversed as a function of the channel of communication.

Judging from the sound track alone, experimenters obtained relatively higher ratings from subjects from whom they expected higher ratings if they were *less* loud.

Judging from the visual channel alone, experimenters who showed less trunk activity, acted less important, and behaved less inconsistently toward their "+5" subjects obtained higher ratings from them than from their "—5" subjects.

In the last chapter the concept of channel discrepancy was described. Because there were observations of behavior based only on the visual channel and observations based only on the auditory channel, a difference could be computed. Such characteristic channel discrepancies were found

TABLE 16—12

Differential Preinstructional Behavior of the Experimenter as Predictor of Subjects' Differential Responding

OBSERVATION CHANNEL

Visual		Auditory		Visual Plus Additory	
Trunk gestures	−.50	Loud	−.49	Loud	+.65
Important-acting	−.48			Hand gestures	+.47
Behaved				Speaks	
inconsistently	−.47			distinctly	+.46
Mean r =	−.48	Mean r =	−.49	Mean r =	+.53
Mean				Mean	
intercorrelation =	+.09		−	intercorrelation =	+.38

to be useful predictors of subsequent expectancy effects. What has not yet been discussed is whether a given experimenter's *changes* in channel discrepancy as a function of the expectancy he has of a given subject's response can be used to predict that subject's subsequent response.

For 17 of the behavioral variables, channel discrepancies could be computed. The mean channel discrepancy an experimenter showed in interacting with a "−5" subject was subtracted from the mean channel discrepancy he showed in interacting with a "+5" subject. The resulting difference scores were correlated with the mean rating of the stimulus photos subsequently given by "−5" subjects subtracted from the mean photo rating given by "+5" subjects. For the preinstructional period alone and for the instructional period alone, 17 correlations were available based on algebraic channel discrepancies (visual minus auditory, retaining the sign of the difference); and 17 correlations were available based on absolute channel discrepancies (visual minus auditory, disregarding the sign of the difference).

Table 16-13 shows the significant ($p \leq .10$) correlations between differences in channel discrepancies in the experimenter's behavior shown toward "+5" as compared to "−5" subjects and differences between these subjects' subsequent photo ratings. Based on observations made in the preinstructional period alone, those experimenters who showed greater absolute channel discordance in their degree of casualness but less discordance in their likability toward their "+5" subjects subsequently obtained the expected higher photo ratings from these subjects ($R = .85$, $p < .001$).

TABLE 16—13

Differential Channel Discrepancies as Predictors of
Subjects' Differential Responding

EXPERIMENTAL PERIOD

Preinstructional			Instructional		
Behavior	r	p	Behavior	r	p
Casual	+.74	.003	Honest*	+.46	.06
Likable	−.57	.04	Dominant	+.41	.10
Multiple R =	.85	.001	Multiple R =	.59	.04

* This was an algebraic discrepancy (visual > auditory). All other
discrepancies were absolute, that is, sign of discrepancy was
ignored.

Based on observations made in the instructional period alone, those
experimenters who showed greater absolute channel discordance in their
degree of dominance, and who showed greater visual than auditory honesty
toward their "+5" than their "−5" subjects, subsequently obtained the
expected higher photo ratings from their "+5" than from their "−5" subjects ($R = .59, p < .04$). It seems best to forego the speculation required
to interpret the specifics of these findings. In general, however, these results
demonstrate the importance of changes in the discrepancies between channels of communication as predictors of subsequent interpersonal influence.

Additional analyses of sound motion pictures of experimenters interacting with their subjects are in progress. We may or may not find more
specific signals by means of which experimenters communicate to their
subjects what it is that is expected of them. Not finding such specific cues
may not mean that there are no such cues but only that we do not yet know
enough about subtle signaling systems to be able to find them. If, in fact,
there were no specific cues to be found, then more molar changes in the
behavior of the experimenter might serve as the nonspecific influencers of
the subjects' behavior. Mention has already been made of these nonspecific
changes in experimenter behavior as antecedents of subjects' subsequent
differential responses. We cannot be sure, however, that these changes in
experimenter behavior are themselves conveyors of information to the subjects as to how they should respond. Possibly, those subjects who later go
on to confirm or disconfirm the experimenter's hypothesis affect the ex-

perimenter differently early in the experiment. The experimenter then behaves differently toward these subjects but without necessarily conveying response-related information to the subject. In other words, differential treatment by the experimenter may be quite incidental to the question of whether a subject goes on to confirm or disconfirm the experimenter's hypothesis. What has been learned that we can accept with confidence is the understatement that interpersonal communication processes are enormously complex and that they may be still more complex when the communication is unintentional.

LEARNING TO COMMUNICATE UNINTENTIONALLY

If, after hundreds of hours of careful observation, no well-specifiable system of unintentional signaling has been uncovered, how do *experimenters* "know" how to influence their subjects unintentionally? Perhaps the knowledge of interpersonal influence processes is a tacit knowledge. As Polanyi (1962) has put it, "There are things that we know but cannot tell" (p. 601). One question that could be answered in part was whether an experimenter "knows" better how to influence his subjects later on in the process of data collection. If an experimenter is more successful in unintentional influencing later than he was earlier, it would be reasonable to think that in part, unintentional influence was a learned phenomenon. That was just what happened in the case of Clever Hans. Pfungst (1911) found that as questioners gained experience in asking Hans to respond they became more successful in unintentionally signaling to Hans when to stop his tapping.

In the chapter dealing with the effects of early data returns, two experiments were described. In both these studies subjects contacted during the last half of the experiment were more influenced by the experimenters' expectancy than were subjects contacted during the first half of the experiment (ps were .02 and .01 respectively). Data collected with Suzanne Haley were similarly analyzed, and later-contacted subjects again showed greater effects of the experimenters' expectancy ($p = .12$). For these three experiments with a total of 54 experimenters, the combined p was less than .001, but it must be mentioned that it was not always possible to be sure that earlier- and later-contacted subjects did not differ in some other ways as well.

In Weick's study reported earlier, there was no increase in expectancy effects when the two experimenters were contacting later as compared to earlier subjects in the sequence. Vikan-Kline's (1962) data, reported two chapters ago, showed no order effect among her lower status experimenters but did show higher status experimenters to increase their expectancy effects as a function of number of subjects contacted ($p = .01$). Although the evidence is not conclusive, it does seem that, on the whole, later-contacted subjects are more influenced by the experimenter's expectancy than earlier-contacted subjects. Over the course of an experiment, experimenters may learn to communicate their expectancies more effectively.

This learning hypothesis is strengthened somewhat by the findings of the studies on experimenter-subject acquaintanceship. The two studies summarized earlier found greater acquaintanceship associated with greater expectancy effects. In part, of course, this may have been due to the greater willingness of people to be influenced by prior acquaintances. In addition, however, acquaintanceship implies a longer joint history with greater opportunity for learning how the interpersonal influence process operates with the specific other. Acquaintances, presumably, not only have greater reinforcement value for each other but probably can better read each other's cues, unintentional as well as intentional.

If the experimenter were indeed learning to increase his unintended influence, who would be the teacher? Most likely, the subject would be the teacher. It seems to be rewarding to have one's expectations confirmed (Aronson, Carlsmith, & Darley, 1963; Carlsmith & Aronson, 1963; Harvey & Clapp, 1965; Sampson & Sibley, 1965). Therefore, whenever the subject responds in accordance with the experimenter's expectancy, the likelihood is increased that the experimenter will repeat any covert communicative behavior that may have preceded the subject's confirming response. Subjects, then, may quite unintentionally shape the experimenter's unintended communicative behavior. Not only does the experimenter influence his subjects to respond in the expected manner, but his subjects may well evoke just that unintended behavior that will lead subjects to respond as expected. As the work of Hefferline (1962) and of Pfungst (1911) suggests, such communication may not fall under what we commonly call "conscious control."

III

METHODOLOGICAL
IMPLICATIONS

SOME THEORETICAL CONSIDERATIONS

**THE CONTROL OF EXPERIMENTER
EXPECTANCY EFFECTS**

17

The Generality and Assessment
of Experimenter Effects

As behavioral scientists, what should be our reaction to the evidence presented in this book? Three different reactions to the presentation of some of the data from this book have actually been observed: (1) the *incredulous*, (2) the *gleeful*, (3) the *realistic*. The *incredulous* reactor (who may not have read this far) feels vaguely that all of this is just so much nonsense and that if it is not completely nonsense, at least it does not apply to him. The *gleeful* reactor (who may have read this far, but may read no further) has "known all along that experiments in the behavioral sciences were riddled with error." He does not do or like empirical research. He is gleeful because, paradoxically, he reads into the experimental evidence presented in this book his justification for his epistemology that knowledge of the world comes through revelation rather than observation. After all, if observation is subject to observer influence, is he not justified in his eschewal of observation? The *realistic* reactor (and the choice of terms is intentionally positively evaluative) has read this far more or less critically and has wondered a bit whether some of his own research might have been affected by his own expectancies or more enduring attributes.

Much of what follows is for that reader who, although skeptical by training, is not incredulous; who, although interested, is not overdeterminedly gleeful; who, although reminiscing about his own research, is not contemplating giving up the scientific enterprise. It is for the reader who agrees with Hyman and his co-authors (1954) when they say: "Let it be noted that the *demonstration* of error marks an advanced state of a science. All scientific inquiry is subject to error, and it is far better to be aware of this, to study the sources in an attempt to reduce it, . . . than to be ignorant of the errors concealed in the data" (p. 4).

THE GENERALITY OF EXPERIMENTER EFFECTS

How pervasive are the unintended effects of the experimenter on the results of his research, and how much ought we to worry about them in our day-to-day research activities? The answer to the first part of this question seems simple. We don't know. No one knows. It seems reasonable to suppose that there may be experimenters doing experiments the results of which are unaffected by the experimenters themselves. Unfortunately, we don't know who they are or which of their experiments, if not all, are immune to their own unintended effect. This lack of specificity in our knowledge suggests the answer to the second part of our question. It seems more prudent to worry than not to worry about experimenter effects in our day-to-day research.

One type of experimenter effect, that of his hypothesis or expectancy, has received our special attention in this book. For this special case of experimenter effect we can sketch out the evidence bearing on the question of its generality. After the manner of Brunswik's conception (1956) of the representative design of experiments, we may specify the sampling domains of experimenters, subjects, tasks, and contexts employed in the experiments described in this book.

Experimenters

Altogether, there have been well over 350 experimenters employed in the studies described. About 90 percent of these were males. All but a handful (faculty experimenters) were graduate or undergraduate students. In all cases, however, experimenters were academically more advanced than were their experimental subjects. Graduate student experimenters were drawn from classes in psychology, education, biology, physics, engineering, and law. Undergraduate student experimenters were drawn primarily from courses in experimental, industrial, and clinical psychology, statistics, and the social sciences. In most cases experimenters were volunteers, but in others the class as a whole was urged by its instructor to participate—a practice that led to essentially nonvolunteer populations (Rosenthal, 1965b). Most experimenter samples were paid for their participation, but many were not.

Thus, although sampling of experimenters has been fairly broad, it has been broad only within various student populations. Does any of the work reported, then, have any real relevance to the "real" experimenter? The *gleeful* reactor mentioned earlier may too quickly say "yes." The *incredulous* reactor may too quickly say "no." In his discussion of the generality of interviewer effects, Hart (obviously a *realistic* reactor) put it this way:

Generalization of our conclusions to researchers of greater maturity and sophistication than these subjects has to be made, therefore, with due and proper caution. It would be dangerous, however, though consoling, for the mature and sophisticated interviewer to assume that he is not equally subject to the operation of the same error-producing factors affecting the varied group of interviewers covered by the studies we are here reporting. As a matter of fact, the available evidence suggests that, while the sophisticated interviewer may be less subject to variable errors of a careless sort, he is probably equally subject to certain biasing errors (1954, pp. ix–x).

Indeed, we can go further than Hart. If anything, our data suggest fairly strongly that more professional, more competent, higher status experimenters are more likely to bias the results of their research than are the more amateurish data collectors.

Most experimenters, like most interviewers, are task-oriented, but the experimenters whom we have studied (and those "real" ones we have known) seem to be much more interested in the subject's response than the survey interviewer apparently is in his respondent's reply (Hyman et al., 1954, p. 270). But that seems not hard to understand. The experimenter, as compared to the survey interviewer, is less of a "hired hand" who, if he performs poorly, can simply take another job. At least to some extent the professional career of the experimenter depends on the responses his subjects give him in the experimental situation. At first glance this may seem far-fetched. Actually it is quite analogous to the situation in the other sciences. The behavior of a noble gas or of heavenly bodies can clearly affect the professional career of the physical scientist interested in such behavior. It gives, or does not give, him something to report or to guide his next experiment or observation.

If the experimenter is not the principal investigator, but a student of the principal investigator, his professional career may still depend, much more than the survey interviewer's, on his subjects' responses. The student bears a much more special relationship to the principal investigator than the interviewer bears to his employing agency. The student is the only employee or one of a handful of employees. The interviewer may be one of thousands of employees. The student experimenter is likely to learn immediately what his employer's reaction is to his subject's responses. The interviewer's feedback may be much delayed or even absent altogether. In short, the experimenter, be he principal investigator or research assistant, has much more at stake than does the interviewer. If he cares so much more about how his subject performs for him in the experimental situation, it seems reasonable to suppose that he may be more likely to communicate something of this concern to his subject than the typical interviewer is likely to do.

At the present time we cannot say with certainty whether very highly experienced professional experimenters are more or less likely to bias their subjects' responses than less experienced experimenters, although all the evidence available suggests that more professional, more competent, higher status experimenters show the greater expectancy effects. In any case, we should note the trend that as experimenters become highly experienced they become less and less likely to contact their subjects directly. As investigators become better established they are more and more likely to acquire more and more assistants who will do the actual data collection. These assistants range from an occasional postdoctoral student through the various levels of graduate students. Increasingly, even undergraduate students are collecting data to be used for serious scientific purposes. Undergraduate research assistants, for example, are the only ones available at many excellent liberal arts colleges with active research programs in the behavioral sciences. For some time original research has been required of at least some undergraduate candidates for honors degrees, and this trend is increasing. More and more we shall probably see undergraduates collecting data for serious purposes under the expanding programs supported by the federal government as part of the movement to encourage the earlier selection of careers in research. The Undergraduate Research Participation Program of the National Science Foundation is a prime example.

With more and more "real" data being collected by less and less experienced experimenters, it appears that our student experimenters are not as unrepresentative of the "real" world of data collection after all. But suppose for a moment that it were indeterminant that there were "real" experimenters in the world who were like the graduate and undergraduate students we employed. How seriously would that restrict the generality of the data presented? Of course, we could not be certain of any answer to that question. But in a relative sense, it does not seem far-fetched to use students as models of student and faculty researchers—certainly much less far-fetched (as Marcia has pointed out in personal communication, 1961) than using a Sprague-Dawley albino rat as the model for man. But we have learned enough of consequence about human behavior from both sophomore and Sprague-Dawley that we do not feel too uncomfortable about even this degree of generalization. If these generalizations seem tenable, then even more does our generalization from student to "real" data collector seem tenable.

Subjects

There have been well over 2,000 human subjects employed in the studies described. About 60 percent have been female. Most of the subjects were undergraduates and were drawn from courses in liberal arts, education, and business. The greatest single contributing course was introductory psychology. Most of the subjects were volunteers, but many were urged by their instructors to participate and so became more like a nonvolunteer population. In some of the studies subjects were paid; usually they were not.

In the case of animal subjects, 80 rats of two different species from two different laboratories were employed. About two thirds were females.

The subjects employed in our research were very much like those typically used in behavior research, and there appears to be little risk in generalizing from our subjects to subjects-in-general. Of course, nonstudent subjects are employed now and then in behavioral research, but this is so relatively rare that McNemar was led to state sadly: "The existing science of human behavior is largely the science of the behavior of sophomores" (1946, p. 333).

Situations

There is no standard way in which we can describe the "situations" in which the experimenter-subject dyads transacted their business in the thirty or so studies that have been carried out. But certainly a part of any experimental situation is the task the subject is asked to perform. The most frequently employed task has been that of rating photos for the degree of success or failure the person pictured has been experiencing. The exact instructions to the subjects, the training of experimenters to administer the task, and the exact mode of administration have all been varied. Nevertheless, in spite of the variations in this task and in spite of the fact that the task is a fairly typical one in psychological research, no single task can be regarded as an adequate sample of the many tasks psychologists have asked their subjects to perform. Accordingly, other tasks have been employed, including verbal conditioning, standardized and projective psychological tests; and for animal subjects, learning in T-mazes and Skinner boxes.

Most of the studies described have been carried out at the University of North Dakota, the Ohio State University, Harvard University, and two smaller universities in Ohio. They were carried out at different times during the academic year and during summer sessions. Length of time elapsing between the contacting of the first and last subjects in a given study has varied from a few hours to several months. In most cases a number of experimenters were simultaneously contacting their subjects, each of whom was individually seen by his experimenter. In other studies, different experimenters contacted their subjects individually but at different times. In one study all subjects were contacted by their experimenter as a group.

The rooms in which experimenter-subject transactions occurred differed considerably. These ranged from a large armory (in which 150 subjects were simultaneously contacted by 30 experimenters) to individual rooms barely large enough for two chairs and a small table. Some of the rooms had one-way-vision mirrors and microphones in view; others did not.

Some of the rooms were furnished so as to convey the impression that the occupant was a person of high status; some were furnished to convey the opposite impression.

Earlier we asked the question of the generality of the effects of the experimenter on the results of his experiment. We are now in a position to conclude, at least for one type of experimenter effect (that of his hypothesis or expectancy), that the phenomenon may well be a fairly general one. This conclusion seems warranted by the variety of experimenter, subject, and situation or context domains sampled and by the fact that expectancy effects have been shown to occur in other than experimental laboratories. Some of this evidence was presented in Part I and some will be touched upon in the final chapter. The generality of the phenomenon of experimenter expectancy effects suggests the need to consider in some detail the implications for psychological research methodology. We will turn our attention first to the problem of the assessment of experimenter effects.

THE ASSESSMENT OF EXPERIMENTER EFFECTS

So far in this book we have found it sufficient to give only very general definitions of certain operating characteristics of the experimenter. In this section we shall see somewhat more formal definitions of some of these characteristics. Whenever we speak here of "an experimenter" or "a subject" we imply that whatever is said applies as well to a homogeneous set of experimenters or subjects unless specifically restricted to the single case.

I. Experimenter Effect

Experimenter effect is defined as the extent to which the datum obtained by an experimenter deviates from the "correct" value. The measure of experimenter effect (or experimenter error) is some function of the sum of the absolute (unsigned) deviations of that experimenter's data about the "correct" value. It is, therefore, a measure of gross or total error.

A. Data. Data are defined as the performance or responses made by the experimenter's subjects. The term "data" may be applied to (1) the "raw" response, (2) the conversion of the raw response to quantitative terms, and (3) any subsequent transformation of the quantitative terms.

1. Response. A subject's response is that behavior of the subject which the experimenter has defined as being of interest. We may use this term to refer to the subject's behavior in both absolute and relative terms, both before and after quantitative transformation. For example, in an experiment comparing one or more experimental groups and one or more "control" groups, a subject's response might be defined as the "raw" (untransformed) response produced or as the difference between that raw response and the mean of any other group.

B. "Correct value." The "correct" or "true" datum is established by reasoned fiat. In some cases there are reasonable bases for the choice of the true or correct value. In a censuslike investigation of age, birth records may serve as the "correct" value against which subjects' responses may be compared. In a study involving college grades the registrar's records may serve as the criterion against which to compare subjects' statements of grades. In both of these examples, we should note, it is entirely possible that the official records are "in error" in some absolute sense and that the subject's response is more accurate. But on the whole, we are more inclined to trust the official bookkeepers of society, not because they are error-free, but because in many situations they seem to have the "best" data most of the time.

But there are no books kept on a given subject's pursuit rotor performance or his political ideology (but affiliation, yes), or sex life, or verbal learning, or small group interaction patterns. We find ourselves hard put to establish a criterion value. In survey research (Hyman et al., 1954) this is often done by sending out more experienced data collectors whose obtained data are then assumed to be more accurate than those collected by more inexperienced data collectors. That this may be so is reasonable but is so far from having been well established that it may be a misleading assumption. Similarly, in anthropological research, it has been suggested that better rapport with informants leads to more accurate data (Naroll, Naroll, & Howard, 1961; Naroll, 1962). This, too, is a reasonable assumption but probably also a risky one. Realistically, we must content ourselves with the fact that in most behavioral research the "true" data are unknown except as we obtain them in behavioral inquiry.

One solution that may serve for the time being is the democratic but not very satisfying one of assuming equal likelihood of error in all experimenters until shown otherwise. On the basis of this assumption, we take the mean data obtained from roughly comparable samples of subjects to be our "true" mean. The more experimenters that have collected such data, in fact, the "truer" will our "true" mean be.

II. Experimenter Bias

Experimenter bias is defined as the extent to which experimenter effect or error is asymmetrically distributed about the "correct" or "true" value. The measure of experimenter bias is some function of the algebraic sum of the deviations of that experimenter's data about the "correct" value. It is, therefore, a measure of net error.

We should note here that for a single subject's score or a single mean we can only judge whether that score or mean is accurate or not if we are given a criterion of "correctness." If the score or mean is accurate, well and good. If it is not accurate, we cannot evaluate whether the inaccuracy is biased or not. In a sense, of course, it *is* biased, since it must represent a net deviation from the correct value. But we would have to have at least one other score or mean to test properly the hypothesis of bias. If a subsequently drawn score or mean were to fall equally distant from, and on the opposite side of, the correct value, we would necessarily reject the notion of a biased data collector.

III. Experimenter Consistency

Experimenter consistency is defined as the extent to which the data obtained by an experimenter from a single subject or sample vary minimally among themselves. The measure of experimenter consistency is some function of the sum of the absolute deviations of that experimenter's obtained data about his mean datum obtained. The commonly used measure in this case would, of course, be the variance or standard deviation.

In the case of experimenter effect and experimenter bias we could take a simple evaluative position: we are likely to be against both. In the case of experimenter consistency the situation is more complex. Whereas we may be against marked inconsistency, we should also worry about hyperconsistency.[1]

If the experimenter is very inconsistent he is inefficient in the sense that he will have to obtain a larger number of responses to establish a reliable mean value. Such inconsistency of obtained responses may be due to random variations in his behavior vis-à-vis his subjects, including minor deviations from both his programmed procedures and his unprogrammed modal "interpersonal style."

If, on the other hand, the experimenter is significantly *under*variable in the data he obtains, his increased "efficiency" is bought at the cost of possible bias. Such possible bias has been well illustrated in the earlier cited study of the error of estimate of blood cell counts (Berkson, Magath, & Hurn, 1940). These workers showed that successive blood counts were significantly undervariable and that this bias could be attributed to an expectancy and desire on the part of the observer for the close agreement of successive counts. Whatever the observer's initial expectancy might be, his counts agree too often with this expectancy. In the absence of any special initial expectancy, it seems reasonable that the early data might have special significance as determinants of subsequent counts. Early data returns, as they influence the central tendencies (rather than the variability) of subsequent data, were discussed in an earlier chapter. It is interesting to note

[1] I want to thank Fred Mosteller for pointing out this problem and for calling my attention to the Berkson et al. (1940) study.

that in the first study described in that chapter (Table 12-1) those experimenters whose early data were biased as to their central tendency (means) obtained subsequent data that were biased not only with respect to central tendency but with respect to variance as well. Variances obtained by experimenters obtaining more biased early returns tended to be significantly smaller than variances obtained by experimenters obtaining relatively unbiased early returns ($F = 4.06$, $df = 6, 3$, $p < .10$). It may be, then, that unusually restricted variance or hyperconsistency can serve as a clue to the possible biasing of central tendencies.

When we speak of "hyper"-consistency or inconsistency we imply that we know the "true" or "correct" variance. The situation for variance is essentially the same as it was for the mean or any other measure of central tendency. We never really know the "true" value, but we can make reasonable choices of a "working-true" value. In a few cases we again can turn to public records from which "true" variances may be computed. We can use as our "true" value the variance obtained by some paragon experimenter or group of experimenters. In our earlier discussion of "correct values" we pointed out some difficulties of this technique, difficulties that apply equally well for variances as for scores or means of scores. For practical purposes, at this stage of our knowledge, we must probably rely on some method of sampling experimenters to arrive at some estimate of a "correct" variance. Such sampling may help us avoid the bias associated with the employment of experimenters who, fortuitously, may be overconsistent or underconsistent.

Before leaving this section, two kinds of experimenter deviation from normality of response distribution will be mentioned. Even assuming a properly consistent and unbiased experimenter, his distribution of obtained responses may contain too many high or low responses (skewness or asymmetry). In addition, his distribution of obtained responses may contain too many or too few responses at or near the mean. When we speak here of "too high" (or low) and of "too many" (or few) we mean it with respect to the normal distribution. Whether the "true" distribution is, in fact, normal is the same sort of question we have asked before when discussing "correct" scores, means, and variances; and our answer is essentially the same.

These two kinds of experimenter deviation from normality of response distribution have been discussed only briefly because, at the present time, we have no evidence that they are in any way serious for the usual conduct of psychological research. It is the rare psychological research paper that deals in any central way with the absolute magnitudes of skewness or kurtosis. It would seem interesting, however, to assess an experimenter's distribution of obtained responses for these characteristics, since in real life situations these deviations may prove to be indicative of error or bias in the means.

A TYPOLOGY OF EXPERIMENTER
OPERATING CHARACTERISTICS

We have emphasized three major concepts dealing with the data-obtaining characteristics of experimenters: effect, bias, and consistency. We may consider these three variables as dichotomous for the sake of simplicity, although recognizing that, in fact, they are continuous variables. The three "concepts" in all possible combinations permit the following seven-category typology of experimenters' operating characteristics:

(1)   I. ACCURATE
      II. INACCURATE
          A. *Unbiased*
(2)   1. Consistent
(3)   2. Inconsistent
          B. *Biased*
              1. Consistent
(4)   a. net high
(5)   b. net low
              2. Inconsistent
(6)   a. net high
(7)   b. net low

Figure 17-1 illustrates each of the seven types of experimenters, each of whom has drawn two samples of N subjects. In each cubicle or semicubicle the two distributions of responses are shown in relation to the "correct" value (indicated by the arrow), and the number corresponding to the

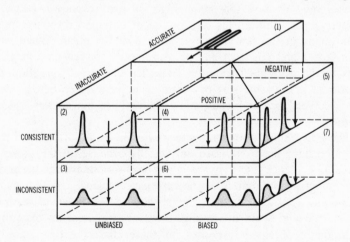

FIGURE 17-1
Schematic Typology of Experimenter Operating Characteristics

experimenter type is shown in the upper right corner. For the sake of clarity we have not considered cases of significantly decreased variability or hyperconsistency.

The type (1) experimenter is accurate; that is, he obtains data that are correctly consistent or variable about the mean of his obtained data, his data vary only negligibly about the "correct" value and, therefore, can be only negligibly biased. We can see from Figure 17-1 that the accurate experimenter is also maximally efficient. He can provide us with the desired estimate of the "correct" value with far fewer responses than can any other experimenter.

All other experimenters [(2) to (7)] are inaccurate, but we vastly prefer the inaccuracy of types (2) and (3), the unbiased experimenters. Their data will, in the long run, also give us a good estimate of the "correct" value. Between experimenters (2) and (3) we prefer (2) because his greater consistency permits us to draw our conclusions with fewer subjects. Among biased experimenters [(4) to (7)] we have no strong preferences. From the point of view of estimating the "correct" value, a positive (net high) [(4) and (6)] bias does not differ from a negative (net low) [(5) and (7)]. There may, however, be a slight preference for the consistent [(4) and (5)] over the inconsistent [(6) and (7)] biased experimenter. Bias can be more quickly determined for the consistent experimenter, and that may be useful information. It may prevent his collecting additional, unusable data.

Let us assume for the moment that most experimenters will show one or another form of bias to a greater or lesser extent. It still seems possible to obtain an unbiased estimate of the "correct" value although the cost will be greater. If we can assume a fairly symmetrical distribution of biases among a population of experimenters, the mean of the data obtained by a number of experimenters is likely to be unbiased. More subjects will be required, and more experimenters, and that is why the cost is greater. If our biased experimenters are consistent [types (4) and (5)], the cost per experimenter will be lower than if they are inconsistent [types (6) and (7)]. We should note that if we employ a set of experimenters of opposite biases, the total variance of subjects' responses, disregarding who their experimenter was, will be quite inflated because the variance attributable to the two types of experimenters will be added to the normal individual difference variance among an individual experimenter's subjects. We shall have more to say later about the important principle of "balancing biases" which was suggested by Mosteller (1944).

BIASED RESPONSE MAGNITUDE VS. BIASED INFERENCE

In our definitions of "data" and "response" we stated that these terms could be used to refer not only to the absolute measure of subjects' behavior but also to the difference between that measure and a comparison measure. Therefore, the data distributions shown in Figure 17-1 may for the sake of generality be viewed either as arrays of raw data obtained from homogeneously treated subjects or as arrays of difference scores arising, for example, from the differences between experimental and control manipulations. What we must consider now is the fact that an experimenter may be very biased in the raw data he obtains and yet be completely unbiased in the inferences his data allow him to make. Put more generally, inaccuracy in the order of magnitude of data obtained may be quite independent of the inaccuracy of the inferences to be drawn from the differences between data obtained from the groups to be compared. We can illustrate this point best by restricting our discussion to the occurrence and nonoccurrence of only one type of inaccuracy: e.g., bias. Tables 17-1, 17-2, 17-3, and 17-4 show the four possible situations:

1. Data magnitude unbiased; inference unbiased
2. Data magnitude unbiased; inference biased
3. Data magnitude biased; inference unbiased
4. Data magnitude biased; inference biased

In Table 17-1 we are interested in comparing E_x's data with the "correct values" as defined by the means of Es $a, b,$ and $c.$ We see in this case that the responses E_x obtained from his subjects are just like those obtained by the criterion experimenters. In addition, the difference between the data obtained from experimental and control group subjects is identical when we compare E_x's value with the "correct value." We conclude that E_x showed no bias in either response magnitude obtained (column III) or inference permissible on the basis of obtained differences (column IV).

TABLE 17—1

Unbiased Response Magnitude and Unbiased Inference

	I Experimental	*II* Control	*III* Sum	*IV* Difference
E_x	1.2	0.8	2.0	0.4
E_a	1.3	0.9	2.2	0.4
E_b	1.2	0.8	2.0	0.4
E_c	1.1	0.7	1.8	0.4
"Correct"	1.2	0.8	2.0	0.4

TABLE 17—2

Unbiased Response Magnitude and Biased Inference

	I	II	III	IV
	Experimental	*Control*	*Sum*	*Difference*
E_x	1.0	1.0	2.0	0.0
E_a	1.3	0.9	2.2	0.4
E_b	1.2	0.8	2.0	0.4
E_c	1.1	0.7	1.8	0.4
"Correct"	1.2	0.8	2.0	0.4

Table 17-2, however, shows that although E_x was unbiased in response magnitude obtained (column III), he *was* biased in the inference permissible from his experiment (column IV). He was the only experimenter not to obtain the "correct" mean difference of 0.4. In this example E_x might have been biased even further in the direction opposite to that of the correct mean difference. That is, he might have obtained significantly higher values from the subjects in his control group than from the subjects in the experimental group. At the same time, his obtained response magnitude might have remained unbiased.

Table 17-3 shows that our protagonist, E_x, has obtained the same dif-

TABLE 17—3

Biased Response Magnitude and Unbiased Inference

	I	II	III	IV
	Experimental	*Control*	*Sum*	*Difference*
E_x	1.7	1.3	3.0	0.4
E_a	1.3	0.9	2.2	0.4
E_b	1.2	0.8	2.0	0.4
E_c	1.1	0.7	1.8	0.4
"Correct"	1.2	0.8	2.0	0.4

ference between his experimental and control subjects that was obtained by the criterion experimenters (column IV). However, the response magnitude he obtained was significantly greater than that obtained by the more "accurate" experimenters (column III). If the purpose of the experiment was simply to establish that the subjects of the experimental group would outperform the subjects of the control group, our E_x has not led us at all astray. However, if there was, in addition to an interest in the experimental-control group difference, an intrinsic interest in the actual values obtained, E_x's data would have been very misleading.

TABLE 17—4

Biased Response Magnitude and Biased Inference

	I	II	III	IV
	Experimental	Control	Sum	Difference
E_x	1.5	1.5	3.0	0.0
E_a	1.3	0.9	2.2	0.4
E_b	1.2	0.8	2.0	0.4
E_c	1.1	0.7	1.8	0.4
"Correct"	1.2	0.8	2.0	0.4

Table 17-4 shows that in this example our E_x has obtained responses of significantly greater magnitude than were obtained by the more "accurate" experimenters (column III). In addition, he found no difference between the subjects of his experimental and control groups and was, with respect to the criterion experimenters, in biased error (column IV). With a given obtained response magnitude, our E_x might have been biased into the opposite direction with his control subjects outperforming his experimental subjects. He might also have been biased if he had obtained, say, a mean difference of 0.8. In this case we would not worry at all if we simply wanted to be able to claim the superiority of the experimental over the control subjects. However, if we had some intrinsic interest in the *magnitude* of the difference favoring the experimental group, we would have been misled. Suppose that our experimental treatment in this case was a very costly surgical procedure, whereas our control treatment was an inexpensive medical procedure. Let us say that a mean difference of 0.4 represents a statistically significant but clinically trivial improvement in patient comfort.

But let us say that a mean difference of 0.8 represents a dramatic clinical improvement in the patient. On the basis of our single experimenter's research, we might institute a surgical procedure that, on balance of cost against utility, is simply not worth it. This is only one example where we might be interested not so much in showing the significance of a difference but in showing its absolute magnitude.

THE PRACTICAL PROBLEM OF ASSESSMENT

Our discussion of the assessment of experimenter effects has been largely theoretical. Now we consider the "real" world of research. Here we have experimenters conducting experiments that, because of differences in subject sampling, instrumentation, and procedure, cannot reasonably be compared directly to any other experiments. How are we to assess the operating characteristics—i.e., the accuracy—of these experimenters? The answer is simple enough—it can't be done. Any data obtained by a single experimenter may be due as much to the experimenter as to his treatment conditions. No experimental data derived from a single experimenter can be considered as anything more than highly provisional unless replicated by at least one other investigator.

We may assume any given experimenter to be accurate until the first replication is carried out. If there is very close agreement between the results of the replication and of the original study, the hypothesis of experimenter accuracy is not discredited, though of course it is not confirmed either. If the results tend to be quite different but not significantly opposite in direction, we may suspend judgment until further replications are carried out. If the results are significantly opposite in direction, we are more assured than ever that the results are biased with respect to each other. Our solution again is to demand further replication. We may find that after a series of replications our original study and the first replication yielded the two most discrepant results, with all subsequent replications filling in the central area of what now begins to look like a normal distribution. Now we, in practice, can conclude (or more accurately, define) the first two studies as each yielding biased data—biased with respect to the grand mean data obtained and opposite in direction. On the other hand, if after our original study and one replication, the next several studies agree clearly with one of the first two, we may decide that the mean of the results of the studies in agreement will constitute our "correct" value in terms of which we define the other earlier study as quite biased. In any case, then, replication is essential not only to assess the accuracy of obtained data but also to help us correct for any inaccuracy of data.

In general, the more discrepant the results from two or more subjects, the more subjects are needed to establish certain parameters. And, in general, the more discrepant the results of two different experiments, the more replications of the entire study by different experimenters are required. In view of the importance of replications to the conclusions we will draw about experimenters' operating characteristics, and ultimately about nature, we will focus our attention further on the problem of replication.

18

Replications and Their Assessment

The crucial role of replication is well established in science generally. The undetected equipment failure, the rare and possibly random human errors of procedure, observation, recording, computation, or report are known well enough to make scientists wary of the unreplicated experiment. When we add to the possibility of the random "fluke," common to all sciences, the fact of individual organismic differences and the possibility of systematic experimenter effects in at least the behavioral sciences, the importance of replication looms larger still to the behavioral scientist.

What shall we mean by "replication"? Clearly the *same* experiment can never be repeated by a different worker. Indeed, the *same* experiment can never be repeated by even the same experimenter (Brogden, 1951). At the very least, the subjects and the experimenter himself are different over a series of replications. The subjects are usually different individuals and the experimenter changes over time, if not necessarily dramatically. But to avoid the not very helpful conclusion that there can be no replication in the behavioral sciences, we can speak of relative replications. We can order experiments on how close they are to each other in terms of subjects, experimenters, tasks, and situations. We can usually agree that *this* experiment, more than *that* experiment, is like a given paradigm experiment. When we speak of replication (and, in a sense, this entire book is an argument that we do so) in this section, we refer to a *relatively* exact repetition of an experiment.

THE REPLICATION SHORTAGE AND
INFERENTIAL MODELS

In the real world we may count two sorts of replications—those carried out and those reported. The latter, unfortunately, are a special case of the former and certainly not a random subsample. The difference in number between replications carried out and those reported is some unknown dark figure—a figure that depends, to some extent at least, on our view of statistical inference. The "null-hypothesis decision procedure" (Rozeboom, 1960), advocated by many statisticians, tends to establish certain critical p values as the definitions of whether a difference has "truly" been obtained. Now this might be nothing more than a semantic convention if it were not for a tendency among authors and editors to prefer publication of results with an associated p value less than some critical point—usually .05 or .01.[1] This tends to result in the publication of a biased sample of experiments (Bakan, 1965; McNemar, 1960; Smart, 1964; Sterling, 1959). It has usually been argued that published experiments are biased in the direction of Type I errors in that record is only made of the ".05 Hits" while the ".06–.99 Misses" are kept off the market. That may well be true. However, it can be argued that Type II errors may also be increased by the adoption of critical p values.

Suppose that a series of experiments has been carried out, all making similar comparisons between an experimental and a control condition. None of the results obtained by the five experimenters were statistically "significant." None are published, and the experimenters may not even be aware of the existence of four replications of their work. Table 18-1 gives the hypothetical results of the five studies. Although even the combined (say, by Fisher's method) probabilities of the five studies may not reach

TABLE 18—1

Hypothetical Results of Five Experiments

Experiment	Experimental	Control	Difference	p
1	8.5	7.0	+1.5	.30
2	7.0	5.5	+1.5	.30
3	9.0	8.0	+1.0	.30
4	9.5	7.5	+2.0	.30
5	7.5	6.0	+1.5	.30
Means	8.3	6.8	+1.5	

[1] A number of other workers have questioned the utility of the accept-reject model of inference (Bakan, 1965; Conrad, 1946; Eysenck, 1960; Wolf, 1961). Evidence that there *are*, psychologically if not statistically, critical p values (or "inferential cliffs") among established investigators as well as the upcoming generation of graduate students has been presented recently (Rosenthal & Gaito, 1963; Beauchamp & May, 1964; Rosenthal & Gaito, 1964).

some conventional level of significance, we note that in each study the experimental group performance exceeds the control group performance, and by a similar amount in each case. Considering these five differences, they are very unlikely to have occurred if the differences between the experimental and control conditions were, in fact, symmetrically distributed about zero ($t = 9.50$, $df = 4$, $p < .001$). There is a sense, then, in which Type II errors can be increased by our tendency to withhold publication of results not achieving a given level of significance (see also, Mosteller & Bush, 1954; Mosteller & Hammel, 1963).

In order to benefit properly from replications actually carried out, it is essential that these be routinely published, even if only as brief notes with fuller reports available from the experimenter, from a university library, or from the American Documentation Institute.[2] Without such availability our efforts to learn about behavioral phenomena in general— and more specifically to the point of this book, our efforts to assess the effects of the experimenter—will continue to be seriously hampered.

It has often been lamented of late that too few investigators concern themselves with more or less precise replications (e.g., Lubin, 1957). As an enterprise, replication, it has been said, lacks status. Who, then, on any large scale will provide us with the necessary replications? McGuigan's (1963) data and Woods' (1961) suggest that there are now enough experiments carried out and reported by multiple authors for there to be no hardships in subdividing these studies into as many complete replicates as there are investigators. The total investment of time would not be increased, but the generality of the results *would* be. Although such replication within projects would help us assess experimenter effects to some extent, we may feel that such replication is not quite the same as a truly "independent" replication carried out by an experimenter in a different laboratory. The problem of the potentially dependent or correlated nature of replicators bears further comment.

CORRELATED REPLICATORS

To begin with, an investigator who has devoted his life to the study of vision, or of psychological factors in somatic disorders, is less likely to carry out a study of verbal conditioning than is the investigator whose interests have always been in the area of verbal learning or interpersonal influence processes. To the extent that experimenters with different research interests are different kinds of people—and if we have shown that different

---

[2] Similar pleas have been made by Wolf (1961), Wolins (1959), and Goldfried and Walters (1959). These last authors have proposed the publication of a special *Journal of Negative Results* patterned after the *Psychological Abstracts*.

kinds of people, experimenters, are likely to obtain different data from their subjects—then we are forced to the conclusion that within any area of behavioral research the experimenters come precorrelated by virtue of their common interests and any associated characteristics. Immediately, then, there is a limit placed on the degree of independence we may expect from workers or replications in a common vineyard. But for different areas of research interest, the degree of correlation or of similarity among its workers may be quite different. Certainly we all know of workers in a common area who obtain data quite opposite from that obtained by colleagues. The actual degree of correlation, then, may not be very high. It may, in fact, even be negative, as with investigators holding an area of interest in common but holding opposite expectancies about the results of any given experiment.

A common situation in which research is conducted nowadays is within the context of a team of researchers. Sometimes these teams consist entirely of colleagues; often they are composed of one or more faculty members and one or more students at various stages of progress toward a Ph.D. Experimenters within a single research group may reasonably be assumed to be even more highly intercorrelated than any group of workers in the same area of interest who are not within the same research group. And perhaps students in a research group are more likely than a faculty member in the research group to be more correlated with their major professor. There are two reasons for this likelihood. The first is a selection factor. Students may select to work in a given area with a given investigator because of their perceived and/or actual similarity of interest and associated characteristics. Colleagues are less likely to select a university, area of interest, and specific project because of a faculty member at that university. The second reason why a student may be more correlated with his professor than another professor might be is a training factor. A student may have had a large proportion of his research experience under the direction of a single professor. Another professor, though he collaborates with his colleagues, has most often been trained in research elsewhere by another person. Although there may be exceptions, even frequent ones, it seems reasonable, on the whole, to assume that student researchers are more correlated with their adviser than another adviser might be.

The correlation of replicators that we have been discussing refers directly to a corrrelation of *attributes* and indirectly to a correlation of *data* these investigators will obtain from their subjects. The issue of correlated experimenters or observers is by no means a new one. Over 60 years ago Karl Pearson spoke of "the high correlation of judgments . . . [suggesting] an influence of the immediate atmosphere, which may work upon two observers for a time in the same manner" (1902, p. 261). Pearson believed the problem of correlated observers to be as critical for the physical sciences as for the behavioral sciences.

REPLICATION ASSESSMENT

What we have had to say about correlated replicators has implications for the assessment of replications. Such assessment may serve two goals; (1) to help us make a general statement of how well studied a given area of inquiry or a specific relationship might be, (2) to help us make a general statement of what the available evidence, taken as a whole, has to say about the nature of the relationship studied. Not only the worker who wants to summarize formally, as in a journal article (e.g., in the *Psychological Bulletin*), what is known of a given relationship but any investigator contemplating work in an area somewhat new to him might profit from some numerical system of replication assessment. Such a system is suggested here.[3]

The basic unit is the single experiment conducted by a single experimenter. Assuming a "perfectly" designed and executed study, we assign a value of 1.00. This would assume for a given research question, and standard sample size, *N,* that the appropriate (as defined by the consensus of colleagues) experimental treatment and control groups were employed, and that the data collector was effectively blind to the treatment group membership of each subject. Now this may seem like vague information with which to assign a numerical value to the soundness of an experiment, but the fact is that we are constantly making judgments of this sort anyway, and sometimes with even less information. There appears to be at least fair agreement on a ranking of the soundness of single studies in formal and informal seminars on research methodology. The really difficult step is the assignment of a numerical value. It should be noted that our interest at the moment is *not* in the assessment of the *experimenter* but of the experiment. Thus, we could find the experimental vs. control comparison in which we were interested regardless of whether the investigator was primarily interested in that particular comparison or not. Certain comparisons of great interest to a given worker are often buried as a few sentences in a report by an investigator who has only an incidental interest in that comparison. In other words, the *intent* of the investigator is irrelevant to our purposes. It is the validity of the comparison that concerns us. Similarly, we are *not* concerned with the conclusion a given investigator draws from his comparison, for such conclusions vary greatly in the degree to which they derive directly from the data. If an investigator finds A > B, it is that inequality which concerns us, not his explanation of how it came about. That explanation may be important, but it is not relevant to the question of replication as we are discussing it.

If we grant that some agreement can be reached on the assessment of the single experiment, we can state the general principle that a replication

[3] I want to thank Fred Mosteller for his helpful discussion of this procedure.

of that experiment which obtains similar results is maximally convincing if it is maximally separated from the first experiment along such dimensions as time, physical distance, personal attributes of the experimenters, experimenters' expectancy, and experimenters' degree of personal contact with each other. The number of dimensions (n) that may prove useful in the future is not known at present, but we can restate our principle in geometric terms. The value of replications with similar results is maximized when the distance between replicates in the n-dimensional space is maximized.

The Replication Index

Now for a concrete example of how we might score a set of replicates to determine how much we know about a given relationship. An investigator conducts a sound study with only some minor imperfections of design or procedure. The mean rating assigned by a seminar of competent methodologists is .80. In a few months he replicates the study and his new score of .80 is added to his old. Now we "know" 1.60's worth. One of his students replicates, and though we have argued that students are likely to be correlated with their professors, the student is a different person. We multiply the student's replication value of .80 by 2 to weight the fact of lessened correlation of replicates. The student's points (1.60) are added to his professor's (1.60) for a total of 3.20 points.

Now, a colleague down the hall replicates the work, a friend, perhaps, who may still not be regarded as uncorrelated but who was trained by other people and who came to the same department for reasons other than working on *this* problem with *this* colleague. Doing the study in a very similar way the colleague earns an .80 for the study, but to credit his presumably lesser correlatedness we multiply that value by 3. He has taught us 2.40's worth. We sum his points with those obtained until now and have 5.60.

If the replication were carried out in a different laboratory by an investigator not known personally to the original worker or his correlated replicators we might want to assign an even higher weight, e.g., 5. Conducted by this stranger, a replication might give us 4.00 points to be added to the previously cumulated total of 5.60.

So far, our hypothetical replicators have all found similar results, and all had no reason to expect otherwise. But now there is a researcher for whom the results, by now reported, make no sense whatever. His theoretical position would postulate just the *opposite* outcomes from those reported. Furthermore, he doesn't know the original investigator personally, or any of the previous replicators, isn't a thing like any of them, and to top it all off, his laboratory is halfway or more across the country. He replicates. His study's basic .80 value gets us 8.00. The weighting of 10, which seems quite large, is due in no small measure to his expectancy, which is opposite to all the other replicators'. We now have a cumulated replication value of

17.60. If we wanted to, we could establish a scale of evaluation such that our score of 17.60 represents a fairly respectable level of replicatedness. We could, for example, call a total of less than 2.00 as hardly representing real replication at all, a total of 5.00 or more might be regarded as a good beginning and values over 10.00 as fairly respectable.

The weighting system described and the particular weights arbitrarily employed in our examples are obviously intended only to be suggestive of the considerations relevant to a more precise system. We can sum up some of the major characteristics of the scoring system:

1. A very badly done experiment profits us little, upon even many replications. As the score per unweighted replicate approaches 0.00, no amount of replication can help us.

2. Replications by different investigators are worth more to us than replications by the same investigator.

3. The more different the replicators are from each other, the more value accrues to the total replicational effort.

The replication index yields a summary statement of how well studied a given problem is, regardless of whether replication results are consistent or inconsistent. However, the index also yields a summary statement of how confident we can be of the specific results obtained if the results are all in the same direction. In the not infrequent situation where some replication results are in opposite directions, we apply the scoring system separately to all those replications yielding results in one direction and then again to those replications yielding results in the opposite direction. The difference between the two scores obtained gives some indication of which result is better established. It is entirely possible that the scoring system suggested can help clarify a set of opposite results. Suppose that of ten experiments five have found A > B and five have found A < B. If one of these sets of five studies was carried out by a single investigator and one or two of his students, whereas the other set was carried out by less correlated experimenters, including some with opposite expectancies, there could be an overwhelming superiority in the points earned by the latter set of replications. This would be especially true if, in addition, there were some reason for assigning a lower score for the individual replicates in the set of studies conducted by the more correlated replicators. At least in some cases, then, it seems more valuable to compare contradictory sets of data on our replication index than to simply say there are five studies "pro" and five studies "con." There may, of course, still be those puzzling situations where the pro studies and con studies each earn high and similar replication index scores.

The Generality Index

We have talked very much as though the replications discussed were virtually "exact." The index of replication can also be applied, however, to only approximate replications. If we were interested in the effects of anxiety on intellectual performance, a more or less "exact" replication would require more or less identical procedures for arousing anxiety and measuring intellectual performance. We could as well apply our index to not-so-exact "replications" in which different arousal procedures and different measures of intellectual functioning were employed. (The less exact the replications, the more the individual study's score for "soundness" may vary.)

A higher score on the replication index for a given research question implies greater generality for the results, assuming these results to be fairly consistent. Because of our special interest in the experimenter, we have dealt primarily with the problem of interexperimenter correlation in our discussion of the assessment of replication. If we were interested in the more general problem of generality, as we often are, we could readily extend our index to include other, nonexperimenter factors increasing the generality of our data. Thus, in the example given earlier of the effect of anxiety on intellectual performance we might give more points on a generality index for a "replication" that employed different methods for arousing anxiety and for measuring intellectual performance. If a sample of males were employed where females had been employed before, or grocery clerks where college students had been employed before, or animals where humans had been employed before, we would weight more heavily the contribution of the "replication" to the generality index. In effect, the generality index can differ from the replication index only to the extent that the replications are only approximately similar experiments.

ANECDOTAL REPLICATION

In order that we not be wasteful of information we must have a place in our replication index or generality index for information derived from sources other than formal experiments. For an appropriate example we may return to our hypothetical study of the effect of anxiety on intellectual performance. Suppose that the experimenter in his role as educator has observed many instances in which students' anxiety has lowered their examination performance. Suppose further that our investigator has never observed an instance in which anxiety (of a given magnitude) led to *improved* examination performance. If other people had also made the same observation and also found no negative instances, we would have some additional evidence for the relationship between anxiety level and intellectual performance. Such evidence we usually regard as *anecdotal,* and that term often carries a negative connotation. On the other hand, however, we can argue that there is a continuity of more and less elegant circumstances of observation which ranges from the fairly crude anecdote to the more elegant anecdotes of the ethologist, the survey researcher, and finally the variable-manipulating experimenter employing control or comparison groups. We can argue further that the most elegant experiment differs from the cruder anecdote only as to the plausibility of the conclusions reached on its basis. Such plausibility, in the final analysis, is defined in psychological terms, such as the degree of belief or conviction it inspires in qualified workers in the area. The well-controlled experiment, then, may be seen as a more formal anecdote, more or less convincing, as with any anecdote, as a function of who "tells" it, how well and carefully it is told, and how relevant it is to the question under study. If we can assign "soundness" points to the experiment, and weight these points to establish a replication or generality index, we ought to be able to do the same thing for the cruder anecdote. The "soundness" points assigned would usually be some value lower than if it were a more systematic anecdote, as is the formal experiment. Arbitrarily, let us assign a score of .10 to any "well-told" ancedote *for which no contrary anecdote can be found* after honest efforts to find them.[4] This search for negative instances is central and can be most usefully pursued by enlisting the reminiscences or observations of workers whose theoretical position would suggest contrary anecdotes. In practice, anecdotes on either side of a theoretical question are likely to cancel each other out. Where they do not, we have fairly powerful sources of additional evidence. The weighting of the soundness scores of anecdotes can be as was described for more formal experiments: more weight given to replicated anecdotes as a function of the noncorrelatedness of the raconteur. Such weights, then, might vary from "1" for a new consistent anecdote by the same teller to "10" for a consistent anecdote told by a very different observer whose theoretical orientation would suggest a contrary anecdote. In order to encourage more systematic observations and discourage an interpretation of these remarks as favorable to a swing to anecdotes as major or even exclusive sources of evidence, we can add the restriction that very informal anecdotes are not scored as greater than zero value in a replication or generality index *unless* the score on that index has already achieved a given level (e.g., a 2.00 score) on the basis of more formal research.

There are situations in which anecdotes of greater or lesser elegance are actually *more* valuable than more formal experiments. Consider some research question that has been well replicated by different experimenters, such that a very respectable replication index score has been achieved. Assume further that the different experiments yield results quite consistent with one another (e.g., A > B). But now suppose that a fair number of less formal anecdotes, including very casual observation, experiments in nature, and field studies, are also quite consistent with each other but incon-

---

[4] For the situation where the anecdote is of the somewhat formal sort—anthropological field reports—Naroll (1962) has made an outstanding contribution through his development of the "observation quality index." This is essentially a method for assessing the reliability of the raconteur.

sistent with the results of the more formal laboratory experiments, such that
A < B always. In such a case it may be that the formal experiments as a set
are biased with respect to more "real-lifelike" situations. This sort of
bias could occur even though the experimenters were completely unbiased
in the sense in which we have used that term. It could well be that the very
laboratory nature of the experimenter-subject interaction systematically so
changes the situation that the more usual extraexperimental response is
quite reversed. This effect of the experimental situation on subjects' responses has been frequently discussed and even labeled (e.g., experimental
back-action or backlash effect). The *demand characteristics of the experimental situation* (Orne, 1962), although varying from experiment to experiment, may have, for a given type of study, such communality that the
results of even an entire set of experiments may be quite biased. For this
reason, and because of other special characteristics of the laboratory experimental situation (Riecken, 1954; Riecken, 1962), there may be occasions on which anecdotes, less formal than the experiment, may be more
valuable than additional laboratory experiments. One view of the more informal source of evidence that emerges in part from what we have said is
that there are phases in systematic inquiry in which more anecdotal evidence
is more likely to have special relevance. Before a program of experiments is
undertaken, informal evidence seems useful in guiding the direction of, or
even in justifying the very existence of, the experimental program. Then
later, at the completion of the program, a systematic search for (preferably
new) anecdotal evidence seems indicated to reassure us that the general
findings of the more formal research program are consistent with more
nearly everyday experience.

Nothing in what we have said about the formal experimental situation
should be so construed that the laboratory setting comes somehow to be regarded as "unreal." Different it is, of course. But at the same time, it is
as real a situation as any other, though perhaps less common than the word
"everyday" implies (Mills, 1962). Whether we can reasonably generalize
from the laboratory to "everyday" life, then, is an empirical question to be
answered by observing both, rather than a philosophical question to be
answered on any a priori grounds.[5]

[5] The same reasoning can be applied to the often-asked question of whether we
can reasonably generalize from studies of animal behavior to human behavior.

19

Experimenter Sampling

Much of this book has been devoted to showing that an experimenter's expectancy may be an unintended determinant of the results of his research. This chapter and those to follow are addressed to the question of what can be done to control the effects of the experimenter's expectancy. A number of strategies will be proposed. Some of these strategies will be recognized as direct attempts to minimize expectancy effects. Somewhat paradoxically, some of these strategies will be recognized as attempts to maximize these effects. In this chapter we shall discuss strategies that seek neither to minimize nor to maximize but rather to randomize and "calibrate" experimenter expectancies. In preceding chapters we have alluded to the advantages accruing from the employment of samples of experimenters rather than the more usual single data collector. In this chapter some of these advantages will be discussed in more detail.

The employment of samples of data collectors is already a common practice in survey research (Hyman et al., 1954). In part this is due to the logistic problem of trying to obtain responses from perhaps thousands, or even millions, of respondents. In part too, however, the practice of sampling data collectors is part of a self-conscious strategic attempt to assess the influence of the data collector on the results of the survey (e.g., Mahalanobis, 1946). In other kinds of psychological research (e.g., laboratory experiments), the number of subjects contacted is low enough for a single experimenter to collect all the data easily. The necessity for employing samples of experimenters in these cases is not logistic but strategic.[1]

It was stated earlier that in principle we cannot assess the experimenter's accuracy at all without having at least one replication to serve as the reference point for the definition of accuracy. And as our sample of experimenters increases in size beyond two, we are in an increasingly good

[1] The practical problem of obtaining samples of data collectors for laboratory research was discussed in the last chapter and has been found not at all insurmountable.

position to assess not only the experimenter's accuracy but his bias and consistency as well.

Subdividing Experiments

With the sample size of subjects fixed, the larger the sample of experimenters, the smaller the subsample of subjects each data collector must contact. Subdivision of the experiment among several experimenters may in itself serve to reduce the potential biasing effects of the experimenter.

Learning to bias. We have suggested that experimenter bias may be a learned phenomenon, and that within a given experiment the experimenter may learn from the subjects' response how to influence subjects unintentionally. This learning process takes time, and with fewer subjects from whom to learn the unintentional communication system there may be less learning to bias. Even if the interpretation of bias as a learned phenomenon were in error, the basic evidence that bias increases as a function of the number of subjects contacted by each experimenter should encourage the use of more experimenters and fewer subjects per experimenter.

Maintaining blindness. A second advantage gained when each experimenter contacts fewer subjects is related particularly to the method of blind contact with subjects. In discussing that method in a subsequent chapter it will be suggested that if enough subjects were contacted, the experimenter might unintentionally "crack the code" and learn which subjects are members of which experimental group and/or the nature of the experimental treatment subjects had received. The fewer subjects each experimenter contacts, the less chance of an unwitting breakdown of the blind procedure.

Early returns. A third advantage of having fewer subjects contacted by each experimenter, a "psychological" advantage, derives from the finding that early data returns may have a biasing effect upon subsequent data. With more experimenters the entire experiment can be completed more quickly if facilities are available for the simultaneous collection of data by different experimenters. With all the results of a study "nearly in" there is less need for the principal investigator to get a glimpse of the early returns and hence less chance for the operation of the biasing effects of these returns.

A limiting case of contacting fewer subjects would, in fact, eliminate entirely the effect of early data returns on the biasing behavior of the data collector. If each experimenter contacted only a single subject in each treatment condition, his obtained data could not, of course, influence the data of any other subject in the same condition. Where there are no later data, there can be no effect of early data returns.

Although there may be some merit to the procedure of allowing each experimenter only a single subject per experimental condition there are two drawbacks. One of these is logistic. It would not be very efficient to train a data collector for a given experiment and have him contact only a single subject per condition. On the other hand, there may be situations in which the utility of the procedure outweighs the increased cost. The other drawback to this procedure is that it provides us with no estimate of individual differences among subjects. The variation among subjects within conditions is confounded with the variation among experimenters. This may not be too serious, however. If we can be satisfied with an estimate of the effect due to the treatment condition and that due to the differences among experimenters, we may be willing to forego the within cells mean square. Even if each experimenter contacts only a single subject in a single condition we could still evaluate the effects of the treatment, although we could get no estimate of the variation among either subjects or experimenters.

Increasing Generalizability

If there were no effect of earlier upon later obtained data, nor indeed any form of experimenter expectancy effect, we would still benefit greatly from the employment of samples of experimenters. As Brunswik (1956) and Hammond (1954) have pointed out, this would greatly increase the generality of our research results. Because of differences in appearance and behavior, different experimenters serve as different stimuli to their subjects, thereby changing to a greater or lesser degree the experimental situation as the subject confronts it.

When only a single experimenter has been employed, we have no way of knowing how much difference it would have made if a different experimenter had been employed. The results of the research are then confounded with the stimulus value of the particular experimenter. We would have little confidence in a prediction of the results of a subsequent experiment employing a different experimenter except the prediction that the result would probably be different. The more experimenters we employ the better, but even the modest addition of a single experimenter helps a great deal. We not only would be able to predict that the result of a subsequent experiment would fall somewhere near the mean of our two experimenters' results but would be able to say something of how much deviation from this value is likely. In other words, with as few as two experimenters we can make a statement of experimenter variance. In principle, of course, this line of reasoning holds only when experimenters are sampled randomly.

A little later, we shall speak of automated data-collection systems (ADCS) and shall stress their value as a means of avoiding differential treatment of subjects. Here it must be added that any ADCS has its own special stimulus value (McGuigan, 1963). We can then regard any given

ADCS with its particular stimulus settings as just another experimenter, although a very "standardized" one. To increase the generality of the obtained results, therefore, we must sample a variety of ADCS's or at least a variety of settings of a single ADCS.

The employment of samples of data collectors, necessitated by their individual differences, may be viewed as a boon to, rather than the price of, behavioral research. Built-in replications, although they bring with them the data collector as a source of variance (which can be measured and handled statistically), also bring a greater robustness to our research findings.[2]

From the point of view now, not so much of generality but of the control of experimenter expectancy effects, there are three conditions involving experimenter sampling which will be discussed in turn. In the first of these conditions, the sampled experimenters' expectancies are unknown and indeterminable. In the second of these conditions, experimenters' expectancies are known before the sampling. In the third condition, experimenters' expectancies are known only after the sampling has occurred.

EXPECTANCIES UNKNOWN

Population Characteristics

There may be experiments in which we decide to employ a sample of experimenters but in which we have no way of assessing the experimenters' expectancies. We may draw such a sample from a variety of populations differing in the number of restrictions imposed. Perhaps the least restrictive population of potential experimenters would be all those who are physically and intellectually capable of serving as experimenters. If we choose such a population we earn perhaps the greatest degree of generalizability of our data, but at the cost of representativeness of the real world or ecological validity. Ecological validity is sacrificed, however, only in the sense that most experimenters who have in the past collected data have been drawn from less broadly defined populations.

Most experimenters in a given experiment are not simply organismically capable of collecting the data. They are further selected on the basis of an interest in research generally and an interest in the particular research question they are trying to answer. They may be further selected on the basis of the expectancy they hold about the outcome. They may, as

[2] It is the name of Brunswik that rightly comes to mind when we speak of the increased generality deriving from the sampling of experimenters and their associated procedural variations. But it would be a mistake to assume that "more classic" or "traditional" workers in the field of experimental design would disagree with Brunswik. R. A. Fisher (1947), for example, though speaking of procedural variation not explicitly associated with different data collectors, makes the same point.

a corollary, be selected for personality characteristics associated with people doing research in a given area of behavioral science and having certain outcome orientations. Because real experimenters are so highly selected—i.e., drawn from such a relatively restricted population of capable data collectors—it might be very difficult to draw a large sample of such experimenters for our purposes.

There is, however, a trend for less highly selected experimenters to collect data for serious scientific purposes. Not only more and more graduate students are collecting behavioral data but undergraduates as well. As this trend continues and accelerates, our employment of less fully professional experimenters will become more and more representative of the "real world" of data collection. At least it seems not at all far-fetched to draw samples of advanced undergraduate students in the behavioral sciences and generalize from their results to what we might expect from advanced undergraduate research assistants. It seems, then, that we may not be sacrificing too much ecological validity, after all, by employing samples of less than fully professional data collectors.

The random assignment of experimenters to experiments gets around the potential problems of self-selection on the basis of hypotheses. Experimenters, naturally enough, spend their time collecting data relevant to a question to which they are likely to expect a given answer. If the investigator, though he may have an expectancy about the outcome, employs a random sample of data collectors, he may protect the data from the effects of his own expectancy. This would be especially true if the sampling of experimenters were combined with some of the control strategies described in subsequent chapters. If indeed there are personality characteristics or other attributes associated with an experimenter's choice of research question, the data collected by that experimenter are likely to show a certain amount of error, though not necessarily bias. The random assignment of experimenters also gets us around this potential problem of self-selection for correlated attributes.

Cancellation of Biases

Simply selecting our experimenters at random does not imply that they will have no expectancies. The expectancies they do have, however, are more likely to be heterogeneous, and the more so as we have not tried to select experimenters very much like the experimenters who have in the past collected data within a given area of research. The more heterogeneous the expectancies, the greater the chance that the effects of expectancies will, at least partially, cancel each other out. The classic discussion of the canceling of biases is that by Mosteller (1944) for the situation of the survey research interviewer, a situation that in principle does not differ from that of the laboratory experimenter.

If we can hope for a canceling of expectancy bias, we can also hope for a canceling of modeling biases. But where the experimenters' expectancies and their own task performances are unknown, we can only hope for such a cancellation. And even if this information were available we could not count on a cancellation. The various expectancies represented in our sample may be held with different intensities, resulting in different magnitudes of expectancy effect. Or particular expectancies may be correlated with personality characteristics or other attributes that are themselves associated with the degree of unintended influence exerted by the experimenter. An example may be helpful.

Suppose we want only to standardize a set of photographs such as those we have often used as to the degree of success or failure reflected by the persons pictured. We select at random 20 experimenters, all enrolled in a course in experimental psychology. For the sake of simplicity let there be only two expectancies among experimenters: (1) that the photos will be rated as successful and (2) that they will be rated as unsuccessful. Let us suppose further that the "true" mean value of the photos is at the exact point of indifference. If ten of our experimenters expect success ratings and ten expect failure ratings, and the magnitudes of their expectancy effects are equal, we obtain a grand mean rating that is quite unbiased. That situation is the one we hope for.

But now suppose that the ten experimenters who expect to obtain success ratings differ from the experimenters expecting failure ratings in being more self-confident, more professional in manner, more businesslike, and more expressive-voiced. These are the experimenters, we have already seen, who are more likely to influence their subjects in the expected direction. The ten experimenters expecting failure ratings do not equitably influence their subjects in the opposite direction. Their mean obtained rating is, therefore, at the point of indifference, and they cannot serve to cancel the biasing effects of our more influential success-expecters. The grand mean rating obtained will be biased in the "success" direction. Troublesome as this situation may be, we should note that it is still better than having employed only a few self-selected, success-expecting experimenters. In this particular example we would have been best served by selecting only those experimenters who could not implement their expectancy. But, of course, in our example we have given ourselves information not ordinarily so readily available.

The hoped-for cancellation of bias may also fail for reasons residing in the experimental task. A good example might involve a "ceiling effect." Suppose a large number of children have been tested on a group administered form of a new perceptual-motor task. The testing was done under those conditions of administration maximizing their performance as the originator of the task intended. Now suppose that to establish the reliability of the task performance all the children are retested, this time with an individually administered alternate form of the task. Again, we employ twenty data collectors, and again they have one of two possible expectancies about the children they will test: (1) that they are very well-coordinated and (2) that they are very poorly coordinated.

By their manner during the interaction with the children, those experimenters expecting poor performance obtain poorer performance. On the average the children's performance on this alternate form retest is lower by some amount than it was on the originally administered test. We can see that this bias cannot be canceled. Controlling for scoring errors, the youngsters tested by experimenters expecting good performance cannot perform any better than they did on the pretest. Regardless of any experimenter characteristics facilitating unintentional influence, organismic limits permit no biasing in the directon of better performance. The grand mean of our obtained retest data has been biased in the low direction by the inability of half the experimenters to exert equivalent and opposite bias. In this case, the retest reliability of the task has also been biased in the low direction. Interestingly enough, if the experimenters expecting very good performance had been able to bias their subjects' performance equivalently there would have been no bias in the grand mean performance obtained, but the correlation between the pretest and posttest would have been even further lowered. If all experimenters showed the same expectancy effect, the grand mean performance would have been maximally biased, but the retest reliability would not, of course, have been affected at all. This assumes, as we have here, that any experimenter of one expectancy exercises the same magnitude of effect as any other experimenter in that same expectancy condition.

An interesting example of asymmetrical effects of bias has been reported by Stember and Hyman (1949). In their analysis of an opinion survey they found that interviewers holding the more common opinion tended to report data that inflated the number of respondents to be found with that same opinion. Interviewers holding the less common opinion, however, inflated the "don't know" category rather than the category of their own opinion. In this case, which we can regard as modeling bias, we again see a failure of the cancellation of bias. The grand mean response was inflated in the more commonly held opinion category. One interpretation of this unexpected finding proposes that an expectancy bias may have been operating simultaneously. Thus, if it is generally known what the majority opinion is, and if it is known also that there is a heavy majority, then all interviewers may have the expectancy that they will obtain majority opinions at least most of the time. This expectancy by itself may inflate the expected majority opinion category.

For interviewers whose own opinion is the majority opinion, their modeling bias may act in conjunction with their expectancy bias to inflate the majority opinion category even more. However, the minority opinion-holding interviewers have a modeling bias which runs counter to their expectancy and serves in fact to cancel it. Left with neither an unopposed modeling bias nor unopposed expectancy, the neutral "don't know" category is inflated. Whether this is what happened in the Stember and Hyman study or not cannot be easily determined. But this analysis does illustrate the possibility that opposing biases within the same experimenter may cancel each other and that consonant biases may reinforce each other. It should be mentioned that the bias in this study could have been one of interpretation or coding rather than a bias affecting the subjects' response, but this does not alter the relevance of the illustration. We have already suggested that the experimenter's attitude toward the results of his research may affect his observation, recording, computation, and interpretation as well as his subjects' responses.

From all that has been said it seems clear that we cannot depend on the complete cancellation of biases in a sample of experimenters. But the argument for sampling experimenters is still strong. At least by sampling experimenters we have the possibility of cancellation of biases, whereas if we use only a single experimenter we can be absolutely certain that no cancellation of bias is possible.

Homogeneity of Results

Employing samples of experimenters will often provide us with considerable reassurance. If all of a sample of experimenters obtain similar data we will not err very often if we assume that no bias has occurred and that, in fact, no effects whatever associated with the experimenter have occurred. On these occasions we have good reason for arguing that only one experimenter would have been required. But, obviously, there is no way of knowing this heartening fact without having first employed experimenter sampling.

The homogeneity of obtained results should not be so reassuring to us if the sampling of experimenters has been very restrictive. If our sample included only data collectors holding one expectancy regarding the data to be obtained, as might occur if we selected only experimenters who had selected a given hypothesis for investigation, our results would be homogeneous still, but biased too. The homogeneity of obtained results is convincing in direct proportion to the heterogeneity of the experimenters' expectancies and other experimenter attributes.

In this section we have discussed the advantages of sampling experimenters even though their expectancies are unknown and indeterminable. Under these circumstances we benefit greatly in terms of the increased generalizability of our data, but our controls for expectancy effects are at best haphazard. No correction formulas can be written to control statistically the effects of experimenter expectancies. To write such corrections we must know what experimenters' expectancies (and related sources of error) are like. In some cases these expectancies may be well known before sampling, and in other cases, although not known before sampling, they can be assessed after sampling. We will discuss next the situation in which experimenter expectancies are generally known before the sampling occurs.

EXPECTANCIES KNOWN BEFORE SAMPLING

In all the sciences there are investigators whose theories and hypotheses are so well known or so easily inferred that there can be wide agreement on the nature of their expectancy for the results of their research. Academic scientist A designs and conducts an experiment in order to demonstrate that his expectancy is warranted. Academic scientist B may design and conduct an experiment in order to demonstrate his expectancy that scientist A's expectancy is unwarranted. This, of course, is scientific controversy at its best—taken into the laboratory for test.

If they are in the behavioral sciences, our two scientists may design and conduct quite different experiments to arrive at their conclusions. Each may obtain the expected results whether or not any unintended biasing effect occurred, and feel his own position to be strengthened. So long as they conducted different experiments, we can have nothing to say about the occurrence of expectancy effects. Sooner or later members of one camp are likely to attempt a more or less exact replication of the other camp's experiment. If they obtain data in agreement with the original data, we are somewhat reassured that the role of expectancy effects in either study was minimal. But if they obtain contradictory data, can we attribute the difference to expectancy effects? Probably not, because geographic and temporal factors, subject population, and experimenter attributes all covaried with the possible expectancy effect.

Collaborative Disagreement

For the resolution of theoretical and empirical issues important enough to engage the interest of two or more competent and disagreeing scientists, it seems worthwhile to coordinate their efforts more efficiently. At the design stage the opponents might profitably collaborate in the production of a research plan which by agreement would provide a resolution of the difference of opinion. At the stage of data collection, too, the opponents may collaborate either in person or by means of assistants provided by both scientists. Conducted at the same place, using a common pool of subjects and the same procedures, the two (or more) replicates should provide similar results. If they do not, we may attribute the difference either to the effects of the differing expectancies or to experimenter variables correlated with the differing expectancies.

Such collaboration of disagreeing scientists has taken place. Disproportionately often this "committee approach" to the resolution of scientific controversy has been applied to controversies involving either "borderline areas" of science or areas having major economic or social implications. Such an approach has been suggested for the investigation of parapsychological phenomena, for alleged cancer cures, and for study of the effects of smoking on the likelihood of developing cancer.

In such cases even the scientific layman can readily infer the scientific "antagonist's" expectancies or at least some potential sources of such expectancies. When the press described the distinguished panel of scientific "judges" preparing the United States Public Health Service report on the effects of smoking, it carefully noted for each member whether he was or was not himself a smoker. Laymen (and some scientists) were forced to reject the hypothesis that the committee's evaluation might have been biased by their expectancies or preferences by noting that its conclusions were uncorrelated with their own smoking habits. On the other hand, when the press reported the dissenting view of scientists employed by the tobacco industry, the report was clearly if implicitly written in the tone of "Well, what else would you expect?" It is, of course, not necessarily true that the expectancy of an industry-employed scientist is due to economic factors. The expectancy may have preceded the employment and indeed may have been a factor in the particular employment sought. But the source of the expectancy may be more relevant to a consideration of ethical rather than scientific questions. The origin of an expectancy may be quite irrelevant to the degree of its effect upon data obtained or upon interpretations of data.

It seems very reasonable that the "committee approach" to scientific investigation has been applied to areas of great interest to the general public. But the more technical, less generally appealing issues to which most scientists direct their attention deserve equal effort to minimize sources of error.

One special problem may arise when established scientists collaborate with a sincere wish to eliminate the effects of their expectancy. In their contacts or their surrogates' contacts with subjects they may bend over backward to avoid biasing the results of their experiment. This "bending over backward," an effect described in an earlier chapter, may lead each investigator to obtain data biased in the direction of his opponents' hypothesis. For this reason, and for even greater control of expectancy effects, the sampling of experimenters with known expectancies is best combined with the control techniques to be described in subsequent chapters.[3]

[3] The analysis of the data collected by disagreeing, collaborating investigators can proceed, in the simple case, in the same way as in any "expectancy-controlled" experiment. In the terminology introduced in the last chapter of this section, one

Another difficulty of the "committee method" of controlling for expectancy effects is that it is likely to involve only a small though well-known sample of experimenters. With a smaller sample of data collectors it becomes more difficult to assess the sources of variation if there is disagreement among the data collected by different investigators.

EXPECTANCIES DETERMINED AFTER SAMPLING

Established investigators involved in a visible scientific difference of opinion are in sufficiently short supply for us to have to turn elsewhere for larger samples of data collectors. If less visible experimenters are to be employed we are unlikely to know their expectancies regarding the outcome of their research. But their expectancies can be determined after they are selected and before they collect any data.[4]

Not only their expectancies but their own task performance may be determined so that modeling effects may also be assessed and controlled. In addition, other experimenter attributes known to affect, or suspected of affecting, subjects' responses may be determined and then controlled. The experimenter's own performance and many other attributes are easy to determine. As part of the training procedure experimenters may be asked to serve as subjects. They learn the procedure they will have to follow while at the same time giving us a measure of their own task performance. Other experimenter attributes, if relevant, can be determined by direct observation (e.g., sex), from public records (e.g., age), by direct questioning (e.g., religion), or by means of standardized tests (e.g., intelligence). Some of these same methods may be used in the determination of experimenters' expectancies, which we now discuss in more detail.

Determination of Expectancies

Inexperienced experimenters. If we are going to employ a fairly large sample of experimenters it is less likely that we can obtain very highly

---

experimenter would be contacting subjects in the A and D cells while his collaborating opponent would be contacting subjects in the B and C cells. The interpretation of various possible outcomes of this 2×2 design would also proceed as described in the chapter dealing with expectancy control groups. The basic logic of employing oppositely expecting experimenters is, of course, the same as that underlying the use of expectancy control groups. The main difference is that in the former case we find the experimenter's expectancy whereas in the latter case we induce it.

[4] If the determination of expectancy or of some other experimenter variable were made after the experimenters' data collection we could not properly regard it as an independent variable. The data collection itself might have influenced the experimenter's expectancy and some (e.g., anxiety) but not all (e.g., birth order) other experimenter attributes. Such contamination renders measures of experimenter variables useless as a means of controlling for their effect by statistical techniques.

experienced data collectors. More inexperienced experimenters such as advanced undergraduates may have no particular expectancy about the result of a given experiment. They may not know enough about the area to have developed an expectancy. For these experimenters we can describe the experiment in detail and ask them to make a "guess" about how subjects will respond. This guess then may serve as the expectancy statement. The form of the guess may vary from an open-ended verbal or written statement, through a ranking of alternatives to an absolute rating of the several alternatives. If there are several possible expectancies or several degrees of one expectancy, we may want to assign to the open-ended statement some numerical value. This can be accomplished by having judges rank or rate these statements on the direction and magnitude of the implied expectancy. Ranking or absolute rating of alternatives by experimenters will give us numerical values of the expectancy in a more direct way and may, therefore, be preferred.

Experienced experimenters. If our sample of experimenters is composed of more sophisticated data collectors there is a greater likelihood that expectancies are better developed. We may still use the methods sketched out for inexperienced experimenters, but we have other alternatives. We may, for example, ask the experimenters' colleagues to rate their expectancies based on their knowledge of the experimenters' theoretical orientations. Or, we can make such judgments ourselves based on reading the reports published by our experimenters or even perhaps their term papers. The reliability of these judgments made of an experimenter's expectancy by his colleagues or from his written documents must, of course, be checked.

With sophisticated experimenters who are already familiar with the research literature, we can ask them to write out or tell us "what previous research has shown" should be the outcome of the experiment and "how well the research was done." This "state of the art" paper or monologue can be quantitatively judged for the expectancy it seems to imply.

Correcting for Expectancy Effect

In some cases we will find expectancies distributed only dichotomously; either a result is expected or it is not. At other times we will have an ordering of expectancies in terms of either ranks or absolute values. In any of these cases we can correlate the results obtained by the experimenters with their expectancies. If the correlation is both trivial in magnitude and insignificant statistically, we can feel reassured that expectancy effects were probably not operating. If the correlation, however, is either large numerically or significant statistically, we conclude that expectancy effects did occur. These can then be "corrected" by such statistical methods as partial correlation or analysis of covariance. These same corrections can be applied if significant and/or large correlations are obtained between the results of the experiment and experimenters' own task performance or other attributes.

20

Experimenter Behavior

In the last chapter some techniques for the control of experimenter expectancy effects were suggested which depended on the determination of experimenter behavior, expectancy, and other attributes before the data collection process began. In this chapter we shall consider some related controls which, however, depend on the determination of experimenter behavior, expectancy, and other attributes during and after the data collection process.

OBSERVATION OF EXPERIMENTER BEHAVIOR

The Public Nature of Science

The public nature of the scientific process is one of its defining characteristics. All we do as scientists is determined in part by our intent that others be able to do it too. All we learn as scientists is intended to be learned as well by any other scientist with appropriate background and interests. Our research reports reflect this intent. We try to make public the reasoning that led to our research, how we conducted the research, what the results were, and how we interpreted these results. We expect scientists to differ in the reasoning that leads to an experiment and in the interpretation of the data. It is because of the public nature of the reasoning and interpretation of scientists that any one may disagree with the reasoning and interpretations of any other.

Not so, however, for the data per se. We must simply accept them as given. With an absolutely complete description of the circumstances of their collection, this would create no problem. But particularly in the behavioral sciences, such a complete description is impossible. We cannot even give a description of some of the most relevant variables affecting our results, because we don't know what they are. In psychological experiments we

344

could give more detailed descriptions than we now do of such variables as temperature, pressure, illumination, the nature and arrangement of the furniture, the physical and personal characteristics of the data collector, and, perhaps most important, his behavior.

We do, of course, describe the experimenter's programmed behavior, but there are literally thousands of experimenter behaviors that are not described. Generally it is not even known that these behaviors have occurred. We have no good vocabulary for describing them if we knew of them. Yet, for all this, these unprogrammed experimenter behaviors do affect the results of the experiment, as has been shown in earlier chapters. These behaviors constitute perhaps the least public stage of the scientific enterprise. They are less serious for occurring "behind closed doors," as Beck (1957) has reminded us, than for having been insufficiently studied and ruled out as sources of unintended variance.

We stand to learn a great deal from making the data collection process more public because it will allow us to define the conditions of the experiment more precisely. We must give other scientists the opportunity of seeing what the experiment was so that, just as in the case of our calculations, our reasoning, and our interpretation, they will be at liberty to disagree with us. They should be free to decide whether the experimental manipulation, which we claim, was or was not successfully implemented. They should be free to decide whether our programmed behavior actually ran according to the program.

Of course, if we knew what relevant variables we were not now reporting, we could simply add that information to our research reports. Since we do not, we must open the data collection process to a wide angle look so that we can learn what variables must in the future also be reported.

Observation Methods

A variety of methods are available for the observation of experimenters' behavior during the data collection process. These methods include the use of various kinds of human and mechanical observers. Each method and each combination of methods has its own special advantages and disadvantages, which each investigator must weigh in deciding on which method to employ.

Subjects as observers. Earlier in this book we have seen how the subjects themselves may be employed as observers. Immediately after the experiment is over for the subject he may be asked to describe his experimenter's behavior. We have most often employed a series of rating scales to help the subject with his description—but open-ended questions, adjective checklists, Q sorts, and other techniques could be employed as well.

More qualitative, less constrained descriptions have the advantage that they may suggest additional categories of experimenter behavior which may prove to be related to unintended sources of variance in the results of the research. For some purposes of control, such qualitative descriptions may have to be quantified, and although it is generally possible to do so, it is not necessarily a convenient or easy matter. Numbered rating scales have the advantage of being easy to work with but presuppose that we have some prior information, or at least guesses, about the relevant categories. Perhaps the most useful method of making observations is to combine the quantitative (e.g., rating scale) and qualitative (e.g., open-ended question). At the very least the qualitative observations can serve as the basis for subsequent, more formal categories.

One question that arises is whether the subject should be told before he contacts the experimenter that he will be asked to describe the experimenter's behavior. If the subject knows he is to describe the experimenter, he may make more careful observations. However, he may also be distracted from the experimental task and therefore perform as a rather atypical subject. In addition, his having been asked by the principal investigator to carefully observe the experimenter may significantly alter the nature of the subject's relationship to his experimenter. The subject may feel himself to be in a kind of collusion with the principal investigator and not at all subordinate in status to the experimenter. His increase in status relative to the status of the experimenter may make him less susceptible to the unintentional influence of the experimenter. The gain of more careful, sensitized observation of experimenter behavior accruing from the subject's set to observe may be offset by the loss of ecological validity arising from the subject's altered concentration on his task and his altered relative status. An empirical evaluation of the gains and losses may be obtained if half the subjects of the experiment are told beforehand to observe the experimenter carefully, and half the subjects are told nothing about their subsequent task of describing the experimenter. The two groups of subjects can then be compared both on their description of the experimenter and on the performance of their experimental task.

The employment of subjects as observers is clearly a case of participant observership, and this is its greatest strength and greatest weakness. Being very much within the experimental situation gives the best opportunity to note what transpired through a variety of communication channels. At the same time the subject as participant is busy with his own task performance and perhaps too deeply involved in the interaction to be "objective." Alternative methods of observation of experimenter behavior, therefore, become important.

Expert observers. Anthropologists, clinical psychologists, psychiatrists, all make their living in part by the careful observation of behavior. These and other experts in observation may be employed to observe the experimenter's behavior. The methods of making the observations may be as described in the case of subjects as observers.

These expert observers may (1) sit in on the experiment; (2) observe through a one-way window; or if not superficially too dissimilar from the subjects of the experiment, (3) serve as "subjects" themselves. In this last case they might, unlike real subjects, be able to retain their "objectivity" in interaction with the experimenter because of the nature of their training, while retaining the greatest possible access to the modalities in which the experimenter can be said to "behave" (e.g., visual, auditory, olfactory, tactual).

Obviously, if the expert sits in on the experiment, the experimenter knows he is being observed. This may alter his behavior in the experiment so that we can no longer learn what his "natural" behavior would be like. Observation of experimenter behavior without the experimenter's knowledge may then be necessary either by covert observation or by the expert's serving as subject. This, of course, raises the question of the propriety of deception for scientific purposes, a question discussed more fully in the chapter describing expectancy control groups. If it were established by careful research that experimenters behave no differently when they believe themselves to be observed, we could in good scientific conscience eliminate the method of covert observation, a method no one really likes to use anyway.

Representative observers. Different observers may see the same behavior in different ways. Since we are primarily interested in the effects of experimenters' behavior on their subjects' performances, we could argue that the observers of the experimenters should be like the subjects of the experimenters. Observers can be drawn from the same population from which subjects are drawn in the hope that they will be responsive to the same aspects of experimenter behavior to which their peer group members, the subjects, were responsive. These subject-representative observers could be asked to function in much the same way as the expert observers. They may miss some behavioral subtleties an "expert" might observe, but they may also attend to the more relevant aspects of the experimenter's behavior.

Other populations of observers that might profitably be employed include colleagues of the experimenter, the principal investigator and his colleagues, randomly selected groups, or specialized groups that might be particularly sensitive to certain aspects of experimenter behavior. Thus, actors, speech teachers, singers; dancers, physical education teachers; photographers and caricaturists may be especially sensitive to verbal, motor, and postural behavior, respectively.

Mechanical "observers." During any given period of the experimental interaction, the experimenter's behavior occurs just once. If any behavior goes unobserved by a human observer it is lost and not recoverable. Fortunately, there are mechanical systems of permanently recording the experimenter's behavior. These mechanical systems, including sound tape recordings, silent film, sound film, and television tapes, are becoming increasingly available, technically more effective, and economically more feasible. These recording systems differ from each other in the completeness of the recording of behavior, in the speed with which the records are available for use, and in their cost.

Tape recording is the most practical system of permanent recording. The machines are readily available, inexpensive, and easy to use. However, they record only that behavior which can be heard, not that which can be seen. Silent film, sound film, and video-tape do record the behavior that can be seen and, in their less elaborate forms, can be surprisingly inexpensive. Silent 8 mm film can be used with a tape recorder to provide a convenient record of behavior which can be both seen and heard. Sound films, while more expensive and less easily available, provide a still better (more synchronized) record.

Developments in photographic technology make it no longer necessary to have studio conditions before good films can be obtained. This seems quite important, since the bright lights and seating arrangements formerly required might significantly affect the experimenter's behavior.

Whether experimenters should be informed that their behavior is being recorded is both a scientific and ethical question, and some of these issues will be discussed later. It goes without saying, of course, that any records of experimenter behavior obtained with or without his knowledge must be treated with utmost confidentiality. An analogy to a clinically privileged communication is appropriate.

None of the systems eliminates the need for the human observers, but they do allow for the more leisurely observation of behavior. The types of judgments made by the observers of the permanently recorded behavior of the experimenter may be the same as those made by a direct observer of the experimental interaction. In addition, however, some more mechanical modes of categorizing are available (e.g., see Mahl & Schulze, 1964).

Observation of a permanent record (on tape or film) of behavior is more "forgiving" than the direct observation of the behavior as it occurs originally. Behavior missed on first observation can be observed on second, third, or fourth observation. Larger groups of observers can simultaneously make their judgments, a logistic advantage that becomes increasingly more important as the judgments of behavior become more difficult or unreliable.

For any observations of experimenter behavior, the reliability among observers must be calculated. In general, more molecular observations (e.g., the experimenter is or is not smiling) will be found to be more reliable than more molar observations (e.g., the experimenter is or is not friendly). However, that does not imply that variations in more molecular experimenter behavior will prove to be better predictors of unintended variation in the data obtained from subjects. On the contrary, experience with both the more molar and the more molecular observations suggests that the former may serve the more useful predictive function. This may be due to the fact that such global judgments as "friendly," although not made as reliably, carry more social meaning than the more molecular observations of glancing or smiling. There may be just too many ways to smile and too many ways to glance, each with a different social meaning. Perhaps by indexing our more molecular observations in future studies—i.e., a friendly glance, a condescending smile—we can increase both the reliability and the predictive value of observations of experimenter behavior.

Before leaving the topic of mechanical recording of experimenters' behavior, mention should be made of the potential value of a very special kind of observer of these records. Milton Rosenberg has suggested in a personal communication (1965) that the experimenter whose behavior was filmed might find it especially instructive to study his own behavior as an experimenter. He might be able to raise questions or hypotheses missed by other, less personally involved observers. There is also the possibility, however, that the experimenter himself would have more to learn than to teach of his own behavior and of its effects on others. The experience of listening to one's own psychotherapy behavior or supervising students' psychotherapy training by means of tape recordings suggests that often the therapist, and perhaps the experimenter too, "is the last to know."

Reduction of Bias by Observer Presence

The question of the effect of an observer's presence on the experimenter's behavior has already been raised. Here we raise the more specific question of the effect of an observer's presence on his unintentional influence on his subjects. It seemed reasonable to suppose that the presence of an observer might reduce the experimenter's unintentional communication of his expectancy to his subjects. An observer's presence might serve to inhibit even those communications from the experimenter of which the experimenter is unaware. Some data are available that provide a preliminary answer to this question (Rosenthal, Persinger, Mulry, Vikan-Kline, & Grothe, 1964a).

In this experiment the standard photo-rating task was administered by 5 experimenters to about 10 subjects each. For half the subjects, experimenters were led to expect ratings of success, and for half the subjects, experimenters were led to expect ratings of failure. For each experimenter, several of his interactions with subjects were monitored by one of the principal investigators who sat in during the experiment.

Table 20-1 shows the effects on magnitude of expectancy effect of the experimenter's having been observed. The numbers in each column repre-

TABLE 20—1

Observer Presence and Expectancy Effects

Experimenter	Unobserved	Observed
A	+2.68	+0.25
B	+2.49	+0.20
C	+1.20	−2.00
D	+0.44	+2.95
E	−0.33	−0.88
Means	+1.30	+0.10

sent the mean photo rating obtained from subjects believed to be low (failure) raters subtracted from the mean photo rating obtained from subjects believed to be high (success) raters. The difference between the grand means might suggest that expectancy effects were reduced by the presence of an observer. Such a conclusion would be misleading, however.

For four of the five experimenters (A, B, C, D) expectancy effects were significantly affected by an observer's presence. Two of the experimenters (A, B) showed a significant reduction of expectancy effects when observed. A third experimenter (C) not only showed a reduction of the expected biasing effect when observed, but actually tended to obtain data significantly opposite to that which he had been led to expect. His bias went into reverse gear. The fourth experimenter (D) tended to obtain unbiased data except when he was observed. At those times, he obtained data significantly biased in the predicted direction.

These somewhat complex results can be interpreted best by postulating that different experimenters interpret an observer's presence in different ways. Those experimenters whose biasing effects disappeared or even reversed in the observer's presence may have interpreted the monitoring as an attempt to guard against subtle differential treatment of the subjects. This interpretation may have led to a reduction or reversal in any such differential treatment. The experimenter whose expectancy effect became more clearly pronounced in the observer's presence may have interpreted the monitoring as an attempt to insure that the experiment would turn out well —i.e., lead to "proper," predicted results. It would seem worthwhile in future experiments to vary systematically the impression conveyed to monitored experimenters as to the real purpose of the observer's presence. This might shed light on whether the hypothesis of different meanings is tenable.

For the present, we cannot draw any simple conclusions about the effects of an observer's presence on the experimenter's expectancy effects.

If our sample of experimenters were larger, we could say, perhaps, that monitoring makes a difference four out of five times, but we could not be sure whether expectancy effects would be significantly increased or decreased among these affected experimenters.

Correcting for Experimenter Behavior

Once we have observed what the experimenter does in the experimental situation, we are in a position to make some correction for those of his unprogrammed behaviors that have affected the results of his research. Suppose that in a certain experiment all subjects were to be treated identically by their experimenter. Suppose further that the observers, who did not know which subjects were in the experimental or control conditions, noted that the experimenter (who might not be blind to subjects' experimental condition) behaved differently toward the subjects of the experimental and control groups. Any difference in the performance of the subjects of the two conditions might then be partially or entirely due to the experimenter's differential behavior. By the use of such techniques as analysis of covariance or partial correlation we can assess the effects of the treatment condition, holding constant that experimenter behavior which was confounded with the subjects' treatment condition.

Individual differences among experimenters in the data they obtain from their subjects can similarly be controlled by knowledge of the experimenters' behavior in the experiment.

Experimenters' behavior may change during the course of an experiment. Practice may change their behavior vis-à-vis their subjects, and so may fatigue or boredom. Even if these phenomena do not bias the results of the experiment in the direction of the experimenter's hypothesis, they may have undesired effects—generally an increase in Type II errors. Variability in experimenter behavior over time associated with variability in subject performance over time will tend to increase (erroneous) failures to reject the null hypothesis.

A fairly extreme correction for unprogrammed experimenter behavior is to drop the data obtained by an experimenter whose behavior was in some way very deviant or unacceptable. An example of such behavior might be an experimenter's unwitting omission of a critical sentence in his instructions to his subject. Such correction by elimination might seem to be an easy matter. In fact, it is not. Experimenters tend to behave in a normally distributed manner, and it will be troublesome to decide that *this* experimenter's behavior (e.g., instruction reading) is barely acceptable while *that* experimenter's behavior is barely unacceptable.

The final decision to drop or not to drop the data obtained by a given experimenter from a given subject is itself highly susceptible to the interpretive bias of the principal investigator. At the very least, such a decision should be made without knowledge of the subject's performance. Ideally, the rules for dropping data will be written before the experiment is begun and the decision to drop made by independent judges whose task is only to decide whether a given behavior violates a given rule. For the near future, at any rate, this will be no easy matter, for we have looked at so few experimental interactions that we hardly have any rules (even of thumb) for what constitutes an adequate, true-to-program set of experimenter behaviors. As Friedman (1964) has pointed out, for the psychological experiment, there is not yet an etiquette.

Although a major deviation of an experimenter's behavior from the behavior intended (usually implicitly) by the principal investigator may significantly alter the intended experimental conditions, such a deviation does not *necessarily* result in either an alteration in the subject's response or in an alteration of the magnitude of the experimenter's expectancy effect. Whether such alterations have occurred can and should be specifically determined for each experiment.

INFERRING EXPERIMENTER BEHAVIOR

Sometimes when there has been no direct observation of the experimenter's behavior we can still make useful inferences about his behavior during the experiment. Such inferences can be based on an analysis of the results of his research and related personal characteristics. Some of these inferences are made on more quantitative bases, others on more qualitative bases.

Quantitative Bases of Inference

In earlier chapters we have emphasized that some replication of an experiment was required in order to assess an experimenter's accuracy. Some such assessment is, however, possible even when only a single experimenter and a single experiment are involved. Replication in this sense involves a partition of the experiment into earlier and later phases. Table 20-2 shows the results of a hypothetical experiment comparing the effects of two teaching methods (one old, one new) on subjects' performance. The experiment has been subdivided into six periods with subjects of both groups represented equally in all periods.

For both teaching methods, subjects who are contacted in later phases of the experiment perform better than do subjects contacted earlier (rho $=$ 1.00, $p = .01$). So long as subjects have been randomly assigned to phases of the experiment, and the possibility of feedback from earlier to later subjects eliminated, we might reasonably infer that the experimenter's behavior has changed over the course of the experiment. He has perhaps be-

TABLE 20—2

Effects of Two Teaching Methods as a Function of Experimental Period

METHODS

Period	Experimental	Control	Difference
1	1.2	1.1	+0.1
2	1.4	1.2	+0.2
3	1.5	1.3	+0.2
4	1.9	1.5	+0.4
5	2.0	1.6	+0.4
6	2.2	1.7	+0.5
Means	1.7	1.4	+0.3

come a better "teacher" or examiner, as it were, and in terms of the hypothesis under test, this need not be of too great concern.

More troublesome is the fact that the superiority of the new teaching method has shown an increase from earlier to later phases of the experiment (rho $= .97$, $p < .02$). It is not easy to interpret this interaction. It may be due to the fact that the new or experimental method becomes more effective when employed by a more effective, more experienced teacher (or when tested by a more effective examiner), which the experimenter has become over time. On the other hand, it is also possible that the experimenter has treated the subjects of the two groups in an increasingly differtial way, and in a way unrelated to the teaching methods themselves. We might suspect this especially if the experimenter was the teacher as well as the examiner or, if he was only the examiner, then one not blind to treatment conditions. If efforts had been made to keep the experimenter-examiner blind, we might suspect a gradual "cracking of the code" by the experimenter. In addition (or alternatively), we might hypothesize that the experimenter was unwittingly learning to bias the results of the experiment or simply becoming a more effective influencer by virtue of his growing professionalness of manner. The nature of the specific experiment may suggest which interpretation of such an order-x-treatment interaction effect is most reasonable.

The method of subdividing experiments is most effective when the experiment is designed specifically for this purpose. Pains can be taken to assign equal or proportional numbers of subjects of all experimental conditions to each phase of the experiment. Pains can also be taken to insure that there will be no feedback of information from earlier- to later-contacted subjects. But the logic of the method can be approximately and usefully applied to experiments that have already been conducted. The subdivision of the experiment can take place on a post hoc basis and can, at the very least, raise interesting questions (e.g., overall significant differences may prove entirely attributable to subjects contacted in only one phase of the experiment).

In our hypothetical example we have used a correlational method of analysis only for the sake of simplicity. The basic method of analysis of subdivided experiments can be a treatment-x-order design, in which we would hope that only the treatment effect would prove significant. Even though the main effect due to order is not significant there may be a significant linear regression which should be checked. Such significant linear regression without significant main effects of order occurs when performance in subsequent phases changes by very small but very regular increments or decrements (see, e.g., Snedecor, 1956, p. 347).

In an earlier chapter it was suggested that significant decreases in the variance of subjects' peformance might serve as a clue to experimenter expectancy effects. Over time an experimenter may unwittingly alter his behavior in some way such as to "shepherd" his subjects' responses into an increasingly narrower range. We can assess the likelihood of this phenomenon in a manner analogous to that described for assessing experimenter effects upon mean performance.

Table 20-3 shows the hypothetical variance of subjects' responses for the experiment on teaching methods described earlier. Later-contacted subjects of both treatment conditions show decreasing variance of performance. This decrease, like the improved performance scores shown in Table 20-2, may be due to the experimenter's increasing skill. Some of his randomly variable behavior may have dropped out, so that he is treating subjects

TABLE 20—3

Performance Variances as a Function of Experimental Period

METHODS

Period	Experimental	Control	Difference
1	15	15	0
2	14	14	0
3	12	14	−2
4	11	13	−2
5	9	12	−3
6	8	12	−4

more consistently. In practice, however, we cannot say whether he began the experiment overly variable in behavior and became more "properly" consistent, or whether he began the experiment "appropriately" variable in behavior and became a more effectively biasing experimenter later on. To help us answer that question, we need additional data of a normative sort about the magnitude of variance ordinarily to be expected.

Perhaps more serious than the systematic decline in subject variability is the differential decline in variability between the two treatment conditions. The decrease in variance of the experimental subjects' performance is proceeding more rapidly than the decrease in performance variance of the control subjects. Whether this is a "natural" consequence of that particular teaching method as a function of experimenter experience, or whether it reflects some phenomenon related to expectancy effects, can be assessed only indirectly, as suggested earlier in the case of differential increments in mean performance. (In general, the reasoning that has been applied to the variability of the experimenter's data may also be applied to its skewness and kurtosis.)

Qualitative Bases of Inference

We have seen that we may be able to make useful inferences about the experimenter's behavior on the basis of the data he has obtained. Crude as this basis of inference may seem, we may at times have even less basis from which to infer something about the experimenter's behavior and yet be *forced* to make such inferences.

Suppose we knew that in a given experiment a large number of computational errors had occurred and that these computational errors were nonrandomly distributed with respect to the hypothesis under test. We might have some weak empirical grounds for inferring that the experimenter's interaction with his subjects was also biased. The research showing a relationship between magnitude of expectancy effects and computational errors has, unfortunately, not yet been replicated (Rosenthal, Friedman, Johnson, Fode, Schill, White, & Vikan-Kline, 1964).

Are we ever justified in using an experimenter's reputation as a basis for inferring what his behavior during an experiment was like? Probably not very often, if at all. There are few scientists who have a clearly documented history of producing data consistently biased by their expectancy. On those occasions when workers are heard to say about a research result, "Oh, you can't believe that, it came out of X's lab," or "Nobody can ever replicate X's work anyway," there is likely to be little documented basis for the statement. In almost a decade of trying to follow up such statements, I have only seldom been personally convinced by the "evidence" that I should believe data less because of the lab or the investigator from whom the data came. Often, perhaps, such a reputational statement means little more than, "They don't get the data *we* get, or which we think they *ought to get.*"

At the present time, then, an investigator's reputation for erring, or more specifically, for obtaining data influenced by his expectancy, does not appear to provide an adequate basis for inferring such error or bias. In principle, however, it could. Not "reputation" in the loose sense, then, but performance characteristics, can be assessed if we are willing to take the trouble. Such assessment will be discussed in the next chapter.

In the present chapter we have discussed the experimenter's behavior in the experiment as the source of expectancy effects and as a vehicle for their control. The methods of observation and of control suggested here are not, of course, intended to substitute for those strategies of control presented in the preceding and following chapters. Rather, they are intended to serve as additional tools for the control of expectancy effects which will sometimes prove especially appropriate and, at other times, especially inappropriate. In general, each investigator interested in controlling for expectancy effects will have to select one or more of the strategies presented in this volume (or others overlooked here) on the basis that it (or they) will best serve the purpose for a given experiment.

21

Personnel Considerations

In the last two chapters suggestions were made which were designed to help control experimenter expectancy effects in specific experiments. In this chapter, which draws upon some of the suggestions made earlier, we shall consider on a possibly more general basis the selection and training of experimenters as an aid to the control of experimenter expectancy effects. If there were certain kinds of data collectors who never influenced their subjects unintentionally, we could make a point of having only these experimenters collect our data. If the amount and type of an experimenter's training were significant predictors of his expectancy effects, we could establish training programs for data collectors such that its graduates' data would be unaffected by their expectancies or hypotheses.

THE SELECTION OF EXPERIMENTERS

The importance of careful selection of data collectors has been recognized by social scientists working in the area of survey research (e.g., Cahalan, Tamulonis, & Verner, 1947; Harris, 1948). Hyman and his collaborators (1954) have an excellent discussion of the personal characteristics of interviewers who are more prone to make various errors during the data collection process. These errors include errors in asking the programmed questions, errors in probing for further information, errors in recording the response, and cheating errors. We may summarize these errors as all being relevant to interviewer competence. More competent interviewers make fewer errors. But lack of competence is probably not the problem when the data collector is a psychological experimenter. Better educated, better motivated, more carefully selected, holding more scientific values, psychological experimenters may well be more competent in the sense of doing what is asked and doing it accurately than are the less highly selected interviewers employed to assist in the conduct of large-scale surveys. Furthermore, more competent, more accurate experimenters are *more,* rather than *less,* likely to show expectancy effects on their subjects' responses, as we saw in an earlier chapter.

Hyman and his co-workers do discuss personal correlates of interviewers who showed a greater biasing effect, but the biasing was usually of the observer bias or interpreter bias variety. As far as could be determined, there have been no studies relating interviewer characteristics to interviewer expectancy bias in which, by independent observation of the respondents' replies, it could be determined that the bias affected the subjects' responses rather than the observation, interpretation, or recording of responses. In fact, as Hyman's group points out, even when the term "bias" includes net errors of observation, recording, and interpretation, "Evidence on what variables might be used as predictors of tendencies to ideological or expectation biases is almost nonexistent" (p. 302). What this literature, so well reviewed by Hyman's group, offers us, then, is a principle rather than a body of information to apply to the situation of the psychological experimenter.

In an earlier chapter are described the personal characteristics of experimenters exerting greater expectancy effects. Although these characteristics were theoretically interesting, the magnitude of their correlation with experimenter bias seems too low to be useful for selection purposes. In any case, it seems unlikely that we would select as experimenters people who are *less* professional, *less* consistent, of *lower* status, *more* tense, and *less* interested. Purposeful selection of such people might lower the degree of bias but at the cost of other, perhaps far more serious, errors. When we read a journal report of an experiment, we put our faith in the experimenter's having been professional, consistent, and competent, or we would doubt that the experiment was conducted as reported. And if we must maintain high standards of competence, we will necessarily have a harder time of developing selection devices that will predict experimenter expectancy effects. As our experimenters become more homogeneous with respect to such variables as intelligence we will find these variables to predict bias less and less well as a simple statistical consequence; i.e., a reduction in the variance of either of two variables to be correlated leads to a reduction in the resulting correlation. What methods, then, can be used to select experimenters?

The Method of Sample Experiments

Hyman and his collaborators (1954) suggest the use of performance tests in the case of interviewer selection, and as employed in survey research organizations, this technique appears to be effective, at least in minimizing coding bias. The ultimate in job sample techniques applied to the situation of the experimenter would involve his actually conducting one or more standard experiments with subjects whose usual responses were known beforehand. For each prospective experimenter, his expectancy of the results of the particular experiment to be conducted could be determined. Subjects would be randomly drawn from a population whose mean response had been determined.[1] Consistent significant deviations in the responses obtained by our prospective experimenter would define him to be a biased data collector. The bias might be in the direction of his expectancy or in the opposite direction. The extent to which his deviations in obtained data could have been occurred by chance would be determined by standard statistical tests.

But what if, for a given experiment, a prospective experimenter showed clearly a propensity to bias the outcome, whereas for another experiment he showed only a propensity for obtaining accurate data? No evidence is available for suggesting whether such is a likely state of affairs. We do not know the degree of generality of experimenters' biasing tendencies over a sample of experiments. Ideally, we would have a large sample of prospective experimenters conduct a series of standard experiments in each of several different areas of research. What we would be likely to discover is that (1) there is a general factor defined by a tendency to bias over a large range of types of experiments, (2) there are group factors defined by a tendency to bias in certain types of experiments, and (3) there are specific factors defined by a tendency to bias in only certain specific experiments. We might find further that some specific experiments or some types of experiments are more commonly free of bias, whereas others are more likely to show biasing effects of experimenters. Figure 21-1 shows the hypothetical profiles of three experimenters who have undergone our somewhat elaborate selection procedure.

Experimenter A shows a tendency to exert expectancy effects in all his research—most especially so in studies of emotional behavior in humans, but less so in studies of perception. Experimenter B tends to bias the results of his learning research only, but for both human and animal subjects. Experimenter C shows the biasing effects of his expectancy only in studies of the emotional behavior of animals. If we had to conduct all eight of these hypothetical experiments using these three data collectors, we would be able to choose one or more to conduct each experiment with some hope of avoiding biasing effects associated with the experimenter's expectancy. In almost every case we would prefer experimenter C, and if we were in the market for a research assistant we would hire him, all other things being equal.

In proposing what amounts to a personal validity index we are suggesting a procedure that, at least in its most ideal form, cannot be appro-

---

[1] The problem of establishing the correct value of the mean response (no small matter) was discussed in the chapter dealing with the assessment of experimenter effect.

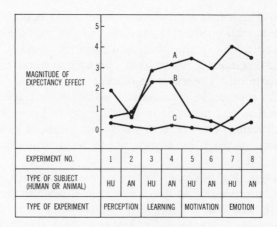

FIGURE 21-1

Expectancy Effects as a Function of Type of Experiment

priately employed by the ordinary principal investigator in search of a research assistant. For one thing, this simply cannot be done to the graduate student or undergraduate who wants to work for a given investigator. Such selection may be educationally inappropriate from the student's point of view. If the experiments are designed only as a selection device there is also a certain indignity involved for the student. The procedure is expensive, time-consuming, and boring. It requires some institutionalized system of implementation. It does, in fact, suggest the creation of a new profession with its own system of selection and training. We shall return to this recommendation later.

Our primary concern in this discussion of the selection of experimenters has been selection for minimal expectancy effects. But the job sample method permits us also to screen out potential experimenters who find it hard to carry out highly programmed procedures. Although there is a correlation between intelligence and accuracy in carrying out instructions, it is not likely to be very high among a selected group of potential experimenters. Yet, we do note individual differences in the skill with which our research assistants carry out their behavior programs. The direct observation or the recording on sound tapes or sound films of the potential experimenter's behavior during the standard sample experiment permits us to assess whether any procedural deviations are too great to tolerate. By the observation, either directly or by way of sound films, of the experimenter's behavior over the course of one or more experiments, we may be able to gauge his ability to learn to behave in that standard fashion we would like.

Ultimately, it may prove feasible to develop tests and questionnaires that will predict an experimenter's proneness to the exertion of expectancy (and related) effects. But the validation of any such instruments requires an ecologically valid criterion. Such a criterion is provided by the job sample method described. The personal validity index, which can be computed separately for each experiment, for related types of experiments, or for all experiments in the standard battery, can simply be correlated with already existing or specially devised instruments. The major advantage of the development of such instruments is, of course, economic. Tests can be administered more quickly and cheaply than experiments can be conducted.

THE TRAINING OF EXPERIMENTERS

In our discussion of the training of experimenters we will define training broadly enough to include the variable of experience as a kind of on-the-job training. Again we find most of the relevant literature to come from the field of survey research.

Amount of Training

Hyman's group (1954), in summarizing a number of studies of interviewer competence and bias, concluded that more experienced interviewers were somewhat more competent and less likely to bias their results. This conclusion, tentatively offered, they tempered by pointing out that selective retention of interviewers might have been operating. The better interviewers may have greater longevity with the research organization—experience may be the dependent rather than the independent variable. Other workers disagree with even the modest conclusion drawn by Hyman et al. Cantril (1944) reported that training did not make much difference in the quality of data obtained. Similarly Eckler and Hurwitz (1958) reported that census interviewers showed no decrease in net errors for at least certain types of questions when additional training was provided.

The lore of psychological research suggests that more experienced experimenters are at least more competent than the more inexperienced. This may well be true. As in the case of the interviewer, there may be a selective retention within the craft of those who can do competent data collection—competent in the sense of following directions. But the lore of psychological research suggests less about the relationship between experimenter's experience and the magnitude of his expectancy effects.[2]

There have been two experiments that, taken together, provide at least some indirect evidence bearing on the effect of experience or training on

[2] The lore of anthropological field research, however, suggests that a better (i.e., professionally) trained observer is less likely to be in error (Naroll, 1962). This certainly seems reasonable, but an experimental demonstration, even if it bore out the lore on the average, would probably show very considerable overlap, with some "amateur" observers erring less than some professionals.

the magnitude of expectancy bias (Rosenthal, Persinger, Mulry, Vikan-Kline, & Grothe, 1964a; 1964b). In one of these studies (a) all experimenters had served as data collectors once before, whereas in the other (b) none had any prior research experience. The two studies were not specifically designed for this comparison, and so any conclusions are tentative, at best. It did appear, however, that magnitude of expectancy effects was not particularly related to the experimenters' experience. If anything, the more experienced experimenters showed a greater biasing effect and were less variable in the degree of their bias. It would even be reasonable to suggest that more experienced experimenters *should* show greater expectancy effects. With more experience, experimenters gain in self-confidence and perhaps behave in a more professional manner. In an earlier chapter we saw that more professional experimenters exerted more biasing influence on their subjects.

Further indirect evidence comes from an examination of the results of the second of the two cited studies (b). Among that group of inexperienced experimenters some were made more conscious of their procedures as determinants of the results of their research. This amounted to a minimal training (or educational) effort. The experimenters who were made minimally more procedure-conscious showed greater biasing effects in the data they obtained from their subjects. The minimal training procedure may have led these experimenters to feel the importance of their role as data collector more keenly. They may have conveyed to their subjects a certain sense of status enhancement, and as we saw in an earlier chapter, experimenters of higher perceived status tend to exert a greater degree of expectancy effect.

In summary, we must be impressed by the absence of well-established findings bearing on the relationship between experimenter expectancy effects and experimenter training and experience. If forced to draw some conclusion from what evidence there is, we might conclude that better trained, more experienced experimenters are likely to be more competent in carrying out their research with minimal procedural deviation. But at the same time, because the more experienced, better trained experimenter is likely to enjoy a higher status in the eyes of his subjects and behave in a more professional manner, those very slight procedural deviations that do occur are more likely to result in the effective communication and influencing effect of the experimenter's expectancy.

Type of Training

There are virtually no data available that would suggest to us how we should train experimenters to maximize their competence generally and to minimize their expectancy effects specifically. There is an undocumented assumption, however, that if only we tell our experimenters about the pitfalls of bias, everything will be all right. What little evidence there is bearing on just this point, however, suggests that this assumption is quite unjustified. Troffer and Tart (1964) showed that fairly experienced experimenters who understood the problem of expectancy effect and presumably tried to guard against it nevertheless treated subjects differently depending on whether subjects were in the experimental or the control condition. There are also some data, collected by Suzanne Haley, which suggest that, if anything, expectancy effects increase when experimenters are asked to try to avoid them.

It seems incongruous that psychologists, who have been so helpful to education, business, industry, and the military in setting up and evaluating training programs, have not turned their attention to the training of psychological experimenters—the members of their own family. We have been like the physician who neglects his own health, the mental health expert who neglects his own family. If we look at procedures currently employed for the training of our research assistants, we find no systematic pattern, not even explicit assumptions about training for data collection. Many experimenters, perhaps most, have never been observed in the data collection process or have even heard a lecture about it. As researchers, then, we lag far behind those "applied" fields, so scorned by some, in the application of the principles of learning.

The clinical psychologist, in contrast, is thoroughly trained in his data collection process. He is observed in his interaction with his patients and given feedback. We may lament the lack of validation of various methods of supervision, but at least the methods exist to be evaluated, and significant research has shown that even very subtle aspects of training and supervision can be empirically investigated (Kelley & Ring, 1961).

In the area of survey research, most organizations have training manuals which, although also unvalidated as to their value in error reduction, at least represent some self-conscious thinking about the problem (Hyman et al., 1954). Perhaps the ultimate in concern with problems of both selection and training of data collectors is reflected in the procedures employed by the Institute for Sex Research (more commonly known as the "Kinsey Group"). Over the several decades of their research they have employed only 3 percent of the applicants who were considered for employment (Pomeroy, 1963). The grand total of nine interviewers employed by the Institute was, then, an extremely carefully selected group. The Institute knew the criteria its interviewers had to meet, and selected accordingly. Although we might wish for an empirical evaluation of the success of their selection and training procedures, we could hardly hope for more caution in the selection of data collectors.

One of the reasons that we, as psychologists, have paid so little attention to our *own* training as experimenters may stem from the combination of a specific belief and a specific value about data collection. The belief is that data collection is simple, if not simple-minded, and that anybody who can reach graduate school can carry out an experimental procedure. The associated value is that data are to be highly prized but data collection is not. The young postdoctoral psychologist can hardly wait to turn the burdens of data collection over to *his* graduate student assistants. Not all psychologists share this belief and the associated value, of course. Extremely sophisticated investigators have pointed out informally that some of their graduate research assistants can, and some cannot, carry out at least some experimental procedures. The fact that some cannot is often learned fairly late in the game, often at some cost to both the experimenter and the principal investigator. Such instances are a tribute to our neglect of both selection and training procedures.

The Professional Experimenter

Science implies observation and the collection of data. The scientist is responsible for the collection of the appropriate data, but it need not be his eye at the telescope or microscope nor his pencil mark indicating how a respondent will vote. In survey research the interviewer is not the scientist. In medical research the laboratory technician is not the scientist. Each of these data collectors is a member of an honorable profession and is perhaps more expert and less biased than the scientist himself. In psychology, however, the scientist himself is commonly the experimenter, or if he has "outgrown" the running of subjects, a scientist-in-training is the collector of the data. This hampers both the selection and training of experimenters who are both competent and unbiased.

What is needed is a new profession, the profession of behavioral experimenter analogous to the professional interviewer and the laboratory technician. The professional experimenter will be well selected, well trained, and well paid. He will enter the profession because he is interested in data collection and not because it is expected as something to be done before an advanced degree can be earned and as something to be delegated quickly to one's own graduate students. Careful, expensive selection and training procedures will be warranted because of the greater longevity of the new professional's data collection career. There will be no conflict between educational and scientific aims as there may be in the case of a brilliant student of science who simply happens to be inept at collecting data in behavioral experiments. At present, such a student may be discouraged from a scientific career because of this one ineptitude. This becomes his loss and ours. There is no reason why he should not conceive of needed experiments, design them, evaluate their results, and report them to the rest of us.

The actual data collection can be turned over to an institute set up at a university or privately, as in the case of various survey research organizations (e.g., National Opinion Research Center).

This proposal does not imply that data collection would no longer be a part of graduate education or that much research would not continue to be done as it now is. But there is no necessary correlation between the educational function of serving as experimenter and the scientific function of data collection. Divisions of labor might sensibly evolve. One very natural division would be between pilot studies and large-scale replications or cross validations. The former would more likely be conducted by the individual investigator and his assistants. The latter might most profitably be contracted to a large research agency which selects and trains professional experimenters and conducts research on contract.

If this proposal should seem radical, we need only remind ourselves that one can already have surveys conducted, tests validated, and experimental animals bred to order. What is proposed here simply extends the limits of the kind of data that could become available on a contract basis.

The details of setting up institutes for the selection and training of professional experimenters and the conduct of behavioral research are complex. They would be expensive and would require the support probably of both universities and interested federal agencies. The various agencies now functioning most nearly like the proposed institutes would need to be consulted so that their experience could be profitably utilized. The "ideal" selection procedure suggested earlier in this chapter could be employed along with others. Different training procedures could be developed with continuing evaluation of their relative effectiveness in increasing experimenter competence and decreasing biased errors. In addition to the development of manuals which may or may not prove to be helpful, more job-related procedures may be introduced. Trainee experimenters could observe the data-collecting behavior of "ideal" experimenters directly or on film. The trainee's own performance could be monitored directly by supervisors or, if on film, by supervisors and by the trainee himself to learn of any procedural deviations.

In the early days of the development of such a new profession, variability of procedures of selection and training would be especially important. Amount and type of the trainee's educational background, intelligence, motor skill, personality variables, and the didactic and performance types of training methods should all be permitted to vary so that the effectiveness of various types of experimenters and training programs may be assessed.

The emotional investment of the professional experimenter would be in collecting the most accurate data possible. That is the performance dimension on which his rewards would be based. His emotional investment would not be in obtaining data in support of his hypothesis. Hypotheses would remain the business of the principal investigator and not of the data collector. There might, in general, be less incentive to obtain biased data by the professional experimenter than by the scientist-experimenter or the graduate student-experimenter. Still, professional experimenters will have or develop hypotheses, and the strategies for the control of expectancy effects described in the last two chapters and in the next two chapters can be employed. In fact, they can be more effectively employed with professional experimenters because there will be less conflict with educational goals. The professional experimenter wants to be kept blind, but the graduate student might properly feel imposed upon if he were kept from knowing what research he was conducting.

Some of the values to be acquired by the professional experimenter are, of course, already found among behavioral scientists, but their increased articulation might have a beneficial feedback effect on those of us back at the universities. We do too often judge a piece of research, not by its careful execution and the data's freedom from error, but by whether the results confirm our expectations. Many universities give implicit recognition to this tendency by protecting their doctoral candidates with a kind of contract. The essence of this contractual procedure is that the soundness of a piece of research is to be judged without reference to the results. If a qualified group of judges (i.e., the doctoral committee) feels that a piece of research is well designed then it must be acceptable no matter how the data fall.[3]

That such contractual arrangements exist is a good and reasonable thing. That such contractual arrangements are necessary is a somewhat sad and sobering situation. It is a situation that suggests we are too often more interested in demonstrating that we already "know" how nature works than in trying to learn how, in fact, she does work.

---

[3] There are, of course, additional reasons for this form of contractual protection of the student, e.g., the possibility of staff turnover, changing standards, and changing interests.

22

Blind and Minimized Contact

BLIND CONTACT

It seems plausible to reason that if the experimenter does not know whether the subject is in the experimental or the control group, then he can have no validly based expectancy about how the subject "should" respond. The experimenter "blind" to the subject's treatment condition cannot be expected unintentionally to treat subjects differentially as a function of their group membership. This is an old and effective idea in the field of pharmacology.

The so-called single blind study refers to the situation in which the patient or subject is kept from knowing what drug has been administered. When both subject and experimenter (physician) are kept from knowing what drug has been administered, the procedure is called "double-blind" (Beecher, 1959; Levitt, 1959; Wilson, 1952).[1] This technique is over 120 years old, having been employed by members of the Vienna Medical Society at least as early as 1844 (Haas, Fink, & Hartfelder, 1963). Haas and his co-authors have recently presented rather convincing evidence that the use of the double-blind study is more than warranted. In a review of nearly 100 placebo studies, involving thousands of subjects and many different disorders, they observed that the placebo works best when the double-blind method has been employed. Apparently, when the experimenter (doctor) does not know that the substance given his subject (patient) is inert, he expects, and gets, a better result.

[1] There is a certain amount of confusion about the exact usage of the term "double-blind." Always the subject is blind, but sometimes the other "blind" person is the subject's personal physician, sometimes the research physician, sometimes the person who actually dispenses the drug, and sometimes several of these. There is talk, too, of triple-blind, quadruple-blind, etc., to add to the confusion. We will adopt a usage in speaking of the psychological experiment such that a double-blind study is one in which no one having direct contact with subjects is permitted to know what the subjects' treatment condition will be, is, or has been, until the experiment is over. "Double-blind" for us will mean "total-blind."

Psychologists have been slow to adopt the double-blind method for other than psychopharmacological research (Shapiro, 1960, p. 125), though Wolf (1964) reports that in 1889 Delboeuf proposed the double-blind method for research in hypnosis. It is the unusual data collector today who does not know whether his subject is a member of the experimental or control group (e.g., Babich, Jacobson, Bubash, & Jacobson, 1965). The suggestion to have experimenters contact their subjects under blind conditions is implied not only logically but empirically as well, if we may draw on the data of the pharmacologists. In addition, it is not a suggestion that would work an impossible hardship on the researcher. More and more data are being collected by less and less sophisticated (or, at least, less academically advanced) student research assistants who could be kept uninformed of the hypothesis and overall design of the experiment, as well as the treatment conditions to which each subject belongs. If these students were too sophisticated, or if the principal investigator preferred to do so from educational and ethical considerations, assistants could be told exactly why they must remain blind. In order to be somewhat more convinced about the efficacy of the double-blind procedure among psychological experimenters, however, it was decided tc try the technique out (Rosenthal, Persinger, Vikan-Kline, & Mulry, 1963).

A Test of Blind Experimentation

Fourteen graduate students (11 males and 3 females) administered the standard person perception experiment to a total of 76 introductory psychology students (about half were males and half were females). As in earlier studies, half the experimenters were led to expect low photo ratings and half were led to expect high photo ratings from their subjects.

Experimenters were told that those who adhered most strictly to the experimental procedure and obtained the "best" data would be awarded "research grants." At the conclusion of this phase of the experiment all experimenters were given small "grants" of $14. Of this amount $10 represented their "salary" for continuing in the role of "principal investigators," and $4 was used to pay their research assistants.

To each of the 13 experimenters who were able to continue in the experiment as "principal investigators" two research assistants were randomly assigned. All but three of these assistants were males. Assistants were trained in the experimental procedure and were paid for their time by the experimenters. Each research assistant then conducted the photo-rating experiment with a new sample of six introductory psychology students. Of the total of 154 subjects contacted by the research assistants, about half were males.

Unlike the original instructions to experimenters, the instructions to the research assistants made no mention of what ratings should be expected from the subjects. Experimenters were led by their instructions to expect their research assistants to obtain data from their subjects of the same sort they had themselves obtained from their earlier-contacted subjects. Experimenters were warned not to leak to their assistants the magnitude of data that experimenters had themselves obtained from their subjects. Research assistants, then, were running "blind."

In spite of the fact that, as a set, these experimenters did not bias their subjects' responses to a very great extent, what bias did exist was transmitted to their research assistants. In spite of the attempt to keep research assistants blind, those whose "principal investigators" had biased their subjects' responses more also biased their own subjects' responses more. The correlation between the magnitude of experimenters' biasing effect and the magnitude of their research assistants' biasing effect was .67 ($p =$ .01).

Here, then, is an interesting case of unintended interpersonal influence once-removed, which has important substantive social psychological implications which will be discussed later on. The methodological implications, however, are clear. Simply not telling our research assistants what to expect from a given subject (i.e., whether they are experimental or control subjects) does not insure real blindness. In some subtle way, by tone and/or gesture, experimenters may unintentionally overinform their research assistants. The principle of the double-blind method is not impugned by our findings; but the difficulty of implementing and maintaining the required experimenter "blindness" is emphasized.[2]

Additional Problems of Maintaining Blindness

We have shown that the principal investigator may be a source of the inadvertent failure of the double-blind method. Here we will show that another source of such failure may be the subject himself. This is well known in pharmacological research.

When active and inert chemical substances are compared, sometimes the active substance has an irrelevant but obvious side effect. Some patients given the "real" drug may change color, for example. Thus the experimenter knows, at least for these subjects, that they are more likely to be in the drug group than the placebo control group.

In psychological experiments, too, such "side effects" may occur. Assume an experiment in which anxiety is the independent variable. People who have just been through an anxiety-arousing experience or who score high on a test of anxiety may behave differently in an experimental situation.

[2] The work of Martin Orne (1962) also suggests that even the "single blind" method is not all that easy to achieve. Although no investigator would tell his subjects what their response "ought" to be, there may be cues from the situation (even if not from the experimenter himself) that unintentionally communicate to the subjects how they are expected to behave.

The "blind" experimenter may then covertly "diagnose" the level of anxiety and, if he knows the hypothesis, bias the results of the experiment in the expected direction or, by bending over backward to avoid bias, "spoil" the study. There are many experimental treatments or measurements that may be assessed unintentionally by the "blind" data collector. A recent example of this derives from a finding that subjects scoring high in need for social approval arrived earlier at the site of the experiment ($r = +.40, p = .003$; Rosenthal, Kohn, Greenfield, & Carota, 1965). In effect, to see a subject arrive is to know something about him that often is meant to remain unknown. Arrival time, overt anxiety, skin color changes, and potentially hundreds of other, more subtle signs may break down the most carefully arranged double-blind study.

Irrelevant Expectancies

Even a truly blind experimenter is likely to have or to develop some expectancy about his subjects' behavior. If he does not know the experimental hypotheses—i.e., how the subjects ought to behave—then his idiosyncratic expectancies are likely to be irrelevant to the hypotheses under investigation. From the point of view of the particular design of the study, however, these more or less "random" idiosyncratic hypotheses may serve to increase the error variance and, from the principal investigator's point of view, increase the likelihood of Type II errors. If the experimenter did not know the hypotheses being tested but *did* know to which group each subject belonged, the results of the study are more likely to be biased in the direction of the hypothesis (or opposite to it) rather than biased irrelevantly with respect to the hypothesis. We can illustrate these considerations by returning to our earlier example of the study of the effects of anxiety on intellectual performance.

Suppose the principal investigator exposes a random half of his subjects to an anxiety-arousing experience, while the remaining subjects are exposed to a situation involving no anxiety arousal. The experimenter who collects the intellectual performance data does not know the hypothesis nor the treatment group membership of any subject. Suppose, however, that the experimenter has the irrelevant covert hypothesis that tall, thin people tend to be unusually bright. He therefore unintentionally treats them somewhat differently, and as a result they obtain higher performance scores.

Table 22-1 illustrates the effect of this irrelevant hypothesis on the results of the experiment. The intellectual performance scores are tabulated as they might occur in each group with and without the effects of the irrelevant expectancy of the data collector. Note that there was only one tall, thin subject in each group whose performance score was affected by the data collector's expectancy. In each case a 5-point effect on these subjects is observed. The table shows that the mean performance scores are barely affected by this particular constant error, that the effect of anxiety (i.e., mean difference) is unchanged, but that the *t* values and *p* levels *are* affected. Even for the relatively minor experimenter effect we have illustrated, the increase in Type II errors is clearly shown. (Particularly damaging, this error, if the principal investigator follows an accept-reject decision model and does not take note of the large mean differences obtained).

TABLE 22—1

Effect of Idiosyncratic Hypothesis on Results of a Double-Blind Study

	TRUE VALUES		AFFECTED VALUES	
	Anxiety	No Anxiety	Anxiety	No Anxiety
	112	117	112	117
	114	119	114	119
	116	121	116	121
	118	123	123*	128*
	120	125	120	125
Means	116	121	117	122
σ^2	8	8	16	16
Mean difference	5.0		5.0	
t	2.50		1.77	
p	< .05		> .10	
Decision	reject		not reject	
Error	none		Type II	

* Affected scores.

If the experimenter is not entirely blind but knows that subjects belong to two groups, and which subjects to which group, the mean difference between groups is more likely to be affected. This is true even though the experimenter does not know what the treatment conditions are. It will be apparent to him that a difference is expected, and he may covertly, and perhaps irrelevantly, hypothesize which group is to be the better performing and behave differently to the subjects of the two groups as a result of his hypothesis. On a chance basis, half the time this should tend to help support the principal investigator's hypothesis and half the time it should tend to weaken it. But, in either case, we can be misled as to the nature of the real state of affairs. It seems, therefore, highly desirable that the experimenter be unaware of which subjects constitute a group even when he does not know what treatments have been administered to any group.

Procedures Helping to Maintain Blindness

We have seen that both subject and principal investigator can serve as sources of unintended cues leading to the breakdown of experimenter blindness. In the next major section of this chapter we shall discuss various strategies that may help maintain blindness by helping to reduce contact between an experimenter and his subject. In this section we shall discuss two strategies designed to help the experimenter maintain blindness in spite of his having some contact with the principal investigator.

Avoiding feedback from the principal investigator. The first of these strategies is implied by the findings described in the chapter dealing with the effects of early data returns (the Ebbinghaus effect): the data collector should not tell the principal investigator the nature of the early returns.

This is a bit of a psychological hardship for a research group eager to learn whether they do or don't "have something." Still, many studies are conducted within a short enough period of time that the hardship would not be excessive.[3] Any contact with the principal investigator, including many unavoidable sorts, is likely to increase the chance of a breakdown of "blindness," but the report of early returns may be especially damaging.

Suppose that over the course of an experiment a blind experimenter is unintentionally having some sort of variable effect on subjects. For example, early in the data collection process he may be smiling more at subjects he sees as more anxious, but later on he smiles somewhat less at them. If the early data returns are reported to the principal investigator there will probably be subtle or overt positive or negative reactions to the news. If the reaction is positive, the principal investigator's pleasure may serve as a reinforcer for the data collector's unprogrammed experimental behavior—in this case his differential smiling. What was a randomly variable bit of unprogrammed behavior coincidentally serving to effect subjects' behavior into the predicted directions, now becomes a systematically biasing behavior on the part of the experimenter which will continue throughout the rest of the data collection process. If the early data returns are in the unpredicted direction and the principal investigator's reaction is negative,

---

[3] Here is another advantage to be gained from employing a large sample of experimenters. An experiment can be completed so much sooner with a number of experimenters, working sometimes even simultaneously, that there is a far less urgent desire on the part of the principal investigator to learn how the data are coming out.

the data collector may *change* his randomly variable unprogrammed behavior possibly to another more "biasing" mode of unprogrammed behavior.[4]

The "total-blind" design. The second strategy to be described is one we have frequently employed and found quite useful in our own research program. This strategy, when applicable (and it often is), gives virtually complete assurance of the maintenance of experimenter blindness, usually so difficult to obtain. Following the terminology of the pharmacological researcher we may call it the "total-blind" method because *no one* knows the treatment condition to which any subject is assigned.

In our simple situation in which half the experimenters are led to expect high photo ratings ($+5$) and half the experimenters are led to expect low photo ratings (-5), these expectations were induced by a written statement of how subjects "would perform." In a small study employing only 10 experimenters a different research room might be assigned to each experimenter. The 10 sets of instructions, five inducing the $+5$ expectancy and five inducing the -5 expectancy, would be randomly and blindly assigned to the 10 rooms. The 10 experimenters then would be randomly assigned to their rooms, where they would read over their "last-minute instructions" which, in fact, were the means for creating the experimental conditions. Not until the conclusion of the experiment, when the experimenters' "last-minute instructions" would be picked up along with the data sheets, would anyone know in what experimental treatment each experimenter (or subject) had been.[5]

In the more complex situation, where there were several different expectancies and other experimental manipulations, the very same procedures were followed. To illustrate the more complex situation, consider an experiment requiring 4 conditions and 6 experimenters per condition. If

[4] The presence and variety of unprogrammed experimenter behaviors during the experiment have been emphasized by Friedman (1964). These unprogrammed behaviors (e.g., smiling or glancing at the subject) cannot be regarded as "wrong" because no one has laid down the ground rules for "right" smiling and glancing or nonsmiling and nonglancing behavior. It would be an error to state simply that none of this behavior should occur in an experiment. The absence of certain socially expected facial, gestural, and tonal behaviors may have a far more unusual, even bizarre, effect upon subjects' behavior than their presence (Rosenthal & Fode, 1963b). In speaking of these unprogrammed interpersonal behaviors of experimenters we should note that they do not necessarily have any implications for biasing the results of an experimental vs. control group comparison. So long as the unprogrammed behavior is either constant or only randomly variable, these behaviors cannot serve to mediate experimenter expectancy effects. Only when subjects are differentially treated with respect to these unprogrammed behaviors as a function of their treatment condition can these behaviors serve to mediate experimenter expectancy effects.

[5] Subjects, of course, were randomly assigned to experimenters (or experimental rooms) but with the restriction that the number of subjects per room be as nearly equal as possible.

we have 4 experimental rooms we divide the experiment into 6 replicates; if we have 8 experimental rooms we divide the study into 3 replicates; if we have 12 experimental rooms we divide the study into 2 replicates, assuming in all cases that we can arrange to have different experimenters contact their subjects simultaneously. Within each replicate each experimental condition is represented equally. Experimental treatments, induced by written "instructions," are put into envelopes, coded, randomly assigned to research rooms, and not associated with any given experimenter until the experiment is over.

Of course, the same logic can be applied even if only one experimental room were available. It is our impression, however, that experimenters (or subjects) who find their way into early vs. later stages of an experiment may be nonrandomly different. Therefore, if we can have early- and later-participating experimenters or subjects equally represented in each treatment condition there may be less confounding of the treatment condition with these temporally associated personal characteristics. If we had only one room available for the data collection process, therefore, we would prefer to have each set of four experimenters represent all four experimental conditions. Random assignment of the four experimenters to the four conditions would have the additional advantage that if there were an unexpected attrition of experimenters toward the end of the experiment, there would be a more nearly equal distribution of experimenters among the various conditions.

All that we have said about our own research employing experimenters can be equally applied to other research employing subjects directly—that is, without intervening experimenters. All those experiments in which a written (or a tape-recorded) communication serves as the experimental manipulation can therefore be run "totally blind." There appear to be few, if any, areas of behavioral research in which this strategy cannot be appropriately employed at least some of the time.

Before leaving the topic of blind contacts, mention should be made of a paradoxical question raised by Milton Rosenberg in a personal communication (1965). He suggested the interesting possibility that experimenters, knowing they were blind, might expect, and therefore obtain, significantly more variable data. The idea is sufficiently intriguing and sufficiently important in terms of leading to increased Type II errors that the implied experiment should clearly be carried out.

MINIMIZED CONTACT

In describing the blind contact strategy in general, we pointed out that it was by no means always easy or even possible to achieve. Therefore, if we could eliminate experimenter-subject contact altogether it would seem that we would then also eliminate the operation of experimenter expectancy effects.

Automated Data Collection

The day may yet come when the elimination of the experimenter, in person, will be a widespread, well-accepted practice. Through the use of computers we may generate hypotheses, sample hypotheses, sample the experimental treatment conditions from a population of potential manipulations, select our subjects randomly, invite their participation, schedule them, instruct them, record and analyze their responses, and even partially interpret and report the results. Even if this fantasy were reality we would not be able to eliminate the experimenter completely. He or his surrogates or colleagues must program the computer and thereby influence the output. However, there would at least be no unprogrammed differential treatment of subjects as a function of their experimental conditions. In short, although experimenter or even machine effects cannot be completely eliminated, we can at least hope for unbiased effects.

Progress is being made along the trail to automation and the elimination of experimenter-subject contact from certain stages of research. Not necessarily because of an interest in reducing expectancy effects, many researchers employing animal subjects have fairly complex automated data-collection systems (McGuigan, 1963). This automation, however, generally applies only to the period of the animal's data production and not to all his pre- and extra-experimental experience (Christie, 1951). Experimenter handling patterns in transporting animals from home cage to the experimental work area and back may vary not only across experimenters but within experimenters as a function of the treatment condition to which the animal belongs.[6] Even if the animals were transported to and from their home cages without human contact there might still be an opportunity to treat differentially the animals of different treatment conditions.

Animals in their home cages may be treated differently as a function of their cage labels even if these labels are in code and the handler is not formally "an experimenter" or data collector. He still knows something of psychological research procedures—i.e., that different behavior is expected of members of different experimental groups. Earlier in this chapter we showed how knowledge of which subjects constitute a treatment group can affect the results of the research even when the hypotheses being tested and the specific treatment conditions are unknown.

Automated data collection, when the subjects are humans, also appears to be on the increase and, as in the case of animal studies, particularly

[6] Such differential handling of animals as a function of their experimental condition was postulated earlier as a major factor in the mediation of experimenter expectancy effects to animal subjects.

among researchers employing operant techniques. Written or tape-recorded instructional methods certainly seem to eliminate experimenter-subject contact. Although these methods should reduce any opportunity for the communication of experimenter expectancy effects, they would not eliminate such opportunity if there were nonblind experimenter-subject contact before the data collection phase of the experiment.

Experiments Requiring Human Interaction

It can be argued that there are experiments that make no sense unless a human interaction can occur between experimenter and subject, situations in which a written communication or tape recording alone simply would not do.

Experimenter constancy. If this must be, then from all we have said the experimenter's behavior should be as nearly constant as possible. There is a way in which we can achieve perfect constancy of experimenter behavior, and that is to employ the identical experimenter's input into each experimenter-subject interaction. This can be accomplished by filming an experimenter's required behavior in the experiment, including sound track. The sound film can then be used to instruct the subject. This alone would be little better than the tape-recorded instruction method if subjects could see that the experimenter was on film. However, where one-way mirrors or a television camera (with or without film) and closed-circuit television monitoring facilities are available, it would be a simple matter to give the impression of a "live" interaction. The situation could be structured for subjects so that they felt they could observe the experimenter and he could observe them via the monitoring system. In this way constancy of experimenter behavior could be assured without sacrificing the impression of "liveness" of interaction which may be crucial in certain experimental conditions.

Restricting cues available to the subject. Where experimenter-subject contact cannot be eliminated completely, it can at least be minimized. Earlier we showed how the reduction of the available channels of communication between experimenter and subject might reduce the effects of the experimenter's expectancy. Thus, interposing a screen between experimenter and subject would reduce the available channels for the communication of expectancy effects from experimenter to subject. However, cues from the subject to the experimenter have also been shown to increase the likelihood of experimenter expectancy effects by serving to break down the experimenter's blindness. It would, therefore, be desirable to restrict cues made available by the subject to the experimenter.

Restricting cues available to the experimenter. Cues to the experimenter tend to increase as he interacts with more subjects and as he interacts more with each subject. An incidental advantage of employing a group of experimenters, then, is that each contacts fewer subjects and therefore has less opportunity unwittingly to "crack the code" of a blind procedure— i.e., to learn which subjects constitute a group and what a subject's experimental condition might have been. In this way the advantages of experimenter blindness may better be maintained.

During his contact with any subject, the experimenter may avoid some important unintentional cues from the subject by having subjects record their own responses. There are many experimental procedures in work with human subjects wherein responses are coded in a fairly simple system. Subjects could then often be requested to record their own response on a clearly laid-out data sheet. If this procedure were followed whenever possible four advantages would accrue: (1) The experimenter's chances of remaining blind would be increased. (2) The experimenter, by simply not looking at the data sheets, could avoid that influence on his subsequent subjects attributable to his knowledge of the early data returns. (3) Experimenters' recording errors, which, though rare, tend to be biased when they do occur, would be virtually eliminated. (4) The amount of interpersonal contact between experimenter and subject would be reduced, thereby reducing the opportunity for the subtle communication of the experimenter's expectancy (or other bias or effect) to his subjects.

Some combined procedures. The use of an ordinary tape recorder may be combined with the use of a screen interposed between experimenter and subject to achieve some of the advantages of using a filmed experimenter to contact the subjects. This alternative procedure requires less expensive equipment than the closed-circuit television monitor. The tape recorder, out of sight of the subject behind the experimenter's screen, could be used to instruct the subject (without the subject's awareness) if earphones were provided. The impression, then, would be that the experimenter was speaking over a telephonelike device. This method assures instructional constancy, elimination of visual cues during the interaction, and when further combined with subjects' self-recording of response, no effects due to early data returns. At the same time the experimenter is physically present, therefore perhaps more "real" as required by some experimental manipulations. The only opportunity for unprogrammed experimenter input would be during the greeting phase of the data collection process before the experimenter retires behind his screen (and even this greeting phase could be eliminated). If the experimenter is also blind to the subject's treatment condition, however, this should not be particularly damaging.

The use of earphones for the subject has the additional advantage that it may help the experimenter maintain his blindness. Suppose the treatment conditions were to be created by the taped instructions. The tape could be constructed so that the different instructions appeared in some random sequence unknown to the experimenter. He would play one segment of the tape after another for sequences of subjects without knowing what instructions the subject had received through the earphones.

Effects of "Absent" Experimenters

We mentioned earlier that the experimenter could never be eliminated completely, even from a fantasied computer-run experiment. We repeat that restriction here. There always are (and always will be) decisions that must be made by the experimenter which may unintentionally affect the subjects' responses. These decisions, however, should have no unprogrammed, differential effect upon the subjects constituting the different experimental conditions.

One sort of research that is erroneously believed to involve no effect of the experimenter is the mail survey. Letters requesting information (often from psychologists themselves) are legion. There is no face-to-face contact between the questioner and the respondent. Yet the wording of the letter may yield different rates of return and, among the respondents, different kinds of responses. Different data collectors interested in the same questions are likely to ask them in different ways, thereby eliciting different responses. The advantage to the mail-survey technique, however, is that there, at least, we can specify exactly what the experimenter's stimulus value was. We can completely capture it simply by having a copy of the letter sent.

Just as letters convey something of the writer, so even more do tapes and films. Experimenter attributes cannot be eliminated. Their effects can only be distanciated, randomized, or held constant over treatment conditions to avoid a bias in the comparison between groups.

At the present time, there is such a dearth, relatively, of studies employing a more or less "absent" experimenter that it is difficult to assess the effect of such absence per se on the subjects' responses. What evidence there is suggests that a more or less "absent" experimenter often does affect subjects' behavior by his absence (Felice, 1961; Masling, 1960). There is at present, however, no reason to assume that an "absent" experimenter can affect his different experimental groups differentially and in the direction of his experimental hypothesis.

The Double Standard for Expectancy Control

Before leaving the topic of minimized contact between experimenter and subject, one further observation must be made. Earlier in this book and elsewhere in more detail (Rosenthal, 1965a) we have reviewed some early attempts to minimize experimenter-subject contact. It is striking that so many of these efforts at greater control occurred in what might be called "borderline" areas of psychology. Even today it would be the rash parapsychologist who would not make every effort to minimize the contact between the experimenter and subject in a study of extrasensory perception. And this is all to the good. Also to the good is the fact that nonparapsychologists would be outraged if such controls against expectancy effects were not employed. But *not* all to the good is the fact that some of these same workers might be outraged if in their own less "borderline" areas of inquiry they were required to institute the same degree of control over their own expectancy effects. Clearly we have a double standard of required degree of control. Those behavioral data found hard to believe are checked and controlled far more carefully than those behavioral data found easier to believe (e.g., Babich et al., 1965). What this amounts to, then, is a widespread interpretive bias which may serve to make it easier to demonstrate easily expected findings and harder to demonstrate intuitively less likely outcomes. In the overall conduct of the business of the behavioral sciences, this may lead to a pervasive bias to support hypotheses in keeping with beliefs of the times. Obviously the solution is not to make it easier to "demonstrate" unlikely events such as clairvoyance, rod-divining, talking animals, or muscle-reading. What is called for is the setting of equally strict standards of control against expectancy effects in the more prosaic, perhaps more important, everyday bread-and-butter areas of behavioral research. There should be no double standard; every area of behavioral inquiry should require the greatest possible control over the potential effects of experimenter expectancy and other sources of scientific error.

23

Expectancy
Control Groups

In the last chapter we discussed some strategies attempting to minimize experimenter expectancy effects. In the present chapter we shall discuss a strategy which essentially attempts to maximize experimenter expectancy effects by the employment of "expectancy control groups."

The logic of the control group was well developed by Mill in 1843 and, according to Boring (1954), had been anticipated a century earlier by Hume and two centuries earlier by Bacon and Pascal.[1] At least since the beginning of this century, psychologists have with increasing frequency employed control groups in their experiments (Solomon, 1949). Expectancy control groups represent a specific set of controls derived directly from the research demonstrating the effects of experimenters' expectancy on the results of their research.

Consider any experiment in which the effects of an experimental and a control treatment are to be compared.[2] The experiment is likely to be

---

[1] Boring tells how Pascal, in 1648, had his brother-in-law, Perier, perform an experiment with the Torricellian tube (barometer). As the tube was carried higher up a mountain the column of mercury dropped lower and lower. A control tube was left at the bottom of the mountain monitored by an observer to note whether there was any change in the level of mercury. A number of readings were made of the mercury level at the top of the mountain and one halfway down. Measures of pressure at any two of the three levels of altitude illustrate Mill's method of difference, and measures at all three points illustrate the more elegant special case of that method: the method of concomitant variation. A much earlier example of the use of control groups comes to us from ancient Egypt (Jones, 1964). That particular research if conducted today might have been titled: "Citron Ingestion as a Determinant of Longevity among Snake-bitten Animals."

[2] Although our example employs an experimental manipulation as the independent variable, the discussion applies as well to any comparison between groups, no matter how they are constituted. For our purpose a comparison between "experimental" and "control" groups does not differ from a comparison between male vs. female subjects, conforming vs. nonconforming subjects, or "high" vs. "low" anxious subjects.

conducted because a difference between the experimental and control group is *expected*.

Table 23-1 shows the generally resultant confounding of experimental treatment conditions with the experimenter's expectancy. Cell A represents the condition in which the experimental treatment is administered to subjects by a data collector who expects the occurrence of the treatment

TABLE 23—1

Confounding of Treatments with Experimenter Expectancy

| | | TREATMENT CONDITIONS | |
		Experimental	Control
EXPECTANCY	Occurrence	A	B
	Nonoccurrence	C	D

effect. Cell D represents the condition in which the absence of the experimental treatment is associated with a data collector who expects the nonoccurrence of the treatment effect. But ordinarily the investigator is interested in the treatment effects unconfounded with experimenter expectancy. The addition of the appropriate expectancy control groups will permit the evaluation of the treatment effect separately from the expectancy effect. A "complete expectancy control" requires the addition of both cells B *and* C, whereas a "partial expectancy control" requires the addition of *either* cell B *or* C. Subjects in cell B are those who will not receive the experimental treatment but who will be contacted by an experimenter who expects a treatment effect. Subjects in Cell C are those who will receive the experimental treatment but who will be contacted by an experimenter who expects no treatment effect.

HYPOTHETICAL OUTCOMES

The results of the case of an experimental vs. a control group comparison with "complete expectancy control" are most simply evaluated by a two-way analysis of variance yielding a main effect attributable to the experimental treatment, a main effect attributable to experimenter expectancy, and an interaction of these two effects. For the sake of simplicity, we may say that any of these three sources of variance can be only (1) significant and large, or (2) significant and small, or (3) insignificant and virtually zero.

Large Treatment Effects

Table 23-2 shows some likely hypothetical results of a complete expectancy-controlled experiment in which the treatment effects are significant statistically and large numerically. The numbers in the cells represent the mean data obtained from the subjects in that condition. For the sake of clarity we may assume that the mean square within cells is so small that any numerical differences are statistically significant.

TABLE 23—2

Expectancy-Controlled Experiments Showing Large Treatment Effects

		TREATMENT CONDITIONS	
Case	Expectancy	Experimental	Control
1	Occurrence	6.0	0.0
	Nonoccurrence	6.0	0.0
2	Occurrence	6.0	1.0
	Nonoccurrence	5.0	0.0
3	Occurrence	6.0	3.0
	Nonoccurrence	3.0	0.0

Case 1 shows that whereas the experimental treatment had a powerful effect upon subjects' performance, experimenter expectancy had neither any effect in itself nor did it enter into interaction with the experimental treatment. A result such as this not only reassures us that our treatment per se "works," but also impugns the generality of experimenter expectancy effects.

Case 2 shows almost the same magnitude of difference between the average performance of experimental vs. control subjects as we found in Case 1. However, experimenter expectancy effects were significant, though small, and trivial relative to the powerful effects of the treatment condition.

Case 3 shows that the treatment effects, although still large and significant, are no greater than the effects of experimenter expectancy.

These first three cases, then, show increasing effects of experimenter expectancy, although in each case we would correctly conclude that the experimental condition had a significant effect with expectancy effects controlled. If we had omitted the expectancy controls, would we have erred seriously? Not if we were interested only in showing that the experimental treatment affected subjects' performance. However, if we were at that more advanced stage of inquiry where we would like to be able to state with some accuracy the *magnitude* of the experimental effect we would have been misled—not, of course, in Case 1, where expectancy had no effect whatever. But in Case 2 we would have overestimated slightly the power of the experimental treatment. And in Case 3 we would have overestimated seriously the power of the treatment under study.

From Table 23-2 we can see that for Case 1 the difference between performances of those experimental and control groups which are normally confounded with expectancy (cell A–cell D) is 6.0 points. This is the same difference obtained by experimenters expecting either the occurrence (cell A–cell B) or the nonoccurrence (cell C–cell D) of the treatment effects. For Case 2 the normally confounded experiment uncontrolled for expectancy would have yielded a difference of 6.0, where only a 5.0 was attributable to treatment unconfounded with expectancy. For Case 3, a 6.0 difference, of which only half was attributable to unconfounded treatment effect, would have been claimed.

Interacting Treatment Effects

The three cases discussed have shown no interaction effects. Cases 4 and 5, shown in Table 23-3, however, both show significant interaction effects in addition to significant main effects. In each case all three sources of variance are equal in magnitude. The main effects of experimental treatment and experimenter expectancy, hence, are not interpretable apart from the interaction effect.

In Case 4 the experimental treatment has an effect on subjects'

TABLE 23—3

Expectancy-Controlled Experiments Showing Interacting Treatment Effects

		TREATMENT CONDITIONS	
Case	Expectancy	Experimental	Control
4	Occurrence	6.0	0.0
	Nonoccurrence	0.0	0.0
5	Occurrence	6.0	6.0
	Nonoccurrence	6.0	0.0

performance only when the experimenter expects such performance. If this outcome were the "true" state of affairs, then the omission of the expectancy control groups would have been quite serious. The experimental treatment would have been regarded as significantly effective and large in magnitude when, in fact, such a conclusion, unqualified, would have been extremely misleading.

Similarly misleading would be conclusions based on the situation shown in Case 5 if expectancy control groups had not been employed. In this case *either* the experimental treatment *or* the experimenter's expectancy was sufficient to affect the subjects' performance in the expected direction, to the same degree, and without any summative effects attributable to the combined effects of treatment and expectancy. (In Case 5 the suspicion might arise that a special instance of Case 3 had occurred where a low ceiling on the dependent variable measure had prevented a higher mean score from being obtained in cell A.)

Small Treatment Effects

In Table 23-4 we see a number of outcomes in which the effects attributable to the experimental treatment are either trivial or absent altogether. Case 6 shows the simplest of all outcomes. Nothing made any difference; not the experimental treatment, not the experimenter's expectancy, and not the interaction. This, like Case 1, is one of the few situations in which an omission of the expectancy control groups would not have increased our errors of interpretation. But as with Case 1, it seems impossible to know beforehand, without our (or someone's) ascertaining empirically that such would be the result.

TABLE 23—4

Expectancy-Controlled Experiments Showing Small Treatment Effects

		TREATMENT CONDITIONS	
Case	Expectancy	Experimental	Control
6	Occurrence	0.0	0.0
	Nonoccurrence	0.0	0.0
7	Occurrence	6.0	6.0
	Nonoccurrence	0.0	0.0
8	Occurrence	6.0	5.0
	Nonoccurrence	1.0	0.0

Case 7 shows only a large and significant expectancy effect. It is like Case 1 in showing only a large main effect, but unlike Case 1 in that the omission of expectancy controls would have caused serious error. Not only would the effect of the treatment have been "significant," but the magnitude of the effect (cell A–cell D) would have been thought to be 6.0, as in Case 1, rather than the zero it really was.

Case 8, somewhat analogous to Case 2, shows a significant and large expectancy effect and a significant but relatively trivial treatment effect. The omission of expectancy controls in this case, as in Case 7, would have greatly misled us as to the magnitude of the treatment effect. Had we been interested only in establishing *any* difference favoring the experimental over the control conditions, however, we would not have been misled by the omission of expectancy controls.

Other Treatment Effects

Only a few of the possible outcomes of expectancy-controlled experiments have been presented. Some of the outcomes not described here in detail make some sort of psychological sense, but many do not. Examples of those that do would be situations in which one main effect is significant and very large relative to the other main effect and interaction, which are small but significant (Table 23-5). Examples of outcomes making less

TABLE 23—5

Expectancy-Controlled Experiments Showing Interpretable Interacting Main Effects

		TREATMENT CONDITIONS	
Case	Expectancy	Experimental	Control
9	Occurrence	6.0	3.0
	Nonoccurrence	6.0	0.0
10	Occurrence	6.0	6.0
	Nonoccurrence	3.0	0.0

psychological sense include those many possible situations in which (1) the means of the control conditions unpredictably exceed the means of the experimental conditions, and/or (2) the means obtained under the expectancy-for-nonoccurrence exceed the means obtained under the expectancy-for-occurrence situation, and/or (3) some interaction of these reversed main effects. To say that some of these outcomes are less sensible psychologically is not to say that they will be rare. The unexpected, reversed finding is quite frequent in the behavioral sciences.

Adding to the likelihood of less sensible findings are some of the data presented earlier in this book demonstrating the "bending-over-backward" effect. Although not the usual result, there are occasions (e.g., when the rewards are psychologically excessive) when experimenters try so hard to avoid letting their expectancy influence their subjects that the subjects are influenced to respond in the direction opposite to that consistent with the experimenter's expectancy. If unexpected treatment effects join synergistically with an experimenter bending over backward to avoid biasing, we may obtain a significant "reversed interaction." In this case, for example, only that cell (D) in the control condition assigned an experimenter not expecting the treatment effect would show the predicted treatment effect.

Partial Expectancy Controls

So far we have discussed only the use of "complete expectancy controls." The use of "partial expectancy controls" (employing *either of* rather than *both* cells B and C) is best considered only if the alternative is to use no expectancy control at all. The relative loss of information incurred, when only partial rather than full expectancy controls are employed, depends on the "true" outcome of the experiment. Thus, although for most outcomes we would be better off to use partial rather than *no* expectancy control, there are "true" outcomes involving interaction effects (e.g., Cases 4, 5, and 10) for which the use of only partial controls could lead to seriously erroneous conclusions about the relative effects of the treatments vs. the effects of the experimenter's expectancy. The problem currently is that we have no good basis for deciding what the true outcome would have been if expectancy had been fully controlled. As complete expectancy control groups are employed more and more, we may accumulate enough information to sensibly decide for what type of study we can afford to omit one (or both) of the expectancy controls.

If for some reason, perhaps logistic, only two of the four cells can be employed, what is our best choice? We may choose either one of the comparisons within rows (cells A vs. B or C vs. D) or one of the comparisons within diagonals (cells B vs. C or A vs. D, the "usual" comparison). By defining the "true" magnitude of the treatment effect as the difference between the column means in the completely controlled expectancy design, the relative merits of the use of within-rows vs. within-diagonal comparisons may be illustrated.

Table 23-6 has been derived from the hypothetical outcomes of the fully controlled experiments shown in Tables 23-2–23-5. For each comparison, the magnitude of error in obtaining the "true" magnitude of the

TABLE 23—6

Magnitude of Error as a Function of Choice of Comparison

COMPARISONS

Case	Within Rows (A-B or C-D)	Within Diagonals (A-D or B-C)
1	0.0	0.0
2	0.0	1.0
3	0.0	3.0
4	3.0	3.0
5	3.0	3.0
6	0.0	0.0
7	0.0	6.0
8	0.0	5.0
9	1.5	1.5
10	1.5	4.5

treatment effect has been listed. It can be seen that the choice of a within-row comparison leads to fewer errors, and none so large as some of those obtained if the choice is of a within-diagonal comparison. Furthermore, errors in obtaining the "true" treatment effect occur in the within-row comparison only in those cases where the completely controlled experiment shows an interaction effect.

It makes no systematic difference which of the two within-rows comparisons we choose (cells A vs. B or cells C vs. D). If we chose to make within-diagonal comparisons, however, it would make a very important systematic difference whether we employed cells B vs. C or cells A. vs. D. The former comparison, except for Cases 1 and 6, *always* underestimates the "true" treatment effect, whereas the latter, more typical comparison *always* overestimates the "true" treatment effect. It seems clear, then, that if for any reason only two cells can be employed, the experimenter should have the same expectancy in both; either favoring the occurrence or the nonoccurrence of the treatment effect.

Although the two-cell, within-row, partial expectancy-controlled experiment is preferable to the ordinary within-diagonal experiment, it is no substitute for the complete expectancy-controlled experiment nor even for the three-cell design (B or C omitted) described. The three-cell design, at least, has the very real advantage of affording us a replication of the usual experiment (cells A vs. D) uncontrolled for expectancy.

IMPLEMENTATION OF EXPECTANCY CONTROLS

We have discussed the general design of expectancy control groups but have had little to say so far about some practical issues raised by this methodological suggestion. For example, we stated at the beginning of this chapter that experimenters' expectancies tended to be preconfounded with their experimental and control conditions. How can we create those conditions in which the experimenters' expectancy runs counter to the predicted effects of the experimental conditions (cells B and C)? A number of methods are available for creating expectancy control groups, and these will be described shortly. However, most of these methods involve the withholding of information from, and giving of false information to, the experimenters. A number of ethical questions are raised by such deception.

Ethical Considerations

Perhaps the major question to ask is whether the distasteful though necessary deception is warranted by the potential importance of the result of the expectancy-controlled experiment. Since virtually no scientific behavioral research can be univocally described as too trivial to warrant adequate controls, it would seem that most research conducted in the behavioral sciences should be expectancy-controlled. It is a moot question whether the deception of data collectors should score lower on an evaluative scale than the production of research results that may be subject to serious error—error that could be assessed by the employment of appropriate controls.

How serious is the deception of data collectors (or subjects) in general? The widespread use of placebo control groups in pharmacological research, especially when conducted under double-blind conditions, suggests that no harmful effects of deception need occur. Placebo and double-blind deceptions have shown themselves to warrant use by the greater knowledge of drug action they have given us. In our own research on experimenter expectancy effects we have employed deception of necessity and have found no harmful effects. Factually erroneous information given data collectors can be quickly (and cognitively) corrected. We have found no hostility (to be affectively corrected) by the data collectors resulting from an explanation of how expectancies had been created. On the contrary, the data collectors seemed intrigued and wondered why expectancy controls were not routinely employed.

Of course, there is no question that hostility can be evoked by the deception of data collectors or subjects. It is my very strong impression—if I may insert here a clinical "footnote"—that such hostility is evoked not by the fact of deception itself but by the manner of deceiving, the personalized nature of the deception, and the manner of subsequent explanation or "de-hoaxing." These variables serve the data collectors (or subjects) as sources of clues to the experimenter's underlying motivation for having employed the deception. If subjects are satisfied that these motivations are primarily rational (e.g., for "science") rather than primarily irrational (e.g., for "fun," to be "cute" or clever, to be hostile), they will re-act with appreciation of the necessity for deception, rather than with hostility *at having been deceived*. Note that we are not speaking here of experimenters' "true" motives in employing (*or not employing*) decep-tion; rather we are speaking of the subjects' perception of these motives. (The general problem of the deception of subjects has been discussed re-cently by Vinacke [1965], by Wolfle [1960], and in most detail, by Kelman [1965].)

The Induction of Experimenter Expectancies

Ascribing subject characteristics. One method for creating experi-menter expectancies calls for a statement of subject characteristics. Subjects assigned to cell B are described to their experimenters as having character-istics such that their response in the experiment will be like that of the subjects in cell A. Subjects assigned to cell C are described to their experi-menters as having characteristics such that their response will be like that of subjects in cell D. If the experiment were one we have described earlier, the effect of anxiety upon intellectual performance among college students, cell B experimenters could be told their subjects were a bit below average intellectually for college students. Cell C experimenters could be told their subjects were a bit above average intellectually. It goes without saying, of course, that subjects are assigned at random to the experimental conditions or equated on intellectual performance.

Ascribing experimental conditions. Another method for generating expectancy control groups is by the labeling of treatment conditions. In those cases where the experimenter does not himself administer the experi-mental treatment, he is told that the cell B subjects have received the ex-perimental treatment and that cell C subjects have received the control "treatment." In the example we have used, cell B experimenters would be told that their subjects had undergone the anxiety-arousing experience, and cell C experimenters would be told that their subjects had not—that they were part of the control group.

Disparagement of treatment effectiveness. A third method of gener-ating expectancy control groups involves a relative disparagement of treat-ment effectiveness. In this method, cell C experimenters are "shown" that the specific experimental treatment of their subjects "could not possibly" have the predicted effect on their behavior. Cell B experimenters are "shown" that, whereas the subjects of the treatment condition may show the predicted response, the subjects of the control group will show that response just as much if not more. Thus, in the example used, cell C experimenters would have pointed out to them that the particular "anxiety-arousal" treatment could not *really* make anyone anxious. Cell B experimenters would have pointed out to them that the particular nature of the "control" condition was such that it might make subjects even more anxious than the "experimental" condition.

Theory reversal. A fourth method of generating expectancy control groups is that of hypothesis or "theory reversal." It can best be used when less academically advanced or less expert data collectors are employed. In this method cell B and cell C experimenters are provided with a plausible rationale (possibly buttressed by "earlier results" or results in the literature that are consistent with the rationale) for expecting just the opposite sort of relative outcome from the experimental and control subjects. In our example, cell B and cell C experimenters might be shown how the usual control situation in an experiment generates anxiety whereas the anxiety-arousing treatment merely puts a "sharp edge" on the subjects, leading to improved intellectual performance.

Although practically none of the outlined methods for creating expectancy control groups have been employed by investigators not specifically interested in the effect of experimenter expectancy, there is an ingenious exception to be found in the work of Rosenhan (1964). In a study of the relationship between hypnosis and conformity Rosenhan (1963) found more hypnotizable subjects to conform more under certain conditions and to conform less under other conditions. He and a research assistant then attempted to replicate these findings. Essentially he assigned himself as an experimenter to cells A and D and the assistant to cells B and C. He employed the technique of "theory reversal" by showing the assistant the results of his earlier study but with the signs preceding the correlation coefficients reversed.

Results of this expectancy-controlled study showed that Rosenhan himself obtained data similar to those he had obtained earlier, but the assistant obtained data similar to the opposite of the data obtained earlier but consistent with her hypothesis. Rosenhan rightly points out that since the two experimenters differed in many ways other than expectancy it cannot be concluded with great certainty that it was the expectancy difference that led to the opposite experimental results. Nevertheless, the results of this expectancy-controlled study showed that experimenter attributes (including expectancy) might account for some of the differences in results reported in the literature.

Intentional influence. A fifth method for the creation of expectancy control groups, and one not requiring the employment of deception, is the "method of intentional influence." This technique can be used with very sophisticated as well as quite unsophisticated experimenters. Experimenters in cell B are quite aware that their subjects are in the control condition, but they are told to try to influence them to respond as though they had received the experimental treatment, but without deviating from the detailed procedure followed by experimenters of cell D. Experimenters in cell C are aware that their subjects are in the experimental condition, but they are told to try to influence them to respond as though they had been in the control condition, but again, without deviating from the detailed procedure followed by experimenters of cell A.

The advantages of this technique have already been mentioned—i.e., that it involves no deception and can be used with experimenters of any degree of sophistication. The major disadvantage of this technique is its lack of symmetry of cells B and C with cells A and D. Experimenters in these last two cells are *not* making any conscious effort to influence their subjects, whereas experimenters in cells B and C *are*. Thus, *intentionality* of influence is confounded with the "primary" (cells A and D) vs. "expectancy control group" (cells B and C) comparison.

Unintentional communication. A sixth method for creating expectancy control groups differs from all those described so far in that no expectancy is ever explicitly communicated to the experimenters of the expectancy control groups. This method is based on the difficulty of maintaining double-blind contact which was documented in the last chapter. Experimenters of cells A and B are trained by experimenters expecting large treatment effects, and experimenters of cells C and D are trained by experimenters expecting no treatment effects. The experimenters serving as trainers are likely to subtly and unintentionally communicate these expectancies to their trainee-experimenters.

The expectancies of the trainer-experimenters can be created by any one of several of the methods described earlier. Another method of creating expectancies in the trainers would be to describe the experiment in which the trainees will be employed without mentioning that cells B and C would be formed as randomly divided subgroups of cell A and cell D trainees. Finally, expectancies may be created in the trainers by having them actually participate as experimenters in cells A and D of the experiment. Cell A trainers, of course, would contact only cell A (and B) trainees, and cell D trainers would contact only cell D (and C) trainees.

Subjects' responses. A final method for creating expectancy control groups is one that also never explicitly communicates an expectancy to the experimenters. It is a method that derives from studies of the effects of early data returns and the finding that experimenter expectancies may be altered by these early returns. Half the experimenters of cell A are, through the use of accomplices, provided with disconfirming early returns, thereby making them more like cell C experimenters. Half the experimenters of cell D are similarly provided with disconfirming data, thereby making them more like cell B experimenters. If only one experimenter is available, we can then employ him in cells A and B or in cells C and D. We saw earlier that this was preferable to employing experimenters in the diagonal conditions (e.g., cells A and D).

More generally, the procedure of providing experimenters with planned early returns can be employed to augment some of the methods described earlier for creating expectancy control groups. Thus, if the "method of ascribing subject characteristics" has been employed, the induced expectancy would be greatly strengthened by the first few subjects' providing the expected data. More details of the procedure for providing confirming or disconfirming early returns through the use of accomplices were presented in the chapter dealing with the effects of early data returns.

In our discussion of various methods for generating expectancy control groups we have tried to be suggestive rather than exhaustive. Entirely different methods, a variety of subtypes of the methods mentioned, or combinations of the several methods may be most useful for a certain area of behavioral research and a specific research question.

Experimenter Assignment

Perhaps the ideal way in which to use expectancy control groups is to take a large and random sample of experimenters and assign them randomly to the various subconditions of the experimental design we have been discussing. The general advantages of a large number of experimenters have already been stressed in earlier chapters. But the absence of such a pool of experimenters does not rule out the use of expectancy-controlled designs.

One experimenter. Even if only a single experimenter is available, experiments can be expectancy-controlled. Subjects in cells A and D would be contacted as in ordinary experimental procedure. By using certain of the methods described earlier for creating expectancies, the same experimenter can also contact subjects in cells B and C. If more than one experimenter is available, all may be employed in each experimental condition. (In such a case the analysis of the data changes from the simple 2×2 [treatment $\times$ expectancy] analysis of variance to the more complex $2 \times 2 \times N$ [treatment $\times$ expectancy $\times$ experimenters] analysis in which each experimenter may be regarded as a replicator of the 2×2 experiment [e.g., Lindquist, 1953] [3].)

[3] For appropriate application, Lindquist (1953) or a comparable text should be consulted with special attention to the fact that error terms in fixed constants models

Two experimenters. If only two experimenters are available it would probably be best if each could contact subjects in all four conditions, but some alternatives are possible and may, for a particular experiment, be necessary. Thus, Rosenhan (1964) could not very well have placed himself into the B and C cells of his expectancy-controlled experiment, nor, by his technique, placed his assistant in the A and D cells.

With two experimenters the four cells can be divided equally in three ways: (1) One experimenter contacts only those subjects to be seen with an expectancy for occurrence of the treatment effect (cells A and B), while the other experimenter contacts the remaining subjects (cells C and D). (2) One experimenter contacts only the treatment condition subjects (cells A and C), while the other contacts only control condition subjects (cells B and D). (3) One experimenter conducts the "basic-uncontrolled" experiment (cells A and D), while the other contacts the subjects in the expectancy control groups (cells B and C).

In each of these three divisions the effect of the experimenter's attributes is confounded with one of the sources of variance.[4] Thus, in division 1 individual differences between the two experimenters could significantly alter the magnitude of the expectancy effect. In division 2 these differences could affect the treatment effect, and in division 3 they could affect the interaction. Divisions 1 and 2 are probably not usable (although their analogue is sometimes employed in research, as when different experimenters contact subjects in the treatment and control conditions).

Division 3 does seem useful. If the effects of experimenters' attributes are constant for the subjects of the two cells contacted by each experimenter, then at least neither of the main effects should be affected, although their interpretation may be complicated by a significant interaction which could far exceed either or both of the main effects. This division, across the diagonals of our basic design, will be remembered as analogous to the expectancy-controlled study conducted by Rosenhan (1964).

More than two experimenters. For samples of experimenters larger than two but smaller than about eight, the best strategy would appear to be either (a) using each experimenter in each cell, or (b) confounding the interaction with experimenter differences as in division 3, above, or perhaps best of all, (c) a combination of a and b such that about half the experimenters available are assigned to each method.

The particular advantage of this method is that it permits a com-

---

are not analogous to error terms in mixed models. The $2 \times 2 \times N$ design, for example, may be regarded as either model depending on what basis was used for the selection of the experimenters.

[4] If two experimenters divided the experiment unequally, it can be seen that the three cells of one experimenter and the single cell of the other would yield results confounded with the experimenter.

parison of the results of the two strategies. Using the results of the replication(s) in which each experimenter functions in all four cells (strategy a) may help us assess whether a large interaction in the results of a replication employing strategy b is due to confounding with experimenters or is more likely to be independent of experimenters. With a small number of experimenters, however, we can never answer that question with great confidence because we will not be able to assess adequately the effects of the orders and sequences in which experimenters contacted the subjects of the different treatment conditions (cells).

More than seven experimenters. If we have eight or more experimenters available, we can begin to think seriously of assigning them at random to one of the four cells of our basic design, thereby eliminating the problem of assessing order and sequence effects.[5] It also becomes more possible to test the significance of the difference in results obtained by experimenters within treatments as well as the effects of the treatment condition, the expectancy condition, and their interaction. If the use of such a "nested" (Winer, 1962) or groups-within-treatments (Lindquist, 1953) analysis shows no significant individual differences between experimenters within cells, we can simply forget that the subjects were contacted by different data collectors and use the individual differences among subjects within cells as the error term against which to evaluate the other sources of variation. Or with samples of experimenters very large, the mean scores obtained by each experimenter may be used as the basic data which can be analyzed by the standard 2×2 analysis of variance.

More Complex Designs

Throughout the discussion of expectancy control groups we have kept the basic design as simple as possible for illustrative purposes. Thus, our basic experiment has been the comparison of a single experimental treatment condition with a control condition. The principle of expectancy control groups can, however, be applied to more complex designs. In some situations the complexity of the expectancy-controlled design increases proportionally to the complexity of the added experimental groups. In other situations, however, the increase in complexity is disproportional.

Proportional increase in complexity. As an example of a proportional increase in complexity, we note that the simple complete expectancy-controlled experiment (2×2) may be subdivided into two subexperiments, each conducted with subjects at one of two levels of some personal charac-

[5] With only four experimenters, if we assigned one to each of the four cells, the effects of cells would be confounded with individual differences among experimenters. With random assignment of experimenters to cells, this confounding is less and less of a problem as our sample of experimenters becomes larger and larger.

teristic (e.g., sex, anxiety, need for achievement). In this case our basic 2×2 design becomes a $2 \times 2 \times 2$ design, assuming that the level of subject characteristic does not in itself affect experimenters' expectancies regarding the effects of the treatment condition. Our four basic groups (A, B, C, D) have become eight groups representing a proportional increase in complexity.

Disproportional increase in complexity. A disproportional increase in complexity may be required by the addition of a single experimental treatment condition if the preexisting expectancy of its effect were opposite to that of the original treatment condition. For illustration we return to our example of a study of the effects of anxiety arousal on intellectual performance. Suppose we add an experimental condition in which subjects are actively reassured about their intellectual performance. The hypothesis might be that this group of subjects would show an improved performance relative to the "no-treatment" control group, whereas the anxious subjects would show an impairment. We may now want to have three conditions or levels of experimenter expectancy rather than the two we have employed in earlier examples. If we did, our basic 2×2 design would become not a 2×3 but rather a 3×3. Our four basic groups, therefore, have become nine groups.

For logistic reasons we may not be able to entertain such a complex design. If this is the case, then what we have said earlier about partial expectancy controls will apply. Therefore, if we can employ only three groups of our design, all three groups should be contacted by experimenters holding the same expectancy. This would represent a within-row comparison rather than the fully uncontrolled (for expectancy) diagonal comparison in which expectancy would be confounded completely with experimental condition.

In any specific experimental situation the basic principle of expectancy control can be applied by the investigator, although the specific form of the design will be determined both by the nature of the research question and by consideration of the resources available for the research.

CONTROLLING FOR SUBJECT EXPECTANCY

In this chapter we have discussed the use of special control groups to control only the effects of experimenter expectancy.[6] In an earlier chapter, however, we showed that, at least in some experimental situations, the subjects' expectancies or outcome orientations could also be unintended de-

---

[6] The control of other experimenter effects, including modeling effects and effects due to various other experimenter attributes, depends on their measurement rather than on their experimental induction; they have been discussed in the chapter dealing with the sampling of experimenters.

terminants of the results of our research. There may be some experiments in which these subject expectancy effects are large and perhaps as important as, or even more important than, experimenter expectancy effects. By employing the principles for generating experimenter expectancy control groups we can control for subjects' expectancy. We can illustrate this best by imagining the following experiment:

We want to learn the effects of alcohol on verbal learning. Our basic design is to have half our randomly assigned subjects consume a given quantity of beverage alcohol while the remaining subjects consume a soft drink. For the sake of simplicity let us suppose that experimenters and subjects alike are convinced that the ingestion of the experimental dosage of alcohol will impair verbal learning. We can control for experimenter expectancy by having experimenters believe that half the subjects in the treatment (alcohol) condition are in the control (soft-drink) condition (cell C). Similarly we could have experimenters in the control condition believe that half of their subjects are in the experimental condition (cell B). So far we have dealt only with our old friends cells A, B, C, and D.

Because subjects believe strongly (let's say) that alcohol impairs their verbal learning, our old A, B, C, D design is confounded by subjects' expectancies. Table 23-7 shows the situation. In our old cell A, subjects

TABLE 23—7

Double Confounding of Treatments with Experimenter and Subject Expectancy

			TREATMENT CONDITIONS	
EXPECTANCY				
Experimenter	Subject	Row	Experimental	Control
Occurrence	Occurrence	1	A	B^1
	Nonoccurrence	2	A^1	B
Nonoccurrence	Occurrence	3	C	D^1
	Nonoccurrence	4	C^1	D

expect the effects of alcohol, but in cell B they do not. In our old cell D, subjects expect no effects of alcohol, but in cell C they do. Our basic experiment of alcohol vs. soft-drink has been doubly confounded. If we used only the basic groups of cell A vs. cell D, any differences might be due to the effect of alcohol, the effect of experimenter expectancies, the effect of subject expectancies, or any of several possible interaction effects.

To control fully for subject expectancy we must add cells A^1, B^1, C^1, and D^1, as shown in Table 23-7. These cells may, for this hypothetical experiment, be generated by the use of a nonalcoholic beverage which has an alcohol-like taste (for cells B^1 and D^1) and the use of an alcoholic beverage which has a nonalcoholic taste (for cells A^1 and C^1).[7] Instead of, or in addition to, the variation of the tastes of the substances ingested, verbal statements to subjects could be used to vary their performance expectancies.

The analysis of the data of this double-expectancy-controlled experiment could proceed as a straightforward $2 \times 2 \times 2$ analysis of variance. We can, therefore, assess the independent effects of the alcohol, the subjects' and the experimenters' expectancies, the interactions between any two of these independent variables, and the interaction of all three.

If all eight groups could not be managed, the design could be cut in half by employing any two rows of cells shown in Table 23-7. Then all experimenters (rows 1 and 2) or none (rows 3 and 4) would expect the effects of alcohol. Or all subjects (rows 1 and 3) or none (rows 2 and 4) would expect the effects of alcohol. Any of these four subdivisions would be helpful, but none would permit a comparison of the effects of experimenter vs. subject expectancy. However, the use of the two rows in which experimenters' and subjects' expectancies disagreed (rows 2 and 3) *would* permit such a comparison.

If the purpose of the experiment were to permit generalization to the real-life social drinking situations in which alcohol was consumed, rather than to evaluate the effects of a chemical upon verbal learning, we would prefer that subdivision of the experiment in which subjects' and experimenters' expectancies were in agreement (rows 1 and 4). In most real-life social drinking situations both the drinker and his "evaluator" are aware of whether alcohol has been consumed, although there are certainly exceptions to this. Employing this subdivision of the full experiment does not permit us to compare the effects of subjects' or experimenters' expectancies. However, we may be less interested in that comparison for some purposes, sacrificing it for the greater ecological validity of this subdivision. Another advantage of this subdivision is that it includes a replicate of the "usual" experiment (cell A vs. cell D).

If, for some reason, we could employ only two of the eight groups, we may choose any one of the four rows, since in each we have equated for both subjects' and experimenters' expectancies. On the grounds of ecological validity, however, we would probably prefer row 1 or row 4 to rows 2 or 3. And because it might be easier to implement practically, we might prefer row 1 over row 4. For any other number of groups to be chosen from the full complement of eight groups, the choice would be made on bases similar to those presented just now and also in the section dealing with partial expectancy controls.

---

[7] It goes without saying that all our subjects are social drinkers and have volunteered to ingest alcohol, though with the understanding that not all volunteers will necessarily receive alcohol.

COMBINING METHODS OF CONTROL

The control group designs described in this chapter can be combined with other methods for the control of experimenter effects which were described in earlier chapters. We can, for example, minimize the contact between experimenters and subjects of expectancy-controlled experiments. This should reduce the communication of our experimenters' expectancy to their subjects, but unless we have an intrinsic interest in these expectancy effects, that is all to the good. As contact with subjects is reduced further and further, in principle we have less and less need for the employment of any expectancy controls at all.

Combining of minimized (or blind) contact with expectancy control groups has a very special advantage. It provides us with an opportunity to assess the success of the minimization (or blindness) of contact. If contact has been successfully minimal (and/or blind), we should find no significant main effect of experimenter expectancies nor any interaction involving experimenter expectancy. Finding such effects would be sufficient evidence for concluding that the minimization (or blind) procedure had been ineffective.

A still more powerful combination of controls for expectancy effects might include sampling experimenters, determining their expectancies, applying the expectancy control group procedure, and maintaining blind and minimized contact. This combination of controls might reduce to an absolute minimum the biasing effect of experimenters' expectancies. The basic 2×2 design described in this chapter could then be extended into a third dimension—the dimension of "idiosyncratic" or "natural" expectancy. If there were only two types of idiosyncratic expectancies, our overall design might become a $2 \times 2 \times 2$ arrangement—the experimental vs. control treatment, the experimenters led to expect a treatment effect vs. those led to expect no treatment effect, and experimenters "naturally" expecting a treatment effect vs. those expecting no treatment effect. If we had a range of idiosyncratic or "natural" expectancies rather than only two, we could elongate the design to have three, four, or even more levels of "natural" expectancy.

One advantage of generating this third dimension of experimenters' "natural" expectancies is that it may help to reduce the variation between experimenters (within cells). Within any one of the basic four cells of our expectancy-controlled experiment, experimenters' obtained data may vary because of variation in initial idiosyncratic expectancies.

Another advantage of generating the dimension of experimenters' idiosyncratic expectancies stems from the finding that expectancy bias is maximized when experimentally induced and idiosyncratic expectancies are in agreement (Rosenthal, Persinger, Vikan-Kline, & Mulry, 1963). In "real" experiments, the data collector has no conflicting expectancies arising from the imposition of an "artificial" expectancy upon the preexisting one. We may, therefore, obtain a more accurate estimate of the upper limits of the effects of expectancy bias as it occurs in "real" data collectors by allowing both types of expectancy to operate jointly.

In addition to the combination of methods for the control of expectancy effects already mentioned we might employ one or more methods of observing experimenters' behavior in interaction with their subjects. Their behavior vis-à-vis their subjects could be regarded as the dependent variable for one analysis. If we found experimenters in the various conditions to show no significant differences in behavior, we would feel more confident in the substantive results of the experiment. If we found significant differences in the behavior of experimenters in different conditions, we would feel more confident that our trouble in setting up the various control conditions was warranted. The experimenters' behavior toward their subjects can also be regarded as an independent variable. If we choose to so regard it, then we will learn something more, not only about methodological matters but about some substantive issues in unintentional interpersonal influence as well.

EXPECTANCY CONTROLS: COST VERSUS UTILITY

In assessing the employment of expectancy control groups we can weigh their cost against their utility. We have already weighed one type of cost—the need to withhold information or give false information to our data collectors. In general, the utility of controlling for experimenter expectancy seems to outweigh heavily the innocuous deception necessitated by most methods of generating expectancy control groups.

What about other costs? The number of subjects required for an experiment is not increased, the time per subject-contact is not increased and, sometimes, the number of data collectors involved is not even increased. The creation of expectancy control groups takes additional time in the planning stages of the experiment and, if more experimenters are employed, in the training stage. But this amount of time is measured in hours and minutes, not in months and weeks, and therefore should prove to be no real obstacle. If a larger number of experimenters is employed there may also be a small increase in the financial cost of the experiment—not because more hours are involved in all, but because an experimenter employed for a total of one hour must usually be paid more per hour than one employed for 50 hours. But this cost, too, is relatively small.[8]

[8] Not really a cost, but a problem associated with the long-term usage of expectancy controls should be made explicit. As Milton Rosenberg has pointed out in a personal communication (1965), it might not take too long before the usual sources of

If a larger number of experimenters is employed than would normally be the case, an additional utility can be achieved if the procedure of simultaneous experimenter-subject contacts is employed, as suggested in the last chapter. The total time from beginning to end of the data collection can be greatly reduced, and this is an efficiency that is not hard to appreciate.

All in all, the total costs of conducting expectancy-controlled experiments seem trivial in relation to the utility of the method. But it can be said that costs are easier to assess than utility. Utility for whom? Are there not areas in the behavioral sciences that just do not require controls for experimenter expectancy? To this it must be said that there may be, but we don't know that to be the case. And if it is the case, we don't know which areas are the immune ones. The employment of expectancy-controlling designs is perhaps the only way in which we can find out. In a sense, we must use these controls to learn whether we can afford to do without them.

---

research assistants are exhausted in the sense that in these circles everyone would know all about expectancy controls. In that case less sophisticated experimenters must be employed, though they will not indefinitely stay unsophisticated. It is for these reasons especially that serious consideration should be given in the near future to the development of the new profession of data collector described earlier.

24

Conclusion

The social situation that comes into being when an experimenter encounters his research subject is one of both general and unique importance to the social sciences. Its general importance derives from the fact that the interaction of experimenter and subject, like other two-person interactions, may be investigated empirically with a view to teaching us more about dyadic interaction in general. Its unique importance derives from the fact that the interaction of experimenter and subject, *un*like other dyadic interactions, is a major source of our knowledge in the social sciences.

To the extent that we hope for dependable knowledge in the social sciences generally, we must have dependable knowledge about the experimenter-subject interaction specifically. We can no more hope to acquire accurate information for our disciplines without an understanding of the data collection situation than astronomers and zoologists could hope to acquire accurate information for their disciplines without their understanding the effects of their telescopes and microscopes. For these reasons, increasing interest has been shown in the investigation of the experimenter-subject interaction system. And the outlook is anything but bleak. It does seem that we can profitably learn of those effects that the experimenter unwittingly may have on the results of his research.

In the last five chapters, a variety of suggestions have been put forward which show some promise as controls for the effects of the experimenter in general and for the effects of his expectancy in particular. In Table 24-1 these suggestions are summarized as ten strategies or techniques. For each one, the consequences of its employment are listed, and for the last three, additional brief summaries are shown in Tables 24-2, 24-3, and 24-4.

THE SOCIAL PSYCHOLOGY OF UNINTENTIONAL INFLUENCE

Quite apart from the methodological implications of research on experimenter expectancy effects there are substantive implications for the

TABLE 24—1

Strategies for the Control of Experimenter Expectancy Effects

1. Increasing the number of experimenters:
   decreases learning of influence techniques
   helps to maintain blindness
   minimizes effects of early data returns
   increases generality of results
   randomizes expectancies
   permits the method of collaborative disagreement
   permits statistical correction of expectancy effects

2. Observing the behavior of experimenters:
   sometimes reduces expectancy effects
   permits correction for unprogrammed behavior
   facilitates greater standardization of experimenter behavior

3. Analyzing experiments for order effects:
   permits inference about changes in experimenter behavior

4. Analyzing experiments for computational errors:
   permits inference about expectancy effects

5. Developing selection procedures:
   permits prediction of expectancy effects

6. Developing training procedures:
   permits prediction of expectancy effects

7. Developing a new profession of psychological experimenter:
   maximizes applicability of controls for expectancy effects
   reduces motivational bases for expectancy effects

8. Maintaining blind contact:
   minimizes expectancy effects (see Table 24-2)

9. Minimizing experimenter-subject contact:
   minimizes expectancy effects (see Table 24-3)

10. Employing expectancy control groups:
    permits assessment of expectancy effects (see Table 24-4)

study of interpersonal relationships. Perhaps the most compelling and most general implication is that people can engage in highly effective and influential unprogrammed and unintended communication with one another and that this process of unintentional influence can be investigated experimentally.

TABLE 24—2

Blind Contact as a Control for Expectancy Effects

A. Sources of breakdown of blindness
    1. Principal investigator
    2. Subject ("side effects")

B. Procedures facilitating maintenance of blindness
    1. The "total-blind" procedure
    2. Avoiding feedback from the principal investigator
    3. Avoiding feedback from the subject

TABLE 24—3

Minimized Contact as a Control for Expectancy Effects

A. Automated data collection systems
    1. Written instructions
    2. Tape-recorded instructions
    3. Filmed instructions
    4. Televised instructions
    5. Telephoned instructions

B. Restricting unintended cues to subjects and experimenters
    1. Interposing screen between subject and experimenter
    2. Contacting fewer subjects per experimenter
    3. Having subjects or machines record responses

A great deal of effort within social psychology has gone into the study of such intentional influence processes as education, persuasion, coercion, propaganda, and psychotherapy. In each of these cases the influencer intends to influence the recipient of his message, and the message is usually encoded linguistically. Without diminishing efforts to understand these processes better, greater effort should be expended to understand the processes of unintentional influence in which the message is often encoded nonlinguistically. The question, in short, is how people "talk" to one another without "speaking."

At the present time we not only do not know the specific signals by which people unintentionally influence one another, we do not even know all the channels of communication involved. There is cause, though, to be

TABLE 24—4

Procedures for Generating Experimenter Expectancies

1. Ascribing subject characteristics
2. Ascribing experimental conditions
3. Disparagement of treatment effectiveness
4. Theory reversal
5. Intentional influence
6. Unintentional communication
7. Early data returns

optimistic. There appears to be a great current increase of interest in nonlinguistic behavior as it may have relevance for human communication
(e.g., Sebeok, Hayes, & Bateson, 1964). Most interest seems to have been
centered in the auditory and visual channels of communication, and those
are the channels investigated in the present research program. Other sense
modalities will bear investigation, however.

For example, Geldard (1960) has brought into focus the role of the
skin senses in human communication and has presented evidence that the
skin may be sensitive to human speech. Even when the sense modality involved is the auditory, it need not be only speech and speech-related stimuli
to which the ear is sensitive. Kellogg (1962) and Rice and Feinstein (1965)
have shown that at least among blind humans, audition can provide a surprising amount of information about the environment. Employing a technique of echo ranging, Kellogg's subjects were able to assess accurately the
distance, size, and composition of various external objects. The implications
for interpersonal communication of these senses and of olfaction or of even
less commonly discussed modalities (e.g., Ravitz, 1950; Ravitz, 1952) are
not yet clear but are worthy of more intensive investigation.

Since expectancies of another person's behavior seem often to be communicated to that person unintentionally, the basic experimental paradigm
employed in our research program might be employed even if the interest
were not in expectancy effects per se. Thus if we were interested in unintentional communication among different groups of psychiatric patients,
some could be given expectancies for others' behavior. Effectiveness of
unintentional influence could then be measured by the degree to which
other patients were influenced by expectancies held of their behavior. There
might be therapeutic as well as theoretical significance to knowing what
kind of psychiatric patients were most successful in the unintentional influence of other psychiatric patients. The following experiment is relevant and
was conducted with Clifford Knutson and Gordon Persinger.

Twelve hospitalized psychiatric patients served as "experimenters." On the basis of their scores on the appropriate MMPI scales, three were classified as schizophrenic, three were classified as paranoid, three as character disorders, and three as neurotics. Each "experimenter" administered the standard photo-rating task to male and female patients, one each in each of the same four diagnostic categories. All subjects were acutely rather than chronically disturbed. From half the subjects in each of the four diagnostic groups, experimenters were led to expect photo ratings of success, and from half they were led to expect ratings of failure.

It was somewhat surprising to find, even with this unusual sample of experimenters and of subjects, that overall expectancy effects were significant. Nine of the 12 experimenters obtained mean ratings from their subjects which were in the direction of their expectancies ($p = .07$), and 65 percent of all subjects gave ratings in the direction their experimenter expected ($p = .002$, $x^2 = 9.05$). Magnitude of expectancy effect was not related directly to the nosology of the experimenter, nosology of the subject, or sex of the subject, though there were some significant interactions. The analysis of the data is not yet completed, but there is a finding that may be illustrative of the type of information such research may yield. Among the psychotic subjects, experimenters exerted greater unintentional influence on schizophrenic subjects if they were themselves schizophrenic, but they exerted less unintentional influence on paranoids if they were themselves paranoid ($p < .10$). Among nonpsychotic subjects, experimenters exerted greater influence on neurotic subjects if they were themselves neurotic, but they exerted less influence on subjects with character disorders if they themselves

TABLE 24—5

Similarity of Experimenter's and Subject's Diagnosis as Determinant of Expectancy Effects: Psychotic Subjects

	EXPERIMENTER'S DIAGNOSIS		
Subject's Diagnosis	Same	Different	Difference
Schizophrenic	+2.53	−0.59	+3.12
Paranoid	−0.65	+1.35	−2.00
Difference	+3.18	−1.94	+5.12*

*$p < .10$ two-tail

had been diagnosed as character disorders ($p < .10$). Tables 24-5 and 24-6 show the magnitudes of expectancy effects for each of these combinations of experimenter and subject nosology. Scores for expectancy effects were defined in the usual manner—i.e., mean ratings obtained from subjects from whom positive ($+5$) ratings were expected minus the mean ratings obtained from subjects from whom negative (-5) ratings were expected. To summarize these preliminary results we might say that schizophrenic and neurotic patients are best "talked to" by patients of their own diagnostic category, whereas paranoid and character disorder patients are least well "talked to" by patients of their own diagnostic category. Of the four diag-

TABLE 24—6

Similarity of Experimenter's and Subject's Diagnosis as Determinant of Expectancy Effects: Nonpsychotic Subjects

	EXPERIMENTER'S DIAGNOSIS		
Subject's Diagnosis	Same	Different	Difference
Neurotic	+3.67	+0.07	+3.60
Character disorder	+0.53	+1.81	−1.28
Difference	+3.14	−1.74	+4.88*

* $p < .10$ two-tail

nostic groups, it is the schizophrenic and neurotic patients who show the greatest degree of overt anxiety and who, perhaps, feel best understood by equally anxious influencers. The paranoid and character disorder patients, both characterized by more overt hostility, may be especially sensitive to and resistant to the hostility of their paranoid and character-disordered influencers.

Findings of the kind described may have implications for the interpersonal treatment of psychiatric disorders. The belief is increasing that an important source of informal treatment is the association with other patients. If, as seems likely, such treatment is more unintentional than intentional, then the grouping of patients might be arranged so that patients are put into contact with those other patients with whom they can "talk" best, even if this "talk" be nonlinguistic.

Perhaps success as an unintentional influencer of another's behavior also has relevance for the selection of psychotherapists to work with certain types of patients. The general strategy of trying to "fit the therapist to the patient" has been employed with considerable success and has aroused considerable interest (e.g., Betz, 1962). That such selection may be made on the basis of unintentional communication patterns may also be suggested. In one recent study, it was found that the degree of hostility in the doctor's speech was unrelated to his success in getting alcoholic patients to accept treatment. However, when the content of the doctor's speech was filtered out, the degree of hostility found in the tone of his voice alone was significantly and negatively related to his success in influencing alcoholics to seek treatment ($r = -.65$, $p = .06$, two-tail [Milmoe, Rosenthal, Blane, Chafetz, & Wolf, 1965]).

EXPECTANCY EFFECTS IN EVERYDAY LIFE

The concept of expectancy has been of central importance for many psychological theorists (e.g., Allport, 1950; Kelly, 1955; Rotter, 1954; Tolman, 1932), and Goldstein (1962) has reviewed the role of expectancy as a construct of interest to psychologists. Expectancy as a determinant of behavior has most often been investigated with an eye to learning the extent to which an individual's expectancy might determine his own subsequent behavior. The construct of expectancy as employed in this book has been more specifically interpersonal. The question, for us, has concerned the extent to which one person's expectancy of another's behavior might serve as determinant of that other's behavior.

In everyday life people do have expectations of how others will behave. These expectations usually are based on prior experience, direct or indirect, with those other people's behavior. Scientist and layman seem agreed that predictions of future behavior are best based on past behavior. If this assumption were untenable there would be no behavioral sciences. If past behavior were unrelated to future behavior, then there could only be the humanist's interest to prompt us to study behavior, not the scientist's. But if expectations are only based upon history how do they influence future events?

It is unpleasant to have one's expectations disconfirmed, though that is not always the case. An unexpected inheritance need not lead to negative feelings. But often it is more pleasant to have one's expectations confirmed than disconfirmed. The evidence for this comes from experiments in which the expectancy is of an event that will befall the "expecter" (Aronson & Carlsmith, 1962; Carlsmith & Aronson, 1963; Festinger, 1957; Harvey & Clapp, 1965; Sampson & Sibley, 1965). The "expecter" seems to behave in such a way as to confirm his expectancy about what will befall him or how he will act (Aronson, Carlsmith, & Darley, 1963). It seems to be not too great an extension to think that if one's expectancy is not of one's own behavior but of another's, one will also behave in such a way as to influence that other to behave in an expected way. Whatever its basis, whether to achieve greater cognitive order, stability, predictability, or to maintain cognitive consonance (Festinger, 1957), there appears to be a motive to fulfill one's interpersonal expectancy.

Interpersonal expectancies in everyday life are likely to be accurate predictors of another's behavior for two reasons. The first reason is that expectancies are often realistic and veridical—i.e., based on prior experience with the other's behavior. The second reason is that, other things being equal, we may behave in such a way as to bring about the accuracy of our interpersonal expectations. If we expect a person to be friendly, it may be "true" because we have experienced him as friendly, or a credible source claims to have experienced him as friendly (Kelley, 1949). In addition to this experience-derived component, however, there is the self-fulfilling prophecy component. Expecting him to be friendly, we may behave in a more friendly fashion and, therefore, evoke a more friendly response.

The fact that there appear to be two components to the accuracy of interpersonal predictions, hypotheses, or expectations has implications for research methods in expectancy effects. If we simply ascertain people's expectations of others' behavior and correlate these with the others' subsequent behavior, the two components of experiential accuracy and self-fulfilling accuracy will be confounded. If we take the appropriate safeguards, however, we can eliminate the self-fulfilling accuracy component (as in asking people to "predict" behavior that has already occurred). We can also randomize the experiential accuracy component by "assigning" expectancies at random, and that is the strategy adopted in much of the research described in this book. What we do not yet know, and what is worth the learning, is the magnitude of expectancy effects, of the self-fulfilling type, in important everyday social interactions.

The experimenter-subject dyad may profitably be viewed as a social influence system different from, but yet similar to, other social influence systems. It seems most fruitful at the present time to emphasize the similarity and to make the working assumption that the principles governing the unintentional influence processes of the experimenter-subject dyad are not different from those governing influence processes of the more commonly investigated type. The experimental approach to the study of unintended social influence process can be extended from the special setting of the scientific experiment to other such special settings as psychotherapy, and to such more general settings as the classroom, industry, and government.

Although we might prefer a more experimental demonstration of the phenomenon, a number of research investigators and practicing clinicians have called attention to the process whereby a psychotherapist's or other healer's expectation of his patient's course in treatment may be communicated to his patient with subsequent effects on the course of the treatment. Goldstein (1962) has given us an excellent picture of what is now known and how much there is yet to be learned in this regard.

In the field of vocational rehabilitation, the staff of the Human Interaction Research Institute concluded that the expectancies of the staff seemed to lead to commensurate client performance. They evaluated a project that attempted to demonstrate that mentally retarded young men could learn to be gainfully employed. "The staff found that when they expected him to assume some personal responsibility, he was able to do so" (Coffey, Dorcus, Glaser, Greening, Marks, & Sarason, 1964, p. 11).

The effect of one person's expectancy on another's behavior has important implications for public policy. In their famous comparison of racially integrated vs. segregated housing patterns, Deutsch and Collins (1952) discussed the social standards of interracial behavior: ". . . people tend to behave as they are expected to behave. The expectations of others in a social situation, particularly if these others are important to the individual, help to define what is the appropriate behavior" (p. 588). This does not surprise social scientists. But what might surprise us is the degree to which the arbitrary definition of "appropriate behavior" can be implicit yet clearly discernable in social interaction by the person who would have these definitions serve as a guide to behavior.

In the educational system a child's reputation precedes him through the succession of classrooms leading from his first school day to his eventual graduation. We need to learn the extent to which that reputation itself serves as the definition for the child of how he should behave in school. If a bright child earns a reputation as bright and then performs brightly, we consider that all is going well. But what if a bright child in some not-at-all impossible way earns a reputation as dull? Will his teachers' perception of him and their expectations of his behavior then lead to duller behavior than need be the case? Or if a duller child, reputed to be bright, is treated as bright in the communication system with his teachers, will he then, in fact, tend to become more bright? We shall return to this question shortly.

The complexity and subtlety of the communication of one's expectancy of another's behavior to that other is well emphasized by reference to that experiment in which expectancy effects were transmitted from the experimenter through his research assistant to the subject (Rosenthal, Persinger, Vikan-Kline, & Mulry, 1963). It appeared from that experiment that in the two-person interaction between subject and research assistant there was a nonpresent third party, the primary experimenter. This nonpresent other appeared to communicate his expectancy through the research assistant but without having simply made the assistant a passive surrogate for himself. The research assistant, while serving as a "carrier" for the nonpresent influencer, was still able to exert his own influence in an additive manner to the influence of the nonpresent participant. This interpersonal influence, once-removed, is no all-or-none phenomenon. The more a person is able to influence others subtly, the more effectively he is able to make other people carriers of his subtle, unplanned influence. How far this chain of subtle interpersonal influence can extend, complicating itself at each link, is not known, nor is the pattern of interpersonal communication of which the chain is woven. But these unknowns lead to fascinating practical and theoretical questions of the extent of interpersonal influence, once-removed. Some of the more obvious ones include:

When the senior psychotherapist or physician believes the more junior healer's patient to have a good or poor prognosis, is the "assessment," whether explicit or implicit, really only an assessment? Or is it really a prophecy which stands a chance of being self-fulfilled?

When the master teacher or school principal believes a junior teacher's pupils to be fast learners, or believes a special group of pupils to be slow learners, is this belief (well founded or not, and verbalized or not) likely to accelerate or decelerate these pupils' educational progress?

Similarly, will the expectancies of performance, explicit or implicit, of civilian and government employers, military commanders, athletic coaches, and symphony orchestra conductors be transmitted ultimately to the employees, the troops, the athletes, and the musicians with a consequent effect on their performance?

THE LAST EXPERIMENT

This is a book primarily *about,* and *of,* research. It seems appropriate, therefore, to end with the description of one more experiment. Several times now there has been mention of the possibility that teachers' expectancies of their pupils' ability might in fact be a partial determinant of those pupils' ability. The experiment to be described was conducted with Lenore Jacobson. The procedure was basically the same as in the experiments on the effects of the experimenter's expectancy.

All of the children in an elementary school were administered a nonverbal group test of intelligence which was disguised as a test that would predict academic "blooming." There were 18 classes, 3 at each of all 6 grade levels. Within each of the grade levels one of the classes was of above average ability children; a second class was of average ability children, and a third class was of below average ability children. A table of random numbers was employed to assign about 20 percent of the children in each of the 18 classes to the experimental condition. Each teacher was given the names of these children "who would show unusual academic development" during the coming school year. That was the experimental manipulation. At the end of the school year the children were retested with the same group intelligence test.

The analysis of the data is not complete, but some of the results can be given. Table 24-7 shows the excess of IQ points gained in each class by the children whose teachers expected such gains when compared to the control subjects. A plus sign preceding an entry means that the children who were expected to show more gain of IQ points did show more gain.

TABLE 24—7

Teacher Expectancy Effects: Gain in IQ of Experimental over Control Groups (after eight months)

INITIAL ABILITY LEVEL

Grades	Higher	Average	Lower	Weighted Means
1	+11.2	+9.6	+24.8**	+15.4***
2	+18.2***	−2.9	+6.1	+9.5*
3	−4.3	+9.1	−6.3	−0.0
4	0.0	+0.2	+9.0	+3.4
5	−0.5	†	+1.2	−0.0
6	−1.3	+1.2	−0.5	−0.7
Weighted means	+3.6	+4.6	+2.8	+3.8*

* $p < .02$ one tail

** $p < .006$ one tail

*** $p < .002$ one tail

† Part of the posttest was inadvertently not administered in this class.

For the 18 classes combined, those children whose teachers expected them to gain in performance showed a significantly greater gain in IQ than did the control children, though the mean relative gain in IQ was small. Teachers' expectancies, it turned out, made little difference in the upper grades. But at the lower levels the effects were dramatic. First graders purported to be bloomers gained 15.4 IQ points more than did the control children, and the mean relative gain in one classroom was 24.8 points. In the second grade, the relative gain was 9.5 IQ points, with one of the classes showing a mean gain of 18.2 points. These effects were especially surprising in view of the large gains in IQ made by the control group, which had to be surpassed by the experimental groups. Thus first graders in the control group gained 12.0 IQ points (compared to the 27.4 points gained by the experimentals) and second graders gained 7.0 IQ points (compared to the 16.5 points gained by the experimentals), somewhat larger than might simply be ascribed to practice effects. It is possible that the entire school was affected to some degree by being involved in an experiment with consequent good effects on the children's performance.

It was somewhat reassuring to find that the gains made by the experimental group children were not made at the expense of the control group children. In fact, the greater the gain made by the experimental group children, the greater the gain made by the control group children in the same class. The rank correlation between gains made by the experimental and control children for the 17 classes that could be compared was $+.57$ ($p = .02$, two-tail).

The teachers had themselves administered the group IQ posttests, so that the question arose whether the gain in IQ of the experimental group might be due to differential behavior of the teacher toward these children during the testing. Three of the classes were retested by a school administrator not attached to the particular school employed. She did not know which of the children were in the experimental conditions. On the average the results of her testing showed somewhat greater effects of the teachers' expectancies. In the class in which the experimental group children had earned a 25 IQ point gain in excess of the control group children's gain, the experimental group children showed an *additional* 8 IQ point gain when retested by the "blind" examiner. It seems unlikely, then, that the IQ gains are attributable only to an examiner effect of the teacher.

That teacher expectancy effects should be more pronounced at the lower grades makes good sense. In the lower grades the children have not yet acquired those reputations that become so difficult to change in the later grades and which give teachers in subsequent grades the expectancies for the pupil's performance. With every successive grade it would be more difficult to change the child's reputation. The magnitude of expectancy effect showed a fairly regular decline from first to sixth grade (rho $= +.83$, $p = .05$, two-tail).

There are important substantive implications for educational practice in the results of this experiment. In addition there are important methodological implications for the design of experiments in education which seek to establish the success of various new educational practices. Such implications will be discussed elsewhere in detail, but for now we can simply call attention to the need for expectancy control groups.

If experimenters can, and if teachers can, then probably healers, parents, spouses, and other "ordinary" people also can affect the behavior of those with whom they interact by virtue of their expectations of what that behavior will be. Of course, we must now try to learn how such communication of expectancies takes place. Considering the difficulties we have had in trying to answer that same question for the case of experimenters, whose inputs into the experimenter-subject interaction could be so relatively easily controlled and observed, we should not expect a quick or an easy solution. But there may be some consolation drawn from the conviction that, at least, the problem is worth the effort.

REFERENCES

Aas, A., O'Hara, J. W., & Munger, M.P.   The measurement of subjective experiences presumably related to hypnotic susceptibility. *Scand. J. Psychol.*, 1962, *3*, 47–64.

Allport, F. H.   *Theories of perception and the concept of structure.* New York: Wiley, 1955.

Allport, G. W.   The role of expectancy. In H. Cantril (Ed.), *Tensions that cause wars.* Urbana, Ill.: Univer. of Illinois Press, 1950. Pp. 43–78.

Allport, G. W., & Vernon, P. E.   *Studies in expressive movement.* New York: Macmillan, 1933.

Anderson, Margaret, & White, Rhea.   A survey of work on ESP and teacher-pupil attitudes. *J. Parapsychol.*, 1958, *22*, 246–268.

Aronson, E., & Carlsmith, J. M.   Performance expectancy as a determinant of actual performance. *J. abnorm. soc. Psychol.*, 1962, *65*, 178–182.

Aronson, E., Carlsmith, J. M., & Darley, J. M.   The effects of expectancy on volunteering for an unpleasant experience. *J. abnorm. soc. Psychol.*, 1963, *66*, 220–224.

Asch, S. E.   *Social psychology.* Englewood Cliffs, N.J.: Prentice-Hall, 1952.

Azrin, N. H., Holz, W., Ulrich, R., & Goldiamond, I.   The control of the content of conversation through reinforcement. *J. exp. anal. Behav.*, 1961, *4*, 25–30.

Babich, F. R., Jacobson, A. L., Bubash, Suzanne, & Jacobson, Ann.   Transfer of a response to naive rats by injection of ribonucleic acid extracted from trained rats. *Science*, 1965, *149*, 656–657.

Back, K. W.   Influence through social communication. *J. abnorm. soc. Psychol.*, 1951, *46*, 9–23.

Bakan, D.   Learning and the scientific enterprise. *Psychol. Rev.*, 1953, *60*, 45–49.

Bakan, D.   A standpoint for the study of the history of psychology. Paper read at Amer. Psychol. Ass., St. Louis, September, 1962.

Bakan, D.   The mystery-mastery complex in contemporary psychology. *Amer. Psychologist*, 1965, *20*, 186–191. (a)

Bakan, D.   The test of significance in psychological research. Unpublished manuscript, Univer. of Chicago, 1965. (b)

Bandura, A., Lipsher, D. H., & Miller, Paula E.   Psychotherapists' approach-avoidance reactions to patients' expression of hostility. *Amer. Psychologist,* 1959, *14,* 335. (Abstract)

BARBER, B. Resistance by scientists to scientific discovery. *Science,* 1961, *134,* 596–602.

BARBER, T. X., & CALVERLEY, D. S. Effect of *E*'s tone of voice on "hypnotic-like" suggestibility. *Psychol. Rep.,* 1964, *15,* 139–144. (a)

BARBER, T. X., & CALVERLEY, D. S. Toward a theory of hypnotic behavior; effects on suggestibility of defining the situation as hypnosis and defining response to suggestions as easy. *J. abnorm. soc. Psychol.,* 1964, *68,* 585–593. (b)

BARNARD, P. G. Interaction effects among certain experimenter and subject characteristics on a projective test. Unpublished doctoral dissertation, Univer. of Washington, 1963.

BARZUN, J., & GRAFF, H. F. *The modern researcher.* New York: Harcourt, Brace & World, 1957.

BATESON, G., JACKSON, D. D., HALEY, J., & WEAKLAND, J. H. Toward a theory of schizophrenia, *Behav. Sci.,* 1956, *1,* 251–264.

BAUCH, M. Psychologische Untersuchungen über Beobachtungsfehler. *Fortschr. Psychol.,* 1913, *1,* 169–226.

BEAN, W. B. An analysis of subjectivity in the clinical examination in nutrition, *J. appl. Physiol.,* 1948, *1,* 458–468.

BEAN, W. B. Cherry angioma—a digression on the longevity of error. *Trans. Assoc. Amer. Physicians,* 1953, *66,* 240–249.

BEAN, W. B. A critique of criticism in medicine and the biological sciences in 1958. *Perspectives in biol. Med.,* 1958, *1,* 224–232.

BEAN, W. B. The natural history of error. *Trans. Assoc. Amer. Physicians,* 1959, *72,* 40–55.

BEAUCHAMP, K. L., & MAY, R. B. Replication report: Interpretation of levels of significance by psychological researchers. *Psychol. Rep.,* 1964, *14,* 272.

BECK, W. S. *Modern science and the nature of life.* New York: Harcourt, Brace & World, 1957.

BEECHER, H. K. *Measurement of subjective responses: Quantitative effects of drugs.* New York: Oxford, 1959.

BELLAK, L. The concept of projection: an experimental investigation and study of the concept. *Psychiat.,* 1944, *7,* 353–370.

BENNEY, M., RIESMAN, D., & STAR, SHIRLEY A. Age and sex in the interview. *Amer. J. Sociol.,* 1956, *62,* 143–152.

BERG, I. A., & BASS, B. M. (Eds.) *Conformity and deviation.* New York: Harper & Row, 1961.

BERGER, D. Examiner influence on the Rorschach. *J. clin. Psychol.,* 1954, *10,* 245–248.

BERKOWITZ, H. Effects of prior experimenter-subject relationships on reinforced reaction time of schizophrenics and normals. *J. abnorm. soc. Psychol.,* 1964, *69,* 522–530.

BERKSON, J., MAGATH, T. B., & HURN, MARGARET. The error of estimate of the blood cell count as made with the hemocytometer. *Amer. J. Physiol.,* 1940, *128,* 309–323.

BERNSTEIN, A. S. Race and examiner as significant influences on basal skin impedance. *J. pers. soc. Psychol.,* 1965, *1,* 346–349.

BERNSTEIN, L. A note on Christie's "Experimental Naiveté and Experiential Naiveté." *Psychol. Bull.,* 1952, *49,* 38–40.

BERNSTEIN, L. The effects of variations in handling upon learning and retention. *J. comp. physiol. Psychol.,* 1957, *50,* 162–167.

BETZ, BARBARA J. Experiences in research in psychotherapy with schizophrenic patients. In H. H. Strupp, & L. Luborsky (Eds.), *Research in psychotherapy.* Washington, D.C.: American Psychological Association, 1962. Pp. 41–60.

BINDER, A., McCONNELL, D., & SJOHOLM, NANCY A. Verbal conditioning as a function of experimenter characteristics. *J. abnorm. soc. Psychol.,* 1957, *55,* 309–314.

BINGHAM, W. V. D., & MOORE, B. V. *How to interview.* (3rd rev.) New York: Harper & Row, 1941.

BIRDWHISTELL, R. L. The kinesic level in the investigation of the emotions. In P. H. Knapp (Ed.), *Expression of the emotions in man.* New York: International Universities Press, 1963. Pp. 123–139.

BIRNEY, R. C. The achievement motive and task performance: A replication. *J. abnorm. soc. Psychol,* 1958, *56,* 133–135.

BLANKENSHIP, A. B. The effect of the interviewer upon the response in a public opinion poll. *J. consult. Psychol.,* 1940, *4,* 134–136.

BORING, E. G. *A history of experimental psychology.* (2nd ed.) New York: Appleton-Century-Crofts, 1950.

BORING, E. G. The nature and history of experimental control. *Amer. J. Psychol.,* 1954, *67,* 573–589.

BORING, E.G. Science and the meaning of its history. *The Key Reporter,* 1959, *24,* 2–3.

BORING, E. G. Newton and the spectral lines. *Science,* 1962, *136,* 600–601. (a)

BORING, E. G. Parascience. *Contemp. Psychol.,* 1962, *7,* 356–357. (b)

BROGDEN, W. J. Animal studies of learning. In S. S. Stevens (Ed.), *Handbook of experimental psychology.* New York: Wiley, 1951. Pp. 568–612.

BROGDEN, W. J. The experimenter as a factor in animal conditioning. *Psychol. Rep.,* 1962, *11,* 239–242.

BROWN, J. M. Respondents rate public opinion interviewers. *J. appl. Psychol.,* 1955, *39,* 96–102.

BRUNSWIK, E. *Perception and the representative design of psychological experiments.* Berkeley: Univer. of California Press, 1956.

BUCKHOUT, R. Need for social approval and dyadic verbal behavior. *Psychol. Rep.,* 1965, *16,* 1013–1016.

BUSS, A. H., & GERJUOY, L. R. Verbal conditioning and anxiety. *J. abnorm. soc. Psychol.,* 1958, *57,* 249–250.

CAHALAN, D., TAMULONIS, VALERIE, & VERNER, HELEN W. Interviewer bias involved in certain types of opinion survey questions. *Int. J. Opin. Attit. Res.,* 1947, *1,* 63–77.

CAHEN, L. S. An experimental manipulation of the "Halo Effect": A study of teacher bias. Unpublished manuscript, Stanford Univer., 1965.

References

CAMPBELL, D. T. Systematic error on the part of human links in communication systems. *Information and Control*, 1958, *1*, 334–369.

CAMPBELL, D. T. Systematic errors to be expected of the social scientist on the basis of a general psychology of cognitive bias. Paper read at Amer. Psychol. Ass., Cincinnati, Sept., 1959.

CANADY, H. G. The effect of "rapport" on the I.Q.: A new approach to the problem of racial psychology. *J. Negro Educ.*, 1936, *5*, 209–219.

CANTRIL, H., & research associates. *Gauging public opinion*. Princeton: Princeton Univer. Press, 1944.

CARLSMITH, J. M., & ARONSON, E. Some hedonic consequences of the confirmation and disconfirmation of expectancies. *J. abnorm. soc. Psychol.*, 1963, *66*, 151–156.

CARLSON, E. R., & CARLSON, RAE. Male and female subjects in personality research. *J. abnorm. soc. Psychol.*, 1960, *61*, 482–483.

CERVIN, V. B., JOYNER, R. C., SPENCE, J. M., & HEINZL, R. Relationship of persuasive interaction to change of opinion in dyadic groups when the original opinions of participants are expressed privately and publicly. *J. abnorm. soc. Psychol.*, 1961, *62*, 431–432.

CHAPANIS, NATALIA P., & CHAPANIS, A. Cognitive dissonance: Five years later. *Psychol. Bull.*, 1964, *61*, 1–22.

CHRISTIE, R. Experimental naiveté and experiential naiveté. *Psychol. Bull.*, 1951, *48*, 327–339.

CLARK, E. L. The value of student interviewers. *J. pers. Res.*, 1927, *5*, 204–207.

CLARK, K. B. Educational stimulation of racially disadvantaged children. In A. H. Passow (Ed.), *Education in depressed areas*. New York: Teachers College, Columbia Univer., 1963. Pp. 142–162.

CLEVELAND, S. The relationship between examiner anxiety and subjects' Rorschach scores. *Microfilm Abstr.*, 1951, *11*, 415–416.

COCHRAN, W. G., & WATSON, D. J. An experiment on observer's bias in the selection of shoot-heights. *Empire J. exp. Agriculture*, 1936, *4*, 69–76.

COFFEY, H. S., DORCUS, R. M., GLASER, E. M., GREENING, T. C., MARKS, J. B., & SARASON, I. G. *Learning to work*. Los Angeles: Human Interaction Research Institute, 1964.

COFFIN, T. E. Some conditions of suggestion and suggestibility. *Psychol. Monogr.*, 1941, *53*, No. 4 (Whole No. 241).

COLBY, K. M. *An introduction to psychoanalytic research*. New York: Basic Books, 1960.

COLE, D. L. The influence of task perception and leader variation on autokinetic responses. *Amer. Psychologist*, 1955, *10*, 343. (Abstract)

CONRAD, H. S. Some principles of attitude-measurement: A reply to "opinion-attitude methodology." *Psychol. Bull.*, 1946, *43*, 570–589.

COOK-MARQUIS, PEGGY. Authoritarian or acquiescent: Some behavioral differences. Paper read at Amer. Psychol. Ass., Washington, D.C., Sept., 1958.

CORDARO, L., & ISON, J. R. Observer bias in classical conditioning of the planarian. *Psychol. Rep.*, 1963, *13*, 787–789.

CRESPI, L. P. The cheater problem in polling. *Publ. Opin. Quart.*, 1945–46, *9*, 431–445.

CRISWELL, JOAN H. The psychologist as perceiver. In R. Tagiuri, & L. Petrullo (Eds.), *Person perception and interpersonal behavior.* Stanford, Calif.: Stanford Univer. Press, 1958. Pp. 95–109.

CROW, LINDA. Public attitudes and expectations as a disturbing variable in experimentation and therapy. Unpublished paper, Harvard University, 1964.

CROWNE, D. P., & MARLOWE, D. *The approval motive.* New York: Wiley, 1964.

CRUMBAUGH, J. C. ESP and flying saucers: A challenge to parapsychologists. *Amer. Psychologist,* 1959, *14,* 604–606.

CRUTCHFIELD, R. S. Conformity and character. *Amer. Psychologist,* 1955, *10,* 191–198.

CUTLER, R. L. Countertransference effects in psychotherapy. *J. consult. Psychol.,* 1958, *22,* 349–356.

DAILEY, J. M. Verbal conditioning without awareness. Unpublished doctoral dissertation, Univer. of Iowa, 1953.

DAS, J. P. Prestige effects in body-sway suggestibility. *J. abnorm. soc. Psychol.,* 1960, *61,* 487–488.

DELBOEUF, J. L. R. *Le magnétisme animal à propos d'une visite à l'école de Nancy.* Paris: Alcan, 1889.

DEMBER, W. N. *The psychology of perception.* New York: Holt, Rinehart and Winston, 1960.

DEUTSCH, M., & COLLINS, MARY E. The effect of public policy in housing projects upon interracial attitudes. In G. E. Swanson, T. M. Newcomb, E. L. Hartley, et al. (Eds.), *Readings in social psychology.* (Rev. ed.) New York: Holt, Rinehart and Winston, 1952. Pp. 582–593.

DULANY, D. E., & O'CONNELL, D. C. Does partial reinforcement dissociate verbal rules and the behavior they might be presumed to control? *J. verb. Learn. verb. Behav.,* 1963, *2,* 361–372.

EBBINGHAUS, H. *Memory: A contribution to experimental psychology.* (1885) Translated by H. A. Ruger, & Clara E. Bussenius. New York: Teachers College, Columbia Univer., 1913.

ECKLER, A. R., & HURWITZ, W. N. Response variance and biases in censuses and surveys. *Bull. de L'Institut International de Statistique,* 1958, *36–2e,* 12–35.

EDITORIAL BOARD, *Consumer Reports.* Food and Drug Administration. *Consumer Reports,* 1964, *29,* 85.

EDITORIAL BOARD, *Science.* An unfortunate event. *Science,* 1961, *134,* 945–946.

EDWARDS, A. L. *Experimental design in psychological research.* New York: Holt, Rinehart and Winston, 1950.

EDWARDS, A. L. Experiments: Their planning and execution. In G. Lindzey (Ed.), *Handbook of social psychology.* Vol. 1. Cambridge, Mass.: Addison-Wesley, 1954.

EHRENFREUND, D. A study of the transposition gradient. *J. exp. Psychol.,* 1952, *43,* 81–87.

EHRLICH, JUNE S., & RIESMAN, D. Age and authority in the interview. *Publ. Opin. Quart.*, 1961, *25*, 39–56.

EKMAN, P., & FRIESEN, W. V. Status and personality of the experimenter as a determinant of verbal conditioning. *Amer. Psychologist*, 1960, *15*, 430. (Abstract)

ERIKSEN, C. W. Discrimination and learning without awareness: a methodological survey and evaluation. *Psychol. Rev.*, 1960, *67*, 279–300.

ERIKSEN, C. W. (Ed.) *Behavior and awareness.* Durham, N.C.: Duke Univer. Press, 1962.

ERIKSEN, C. W., KUETHE, J. L., & SULLIVAN, D. F. Some personality correlates of learning without verbal awareness. *J. Pers.*, 1958, *26*, 216–228.

ESCALONA, SIBYLLE, K. Feeding disturbances in very young children. *Amer. J. Orthopsychiat.*, 1945, *15*, 76–80. Also in G. E. Swanson, T. M. Newcomb, & E. L. Hartley et al. (Eds.), *Readings in Social Psychology.* (Rev. ed.) New York: Holt, Rinehart and Winston, 1952. Pp. 29–33.

EXLINE, R. V. Explorations in the process of person perception: Visual interaction in relation to competition, sex, and need for affiliation. *J. Pers.*, 1963, *31*, 1–20.

EXLINE, R. V., GRAY, D., & SCHUETTE, DOROTHY. Visual behavior in a dyad as affected by interview content and sex of respondent. *J. pers. soc. Psychol.*, 1965, *1*, 201–209.

EYSENCK, H. J. The concept of statistical significance and the controversy about one-tailed tests. *Psychol. Rev.*, 1960, *67*, 269–271.

FEINSTEIN, A. R. The stethoscope: a source of diagnostic aid and conceptual errors in rheumatic heart disease. *J. chronic Dis.*, 1960, *11*, 91–101.

FELICE, A. Some effects of subject-examiner interaction on the task performance of schizophrenics. *Dissert. Abstr.*, 1961, *22*, 913–914.

FELL, HONOR B. Fashion in cell biology. *Science*, 1960, *132*, 1625–1627.

FERBER, R., & WALES, H. G. Detection and correction of interviewer bias. *Publ. Opin. Quart.*, 1952, *16*, 107–127.

FERGUSON, D. C., & BUSS, A. H. Operant conditioning of hostile verbs in relation to experimenter and subject characteristics. *J. consult. Psychol.*, 1960, *24*, 324–327.

FESTINGER, L. *A theory of cognitive dissonance.* New York: Harper & Row, 1957.

FESTINGER, L., & CARLSMITH, J. M. Cognitive consequences of forced compliance, *J. abnorm. soc. Psychol.*, 1959, *58*, 203–210.

FILER, R. M. The clinician's personality and his case reports. *Amer. Psychologist*, 1952, *7*, 336. (Abstract)

FINE, B. J. Conclusion-drawing, communication, credibility, and anxiety as factors in opinion change. *J. abnorm, soc. Psychol.*, 1957, *54*, 369–374.

FISHER, R. A. Has Mendel's work been rediscovered? *Ann. Sci.*, 1936, *1*, 115–137.

FISHER, R. A. *The design of experiments.* (4th ed.) Edinburgh and London: Oliver & Boyd, 1947.

FODE, K. L. The effect of non-visual and non-verbal interaction on experimenter bias. Unpublished master's thesis, Univer. of North Dakota, 1960.

FODE, K. L. The effect of experimenters' and subjects' anxiety and social desirability on experimenter outcome-bias. Unpublished doctoral dissertation, Univer. of North Dakota, 1965.

FOSTER, R. J. Acquiescent response set as a measure of acquiescence. *J. abnorm. soc. Psychol.,* 1961, *63,* 155–160.

FOSTER, W. S. Experiments on rod-divining. *J. appl. Psychol.,* 1923, *7,* 303–311.

FRANK, J. Discussion of Eysenck's "The effects of psychotherapy." *Int. J. Psychiat.,* 1965, *1,* 150–152.

FREIBERG, A. D., VAUGHN, C. L., & EVANS, MARY C. Effect of interviewer bias upon questionnaire results obtained with a large number of investigators. *Amer. Psychologist,* 1946, *7,* 243. (Abstract)

FRIEDMAN, N. The psychological experiment as a social interaction. Unpublished doctoral dissertation, Harvard Univer., 1964.

FRIEDMAN, N., KURLAND, D., & ROSENTHAL, R. Experimenter behavior as an unintended determinant of experimental results. *J. proj. Tech. pers. Assess.,* 1965, *29,* 479–490.

FRIEDMAN, PEARL. A second experiment on interviewer bias. *Sociometry,* 1942, *5,* 378–379.

FROMM-REICHMANN, FRIEDA. *Principles of intensive psychotherapy.* Chicago: Univer. of Chicago Press, 1950.

FRUCHTER, B. *Introduction to factor analysis.* Princeton, N.J.: Van Nostrand, 1954.

FUNKENSTEIN, D. H., KING, S. H., & DROLETTE, MARGARET E. *Mastery of stress.* Cambridge, Mass.: Harvard Univer. Press, 1957.

GANTT, W. H. Autonomic conditioning. In J. Wolpe, A. Salter, & L. J. Reyna (Eds.), *The conditioning therapies.* New York: Holt, Rinehart, and Winston, 1964. Pp. 115–126.

GARFIELD, S. L., & AFFLECK, D. C. Therapists' judgments concerning patients considered for therapy. *Amer. Psychologist,* 1960, *15,* 414. (Abstract)

GARRETT, H. E. On un-American science reporting. *Science,* 1960, *132,* 685.

GELDARD, F. A. Some neglected possibilities of communication. *Science,* 1960, *131,* 1583–1588.

GELFAND, DONNA M., & WINDER, C. L. Operant conditioning of verbal behavior of dysthymics and hysterics. *J. abnorm. soc. Psychol.,* 1961, *62,* 688–689.

GEORGE, W. H. *The scientist in action: A scientific study of his methods.* New York: Emerson, 1938.

GILLISPIE, C. C. *The edge of objectivity.* Princeton: Princeton Univer. Press, 1960.

GLUCKSBERG, S., & LINCE, D. L. The influence of military rank of experimenter on the conditioning of a verbal response. *Tech. Mem. 10–62,* Human Engineering Lab., Aberdeen Proving Ground, Maryland, 1962.

GOLDBERG, S., HUNT, R. G., COHEN, W., & MEADOW, A. Some personality correlates of perceptual distortion in the direction of group conformity. *Amer. Psychologist,* 1954, *9,* 378. (Abstract)

GOLDFRIED, M. R., & WALTERS, G. C. Needed: Publication of negative results. *Amer. Psychologist,* 1959, *14,* 598.

GOLDSTEIN, A. P. Therapist and client expectation of personality change in psychotherapy. *J. counsel. Psychol.,* 1960, *7,* 180–184.

GOLDSTEIN, A. P. *Therapist-patient expectancies in psychotherapy.* New York: Pergamon Press, 1962.

GORANSON, R. E. Effects of the experimenter's prestige on the outcome of an attitude change experiment. Paper read at Midwest. Psychol. Assoc., Chicago, May, 1965.

GORDON, L. V., & DUREA, M. A. The effect of discouragement on the revised Stanford Binet Scale. *J. genet. Psychol.,* 1948, *73,* 201–207.

GRAHAM, S. R. The influence of therapist character structure upon Rorschach changes in the course of psychotherapy. *Amer. Psychologist,* 1960, *15,* 415. (Abstract)

GREENBLATT, M. Controls in clinical research. Unpublished paper. Tufts Univer. School of Medicine, 1964.

GRIFFITH, R. Rorschach water percepts: A study in conflicting results. *Amer. Psychologist,* 1961, *16,* 307–311.

GRUENBERG, B. C. *The story of evolution.* Princeton, N.J.: Van Nostrand, 1929.

GUILFORD, J. P. *Psychometric methods.* (2nd ed.) New York: McGraw-Hill, 1954.

GUTHRIE, E. R. *The psychology of human conflict.* New York: Harper & Row, 1938.

HAAS, H., FINK, H., & HÄRTFELDER, G. The placebo problem. *Psychopharmacol. Serv. Cent. Bull.,* 1963, *2,* 1–65.

HAMMOND, K. R. Representative vs. systematic design in clinical psychology. *Psychol. Bull.,* 1954, *51,* 150–159.

HANER, C. F., & WHITNEY, E. R. Empathic conditioning and its relation to anxiety level. *Amer. Psychologist,* 1960, *15,* 493. (Abstract)

HANLEY, C., & ROKEACH, M. Care and carelessness in psychology. *Psychol. Bull.,* 1956, *53,* 183–186.

HANSON, N. R. *Patterns of discovery.* Cambridge, England: Cambridge Univer. Press, 1958.

HANSON, R. H., & MARKS, E. S. Influence of the interviewer on the accuracy of survey results. *J. Amer. Statist. Assoc.,* 1958, *53,* 635–655.

HARARI, C., & CHWAST, J. Class bias in psychodiagnosis of delinquents. *Amer. Psychologist,* 1959, *14,* 377–378. (Abstract)

HARLEM YOUTH OPPORTUNITIES UNLIMITED, INC. *Youth in the ghetto.* New York: Author, 1964.

HARRIS, NATALIE. Introducing a symposium on interviewing problems. *Int. J. Opin. Attit. Res.,* 1948, *2,* 69–84.

HART, C. W. Preface to H. H. Hyman, W. J. Cobb, J. J. Feldman, C. W. Hart, & C. H. Stember, *Interviewing in social research.* Chicago: Univer. of Chicago Press, 1954.

HARVEY, O. J., & CLAPP, W. F. Hope, expectancy, and reactions to the unexpected. *J. pers. soc. Psychol.,* 1965, *2,* 45–52.

HARVEY, S. M. A preliminary investigation of the interview. *Brit. J. Psychol.,* 1938, *28,* 263–287.

HEFFERLINE, R. F. Learning theory and clinical psychology—an eventual symbiosis? In A. J. Bachrach (Ed.), *Experimental foundations of clinical psychology.* New York: Basic Books, 1962. Pp. 97–138.

HEILIZER, F. An exploration of the relationship between hypnotizability and anxiety and/or neuroticism. *J. consult. Psychol.,* 1960, *24,* 432–436.

HEINE, R. W., & TROSMAN, H. Initial expectations of the doctor-patient interaction as a factor in continuance in psychotherapy. *Psychiatry,* 1960, *23,* 275–278.

HELLER, K., DAVIS, J. D., & SAUNDERS, F. Clinical implications of laboratory studies of interpersonal style. Paper read at Midwest. Psychol. Assoc., St. Louis, May, 1964.

HELLER, K., & GOLDSTEIN, A. P. Client dependency and therapist expectancy as relationship maintaining variables in psychotherapy. *J. consult. Psychol.,* 1961, *25,* 371–375.

HELLER, K., MYERS, R. A., & VIKAN-KLINE, LINDA. Interviewer behavior as a function of standardized client roles. *J. consult. Psychol.,* 1963, *27,* 117–122.

HELSON, H. *Adaptation-level theory.* New York: Harper & Row, 1964.

HOMANS, G. C. *Social behavior: Its elementary forms.* New York: Harcourt, Brace & World, 1961.

HOMME, L. E., & KLAUS, D. J. *Laboratory studies in the analysis of behavior.* Pittsburgh: Lever Press, 1957.

HONIGFELD, G. Non-specific factors in treatment. *Dis. nerv. Syst.,* 1964, *25,* 145–156, 225–239.

HOVLAND, C. I., & JANIS, I. L. (Eds.) *Personality and persuasibility.* New Haven, Conn.: Yale Univer. Press, 1959.

HOVLAND, C. I., & WEISS, W. The influence of source credibility on communication effectiveness. *Publ. Opin. Quart.,* 1951 *15,* 635–650.

HYMAN, H. H., COBB, W. J., FELDMAN, J. J., HART, C. W., & STEMBER, C. H. *Interviewing in social research.* Chicago: Univer. of Chicago Press, 1954.

ISMIR, A. A. The effects of prior knowledge of the TAT on test performance. *Psychol. Rec.,* 1962, *12,* 157–164.

ISMIR, A. A. The effect of prior knowledge, social desirability, and stress upon the Thematic Apperception Test performance. Unpublished doctoral dissertation, Univer. of North Dakota, 1963.

JAHN, M. E., & WOOLF, D. J. (Eds.) *The lying stones of Dr. Johann Bartholomew Adam Beringer, being his Lithographiae Wirceburgensis.* Berkeley: Univer. of California Press, 1963.

JAMES, W. *Essays in pragmatism.* New York: Hafner, 1948.

JANIS, I. L. Anxiety indices related to susceptibility to persuasion. *J. abnorm. soc. Psychol.,* 1955, *51,* 663–667.

JASTROW, J. *Fact and fable in psychology.* Boston: Houghton Mifflin, 1900.

JENNESS, A. The role of discussion in changing opinions regarding a matter of fact. *J. abnorm. soc. Psychol.,* 1932, *27,* 279–296.

JOEL, W. The interpersonal equation in projective methods. *J. proj. Tech.*, 1949, *13*, 479–482.

JOHNSON, H. M. Audition and habit formation in the dog. *Behav. Monogr.*, 1913, *2*, No. 3 (Serial No. 8).

JOHNSON, M. L. Seeing's believing. *New Biology*, 1953, *15*, 60–80.

JONES, E. E. Conformity as a tactic of ingratiation. *Science*, 1965, *149*, 144–150.

JONES, E. E., & THIBAUT, J. W. Interaction goals as bases of inference in interpersonal perception. In R. Tagiuri & L. Petrullo (Eds.), *Person perception and interpersonal behavior*. Stanford, Calif.: Stanford Univer. Press, 1958. Pp. 151–178.

JONES, F. P. Experimental method in antiquity. *Amer. Psychologist*, 1964, *19*, 419.

JONES, R. H. Physical indices and clinical assessments of the nutrition of school children. *J. Royal Statist. Soc.*, Part I, 1938, *101*, 1–34.

JORDAN, N. The mythology of the non-obvious—autism or fact? *Contemp. Psychol.*, 1964, *9*, 140–142.

KAGAN, J., & MOSS, H. J. *Birth to maturity*. New York: Wiley, 1962.

KANFER, F. H., & KARAS, SHIRLEY C. Prior experimenter-subject interaction and verbal conditioning. *Psychol. Rep.*, 1959, *5*, 345–353.

KATZ, D. Do interviewers bias poll results? *Publ. Opin. Quart.*, 1942, *6*, 248–268.

KATZ, I. Review of evidence relating to effects of desegregation on the intellectual performance of Negroes. *Amer. Psychologist*, 1964, *19*, 381–399.

KATZ, I., ROBINSON, J. M., EPPS, E. G., & WALY, PATRICIA. The influence of race of the experimenter and instructions upon the expression of hostility by Negro boys. *J. soc. Issues*, 1964, *20*, 54–59.

KATZ, R. Body language: A study in unintentional communication. Unpublished doctoral dissertation, Harvard Univer., 1964.

KELLEY, H. H. The effects of expectations upon first impressions of persons. *Amer. Psychologist*, 1949, *4*, 252. (Abstract)

KELLEY, H. H., & RING, K. Some effects of "suspicious" versus "trusting" training schedules. *J. abnorm. soc. Psychol.*, 1961, *63*, 294–301.

KELLOG, W. N. *Porpoises and sonar*. Chicago: Univer. of Chicago Press, 1961.

KELLOG, W. N. Sonar system of the blind. *Science*, 1962, *137*, 399–404.

KELLY, G. A. *The psychology of personal constructs*. New York: Norton, 1955.

KELMAN, H. C. Attitude change as a function of response restriction. *Hum. Relat.*, 1953, *6*, 185–214.

KELMAN, H. C. The human use of human subjects: The problem of deception in social-psychological experiments. Paper read at Amer. Psychol. Assoc., Chicago, September, 1965.

KENNEDY, J. L. Experiments on "unconscious whispering." *Psychol. Bull.*, 1938, *35*, 526. (Abstract)

KENNEDY, J. L. A methodological review of extra-sensory perception. *Psychol. Bull.*, 1939, *36*, 59–103.

KENNEDY, J. L., & UPHOFF, H. F. Experiments on the nature of extra-sensory perception: III. The recording error criticism of extra-chance scores. *J. Parapsychol.*, 1939, *3*, 226–245.

KETY, S. S.   Biochemical theories of schizophrenia, Part I. *Science*, 1959, *129*, 1528–1532; Part II, 1590–1596.

KIMBLE, G. A.   Classical conditioning and the problem of awareness. *J. Pers.*, 1962, *30*, Supplement: C. W. Eriksen (Ed.), *Behavior and awareness*, 27–45.

KLEIN, G. S.   Perception, motives and personality. In J. L. McCary (Ed.), *Psychology of personality: Six modern approaches*. New York: Logos, 1956. Pp. 121–199.

KOESTLER, A.   *The act of creation*. New York: Macmillan, 1964.

KRAMER, E., & BRENNAN, E. P.   Hypnotic susceptibility of schizophrenic patients. *J. abnorm. soc. Psychol.*, 1964, *69*, 657–659.

KRASNER, L.   Studies of the conditioning of verbal behavior. *Psychol. Bull.*, 1958, *55*, 148–170.

KRASNER, L.   The therapist as a social reinforcement machine. In H. H. Strupp & L. Luborsky (Eds.), *Research in psychotherapy*. Washington, D.C.: Amer. Psychol. Ass., 1962. Pp. 61–94.

KUBIE, L. S.   The use of psychoanalysis as a research tool. *Psychiat. Res. Rep.*, 1956, *6*, 112–136.

KUETHE, J. L.   Acquiescent response set and the psychasthenia scale: An analysis via the *aussage* experiment. *J. abnorm. soc. Psychol.*, 1960, *61*, 319–322.

LANE, F. W.   *Kingdom of the octopus*. New York: Sheridan House, 1960.

LEFKOWITZ, M., BLAKE, R. R., & MOUTON, JANE S.   Status factors in pedestrian violation of traffic signals. *J. abnorm. soc. Psychol.* 1955, *51*, 704–706.

LEVIN, S. M.   The effects of awareness on verbal conditioning. *J. exp. Psychol.*, 1961, *61*, 67–75.

LEVITT, E. E.   Problems of experimental design and methodology in psychopharmacology research. In R. H. Branson (Ed.), *Report of the conference on mental health research*. Indianapolis: Assoc. Advance. Ment. Hlth. Res. Educ., 1959.

LEVITT, E. E., & BRADY, J. P.   Expectation and performance in hypnotic phenomena. *J. abnorm. soc. Psychol.*, 1964, *69*, 572–574.

LEVY, L. H., & ORR, T. B.   The social psychology of Rorschach validity research. *J. abnorm. soc. Psychol.*, 1959, *58*, 79–83.

LIDDELL, H. S.   The alteration of instinctual processes through the influence of conditioned reflexes. In S. S. Tomkins, *Contemporary psychopathology*. Cambridge, Mass: Harvard Univer. Press, 1943.

LINDQUIST, E. F.   *Design and analysis of experiments in psychology and education*. Boston: Houghton Mifflin, 1953.

LINDZEY, G.   A note on interviewer bias. *J. appl. Psychol.*, 1951, *35*, 182–184.

LONDON, P., & FUHRER, M.   Hypnosis, motivation, and performance. *J. Pers.*, 1961, *29*, 321–333.

LORD, EDITH.   Experimentally induced variations in Rorschach performance. *Psychol. Monogr.*, 1950, *64*, No. 10.

LUBIN, A.   Replicability as a publication criterion. *Amer. Psychologist*, 1957, *12*, 519–520.

LUFT, J. Interaction and projection. *J. proj. Tech.*, 1953, *17*, 489–492.

LYERLY, S. B., ROSS, S., KRUGMAN, A. D., & CLYDE, D. J. Drugs and placebos: The effects of instructions upon performance and mood under amphetamine sulphate and chloral hydrate. *J. abnorm. soc. Psychol.*, 1964, *68*, 321–327.

MACCOBY, ELEANOR E., & MACCOBY, N. The interview: A tool of social science. In G. Lindzey (Ed.), *Handbook of social psychology*. Vol. I. Cambridge, Mass.: Addison-Wesley, 1954. Pp. 449–487.

MACDOUGALL, C. D. *Hoaxes*. New York: Macmillan, 1940.

MACKINNON, D. W. The nature and nurture of creative talent. *Amer. Psychologist*, 1962, *17*, 484–495.

MAHALANOBIS, P. C. Recent experiments in statistical sampling in the Indian Statistical Institute. *J. Royal Statist. Soc.*, 1946, *109*, 325–370.

MAHL, G. F., & SCHULZE, G. Psychological research in the extralinguistic area. In T. A. Sebeok, A. S. Hayes, & Mary C. Bateson (Eds.), *Approaches to semiotics*. The Hague: Mouton, 1964. Pp. 51–124.

MAIER, N. R. F. Frustration theory: Restatement and extension. *Psychol. Rev.*, 1956, *63*, 370–388.

MAIER, N. R. F. Maier's law. *Amer. Psychologist*, 1960, *15*, 208–212.

MARCIA, J. Hypothesis-making, need for social approval, and their effects on unconscious experimenter bias. Unpublished master's thesis, Ohio State Univer., 1961.

MARINE, EDITH L. The effect of familiarity with the examiner upon Stanford-Binet test performance. *Teach. Coll. contr. Educ.*, 1929, *381*, 42.

MARKS, M. R. How to build better theories, tests and therapies: The off-quadrant approach. *Amer. Psychologist*, 1964, *19*, 793–798.

MARWIT, S., & MARCIA, J. Tester-bias and response to projective instruments. Unpublished paper. State Univer. of New York at Buffalo, 1965.

MASLING, J. The effects of warm and cold interaction on the administration and scoring of an intelligence test. *J. consult. Psychol.*, 1959, *23*, 336–341.

MASLING, J. The influence of situational and interpersonal variables in projective testing. *Psychol. Bull.*, 1960, *57*, 65–85.

MASLING, J. Differential indoctrination of examiners and Rorschach responses. *J. consult. Psychol.*, 1965, *29*, 198–201.

MATARAZZO, J. D., SASLOW, G., & PAREIS, E. N. Verbal conditioning of two response classes: Some methodological considerations. *J. abnorm. soc. Psychol.*, 1960, *61*, 190–206.

MATARAZZO, J. D., WIENS, A. N., & SASLOW, G. Studies in interview speech behavior. In L. Krasner & L. P. Ullman (Eds.), *Research in behavior modification: New developments and implications*. New York: Holt, Rinehart and Winston, 1965. Pp. 181–210.

MAUSNER, B. Studies in social interaction: III. Effect of variation in one partner's prestige on the interaction of observer pairs. *J. appl. Psychol.*, 1953, *37*, 391–393.

MAUSNER, B. The effect of one partner's success or failure in a relevant task on the interaction of observer pairs. *J. abnorm. soc. Psychol.*, 1954, *49*, 557–560.

MAUSNER, B., & BLOCH, BARBARA L. A study of the additivity of variables affecting social interaction. *J. abnorm. soc. Psychol.*, 1957, *54*, 250–256.

McCLELLAND, D. C. Wanted: A new self-image for women. In R. J. Lifton (Ed.), *The woman in America.* Boston: Houghton Mifflin, 1965. Pp. 173–192.

McFALL, R. M. "Unintentional communication": The effect of congruence and incongruence between subject and experimenter constructions. Unpublished doctoral dissertation, Ohio State Univer., 1965.

McGUIGAN, F. J. The experimenter: A neglected stimulus object. *Psychol. Bull.*, 1963, *60*, 421–428.

McNEMAR, Q. Opinion-attitude methodology. *Psychol. Bull.*, 1946, *43*, 289–374.

McNEMAR, Q. At random: Sense and nonsense. *Amer. Psychologist*, 1960, *15*, 295–300.

McTEER, W. Observational definitions of emotion. *Psychol. Rev.*, 1953, *60*, 172–180.

MERTON, R. K. The self-fulfilling prophecy. *Antioch Rev.*, 1948, *8*, 193–210.

MILLER, J. G. *Unconsciousness.* New York: Wiley, 1942.

MILLS, J. Changes in moral attitudes following temptation. *J. Pers.*, 1958, *26*, 517–531.

MILLS, T. M. A sleeper variable in small groups research: The experimenter. *Pacific sociol. Rev.*, 1962, *5*, 21–28.

MILMOE, SUSAN, ROSENTHAL, R., BLANE, H. T. CHAFETZ, M. E., & WOLF, I. The doctor's voice: Postdictor of successful referral of alcoholic patients. Unpublished paper, Harvard Univer., 1965. (*J. abnorm. Psychol.*, 1966, in press.)

MINTZ, N. On the psychology of aesthetics and architecture. Unpublished paper, Brandeis Univer., 1957.

MOLL, A. *Hypnotism.* (4th ed.) New York: Scribner, 1898.

MOLL, A. *Hypnotism.* Translated by A. F. Hopkirk. (4th enlarged ed.) London: Walter Scott; New York: Scribner, 1910.

MORROW, W. R. Psychologists' attitudes on psychological issues: I. Constrictive method-formalism. *J. gen. Psychol.*, 1956, *54*, 133–147.

MORROW, W. R. Psychologists' attitudes on psychological issues: II. Static-mechanical-elementarism. *J. gen. Psychol.*, 1957, *57*, 69–82.

MOSTELLER, F. Correcting for interviewer bias. In H. Cantril, *Gauging public opinion.* Princeton: Princeton Univer. Press, 1944. Pp. 286–288.

MOSTELLER, F., & BUSH, R. R. Selected quantitative techniques. In G. Lindzey (Ed.), *Handbook of social psychology.* Cambridge, Mass.: Addison-Wesley, 1954. Pp. 289–334.

MOSTELLER, F., & HAMMEL, E. A. Review of Naroll, R. *Data quality control —a new research technique.* New York: Macmillan, 1962. *J. Amer. Statist. Assoc.*, 1963, *58*, 835–836.

MULRY, R. C. The effects of the experimenter's perception of his own performance on subject performance in a pursuit rotor task. Unpublished master's thesis, Univer. of North Dakota, 1962.

MUNN, N. L. *Handbook of psychological research on the rat.* Boston: Houghton Mifflin, 1950.

Murphy, G. Science in a straight jacket? *Contemp. Psychol.,* 1962, *7,* 357–358.

Murray, H. A. Techniques for a systematic investigation of fantasy. *J. Psychol.,* 1937, *3,* 115–143.

Naroll, Frada, Naroll, R., & Howard, F. H. Position of women in childbirth. *Amer. J. Obstetrics Gynecol.,* 1961, *82,* 943–954.

Naroll, R. *Data quality control—a new research technique.* New York: Macmillan, 1962.

Newcomb, T. M. *The acquaintance process.* New York: Holt, Rinehart and Winston, 1961.

Noltingk, B. E. *The human element in research management.* Amsterdam: Elsevier, 1959.

Norman, R. D. A review of some problems related to the mail questionnaire technique. *Educ. psychol. Measmt.,* 1948, *8,* 235–247.

Orne, M. T. The nature of hypnosis: Artifact and essence. *J. abnorm. soc. Psychol.,* 1959, *58,* 277–299.

Orne, M. T. On the social psychology of the psychological experiment: With particular reference to demand characteristics and their implications. *Amer. Psychologist,* 1962, *17,* 776–783.

Palmer, L. R. New evidence in Knossos affair. London: *The Sunday Observer,* 1962 (Feb. 11).

Parsons, T. The American family: Its relations to personality and to the social structure. In T. Parsons, & R. F. Bales, *Family, socialization and interaction process.* New York: Free Press, 1955. Pp. 3–33.

Parsons, T., & Bales, R. F. *Family, socialization and interaction process.* New York: Free Press, 1955.

Parsons, T., Bales, R. F., & Shils, E. A. *Working papers in the theory of action.* New York: Free Press, 1953.

Pearson, K. On the mathematical theory of errors of judgment with special reference to the personal equation. *Phil. Trans. Roy. Soc. London,* 1902, *198,* 235–299.

Persinger, G. W. The effect of acquaintanceship on the mediation of experimenter bias. Unpublished master's thesis, Univer. of North Dakota, 1962.

Pflugrath, J. Examiner influence in a group testing situation with particular reference to examiner bias. Unpublished master's thesis, Univer. of North Dakota, 1962.

Pfungst, O. *Clever Hans (the horse of Mr. von Osten): A contribution to experimental, animal, and human psychology.* (Translated by C. L. Rahn.) New York: Holt, 1911.

Polanyi, M. *Personal knowledge.* Chicago: Univer. of Chicago Press, 1958.

Polanyi, M. Tacit knowing: Its bearing on some problems of philosophy. *Reviews of Modern Physics,* 1962, *34,* 601–616.

Polanyi, M. The potential theory of adsorption. *Science,* 1963, *141,* 1010–1013.

POMEROY, W. B. Human sexual behavior. In N. L. Farberow (Ed.), *Taboo topics*. Englewood Cliffs, N.J.: Prentice-Hall, 1963. Pp. 22–32.

PRINCE, A. I. Relative prestige and the verbal conditioning of children. *Amer. Psychologist*, 1962, *17*, 378. (Abstract)

QUART. J. STUD. ALCOHOL, EDITORIAL STAFF. Mortality in delirium tremens. *No. Dak. Rev. Alcoholism*, 1959, *4*, 3. Abstract of Gunne, L. M. Mortaliteten vid delirium tremens. *Nord. Med.*, 1958, *60*, 1021–1024.

RANKIN, R., & CAMPBELL, D. Galvanic skin response to Negro and white experimenters. *J. abnorm. soc. Psychol.*, 1955, *51*, 30–33.

RAPP, D. W. Detection of observer bias in the written record. Unpublished manuscript, Univer. of Georgia, 1965.

RAVEN, B. H., & FRENCH, J. R. P., JR. Group support, legitimate power and social influence. *J. Pers.*, 1958, *26*, 400–409.

RAVITZ, L. J. Electrometric correlates of the hypnotic state. *Science*, 1950, *112*, 341–342.

RAVITZ, L. J. Electrocyclic phenomena and emotional states. *J. clin. exp. Psychopathol.*, 1952, *13*, 69–106.

RAZRAN, G. Pavlov the empiricist. *Science*, 1959, *130*, 916.

REECE, M. M., & WHITMAN, R. N. Expressive movements, warmth, and verbal reinforcements. *J. abnorm. soc. Psychol.*, 1962, *64*, 234–236.

REIF, F. The competitive world of the pure scientist. *Science*, 1961, *134*, 1957–1962.

RHINE, J. B. How does one decide about ESP? *Amer. Psychologist*, 1959, *14*, 606–608.

RICE, C. E., & FEINSTEIN, S. H. Sonar system of the blind: Size discrimination. *Science*, 1965, *148*, 1107–1108.

RICE, S. A. Contagious bias in the interview: A methodological note. *Amer. J. Sociol.*, 1929, *35*, 420–423.

RIDER, P. R. Criteria for rejection of observations. *Washington Univer. Stud.*: New Ser., Sci. Tech., 1933, *8*.

RIECKEN, H. W. A program for research on experiments in social psychology. In N. F. Washburne (Ed.), *Decisions, values and groups*. Vol. II. New York: Pergamon Press, 1962. Pp. 25–41.

RIECKEN, H. W., et al. Narrowing the gap between field studies and laboratory experiments in social psychology: A statement by the summer seminar. *Items, Soc. Sci. Res. Council*, 1954, *8*, 37–42.

RINGUETTE, E. L., & KENNEDY, GERTRUDE L. An experimental investigation of the double-bind hypothesis. *Amer. Psychologist*, 1964, *19*, 459. (Abstract)

ROBINSON, D., & ROHDE, S. Two experiments with an anti-Semitism poll. *J. abnorm. soc. Psychol.*, 1946, *41*, 136–144.

ROBINSON, J., & COHEN, L. Individual bias in psychological reports. *J. clin. Psychol.*, 1954, *10*, 333–336.

RODNICK, E. H., & KLEBANOFF, S. G. Projective reactions to induced frustration as a measure of social adjustment. *Psychol. Bull.*, 1942, *39*, 489. (Abstract)

ROE, ANN. Man's forgotten weapon. *Amer. Psychologist*, 1959, *14*, 261–266.

ROE, ANN. The psychology of the scientist. *Science,* 1961, *134,* 456–459.

ROKEACH, M. *The open and closed mind.* New York: Basic Books, 1960.

ROSENBERG, M. J. When dissonance fails: On eliminating evaluation apprehension from attitude measurement. *J. pers. soc. Psychol.,* 1965, *1,* 28–42.

ROSENHAN, D. Hypnosis, conformity, and acquiescence. *Amer. Psychologist,* 1963, *18,* 402. (Abstract)

ROSENHAN, D. On the social psychology of hypnosis research. *Educat. Test. Serv. Research Memo.* Princeton, N.J.: Educ. Test. Serv., March, 1964. Also to appear as Chapter 13 in J. E. Gordon (Ed.), *Handbook of experimental and clinical hypnosis.*

ROSENTHAL, R. An attempt at the experimental induction of the defense mechanism of projection. Unpublished doctoral dissertation, Univer. of California at Los Angeles, 1956.

ROSENTHAL, R. Projection, excitement, and unconscious experimenter bias. *Amer. Psychologist,* 1958, *13,* 345–346. (Abstract)

ROSENTHAL, R. Variation in research results associated with experimenter variation. Unpublished paper, Harvard Univer., 1962.

ROSENTHAL, R. Experimenter attributes as determinants of subjects' responses. *J. proj. Tech. pers. Assess.,* 1963, *27,* 324–331. (a)

ROSENTHAL, R. Experimenter modeling effects as determinants of subject's responses. *J. proj. Tech. pers. Assess.,* 1963, *27,* 467–471. (b)

ROSENTHAL, R. On the social psychology of the psychological experiment: The experimenter's hypothesis as unintended determinant of experimental results. *Amer. Scient.,* 1963, *51,* 268–283. (c)

ROSENTHAL, R. Subject susceptibility to experimenter influence. Unpublished paper, Harvard Univer., 1963. (d)

ROSENTHAL, R. The effect of the experimenter on the results of psychological research. In B. A. Maher (Ed.), *Progress in experimental personality research.* Vol. I. New York: Academic Press, 1964. Pp. 79–114. (a)

ROSENTHAL, R. Experimenter outcome-orientation and the results of the psychological experiment. *Psychol. Bull.,* 1964, *61,* 405–412. (b)

ROSENTHAL, R. Clever Hans: A case study of scientific method. Introduction to Pfungst, O., *Clever Hans.* New York: Holt, Rinehart and Winston, 1965. Pp. ix–xlii. (a)

ROSENTHAL, R. The volunteer subject. *Hum. Relat.,* 1965, *18,* 389–406. (b)

ROSENTHAL, R. Covert communications and tacit understandings in the psychological experiment. Paper read at Amer. Psychol. Assoc., Chicago, September, 1965. (c)

ROSENTHAL, R., & FODE, K. L. The problem of experimenter outcome-bias. In D. P. Ray (Ed.), *Series research in social psychology.* Symposia studies series, No. 8, Washington, D.C.: National Institute of Social and Behavioral Science, 1961.

ROSENTHAL, R., & FODE, K. L. The effect of experimenter bias on the performance of the albino rat. *Behav. Sci.,* 1963, *8,* 183–189. (a)

ROSENTHAL, R., & FODE, K. L. (Psychology of the scientist: V) Three experiments in experimenter bias. *Psychol. Rep.,* 1963, *12,* 491–511. (b)

ROSENTHAL, R., FODE, K. L., FRIEDMAN, C. J., & VIKAN-KLINE, LINDA. Subjects' perception of their experimenter under conditions of experimenter bias. *Percept. mot. Skills*, 1960, *11*, 325–331.

ROSENTHAL, R., FODE, K. L., & VIKAN-KLINE, LINDA L. The effect on experimenter bias of varying levels of motivation of *E*s and *S*s. Unpublished manuscript, Harvard Univer., 1960.

ROSENTHAL, R., FODE, K. L., VIKAN-KLINE, LINDA, & PERSINGER, G. W. Verbal conditioning: Mediator of experimenter expectancy effects? *Psychol. Rep.*, 1964, *14*, 71–74.

ROSENTHAL, R., FRIEDMAN, C. J., JOHNSON, C. A., FODE, K. L., SCHILL, T. R., WHITE, C. R., & VIKAN-KLINE, LINDA L. Variables affecting experimenter bias in a group situation. *Genet. Psychol. Monogr.*, 1964, *70*, 271–296.

ROSENTHAL, R., FRIEDMAN, N., & KURLAND, D. Instruction-reading behavior of the experimenter as an unintended determinant of experimental results. Paper read at East. Psychol. Ass., Atlantic City, April, 1965. (*J. exp. Res. Pers.*, 1966, in press.)

ROSENTHAL, R., & GAITO, J. The interpretation of levels of significance by psychological researchers. *J. Psychol.*, 1963, *55*, 33–38.

ROSENTHAL, R., & GAITO, J. Further evidence for the cliff effect in the interpretation of levels of significance. *Psychol. Rep.*, 1964, *15*, 570.

ROSENTHAL, R., & HALAS, E. S. Experimenter effect in the study of invertebrate behavior. *Psychol. Rep.*, 1962, *11*, 251–256.

ROSENTHAL, R., KOHN, P., GREENFIELD, PATRICIA M., & CAROTA, N. Experimenters' hypothesis-confirmation and mood as determinants of experimental results. *Percept. mot. Skills*, 1965, *20*, 1237–1252.

ROSENTHAL, R., KOHN, P., GREENFIELD, PATRICIA M., & CAROTA, N. Data desirability, experimenter expectancy, and the results of psychological research, *J. Pers. soc. Psychol.*, 1966, *3*, 20–27.

ROSENTHAL, R., & LAWSON, R. A longitudinal study of the effects of experimenter bias on the operant learning of laboratory rats. *J. Psychiat. Res.*, 1964, *2*, 61–72.

ROSENTHAL, R., & PERSINGER, G. W. Let's pretend: Subjects' perception of imaginary experimenters. *Percept. mot. Skills*, 1962, *14*, 407–409.

ROSENTHAL, R., PERSINGER, G. W., & FODE, K. L. Experimenter bias, anxiety, and social desirability. *Percept. mot. Skills*, 1962, *15*, 73–74.

ROSENTHAL, R., PERSINGER, G. W., MULRY, R. C., VIKAN-KLINE, LINDA, & GROTHE, M. A motion picture study of 29 biased experimenters. Unpublished data, Harvard Univer., 1962.

ROSENTHAL, R., PERSINGER, G. W., MULRY, R. C., VIKAN-KLINE, LINDA, & GROTHE, M. Changes in experimental hypotheses as determinants of experimental results. *J. proj. Tech. pers. Assess.*, 1964, *28*, 465–469. (a)

ROSENTHAL, R., PERSINGER, G. W., MULRY, R. C., VIKAN-KLINE, LINDA, & GROTHE, M. Emphasis on experimental procedure, sex of subjects, and the biasing effects of experimental hypotheses. *J. proj. Tech. pers. Assess.*, 1964, *28*, 470–473. (b)

ROSENTHAL, R., PERSINGER, G. W., VIKAN-KLINE, LINDA, & FODE, K. L. The effect of early data returns on data subsequently obtained by outcome-biased experimenters. *Sociometry*, 1963, *26*, 487–498. (a)

ROSENTHAL, R., PERSINGER, G. W., VIKAN-KLINE, LINDA, & FODE, K. L. The effect of experimenter outcome-bias and subject set on awareness in verbal conditioning experiments. *J. verb. Learn. verb. Behav.*, 1963, *2*, 275–283. (b)

ROSENTHAL, R., PERSINGER, G. W., VIKAN-KLINE, LINDA, & MULRY, R. C. The role of the research assistant in the mediation of experimenter bias. *J. Pers.*, 1963, *31*, 313–335.

ROSTAND, J. *Error and deception in science.* New York: Basic Books, 1960.

ROTTER, J. B. *Social learning and clinical psychology.* Englewood Cliffs, N.J.: Prentice-Hall, 1954.

ROTTER, J. B., & JESSOR, SHIRLEY. The problem of subjective bias in TAT interpretation. Unpublished manuscript, Ohio State Univer. (undated, circa 1947).

ROZEBOOM, W. W. The fallacy of the null-hypothesis significance test. *Psychol. Bull.*, 1960, *57*, 416–428.

RUSSELL, B. *Philosophy.* New York: Norton, 1927.

SACKS, ELEANOR L. Intelligence scores as a function of experimentally established social relationships between child and examiner. *J. abnorm. soc. Psychol.*, 1952, *47*, 354–358.

SAMPSON, E. E., & FRENCH, J. R. P. An experiment on active and passive resistance to social power. *Amer. Psychologist,* 1960, *15*, 396. (Abstract)

SAMPSON, E. E., & SIBLEY, LINDA B. A further examination of the confirmation or nonconfirmation of expectancies and desires. *J. pers. soc. Psychol.*, 1965, *2*, 133–137.

SANDERS, R., & CLEVELAND, S. E. The relationship between certain examiner personality variables and subject's Rorschach scores. *J. proj. Tech.*, 1953, *17*, 34–50.

SANFORD, R. N. The effects of abstinence from food upon imaginal processes: A preliminary experiment. *J. Psychol.*, 1936, *2*, 129–136.

SAPOLSKY, A. Effect of interpersonal relationships upon verbal conditioning. *J. abnorm. soc. Psychol.*, 1960, *60*, 241–246.

SARASON, I. G. Interrelationships among individual difference variables, behavior in psychotherapy, and verbal conditioning. *J. abnorm, soc. Psychol.*, 1958, *56*, 339–344.

SARASON, I. G. Individual differences, situational variables, and personality research. *J. abnorm. soc. Psychol.*, 1962, *65*, 376–380.

SARASON, I. G. The human reinforcer in verbal behavior research. In L. Krasner & L. P. Ullman (Eds.), *Research in behavior modification: New developments and implications.* New York: Holt, Rinehart and Winston, 1965. Pp. 231–243.

SARASON, I. G., & HARMATZ, M. G. Test anxiety and experimental conditions. *J. pers. soc. Psychol.*, 1965, *1*, 499–505.

SARASON, I. G., & MINARD, J. Interrelationships among subject, experimenter, and situational variables. *J. abnorm. soc. Psychol.*, 1963, *67*, 87–91.

SARASON, S. B. The psychologist's behavior as an area of research. *J. consult. Psychol.*, 1951, *15*, 278–280.

SARASON, S. B., DAVIDSON, K. S., LIGHTHALL, F. F., WAITE, R. R., & RUEBUSH, B. K. *Anxiety in elementary school children.* New York: Wiley, 1960.

SCHACHTER, S. *The psychology of affiliation.* Stanford, Calif.: Stanford Univer. Press, 1959.

SCHMEIDLER, GERTRUDE, & MCCONNELL, R. A. *ESP and personality patterns.* New Haven: Yale Univer. Press, 1958.

SCHULTZ, D. P. Time, awareness, and order of presentation in opinion change. *J. appl. Psychol.,* 1963, *47,* 280–283.

Science and Politics: AMA attacked for use of disputed survey in "Medicare" lobbying, *Science,* 1960, *132,* 604–605.

SEBEOK, T. A., HAYES, A. S., & BATESON, MARY C. (Eds.) *Approaches to semiotics.* The Hague: Mouton, 1964.

SHAPIRO, A. K. A contribution to a history of the placebo effect. *Behav. Sci.,* 1960, *5,* 109–135.

SHAPIRO, A. K. Factors contributing to the placebo effect. *Amer. J. Psychother.,* 1964, *18,* 73–88.

SHAPIRO, A. K. Iatroplacebogenics. Unpublished paper, Montefiore Hospital, New York City, 1965.

SHAPIRO, A. P. The investigator himself. In S. O. Waife & A. P. Shapiro, (Eds.), *The clinical evaluation of new drugs.* New York: Hoeber-Harper, 1959. Pp. 110–119.

SHEFFIELD, F. D., KAUFMAN, R. S., & RHINE, J. B. A PK experiment at Yale starts a controversy. *J. Amer. Soc. Psychical Res.,* 1952, *46,* 111–117.

SHERIF, M., & HOVLAND, C. I. *Social judgment.* New Haven: Yale Univer. Press, 1961.

SHINKMAN, P. G., & KORNBLITH, CAROL L. Comment on observer bias in classical conditioning of the planarian. *Psychol. Rep.,* 1965, *16,* 56.

SHOR, R. E. Shared patterns of nonverbal normative expectations in automobile driving. *J. soc. Psychol.,* 1964, *62,* 155–163.

SILVERMAN, I. In defense of dissonance theory: Reply to Chapanis and Chapanis. *Psychol. Bull.,* 1964, *62,* 205–209.

SILVERMAN, I. Motives underlying the behavior of the subject in the psychological experiment. Paper read at Amer. Psychol. Ass., Chicago, September, 1965.

SIMMONS, W. L., & CHRISTY, E. G. Verbal reinforcement of a TAT theme. *J. proj. Tech.,* 1962, *26,* 337–341.

SMART, R. G. The importance of negative results in psychological research. *Canad. Psychologist,* 1964, *5a,* 225–232.

SMITH, E. E. Relative power of various attitude change techniques. Paper read at Amer. Psychol. Ass., New York, September, 1961.

SMITH, H. L., & HYMAN, H. H. The biasing effect of interviewer expectations on survey results. *Publ. Opin. Quart.,* 1950, *14,* 491–506.

SNEDECOR, G. W. *Statistical methods.* (5th ed.) Ames, Iowa: Iowa State University Press, 1956.

SNOW, C. P. *The Affair.* London: Macmillan, 1960.

SNOW, C. P. The moral un-neutrality of science. *Science,* 1961, *133,* 256–259.

SOLOMON, R. L. An extension of control group design. *Psychol. Bull.,* 1949, *46,* 137–150.

SPENCE, K. W. Anxiety (drive) level and performance in eyelid conditioning. *Psychol. Bull.,* 1964, *61,* 129–139.

SPIELBERGER, C. D., BERGER, A., & HOWARD, KAY.   Conditioning of verbal behavior as a function of awareness, need for social approval, and motivation to receive reinforcement. *J. abnorm. soc. Psychol.,* 1963, *67,* 241–246.

SPIELBERGER, C. D., & DE NIKE, L. D.   Descriptive behaviorism versus cognitive theory in verbal operant conditioning. *Psychol. Rev.,* 1966, *73,* in press.

SPIRES, A. M.   Subject-experimenter interaction in verbal conditioning. Unpublished doctoral dissertation, New York Univer., 1960.

STANTON, F.   Further contributions at the twentieth anniversary of the Psychological Corporation and to honor its founder, James McKeen Cattel. *J. appl. Psychol.,* 1942a, *26,* 16–17.

STANTON, F., & BAKER, K. H.   Interviewer bias and the recall of incompletely learned materials. *Sociometry,* 1942, *5,* 123–134.

STAR, SHIRLEY A.   The screening of psychoneurotics: comparison of psychiatric diagnoses and test scores at all induction stations. In S. A. Stouffer, L. Guttman, E. A. Suchman, P. F. Lazarsfeld, Shirley A. Star, & J. A. Clausen, *Measurement and prediction.* Princeton: Princeton Univer. Press, 1950. Pp. 548–567.

STEMBER, C. H., & HYMAN, H. H.   How interviewer effects operate through question form. *Int. J. Opin. Attit. Res.,* 1949, *3,* 493–512.

STEPHENS, J. M.   The perception of small differences as affected by self interest. *Amer. J. Psychol.,* 1936, *48,* 480–484.

STERLING, T. D.   Publication decisions and their possible effects on inferences drawn from tests of significance—or vice versa. *J. Amer. Statist. Assoc.,* 1959, *54,* 30–34.

STEVENS, S. S.   To honor Fechner and repeal his law. *Science,* 1961, 133, 80–86.

STEVENSON, H. W.   Social reinforcement with children as a function of CA, sex of *E,* and sex of *S. J. abnorm. soc. Psychol.,* 1961, *63,* 147–154.

STEVENSON, H. W.   Social reinforcement of children's behavior. In L.P. Lipsitt & C. C. Spiker, (Eds.), *Advances in child development and behavior.* Vol. 2. New York: Academic Press, 1965.

STEVENSON, H. W., & ALLEN, SARA.   Adult performance as a function of sex of experimenter and sex of subject. *J. abnorm. soc. Psychol.,* 1964, *68,* 214–216.

STEVENSON, H. W., KEEN, RACHEL, & KNIGHTS, R. M.   Parents and strangers as reinforcing agents for children's performance. *J. abnorm. soc. Psychol.,* 1963, *67,* 183–186.

STEVENSON, H. W., & KNIGHTS, R. M.   Social reinforcement with normal and retarded children as a function of pretraining, sex of *E,* and sex of *S. Amer. J. ment. Defic.,* 1962, *66,* 866–871.

STEVENSON, H. W., & ODOM, R. D.   Visual reinforcement with children. Unpublished manuscript, Univer. of Minnesota, 1963.

STRATTON, G. M.   The control of another person by obscure signs. *Psychol. Rev.,* 1921, *28,* 301–314.

STRUPP, H. H.   Toward an analysis of the therapist's contribution to the treatment process. *Amer. Psychologist,* 1959, *14,* 336. (Abstract)

STRUPP, H. H., & LUBORSKY, L. (Eds.)   *Research in psychotherapy.* Washington, D.C.: Amer. Psychol. Ass., 1962.

SULLIVAN, H. S.   A note on the implications of psychiatry, the study of inter-personal relations, for investigations in the social sciences. *Amer. J. Sociol.,* 1936–37, *42,* 848–861.

SUMMERS, G. F., & HAMMONDS, A. D.   Toward a paradigm of respondent bias in survey research. Unpublished paper, Univer. of Wisconsin, 1965.

SYMONS, R. T.   Specific experimenter-subject personality variables pertinent to the influencing process in a verbal conditioning situation. Unpublished doc-toral dissertation, Univer. of Washington, 1964.

Symposium: Survey on problems of interviewer cheating. *Int. J. Opin. attit. Res.,* 1947, *1,* 93–106.

TAFFEL, C.   Anxiety and the conditioning of verbal behavior. *J. abnorm. soc. Psychol.,* 1955, *51,* 496–501.

TAYLOR, JANET A.   A personality scale of manifest anxiety. *J. abnorm. soc. Psychol.,* 1953, *48,* 285–290.

TOLMAN, E. C.   *Purposive behavior in animals and men.* New York: Century, 1932.

TROFFER, SUZANNE A., & TART, C. T.   Experimenter bias in hypnotist per-formance. *Science,* 1964, *145,* 1330–1331.

TUDDENHAM, R. D.   The view from Hovland Headland. *Contemp. Psychol.,* 1960, *5,* 150–151.

TUKEY, J. W.   Data analysis and the frontiers of geophysics. *Science,* 1965, *148,* 1283–1289.

TURNER, G. C., & COLEMAN, J. C.   Examiner influence on thematic appercep-tion test responses. *J. proj. Tech.,* 1962, *26,* 478–486.

TURNER, J.   On being fair though one-sided. *Science,* 1961, *134,* 585. (a)

TURNER, J.   What laymen can ask of scientists. *Science,* 1961, *133,* 1195. (b)

UDOW, A. B.   The "interviewer effect" in public opinion and market research surveys. *Arch. Psychol.,* 1942, *39,* No. 277.

VEROFF, J.   Anxious first-borns. *Contemp. Psychol.,* 1960, *5,* 328–329.

VERPLANCK, W. S.   The control of the content of conversation: Reinforcement of statements of opinion. *J. abnorm. soc. Psychol.,* 1955, *51,* 668–676.

VIKAN-KLINE, LINDA L.   The effect of an experimenter's perceived status on the mediation of experimenter bias. Unpublished master's thesis, Univer. of North Dakota, 1962.

VINACKE, W. E.   Laboratories and lives. Paper read at Amer. Psychol. Ass., Chicago, September, 1965.

WALLACH, M. S., & STRUPP, H. H.   Psychotherapist's clinical judgments and attitudes toward patients. *J. consult. Psychol.,* 1960, *24,* 316–323.

WALLIN, P.   Volunteer subjects as a source of sampling bias. *Amer. J. Sociol.,* 1949, *54,* 539–544.

WALTERS, CATHRYN, PARSONS, O. A., & SHURLEY, J. T.   Male-female dif-ferences in underwater sensory isolation. *Brit. J. Psychiat.,* 1964, *109–110,* 290–295.

WALTERS, CATHRYN, SHURLEY, J. T., & PARSONS, O. A.   Differences in male and female responses to underwater sensory deprivation: An exploratory study. *J. nerv. ment. Dis.*, 1962, *135*, 302–310.

WARE, J. R., KOWAL, B., & BAKER, R. A., JR. The role of experimenter attitude and contingent reinforcement in a vigilance task. Unpublished paper, U.S. Army Armor Human Research Unit, Fort Knox, Kentucky, 1963.

WARNER, L., & RAIBLE, MILDRED. Telepathy in the psychophysical laboratory. *J. Parapsychol.*, 1937, *1*, 44–51.

WARTENBERG-EKREN, URSULA. The effect of experimenter knowledge of a subject's scholastic standing on the performance of a reasoning task. Unpublished master's thesis, Marquette Univer., 1962.

WEICK, K. E. When prophecy pales: The fate of dissonance theory. *Psychol. Rep.*, 1965, *16*, 1261–1275.

WEITZENHOFFER, A. M., & HILGARD, E. R. *Stanford Hypnotic Susceptibility Scale: Form C*. Palo Alto, California: Consulting Psychologists Press, 1962.

WHITE, C. R. The effect of induced subject expectations on the experimenter bias situation. Unpublished doctoral dissertation, Univer. of North Dakota, 1962.

WHITMAN, R. M. Drugs, dreams and the experimental subject. *J. Canad. Psychiat. Assoc.*, 1963, *8*, 395–399.

WHYTE, W. F. *Street corner society*. Chicago: Univer. Chicago Press, 1943.

WILLIAMS, F., & CANTRIL, H. The use of interviewer rapport as a method of detecting differences between "public" and "private" opinion. *J. soc. Psychol.*, 1945, *22*, 171–175.

WILLIAMS, J. A. Interviewer-respondent interaction: A study of bias in the information interview. *Sociometry*, 1964, *27*, 338–352.

WILLIAMS, L. P. The Beringer hoax. *Science*, 1963, *140*, 1083.

WILSON, A. B. Social stratification and academic achievement. In A. H. Passow (Ed.), *Education in depressed areas*. New York: Teachers College, Columbia Univer., 1963. Pp. 217–235.

WILSON, E. B. *An introduction to scientific research*. New York: McGraw-Hill, 1952.

WINER, B. J. *Statistical principles in experimental design*. New York: McGraw-Hill, 1962.

WINKEL, G. H., & SARASON, I. G. Subject, experimenter, and situational variables in research on anxiety. *J. abnorm. soc. Psychol.*, 1964, *68*, 601–608.

WIRTH, L. Preface to K. Mannheim, *Ideology and utopia*. New York: Harcourt, Brace & World, 1936.

WOLF, I. S. Perspectives in psychology, XVI. Negative findings. *Psychol. Rec.*, 1961, *11*, 91–95.

WOLF, S. Human beings as experimental subjects. In S. O. Waife, & A. P. Shapiro (Eds.), *The clinical evaluation of new drugs*. New York: Hoeber-Harper, 1959. Pp. 85–99.

WOLF, THETA H. An individual who made a difference. *Amer. Psychologist*, 1961, *16*, 245–248.

WOLF, THETA H. Alfred Binet: A time of crisis. *Amer. Psychologist*, 1964, *19*, 762–771.

WOLFLE, D. Research with human subjects. *Science*, 1960, *132*, 989.

WOLINS, L. Needed: Publication of negative results. *Amer. Psychologist,* 1959, *14,* 598.

WOLINS, L. Responsibility for raw data. *Amer. Psychologist,* 1962, *17,* 657–658.

WOOD, F. G. Pitfall. *Science,* 1962, *135,* 261.

WOODS, P. J. Some characteristics of journals and authors. *Amer. Psychologist,* 1961, *16,* 699–701.

WOOSTER, H. Basic research. *Science,* 1959, *130,* 126.

WUSTER, C. R., BASS, M., & ALCOCK, W. A test of the proposition: We want to be esteemed most by those we esteem most highly. *J. abnorm. soc. Psychol.,* 1961, *63,* 650–653.

WYATT, D. F., & CAMPBELL, D. T. A study of interviewer bias as related to interviewers' expectations and own opinions. *Int. J. Opin. Attit. Res.,* 1950, *4,* 77–83.

YOUNG, R. K. Digit span as a function of the personality of the experimenter. *Amer. Psychologist,* 1959, *14,* 375. (Abstract)

YULE, G. U. On reading a scale. *J. Roy. statist. Soc.,* 1927, *90,* 570–587.

YULE, G. U., & KENDALL, M. G. *An introduction to the theory of statistics.* (14th ed.) New York: Hafner, 1950.

ZELDITCH, M. Role differentiation in the nuclear family: A comparative study. In T. Parsons & R. F. Bales, *Family, socialization and interaction process.* New York: Free Press, 1955. Pp. 307–351.

ZILLIG, MARIA. Einstellung und Aussage. *Z. Psychol.,* 1928, *106,* 58–106. (Translated by Irene Jerison.)

ZIRKLE, C. Citation of fraudulent data. *Science,* 1954, *120,* 189–190.

ZIRKLE, C. Pavlov's beliefs. *Science,* 1958, *128,* 1476.

ZIRKLE, C. A conscience in conflict. Book review in *Science,* 1960, *132,* 890.

ZIRKLE, G. A. Some potential errors in conducting mental health research. In R. H. Branson (Ed.), *Report of the conference on mental health research.* Indianapolis: Assoc. Advance. Ment. Hlth. Res. Educ., 1959.

ZNANIECKI, F. *The social role of the man of knowledge.* New York: Columbia Univer. Press, 1940.

Interpersonal Expectancy Effects: A Follow-up

Contents

Interpersonal Expectancy
Effects: A Follow-up

Consistency Over Time

In 1969, just three years after the original appearance of the present volume, a provisional summary of the literature on interpersonal expectations was published which listed and surveyed 105 studies of interpersonal expectations (Rosenthal, 1969). Table 1 shows an overall comparison of the results of these early 105 studies with the results of 206 subsequent studies. The first two columns show the number of studies conducted within each of eight areas of research as these areas were defined by the earlier review (Rosenthal, 1969). An analysis of the proportion of all studies conducted in each time period falling into each research area showed that, overall, there was a large shift in the areas receiving research attention ($\chi^2 = 42.9$, $df = 7$, $p < .001$). Most of this shift was due to changes in two of the eight research areas. Studies of person perception decreased dramatically from 53% of all studies conducted up to 1969 to only 27% of all studies conducted since 1969. Studies of everyday life situations, including studies of teacher expectations, increased dramatically from 10% of all studies conducted up to 1969 to 41% of all studies conducted since 1969.

The third and fourth columns of Table 1 show the proportion of studies reaching the .05 level of significance for each of the eight research areas. All of the research areas both before and after 1969 show very substantially higher proportions of significant results than the proportion of .05 that would be expected by chance. Considering the research areas separately, none of them show a significant ($p = .10$, two-tail) change in the proportion of results reaching significance before 1969 as compared to after 1969. For both the older and the newer studies, about one-third reach the .05 level, about seven times more than we would expect if there were in fact no significant relationship between experimenters' or teach-

TABLE 1

Overall Comparison of Results of Studies Before and After 1969

	Number of Studies		Proportion Reaching p ≤.05	
Research Area	To 1969	Since 1969	To 1969	Since 1969
Reaction Time	3	3	.33	.33
Inkblot Tests	4	5	.75	.20
Animal Learning	9	5	.89	.40
Laboratory Interviews	6	16	.33	.38
Psychophysical Judgments	9	14	.33	.50
Learning and Ability	9	24	.22	.29
Person Perception	57	57	.25	.30
Everyday Situations	11	85	.36	.38
Median	9	15	.33	.36
Total	108[a]	209[a]	.35	.35

[a]Three of these entries are nonindependent i.e., they occur in more than one area.

ers' expectations and their subjects' or pupils' subsequent behavior. Results so striking could essentially never occur if there were really no such relationship ($\chi^2 = 585$, $z = 24.2$.)

A Brief Overview

Table 2 summarizes the results of all the studies, published and unpublished, that I was able to find up to the time of this writing. The first column gives the total number of studies that fall into each of the eight research areas that were defined for convenience in tabulating results (Rosenthal, 1969). Adding over all eight areas yields a grand total of 317 studies. Six of those studies, however, were not independent but involved dependent variables that fell into more than one research area. The total net number of independent studies, therefore, was 311. The second column of Table 2 shows the approximate number of degrees of freedom upon which the average study in that area was based. These data are included to give some feel for the typical size of the studies conducted in each area. The range of these means over the eight research areas was from 21 to 124 with a median of 48.5. All the values are reasonably homogeneous except for the mean of 124 *df* for the reaction time studies. That appears to be significantly larger than the remaining seven values

TABLE 2

Expectancy Effects in Eight Research Areas

Research Area	Number of Studies	Estimated Mean df for t	Proportion of Studies Reaching p ≤ .05	Estimated Mean Effect Size (σ)	Estimated z Standard Normal Deviate Random	Estimated z Standard Normal Deviate Truncated
Reaction Time	6	124	.33	0.23	+ 3.11	+ 2.62
Inkblot Tests	9	28	.44	0.84	+ 4.23	+ 4.05
Animal Learning	14	21	.64	1.78	+ 6.96	+ 7.56
Laboratory Interviews	22	52	.36	0.27	+ 6.21	+ 5.80
Psychophysical Judgments	23	34	.43	1.31	+ 9.02	+ 6.61
Learning and Ability	33	52	.27	0.72	+ 3.82	+ 4.60
Person Perception	114	54	.27	0.51	+ 3.82	+ 6.55
Everyday Situations	96	45	.38	1.44	+ 5.92	+11.70
Median	22.5[a]	48.5	.37[b]	0.78[c]	+ 5.08	+ 6.18

[a]Six entries occur in more than one area.

[b]These proportions do not differ significantly from each other $X^2 = 9.7$, $df = 7$, $p > .20$.

[c]The correlation between columns 3 and 4 was .778, $p = .012$.

and can be classified a statistical outlier at $p < .05$ (Snedecor and Cochran, 1967, p. 323). Examination of the six studies of reaction time suggested no hypothesis as to why these studies should be so substantially larger than those of other areas of research.

The third column of Table 2 shows the proportion of studies reaching the .05 level of significance in the predicted direction. The range of these proportions was from .27 to .64 with a median proportion .37. These eight proportions did not differ significantly from each other ($\chi^2 = 9.7$, $df = 7$, $p > .20$). Thus, as we learned earlier from Table 1, about one-third of the studies investigating the effects of interpersonal expectations show such effects to occur at the .05 level of significance and one-third is a reasonable estimate regardless of the particular area of inquiry.

Effect Size

In the earlier follow-up to the present book (Rosenthal, 1969) over a hundred studies were listed; some of them were described in some detail, and it was shown that the number of significant results occurring ruled out the possibility that sampling fluctuations or capitalization on chance could account for the large number of significant results obtained. Some effort was also made in that earlier follow-up to give estimates of the size of the effects of interpersonal expectations. It appears to me now, however, that the issue of effect size was not well handled. Since the preparation of the earlier overview Cohen's (1969) superb book *Statistical Power Analysis for the Behavioral Sciences* was published, and its treatment of effect sizes in relation to power considerations made a lasting impression. In the present follow-up, therefore, an effort was made to provide estimates of effect size more useful than those provided in the earlier review.

The primary index of effect size employed in the present study is the statistic *"d"* defined as the difference between the means of the two groups being compared, divided by the standard deviation common to the two populations (Cohen, 1969, p. 18). The great advantage of this index is that it permits us to compare the magnitudes of effects for a large variety of measures. It frees us from the particular scale of measurement and allows us to speak of effects measured in standard deviation (σ) units. There are many different measures of effect size that could have been employed in the present follow-up, each with its special advantages and disadvantages. The measure *"d"* was chosen for its simplicity and because such a large proportion of the studies of interpersonal expectancy effects involve simply a comparison of an experimental with a control group by means of a test (or F with $df = 1$ for the numerator), and d is particularly useful for that situation both conceptually and computationally. (For a recent example of the extensive use of *"d"* as an index of effect size in the behavioral sciences see Rosenthal and Rosnow, 1975.)

Ideally it would have been best to go back to the over 300 studies of interpersonal expectations and to compute for each one the effect size in σ units. For the present follow-up, which is to some degree provisional, it was not possible to be exhaustive. Instead, a doubly stratified random sample (with planned oversampling) of 75 studies was chosen to permit the estimation of effect sizes. The first stratification was on the dimension of research area. For the two areas with fewer than 10 studies, reaction time and inkblot tests, all studies were included. For the remaining six areas, ten studies were included for each area. Thus, areas with fewer studies were oversampled in comparison to areas with more studies. In the area of animal learning, for example, 71% of the studies were included while in the area of person perception only 9% of the studies were included.

The second stratification was on the statistical significance of the primary result of the studies in each area. Arbitrarily, the five most significant studies were included for each area, and five studies were selected at random from the remaining studies in each area. The latter five studies, of course, were weighted in proportion to the size of the population of available studies so that there would be no bias favoring studies of greater statistical significance. An example will be useful. There were 33 studies of the effects of experimenter expectations on the learning and ability scores of their subjects. The mean effect size of the five most significant studies was 1.25σ. The mean effect size of the five studies randomly selected from the remaining 28 studies was 0.63σ. The estimated effect size for all 33 studies was 0.72σ, a value much closer to that of the random five studies mean than to that of the high significance five studies' mean. The means are weighted by 5 and N-5, respectively, so that the overall estimated effect size is given by $[5\ \overline{X}\ \text{Top} + (N - 5)\overline{X}\ \text{Random}]/N$, where N is the total number of studies conducted in that area.

The fourth column of Table 2 shows these estimated effect sizes for each of the eight research areas. The range is from 0.23σ for studies of reaction time to 1.78σ for studies of animal learning, with a median effect size of 0.78σ. In Cohen's terminology, then, these effect sizes range from small ($.20\sigma$) through medium ($.50\sigma$) to large ($.80\sigma$) and, for three of the research areas, to very large (Cohen, 1969, p. 38). It is interesting to note that there was a large and significant correlation of .78 between the estimated effect size and the proportion of studies reaching significance in the various areas of research.

The fifth column of Table 2 shows the standard normal deviate (z) associated with the combined results of each of the eight areas of research according to the method of Mosteller and Bush (1954) and as employed in the earlier follow-up (Rosenthal, 1969). For each of the studies sampled, the obtained level of significance was converted to its associated algebraic standard normal deviate with a positive sign indicating that the result was in the direction of the hypothesis of interpersonal expectancy effects. The combined z was then computed according to the formula: $[5 \bar{z} \text{ Top} + (N - 5) \bar{z} \text{ Random}]/\sqrt{N}$. It is clear from column five of Table 2 that all areas of research showed overall significant effects of interpersonal expectancy. The final column of Table 2 shows the standard normal deviates of the combined results based not on sampling the studies of each research area but on the direct computation of the standard normal deviate for all studies in each area. In order to be consistent with the procedure of the earlier review (Rosenthal, 1969), however, any z falling between -1.27 and $+1.27$ was entered as zero, a procedure which tends to lead to combined results that are too conservative. The results shown in this column also show significant overall effects of interpersonal expectancies in all research areas.

In order to get a better understanding of the probable ranges of effect sizes for the various areas of research, confidence intervals were computed and these are shown in columns five and six of Table 3. For each area of research the 95% confidence interval suggests the likely range of the effect size for that area. If we claim that the effect size falls within the range given we will be correct 95% of the time. The confidence intervals are wide because their computation was based on such small samples of studies (i.e., 6, 9, or 10). When each of the eight confidence intervals is compared with all other confidence intervals we find that only two of the 28 comparisons show non-overlapping confidence intervals. The reaction time confidence interval is lower than the confidence intervals for animal learning and psychophysical judgments. Studies of reaction time appear to have a particularly narrow confidence interval but this result could have occurred by chance. The standard error of the mean effect size for the reaction time research is not a significant outlier, nor is the standard error of the mean effect size for any other research area.

When we consider the total set of 75 studies sampled, we find the 95% confidence interval to lie between an effect size of 0.62 and 1.22, corresponding to effect magnitudes ranging from medium to very large in Cohen's (1969) terminology.

The first three columns of Table 3 show the various ingredients required for the computation of the confidence interval, the number of studies sampled, the estimated standard deviation, and the standard error of the mean. The last column of Table 3 reports the correlations obtained within each research area between the effect size measured in σ units and the degree of statistical significance measured in standard normal deviates. These correlations were overwhelmingly positive ranging from $+.38$ to $+.87$ with a median correlation of $+.74$. Such high correlations are what we would expect as long as the sample sizes employed within the various research areas are relatively homogeneous.

TABLE 3

Confidence Intervals for Mean Effect Sizes in Eight Research Areas

Research Area	Number of Studies Sampled	Estimated S	Standard Error of the Mean	Mean Effect Size	95% Confidence Interval From	To	Correlations Between Effect Size and Level of Significance (z)
Reaction Time	6	0.11	.04	0.23	+ 0.13	0.33	.82
Inkblot Tests	9	1.17	.39	0.84	- 0.06	1.74	.85
Animal Learning	10	1.69	.53	1.78	+ 0.58	2.98	.69
Laboratory Interviews	10	0.94	.30	0.27	- 0.41	0.95	.87
Psychophysical Judgments	10	1.15	.36	1.31	+ 0.50	2.12	.38
Learning and Ability	10	1.49	.47	0.72	- 0.34	1.78	.60
Person Perception	10	0.87	.28	0.51	- 0.12	1.14	.79
Everyday Situations	10	2.74	.87	1.44	- 0.53	3.41	.51
Median	10	1.16	.38	0.78	- 0.09	1.76	.74
Total	75	1.33	.15	0.92	0.62	1.22	.68

Alternative Indices

So far we have reported effect sizes only in σ units. In earlier reviews, however, effect sizes were reported in terms of the percentage of experimenters or teachers who obtained responses from their subjects or students in the direction of their expectations (Rosenthal, 1969, 1971). If there were no effect of interpersonal expectations we would expect about half the experimenters or teachers to obtain results in the direction of their expectation while the remaining half obtained results in the opposite direction. The results of the earlier reviews, based on over 60 studies, suggested that about two-thirds of the experimenters and teachers, the "expecters," obtained results in the predicted direction. For purposes of comparison with those earlier analyses, Table 4 was prepared. The first column shows that for 87 studies of experimenter expectations about two-thirds of the experimenters obtained results in the direction of their expectation. The second column of Table 4 shows that the results for studies of teacher expectations were about the same, with the obtained percentages of biased experimenters or teachers corresponding to an effect size of about one standard deviation (Cohen, 1969; Friedman, 1968). Although these estimates are based on 117 studies, we should not have any greater confidence in them than in the estimates based on the 75 studies that were sampled more randomly and with stratification. The reason for extra caution in the case of the percentages of biased "expecters" is that these studies were not chosen at random but rather because sufficient data were available in these studies to permit the convenient calculation of the percentage of biased "expecters." We cannot tell how these studies might differ from the remaining studies. However, the results obtained from these 117 studies were very much in line with the results obtained from the more systematically sampled set of 75 studies. Several of the research areas showed larger average effect sizes, and several showed smaller average effect sizes than those obtained from the potentially less representative 117 studies, and these latter results fall well within the 95% confidence interval of the mean effect size based on the more systematically sampled studies. There was, of course, considerable overlap between these two sets of studies.

The third and fourth columns of Table 4 report the analogous data from the point of view of the subjects of biased experimenters and the pupils of biased teachers. Once again we expect that if no expectancy effects are operating, half the subjects or pupils will respond in the direction of their "expecter's" induced expectation while half will respond in the opposite direction. For both subjects and pupils just under two-thirds show the predicted expectancy bias, a rate of bias equivalent to approximately three-quarters of a standard deviation. There may be a somewhat greater degree of sampling bias in the studies of "expectees" than in the studies of "expecters" simply because far fewer studies re-

TABLE 4

Percentages of Experimenters, Teachers, Subjects and Pupils
Showing Expectancy Effects

	"Expecter"		"Expectee"	
	Experimenters	Teachers	Subjects	Pupils
Number of Studies	87	30	52	13
Median z (approximation)	1.25	1.32	1.28	1.97
Number of Es, Ts, Ss, or Ps.	909	340	2,748	515
Mean N per Study	10	11	53	40
Weighted Percent of Biased Es, Ts, Ss, or Ps.	66%	69%	60%	63%
Median Percent of Biased Es, Ts, Ss, or Ps.	69%	70%	64%	65%
Approximate Effect Size in σ units of Median Percent of Biased Persons[a]	1.01	1.06	0.71	0.75

[a]See Table 1 of Friedman, 1968.

ported results in sufficient detail to permit an analysis of "expectee" bias rates. Still, the results of these studies are very consistent with the results of the studies sampled more systematically, falling well within the 95% confidence interval of the mean effect size based on the more systematically sampled studies.

Expectancy Control Groups

Chapter 23 dealt in detail with the utilization of expectancy control groups which permit the comparison of the effect size of the variable of interpersonal expectancy with the effect size of some other variable of psychological interest which is not regarded as an "artifact" variable. Chapter 23 was exclusively theoretical in the sense that there were no studies available that had employed the suggested paradigm. That situation has changed, and there are now a number of studies available that permit a direct comparison of the effects of experimenter expectancy with such other psychological effects as brain lesions, preparatory effort, and persuasive communications.

The first of these was conducted by Burnham (1966). He had 23 experimenters each run one rat in a T-maze discrimination problem.

About half the rats had been lesioned by removal of portions of the brain, and the remaining animals had received only sham surgery which involved cutting through the skull but no damage to brain tissue. The purpose of the study was explained to the experimenters as an attempt to learn the effects of lesions on discrimination learning. Expectancies were manipulated by labeling each rat as lesioned or nonlesioned. Some of the really lesioned rats were labeled accurately as lesioned but some were falsely labeled as unlesioned. Some of the really unlesioned rats were labeled accurately as unlesioned but some were falsely labeled as lesioned. Table 5 shows the standard scores of the ranks of performance in each of the four conditions. A higher score indicates superior performance. Animals that had been lesioned did not perform as well as those that had not been lesioned, and animals that were believed to be lesioned did not perform as well as those that were believed to be unlesioned. What makes this experiment of special interest is that the effects of experimenter expectancy were actually larger than those of actual removal of brain tissue although this difference was not significant.

Ten major types of outcomes of expectancy-controlled experiments were outlined in Chapter 23, and Burnham's result fits most closely that outcome labeled as Case 3 (p. 382). If an investigator interested in the effects of brain lesions on discrimination learning had employed only the two most commonly employed conditions, he could have been seriously misled by his results. Had he employed experimenters who believed the rats to be lesioned to run his lesioned rats and compared their results to those obtained by experimenters running unlesioned rats and believing them to be unlesioned, he would have greatly overestimated the effects on discrimination learning of brain lesions. For the investigator interested in assessing for his own specific area of research the likelihood and magnitude of expectancy effects, there appears to be no fully adequate substitute for the employment of expectancy control groups. For the investigator interested only in the reduction of expectancy effects, other techniques such as blind or minimized experimenter-subject contact or automated experimentation are among the techniques that may prove to be useful (see Chapters 19-22).

The first of the experiments to compare directly the effects of experimenter expectancy with some other experimental variable, employed animal subjects. The next such experiment to be described employed human subjects. Cooper, Eisenberg, Robert, and Dohrenwend (1967) wanted to compare the effects of experimenter expectancy with the effects of effortful preparation for an examination on the degree of belief that the examination would actually take place.

Each of ten experimenters contacted ten subjects; half of the subjects were required to memorize a list of 16 symbols and definitions that were claimed to be essential to the taking of a test that had a 50-50 chance of

TABLE 5

Discrimination Learning as a Function of Brain Lesions and Experimenter Expectancy: After Burnham.

Actual Brain State	Experimenter Expectancy		Σ	Statistics of Difference		
	Lesioned	Unlesioned		t	p	Effect Size
Lesioned	46.5	49.0	95.5	1.62	.06	0.71σ
Unlesioned	48.2	58.3	106.5			
Σ	94.7	107.3				
Statistics	t	2.19				
of Difference	p	.02				
	Effect Size	0.95σ				

TABLE 6

Certainty of Having to Take a Test as a Function of Preparatory Effort and Experimenter Expectancy: After Cooper et al.

Effort Level	Experimenter Expectancy		Σ	Statistics of Difference		
	High	Low		t	p	Effect Size
High	+ .64	− .40	+ .24	0.33	.37	0.07σ
Low	+ .56	− .52	+ .04			
Σ	+ 1.20	− .92				
Statistics	t	3.48				
of Difference	p	.0004				
	Effect Size	0.71σ				

being given, while the remaining subjects, the "low effort" group, were asked only to look over the list of symbols. Half of the experimenters were led to expect that "high effort" subjects would be more certain of actually having to take the test, while half of the experimenters were led to expect that "low effort" subjects would be more certain of actually having to take the test.

Table 6 gives the subjects' ratings of their degree of certainty of having to take the test. There was a very slight tendency for subjects who had exerted greater effort to believe more strongly that they would be taking the test. Surprising in its relative magnitude was the finding that experimenters expecting to obtain responses of greater certainty obtained such responses to a much greater degree than did experimenters expecting responses of lesser certainty. The size of the expectancy effect was ten times greater than the size of the effort effect. In the terms of the discussion of expectancy control groups, these results fit well the so-called case 7 (p. 384). Had this experiment been conducted employing only the two most commonly encountered conditions, the investigators would have been even more seriously misled than would have been the case in the earlier mentioned study of the effects of brain lesions on discrimination learning. If experimenters, while contacting high effort subjects, expected them to show greater certainty, and if experimenters, while contacting low effort subjects, expected them to show less certainty, the experimental hypothesis might quite artifactually have appeared to have earned strong support. The difference between these groups might have been ascribed to effort effects while actually the difference seems due almost entirely to the effects of the experimenter's expectancy.

As part of a very large research undertaking involving 780 subjects, Miller (1970) conducted three sub-studies that permitted the comparison of the effects of persuasive communications (pro vs con) with the effects of experimenters' expectations. Table 7 gives the results of the comparisons. In two of the three analyses the effects of pro vs con persuasive communications were greater than the effects of the experimenters' expectancies, and the average effect size for persuasive communications was somewhat larger than the average effect size of experimenters' expectations (.86 σ vs .60 σ). When we consider all five analyses together, those of Burnham and Cooper et al. as well as those of Miller, we find that the median size of the effects of experimenter expectations was just as large as the median size of the effects of the psychological variables against which expectancy effects had been pitted, .71σ in both cases.

Five studies are not very many upon which to base any but the most tentative conclusions. Nevertheless, it does seem that it can no longer be said without considerable new evidence that the effects of interpersonal expectations, while "real", are trivial in relation to "real" psychological variables.

TABLE 7

Results of Three Comparisons of the Effects of Persuasive
Communications with the Effects of Experimenters' Expectancy:
After Miller

Study	Statistics of Difference	Pro vs Con Communication	Experimenter Expectancy
	t	5.30	1.58
I (df = 76)	p	.0001	.06
	Effect Size (σ)	1.22	0.36
	t	1.97	3.56
II (df = 76)	p	.03	.0002
	Effect Size (σ)	0.45	0.82
	t	4.04	2.69
III (df = 76)	p	.0001	.004
	Effect Size (σ)	0.93	0.62
	t	3.77	2.61
Mean	p	.0001	.005
(Miller only)	Effect Size (σ)	0.86	0.60
	t	1.97	2.69
Median	p	.03	.004
(Miller, Burnham,	Effect Size (σ)	0.71	0.71
Cooper, et al.)			

An Analysis of Doctoral Dissertations

In our overview of research on interpersonal expectations the results
of 311 independent studies were summarized. These studies were all the
ones I could locate employing the usual formal and informal bibliographic
search procedures. *Psychological Abstracts, Dissertation Abstracts International,* programs of conventions of national and regional psychological,
sociological, and educational conventions, various computer assisted
searches, and word of mouth were all employed to maximize the chances
of finding all studies of interpersonal expectancy effects. Nevertheless,
it was possible that many studies could not be retrieved because they
were regarded by their authors as uninteresting or counter-intuitive, or
overly complex, or whatever. Such studies may have shown preponder-
antly negative results. Could it be that the studies that were retrievable
represented roughly the 5% of the results that by chance might have been
significant at the 5% level, while the studies that were not retrievable
represented roughly the 95% of the studies that showed no effect (see page

322)? That seems unlikely. Since 109 studies were found showing expectancy effects at $p \leqslant .05$ and 202 studies were found not showing expectancy effects at $p \leqslant .05$ it would mean that if 1,549 studies had been conducted but not reported, or at least not found by the present search, and if all 1,549 showed no significant effects, there would *still* be an overall significant effect of interpersonal expectancy. To make the point a bit more strongly we take into account the actual significance levels of the 311 studies collected, rather than just whether they did or did not reach the .05 level. The sum of the standard normal deviates associated with the significance levels of the 311 studies was about +367. Adding 49,457 new studies with a mean standard normal deviate of zero would lower the overall combined standard normal deviate to +1.645 ($p = .05$). It seems unlikely that there are file drawers crammed with the unpublished results of nearly 50,000 studies of interpersonal expectations!

Sampling bias, then, cannot reasonably explain the overall significant results of studies of interpersonal expectancies. Nevertheless the studies that could be found might still differ in various ways from the studies that could not be found. It would be quite useful to examine any subset of studies for which we could be more sure of having found all the research performed. Such a situation exists to some extent in the case of doctoral dissertations. If the dissertation is accepted by the university where it is conducted it can be well-retrieved through *Dissertation Abstracts International* (DAI). Dissertations not accepted because the results are "nonsignificant" (see page 366) or in a direction displeasing to one or more members of the student's committee, will not of course be retrievable. Even if we could get a very large proportion of all dissertation research results through DAI we could not assume an unbiased sample of research studies. Sampling bias might be reduced, but other biases might be operating. Dissertation researchers may be less experienced investigators, less prestigeful in the eyes of their research subjects, and less competent in the conduct of their research. All of these factors have been implicated as variables moderating the effects of interpersonal expectancies. Despite these difficulties it was felt to be worthwhile to compare the results obtained in the dissertation vs non-dissertation research included in our stratified random sample of 75 studies.

Table 8 shows the results of this comparison. The first two columns show the number of studies in each research area that were dissertations or non-dissertations. Just over one-third (35%) of all the studies were doctoral dissertations, and the proportion of dissertations did not vary significantly from research area to research area ($\chi^2 = 6.56$, $df = 7$, $p \doteq .50$). The third and fourth columns of Table 8 show the mean effect sizes in σ units of the dissertations and non-dissertations of each research area, and the fifth column shows the weighted mean effect size for all studies in that research area. The effect sizes of columns 3 and 4 are too large,

TABLE 8

Mean Effect Sizes Estimated Separately for Dissertations and Non-Dissertations

| Research Area | Number of Studies | | Uncorrected Effect Size | | Mean Effect Size | Corrected Effect Size | | Difference |
	Diss. $(W_D)^a$	Non-Diss. $(W_O)^b$	Diss. $(E_D)^c$	Non-Diss. $(E_O)^d$	$(E_T)^e$	Diss. $(X)^f$	Non-Diss. $(Y)^g$	$(Y-X)$
Reaction Time	3	3	0.21	0.25	0.23	0.21	0.25	+0.04
Inkblot Tests	3	6	0.53	1.00	0.84	0.53	1.00	+0.47
Animal Learning	1	9	0.44	2.22	1.78	0.38	1.94	+1.56
Laboratory Interviews	4	6	0.74	0.33	0.27	0.40	0.18	-0.22
Psychophysical Judgments	2	8	1.86	1.56	1.31	1.50	1.26	-0.24
Learning and Ability	3	7	0.44	1.16	0.72	0.34	0.89	+0.55
Person Perception	5	5	2.74	3.96	0.51	0.42	0.60	+0.18
Everyday Situations	5	5	1.38	2.42	1.44	1.05	1.83	+0.78
Median	3	6	0.64	1.36	0.78	0.41	0.94	+0.32
Total	26	49	1.20	1.66	0.92	0.74	1.02	+0.28

[a] Number of dissertations in sample.

[b] Number of non-dissertations in sample.

[c] Estimated effect size based on dissertations only, uncorrected for oversampling of studies with large effect sizes.

[d] Estimated effect size based on non-dissertations only, uncorrected for oversampling of studies with large effect sizes.

[e] Estimated total effect size based on stratified random sampling.

[f] Estimated effect size based on dissertations only, corrected for oversampling of studies with large effect sizes:

$$X = \frac{E_D \, (W_D + W_O) \, E_T}{E_D \, W_D + E_O \, W_O}$$

[g] $Y = (E_O / E_D) \, X$

however, because of the oversampling of studies showing more significant results. The sixth column of Table 8, therefore, shows the estimated mean effect size of the doctoral dissertations after correction for the oversampling of more statistically significant outcomes. The corrected effect size (X) was computed according to the formula:

$X = [E_D (W_D + W_0) E_T] / [E_D W_D + E_0 W_0]$. The seventh column of Table 8 shows the estimated mean effect size of the non-dissertations after correction for the oversampling of more significant outcomes. The corrected effect size (Y) was computed according to the formula:

$Y = (E_0/E_D) X$ with X defined as above. The final column of Table 8 shows that over the eight research areas the differences in effect sizes between dissertations and non-dissertations ranged from about a quarter of a σ favoring the dissertations to about one-and-a-half σ favoring the non-dissertations with a median difference favoring the non-dissertations by about one-third of a σ unit. The differences in effect sizes between dissertations and non-dissertations are not significant statistically, and median or mean effect sizes for either dissertations or non-dissertations fall very comfortably within the 95% confidence intervals for medians or means of the 75 studies as shown in the bottom two rows of Table 3. The tendency for dissertations to show somewhat smaller effect sizes might be due to a reduction in sampling bias in retrieving dissertations as compared to non-dissertations, or it might be due to the introduction of one or more biases associated with dissertation research e.g. less experienced, less prestigeful, and less skilled investigators. A potentially powerful biasing factor might be introduced by dissertation researchers if they were unusually procedure-conscious in the conduct of their research. There are indications that such researchers may tend to obtain data that are substantially biased in the direction *opposite* to their expectations (Rosenthal, 1969, page 234).

Controls For Cheating and Recording Errors

Elsewhere it has been shown that although the occurrence of cheating or recording errors on the part of experimenters and teachers cannot be definitively ruled out, the occurrence of such intentional or unintentional errors can not reasonably account for the overall obtained effects of interpersonal expectations (Rosenthal, 1969, Pages 245-249). Indeed, experiments were described that showed major effects of interpersonal expectations despite the impossibility of the occurrence of either cheating or recording errors.

More recently in two ingenious experiments, Johnson and Adair (1970; 1972) were able to assess the relative magnitudes of intentional and/ or recording errors. In both experiments the overall effects of interpersonal expectations were modest ($.30\sigma$ and $.33\sigma$) and cheating or recording errors accounted for 30% of these effects ($.09\sigma$ and $.10\sigma$, respectively). Thus, even where cheating and/or recording errors can and do occur, they can not reasonably be invoked as an "explanation" of the effects of interpersonal expectations.

In the process of reviewing the procedures employed in the 311 studies under review here, it was possible to identify a subset of 36 studies that employed special methods for the elimination or control of cheating or observer errors or permitted an assessment of the possibility of intentional or unintentional errors. These methods included employing tape recorded instructions, data recording by blind observers, and videotaping of the interaction between the subject and the data-collector. The results of these 36 studies that had employed such safeguards were of special interest. If cheating and recording errors really played a major role in "explaining" interpersonal expectancy effects, then we would expect

TABLE 9

Effects of Special Controls Against Cheating on the Proportion of Studies Reaching Given Levels of Significance

	z	Expected Proportion	Special Controls (N = 36)	Other Studies (N = 275)	Total (N = 311)
Unpredicted	- 3.09	.001	.00	.00	.00
Direction	- 2.33	.01	.00	.01	.01
	- 1.65	.05	.06	.04	.04
Not Significant	- 1.64 to + 1.64	.90	.39[a]	.64[b]	.61[c]
Predicted	+ 1.65	.05	.56[d]	.32[d]	.35
Direction	+ 2.33	.01	.33	.17	.19
	+ 3.09	.001	.19	.11	.12
	+ 3.72	.0001	.17	.05	.07
	+ 4.27	.00001	.11	.04	.05
	+ 4.75	.000001	.06	.03	.04
	+ 5.20	.0000001	.06	.02	.02

[a] Mean z = + 1.72.   [b] Mean z = + 1.11.   [c] Mean z = 1.18.

[d] χ^2 that these proportions differ = 6.54, p = .01.

that studies guarding against such errors would show no effects of interpersonal expectation or at least would show only a very diminished likelihood of obtaining such effects.

Table 9 shows the proportion of these special 36 studies reaching various levels of significance in the unpredicted and predicted directions compared to the analogous proportion of the remaining 275 studies. The results are unequivocal. The more carefully controlled studies are *more* likely ($p = .01$) rather than less likely to show significant effects of interpersonal expectations than the studies permitting at least the possibility of cheating and/or recording errors. The mean standard normal deviate for the specially controlled studies was $+1.72$ while that for the remaining studies was $+1.11$. Just why these specially controlled studies should be more likely than the remaining studies to yield significant effects is not immediately obvious. The median sample sizes employed in these studies was about the same as the median sample size employed in all 311 studies. Perhaps those investigators careful enough to institute special safeguards against cheating and/or observer errors are also careful enough to reduce nonsystematic errors to a minimum thereby increasing the precision and power of their experiments.

A subgroup of the 36 specially controlled studies was of special interest; that subgroup was the set of 18 that were also doctoral dissertations. Examination of the effect sizes of these studies might permit a reasonable estimate of the effect sizes obtained in studies that were both error-controlled and less susceptible to sampling bias since it does appear that dissertations are more retrievable than non-dissertations. Other biases might, of course, be introduced such as the possible lower levels of experience and prestige of dissertation researchers. Still, examination of the subgroup of specially controlled dissertations at least focusses on careful dissertation researchers or on dissertation researchers whose committee members are careful.

Table 10 lists the 18 studies of this subgroup along with the effect size obtained in each. The mean and median effect sizes of these specially controlled dissertations are slightly larger than those found for the 26 dissertations examined in Table 8; (that set of dissertations includes some of the 18 dissertations of Table 10.) The 95% confidence interval around the mean effect size runs from $0.26\,\sigma$ to $+1.30\,\sigma$ or from small to very large indeed. This confidence interval includes completely the confidence interval estimated for all 311 studies and based upon the 75 studies of Table 3.

Whereas 35% of all 311 studies were significant at the .05 level in the predicted direction, 56% of these specially controlled dissertations were significant at the .05 level. This was not due to any tendency for these studies to employ larger sample sizes. The median df for all 311 studies was 48 and the median df for these specially controlled dissertations was also 48. The mean standard normal deviate for these 18 studies was $+1.86$ (median $= +1.84$).

TABLE 10

Effect Sizes of Doctoral Dissertations Employing Special Controls
for Cheating and Observer Errors

Area	Study	Effect Size (σ)
Everyday Situations		
	Anderson, 1971 I	- 0.43
	Anderson, 1971 II	- 0.20
	Beez, 1970	+ 1.89
	Carter, 1969	+ 0.53
	Keshock, 1970	+ 1.55
	Maxwell, 1970	+ 0.81
	Seaver, 1971	+ 0.44
	Wellons, 1973	+ 4.08
Person Perception		
	Blake (and Heslin) 1971	+ 0.55
	Hawthorne, 1972	+ 0.21
	Mayo, 1972	+ 0.15
	Todd, 1971	+ 1.16
Learning and Ability		
	Johnson, 1970 I	+ 0.19
	Johnson, 1970 II	+ 0.28
	Page, 1970	+ 1.74
	Yarom, 1971	+ 0.04
Laboratory Interviews		
	Gravitz, 1969	+ 0.19
Inkblot Tests		
	Marwit, 1968	+ 0.90
	Median	+ 0.48
	Mean	+ 0.78
	95% Confidence Interval	+ 0.26 to + 1.30

Correcting Errors of Data Analysis

Although there is reason to believe that this sample of 18 specially
controlled doctoral dissertations reflected the work of unusually careful
researchers, it must be noted that errors of data analysis occurred with
some frequency in this special sample as they did in the remainder of the
311 studies we have surveyed. Sometimes these errors were trivial and
sometimes they were large. Sometimes the errors were such that expectancy effects were claimed to be significant when they were not, and

sometimes the errors were such that expectancy effects were claimed to be not significant when they were very significant. Such was the case in the otherwise excellent experiment by Keshock (1970) listed in Table 10.

The pupils were 48 Black inner city boys aged 7 to 11 and in grades 2 to 5. Within each grade level half the children were reported to their teachers as showing an ability level one σ greater than their actual scores. For control group children the actual scores were reported to the teachers. There were three dependent variables: intelligence, achievement, and motivation. The data analysis for intelligence and for motivation employed the appropriate blocking on grade level and showed no effects of teacher expectations on intelligence but a very large effect ($+1.55\sigma$) on motivation. However, in the analysis of the achievement data, no blocking was employed despite a correlation (eta) between grade level and total achievement of .86. In short, the massive effects of grade level were inadvertently pooled into the within condition error term instead of being removed from the error term by blocking. Accordingly, the effects of teacher expectations were claimed to be non-significant. Fortunately, Keshock wisely provided the raw gain scores for all children for the achievement variables so that a desk calculator re-analysis was a simple matter. The components of the total achievement gain scores were a reading gain score (grand mean $= +3.1, S = 7.0$) and an arithmetic gain score (grand mean $= +2.1, S = 6.8$); these components were substantially correlated, $r = +.59$, a correlation higher than that often found between subtests of ability tests (e.g., $r = .43$ for TOGA; Rosenthal and Jacobson, 1968, Page 68).

Table 11 shows the results of the reanalysis. Gains in performance were substantially greater for the children whose teachers had been led to expect greater gains in performance. The sizes of the effects varied across the four grades from nearly half a σ unit to nearly four σ units.

TABLE 11

Excess of Gains in Achievement of Experimental Over
Control Group Pupils Due to Favorable Teacher Expectations:
After Keshock

Grade	Reading	Arithmetic	Total	z	Effect Size (σ)
2	9.99	11.67	21.66	+ 5.20	+ 3.85
3	6.33	6.84	13.17	+ 3.72	+ 2.34
4	1.16	1.50	2.66	+ 0.81	+ 0.47
5	4.67	3.66	8.33	+ 2.45	+ 1.48
Mean	5.54	5.92	11.46	+ 5.70	+ 2.04

For all subjects combined, the effect size was over two standard deviations. The entry for this study in Table 10 shows the median effect size obtained for the three dependent variables.

Interestingly, in another carefully conducted doctoral dissertation carried out by a colleague of Keshock's at about the same time, at the same university, under the same committee members in part, significant effects of teacher expectations on intelligence (Binet) were obtained although effects on achievement were not found to be significant (Maxwell, 1970). An enlightening footnote on the sociology of science is provided by the fact that a faculty member serving on both doctoral committees, subsequently published a study of her own reporting no significant expectancy effects. In her report neither of her own students' doctoral dissertations was cited although other research reporting no significant expectancy effects *was* cited, including an article published in the year following the completion of both dissertations.

The External Validity of Interpersonal Expectancy Effects

The book for which this is the epilogue ended with the description of an experiment designed to extend the external validity of the construct of the interpersonal self-fulfilling prophecy to everyday life situations. This experiment came to be known as the Pygmalion Experiment and it was reported in detail by Rosenthal and Jacobson (1968). Although a wealth of subsequent research has considerably weakened the impact of criticism of the Pygmalion research, it should be noted here for the sake of completeness that such criticism was forthcoming, with vigor, from several educational psychologists. Before proceeding we must examine at least the more famous of these criticisms.

In his well-known article in the *Harvard Educational Review*, Jensen (1969) makes three criticisms.

The first of these is that the child had been employed as the unit of analysis rather than the classroom, and that if the classroom had been employed the analysis would have yielded only negligible results. That was an unfortunate criticism for several reasons. First, because analyses by classrooms had not only been performed but quite clearly reported (page 95), and second, because for total IQ the significance level changed only trivially in going from a "per child" to a "per classroom" analysis, specifically from a probability of 2% to a probability of 3%! For reasoning IQ, incidentally, the per classroom analysis led to even more significant results than had the per child analysis. That fact, however, also printed on page 95, was not mentioned by Jensen.

Jensen's second criticism was that the same IQ test had been employed both for the pretest and for the post-test and that practice effects were thus maximized. Regrettably, Jensen did not state how the results of a randomized experiment could be biased by practice effects. If practice effects were so great as to drive everyone's performance up to the upper limit, or ceiling, of the test, then practice effects could operate to *diminish* the effects of the experimental manipulation, but they could not operate to increase the effects of the experimental manipulation.

Jensen's third criticism was that the teachers themselves administered the group tests of IQ. This criticism was unfortunate for two reasons. First, because Jensen neglected to mention to his readers what Rosenthal and Jacobson had mentioned to *theirs*, namely, that when the children were retested by testers who knew nothing of the experimental plan, the effects of teacher expectations actually increased, rather than decreased. Second, Jensen implied that teacher administered tests are unreliable compared to individually administered tests of intelligence (which is true) and that, therefore, the excess in IQ gain of the experimental over the control group children might be due to test undependability (which is not true). In fact, decreased test reliability makes it harder, not easier, to obtain significant differences between experimental and control groups when such differences are real. In short, Jensen's "criticism" would have served to account for the failure to obtain differences between the experimental and control group children if no differences had been found. In no way can such a criticism be used to explain away an obtained difference no matter how uncongenial to one's own theoretical position.

Another critique of the Pygmalion experiment was published by R. L. Thorndike (1968), but since that review has been answered point for point elsewhere (Rosenthal, 1969a), we can summarize it here quite briefly. The general point was that the IQ of the youngest children was badly measured by the test employed and, therefore, that any inference based on such measurement must be invalid. The facts, however, are these: (a) that the validity coefficient of the reasoning IQ subtest regarded as worthless by Thorndike in fact was .65, a value higher than that often advanced in support of the validity of IQ tests. The calculation of validity reported here was based on data readily available in the report of Pygmalion, and the calculation could have been made by any interested reader. (b) Even if the IQ measure had been seriously unreliable, Thorndike failed to show how unreliability could have led to spuriously significant results. As we saw earlier in the discussion of Jensen's critique, unreliability could make it harder to show significant differences between the experimental and control groups but it could not make it easier as Thorndike erroneously implied. (c) Even if the reasoning IQ data for the youngest children had been omitted from the analysis there would still have been a significant effect of teacher expectations for the remaining classrooms as measured by reasoning IQ ($p = .001$).

By far the most ambitious critique of Pygmalion was undertaken in a long-term study and re-analysis of the basic data by Elashoff and Snow (1970, 1971). That critique was actually published as a book and has been answered by Rosenthal and Rubin (1971).[1] The gist of the critique and of the reply can be given briefly. Elashoff and Snow transformed the data of Pygmalion in various ways some of which were very seriously biased. Yet despite the use of eight transformations not employed by Rosenthal and Jacobson, not a single transformation gave a noticeably different result from any reported by Rosenthal and Jacobson. Thus, for total IQ every transformation employed by Elashoff and Snow for all children of the experiment gave a significant result when a significant result had been claimed by Rosenthal and Jacobson, and no transformation gave a significant result when no significant result had been claimed by Rosenthal and Jacobson (Rosenthal and Rubin, 1971, page 142). When verbal and reasoning IQ were also considered, the various transformations employed by Elashoff and Snow in fact turned up more significant effects of teacher expectations than had been claimed by Rosenthal and Jacobson.

Table 12 compares the excess of gain in IQ by experimental over control group children as defined by Rosenthal and Jacobson and as

TABLE 12

Comparison of Expectancy Advantage Scores in Total, Verbal, and Reasoning IQ Employed in Rosenthal and Jacobson vs. the Median of Nine Scores Employed in Elashoff and Snow

	Total IQ		Verbal IQ		Reasoning IQ	
	RJ	ES	RJ	ES	RJ	ES
Grades						
1 & 2	11.0*	10.8*	10.1*	8.7*	12.6	12.6
3 & 4	1.8	1.8	-4.6	-5.6	8.7	8.5*
5 & 6	.2	.1	2.0	1.0	4.8	.5
Total	3.8*	†	2.1	†	7.1**	†

*Two-tailed $p \leqslant .05$

**Two-tailed $p \leqslant .01$

†Not reported by ES.

[1]The reply by Rosenthal and Rubin was written in response to the Elashoff and Snow monograph dated 1970. The preparation of the various drafts of that monograph occupied several years but Rosenthal and Rubin were asked to prepare their reply in two weeks. In addition, Rosenthal and Rubin were shown only the 1970 version of the monograph and were not permitted to respond to the 1971 version which included the deletion of some information particularly damaging to the Elashoff and Snow position (e.g., in Tables 23 and 24 of their widely circulated 1970 monograph).

defined by the median of the nine measures analyzed by Elashoff and Snow. The comparisons are based on data provided by Elashoff and Snow's Tables 20, 21, and 22 (1971). The very high degree of agreement between the original measure employed and the median of the transformation measures is evident in the table by inspection and is supported by the 0.95 Pearson product moment correlation and the 0.93 Spearman rank correlation between the original and the transformed measures. For all the effort expended, the re-analyses by Elashoff and Snow changed nothing as Table 12 shows.

Many studies of teacher expectation effects have been conducted since the Pygmalion Experiment (Rosenthal, 1973). However, the bulk of the 311 studies we have surveyed in this epilogue have been studies of interpersonal expectation effects in laboratory situations rather than in such everyday situations as schools, clinics, or industries. We can best examine the external validity, or generality, of the interpersonal expectancy effect by comparing the results of those studies conducted in laboratories with those studies conducted in more "real-life" situations. Such comparisons have been made implicitly in Tables 1, 2, 3, 4, 8, and 10 but now we address the question explicitly.

Table 13 compares the results of studies of interpersonal expectancy effects in laboratory situations with everyday situations, using data drawn

---

TABLE 13

Comparison of Studies of Interpersonal Expectancy Effects
in Everyday Situations with Laboratory Situations

	Laboratory Situations	Everyday Situations	Combined Situations
Mean df	52	45	48
% Biased			
"Expecters"	69%	70%	69%
"Expectees"	64%	65%	64%
Effect Size (σ)			
Sampled Dissertations (n = 26)	0.40	1.05	0.74
Specially Controlled Dissertations (n = 18)	0.54	1.08	0.78
Estimated Total: All Studies (N = 311)	0.72	1.44	0.92
Estimated S of Effect Size	1.15	2.74	1.33
95% Confidence Interval of Total ES	−0.06	−0.53	+0.62
to:	+1.74	+3.41	+1.22

from earlier tables. The two kinds of studies are similar in average size of study and in the percentages of experimenters or teachers (and subjects or pupils) showing the biasing effects of interpersonal expectations. Effect sizes as measured in σ units tend to be larger, on the average, for everyday situations than in laboratory situations, but they are also substantially more variable so that the effect size expected for any single study can be less accurately predicted. A final comparison is given in Table 14 which gives the proportion of studies reaching various levels of significance in the predicted and unpredicted directions for studies conducted in laboratory vs everyday situations. Results for the two types of studies are in close agreement with studies conducted in everyday situations showing significant results in the predicted direction slightly more often.

The results shown in Tables 13 and 14 strongly support the conclusion that interpersonal expectancy effects are at least as likely to occur in everyday life situations as in laboratory situations. That conclusion is

TABLE 14

Proportion of Studies Reaching Given Levels of Significance

| | | | Type of Study | | |
| | | | Laboratory Situations (N = 215) | Everyday Situations (N = 96) | Total (N = 311) |
	z	Expected Proportion			
	– 3.09	.001	.00	.00	.00
Unpredicted	– 2.33	.01	.01	.00	.01
Direction	– 1.65	.05	.05	.01	.04
Not Significant	– 1.64 to + 1.64	.90	.61	.61	.61[a]
Predicted	+ 1.65	.05	.34	.38	.35[b]
Direction	+ 2.33	.01	.19	.19	.19
	+ 3.09	.001	.11	.14	.12
	+ 3.72	.0001	.05	.10	.07
	+ 4.27	.00001	.03	.08	.05
	+ 4.75	.000001	.03	.05	.04
	+ 5.20	.0000001	.02	.03	.02

[a]Grand mean of all zs = +1.18.

[b]χ^2 that this exceeds expected proportion = 585, z = 24.2.

based on evidence from so many studies that dozens of additional studies cannot appreciably alter the conclusion without their showing very significant *reverse* effects of interpersonal expectations. The phenomenon is general across many situations, and it is not necessarily small in magnitude. Often it is very large.

Future Research

What, then, is there left for us to find out? Almost everything of consequence. What are the factors increasing or decreasing the effects of interpersonal expectations, i.e., what are the moderating variables? What are the variables serving to mediate the effects of interpersonal self-fulfilling prophecies? Only some bare beginnings have been made to address these questions. The role of moderating variables has been considered elsewhere and is being actively surveyed at the present time (Rosenthal, 1969). The variables serving to mediate the effects of interpersonal expectancies have also been considered elsewhere, and for the teacher-pupil interaction a four factor "theory" has been proposed (Rosenthal, 1969; 1973). This "theory" suggests that teachers, counselors, and supervisors who have been led to expect superior performance from some of their pupils, clients, or trainees, appear to treat these "special" persons differently than they treat the remaining not-so-special persons in roughly four ways:

Climate. Teachers appear to create a warmer socio-emotional climate for their "special" students.

Feedback. Teachers appear to give to their "special" students more differentiated feedback as to how these students have been performing.

Input. Teachers appear to teach more material and more difficult material to their "special" students.

Output. Teachers appear to give their "special" students greater opportunities for responding.

Work on this four factor theory is currently in progress.

Much of the research on interpersonal expectancies has suggested that mediation of these expectancies depends to some important degree on various processes of nonverbal communication (Rosenthal, 1969; 1973). Moreover, there appear to be important differences among experimenters, teachers, and people generally in the clarity of their communication through different channels of nonverbal communication. In addition, there appear to be important differences among research subjects, pupils, and people generally, in their sensitivity to nonverbal communications transmitted through different nonverbal channels. If we knew a great deal more about differential sending and receiving abilities we might be in a much better position to address the general question of what kind of person (in terms of sending abilities) can most effectively influence covertly what kind of other person (in terms of receiving abilities). Thus, for example, if those teachers who best communicate their expectations for children's intellectual performance in the auditory channel were assigned children whose best channels of reception were also auditory, we would predict greater effects of teacher expectation than we would if those same teachers were assigned children less sensitive to auditory channel nonverbal communication.

Ultimately, then, what we would want would be a series of accurate measurements for each person describing his or her relative ability to send and to receive in each of a variety of channels of nonverbal communication. It seems reasonable to suppose that if we had this information for two or more people we would be better able to predict the outcome of their interaction regardless of whether the focus of the analysis were on the mediation of interpersonal expectations or on some other interpersonal transaction.

Our model envisages people moving through their "social spaces" carrying two vectors or profiles of scores. One of these vectors describes the person's differential clarity in sending messages over various channels of nonverbal communication. The other vector describes the person's differential sensitivity to messages sent over various channels of nonverbal communication. Diagrammatically for any given dyad:

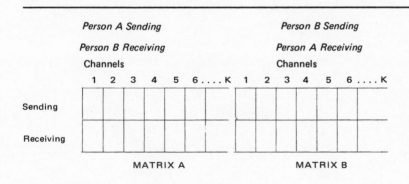

Within each of the two matrices the scores on channels of sending of the sender can be correlated with the scores of channels of receiving of the receiver. Given a fixed average performance level for senders and receivers, a higher correlation reflects a greater potential for more accurate communication between the dyad members since the receiver is then better at receiving the channels which are the more accurately encoded channels of the sender. The mean (arithmetic, geometric, or harmonic) of the correlations between Matrix A and Matrix B reflects how well the dyad members "understand" each other's communications. That mean correlation need not reflect how well the dyad members like each other, however, only that A and B should more quickly understand each others' intended and unintended messages including how they feel about one another.

As a start toward the goal of more completely specifying accuracy of sending and receiving nonverbal cues in dyadic interaction we have been developing an instrument designed to measure differential sensitivity to various channels of nonverbal communication: *The Profile of Nonverbal Sensitivity* or PONS (Rosenthal, Archer, DiMatteo, Koivumaki, and Rogers, 1976). It is our hope that research employing the PONS and related measures of skill at sending and receiving messages in various channels of nonverbal communication along with related research will help us to unravel the mystery of the mediation of interpersonal expectancy effects. That is the hope; but the work lies ahead.

References

ANDERSON, D. F. Mediation of teachers' expectancy with normal and retarded children. Unpublished doctoral dissertation, Harvard University, 1971.

BEEZ, W. V. Influence of biased psychological reports on "teacher" behavior and pupil performance. Unpublished doctoral dissertation, Indiana University, 1970.

BLAKE, B. F., and HESLIN, R. Evaluation apprehension and subject bias in experiments. *Journal of Experimental Research in Personality*, 1971, *5*, 57-63.

BURNHAM, J. R. Experimenter bias and lesion labeling. Unpublished manuscript, Purdue University, 1966.

CARTER, R. M. Locus of control and teacher expectancy as related to achievement of young school children. Unpublished doctoral dissertation, Indiana University, 1969.

COHEN, J. *Statistical power analysis for the behavioral sciences*. New York: Academic Press, 1969.

COOPER, J., EISENBERG, L., ROBERT, J., and DOHRENWEND, B. S. The effect of experimenter expectancy and preparatory effort on belief in the probable occurrence of future events. *Journal of Social Psychology*, 1967, *71*, 221-226.

ELASHOFF, J. D., and SNOW, R. E. A case study in statistical inference: Reconsideration of the Rosenthal-Jacobson data on teacher expectancy. Technical Report No. 15, Stanford Center for Research and Development in Teaching, School of Education, Stanford University, December, 1970.

ELASHOFF, J. D., and SNOW, R. E. (Eds.) *Pygmalion Reconsidered*. Worthington, Ohio: Charles A. Jones, 1971.

FRIEDMAN, H. Magnitude of experimental effect and a table for its rapid estimation. *Psychological Bulletin*, 1968, *70*, 245-251.

GRAVITZ, H. L. Examiner expectancy effects in psychological assessment: The Bender Visual Motor Gestalt Test. Unpublished doctoral dissertation, University of Tennessee, 1969.

HAWTHORNE, J. W. The influence of the set and dependence of the data collector on the experimenter bias effect. Unpublished doctoral dissertation, Duke University, 1972.

JENSEN, A. R. How much can we boost IQ and scholastic achievement? *Harvard Educational Review*, 1969, *39*, 1-123.

JOHNSON, R. W. Inducement of expectancy and set of subjects as determinants of subjects' responses in experimenter expectancy research. Unpublished doctoral dissertation, University of Manitoba, 1970.

JOHNSON, R. W., and ADAIR, J. G. The effects of systematic recording error vs, experimenter bias on latency of word association. *Journal of Experimental Research in Personality*, 1970, *4*, 270-275.

JOHNSON, R. W. and ADAIR, J. G. Experimenter expectancy vs. systematic recording error under automated and nonautomated stimulus presentation. *Journal of Experimental Research in Personality*, 1972, *6*, 88-94.

KESHOCK, J. D. An investigation of the effects of the expectancy phenomenon upon the intelligence, achievement and motivation of inner-city elementary school children. Unpublished doctoral dissertation, Case Western Reserve University, 1970.

MARWIT, S. J. An investigation of the communication of tester-bias by means of modeling. Unpublished doctoral dissertation, State University of New York at Buffalo, 1968.

MAXWELL, M. L. A study of the effects of teacher expectation on the I.Q. and academic performance of children. Unpublished doctoral dissertation, Case Western Reserve University, 1970.

MAYO, C. C. External conditions affecting experimental bias. Unpublished doctoral dissertation, University of Houston, 1972.

MILLER, K. A. A study of "experimenter bias" and "subject awareness" as demand characteristic artifacts in attitude change experiments. Unpublished doctoral dissertation, Bowling Green State University, 1970.

MOSTELLER, F., and BUSH, R. R. Selected quantitative techniques. In G. Lindzey (Ed.) *Handbook of social psychology,* Vol. I. Cambridge, Mass.: Addison-Wesley, 1954. Pp. 289-334.

PAGE, J. S. Experimenter-subject interaction in the verbal conditioning experiment. Unpublished doctoral dissertation, University of Toronto, 1970.

ROSENTHAL, R. Interpersonal expectations: Effects of the experimenter's hypothesis. In R. Rosenthal and R. L. Rosnow (Eds.) *Artifact in behavioral research*. New York: Academic Press, 1969. Pp. 181-277.

ROSENTHAL, R. Empirical vs. decreed validation of clocks and tests. *American Educational Research Journal,* 1969, *6*, 689-691. (a)

ROSENTHAL, R. Teacher expectations and their effects upon children. In G. S. Lesser (Ed.), *Psychology and educational practice*. Glenview, Ill.: Scott, Foresman, 1971. Pp. 64-87.

ROSENTHAL, R. *On the social psychology of the self-fulfilling prophecy: Further evidence for Pygmalion effects and their mediating mechanisms*. New York: MSS Modular Publication, Module 53, 1973.

ROSENTHAL, R., ARCHER, D., DIMATTEO, M. R., KOIVUMAKI, J. H., and ROGERS, P. L. *Measuring sensitivity to nonverbal communication: The PONS Test*. Unpublished manuscript, Harvard University, 1976.

ROSENTHAL, R., and JACOBSON, L. *Pygmalion in the classroom*. New York: Holt, Rinehart and Winston, 1968.

ROSENTHAL, R., and ROSNOW, R. L. *The volunteer subject*. New York: Wiley-Interscience, 1975.

ROSENTHAL, R., and RUBIN, D. B. Pygmalion reaffirmed. In J. D. Elashoff, and R. E. Snow (Eds.) *Pygmalion reconsidered*. Worthington, Ohio: Charles A. Jones, 1971. Pp. 139-155.

SEAVER, Jr., W. B. Effects of naturally induced teacher expectancies on the academic performance of pupils in primary grades. Unpublished doctoral dissertation, Northwestern University, 1971.

SNEDECOR, G. W., & COCHRAN, W. G. *Statistical methods*. (6th ed.) Ames, Iowa: Iowa State University Press, 1967.

THORNDIKE, R. L. Review of Pygmalion in the classroom. *American Educational Research Journal,* 1968, *5,* 708-711.

TODD, J. L. Social evaluation orientation, task orientation, and deliberate cuing in experimenter bias effect. Unpublished doctoral dissertation, University of California, Los Angeles, 1971.

WELLONS, K. W. The expectancy component in mental retardation. Unpublished doctoral dissertation, University of California, Berkeley, 1973.

YAROM, N. Temporal localization and communication of experimenter expectancy effect with 10-11 year old children. Unpublished doctoral dissertation, University of Illinois, 1971.

Index of Names

Subject Index